Computer Communications:
Architectures, Protocols, and Standards
Third Edition

Third Edition

Tutorial

Computer Communications
Architectures, Protocols, and Standards

William Stallings

 IEEE Computer Society Press   ✦ The Institute of Electrical and Electronics Engineers, Inc.

Computer Communications:
Architectures, Protocols, and Standards
Third Edition

by William Stallings

IEEE Computer Society Press
Los Alamitos, California
Washington • Brussels • Tokyo

IEEE Computer Society Press Tutorial

Library of Congress Cataloging-in-Publication Data

Computer communications: architectures, protocols, and standards /
[edited] by William Stallings.—3rd ed.
  p.   cm.—(IEEE Computer Society Press tutorial)
Includes bibliographical references (p.   ).
"IEEE Computer Society Press order number 2712"—T.p. verso.
"IEEE catalog number EH0347-5"—T.p. verso.
ISBN 0-8186-2711-5 (microfiche).—ISBN 0-8186-2712-3 (case)
  1. Computer network architectures. 2. Computer network protocols.
 3. Computer networks—Standards. I. Stallings, William.
 II. Series.
TK5105.5.C6375   1992   92-6850
004.6—dc20   CIP

Published by the
IEEE Computer Society Press
10662 Los Vaqueros Circle
PO Box 3014
Los Alamitos, CA 90720-1264

© 1992 by the Institute of Electrical and Electronics Engineers, Inc. All rights reserved.

Copyright and Reprint Permissions: Abstracting is permitted with credit to the source. Libraries are permitted to photocopy beyond the limits of US copyright law, for private use of patrons, those articles in this volume that carry a code at the bottom of the first page, provided that the per-copy fee indicated in the code is paid through the Copyright Clearance Center, 27 Congress Street, Salem, MA 01970. Instructors are permitted to photocopy isolated articles, without fee, for non-commercial classroom use. For other copying, reprint, or republication permission, write to IEEE Copyrights Manager, IEEE Service Center, 445 Hoes Lane, PO Box 1331, Piscataway, NJ 08855-1331.

IEEE Computer Society Press Order Number 2712
Library of Congress Number 92-6850
IEEE Catalog Number EH0347-5
ISBN 0-8186-2711-5 (microfiche)
ISBN 0-8186-2712-3 (case)

Additional copies can be ordered from

IEEE Computer Society Press	IEEE Service Center	IEEE Computer Society	IEEE Computer Society
Customer Service Center	445 Hoes Lane	13, avenue de l'Aquilon	Ooshima Building
10662 Los Vaqueros Circle	PO Box 1331	B-1200 Brussels	2-19-1 Minami-Aoyama
PO Box 3014	Piscataway, NJ 08855-1331	BELGIUM	Minato-ku, Tokyo 107
Los Alamitos, CA 90720-1264			JAPAN

Editorial production: Catherine Harris
Cover design: Joseph Daigle
Printed in the United States of America by Braun-Brumfield, Inc.

   THE INSTITUTE OF ELECTRICAL AND ELECTRONICS ENGINEERS, INC.

Contents

Preface ix

Chapter 1: Communications Architectures 1

Implementing OSI Systems 11
    L. Svobodova *(IEEE Journal on Selected Areas in Communications,* September 1989,
    pp. 1115–1130)

Performance Modeling of Multi-Layered OSI Communication Architectures 27
    A. Conway *(Proc. IEEE International Conference on Communications,* June 1989,
    pp. 651–657)

A Network Security Primer 34
    W. Stallings *(ComputerWorld,* January 29, 1990, pp. 63–70)

The Reality of OSI Management 40
    W. Collins and K. Korostoff *(Network World,* October 9, 1989, p.1 and pp. 37–42, and October
    16, pp. 53–66)

The DARPA Internet Protocol Suite 48
    B. Leiner, R. Cole, J. Postel, and D. Mills *(IEEE Communications Magazine,* March 1985,
    pp. 29–34)

The Design Philosophy of the DARPA Internet Protocols 54
    D. Clark *(Proc. SIGCOMM '88 Symposium,* August 1988, pp. 106–114)

Relationship of the Signaling System No. 7 Protocol Architecture to the OSI
Reference Model 63
    N. Mitra and S. Usiskin *(IEEE Network,* January 1991, pp. 26–37)

Chapter 2: Physical and Data Link Protocols 73

Unraveling RS-232 76
    G. Kessler *(LAN Magazine,* August 1988, pp. 119–124)

CCITT Standardization of Network Node Interface of Synchronous
Digital Hierarchy 80
    K. Asatani, K. Harrison, and R. Ballart *(IEEE Communications Magazine,* August 1990,
    pp. 15–20)

A Tutorial on the IEEE 802 Local Network Standard 86
    W. Stallings *(Local Area and Multiple Access Networks,* 1986, pp. 1–30)

IEEE 802.6 MAN 109
    G. Kessler *(LAN Magazine,* April 1990, pp. 102–116)

Frame Relaying Service: An Overview 116
    W. Lai *(IEEE INFOCOM '89,* April 1989, pp. 668–673)

Chapter 3: Network Access Protocols 123

X.25: An Interface to Public Packet Networks 126
    C. Dhas and V. Konangi *(IEEE Communications Magazine,* September 1986,
    pp. 18–25)

The Internal Organization of the Network Layer: Concepts, Applications, and Issues 134
    C. Hemrick *(Journal of Telecommunications Networks,* Fall 1984, pp. 15–22)

OSI Addressing Strategies 145
    K. Jakobs *(Computer Communications Review,* July/August 1987, pp. 7–12)

ISDN Protocols for Connection Control 151
    W. Harman and C. Newman *(IEEE Journal on Selected Areas in Communications,*
    September 1989, pp. 1034–1042)

Chapter 4: Internetworking **161**
Network Interconnection and Gateways 167
    C. Sunshine *(IEEE Journal on Selected Areas in Communications,* January 1990,
    pp. 4–11)
Networking of Networks: Interworking According to OSI 175
    F. Burg and N. Di Iorio *(IEEE Journal on Selected Areas in Communications,*
    September 1989, pp. 1131–1142)
Design of Inter-Administrative Domain Routing Protocol 187
    L. Breslau and D. Estrin *(Proc. SIGCOMM '90 Symposium,* September 1990,
    pp. 231–241)
Internetworking ISDN with LANs 199
    J. Tao, R. Martinez, C. Jiron, and P. Afsharnejad *(Proc. Ninth Annual Int'l Phoenix*
    Conference on Computers and Communications, March 1990, pp. 202–207)

Chapter 5: Transport and Session Protocols **205**
A Primer: Understanding Transport Protocols 208
    W. Stallings *(Data Communications,* November 1984, pp. 201–215)
Architectures, Features, and Implementation of High-Speed Transport Protocols 217
    T. La Porta and M. Schwartz *(IEEE Network,* May 1991, pp. 14–22)
Hints for the Interpretation of the ISO Session Layer 226
    F. Caneschi *(Computer Communications Review,* July/August 1986, pp. 34–72)

Chapter 6: Presentation and Application Protocols **265**
Components of OSI: The Presentation Layer 266
    D. Chappell *(Connexions,* November 1989, pp. 16–23)
ASN.1 and ROS: The Impact of X.400 on OSI 274
    J. White *(IEEE Journal on Selected Areas in Communications,* September 1989,
    pp. 1060–1072)
File Transfer Protocols 287
    P. Linington *(IEEE Journal on Selected Areas in Communications,*
    September 1989, pp. 1052–1059)
The Development of Office Document Architecture (ODA) 295
    W. McDonald *(Open Systems Data Transfer,* October 1990, pp. 1–8)
X.400 MHS: First Steps Toward an EDI Communication Standard 303
    G. Genilloud *(Computer Communications Review,* April 1990, pp. 72–86)
Telecommunication Services and Distributed Applications 318
    C. Chabernaud, and B. Vilain *(IEEE Network,* November 1990, pp. 10–13)
Distributed Multimedia Information Handling and Processing 322
    G. Schurmann and U. Holzmann-Kaiser *(IEEE Network,* November 1990, pp. 23–31)

Chapter 7: Glossary **331**

Chapter 8: Bibliography **333**

Author Profile **342**

Figures

1-1	A simplified architecture for file transfer	1
1-2	Communications architectures and networks	2
1-3	Protocols in a simplified architecture	3
1-4	Protocol data units	3
1-5	Operation of a communications architecture	4
1-6	The OSI environment	7
1-7	The use of a relay	7
2-1	Generic interface to transmission medium	73
3-1	Communication across a network	123
3-2	OSI configurations for circuit-switched communication	124
3-3	OSI configuration for packet-switched communication	125
4-1	Internetworking approaches	163
4-2	Internetwork architectures	164
4-3	Network-layer addressing	165
5-1	Session delimited data units	207

Tables

1-1	The OSI layers	6
4-1	Internetworking terms	161

Preface

In the early 1970s, networks that interconnected computers and terminals began to apppear. These networks were developed primarily to share expensive computing resources and to minimize data transmission costs. Since that time, the rapid proliferation of minicomputers and personal computers has increased the demand for data communication beween computers, between terminal and computer, and between terminals. Such communication is accomplished by means of protocols. Typically, the task is too complex for a single protocol, so a structured set of protocols forming a communications architecture is used instead.

Tutorial focus

The focus of this tutorial is twofold. First, it presents the motivating factors and design principles of a communications architecture. Considerable attention is devoted to the open systems interconnection (OSI) model, which has achieved near-universal acceptance. This model provides the framework used to develop protocols and the terms of reference used to discuss communication system design. In addition, a somewhat dissimilar view of communications architecture that is evolving out of the ARPANET experience is examined. The contrast between the OSI and ARPANET viewpoints serves to highlight the important design issues for a communications architecture.

Second, this tutorial presents a broad overview of communication protocols. It explores key issues in the field in the following general categories:

- *Principles:* This tutorial provides an understanding of protocols in general and explores the design principles common to all protocols.
- *Services and mechanisms:* A protocol provides services to its user, which is generally a higher-level protocol. To provide these services, a set of mechanisms is implemented. This tutorial examines the services and mechanisms of various protocols.
- *Standards:* It is essential to use standard protocols to allow the greatest possible degree of interoperability among systems, a view that has now been accepted by suppliers as well as users. This tutorial presents the nature and current status of protocol standards.

This tutorial strives for breadth rather than depth. Both the Bibliography (Chapter 8) and the references contained in each paper suggest additional sources for the interested reader.

Intended audience

This tutorial is intended for a broad range of readers interested in the architecture and protocols of computer-communications architecture, including:

- *Students and professionals in data processing and data communications.* This tutorial provides a convenient means of reviewing some of the important papers in the field. Both the organization of the papers and the content of the new material will aid the reader in understanding this exciting area of data processing and data communications.
- *Protocol designers and implementers.* This tutorial discusses critical design issues and explores approaches to meeting communications requirements.
- *Computer system customers and managers.* This tutorial helps the reader understand what features and structures are needed in a communications capability, and provides information about current and evolving standards to enable the reader to assess a specific vendor's offering.

Most of the material can be comfortably read by those with no background in data communications. The original material and the glossary provide supporting information for the reprinted papers.

Organization of the material

This tutorial is a combination of original material and reprinted papers. Because the OSI model has become the almost universally accepted context both for designing protocols and for conducting professional discourse on computer communications, the structure of this tutorial is based on that model. The organization of the chapters is as follows:

(1) *Communications architectures:* A communications architecture is a structured set of protocols that performs the communications task. Although the OSI model is almost universally accepted as the framework for discourse in this area, there is another point of view that grows out of the extensive research and practical experience of ARPANET. Both points of view are presented in this chapter.
(2) *Physical and data link protocols:* The physical and data link layers (Layers 1 and 2) are concerned with providing a direct communications path between two devices. This chapter looks at some of the key protocol standards at these two layers, including one of the newest data link protocols, frame relay.
(3) *Network access protocols:* Network access protocols provide an interface through which devices may access a communications network. One of the most important standards at this level is X.25. In addition to a paper on this topic, this chapter includes several papers on the OSI network layer, and one on the control interface to ISDN.
(4) *Internetworking:* Increasingly, there is a requirement for communication across multiple interconnected networks. The OSI model does not easily accommodate this requirement, which seems to call for a protocol between Layers 3 and 4. This chapter covers various aspects of the internetworking function.
(5) *Transport and session protocols:* The transport and session layers (Layers 4 and 5) provide an end-to-end communication service. This chapter looks at these two layers and includes a paper on lightweight transport protocols, one of the newest approaches to transport protocol design.
(6) *Presentation and application layers:* For Layers 5 (session) and below, there are relatively few distinct protocols at each layer. However, at the presentation and application layers, (Layers 6 and 7) there are a variety of protocols to provide a broad range of user-oriented services. This chapter includes an overview of these protocols, plus some representative examples.
(7) *Glossary:* The Glossary includes definitions for most of the key terms appearing in the text.
(8) *Bibliography:* The Bibliography provides a guide to further reading.

Related materials

Data and Computer Communications, third edition (Macmillan, 1991), by William Stallings, covers the same topics as this tutorial text, with an emphasis on the technology of computer communications. *The Handbook of Computer Communication Standards, Volume I: The Open Systems Interconnection (OSI) Model and OSI-Related Standards,* second edition (Howard W. Sams, 1990), also by William Stallings, provides a detailed description of the OSI model and standards at each layer of the model. In addition, the author has prepared a videotape course that can be used with this tutorial text. It is available from Professional Development Video Programs, The Media Group, Boston University, 565 Commonwealth Avenue, Boston, Massachusetts 02215; telephone (617) 353-3227.

The third edition

In the three years since the second edition of this book was published, the computer communications field has continued to evolve and expand, as evidenced by the makeup of this third edition, in which 24 of the 29 papers are new. Among the most noteworthy additions are papers on Signaling System Number 7, frame relay, and ISDN call control, which reflect the increasing importance of ISDN. Other new topics include the IEEE 802.6 Metropolitan Area Network (MAN) standard, lightweight transport protocols, and internetwork routing protocols. New papers are included on application-level protocols and standards, and more current papers on a number of protocols have replaced earlier versions from the second edition.

This third edition of *Computer Communications: Architectures, Protocols, and Standards* constitutes a major revision which should provide a balanced and comprehensive survey of this fascinating field.

William Stallings
March, 1992

Chapter 1
Communications Architectures

The need for a communications architecture

When computers, terminals, and other data processing devices exchange data, the procedures involved can be quite complex. Consider the transfer of a file between two computers attached to a network. Some of the typical tasks to be performed are:

(1) The source system must inform the network of the identity of the desired destination system.
(2) The source system must determine that the destination system is prepared to receive data.
(3) The file transfer application on the source system must determine that the file management program on the destination system is prepared to accept and store the file from this particular user.
(4) One of the two systems must perform a format translation function if the file formats used on the two systems are incompatible.

It is clear that there must be a high degree of cooperation between the two computers. Instead of implementing the logic for this as a single module, the task is broken up into subtasks, each of which is implemented separately. Figure 1-1 suggests the way in which a file-transfer facility could be implemented. Three modules are used. Tasks 3 and 4 in the preceding list could be performed by a file transfer module. The two modules on the two systems exchange files and commands. However, rather than requiring the file transfer module to deal with the details of actually transferring data and commands, the file transfer modules each rely on a communications service module. This module is responsible for making sure that the file transfer commands and data are reliably exchanged between systems. Among other things, this module would perform Task 2. Now the nature of the exchange between systems is independent of the nature of the network that interconnects them. Therefore, rather than building details of the network interface into the communications service module, it makes sense to have a third module, the network access module, that performs Task 1 by interacting with the network.

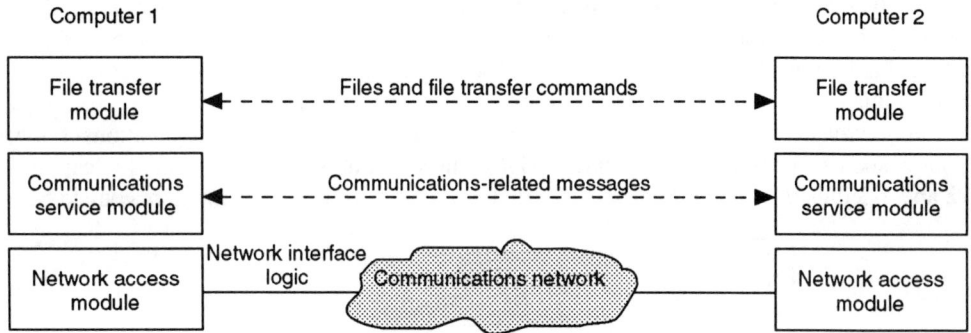

Figure 1-1. A simplified architecture for file transfer.

Let us try to summarize the motivation for the three modules in Figure 1-1. The file-transfer module contains all of the logic that is unique to the file transfer application, such as transmitting passwords, file commands, and file records. These files and commands must be transmitted reliably; however, the same sorts of reliability requirements are relevant to a variety of applications (e.g., electronic mail and document transfer). A separate communications service module that can be used by a variety of applications better meets these requirements. This communications service module has two concerns: assuring that the two computer systems are active and ready for data transfer, and tracking the data that are being exchanged to assure delivery. Since these tasks are independent of the type of network that is being used, the logic for actually dealing with the network is separated out into a separate network access module. That way, if the network to be used is changed, only the network access module is affected.

Thus, instead of a single module for performing communications, there is a structured set of modules that implements the communications function. That structure is referred to as a communications architecture. In the remainder of this section, we generalize the preceding example to present a simplified communications architecture.

A simple communications architecture

In very general terms, communications can be said to involve three agents: applications, computers, and networks. The applications that we are concerned with here are distributed applications that involve the exchange of data between two computer systems; examples are electronic mail and file transfer. These applications, and others, execute on computers that are multiprogrammed to support multiple concurrent applications. Computers are connected to networks, and the data to be exchanged are transferred by the network from one computer to another. Thus, the transfer of data from one application to another involves first getting the data to the computer in which the application resides and then getting it to the intended application within the computer. With these concepts in mind, it appears natural to organize the communications task into three relatively independent layers:

- Network access layer.
- Transport layer.
- Application layer.

The *network access layer* is concerned with the exchange of data between a computer and the network to which it is attached. The sending computer must provide the network with the address of the destination computer, so that the network may route the data to the appropriate destination. The sending computer may wish to invoke certain services, such as priority, that might be provided by the network. The specific software used at this layer depends on the type of network to be used; different standards have been developed for circuit-switching, packet-switching, local area networks, and others. For example, X.25 is a standard that specifies the access to a packet-switching network. Thus it makes sense to separate those functions having to do with network access into a separate layer. By doing this, the remainder of the communications software above the network access layer need not be concerned about the specifics of the network to be used. The same higher-layer software should function properly regardless of the particular network to which the computer is attached.

Regardless of the nature of the applications that are exchanging data, there is usually a requirement that data be exchanged reliably; that is, we would like to be assured that all of the data arrive at the destination application, and also that the data arrive in the same order in which they were sent. Since the mechanisms for providing reliability are essentially independent of the nature of the applications, it makes sense to collect those mechanisms in a common layer shared by all applications; this is referred to as the *transport layer*.

Finally, the *application layer* contains the logic needed to support the various user applications. For each different type of application, such as file transfer, a separate module is needed that is peculiar to that application.

Figures 1-2 and 1-3 illustrate this simple architecture. Figure 1-2 shows three computers connected to a network.

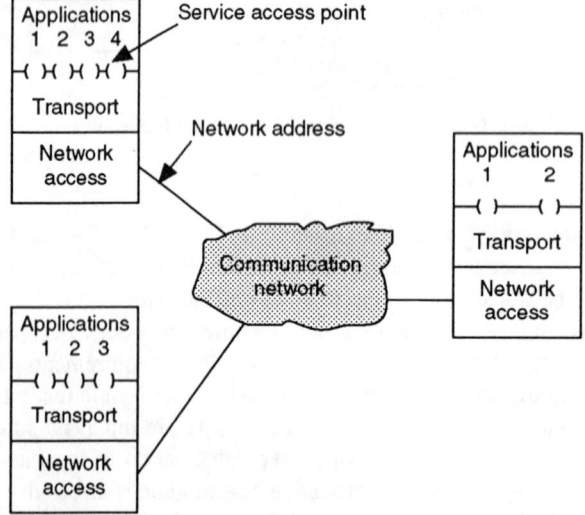

Figure 1-2. Communications architectures and networks.

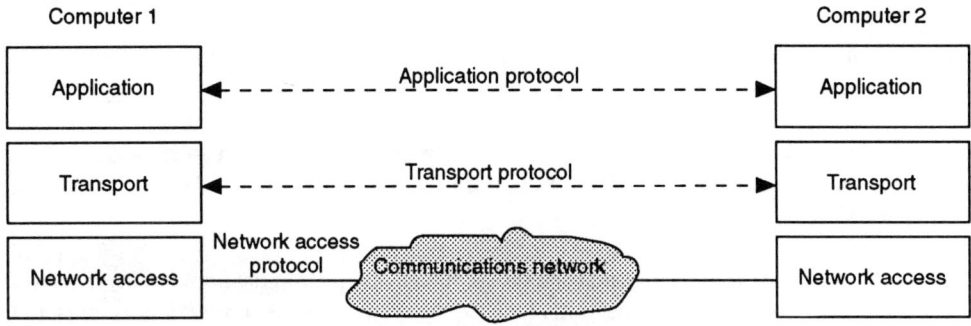

Figure 1-3. Protocols in a simplified architecture.

Each computer contains software at the network access and transport layers, and software at the application layer for one or more applications. For successful communication, every entity in the overall system must have a unique address. Actually, two levels of addressing are needed. Each computer on the network must have a unique network address; this allows the network to deliver data to the proper computer. Each application on a computer must have an address that is unique within that computer; this allows the transport layer to deliver data to the proper application. These latter addresses are known as *service access points* (SAPs), connoting the fact that each application individually accesses the services of the transport layer.

Figure 1-3 shows how modules at the same level on different computers communicate with each other by means of a protocol. A protocol is the set of rules or conventions governing the way in which two entities cooperate to exchange data. A protocol specification details the control functions that may be performed, the formats and control codes used to communicate those functions, and the procedures that the two entities must follow.

Let us trace a simple operation. Suppose that an application, associated with SAP 1 at computer A, wishes to send a message to another application, associated with SAP 2 at computer B. The application at A hands the message over to its transport layer with instructions to send it to SAP 2 on computer B. The transport layer hands the message over to the network access layer, which instructs the network to send the message to computer B. Note that the network need not be told the identity of the destination service access point. All that it needs to know is that the data are intended for computer B.

To control this operation, control information and user data must be transmitted as suggested in Figure 1-4. Let us say that the sending application generates a block of data and passes this to the transport layer. The transport layer may break this block into two smaller pieces to make it more manageable. To each of these pieces the transport layer appends a transport header, containing protocol control information. The combination of data from the next higher layer and control information is known as a protocol data unit (PDU); in this case, it is referred to as a transport protocol data unit. The header in each transport PDU contains control information to be used by the peer transport protocol at computer B. Examples of items that may be stored in this header include:

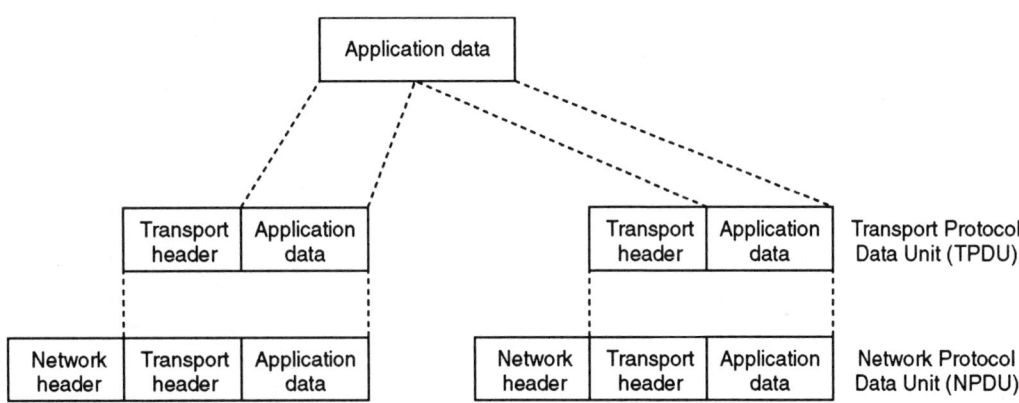

Figure 1-4. Protocol data units.

- *Destination SAP:* When the destination transport layer receives the transport protocol data unit, it must know to whom the data are to be delivered.
- *Sequence number:* Since the transport protocol is sending a sequence of protocol data units, it numbers them sequentially so that if they arrive out of order, the destination transport entity may reorder them.
- *Error-detection code:* The sending transport entity may calculate and insert an error-detecting code so that the receiver can determine if an error has occurred, discard the protocol data unit, and request its retransmission.

The next step is for the transport layer to hand each protocol data unit over to the network layer, with instructions to transmit it to the destination computer. To satisfy this request, the network access protocol must present the data to the network with a request for transmission. As before, this operation requires the use of control information. In this case, the network access protocol appends a network access header to the data it receives from the transport layer, creating a network-access PDU. Examples of the items that may be stored in the header include:

- *Destination computer address:* The network must know to whom (which computer on the network) the data are to be delivered.
- *Facilities requests:* The network access protocol might want the network to make use of certain facilities, such as priority.

Figure 1-5 puts these concepts together and shows the interaction between modules to transfer one block of data. Let us say that the file transfer module in computer X tranfers a file one record at a time to computer Y. Each record is handed over to the transport layer module. We can picture this action as being in the form of a command or procedure call, A-SEND (application-send). The arguments of this procedure call include the destination computer address, the destination service access point, and the record. The transport layer appends the destination service access point and other control information to the record to create a transport PDU. This is then handed down to the network access layer in a T-SEND command. In this case, the arguments for the command are the destination computer address and the transport protocol data unit. The network access layer uses this information to construct a network PDU. Suppose the network is an X.25 packet-switching network. In this case, the network protocol data unit is an X.25 data packet. The transport protocol data unit is the data field of the packet, and the packet header includes the virtual circuit number for a virtual circuit connecting X and Y.

The network accepts the data packet from X and delivers it to Y. The network access module in Y receives the packet, strips off the packet header, and transfers the enclosed transport protocol data unit to X's transport layer module. The

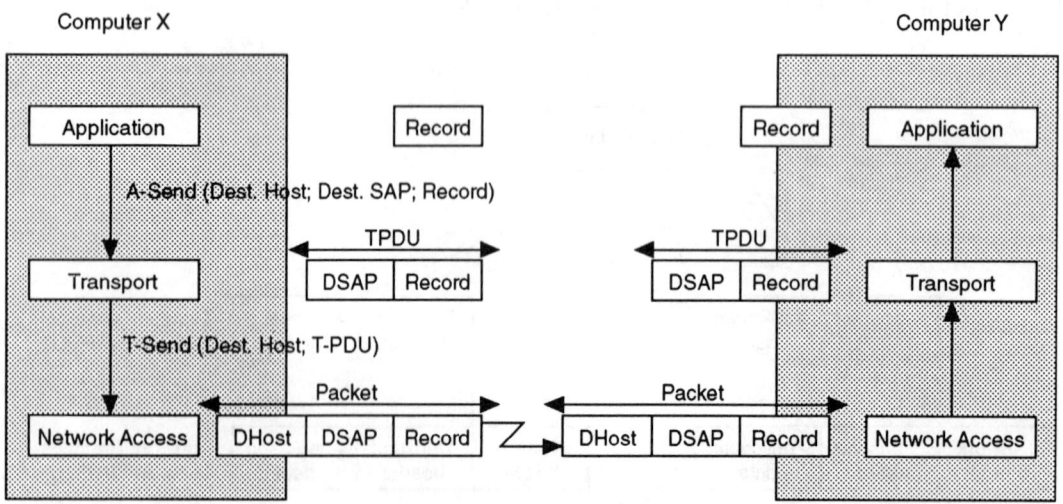

Figure 1-5. Operation of a communications architecture.

transport layer examines the transport protocol data unit header and, on the basis of the SAP field in the header, delivers the enclosed record to the appropriate application, in this case the file transfer module in Y.

This "simple communications architecture" will repay close study. The remainder of this chapter describes a more complex communications architecture that is based on the same principles and mechanisms as the preceding simple communications architecture.

The OSI architecture

When communication is desired among computers from different vendors, the software development effort can be a nightmare. Different vendors use different data formats and data exchange protocols. Even within one vendor's product line, different models of computers may communicate in unique ways.

As the use of computer communications and computer networking proliferates, a one-at-a-time, special-purpose approach to communications software development is too costly to be acceptable. The only alternative is for computer vendors to adopt and implement a common set of conventions. For this to happen, international standards are needed. Such standards would have two benefits:

(1) Wide usage of the standards will encourage more vendors to implement them to keep their products marketable.
(2) Customers will be in a position to require that the standards be implemented by any vendor wishing to propose equipment to them.

This line of reasoning led the International Organization for Standardization (ISO) to develop a communications architecture known as the Open Systems Interconnection (OSI) model. The model is a framework for defining standards for linking heterogeneous computers. The term *open* denotes the ability of any two systems conforming to the architecture and the associated standards to communicate.

The concept of open systems

Open Systems Interconnection is based on the concept of cooperating distributed applications. In the OSI model, a system consists of a computer, all of its software, and any peripheral devices attached to it, including terminals. A distributed application is any activity that involves the exchange of information between two open systems. Examples of such activities include:

- A user at a terminal on one computer logs on to an application such as transaction processing on another computer.
- A file management program on one computer transfers a file to a file management program on another computer.
- A user sends an electronic mail message to a user on another computer.
- A process-control program sends a control signal to a robot.

OSI is concerned with the exchange of information between a pair of open systems and not with the internal functioning of each individual system. Specifically, it is concerned with the capability of systems to cooperate in the exchange of information and in the accomplishment of tasks.

The objective of the OSI effort is to define a set of standards that will enable open systems located anywhere in the world to cooperate by interconnecting through some standardized communications facility and executing standardized OSI protocols.

An open system may be implemented in any way provided that it conforms to a minimal set of standards that allows communication to be achieved with other open systems. An open system consists of a number of applications, an operating system, and system software such as a data base management system and a terminal handling package. It also includes the communications software that turns a closed system into an open system. Different manufacturers will implement open systems in different ways to achieve a product identity that will increase their market share or create a new market. However, virtually all manufacturers are now committed to providing communications software that behaves in conformance with OSI in order to provide their customers with the ability to communicate with other open systems.

The OSI model

The OSI model of computer-communications architecture uses layering, a widely accepted structuring technique that partitions communications functions into a hierarchical set of layers. Each layer performs a related subset of the functions required to communicate with another system. It relies on the next lower layer to perform more primitive functions and to conceal the details of those functions. It provides services to the next higher layer. Ideally, the layers should be defined so that changes in one layer do not require changes in the other layers. Thus we have decomposed one problem into a number of more manageable subproblems.

The task of ISO was to define a set of layers and the services performed by each layer. The partitioning should group functions logically, and should have enough layers to make each layer manageably small, but should not have so many layers that the processing overhead imposed by the collection of layers is burdensome. The resulting OSI architecture has seven layers, which are listed with a brief definition in Table 1-1.

TABLE 1-1. The OSI Layers.

1	*Physical*	Concerned with transmission of unstructured bit stream over physical link; involves such parameters as signal voltage level and bit duration; deals with mechanical, electrical, and procedural characteristics to establish, maintain, and deactivate physical link.
2	*Data Link*	Provides for the reliable transfer of data across the physical link; sends blocks of data (frames) with the necessary synchronization, error control, and flow control.
3	*Network*	Provides upper layers with independence from the data transmission and switching technologies used to connect systems; responsible for establishing, maintaining, and terminating connections.
4	*Transport*	Provides reliable, transparent transfer of data between end points; provides end-to-end error recovery and flow control.
5	*Session*	Provides the control structure for communication between applications; establishes, manages, and terminates connections (sessions) between cooperating applications.
6	*Presentation*	Performs generally useful transformations on data to provide a standardized application interface and to provide common communications services; examples: encryption, text compression, reformatting.
7	*Application*	Provides services to users of the OSI environment; examples: transaction server, file transfer service, network management.

Figure 1-6 illustrates the OSI architecture. Each computer contains the seven layers. Communication is between applications in the two computers, labeled application X and application Y in the figure. If application X wishes to send a message to application Y, it invokes the application layer (layer 7). Layer 7 establishes a peer relationship with layer 7 of the target computer, using a layer-7 protocol (application protocol). This protocol requires services from layer 6, so the two layer-6 entities use a protocol of their own, and so on down to the physical layer, which actually transmits bits over a transmission medium.

The figure also illustrates the way in which the protocols at each layer are realized. When application X has a message to send to application Y, it transfers those data to an application layer module. That module appends an application header to the data; the header contains the control information needed by the peer layer on the other side. The original data plus the header, referred to as an application PDU, is passed as a unit to layer 6. The presentation module treats the whole unit as data and appends its own header. This process continues down through layer 2, which generally adds both a header and a trailer. This layer-2 protocol data unit, usually called a *frame*, is then transmitted by the physical layer onto the transmission medium. When the frame is received by the target computer, the reverse process occurs. As we ascend the layers, each layer strips off the outermost header, acts on the protocol information contained therein, and passes the remainder up to the next layer.

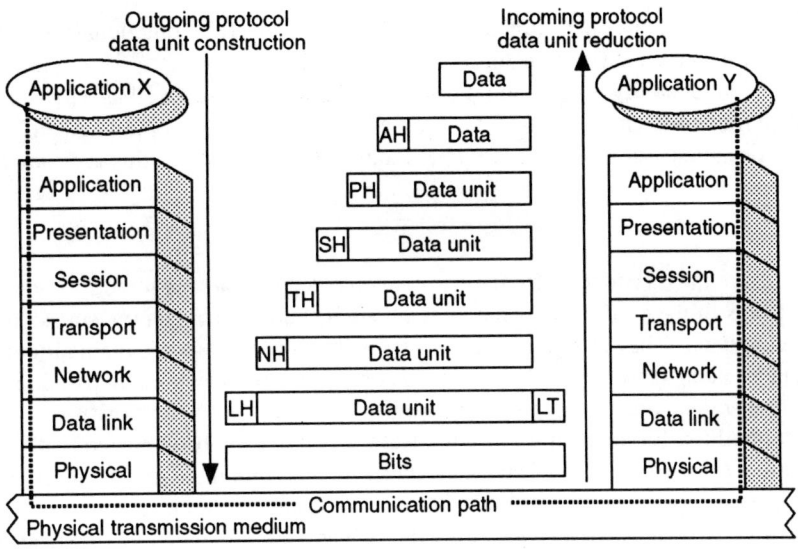

Figure 1-6. The OSI environment.

The OSI layers

The principal motivation for the development of the OSI model was to provide a framework for standardization. Within the model, one or more protocol standards can be developed at each layer. The model defines in general terms the functions to be performed at that layer and facilitates the standards-making process in two ways:

- Since the functions of each layer are well defined, standards can be developed independently and simultaneously for each layer. This speeds up the standards-making process.
- Since the boundaries between layers are well defined, changes in standards in one layer need not affect already existing software in another layer. This makes it easier to introduce new standards.

We now turn to a brief description of each layer and discuss some of the standards that have been developed for each layer.

Physical layer

The physical layer covers the physical interface between a data transmission device and a transmission medium and the rules by which bits are passed from one to another. The physical layer has four important characteristics:

- *Mechanical:* pertains to the point of demarcation. Typically, this is a pluggable connector with a specified number of pins to support a number of signal-carrying wires across the interface.
- *Electrical:* have to do with the voltage levels and timing of voltage changes that define bits. These characteristics determine the data rates and distances that can be achieved.
- *Functional:* specify the functions that are performed by assigning meaning to various wires. For example, one or more circuits may carry data, while others carry control signals.
- *Procedural:* specify the sequence of events for transmitting data, based on the functional characteristics. For example, a control signal from one side may be followed by a companion control signal from the other side.

One of the most common physical interface standards is RS-232-C, and its follow-on version, EIA-232-D. The physical interface to a local area network is specified in a set of standards referred to as ISO 8802.

Data link layer

The physical layer provides only a raw bit stream service. The data link layer attempts to make the physical link reliable and provides the means to activate, maintain, and deactivate the link. The principal service provided by the data link layer to higher layers is that of error detection and control. Thus, with a fully functional data link layer protocol, the next higher layer may assume error-free transmission over the link.

The approach taken to provide reliability is to communicate control information as well as data over the link. Data is transmitted in blocks called frames. Each frame consists of a header, a trailer, and an optional data field. The header and trailer contain control information used to manage the link. Examples of standards at this layer are HDLC, LAPB, LAPD, and LLC.

Network layer

The network layer provides for the transfer of information between computers across some sort of communications network. It relieves higher layers of the need to know anything about the underlying data transmission and switching technologies used to connect systems. The network service is responsible for establishing, maintaining, and terminating connections across the intervening network. At this layer, the computer system engages in a dialogue with the network to specify the destination address and to request certain network facilities, such as priority.

There is a spectrum of possibilities for intervening communications facilities to be managed by the network layer. At one extreme, there is a direct point-to-point link between stations. In this case, there may be no need for a network layer because the data link layer can perform the necessary function of managing the link.

Next, the systems could be connected across a single network, such as a circuit-switching or packet-switching network. As an example, the packet level of the X.25 standard is a network layer standard for this situation. Figure 1-7 shows how the presence of a network affects the OSI architecture. The lower three layers are concerned with attaching to and communicating with the network. The packets (layer 3 protocol data units) that are created by the end system pass through one or more network nodes that act as relays between the two end systems. The network nodes implement layers 1–3 of the architecture. In the figure, two end systems are connected through a single network node. Layer 3 in the node performs a switching and routing function. Within the node, there are two data link layers and two physical layers, corresponding to the links to the two end systems. Each data link (and physical) layer operates independently to provide service to the network layer over its respective link. The upper four layers are "end-to-end" protocols between the attached computers.

At the other extreme, two stations might wish to communicate that are not even connected to the same network; rather, they are connected to networks that directly or indirectly are connected to each other. This case requires the use of some sort of internetworking technique. In essence, packets are still used, but the logic involved includes functions for routing between networks as well as routing within networks.

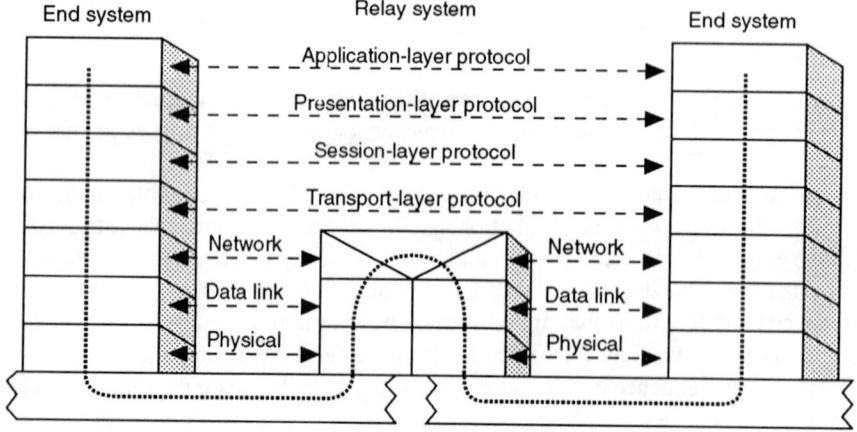

Figure 1-7. The use of a relay

Transport layer

The transport layer provides a reliable mechanism for the exchange of data between computers. It ensures that data are delivered error-free, in sequence, with no losses or duplications. The transport layer may also be concerned with optimizing the use of network services and providing a requested quality of service. For example, the session layer may specify maximum delay, priority, and security features.

The mechanisms used by the transport protocol to provide reliability are very similar to those used by data link control protocols such as HDLC: the use of sequence numbers, error-detecting codes, and retransmission after timeout. The reason for this apparent duplication of effort is that the data link layer only deals with a single, direct link, whereas the transport layer deals with a chain of network nodes and links. Although each link in that chain is reliable because of the use of HDLC, a node along that chain may fail at a critical time. Such a failure will affect data delivery, and it is the transport protocol that addresses this problem.

The size and complexity of a transport protocol depend on how reliable or unreliable the underlying network and network layer services are. Accordingly, ISO has developed a family of five transport protocol standards, each oriented toward a different underlying service.

Session layer

The session layer provides the mechanism for controlling the dialogue between two end systems. In many cases, there will be little or no need for session-layer services, but for some applications, such services are used. The key services provided by the session layer include:

- *Dialogue discipline:* This can be two-way simultaneous (full duplex) or two-way alternate (half duplex).
- *Grouping:* The flow of data can be marked to define groups of data. For example, if a retail store is transmitting sales data to a regional office, the data can be marked to indicate the end of the sales data for each department. This would signal the host computer to finalize running totals for that department and start new running counts for the next department.
- *Recovery:* The session layer can provide a checkpointing mechanism, so that if a failure of some sort occurs between checkpoints, the session entity can retransmit all data since the last checkpoint.

ISO has issued a standard for the session layer that includes those services just described as options.

Presentation layer

The presentation layer defines the format of the data to be exchanged between applications and offers application programs a set of data transformation services. For example, data compression or data encryption could occur at this level.

Application layer

The application layer provides a means for application programs to access the OSI environment. This layer contains management functions and generally useful mechanisms to support distributed applications. In addition, general-purpose applications such as file transfer, electronic mail, and terminal access to remote computers are considered to reside at this layer.

Summary

"Implementing OSI Systems" provides a practical look at the problems of actually using OSI as the basis for communications. The problems of implementing a multilayer protocol architecture and achieving interoperability with other systems are examined. "Performance Modeling of Multi-Layered OSI Communication Architectures" examines the performance implications of OSI.

The next two papers examine issues related to OSI that must be addressed to provide for a full-functioned OSI-based distributed system. "A Network Security Primer" presents the security architecture specified by ISO as an integral part of the OSI architecture. Security requirements and functions are examined. "The Reality of OSI Management" provides an overview of the complex set of standards issued by ISO to specify the network management function in OSI-based systems.

The next two papers present the somewhat different perspective on communications architecture growing out of the ARPANET research. "The DARPA Internet Protocol Suite" defines an architecture and set of protocols that have been standardized by the U.S. Department of Defense, and that have achieved widespread use in commercial as well as military and other government applications. "The Design Philosophy of the DARPA Internet Protocols" is an insightful look at the design approach and the design decisions that resulted in this set of protocols and this architecture.

The final paper looks at a very different sort of communications architecture, one that is used for the internal functioning of a telecommunications network. Thus the protocols are among telecommunications switches and network management centers rather than end user computers. "Relationship of the Signaling System No. 7 Protocol Architecture to the OSI Reference Model" presents the SS7 architecture and describes the protocols at each layer.

Implementing OSI Systems

LIBA SVOBODOVA

Abstract—In order to realize the objectives of OSI, it is necessary to implement the OSI standards on a large variety of real systems. Implementation of complete OSI systems comprising the specified multiple layers of complex protocols is a challenging task. Above all, the implementation must be *correct:* it must conform to the published specifications and interact correctly with its local environment. Second, the implementation should be *efficient:* the communication subsystem should provide low delays and high throughput. Furthermore, the implementers must consider how *general* the implementation ought to be: should it be optimized for a particular usage? Should it be usable in different hardware/software environments? In the framework of these objectives, this paper examines the specification, design, and implementation issues and approaches at two levels: 1) the realization of the individual protocols, and 2) the construction of complete multilayer communication systems.

I. INTRODUCTION

THIS paper deals with the problem of how to implement an OSI communication subsystem, starting from the documents that define the individual protocol layers. Such a communications subsystem, which will be called *OSI system* for short, is a facility composed of all the OSI protocols required to support multiple applications over one or more subnetworks to which the real system is attached. It is assumed that such a facility does not include the OSI specific application services such as MHS (message handling system) or FTAM (file transfer, access and management). An OSI system, in the sense used here, is thus a subsystem of a real open system.[1]

The existence of concrete standards for each of the individual layers does not make the design of an OSI system straightforward. First, more than one kind of service and/or multiple protocols have been defined for most of the layers. The network and transport layers are a well-known case: the ISO network-layer standards permit both connection-mode and connectionless-mode service; the ISO transport-layer standards define five protocol classes to support connection-mode service in different network environments.[2] Furthermore, a particular service and protocol may include a large number of options, in the upper layers, different functional subsets exist. Appropriate choice of the type of service, protocol class, functional units, and options requires not only a thorough understanding of the standards, but also mutual agreement with other implementers. Various users and manufacturer groups, government institutions, and standards organizations around the world are involved in defining the functional groupings and options to be supported in specific environments [2]. The NIST (National Institute of Standards and Technology)[3] Workshop for Implementors of OSI [3] has defined functional standards that form basis of MAP/TOP (Manufacturing Automation Protocol, Technical and Office Protocols) [4] and of U.S. GOSIP (Government Open Systems Interconnection Profile) [5]. In Europe, the functional standards are being defined by ITSTC (Information Technology Common Steering Committee) formed by the CEN/CENELEC (European standards bodies) together with CEPT (Conference of European PTT's), and by EWOS (European Workshop on Open Systems) [6]. In Japan, work on functional standards is done under POSI (Conference for the Promotion of OSI) and INTAP (Interoperability Technology Association for Information Processing) [7]; Japan participates also in OSI Asia-Oceania Workshop (AOW). The functional standards emerging from these different sources are being "internationally harmonized;" a special group was established within ISO to develop such harmonized agreements to International Standardized Profiles (ISP's) [2], [6].

The functional agreements still are, however, far from defining a complete communication architecture. The nature of the interlayer interfaces, the layer management, and overall resource management in an OSI system are a "local implementation matter," which remains to be resolved by the implementers. Moreover, even some protocol mechanisms are not completely specified (for example, generation of acknowledgments), leaving open the possibility of different design choices, with the danger that the choices made in different implementations might be incompatible (see Section III-C).

In summary, correct implementation of OSI systems requires a substantial investment in understanding the standards specifications and assessing the implications of different design choices.

A. What New Implementation Issues are Posed by OSI?

OSI is neither the only nor the first complex layered communication model. The IBM System Network Archi-

---

Manuscript received May 10, 1988; revised March 20, 1989. This paper was presented in part at CIPS '88 (Canadian Information Processing Society), Edmonton, Alta., November 15-17, 1988.

The author is with the IBM Research Division, Zurich Research Laboratory, 8803 Rüschlikon, Switzerland.

IEEE Log Number 8929690.

[1] The OSI Reference Model defines a real open system as "a real system which complies with the requirements of OSI standards in its communication with other real systems" ([1, Section 4.1.2]).

[2] Connectionless service and protocol have also been defined for the transport layer, but the use of connectionless versus connection-mode transport service has not yet become an important argument.

[3] Formerly National Bureau of Standards (NBS).

Reprinted from *IEEE Journal on Selected Areas in Communications,* September 1989, pp. 1115–1130. Copyright © 1989 by The Institute of Electrical and Electronics Engineers, Inc. All rights reserved.

tecture (SNA) [8], [9] and the Internet protocol suite [10], [11] are well-known examples of multilayer protocols, defined long before OSI and implemented on many different systems. In this section, we look briefly at how SNA and the Internet suite are defined, with an attempt to answer the questions: what is different, and what new problems are encountered in implementing OSI?

SNA is a complete architecture, which specifies not only the exact protocols in the individual layers, but also the interlayer interactions as well as the management of the resources needed by the protocols and applications. In fact, the SNA APPC (Advanced Program-to-Program Communication) has been described as a framework for a *distributed operating system*, managing not just the communication resources (sessions) for its users, but also files and I/O devices [9]. SNA is defined by means of a machine-independent unambiguous *meta-implementation* [12], [13], which is being specified in an executable language FAPL [14]. Most of the difficult design issues including how to construct a complete SNA system (called SNA node) are resolved in the meta-implementation; the meta-implementation serves as a reference for actual implementations. The FAPL code is for IBM's internal use only, but all the details necessary to implement an SNA node correctly have been published in so-called structured prose. This contrasts with the OSI specifications that profess to define only those aspects of the services and protocols necessary to ensure correct communication between (independently developed) peer entities.

The Internet suite is significantly simpler than either OSI or SNA. It consists of essentially four layers: Network, Internet, Service protocols (transport service), and applications [11]. The Network layer comprises the physical, link, and (sub)network protocols. The Application protocols incorporate the necessary session and presentation functions. The Internet protocols are specified only informally, but the specifications are concrete in the sense that they already embody the agreement of what must be implemented. Furthermore, very detailed descriptions of implementations of the Internet protocols are widely available (even including the source code); they can serve as guidelines for other implementers [15]. In the OSI arena, the NIST, besides playing a very active role in drawing up the implementation agreements, also issued some implementation guidelines [16]. However, open presentations and analyses of concrete OSI implementations are still rare [17], [18]. The published studies of the commercial products have been limited to the externally observable behavior [19]–[23].

Although both SNA and Internet consist of multiple functional layers, a layer in OSI is defined as a concept on its own (Fig. 1). The layer abstraction not only provides a unified framework for defining the specific services and protocols, but also appears to be the basic building block of an OSI system, with the Service Access Point (SAP) as the basic mechanism for tying the layers together. It seems natural to carry the regular conceptual architecture defined by the OSI Reference Model [1] into

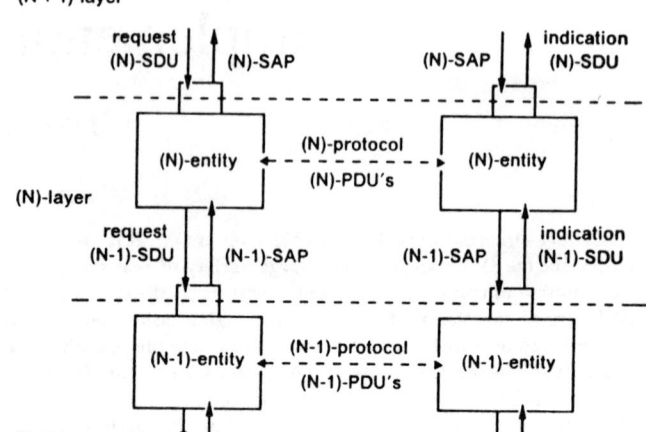

Fig. 1. OSI concept of a layer and interlayer communication.

the real system, in fact, to provide a special kind of operating system environment that would facilitate "plugging in" the individual layers with different combinations of protocols [24]. However, an OSI system can be structured in many different ways, such as by grouping layers in a way similar to the Internet model.

Overall, the problems encountered in the design and implementation of OSI systems are not fundamentally new. It is the number of distinct, separately specified layers the OSI implementers have to deal with, the amount of the "local implementation matter" in each layer that needs to be resolved in an implementation, and the sometimes ambiguous nature of the specifications that make a correct and efficient implementation of an OSI system a difficult task. Formal specifications (see Section II) should remove the ambiguities, but OSI standards will remain "implementation-independent." Implementers starting from the specifications of the standards have to develop their own detailed specifications of an OSI *system*. But, since many of the system-level issues are independent of the actual protocols used, OSI implementers can benefit from the experiences gained in designing detailed specifications for and implementing other kinds of communication systems.

B. General Implementation Considerations

The introductory discussion has brought up two aspects of "implementing OSI:" the realization of the individual selected protocols, and the construction of a complete multilayer communication system. Besides *correctness*, the main issues governing the implementation at both of these levels are *efficiency* and *generality*, and their trade-offs.

OSI, and layered communication models in general, are frequently criticized as having implicit performance drawbacks. Each layer represents an added overhead. First, each layer has its own peer protocol, which usually generates additional control messages not directly related to the communication at the application level. Second, each layer has to construct appropriate message headers on the sending side, and analyze these headers on the receiving side. Last, but not least, the interlayer interfaces can have a significant impact on performance. It is a true challenge to implement a high-performance multilayer communication system.

The generality considerations are twofold. The first consideration is whether the implementation must be able to support diverse applications and networks, or whether it can be optimized for some *a priori* restricted usage, for example, to operate only in a single local-area network or to support only a particular sort of application. Such tailoring may be particularly important for small systems such as personal computers [25]. The other consideration is *portability* of the communication subsystem or even *reusability* of the individual protocol layers in different environments.

The efficiency and generality considerations must not jeopardize the *conformance* of the implementation to agreed-upon standards. Here the issue is correct interpretation of the specifications and correct realization of the specifications in a specific hardware/software environment. To ensure correct interpretation, the best solution would be to derive the code for the target system from the specification in an automated or at least semi-automated way. This would be also the most natural way to achieve reusability.

The rest of the paper will address these points. Section II discusses the use of formal specification methods and the feasibility of automated derivation of implementations from the formal specifications. The following two sections concentrate on various design details not resolved in the standard specifications, with emphasis on the efficiency of the implementation: Section III deals primarily with the implementation and use of various mechanisms found in protocols, Section IV addresses the issues concerning construction of a multilayer communication system. Section V presents concluding remarks.

II. From Specification to Implementation

In general, the OSI standards for each individual layer or, more broadly, for each service, are presented in two documents: the service definition and the protocol specification. These documents consist of an informal description of the functions, definitions of variables, predicates and actions, and of state tables representing the service and protocol in the form of extended finite-state machines. These are *universal* specifications that define only those aspects that must be satisfied by all implementations in order to be able to communicate. Additional aspects that allow different implementation choices may be explicitly pointed out in these specifications as so-called *local implementation matter*, but no suggestion on how to resolve them is included. The universal specifications of the individual layers must be refined to a comprehensive *design* specification that includes the layer-specific local implementation matter as well as the aspects concerning how these layers are to form a well-functioning system together. One approach is to aim this design specification directly at a precise real system environment. However, when implementations on more than one real system are anticipated, it is advantageous to produce first a design specification that is still independent of the real environment; the SNA meta-implementation belongs to this category [12], [13]. The first step, however, is to comprehend the universal specifications. The informal text of the present OSI specifications is often imprecise or even incomplete; [26] provides an illustrative example.

A. Development of Formal Specifications

The ISO Formal Description Techniques (FDT's) LOTOS [27], [28] and Estelle [29]–[31] are becoming stable, and in the future, OSI standards are expected to be specified using these techniques. In fact, draft specifications in LOTOS and/or Estelle have already been produced for a variety of OSI services and protocols [28], [31]. The CCITT formal description technique, SDL [32], [33], already in wide use, is another strong candidate as an FDT for OSI standards. So, the natural question is, how will the availability of formal specifications impact implementations of OSI systems?

The primary role of formal specifications is to provide a precise and definitive reference that prevents different interpretations and consequently incompatible implementations. In the spirit of OSI, the main requirement set for the ISO formal description techniques is to allow *implementation-independent* specifications of OSI services and protocols [34].[4] However, producing specifications that do not suggest any implementation choices is not an easy task. In general, some internal structure and a form of interactions with the environment have to be assumed in the specification expressed in an FDT; both have implementation connotations. Such implementation connotations in a specification are not just a result of how an FDT is applied, but stem from the FDT itself; several illuminating examples comparing specifications of different mechanisms in Estelle and LOTOS can be found in [36]. In particular, some of the Estelle features have been criticized as being too implementation oriented, thus leading to overspecifications [36], [37]. On the other hand, these implementation-oriented features are still too weak to produce a real implementation [16], [37]. It seems that more work is needed to find the optimal specification constructs and style for producing truly universal specifications [37]–[41].

An important issue studied by the FDT working groups concerns the precise definition of the basic architectural concepts and their reflection in FDT's, referred to as the *architectural semantics* [42]. In the pursuit of implementation-independent definitions, the OSI Reference Model

---

[4]SDL was developed with a rather different objective: the standardization of interfaces between organizations; the implementation-independent representation was only a secondary goal [35].

[1] fails to define clearly the fundamental architectural concepts such as SAP (Service Access Point) and CEP (Connection End Point). This presents a problem for those attempting to formally specify layer services and inter-layer interactions as well as for the implementers; in fact, the specific difficulties highlighted in the context of experiments with FDT's [36], [37] also represent the main difficulties encountered by the implementers. However, precise architectural semantics for the basic OSI concepts alone will not solve the problem of how to construct a complete OSI *system*. First, it remains necessary to select or design specific means for realizing these still abstract mechanisms in a given system environment. Second, the universal specifications have to be extended to include management of the internal resources and other supervisory functions necessary for effective operation of a complete OSI system.

B. Automated Generation of Implementations

Automated derivation of an actual implementation from a formal specification would not only ensure that the implementation does indeed conform to the specification but also speed up the implementation process. However, there are still many problems to be solved before such an automated implementation process becomes widely feasible.

Thus far, automated generation of executable code from protocol specifications has focused on a single layer [13], [24], [43]–[50]. The interfaces to the surrounding environment have always been hand-coded. The hand-coded part, which usually includes the generation and analysis of PDU's (Protocol Data Units), can amount to more than 50 percent of the total code. However, some of the hand-coded support could be reused for other layers, that is, become part of the common run-time support.

For real products, the efficiency of implementations generated directly from specifications must be close to what could be achieved by careful design and coding for a specific system environment. Comparative studies of automatically-generated versus hand-coded implementations of the OSI transport protocols confirmed that the hand-coded implementations are both smaller and faster [46]–[48], but the automatically-generated code was found to be better structured, easier to maintain, and highly portable [48]. Smith and West [13] described a successful product code generation from the SNA meta-implementation. No comparative study with hand-coded implementation was made, but the path-length and size of the generated code were found acceptable.

These results are encouraging, but more work is needed to increase the proportion and efficiency of the implementation that can be generated directly from the specifications. The former requires that more details, including assumptions about the environment, be incorporated into the formal specifications of the communication entities. In order to keep the specifications independent of the idiosyncrasies of any particular real systems, a possible approach is to specify a *generic environment* that a given class of real systems is expected to support. Of course, when such a required environment is defined, it is necessary to implement its support on the real systems. How much can be saved on the implementation effort compared to working with less complete specifications that have to be interfaced on case-by-case basis to the real environment will depend on the degree of mismatch between required and real environments [13]. On the other hand, the specification of an environment well-suited for layered communication software can also drive a design of a real environment to support it. This is one of the objectives of the programming infrastructure projects of the RACE program [51].

Finally, let us look at the tools needed for the design and implementation process. Tools to aid in systematic stepwise refinement are needed to progress from the universal OSI specification to detailed specifications. To produce efficient implementations, optimizing compilers for the FDT's are clearly needed. Sets of tools for both Estelle and LOTOS have been developed. For Estelle, this includes compilers that produce code in an intermediate language (mainly C) [31], [52]. For LOTOS, a collection of tools called LIW (LOTOS Implementation Workbench) exists [28], [53]. LIW supports interactive refinement by transformations performed on the LOTOS specifications, and by so-called annotations that define functions difficult to express in LOTOS; annotations are mapped directly into program fragments in the C language. A true compiler for LOTOS is a long-term project. Another possible way to aid in deriving implementations from LOTOS specifications is to convert the LOTOS behavioral expressions into a finite-state machine form, which could be then expressed in Estelle or any common procedural language [54].

High-quality tools are fundamental to working with formal specifications, but tools alone will not produce high-quality implementations. How the various local implementation matter is handled in the detailed design specifications remains important; this subject is treated in the following sections.

III. IMPLEMENTATION AND USE OF PROTOCOL FUNCTIONS AND MECHANISMS

This section focuses on efficient implementation of the basic protocol functions and effective use of various protocol mechanisms. Efficiency on an implementation is a combination of the number of instructions it takes to execute the different protocol functions, the number of messages needed to transfer a given amount and type of information, and the various delays due to imperfect synchronization between the peer entities. Optimizations along these lines are mostly protocol-dependent: they concern implementation options and layer management functions allowed by the universal specifications (local implementation matter). However, some implementation issues are common to essentially all communication protocols: the representation of the protocol "logic," and composition and decomposition of protocol data units.

It should be emphasized that this section does not attempt to define which issues should be resolved in the formal specifications, and how. Its objective is to highlight where implementation choices must be made and the implications of particular choices; this may concern the universal specifications, refined design specifications, runtime support, or very specific optimizations for a particular system environment.

Section III-A discusses implementation of the basic elements of communication protocols. Section III-B looks at the impact of the various mappings between service data units and protocol data units. Section III-C addresses the protocol-specific optimizations in the lower layers, with focus on the Class 4 transport protocol. Section III-D discusses connection establishment and management throughout the layers.

A. Basic Elements of Communication Protocols

A protocol consists of procedural rules for dialogue and precisely defined formats for each type of protocol data unit (PDU) that can be used within the protocol. The procedural rules (protocol logic) are usually expressed and implemented as one or a set of cooperating finite-state machines (FSM's). Thus, it desirable to have suitable mechanisms in the source language to represent FSM's as well as an efficient implementation of these mechanisms in the real environment. The PDU's consist of a header and (possibly) a data part, which comes from or has to be delivered to the next higher layer. The header has to be properly constructed on the sending side and analyzed on the receiving side. We will now look at the possible implementations of these two basic parts of communication protocols.

1) Representation of FSM's: In the official semi-formal OSI specifications, the finite-state machines are represented by state tables that have a form of a matrix of the type *event × state*. For each possible combination of an event and a state, additional conditions may be specified in form of predicates, and, for each condition, the actions to be taken and the next state. Estelle provides special constructs for defining finite-state machine transitions with the enabling conditions and associated actions [29]–[31]. In FAPL, an FSM is a special type of procedure; in its body, the FSM transitions are represented in a state-table form [14]. Similarly, a state-table form could be used in a hand-coded implementation in a common programming language, or derived from another formal form [44]. A more common implementation approach, however, is to express the states and transitions directly in code, using nested select statements to identify the state/event combination, or even using explicit branches to move to the next state [24]. The coded FSM's tend to run faster, since the state-table form is a data structure that has to be interpreted. However, experiments in automated generation of protocol code demonstrated that representing FSM's as data not only might require much less storage than a coded representation, but may even be better in the execution time [55]. The ultimate representation form and efficiency also depend on the compiler for the implementation language, or the intermediate language used when starting from formal specifications.

2) Composition and Decomposition of Protocol Headers: In an actual implementation, the (N)-entity, that is, the active element of the (N)-layer in a given system, must compose outgoing (N)-PDU's and decompose and analyze the incoming (N)-PDU's. An (N)-PDU consists of the (N)-PCI (Protocol Control Information) and possibly of $(N+1)$-user-data. The (N)-PCI, usually called the header, consists of several fields of different lengths, where the exact number of fields may depend on the type of (N)-PDU and the options in effect.

Processing of headers can be time consuming, especially on the receiving side [56]. Possible optimizations consist of using partially prefilled header templates [25], [57] or even various hints on what is the most likely header for the next PDU [58]. Furthermore, it is desirable to check the consistency and content of the header as early as possible, to avoid wasting processor cycles on working with PDU's that will have to be discarded anyway. Specifically, the checks that are independent of the current state of the receiver should be performed before the respective FSM has been located and scheduled to run. The separation into state-independent and state-dependent checks can be defined in the universal formal specification of the protocol. Use of header templates and predictions are very specific optimizations that have to be done by hand.

Hardware support for composing and decomposing headers and checking the individual fields could be very valuable. Krishnakumar *et al.* describe a design of an experimental VLSI chip for assembling and disassembling PDU's, customizable for different protocols [59]. The customizing is driven by a formal specification of the PCI structure for the particular protocol. This component can check whether the structure of the PDU is correct (number of fields, field lengths), and calculate the checksum, when supported. However, checking the content of the individual fields is more involved, since it relates to the semantics of the protocol.

In the application layer, the PDU's, including the header, are described in ASN.1 (Abstract Syntax Notation One) [60] as a collection of built-in and defined data types. The presentation layer is responsible for the encoding and decoding between the local representation of the data types described by the abstract syntax and the *transfer syntax* [61], which defines a globally unique bit-level representation for each data type, suitable for transmission over a network. The processing of protocol headers of application layer protocols is thus more involved; automated tools are needed to handle the translations [62]–[65]. Thus far, the efficiency of such translators has received only limited attention [65].

B. Mapping Between SDU's and PDU's

The unit of information to be transferred between $(N+1)$-entities via (N)-service is called the (N)-ser-

vice-data-unit, or (N)-SDU. In the simplest case, the whole (N)-SDU fits into the user data field on the (N)-PDU, and (N)-PDU's map one-to-one into (N−1)-SDU's. However, the relationship between these three data units can be more complex. The OSI Reference Model defines three mappings:
- segmenting/reassembling, where one (N)-SDU is mapped into multiple (N)-PDU's;
- blocking/deblocking, where multiple (N)-SDU's are mapped into a single (N)-PDU;
- concatenation/separation, where multiple (N)-PDU's are mapped into a single (N−1)-SDU.

In general, blocking and concatenation improve performance: they reduce the number of (N−1)-SDU's needed to transfer the (N)-SDU's and various control (N)-PDU's and consequently the processing overhead in layers (N−1) and below. Segmentation, however, has been shown to degrade performance [17], [20], [21], [66]-[69]. First, segmentation can cause fragmentation. Assume the worst case where (N)-SDU is only one byte larger than the user data field of the (N)-PDU: unless segments from consecutive (N)-SDU's can be mixed in the same (N)-PDU (not included in the mappings defined by the OSI Reference Model), every second (N)-PDU will carry only one byte of data! Clearly, the performance will suffer; see, for example, the measurements reported in [20] and [21]. Second, segmentation has important consequences for buffer management; this problem will be discussed in more detail in Section IV-B. Segmentation can be avoided by restricting the size of SDU's, that is, by making the service less general; this "solution" only pushes the problem up to the higher layers, and ultimately to the applications. Thus, to minimize constraints on the applications, segmentation needs to be supported in the lower layers, but it is desirable to perform it at most once per application SDU. In OSI, segmentation may be performed in the session, transport, and network layers. A careful *system* design is needed to avoid segmentation in all three layers.

Concatenation is defined in the transport and session layers, but when to use it is not included in the specifications.

C. Implementation Issues and Options in the Transport Service

The OSI Reference Model defines the purpose of the transport service in the following way. "The transport service provides transparent transfer of data between session entities and relieves them from any concern with the detailed way in which reliable and cost effective transfer of data is achieved" [1, Section 7.4.2]. The transport service [70] has to provide efficient support to many different applications in many different network environments, be it single subnetworks or concatenated subnetworks of different capacity, delays, and reliability. Furthermore, the transport service should ensure an optimal level of performance with respect to the actual processing capacities of sender and receiver. The flow and error-control procedures in the data-link, network, and transport protocols that together provide the transport service are the basic mechanisms for achieving these goals. Actual implementation of these mechanisms and the values of their control parameters have an important impact on throughput and delays of transport connections, and consequently on the quality of service provided to the applications. Thus, an efficient implementation of the transport service is of utmost importance.

In the following, we will focus on the OSI transport protocol class 4 (TP4) [71] or, more specifically, on the data transfer phase of TP4. The combination of TP4 and CLNS (Connectionless Network Service [72], [73]) was chosen for MAP/TOP [4] and U.S. GOSIP [5], and endorsed by the NIST Workshop for the Implementors of OSI for general communication between private systems [3]. This combination is similar to the widely supported TCP/IP of the Internet suite [74], [75]. Thus, the experience with operating TCP/IP protocols in different networks can be utilized in implementing TP4/CLNS. A comparison of TP4 and TCP can be found in [17], [76]-[78].

TP4 is called the "error detection and recovery class." TP4 makes no assumptions about the reliability of the underlying network service; it provides its own mechanisms to handle lost, duplicated, out-of-sequence, and corrupted TPDU's (Transport Protocol Data Units). Sequence numbers in TPDU's are used to detect the second and third type of errors, a checksum to detect corrupted TPDU's. The receiver discards duplicated and corrupted TPDU's; corrupted TPDU's thus turn into lost TPDU's. Lost TPDU's must be retransmitted. A TPDU is assumed to have been lost if the sender does not receive an appropriate response from the receiver within a certain time, measured by a retransmission timer set by the sender. For a DT-TPDU (data TPDU), the response required is an AK-TPDU (acknowledgment TPDU) bearing a higher sequence number than that DT-TPDU. At the same time, AK-TPDU's are used also for flow control: the sequence number in the AK-TPDU determines the lower edge of the sender's transmit window, the credit value in the AK-TPDU determines the current window size and thus the upper window edge. The sender is allowed to transmit only DT-TPDU's with sequence numbers within this window. The receiver can completely close the window by issuing an AK-TPDU with zero credit, and reopen it later using another AK-TPDU. Since AK-TPDU's may get lost, TP4 also includes procedures for retransmitting AK-TPDU's. However, the universal specification of TP4 [71] still leaves considerable freedom in how to implement and use the basic mechanisms.

The use of AK-TPDU's is one area where implementation optimizations are possible. An AK-TPDU bearing sequence number k acknowledges all DT-TPDU's with sequence numbers $k − 1$ and lower sent on that particular connection. Thus, it is not necessary to generate an explicit acknowledgment for every DT-TPDU received; as long as DT-TPDU's are received in sequence, the receiver can "accumulate" acknowledgments for several DT-TPDU's, that is, generate an AK-TPDU only for every nth DT-TPDU, where $1 < n \leq w$ and w is the window size. In many networks, acknowledgment accumulation (also called acknowledgment withholding) can improve throughput significantly [17], [68], [79]; however, in networks subject to congestion, frequent acknowledgments are very important.

Another implementation optimization concerns the management of timers. In principle, a retransmission timer needs to be associated with each DT-TPDU[5] transmitted. In an implementation, one timer can be used to protect several sequentially transmitted DT-TPDU's; in particular, it is possible to use only one retransmission timer per transport connection. This reduces the number of timers that need to be maintained, and thus the cost of setting and canceling timers [17], [80], [81]. However, when a single retransmission timer is "shared" by several DT-TPDU's, it is difficult to set its value optimally; this issue is discussed in more detail below. Efficient schemes for managing a large number of timers have been developed; such a timer facility, especially when realized in hardware [81], would make sharing of retransmission timers unnecessary.

When a retransmission timer expires, the sending entity must resend the oldest but it can resend all unacknowledged DT-TPDU's that are within the current transmit window.[6] In particular, when several DT-TPDU's are protected by the same timer, the simplest course of action is to resend the subset. When the receiving entity receives a DT-TPDU with a higher sequence number than expected, it can store such an out-of-sequence DT-TPDU internally until it receives the missing DT-TPDU (to the transport service user, the data must be passed in the correct sequence), or discard it on the assumption that the expected DT-TPDU has been lost and that both it and the higher-numbered DT-TPDU's will be retransmitted. The latter strategy may reduce the amount of buffer space needed in the receiver and simplify the handling of DT-TPDU's. However, when the sending entity uses the "oldest-TPDU-only" retransmission strategy, the higher-numbered DT-TPDU's would not have to be retransmitted if they were not discarded by the receiver. Furthermore, they will be retransmitted only when *their* timer expires, which may cause unnecessary delays. Thus, the optimizations made in one implementation may be countered by the choices made in another implementation. Furthermore, the "best" choice depends on the characteristics of the network environment. In a single LAN, the combination of "retransmit all/retain out-of-sequence DT-TPDU's" was found to yield the best throughput [79].

[5]In fact, a retransmission timer needs to be associated with any TPDU that requires some sort of response from the peer entity.
[6]The transmit window could have been reduced by the receiver after all or some of the unacknowledged DT-TPDU's were transmitted. The retransmission of those DT-TPDU's that are outside of the current window can take place only after the sender has received a new, sufficiently large, credit from the receiver.

However, in a congested network, the "retransmit all" strategy is very bad, even when the receiver does not retain out-of-sequence DT-TPDU's.

In order to minimize the delay needed to resynchronize after a loss of a DT-TDPU, the optimal value of the retransmission timer should not be much longer than the time needed to send and process a DT-TPDU and generate and receive the corresponding AK-TPDU. The DT-TPDU/AK-TPDU roundtrip delay includes the queueing delays in the sending and receiving nodes, and network delays in both directions. Both these components and thus the optimal values for the retransmission timers are subject to load variations. The timers could be set to a value sufficiently large to make false retransmissions unlikely even in high-load situations, but this could make recovery from lost DT-TPDU's rather inefficient. An alternative approach is to dynamically adjust the timer value to the situation. The TCP specification includes a procedure for calculating the value of the retransmission timer from an estimate of the current roundtrip delay; this estimate is calculated cumulatively from the observed roundtrip delays [74]. The NIST Implementation Agreements for OSI Protocols recommend the same procedure [3]. However, such a procedure has to be used with caution. When a DT-TPDU is retransmitted, it is not possible to measure correctly the corresponding roundtrip delay; specifically, when the sender finally receives an acknowledgment for a DT-TPDU that has been retransmitted one or more times, it cannot determine which instance of that DT-TPDU triggered that acknowledgment. Depending on how the round-trip delay is measured in such a case, the roundtrip delay estimate may diverge either to too large or too small values; both are likely to cause severe performance degradations [82]-[85].[7] Improved algorithms for calculating the retransmission timer value are reported in [84] and [85].

Tuning the retransmission timer to the current roundtrip delay is not sufficient to ensure optimal performance in complex networks. Another important mechanism is dynamic adjustment of the transmit window [85]. The TP4 specification includes only a mechanism by which the *receiver* can control the sender's transmit window; this mechanism, the credit value in the AK-TPDU, reflects only the available resources and processing capability of the receiver. The adjustment to the varying load and occasional congestion in the network must be handled by the *sender*. Such a procedure has been applied in TCP, with very good results [85]. This sort of control of the transmit window by the sender does not require any support from the peer entity; thus, it can be considered a local implementation matter, and included in any TP4 implementation.

Besides the retransmission timer, several other timers drive the flow-control and error-recovery mechanisms of

[7]Acknowledgment accumulation by the receiver also interferes with correct measurements of the roundtrip delay, but its effect is not as serious as the problem just described.

TP4: the persistence timer, the window timer, and the inactivity timer. Inappropriate setting of these timers may cause not only performance degradation, but could also make it impossible to maintain a connection with another implementation. In particular, the latter problem may arise when the window timer value used in one implementation is longer than the inactivity timer value used by the peer. A solution to this problem is described in the NIST agreements [3].

The final point concerning TP4 is the calculation of the optional checksum, which is the principal mechanism for detecting corrupted TPDU's. Severe performance degradation has been reported with the straightforward implementation of the algorithm presented in the ISO standard [17], [23]. Efficient algorithms for different classes of processor are presented in [86] and [87]. Clearly, such optimizations will remain a local implementation matter.

D. Connection Management

One of the frequently criticized aspects of OSI is the necessity to establish an explicit connection at each individual layer (unless, of course, the layer provides a connectionless-mode service). Two (N)-PDU's are needed to convey the (N)-CONNECT request and (N)-CONNECT confirm that establish an (N) connection; cascaded over several layers, this may become an important overhead. However, this problem has been recognized and mechanisms exist to minimize this overhead. In the lower layers up to the transport layer, connections can be reused. In the upper layers, there is one-to-one mapping between the association at the application layer and the presentation and session connections, and they are established simultaneously: the ASSOCIATE request is embedded in the user data field of the *P*-CONNECT request, which is carried in the user data field of the *S*-CONNECT request; the confirmation is handled in the same fashion. Thus, only two messages need be exchanged on an existing transport connection to establish an application-level association.

Let us now look at the connection management in the lower layers. In the case of connection-mode network service, two or more transport connections can be multiplexed onto a single network connection (supported by the transport protocol classes 2, 3, and 4), or a single transport connection can be mapped onto two or more network connections (with the transport protocol class 4 only). A new network connection must be established for a new transport connection if no network connection exists to the destination node or if the existing network connections to the destination node are not sufficient to support the quality of service required by the new and the existing transport connections. A separate Network Connection Management Subprotocol has been defined as an addendum to the transport protocol standard to facilitate flexible assignment and reassignment of transport connections to network connections [88]. However, the actual *policy* when to share, retain, and reuse network connections to provide the quality of service required by the transport connections is not specified; such a policy has to take into consideration also the pricing policy for establishing and maintaining network connections in a particular network.

Finally, while a transport connection cannot be multiplexed among multiple-session connections, it does not have to be released when the current session connection terminates, and thus a new session connection could be associated with it later, provided that it does not require a different quality of service. The ability to reuse a transport connection can be quite important, especially if application associations are of short duration. The session protocol specification includes a procedure for retaining a transport connection after termination of the current session connection, but the actual algorithm when to retain and reuse a transport connection in a particular environment is again left to the implementers.

Another aspect of connection management in the association of (N)-SDU's and (N)-PDU's to the appropriate (N)-connections within the (N)-entity. An (N)-connection is uniquely identified by a pair of (N)-SAP, (N)-CEP (Service Access Point, Connection End Point). This connection reference is used to find the context in which the (N)-SDU or (N)-PDU received by the (N)-entity is to be processed. There are various ways to represent a connection within a layer entity, and various ways to maintain the set of the active connection contexts (see also Section IV-A). One of the simplest ways is to represent a connection by a control block, and link the control blocks together. A more efficient approach is to use the connection reference as an index to an array of control blocks; since the references can be rather large, it may be necessary to apply first some hashing function. It has been demonstrated that an additional performance improvement can be realized when the (N)-entity caches the control block of the (N)-connection identified by the most recently received (N)-PDU on the assumption that the next (N)-PDU will belong to the same (N)-connection; even in case of a shared server, a surprisingly high hit ratio has been observed [58].

IV. System Design Issues

We will now turn our attention to the *system design* issues, that is, issues concerning design of a multilayer communication subsystem for a specific hardware/software environment. Such a subsystem can run on the same processor as the applications or be confined to a front-end processor. In the former case, it can be embedded in the operating system kernel, or implemented as one or several user-level processes. In fact, these approaches are frequently combined: the lower layers are implemented in the kernel or on a front-end processor, the upper layers run in a user process, sometimes together with the actual application. A discussion of the advantages and disadvantages of these approaches can be found in [16] and [56]. Here we shall focus on the internal structure of such a subsystem.

Section IV-A discusses the relationship between layer entities and processes, and the possible realizations of the different models in common multiprocessing operating systems. Section IV-B focuses on the passing of data between layer entities and the underlying buffer management.

A. Layer Entities Versus Processes

The OSI Reference Model prescribes *functional* layering, but does not prescribe that individual layer entities must be distinct modules in the implementation, and that a clean service interface be provided for each layer. Hence, for performance reasons, it may be preferable to tie two or more layer entities together in a single module. However, a concrete service interface for each layer may be required for *conformance testing* [89], [90]. Multilayer testing, which allows "black-box" testing of several layers together, is still an unsolved problem. Furthermore, when a layer entity is implemented as a well-defined module, it is possible to change the protocol implementation or even the protocol itself (provided that the new protocol realizes the same service) without impact on the users. We assume that each layer entity is to be implemented as a distinct module, and will investigate how these modules relate to processes.

There are two basic models of how to use processes to implement a multilayer communication system: we will call them a *server* model and an *activity-thread* model. In the server model, each (N)-entity consists of a single process or multiple processes (a process cluster); the layer entities communicate via messages. In the activity-thread model, a process is not associated with a specific layer, but is used as a general "worker" to process an incoming or outgoing request through several layers; the interlayer communication has a form of procedure calls. In these models, a process is essentially a thread of execution; in discussing how these models can be realized, a process is a unit for processor scheduling administered by the operating system.

1) Server model: There are essentially two types of server model: a multiprocess server with a distinct process per connection, and a single-process server which handles concurrent connections with additional internal mechanisms. In the multiprocess server, a process may be created and destroyed with the connection, or the server may contain a fixed number of processes, each of which can be assigned to at most one connection at a time. In both cases, some mechanism such as a permanent supervisor process is needed to accept CONNECT requests and indications, and to create or assign a connection process to handle the newly established connection (Fig. 2). This type of server is often used at the specification level [16], [24], [91]. The single-process server model is often used in implementations [18], [43], [46]–[48].[8]

---
[8]Another possible type of server is a multiprocess server where any process can handle any request belonging to any connection, but such a server does not present any advantages from either the specification or implementation point of view.

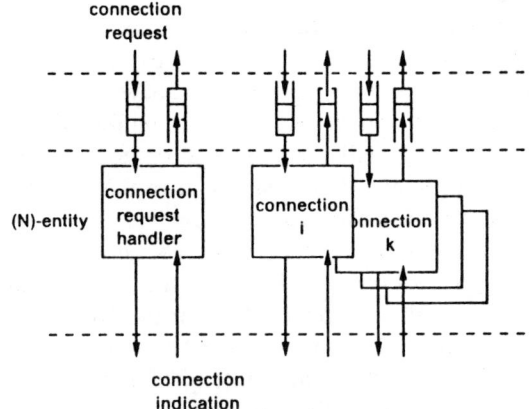

Fig. 2. Multiprocess server model.

The interlayer communication, that is, the communication between servers for adjacent layers, can be either asynchronous or synchronous. Asynchronous communication of the (N)-entity with the $(N+1)$-entity and $(N-1)$-entity is usually modeled by paired (input/output) message queues. The multiprocess server model usually assumes a pair of queues per connection in each direction. However, the way in which the interlayer communication takes place in an actual implementation depends on the interprocess communication (IPC) facilities offered by the programming language used and the local operating system. For example, when a process may have only a single input queue (port), additional procedures are needed to sort out the queued messages according to the layer they come from (above or below), and to associate them with the correct connection.

Asynchronous interfaces pose two problems: interlayer flow control and atomic execution of certain events. Interlayer flow control between $(N+1)$-entity and (N)-entity is a necessary complement of the *peer* flow control in the (N)-layer (that is, in the (N)-protocol) or some layer below. It prevents the $(N+1)$-entity from generating requests to the (N)-entity faster than the (N)-entity can dispose of them, and similarly for the indications from the (N)-entity to the $(N+1)$-entity. An effective interlayer flow control can be achieved through the use of direct *finite* input queues for each (N)-connection, one queue for the requests from the $(N+1)$-entity, the other for the indications from the $(N-1)$-entity. The process representing an (N)-connection may have to stop sending (N)-PDU's because of the (N)-protocol flow control or because the input queue for the $(N-1)$-connection to which this (N)-connection is mapped is full; at this point, the process can stop receiving from its input queue serving the $(N+1)$-entity. Thus, this so-called back-pressure propagates effectively to the application layer. The other direction is similar. In the case where the input queues are unlimited or where a single input queue is used for multiple connections, additional interface primitives are needed that, similar to flow control procedures found in lower level protocols (transport, network, and data link), convey the credit available to the source, that is, the number of requests/indications or the amount of data a layer entity or a connection process can queue for another layer entity or connection process. Such an explicit interlayer flow control can be very complex. Another possible solution is to control interlayer flow via buffer allocation. $(N+1)$-connection will have only a limited amount of send buffers in which it can pass data to the (N)-entity; the (N)-entity must eventually return the buffers, but it can delay this step until after the contents have been successfully passed to the $(N-1)$-entity. In the other direction, the (N)-entity can queue data for the $(N+1)$-entity only in the buffers provided by the $(N+1)$-entity. This approach effectively simulates finite queues. Concrete implementations of both of these techniques are presented in [18].

The second problem posed by asynchronous interfaces can be demonstrated by an example of a disconnected request. According to the specification, the initiator of a disconnect request can assume that once the request has been executed, the respective connection no longer exists. However, it is not sufficient to assume that a disconnect request issued in the $(N+1)$-entity has been fully executed once it has been placed in the input queue of the (N)-entity, since there may still be outstanding messages for this connection queued in the opposite direction. The possible solutions to this problem again are discussed in [18].

Synchronous interlayer communication provides a natural solution of both problems discussed above, but limits potential concurrency. Especially, it is not suitable for a single-process server.

The general concern with the server model is the number of context switches that need to be performed in the course of sending and receiving messages on behalf of the applications. In most operating systems, interprocess communication represents significantly higher overhead than procedure calls. Another problem is the overall process scheduling strategy. Assume a situation in which processes are assigned static priorities according to the layer: the lower the layer, the higher the priority. The (N)-entity, in processing a single (N)-SDU, may generate several $(N-1)$-SDU's. If each $(N-1)$-SDU is passed immediately to the $(N-1)$-entity, it will trigger a chain of process switches until that $(N-1)$-SDU has been passed to the physical network attachment, and eventually a switch back to the (N)-entity process to generate the next $(N-1)$-SDU. One possible approach to avoid this sort of switching is to pass the whole set of outputs in a single atomic step, but such a feature usually is not supported by IPC mechanisms. Better, scheduling should not be based on some fixed priority of individual processes, but on the importance of the events they must handle. In other words, the dispatching priority of a process should be determined dynamically, according to the most important event waiting to be handled by this and other eligible processes. Again, this may not be possible to realize in a general-purpose multiprocessing operating system.

2) Activity-Thread Model: The simplest form of the activity-thread model is a synchronous execution of a user request or an incoming network message through all the relevant intermediate layers, one such activity at a time. This form has been used in systems lacking efficient multitasking facilities. Several years ago, Clark suggested a new structuring method based on two concepts: multitask modules and upcalls [92]. A protocol layer implemented as a multitask module is basically a collection of subroutines that may be executed concurrently by several tasks (processes). The processing of an incoming or outgoing message through multiple layers is handled, as far as possible, within a single process (Fig. 3). The interlayer communication takes the form of procedure calls. There are two types of interlayer calls: an *upcall*, which is a call from the (N)-entity to the $(N+1)$-entity, and *downcalls* from the $(N+1)$-entity to the (N)-entity. Downcalls are used primarily as "arming" calls, to indicate to the (N)-entity that a certain service is desired, for example, that the $(N+1)$-entity has data to send. When the (N)-entity is ready to peform the service, it will obtain the data via an upcall to the entry within the $(N+1)$-layer specified in the previous downcall. The objective of this upcall-downcall paradigm is to match the natural flow of control in the system. In addition, the upcall mechanism can be used to receive specific information about the $(N + 1)$-layer that might assist the (N)-layer in optimizing its behavior. An operating system kernel called Swift was designed to support this structuring method [92]. Swift implements preemptive priority scheduling where the priority of a process changes dynamically, depending on the importance of its task, expressed in terms of deadline. An experiment with different realizations of upcalls in another environment is described in [93].

The structuring approach described above has yielded encouraging results, but programming with upcalls poses many problems. The activity-thread model, however, can be developed into a clean software-engineering method. BASE, the OSI implementation environment described in [24], supports interlayer communication through structured control blocks representing SAP's and CEP's. Both downward and upward communications between layers are handled in the same way: the originating layer prepares a work request and associates it with the appropriate SAP/CEP. The target layer will eventually be called by BASE to process the work request. Once a given work request has been processed, the layer returns control to BASE. The thread of related requests generated by a work request from either end (application or network) or some intermediate layer (e.g., an acknowledgment) is executed in a synchronous manner. BASE supports multiple concurrent threads. On the whole, BASE provides the layers with the necessary operating system services in a way independent of the native operating system; thus, the porting of such a communication system to different operating system environments reduces to the porting of BASE.

3) Binding Between Layer Entities: In the OSI Reference Model, communication between the $(N + 1)$-entity and the (N)-entity is defined to occur at a specific

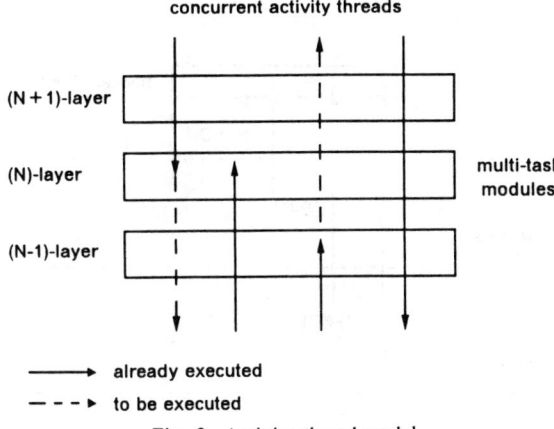

Fig. 3. Activity-thread model.

(N)-SAP. Several (N)-SAP's may be defined for a single (N)-entity, and an ($N+1$)-entity can use more than one (N)-SAP. However, only a single ($N+1$)-entity can be attached to a specific (N)-SAP; the (N)-SAP *address* thus identifies the ($N+1$)-entity attached to that (N)-SAP. Several (N)-connections can be established through a particular (N)-SAP. Each (N)-connection is represented by an (N)-CEP, associated with that (N)-SAP; an (N)-CEP has an identifier unique with the (N)-SAP. The (N)-SAP address and (N)-CEP-identifier together uniquely identify the (N)-connection within both the (N)-entity and the ($N+1$)-entity.

In both the OSI Reference Model and the ISO standards for the individual layers, SAP and CEP are defined only as conceptual rather than architectural elements. How SAP's and CEP's are realized depends on the process model chosen and the nature of the interprocess communication mechanism. In all cases, it is necessary to decide how SAP addresses and CEP identifiers are to be assigned and used to bind the service provider and the service user. In particular, (N)-CEP identifiers need to be assigned for (N)-CONNECT requests originating from the ($N+1$)-entity as well as for (N)-CONNECT indications generated by the (N)-entity in response to a remote(N)-CONNECT request. Since requests and indications for different connections at the same (N)-SAP can occur simultaneously, some mechanism is needed to ensure that the same identifier is not assigned more than once. This problem can be solved without a common id manager by using *pairs* of identifiers, one of which is assigned by the service provider, the other by the user. Finally, additional interface primitives to *register* and *deregister* an ($N+1$)-entity at a specific(N)-SAP are useful for setting up the binding between layers [16].

4) Use of the Different Models: The multiprocess server model with separate input/output channels per connection provides the cleanest structural model of a layer and interlayer communication. As mentioned earlier, this model is often used in the layer specification. In order to support this model efficiently, the interprocess communication and process scheduling need to be designed with the behavior and requirements of multilayer communication systems in mind. Usually, this model is converted into a single-server model in the implementation step: the connection processes become procedures called by a supervisor component which now also handles all communication with the surrounding layers [43], [46]–[48]. This supervisor component is written by hand. In fact, the very same approach can be used to generate layer entities for the activity-thread model [24]. The conversion could be facilitated further if the interlayer communication were specified in a more implementation-independent way, which brings us back to the need to define SAP and CEP as precise architectural elements. The functional port-class concept presented in [94] could be the right foundation.

It should also be pointed out that the server model and activity-thread model can be combined in the same system. Specifically, the activity-thread model is better suited for the upper layers than the server model: there is no need for asynchronous interfaces between the session, presentation, and application layers. The structure of the application layer, however, can be quite complex [95]. A particular application may require several different Application Service Elements (ASE's); in fact, an application may use different types of application associations, where each type consists of a different subset of ASE's. Each application association is modeled by a distinct SAO (Single Association Object), within which the multiple ASE's are coordinated by SACF (Single Association Control Function). Furthermore, the application layer includes the concept of MACF (Multiple Association Coordination Function) for coordinating related activities on several application associations. Configuration of SAO's for specific applications and realization of MACF are still open questions [96].

B. Buffer Allocation and Management

In principle, buffers are needed to hold SDU's passed across a service interface,[9] and to construct outgoing and process incoming PDU's within a protocol entity. In Section III-B, we discussed different mappings between SDU's and PDU's: an (N)-entity may have to perform segmentation and reassembly when the (N)-SDU's are too large; it may use blocking/deblocking when (N)-SDU's are too small, or concatenation/separation to mix different small (N)-PDU's in a single ($N-1$)-SDU. In all three cases, an (N)-PDU is fully contained within an ($N-1$)-SDU. Thus, for each (N)-layer, it is sufficient to provide only buffers suitable to hold($N-1$)-SDU's.

The main issues concerning buffer allocation and management are: 1) how to pass buffers between layers, 2) whether to use a single consecutive buffer or a structure consisting of several buffer elements, and 3) how to manage the buffer pool.

---

[9]In fact, the unit of information transferred across an (N)-SAP in single interaction is the (N)-interface-data-unit, which may contain the whole or only part of an (N)-SDU. For simplicity, we will not elaborate on the latter case.

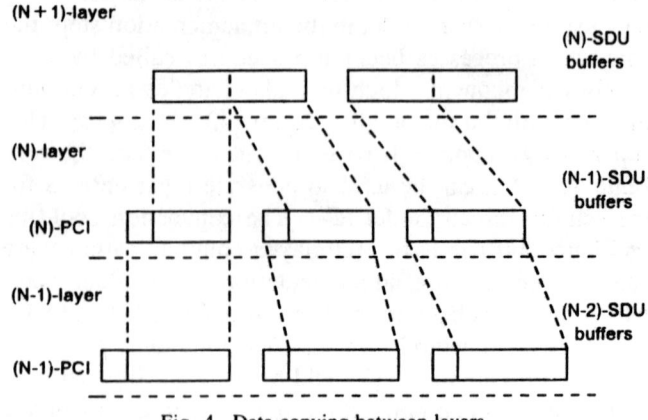

Fig. 4. Data copying between layers.

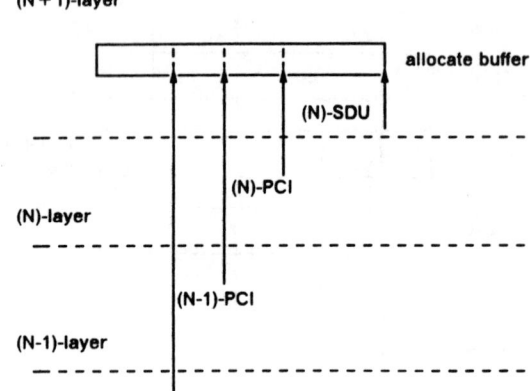

Fig. 5. Buffer passing between layers with off-setting.

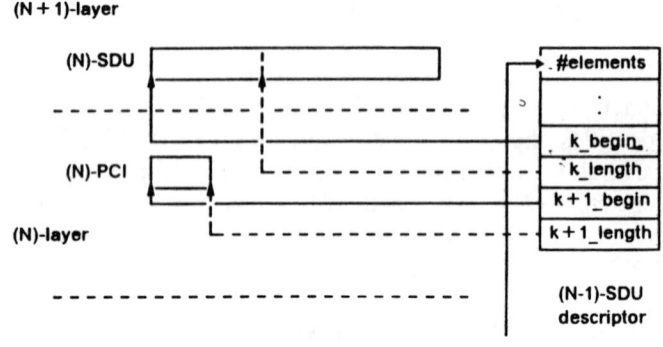

Fig. 6. Use of noncontiguous buffer elements.

The most straightforward approach to buffer management is to provide a distinct buffer pool in each layer and to copy (N)-SDU's from the $(N+1)$-layer buffers to the (N)-layer buffers, and vice versa. All three mappings between SDU's and PDU's can be supported in this way; Fig. 4 illustrates SDU copying with segmentation. This approach also makes the individual layers independent of each other, which is an important prerequisite for portability of the individual layer entities.

Copying data to and from buffers between protocol layers in general represents significant overhead [66], [67], [97]; it has been one of the most widely publicized "don'ts" in the design of multilayer communication systems. An alternative is to pass (N)-SDU's between the $(N+1)$-layer and the (N)-layer by reference, provided the respective protocol entities have access to common memory. However, implementation of the various mappings, in particular, of segmentation, becomes much more complicated.

Consider first the simplest case in which, for every layer, an (N)-SDU is always mapped into a single unique (N)-PDU. For outbound traffic, the (N)-entity only needs to prefix the appropriate (N)-PCI (header) to each (N)-SDU passed to it by the $(N+1)$-entity; for inbound traffic, it has to remove the (N)-PCI from the $(N-1)$-SDU passed to it by the $(N-1)$-entity. This can be accomplished in two ways: by off-setting or by a gather/scatter technique. To use the off-setting approach, the buffers must be large enough to hold the highest layer SDU plus the headers of all the lower layers. (The highest layer is not always the application layer; this scheme has to accommodate also the various control PDU's of lower layer protocols.) An (N)-entity is passed a pointer to the proper location in the buffer where it should put or where it finds the (N)-PCI; the application entity gets a pointer to where it should put its data (Fig. 5). However, this approach may not work well in the situations where somewhere along the path the data must be aligned on a certain address boundary (e.g., page boundary).[10]

The other approach is to construct the individual headers in separate (noncontiguous) buffers. An $(N-1)$-SDU is then represented by a descriptor containing pointers to the original data and the headers added by each layer above and including the (N)-layer (Fig. 6). Ultimately, these elements must be "gathered" together into one physical SDU at the transmission time, but this can happen earlier, for example, between the main processor and the network attachment device. For incoming messages, separation of the headers from the data by "scattering," the reverse of "gathering," is more difficult if at all possible, since the size of the individual headers and thus the beginning of the actual data are not known at the network attachment point; only the (N)-layer can determine what part of a given $(N-1)$-SDU represents the (N)-PCI.[11]

The gather/scatter technique can also be used for a rather different purpose, namely, to simplify memory allocation for buffers. Rather than supporting contiguous buffers of many different sizes, it is a frequent practice to use small buffers of the same size and chain them together as needed [66], [67], [97]. In this usage, the gather/scatter technique works well in both directions.

Let us now look at the case when an (N)-layer per-

---

[10] A desired alignment can be achieved with the gather/scatter technique, or when the headers are *appended* to the end of the data; the TCP protocol includes such an option [67].

[11] A possible albeit nonstandard solution is to insert a special mark between the data and the headers when the network attachment device gathers its SDU. This mark is then used by the receiving network attachment to channel the headers and the data to separate buffers [98].

forms segmentation and reassembly of (N)-SDU's. For the outbound direction, the individual (N)-SDU segments can either be copied into separate buffers with enough space for the headers of the (N)-layer and below, or the "gathering" approach can be used to pull out these segments directly from the buffer holding the (N)-SDU. To reassemble a segmented (N)-SDU, it might be best to copy the segments into an $(N+1)$-layer buffer of suitable size, especially when the application expects its SDU in a contiguous block of memory. An alternative solution would be to use off-setting to separate the headers of the (N)-layer and below, and then chain the segments of the (N)-SDU together. The possible solutions avoiding copying become substantially more complicated when segmentation and reassembly must be supported in more than one layer. In the end, copying might be more efficient than operations on complex structures of noncontiguous buffer elements.

When data are passed between layers in global buffers, it is necessary to develop procedures for proper deallocation of the buffers. In most cases, a buffer allocated by one layer will find its final use in another layer. A buffer allocated for a PDU received from the network can be deallocated once the application data have been copied into the allocation buffers. In the opposite direction, however, the situation is more complicated. Once the content of a buffer has been transferred into the network adapter, the buffer cannot be deallocated if some higher layer might need to retransmit the PDU contained in that buffer.

A well-designed set of procedures for constructing (N)-PDU's (and further $(N-1)$-SDU's) from (N)-SDU's and reclaiming (N)-SDU's from (N)-PDU's that hide the actual mapping of the (N)-SDU's and (N)-PDU's into physical buffers is needed to ensure that all layers perform these operations consistently. Such an abstraction is also necessary to make the layer entities portable between environments that put different constraints on buffer sizes and buffer sharing.

The final point on buffer management to be discussed here is the allocation of buffers to connections. The amount of buffer space available to a connection impacts the achievable throughput on that connection [17], [19]. So, the first question is how much buffer space is needed for optimal performance. The required amount of buffer space can either be reserved per connection, or allocated from a common pool as required. The common pool approach can save on the total buffer space, but is more complex. Next, buffer allocation needs to be tied to both interlayer flow control and peer flow control between the sending and receiving nodes. Moreover, to prevent deadlocks, the (N)-entity should always be able to send and receive certain control (N)-PDU's. For example, a transport entity implementing the class 4 protocol should be able to receive an acknowledgment at any time, and especially when it has many unacknowledged DT-TPDU's that tie up most of its data buffers, since it cannot release any of these buffers until the respective TPDU's have been acknowledged. When buffers are to be shared between layers, the buffer-allocation scheme has to be designed with great care, both to prevent deadlocks and to ensure equitable allocation of buffers to the different activities in the whole multilayer system.

The various aspects of buffer management discussed above have been studied in many different contexts, but a comprehensive model of their interactions in a multilayer system is still missing.

V. Concluding Remarks

Implementation of a complete OSI system is a difficult undertaking. The published standards specify the protocols for the individual layers in detail, but deliberately avoid guidelines on how to construct a complete multilayer system. Although the problems encountered in the design and implementation of an OSI system are not fundamentally new compared to other multilayer communication models, the number of distinct, separately specified layers combined with the implementation-independent and sometimes ambiguous nature of the specifications make it a very complex task.

This paper examined many different aspects concerning implementation of individual protocols and construction of multilayer OSI systems, but no claim is made that this exposition is exhaustive. First, very little attention has been given to the implementation issues specific to the application layer, specifically, to the configuration and coordination of multiple application service elements for different applications. However, the work in this area is not yet sufficiently advanced. Second, the overall management of network and system resources has been treated only superficially. It is not sufficient to optimize performance on a single connection; the whole system must be well balanced to be able to provide the performance required by many diverse applications. This is possibly the most difficult implementation issue.

The final remark pertains to conformance and compatibility of different implementations. Precise formal specifications and tools facilitating automated derivation of code for the target system would not only speed up implementation process, but also ensure that the implementations conform to the specification. However, full interoperability is a more complicated issue; it requires not just correct implementation of those protocol features that have been included in the universal specifications, but also compatible choices concerning some of the "local implementation matters."

Acknowledgment

I would like to acknowledge the intangible but essential contributions of many colleagues from our laboratory who made me aware of and helped me understand some of the implementation issues discussed in this paper. Special recognition is due to D. Gantenbein, R. Hauser, E. Mumprecht, and A. Wittmann, who designed and implemented an OSI transport service in two different operating system environments, and in the course exposed various shortcomings in the relevant standards and the influence of the real environment on the design of a multilayer communication system.

References

[1] "Information processing systems—Open systems interconnection—basic reference model," International Organization for Standardization, International Standard ISO 7498.
[2] B. Wood, "Standards for OSI—Present status, future plans," *Telecommunications*, pp. 32–36, Mar. 1988.
[3] "Stable Implementation agreements for open systems interconnection protocols," Version 1, Ed. 2, U.S. Dept. of Commerce, National Bureau of Standards, Gaithersburg, MD, May 1988.
[4] V. C. Jones, *MAP/TOP Networking*. New York: McGraw-Hill, 1988.
[5] S. M. Radack, "US government moves toward implementing OSI standards," *IEEE Computer Mag.*, vol. 21, no. 6, pp. 82–83, June 1988.
[6] *The Open Systems Newsletter*, vol. 1, no. 9, Nov. 1987, Technology Appraisals Ltd., U.K., pp. 1–13.
[7] Y. Maruyama, "Current status and future plans of the development of implementation specifications in INTAP," in *Proc. 2nd Int. Symp. Interoperable Inform. Syst.*, Tokyo, Japan, Nov. 1988, pp. 37–44.
[8] R. J. Sundstrom and G. D. Schult, "The SNA's first six years," in *Proc. Fifth Int. Conf. Comput. Commun.*, Atlanta, GA, Oct. 1980, pp. 578–585.
[9] J. P. Gray, P. J. Hansen, P. Holman, M. A. Lerner, and M. Pozefsky, "Advanced program-to-program communication in SNA," *IBM Syst. J.*, vol. 22, no. 4, pp. 298–318, 1983.
[10] J. Reynolds and J. Postel, "Official Internet protocols," Network Inform. Center RFC 1011, SRI International, Menlo Park, CA, May 1987.
[11] B. M. Leiner, R. Cole, J. Postel, and D. Mills, "The DARPA Internet protocol suite," *IEEE Commun. Mag.*, vol. 23, pp. 29–34, Mar. 1985.
[12] G. D. Schultz, D. B. Rose, C. W. West, and J. P. Gray, "Executable description and validation of SNA," *IEEE Trans. Commun.*, vol. COM-28, pp. 661–677, Apr. 1980.
[13] F. D. Smith and C. H. West, "Technologies for network architecture and implementation," *IBM J. Res. Develop.*, vol. 27, pp. 68–78, Jan. 1983.
[14] S. C. Nash, "Format and protocol language (FAPL)," *Comput. Networks ISDN Syst.*, vol. 14, no. 1, pp. 61–77, 1987.
[15] C. Kline, "Supercomputers on the Internet: A case study," in *Proc. ACM SICCOMM'87 Workshop*, Stowe, VT, Aug. 1987; *ACM Comp. Commun. Rev.*, vol. 17, no. 5, Special Issue, pp. 27–33.
[16] W. McCoy, K. Mills, and R. Collela, "Implementation guide for ISO transport protocols," ICST/SN85-18, U.S. Dept. of Commerce, National Bureau of Standards, Gaithersburg, MD, Dec. 1985.
[17] A. Bricker, L. Landweber, T. Lebeck, and M. Vernon, "ISO transport protocol experiments," MTR-8600002, MITRE Corp., McLean, VA, Jan. 1986.
[18] D. Gantenbein, R. Hauser, and E. Mumprecht, "Implementation of the OSI transport service in a heterogeneous environment," in *HECTOR, Vol. II: Basic Projects*, G. Krüger and G. Müller, Eds. Berlin, Germany: Springer-Verlag, 1988, pp. 215–241.
[19] A. Aronoff, K. Mills, and M. Wheatley, "Transport layer performance tools and measurement," *IEEE Network*, vol. 1, no. 3, pp. 21–31, July 1987.
[20] S. Heatley and D. Stokesberry, "Measurement of a transport implementation over an IEEE 802.3 local area network," in *Proc. IEEE Computer Networking Symp.*, Washington, Apr. 1988, pp. 34–43.
[21] W. T. Strayer and A. C. Weaver, "Performance measurement of data transfer services in MAP," Comput. Sci. Rep. TR-88-04, Univ. of Virginia, Charlottesville, VA, Feb. 1988.
[22] —, "Performance measurements of Motorola's implementation of MAP," in *Proc. 13th Local Comput. Networks Conf.*, Minneapolis, MN, Oct. 1988. Also Comput. Sci. Rep. TR-88-17, Univ. of Virginia, Charlottesville, VA, July 1988.
[23] W. T. Strayer, M. Mitchell, and A. C. Weaver, "ISO protocol performance measurements," in *Proc. Int. Symp. on Mini- and Microcomput.*, Miami Beach, FL, Dec. 1988.
[24] A. Fleischmann, S. T. Chin, and W. Effelsberg, "Specification and implementation of an ISO session layer," *IBM Syst. J.*, vol. 26, no. 3, pp. 255–275, 1987.
[25] J. H. Saltzer, D. D. Clark, J. L. Romkey, and W. L. Gramlich, "The desktop computer as network participant" *IEEE J. Select. Areas Commun.*, vol. SAC-3, no. 3, pp. 468–478, May 1985.
[26] F. Caneschi, "Hints for the interpretation of the ISO session layer," *ACM SIGCOMM Comput. Commun. Rev.*, vol. 16, no. 4, pp. 34–72, July/Aug. 1986.
[27] T. Bolognesi and E. Brinksma, "Introduction to the ISO specification language LOTOS," *Comput. Newtworks ISDN Syst.*, vol. 14, no. 1, pp. 25–59, 1987.
[28] P. H. J. van Eijk, C. A. Vissers, and M. Diaz, Eds., *The Formal Description Technique LOTOS*. Amsterdam, The Netherlands: North-Holland, (Elsevier Science Publishers B.V.), 1989.
[29] S. Budkowski and P. Dembinski, "An introduction to Estelle: A specification language for distributed systems," *Comput. Networks ISDN Syst.*, vol. 14, no. 1, pp. 3–23, 1987.
[30] R. L. Linn, "The features and facilities of Estelle," in *Protocol Specification, Testing, and Verification*, V. M. Diaz, Ed. Amsterdam, The Netherlands: North-Holland (Elsevier Science Publishers B.V.), 1986, pp. 271–297.
[31] M. Diaz, J.-P. Ansart, J.-P. Courtiat, P. Anzema, and V. Chari, Eds. *The Formal Description Technique Estelle*. Amsterdam, The Netherlands: North-Holland, (Elsevier Science Publishers B.V.), 1989.
[32] "Course on SDL: The CCITT specification and description language," in *Proc. 7th IFIP Int. Symp. Protocol Specification, Testing and Verification* (Tutorial Notes), Zurich, Switzerland, May 1987.
[33] R. Saracco and P. A. J. Tilanus, "CCITT SDL: Overview of the language and its applications," *Comput. Networks ISDN Syst.*, vol. 13, no. 2, pp. 65–74, 1987.
[34] C. Vissers, "Standardization of formal description techniques for communication protocols," in *Information Processing 86*, H.-J. Kugler, Ed. Amsterdam, The Netherlands: Elsevier Science, 1986, pp. 321–328.
[35] R. Saracco, "Standardization of formal description techniques for communication protocols," in *Information Processing 86*. H.-J. Kugler, Ed. Amsterdam, The Netherlands: Elsevier Science, 1986, pp. 329–333.
[36] C. A. Vissers and G. Scollo, "Formal specification in OSI," in *Networking in Open Systems*, Lecture Notes in Computer Science, 248, G. Müller and R. P. Blanc, Eds. Berlin, Germany: Springer-Verlag, 1987, pp. 338–372.
[37] J.-P. Courtiat, "How could Estelle become a better FDT?" in *Protocol Specification, Testing, and Verification, VII*, H. Rudin and C. H. West, Eds. Amsterdam, The Netherlands: North-Holland, (Elsevier Science Publishers B.V.), 1987, pp. 43–60.
[38] —, "Estelle*: A powerful dialect of Estelle for OSI protocol description," *Protocol Specification, Testing, and Verification, VIII*. S. Aggarwal and K. Sabnani, Eds. Amsterdam, The Netherlands: North-Holland (Elsevier Science Publishers B.V.), 1988, pp. 171–186.
[39] P. D. Amer, A. Pridor, and J. Schmidt, "Expansion of transitions in Estelle formal specifications," in *Protocol Specification, Testing, and Verification, VIII*, S. Aggarwal and K. Sabnani, Eds. Amsterdam, The Netherlands: North-Holland (Elsevier Science Publishers B.V.), 1988, pp. 159–170.
[40] J. Quemada and A. Fernandez, "Introduction of quantitative relative time into LOTOS," in *Protocol Specification, Testing, and Verification, VII.*, H. Rudin and C. H. West, Eds. Amsterdam, The Netherlands: North-Holland (Elsevier Science Publishers B.V.), 1987, pp. 105–122.
[41] G. J. Leduc, "The intertwining of data types and processes in LOTOS," in *Protocol Specification, Testing, and Verification, VII*. H. Rudin and C. H. West, Eds. Amsterdam, The Netherlands: North-Holland (Elsevier Science Publishers B.V.), 1987, pp. 123–136.
[42] K. J. Turner, "An architectural semantics for LOTOS," in *Protocol Specification, Testing, and Verification, VII*, H. Rudin and C. H. West, Eds. Amsterdam, The Netherlands: North-Holland (Elsevier Science Publishers B.V.), 1987, pp. 15–28.
[43] T. P. Blumer and R. L. Tenney, "A formal specification technique and implementation method for protocols," *Comput. Networks* vol. 6, pp. 201–217, July 1982.
[44] T. P. Blumer and D. S. Sidhu, "Mechanical verification and automatic implementation of communication protocols," *IEEE Trans. Software Eng.*, vol. SE-12, pp. 827–843, Aug. 1986.
[45] S. C. Nash, "Automated implementation and SNA communication

protocols," in *Proc. Int. Conf. Commun.*, Boston, MA, June 1983, pp. 1316-1322.

[46] J.-M. Serre, E. Cerny, and G. V. Bochmann, "A methodology for implementing high level communication protocols," in *Proc. 19th Hawaii Int. Conf. Syst. Sci.*, Hawaii, Jan. 1986, pp. 744-754.

[47] G. v. Bochmann, G. Gerbert, and J. M. Serre, "Semiautomatic implementation of communication protocols," *IEEE Trans. Software Eng.*, vol. SE-13, pp. 989-999, Sept. 1987.

[48] S. T. Vuong, A. C. Lau, and R. I. Chan, "A semiautomatic implementation of protocols using an Estelle-C compiler," *IEEE Trans. Software Eng.*, vol. 14, no. 3, pp. 384-393, Mar. 1988.

[49] R. J. Linn, Jr., "Testing to assure interworking of implementations of ISO/OSI protocols," *Comput. Networks ISDN Syst.*, vol. 11, no. 4, pp. 277-286, Apr. 1986.

[50] C. H. West, "A validation of the OSI session layer protocol," *Comput. Networks ISDN Syst.*, vol. 11, no. 3, pp. 173-182, Mar. 1986.

[51] The SPECS Consortium and J. Bruijning, "Evaluation and integration of specification languages," *Comput. Networks ISDN Syst.*, vol. 13, no. 2, pp. 75-89, 1987.

[52] S. T. Vuong, R. I. Chan, and W. Y. L. Chan, "An Estelle-C compiler for automatic protocol implementation," in *Protocol Specification, Testing, and Verification, VIII*, S. Aggarwal and K. Sabnani, Eds. Amsterdam, The Netherlands: North-Holland (Elsevier Science Publishers B.V.), 1988, pp. 387-398.

[53] J. A. Mañas and H. v. Thienen, "The implementation of a specification language for OSI systems," in *Proc. 1988 Int. Zurich Seminar Digital Commun.*, Zurich, Switzerland, Mar. 1988, pp. 103-107.

[54] G. Karjoth, "Implementing process algebra specifications by state machines," in *Protocol Specification, Testing, and Verification, VIII*, S. Aggarwal and K. Sabnani, Eds. Amsterdam, The Netherlands: North-Holland (Elsevier Science Publishers B.V.), 1988, pp. 47-60.

[55] A. Fleischman, "PASS—The parallel activity specification scheme," Tech. Rep. 43.8715, IBM European Networking Center, Heidelberg, West Germany, 1988.

[56] D. Clark, "Modularity and efficiency in protocol implementation," *Internet Protocol Implementation Guide*, Network Information Center, SRI International, Menlo Park, CA, Aug. 1982.

[57] P. Sjödin, "Optimizing protocol implementations for performance—A case study," SICS R87009, Swedish Instit. of Comput. Science, Spånga, Sweden, 1987.

[58] D. D. Clark, V. Jakobson, J. Romkey, and H. Salwen, "An analysis of TCP processing overhead," *IEEE Commun. Mag.*, vol. 27, no. 6, June 1989 (in press).

[59] A. S. Krishnakumar, B. Krishnamurthy, and K. Sabnani, "Translation of formal protocol specifications to VLSI design," in *Protocol Specification, Testing, and Verification, VII*, H. Rudin and C. H. West, Eds. Amsterdam, The Netherlands: North-Holland (Elsevier Science Publishers B.V.), 1987, pp. 375-390.

[60] Information Processing Systems—Open Systems Interconnection—Specification of Abstract Syntax Notation One (ASN.1), International Organization for Standardization, International Standard ISO 8824.

[61] Information Processing Systems—Open Systems Interconnection—Specification of Basic Encoding Rules for Abstract Syntax Notation One (ASN.1), International Organization for Standardization, International Standard ISO 8825.

[62] C. Cleghorn, S. Gallouzi, and H. Ural, "On the use of invertible execution of ASN.1 encoding rules," in *Proc. CIPS'87*, Edmonton, Alta., Canada, Nov. 1987, pp. 289-294.

[63] F. Caneschi and E. Merelli, "An architecture for an ASN.1 encoder/decoder," *Comput. Networks ISDN Syst.*, vol. 14, no. 2-5 (Special Issue, *Conf. Commun. and Data Commun.*), pp. 297-303, 1987.

[64] M. Bever and M. Zimmermann, "Data translation in heterogeneous computer networks," Tech. Rep. 43.8806, IBM European Networking Center, Heidelberg, West Germany, 1988.

[65] T. Nakawaji, K. Katsuyama, N. Miyauchi, and T. Mizuno, "Development and evaluation of APRICOT (tools for abstract syntax notation one)," in *Proc. 2nd Int. Symp. Interoperable Inform. Syst.*, Tokyo, Japan, Nov. 1988, pp. 55-62.

[66] L.-P. Cabrera, E. Hunter, M. J. Karels, and D. A. Mosher, "User-process communication performance in networks of computers," *IEEE Trans. Software Eng.*, vol. 14, no. 1, pp. 38-53, Jan. 1988.

[67] L.-P. Cabrera, "Improving network subsystem performance in a distributed environment. A Berkeley Unix case study," Res. Rep. RJ5719, IBM Res. Division, Almaden Research Center, June 1987.

[68] E. Vazquez, R. Colella, J. Vinyes, J. Fox, and J. Berrocal, "Performance of OSI transport over ACCUNET and IBERPAC," in *Proc. IEEE INFOCOM'88*, New Orleans, LA, Mar. 1988, pp. 651-659.

[69] C. A. Kent and J. C. Mogul, "Fragmentation considered harmful," in *Proc. ACM SICCOMM'87 Workshop*, Stowe, VT, Aug. 1987; *ACM Comput. Commun. Rev.*, vol. 17, no. 5, Special Issue, pp. 390-401.

[70] "Information Processing Systems—Open Systems Interconnection—Transport Service Definition," International Organization for Standardization, International Standard ISO 8072.

[71] "Information Processing Systems-Open Systems Interconnection—Connection Oriented Transport Protocol Specification," International Organization for Standardization, International Standard ISO 8073.

[72] "Information Processing Systems—Data Communications—Network Service Definition, Addendum 1: Connectionless-mode transmission," International Organization for Standardization, International Standard ISO 8348/AD1.

[73] "Information Processing Systems—Data Communications—Protocol for Providing the Connectionless-Mode Network Service," International Organization for Standardization, International Standard ISO 8473.

[74] J. B. Postel, "Transmission Control Protocol, DARPA," Internet Program Protocol Specification, Network Information Center RFC 793, SRI International, Menlo Park, CA, Sept. 1981.

[75] ——, "Internet Protocol, DARPA," Internet Program Protocol Specification, Network Information Center RFC 791, SRI International, Menlo Park, CA, Sept. 1981.

[76] I. Groenbaek, "Conversion between the TCP and ISO transport protocols as a method of achieving interoperability between data communications systems," *IEEE J. Select. Areas Commun.*, vol. SAC-4, no. 2, pp. 288-296, Mar. 1986.

[77] W. Stallings, "A primer: Understanding transport protocols," *Data Commun.*, vol. 13, pp. 201-215, Nov. 1984.

[78] A. S. Tanenbaum, *Computer Networks*. Englewood Cliffs, NJ: Prentice-Hall, 1988.

[79] B. Meister, "A performance study of the ISO transport protocol," in *Proc. 7th Int. Conf. Distrib. Comput. Syst.*, Berlin, West Germany, Sept. 1987, pp. 398-405.

[80] E. Mumprecht, D. Gantenbein, and R. Hauser, "Timers in OSI protocols—specification versus implementation," in *Proc. 1988 Int. Zurich Seminar Digital Commun.*, Zurich, Switzerland, Mar. 1988, pp. 93-98.

[81] G. Varghese and T. Lauck, "Hashed and hierarchical timing wheels: Data structures for the efficient implementation of a timer facility," in *Proc. 11th ACM SIGOPS Symp. Oper. Syst. Principles*, Austin, TX, Nov. 1987, pp. 25-38.

[82] R. Jain, "Divergence of timeout algorithms for packet retransmission," in *Proc. 5th Int. Phoenix Conf. Comput. Commun.*, Scottsdale, AZ, Mar. 1986, pp. 174-179.

[83] L. Zhang, "Why TCP timers don't work well," in *Proc. ACM SIGCOM'86 Symp. Commun. Architectures Protocols*, Stowe, VT, Aug. 1986, pp. 397-405.

[84] P. Karn and C. Partridge, "Improving round-trip time estimates in reliable transport protocols," in *Proc. ACM SICCOMM'87 Workshop*, Stowe, VT, Aug. 1987; *ACM Comput. Commun. Rev.*, vol. 17, no. 5, Special Issue, pp. 2-7.

[85] V. Jacobson, "Congestion avoidance and control," in *Proc. ACM SICCOMM'88 Symp.*, Stanford, CA, Aug. 1988; *ACM Comput. Commun. Rev.*, vol. 18, no. 4, pp. 314-329.

[86] A. Nakassis, "Fletcher's error detection algorithm, How to implement it efficiently and how to avoid most common pitfalls," ICST/SN86-4, Systems and Network Architecture Division, Institute for Computer Science and Technology, National Bureau of Standards, Gaithersburg, MD, Jan. 1986.

[87] A. Cockburn, "Efficient implementation of the OSI transport protocol checksum algorithm using 8/16-bit arithmetic," in *Proc. ACM SIGCOMM Comp. Commun. Rev.*, vol. 17, no. 3, July/Aug. 1987, pp. 13-20.

[88] "Information Processing Systems—Open Systems Interconnection—Connection Oriented Transport Protocol Specification—Addendum 1: Network Connection Management Subprotocol," International Organization for Standardization, International Standard ISO 8073/AD1.

[89] I. Davidson, "Testing conformance to OSI standards," *Comput. Commun.*, vol. 8, no. 4, pp. 170-179, Aug. 1985.

[90] ——, "OSI protocol testing at the Corporation for Open Systems," in *Protocol Specification, Testing, and Verification, VII*. H. Rudin

and C. H. West, Eds. Amsterdam, The Netherlands: North-Holland (Elsevier Science Publishers B.V.), 1987, pp. 3-12.
[91] H. J. Burkhardt and H. Eckert, "From protocol specification to implementation and test," in *Networking in Open Systems Lecture Notes in Computer Science 248*, G. Müller and R. P. Blanc, Eds. Berlin, Germany: Springer-Verlag, 1987, pp. 373-399.
[92] D. Clark, "The structuring of systems using upcalls," in *Proc. 10th ACM SIGOPS Symp. Oper. Syst. Principles*, Orcas Island, WA, Dec. 1985, pp. 171-180.
[93] M. S. Atkins, "Experiments in SR with different upcall program structures," *ACM Trans. Comput. Syst.*, vol. 6, no. 4, pp. 365-392, Nov. 1988.
[94] K. Rothermel, "A communication mechanism supporting actions," *Comput. Networks ISDN Syst.*, vol. 15, pp. 97-108, 1988.
[95] "Information Processing Systems—Open Systems Interconnection—Application Layer Structure," International Organization for Standardization, Draft International Standard ISO DIS 9545.
[96] M. Bever, "OSI application layer—Entwicklungsstand und Tendenzen," Tech. Rep. 43.8901 (in German), IBM European Networking Center, Heidelberg, West Germany, 1989.
[97] V. Lasker, M. Lein, and E. Benhamou, "An architecture for high performance protocol implementations," in *Proc. IEEE INFOCOM 84*, San Francisco, CA, Apr. 1984.
[98] P. J. Leach, P. H. Levine, B. P. Douros, J. A. Hamilton, D. L. Nelson, and B. L. Stumpf, "The architecture of an integrated local network," *IEEE J. Select. Areas Commun.*, vol. SAC-1, no. 5, pp. 842-857, Nov. 1983.

Liba Svobodova was born in Prague, Czechoslovakia, where she studied electrical engineering at the Czech Institute of Technology (CVUT). She received the M.S. degree in 1970 and the Ph.D. degree in 1974, both from Stanford University, Stanford, CA. Her doctoral thesis was in the area of computer performance evaluation.

She is a manager of Communication Architecture and Software Technology group at IBM's Zurich Research Laboratory, Rüschlikon, Switzerland. The group conducts research in the areas of specification, validation, implementation, and testing of communication protocols. Prior to joining IBM, she was an Assistant Professor at the Department of Electrical Engineering and Computer Science and a member of the Laboratory for Computer Science at the Massachusetts Institute of Technology, Cambridge, where her primary research area was resilient distributed systems. She published a book on computer performance measurement and evaluation methods, and a number of articles on distributed systems, servers, and communication issues.

Dr. Svobodova is a member of the Association for Computing Machinery and of the IEEE Computer Society.

Performance Modeling of Multi-Layered OSI Communication Architectures

Adrian E. CONWAY

GTE Laboratories Incorporated
40 Sylvan Road
Waltham, Massachusetts

Abstract: A generic queueing network model is formulated for the analytical performance evaluation of communication networks which are layered according to the OSI Reference Model. The proposed model, based directly on the generic specifications of the Reference Model, may be used to quantitatively evaluate end-to-end mean performance measures taking into account multiple layers of protocol, a multitude of open connections across the network, the underlying topology, and the manner in which the processing capacity is distributed among the various entities. For the solution of the model, a computationally efficient iterative decomposition algorithm is formulated. To justify the methodology formulated here, we review previous work in the area of the analysis of layered systems and expose the limitations of hitherto proposed performance evaluation methodologies.

1. Introduction

In recent years, a number of organizations and researchers have become concerned with the processing overheads that are associated with the OSI suite of protocols [OSI1] and the effect of this on system performance, as perceived by end-users or processes [STR1]. The complexity of OSI protocols is viewed as a communications processing bottleneck that limits the achievable information throughput in the upper layers of the OSI Reference Model. As a result, for certain applications, the need has been identified to simplify, or 'streamline', the OSI protocols, both in the interest of reducing the required processing overheads and also to enable, in the future, their efficient implementation in VLSI [CHE1].

The effects of the processing overheads and of the layering of protocols on the performance of a system are, at present, little understood quantitatively. Most analytic performance studies for systems have been focussed on the analysis of specific communication mechanisms in isolation, such as particular link layer and transport layer protocols [KUH1,REI1]. This has been due to the mathematical difficulties which are encountered when two or more layers of protocol are considered together. Relatively little work has appeared in the literature on the performance evaluation of systems with a *multi-layered* protocol structure.

In this paper, we propose a new methodology for the analytical evaluation of end-to-end mean performance measures in communication networks with a multi-layered architecture. The proposed model is based directly on the structure and specifications of the seven-layer OSI Reference Model and takes into account

(1) the network topology,
(2) the layering of protocols,
(3) the functions that may be carried out by the entities in the various layers at the nodes of the network,
(4) the processing overheads incurred, and
(5) the presence of multiple open connections across the network.

For the efficient solution of the model, we formulate an approximate *iterative decomposition technique* [SOU1]. The generic model and the solution technique developed here may be applied to analyze large and complex layered networks in a relatively efficient manner.

This paper is organized as follows. In the following section, we survey the various performance models that have appeared in the literature for the analysis of networks with a *layered* protocol structure and briefly review the main performance evaluation methodologies that have been proposed (a more comprehensive review may be found in [CON2]). This serves to justify the methodology proposed here. In Section 3, we summarize the functions of the various layers that may be taken into account in our model. In Section 4, we describe how we model processing overheads and the elemental functions considered in Section 3. The overall generic model for layered OSI networks is formulated in Section 5. The iterative decomposition algorithm for the solution of this model is summarized in Section 6. Aspects of the implementation are described in Section 7. Finally, in the concluding section, we describe the directions in which the present work is being continued.

2. Multi-Layered Performance Models

The development of queueing network based performance models for systems with a layered protocol structure has been motivated by a number of different applications. Within the context of local area networks (LANs), several approximate analytical performance models have been proposed. Wong et al [WON1] formulated a three-layer model for file transfers on a LAN. Mitchell and Lide [MIT1] formulated a three-layer generic model for LAN systems. A two-layer model for LAN systems has been developed by Murata and Takagi [MUR1]. In [FDI1], a hierarchical queueing model is formulated to analyze the end-to-end delays in a concatenated network. In [FDI2], a case study of the X.25 protocol, with two levels of flow control, is presented. In [KAT1], an analytical queueing model is developed for the combination of a session layer and a transport layer. Simulation methods have also been applied to the analysis of multi-layered models [MEI1,MEI2,GEO1,SAI1].

Several papers may be found that are orientated towards the problem of analyzing architectures with a full *seven-layer* structure. In [FAR1], the performance evaluation and optimization of layered communication architectures is discussed in general terms. In [PUJ1], a general solution methodology, based on 'semaphore' queues [FDI3], is presented for the analysis of nested window flow controls. In [GIH1], an overview is given of a hierarchical decomposition and aggregation (D/A) [COU1] technique which is orientated towards the seven-layer OSI Reference Model. In [KUH2] and [WIL1], a hierarchical D/A method is proposed for the analysis of common-channel signalling networks.

An alternative to constructing queueing network models is to attempt to predict performance directly from the formal specifications of the protocols which are employed. There are two main avenues that may be followed in this direction, namely, simulation and analysis [RUD1,RUD4]. In the simulation approach, a simulation program is compiled directly from a machine-readable specification of the protocol and the performance of the protocol is evaluated statistically [BAU1]. The idea of *analytically* predicting protocol performance, directly from the formal specification of a protocol, may be attributed to Rudin [RUD2,RUD3]. Given a finite-state machine (FSM) representation of a protocol, one may label the arcs of the associated FSM state-transition graph with transition probabilities and delays. The resulting model is isomorphic to a continuous-time Markov chain. Kritzinger [KRI1] developed this approach to analyze the efficiency of single-layer protocols. The approach is equivalent fundamentally to the analysis of protocol performance using Stochastic Petri Nets (SPN) [MOL1,KRI1]. In a later work [KRI2], Kritzinger extended the method developed in [KRI1] to accommodate multiple-layers of protocol and multiple connections. The model developed in [KRI2] also takes into account how the available processing capacity is shared between the various layers. The resulting model is isomorphic to a two-queue closed *multiple-chain* product-form queueing network [LAV1].

Among the works summarized above, the two main *generic* performance evaluation methodologies that have been proposed for systems with a full seven-layer protocol structure may be considered to be the ones of Kritzinger [KRI2] and of Gihr, Kuhn and Willmann [GIH1,KUH1,KUH2,WIL1]. One limitation of the method of Kritzinger is that it does not take into account the coupling that exists between the states of entities in adjacent layers. Another limitation is that the model requires the *a priori* specification of the transition probabilities and mean holding times for the states of the so-called 'transition-relation' graph [KRI2] associated with each entity in every layer. If these quantities are not available from some measurement experiments or from simulations, then they must somehow be estimated. It appears, however, that for realistic protocols the estimation of a large number of parameters ceases to maintain credibility. This same limitation may also be said to be inherent in SPN models where firing rates must be assigned to the transitions.

In the analytical method considered by Gihr, Kuhn and Willmann, on the other hand, queueing submodels are constructed for each layer. For the solution of the model, a hierarchical D/A approximation technique is proposed. There are several practical problems that may be encountered with this method. The first is that the solution of the submodel of each layer may be quite complicated since it involves the analysis of a queueing network with features that, in general, violate the conditions of a product-form queueing network. Furthermore, the flow-equivalent queues arising in the D/A method complicate the analysis further. The method also requires the solution of the submodels as a function of $k^{(n)}$, for $0 \leq k^{(n)} \leq K^{(n)}$, where $k^{(n)} = (k_1^{(n)},...,k_R^{(n)})$, $K^{(n)} = (K_1^{(n)},...,K_R^{(n)})$, and $K_r^{(n)}$ is the population of the r'th routing chain at layer n. This implies that the overall computational costs are at least of the order of

$$\text{Max} \{ \prod_{r=1}^{R} (K_r^{(n)}+1) \mid n = 1,...,7 \}.$$

This factor precludes the solution of submodels in which there are a large number of routing chains or large chain populations.

The new methodology that we propose here for the evaluation of networks with a full seven-layer architecture is designed to avoid the difficulties outlined above. The approach we adopt is similar to that of Gihr, Kuhn and Willmann, in that we construct a queueing network model. This avoids the difficulties that we have identified in the approach of Kritzinger. For the solution of the model, however, we formulate an approximate iterative decomposition technique. This avoids the potentially high computational costs associated with the D/A approach. An overriding concern in the development of our methodology has been to balance the tradeoff between modeling fidelity, accuracy, and computational requirements.

3. Structure and Functions of the OSI Reference Model

In the Reference Model, the offered services and the protocols employed in a network are organized into seven *layers* of increasing abstraction. Within each layer there are *entities* that carry out certain functions. The entities in adjacent layers are interconnected through *Service Access Points* (SAPs). *Service Data Units* (SDUs) are passed between adjacent entities through the SAPs. Peer entities, in possibly different geographical locations, are associated by connections and cooperate according to established protocols to achieve the functions that are necessary to support the services offered by the layer.

The generic model that we shall formulate in Section 5 takes into account a number of the possible functions that may be carried out by peer entities in each of the seven layers of the Reference Model. The functions that may be employed in each layer may be found summarized in [STA1, App. A]. In the following, we enumerate those that may be taken into account explicitly in the model to be developed here.

In the **Physical Layer**, the only functions that we shall consider modeling are those of *transmission* and *relaying*. With these functions, we can take into account a physical connection that may be provided by the interconnection of a number of data circuits.

In the **Data Link Layer**, the functions that may be taken into account in the performance model are *splitting* and *recombining*, *error detection* and *recovery*, and *flow control*.

The functions in the **Network Layer** that may be taken into account include *relaying* of network connections through intermediate network entities, *multiplexing* and *demultiplexing*, *segmentation* and *reassembly*, *blocking* and *deblocking*, *error detection* and *recovery*, *flow control*, *expedited data transfer* and certain forms of *routing*. We may also take into account concatenated sets of tandem subnetwork connections.

In the **Transport Layer**, the functions that may be taken into account include *normal data transfer*, *expedited data transfer*, *multiplexing* and *demultiplexing*, *error detection* and *recovery*, *segmentation* and *reassembly*, *blocking* and *deblocking*, and *concatenation* and *separation*.

The functions of the **Session Layer** that may be taken into account include *normal data exchange*, *expedited data exchange*, *flow control*, *multiplexing* and *demultiplexing*, and *splitting* and *recombining*. Although the functions of *multiplexing* and *demultiplexing* and *splitting* and *recombining* are not included in the session layer as defined by the CCITT [OSI1], for the sake of generality we allow for their inclusion in the generic model since in some systems these functions may be desirable.

In the **Presentation Layer**, the functions that we may take into account are the *transformation of syntax* and *data transfer*. The modeling of the transformation of syntax, however, is done simply by taking into account the processing overhead that is incurred in carrying out this function.

In our performance model, the functions carried out in the **Application Layer** are not modeled explicitly since they are, by definition, largely application dependent. Rather, we assume that in the network of open systems there are a number of application entities between which there are connections and certain traffic flows. The actual flows in the model and the queueing models for the application entities themselves depend on the specific applications that are under consideration.

There are also two types of flow control defined in the OSI Reference Model that may be taken into account in our model, namely, *Peer Flow Control*, which regulates the rate at which Protocol Data Units (PDUs) are sent to peer entities over a connection and *Interface Flow Control* which regulates the rate at which interface data is passed between an (n+1)-entity and an (n)-entity.

4. Modeling of OSI Functions and Processing Overheads

The generic model, to be formulated, takes into account the processing overheads associated with the protocols and the functions of the Reference Model that we have enumerated in Section 3. In this section, we describe how these elemental functions and effects are represented.

In the generic model, a routing chain [LAV1] is associated with each open connection across the network that exists between application layer entities. The chain specifies the path that the PDUs associated with the connection follow through the SAPs, processing elements, and entities of the system. Several routing chains are illustrated schematically in Fig. 1(a). Depending on the applications that are being modeled, the routing chains and the sources that feed them may take on different forms. An *open source* corresponds to a Poisson source of customers (jobs, tasks, PDUs, etc.) that are transferred across the network to some destination. A *closed source* consists of a finite number of customers that circulate continuously through the routing chain. The return path for a closed chain may either pass through the underlying entities or directly back to the source through a delay (IS) queue.

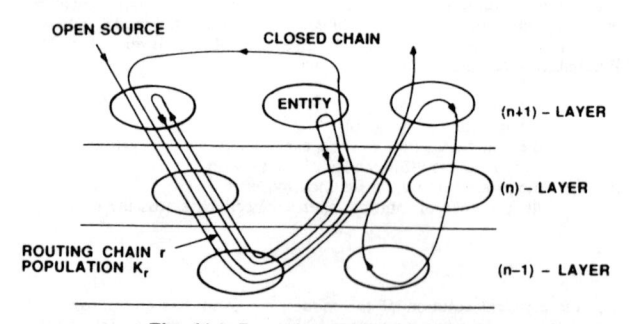

Fig. 1(a). Examples of Routing Chains

A potential problem arises as a result of the inclusion of open sources in the model. When there are open sources, the state-space of the model may, in theory, be countably infinite and it is, in general, difficult to ascertain *a priori* if the model will be stable, in the sense of the existence of an equilibrium distribution. To circumvent this difficulty, we replace each open chain by a closed chain having a relatively large population and introduce an auxiliary input queue having a service rate that is equal to the rate of the original open source.

The most basic function employed in the Reference Model is the transmission of PDUs through a data transmission channel. This may be represented by a queue of the M/M/1, M/M/K or Processor Sharing (PS) type. In the network model, we have one such queue for each link in the network. Full-duplex channels are represented by pairs of such queues.

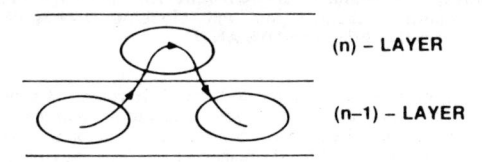

Fig. 1(b). Relaying of PDUs

The *relaying* of customers is illustrated in Fig. 1(b). The required relaying through entities is specified by appropriate routing transition probabilities. The modeling of the *splitting* and *recombining* of connections is carried out by placing a probabilistic split in the routing chain of a connection.

In practice, there are several types of *error detection* and *recovery* schemes that may be employed. Selective-repeat may be modeled in a simple manner by incorporating a return path, as illustrated in Fig. 1(c), which customers must follow if an error is detected. With probability p_e, the probability of error, the customer returns back to its point of origination for retransmission. The return path may pass through an IS queue to take into account the delay that is incurred between detection and retransmission. In the future, we intend to incorporate other schemes such as Go-back-N (as will be seen in Section 6, the modularity of the solution algorithm allows for this to be done in a relatively straightforward manner).

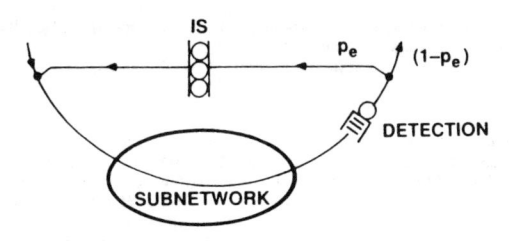

Fig. 1(c). Modeling of Error Detection and Recovery

In the Reference Model, there are two types of flow control, namely, peer flow control and interface flow control. In practice, there are a number of peer flow control schemes that are used. In the present model, we only consider the function of *window flow control*. Other types of peer flow control, such as pacing, may possibly be incorporated into the generic model in the future (in Section 6, we mention how this may be done). The function of window flow control may be modeled by having allocate and deallocate points through which the routing chain associated with a connection must pass. The mechanism of window flow control is illustrated schematically in Fig. 1(d).

The function of *interface flow control* is modeled in a simple manner using a single-server M/M/1 type queue, as illustrated in Fig. 1(e). The routing chains associated with different connections may pass through the same interface flow control queue.

The function of *routing* is carried out in the network layer. In our generic model we limit ourselves to the general class of routing schemes that is allowed in queueing networks of the BCMP type [LAV1]. By appropriate choice of the routing matrix and using the *class-switching* feature of BCMP networks, we can realize a variety of different routing schemes.

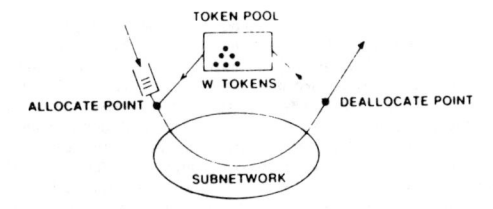

Fig. 1(d). Modeling of Peer Window Flow Control

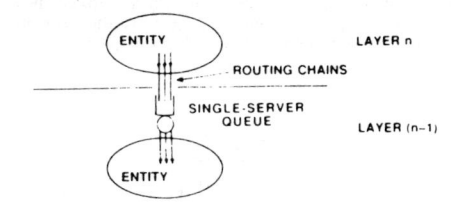

Fig. 1(e). Modeling of Interface Flow Control

The modeling of the functions of *multiplexing* and *demultiplexing* may be carried out by assuming that the customers associated with the multiplexed connections follow the same routing chain through the underlying entities. The function of *segmentation* is modeled by having segmentation points at which PDUs are broken up into a number of smaller data units. The function of *reassembly* is modeled by having a reassembly point at which PDUs wait until a complete PDU is formed. The functions of *concatenation* and *separation* are treated in the opposite way as segmentation and reassembly. If several chains pass through a single concatenation point, then it is assumed that the PDUs associated with the various chains may be mixed together in a single concatenated PDU. The function of *blocking* and *deblocking* is treated here in the same manner as concatenation and separation although, in the standards literature [OSI1] there is a minor technical difference between these two functions. The function of *expedited data transfer* is taken into account by introducing priorities into the queueing network model. The priorities may either be of the *head-of-line* or *preempt-resume* types. Expedited data may be allowed to bypass flow control mechanisms.

In the generic model, *processing overheads* are taken into account by assuming that in the network model there are a set of processing queues that are distributed in a specified way over the open systems that exist in the network. The processor(s) in an open system at a particular geographical location may be shared between the entities of different layers. Whenever an entity processes a PDU, we assume that the PDU visits the set of processing queues, as illustrated in Fig. 1(f).

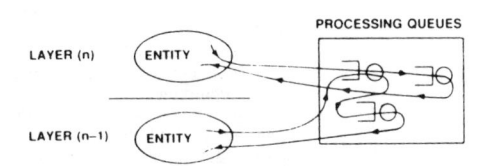

Fig. 1(f). Modeling of Processing Overheads

The functions of the application layer are dependent on particular applications. For the modeling of such functions, the general approach taken here is to consider that in the network of open systems there exist instances of associated application layer entities between which there are certain traffic flows. These traffic flows are assumed to follow the paths specified by the routing chains which are associated with the connections that exist between the application layer entities.

5. A Generic Model for Multi-Layered OSI Architectures

In the generic model, we consider the network as a whole, as illustrated in Fig. 2. In this 'global' model, it is assumed that at each open system in the network there are entities in the seven layers that are interconnected through SAPs. The open systems at different geographical locations are interconnected through the entities of the physical layer. The entities in the application layer are assumed to be fed by open and closed sources, as described in Section 4. Open sources are assumed to be replaced by closed ones. At the SAPs, we may have interface flow control queues. Each entity may carry out a number of functions. Within an entity we may have allocate and deallocate points for peer flow control, segmentation and reassembly points, concatenation and separation points, blocking and deblocking points, relaying, splitting and recombining, error detection and recovery, routing, multiplexing and demultiplexing, and priorities. In addition, it is assumed that there is a set of processing queues that are distributed geographically over the nodes of the network (these queues are not illustrated in Fig. 2). Associated with each closed source r is a closed routing chain r that follows some path through the entities and processing queues of the network. The path is defined by a transition matrix $P^{(r)} = [p_{ic;jd}^{(r)}]$, where $p_{ic;jd}^{(r)}$ is the probability that a customer of chain r at queue i in class c moves to queue j in class d.

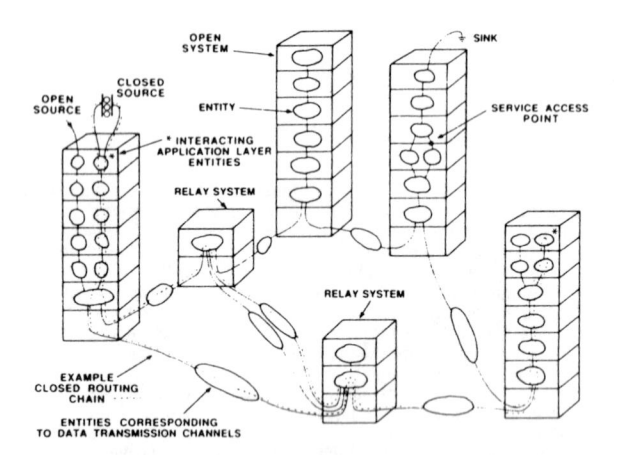

Fig. 2. Global Network Model Composed of Open Systems, Entities, and Sources

The global model may be described as a multiple-chain closed queueing network with the following parameters. There are a total of **NTOT** queues (this does not include *points* at which functions such as segmentation take place), including the processing queues. Nodes (NTOT-PTOT+1),...,NTOT are assumed to be processing queues, where **PTOT** is the total number of processing points in the model. The number of closed routing chains is **RTOT**. The number of possible class memberships that a customer of chain r may take on is **CTOT**(r). The transition probability $p_{ic;jd}^{(r)}$ is denoted by **PTRANS**(i,c,j,d,r). The type of a queue i is specified by **INDOR**(i), as follows:

INDOR(i) =
1	IS (delay),
2	PS or LCFSPR single-server BCMP,
3	FCFS single-server BCMP,
4	FCFS multi-server BCMP,
5	FCFS multi-server with chain-dependent service-requirements,
6	single-server preempt-resume priority,
7	single-server head-of-line priority,
8	FCFS single-server with chain-dependent service-requirements.

At FCFS queues of the BCMP type, the service-requirements for all customers must be exponential and identically distributed. At PS and LCFSPR queues, the mean service-requirements for different chains may be different and the distributions may take on arbitrary forms. At the other types of queues, the service-requirements are assumed to be exponentially distributed. The number of servers at node i, in the case that INDOR(i) = 4 or 5, is **IOS**(i). At a priority queue i, chain r has priority over chain s if the parameter **IPRIO**(i,r) < IPRIO(i,s). We assume that no priority distinction is made between customers of different classes c that belong to the *same* routing chain r.

We now define the type of so-called 'point-pairs' at which functions such as segmentation and reassembly may take place. The type of the point-pair p is specified by **TTYPE**(p), as follows:

TTYPE(p) =
1	window flow control,
2	segmentation/reassembly,
3	concatenation/separation,
4	blocking/deblocking.

It is to be noted that we only allow one function to be carried out at a single point. The functions specified by TTYPE may, however, be nested to an arbitrary degree. If TTYPE(p) = 1, then the window size for point-pair p is given by **PARA**(p). If TTYPE(p) = 2, then the number of segments into which a PDU is broken up is given by **PARA**(p). If TTYPE(p) = 3, then the number of PDUs which are concatenated is given by the parameter **PARA**(p). If TTYPE(p) = 4, then the number of PDUs which are blocked together is specified by **PARA**(p). The total number of point-pairs in the model is denoted by **ITTOT**. The number of customers in closed routing chain r is denoted by **RPOP**(r). This is considered to be the *nominal* chain population. At lower layers in the model, functions such as concatenation, segmentation and peer flow control may give rise to lower or higher populations that depend on the parameters PARA. The mean service-requirement for a customer of chain r in class c at node i is denoted by **DMEAN**(i,r,c). This, again, is regarded as a nominal service-requirement since the functions of segmentation, concatenation and blocking may give rise to requirements that differ from DMEAN.

We now introduce the concept of the control of a customer. A customer of chain r in class c at node i is said to be *controlled* by point p if, in order for it to have arrived at node i in class c, it must have passed through the input point of the point-pair p. Once the customer passes through the output point of point-pair p, it is no longer considered to be controlled by p. If a customer of chain r in class c is controlled by p at node i, then **ICONT**(i,c,r,p) = 1, or 0 otherwise.

The complete specification of the generic model is given by the parameters **NTOT**, **PTOT**, **RTOT**, **CTOT**(r), **PTRANS**(i,c,j,d,r), **INDOR**(i), **IOS**(i), **IPRIO**(i,r), **TTYPE**(p), **PARA**(p), **ITTOT**, **RPOP**(r), **DMEAN**(i,r) and **ICONT**(i,c,r,p). The functions of routing, multiplexing and demultiplexing, splitting and recombining and error detection and recovery are assumed to be specified implicitly by PTRANS.

6. Iterative Decomposition Algorithm for the Generic Model

The generic model is a complex multiple-chain closed queueing network with a variety of features that do not support a product-form distribution. For its solution, we formulate an approximate iterative decomposition technique which is related to the one that has been formulated in [SOU2] for networks that contain nested flow controls. The algorithm formulated here is, however, more general since we accommodate

(1) the various types of queueing disciplines specified by INDOR(i),
(2) the class-switching feature, and
(3) the variety of functions specified by TTYPE(p).

Apart from these extensions, to reduce the overall computational costs, we also employ computational procedures which are different from those used in [SOU2]. The iterative algorithm in [SOU2] involves the successive solution of a set of *reduced networks* that are each solved individually by a *recursive* Mean Value Analysis (MVA) [LAV1] based method. The computational requirements of this method are exponential in the number of closed chains in a reduced network. This precludes the analysis of networks with many chains in a particular reduced network. The solution algorithm formulated here also involves the successive solution of a set of reduced networks but, to circumvent the potential computational bottleneck in the solution of the reduced networks, we employ an iterative Linearizer [CHA1] based method which is an extension of the one developed in [CON1]. The storage space requirements and the computational costs of this method are of the order of NR^2 and NR^3, respectively, where N is the number of queues and R is the number of chains in a reduced network. This allows for the solution of large complex models with many routing chains. In the following, we describe the main elements of the iterative decomposition algorithm that has been developed. Further details are provided in [CON2].

Decomposition into a Set of Subsystems

In the solution algorithm, the original queueing model M is first decomposed into a set S of *subsystems*. The subsystem to which a particular queue i belongs is determined by its so-called *depth*, to be defined. Queues NTOT-PTOT+1,...,NTOT are assumed to be in the *processing subsystem*. A queue is considered to be at depth d if

$$\text{Max}\{ \sum_{p=1}^{ITTOT} ICONT(i,c,r,p) \mid c = 1,...,CTOT(r), r = 1,...,RTOT \} = d.$$

In words, the depth of a queue i is the maximum number of point-pairs that control a chain which visits queue i. All queues in the processing subsystem are, by definition, considered to be at depth -1.

The number of depths in the model is denoted by **IDPM** and the depth of node i is **DEPTH**(i). The number of depths does not include depth -1. It also does not include depth 0 which consists of those queues which are not controlled by any point-pairs and which are not in the processing subsystem. We let **TOKD2**(p,d) = 1, if point-pair p controls a queue at depth d and none at depth (d-1), and 0, otherwise. The total number of point-pairs that control queues at depth d and none at depth (d-1) is defined to be **TOKN**(d).

Construction of the Reduced Networks

Having partitioned M into the set of subsystems S, where $S = \{M_s \mid -1 \leq s \leq IDPM\}$ and $M_s = \{ i \mid DEPTH(i) = s, 1 \leq i \leq NTOT \}$, as illustrated in Fig. 3, the next step is to construct a *reduced network* around each subsystem M_s. This is done by replacing the part of the network which is complementary to M_s by certain 'flow-equivalent' queues, as illustrated in Fig. 4. The service-time requirements at the flow-equivalent queues are meant to represent the delays incurred by customers in traversing through the complementary parts of the network.

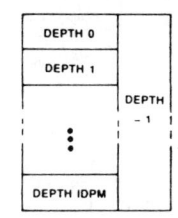

Fig. 3. Partitioning into Depths

We now first consider the construction of the reduced network around M_d, where $1 \leq d \leq IDPM$. Let P_d be the set of point-pairs that lie at the interface between depths d and (d+1). We have

$P_d = \{ p \mid 1 \leq p \leq ITTOT, TOKD2(p,d+1) = 1\}.$

Each point-pair p, $p \in P_d$, may be visited by a number of chains that traverse from depth d to (d+1). In addition, there may be a number of chains which traverse from depth d to (d+1) without passing through any controlling point-pair. For those chains r that cross from depth d into depth (d+1) without passing through any point-pair, we represent the delay incurred in traversing depth (d+1) by a queue of the IS type. For those chains r that pass through a window flow control point in passing into and out of depth (d+1), we represent the delay incurred by a queue of the multi-server chain-dependent FCFS type. The number of servers is set equal to the window size. For those chains r that pass through point-pairs p for which TTYPE(p) = 2, 3 or 4, we represent the delay incurred by queues of the IS type. Since the number of controlling point-pairs used at depth (d+1) and not at depth d is TOKN(d+1), in the reduced network constructed around M_d we have, in total, TOKN(d+1)+1 flow-equivalent queues to represent the delays incurred by chains in passing into and out of depth (d+1). We call these queues the *higher-depth* flow-equivalents.

Delays are also incurred by routing chains in passing through the set of processing queues at depth -1. For those chains r at depth d that pass into and out of depth -1, we represent the overall processing delays by a queue of the IS type. Point-pairs are not allowed to reside at the interface to depth -1. Also, for routing chains at depth d which actually originate from depth (d-1), the delay as perceived from depth d to travel through depth (d-1) and back into depth d is also represented by an IS queue. We call this queue the *lower-depth* flow-equivalent.

In the reduced system constructed around M_d, we label the lower-depth flow-equivalent queue as (**NTOT+1**), we label the TOKN(d+1)+1 higher-depth flow-equivalents as (**NTOT+2**), ..., (**NTOT+TOKN(d+1)+2**) and we label the processing-system flow-equivalent as (**NTOT+TOKN(d+1)+3**). The IS queue used to represent the delay at depth (d+1) for chains that do not pass through any point-pair in traversing into and out of depth (d+1) is assumed to be the one labelled **NTOT+TOKN(d+1)+2**. Fig. 5 illustrates the details of the construction of a reduced network around M_d, where $1 \leq d \leq IDPM-1$. The construction of the reduced network around M_{IDPM} is the same as for M_d, where $1 \leq d \leq IDPM-1$, except that the higher depth flow-equivalents are not used. The construction of the reduced network around M_0 is the same as for M_d, $1 \leq d \leq IDPM$, except that the queue labelled (**NTOT+1**) is not used. In the reduced network constructed around M_{-1}, only one flow-equivalent queue of the IS type is used. This queue, labelled NTOT+1, represents the delay, as perceived from the processing subsystem, that customers incur in travelling from depth -1 into depth d, where $0 \leq d \leq IDPM$, and then back into depth -1 from depth d.

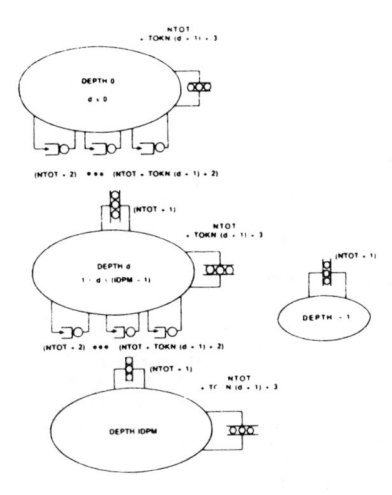

Fig. 4. Illustration Showing Reduced Systems in the Various Depths

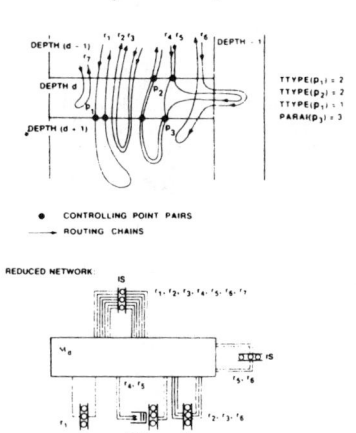

Fig. 5. Illustration of the Contruction of a Reduced Network

Iterative Solution of the Reduced Networks

Having partitioned M into a set of subsystems and constructed a reduced network around each one, the mean performance measures for the network are obtained iteratively. The iterative algorithm is summarized below. In the following, we use R_d to denote the reduced network constructed around M_d.

Iterative Solution of the Generic Queueing Network M

Initializations
Partition the original queueing network model M into the set of subsystems S.
For d = -1,0,1,...,IDPM:
 Construct the reduced network R_d around M_d.
 Initialize the mean performance measures for R_d.

Main Iteration
While Not Converged DO:
 For d = 0,1,...,IDPM:
  Update the service-time requirements at the flow-equivalent queues in R_d.
  Solve the reduced network R_d for the mean performance measures using the Linearizer based algorithm
  Update the service-time requirements at the flow-equivalent queue in R_{-1}.
  Solve the reduced system R_{-1} for the mean performance measures using the Linearizer based algorithm

We now describe (1) how we update the service-requirements at the flow-equivalents and (2) how we solve the reduced networks. Other details, including the initialization of the performance measures for R_d and the convergence criteria, are described in [CON2].

Updating of the Service-Requirements at Flow-Equivalents

The service-requirements at the flow-equivalent queues are updated prior to the successive solution of each reduced network. Consider the updating of the service-requirements at the queue labelled (NTOT+TOKN(d+1)+3) in R_d, where $0 \leq d \leq$ IDPM, and consider a particular chain r that visits this queue. Let **DMACD**(d,i,r) denote the service-requirement for chain r at node i in R_d, where $-1 \leq d \leq$ IDPM. The mean service-requirement for a customer of chain r at (NTOT+TOKN(d+1)+3) is meant to represent the delay that a customer of chain r experiences in making a tour through depth -1. Let this delay be denoted by $\Delta_r(d,-1)$. Hence, we let

DMACD(d,NTOT+TOKN(d+1)+3,r) = $\Delta_r(d,-1)$.

Consider now the updating of the service-requirements at the queue labelled (NTOT+1) in R_{-1} and suppose that chain r visits (NTOT+1). This chain may originate from any one of the depths 0,1,2,...,IDPM. Let δ be the depth from which the chain originates and let $\Delta_r(-1,δ)$ represent the delay incurred by a customer of chain r in making a tour through the part of the network which is complementary to depth -1. In this case, we let

DMACD(-1,NTOT+1,r) = $\Delta_r(-1,δ)$.

We now determine the service-requirements at the queues labelled (NTOT+2),...,(NTOT+TOKN(d+1)+2) in the reduced network R_d, where $0 \leq d \leq$ (IDPM-1). Consider initially the queue labelled (NTOT+TOKN(d+1)+2). This is used to represent the delay $\Delta_r^*(d,d+1)$ incurred by a customer that does not pass through a point-pair in traversing the interface between depths d and (d+1) in making a tour through depth (d+1). For a chain r that visits node (NTOT+TOKN(d+1)+2), we let

DMACD(d,NTOT+TOKN(d+1)+2,r) = $\Delta_r^*(d,d+1)$.

Now consider queue i such that (NTOT+2) $\leq$ i $\leq$ (NTOT+TOKN(d+1)+1). In this case, there are several situations that must be distinguished depending on the parameter TTYPE(p), where p is the number of the point-pair associated with queue i. Depending on the value of TTYPE(p), the queue i represents the complementary part of the network (higher depths) for chains r that are either subject to window flow control, segmentation, concatenation or blocking. In these various cases, the service-requirements at the flow-equivalents are updated in different ways.

In the case that TTYPE(p) = 1 (window flow control), we let

DMACD(d,i,r) = $\Delta_r(d,d+1)$,

where $\Delta_r(d,d+1)$ represents the delay incurred by a customer of chain r in making a tour through depth (d+1). In the cases that TTYPE(p) = 2, 3, or 4, the determination of the service-requirements at the flow-equivalents is more involved and will be considered in the following subsection.

We consider now the specification of the service-requirements at the IS queue labelled (NTOT+1) in R_{d+1}, where $0 \leq d \leq$ IDPM-1. Let the set of all chains r that visit (NTOT+1) in R_{d+1} and which are controlled by point-pair p, such that TOKD2(p,d+1) = 1, be denoted by $C_{(d+1)p}$ and suppose that node i (at depth d) is the flow-equivalent associated with point-pair p. In the case that TTYPE(p) = 1, we let

DMACD(d+1,NTOT+1,r) = $\Delta_r(d+1,d)$,

where r $\in C_{(d+1)p}$ and $\Delta_r(d+1,d)$ is the mean time from when a customer of chain r leaves node i until it enters *service* at node i in M_d. The determination of DMACD(d+1,NTOT+1,r), for r $\in C_{(d+1)p}$, in the case that TTYPE(p) = 2, 3, or 4, is considered in the following subsection.

Updating when TTYPE(p) = 2,3,4

We now consider the determination of DMACD(d,i,r) at queue i in R_d, where (NTOT+2) $\leq$ i $\leq$ (NTOT+TOKN(d+1)+1), for all chains r that visit queue i, in the case that TTYPE(p) = 2, 3, or 4, where p is the point-pair associated with queue i. These service-requirements are found by solving a small *equivalent queueing network* constructed around point-pair p, as illustrated in Fig. 6. The equivalent network is made up of two IS queues, labelled Q_1 and Q_2, and a controlling point-pair p that carries out either a function of segmentation and reassembly, concatenation and separation, or blocking and deblocking, depending on the value of TTYPE(p). The mean service-requirement for a customer of chain r at queue Q_i, i = 1,2, is denoted by $\tau_{Q_i}(r)$. The quantity $\tau_{Q_1}(r)$ is the mean time from when a customer of chain r enters depth d from depth (d+1) to when it leaves depth d to enter depth (d+1), as illustrated in Fig. 7. The definition of $\tau_{Q_2}(r)$ is also illustrated in Fig. 7. The quantities $\tau_{Q_1}(r)$ and $\tau_{Q_2}(r)$ are determined from the current values of the performance measures for R_d and R_{d+1}, respectively. The delay DMACD(d,i,r), where (NTOT+2) $\leq$ i $\leq$ (NTOT+TOKN(d+1)+1), is illustrated in Fig. 6 and may be computed by solving the network illustrated in Fig. 6. Depending on the cardinality of the set $C_{(d+1)p}$ and the specific function that is carried out by point-pair p, the equivalent network may be solved using either analytic or matrix methods.

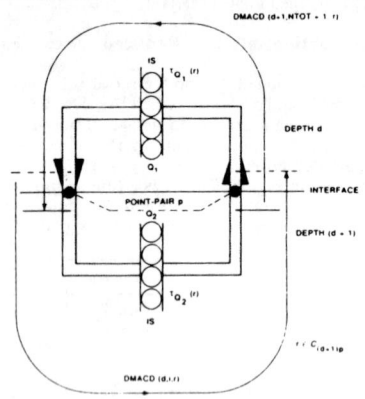

Fig. 6. Illustration of the Equivalent Queueing Network Constructed around Point-Pair p

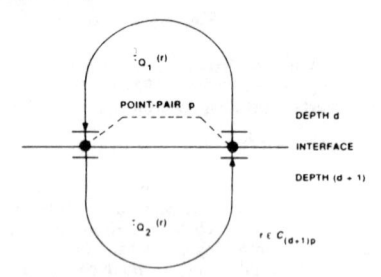

Fig. 7. Illustration of τ_{Q_1} and τ_{Q_2}

Finally, consider the updating of DMACD(d+1,NTOT+1,r), for r $\in C_{(d+1)p}$, in the case that TTYPE(p) = 2, 3 or 4. This quantity represents the mean delay between when a chain r customer leaves depth (d+1) to enter depth d through the *output* point of the point-pair p and when it enters depth (d+1) from depth d through the input point of point-pair p, as also illustrated in Fig. 6. The quantity DMACD(d+1,NTOT+1,r) is obtained by solving the same equivalent network as that used to determine DMACD(d,i,r) for (NTOT+2) $\leq$ i $\leq$ (NTOT+TOKN(d+1)+1).

One advantage of adopting the approach of constructing an equivalent network centered on particular point-pairs is that it facilitates the future incorporation of other functions such as, for example, pacing controls and the Go-back-N error recovery scheme. To accommodate such extensions, we need only alter the algorithm employed in the solution of the equivalent network. This modularity facilitates the introduction of future extensions to the present generic model.

Linearizer Based Algorithm for the Reduced Networks

In [CON1], an efficient iterative Linearizer [CHA1] based solution algorithm has been developed for closed multiple-chain BCMP queueing networks that contain multi-server chain-dependent FCFS queues. The iterative algorithm that we employ here to solve each reduced network R_d is essentially the same as that presented in [CON1] except that extensions are made to accommodate the queueing disciplines of types 6, 7 and 8. In order to accommodate queues of type 6, we use the approximate MVA waiting-time equation of Reiser [REI2, eq. 3.28]. For queues of type 7 and 8, we use the 'BKT' MVA waiting-time equations given in [BRY1]. These waiting-time equations are inserted directly into eq. 2.1 in [CON1].

7. Aspects of the Implementation

The solution algorithm for the generic model has been programmed in FORTRAN. In the implementation, use is made of sparse matrix storage techniques so as to avoid matrices with many dimensions. The implementation also takes advantage of the possible reducibility of reduced networks into sets of smaller independent queueing networks. By solving the independent networks separately, we may, in general, reduce the overall computational costs to solve the reduced networks.

8. Conclusions

In this paper, we have formulated a generic queueing network model for communication architectures that are layered according to the specifications of the seven-layer OSI Reference Model. In its present form, the model can take into account many of the functions that are defined in the standards literature. The model is a 'global' one since, rather than concentrating on a particular connection in isolation, it treats the network as a whole. This enables the quantitative evaluation of end-to-end mean performance measures taking into account the layering of functions, the underlying topology and physical resources of the data transmission network, the existence of multiple simultaneous connections across the network and the manner in which the processing capacity is distributed among the open systems and layers of the network. To solve the generic model, we have formulated an iterative decomposition technique with relatively low computational costs. This enables the solution of relatively large and complex communication network models. In this paper, we have also reviewed previous work in the area of the analytical performance evaluation of systems with a multi-layered structure. We exposed the inherent theoretical and practical limitations of the main hitherto proposed methodologies and used this to justify the approach taken here.

There are several directions in which the work is being continued. Currently, we are investigating the numerical properties and the accuracy of the iterative decomposition technique. We are also developing a *dynamic* model based on quasi-static assumptions to take into account the dynamics of connection establishment, data transfer and release [CON2]. In the future, we intend to extend the functions that are currently available in the model.

9. Acknowledgment

We would like to thank Dr. P. O'Reilly for helpful suggestions and discussions relating to this work.

10. References

[BAU1] W.L. Bauerfeld, Performance Prediction of Computer Network Protocols, *Int. Conf. on Communications*, pp. 1311-1315, Boston, MA, 1983.

[BRY1] R.M. Bryant, A.E. Krzesinski, M.S. Lakshmi, and K.M. Chandy, The MVA Priority Approximation, *ACM Trans. Computer Systems*, 2, 4, pp. 335-359, 1984.

[CHA1] K.M. Chandy, and D. Neuse, Linearizer: A Heuristic Algorithm for Queueing Network Models of Computing Systems, *Commun. ACM*, 25, 2, pp. 126-134, 1982.

[CHE1] G. Chesson, The Protocol Engine Project, *Unix Review*, pp. 70-77, Sept., 1987.

[CON1] A.E. Conway, Fast Approximate Solution of Queueing Networks with Multi-Server Chain-Dependent FCFS Queues, *4th Int. Conf. on Modelling Techniques and Tools for Computer Performance Evaluation*, pp. 455-472, Palma de Mallorca, Spain, Sept. 1988.

[CON2] A.E. Conway, A Generic Performance Model for Layered OSI Communication Architectures, Technical Memorandum, TM-0069-10-88-414.17, GTE Laboratories Incorporated, Oct. 1988.

[COU1] P.J. Courtois, *Decomposability: Queueing and Computer System Applications*, Academic Press, New York, 1977.

[FAR1] A. Faro, and G. Messina, A Layered Approach for Performance Evaluation of Computer Networks, in *Proc. 10th IMACS World Congress on System Simulation and Scientific Computation*, 4, pp. 288-291, Montréal, Canada, Aug. 1982.

[FDI1] S. Fdida, U. Korner, H. Perros, and G. Shapiro, End to End Delays in a Catenet Environment, in Proc. *3rd. Int. Conf. on Data Commun. Syst. and their Performance*, Rio de Janeiro, Brazil, June 1987.

[FDI2] S. Fdida, A. Wilk, and H. Perros, Semaphore Queues: Modelling Window Flow Control Mechanisms, *Research Report 181*, Lab. MASI, Univ. P. et M. Curie (Paris 6), Paris, France, May 1987.

[FDI3] S. Fdida, G. Pujolle, and D. Mailles, Réseaux de Files d'Attente avec Sémaphores, *Technique et Science Informatique*, 3, pp. 187-196, 1986.

[GEO1] N. Georganas, and N. Naffah, Integrated Office Systems over LANs - A Performance Study, *Computer Communications*, 10, 6, pp. 291-296, 1987.

[GIH1] O. Gihr, and P.J. Kuhn, Comparison of Communication Services with Connection-Oriented and Connectionless Data Transmission, *Computer Networking and Performance Evaluation*, T. Hasegawa, H. Takagi, and Y. Takahashi (Eds.), Elsevier Science Publishers B.V. (North-Holland), 1986.

[KAT1] S. Katz, and I. Rubin, Performance of Combined Session Level and Message Level Flow Control Schemes for a Multi-Node Network, in *Proc. of the 7th. IEEE Conference on Computer Communications (INFOCOM '88)*, pp. 418-426, 1988.

[KRI1] P.S. Kritzinger, Analyzing the Time Efficiency of a Communication Protocol, *Protocol Specification, Testing, and Verification*, 4, Y. Yemini, R. Strom, and S. Yemini (Eds.), Elsevier Science Publishers B.V. (North-Holland), 1985.

[KRI2] P.S. Kritzinger, A Performance Model of the OSI Communication Architecture, *IEEE Trans. Communications*, 34, 6, pp. 554-563, 1986.

[KUH1] P.J. Kuhn, Modelling of New Services in Computer and Communication Networks, *Computer Networking and Performance Evaluation*, T. Hasegawa, H. Takagi, and Y. Takahashi (Eds.), Elsevier Science Publishers B.V. (North-Holland), 1986.

[KUH2] P.J. Kuhn, Modelling Signalling Networks for the Integrated Services Digital Network, Extended Abstract, *ORSA/TIMS Conference on Queueing Networks and their Applications*, New Brunswick, NJ, Jan. 1987.

[LAV1] S.S. Lavenberg (Ed.), *Computer Performance Modeling Handbook*, Academic Press, New York, 1983.

[MEI1] B.W. Meister, P.A. Jason, and L. Svobodova, Connection-Oriented Versus Connectionless Protocols: A Performance Study, *IEEE Trans. Computers*, 34, 12, pp. 1164-1173, 1985.

[MEI2] B. Meister, A Performance Study of the ISO Transport Protocol, in *Proc. of the 7th Int. Conf. on Distributed Computing Systems*, Berlin, West Germany, pp. 398-405, Sept. 1987.

[MIT1] L.C. Mitchell, and D.A. Lide, End-to-End Performance Modeling of Local Area Networks, *IEEE J. Select. Areas in Comm.*, 4, 6, pp. 975-985, 1986.

[MOL1] M.K. Molloy, Performance Analysis Using Stochastic Petri Nets, *IEEE Trans. on Computers*, 31, 9, pp. 913-917, 1982.

[MUR1] M. Murata, and H. Takagi, Two-Layer Modeling for Local Area Networks, *IEEE Trans. Communications*, 36, 9, pp. 1022-1034, 1988.

[OSI1] *Data Communications Networks Systems Interconnection (OSI) System Description Techniques*, Red Book, Vol. 8, Fasc. 8.5, CCITT, Geneva, 1985.

[PUJ1] G. Pujolle, and S. Fdida, General Resource Sharing Systems, *Teletraffic Analysis and Computer Performance Evaluation*, O.J. Boxma, J.W. Cohen, and H.C. Tijms (Eds.), Elsevier Science Publishers B.V. (North-Holland), 1986.

[REI1] M. Reiser, Communication-System Models Embedded in the OSI Reference Model: A Survey, *Computer Networking and Performance Evaluation*, T. Hasegawa, H. Takagi, and Y. Takahashi (Eds.), Elsevier Science Publishers B.V. (North-Holland), pp. 85-111, 1986.

[REI2] M. Reiser, A Queueing Network Analysis of Computer Communication Networks with Window Flow Control, *IEEE Trans. Communications*, 27, pp. 1199-1209, 1979.

[RUD1] H. Rudin, The ICC '83 Communication Protocols Session: An Overview, *Int. Conf. on Communications*, pp. 1291-1295, Boston, MA, 1983.

[RUD2] H. Rudin, From Formal Protocol Specification Towards Automated Performance Prediction, *Protocol Specification, Testing, and Verification*, 3, H. Rudin, and C.H. West (Eds.), Elsevier Science Publishers B.V. (North-Holland), 1983.

[RUD3] H. Rudin, An Improved Algorithm for Estimating Protocol Performance, *Protocol Specification, Testing, and Verification*, 4, Y. Yemini, R. Strom, and S. Yemini (Eds.), Elsevier Science Publishers B.V. (North-Holland), 1985.

[RUD4] H. Rudin, An Informal Overview of Formal Protocol Specification, *IEEE Communications Magazine*, 23, 3, pp. 46-52, 1985.

[SAI1] T. Saito, H. Aida, A. Shirahata, M. Hamaogi, W. Takahashi, and H. Ishihara, A Performance Evaluation of Computer Network using Multi-Layered Protocol, *12th International Teletraffic Congress* (ITC), pp. 5.3B.4.1 - 5.3B.4.7, Torino, Italy, June 1988.

[SOU1] E. de Souza e Silva, S.S. Lavenberg, and R.R. Muntz, A Perspective on Iterative Methods for the Approximate Analysis of Closed Queueing Networks, *Mathematical Computer Performance and Reliability*, G. Iazeolla, P.J. Courtois, and A. Hordijk (Eds.), Elsevier Science Publishers B.V. (North-Holland), 1984.

[SOU2] E. de Souza e Silva, and R.R. Muntz, Approximate Solutions for a Class of Non-Product Form Queueing Network Models, *Performance Evaluation*, 7, pp. 221-242, 1987.

[STA1] W. Stallings, *Handbook of Computer Communications Standards: Volume 1*, Macmillan, New York, 1987.

[STR1] P. Strauss, OSI Throughput: Breakthrough or Bottleneck?, *Data Communications*, pp. 53-56, May 1987.

[WIL1] G. Willmann, Modelling and Performance Evaluation of Multi-Layered Signalling Networks Based on the CCITT No. 7 Specification, *12th International Teletraffic Congress* (ITC), Torino, Italy, pp. 2.4A.3.1-2.4 A.3.11, June 1988.

[WON1] J.W. Wong, J.A.B. Moura, and J.A. Field, Hierarchical Modelling of File Transfers on Local Area Networks, *Comput. and Elect. Engng.*, 10, 3, pp. 191-207, 1983.

A network security primer

OSI guidelines can help you plan and build more secure systems

BY WILLIAM STALLINGS

Last week's conviction of Robert T. Morris, only days after a federal indictment of three former SRI International co-workers for breaking into government and Pacific Bell computers, undoubtedly rattled countless IS managers—with good reason. Incidents such as these are reminders that network security is far from a theoretical problem.

The introduction of distributed systems and use of networks and communications facilities for carrying data have increased the need for network security measures to protect data during its transmission. Are your networks secure?

To assess the security needs of an organization effectively and evaluate and choose various security products and policies, information systems managers need a systematic method of defining security requirements and solutions. This is difficult enough in a centralized data processing environment; local- and wide-area networks greatly compound the problem.

Fortunately, such an approach has been developed by the International Standards Organization (ISO) as part of its standard for an Open Systems Interconnect (OSI) communications architecture.

The document, called "DIS 7498-2, OSI Reference Model Part 2: Security Architecture," can greatly help IS managers in several ways. The document provides a checklist of the most important network security features. The OSI security architecture can help managers organize the task of providing security while also providing immediate guidance to implementors and purchasers. Because the document does not dictate a specific implementation, vendors and customers are free to configure a set of services and mechanisms that meet their specific requirements. The scheme also is a way of standardizing security implementations.

The ISO standard serves two purposes: It provides a functional assignment of security features to OSI layers that will guide standards makers in future enhancements of OSI-based standards, and it provides a structured

Copyright © 1990 by CW Publishing, Inc., Framingham, MA 01701.
Reprinted from *Computerworld*.

Safe and sound
Mainframe/minicomputer access control outpaces other security technologies

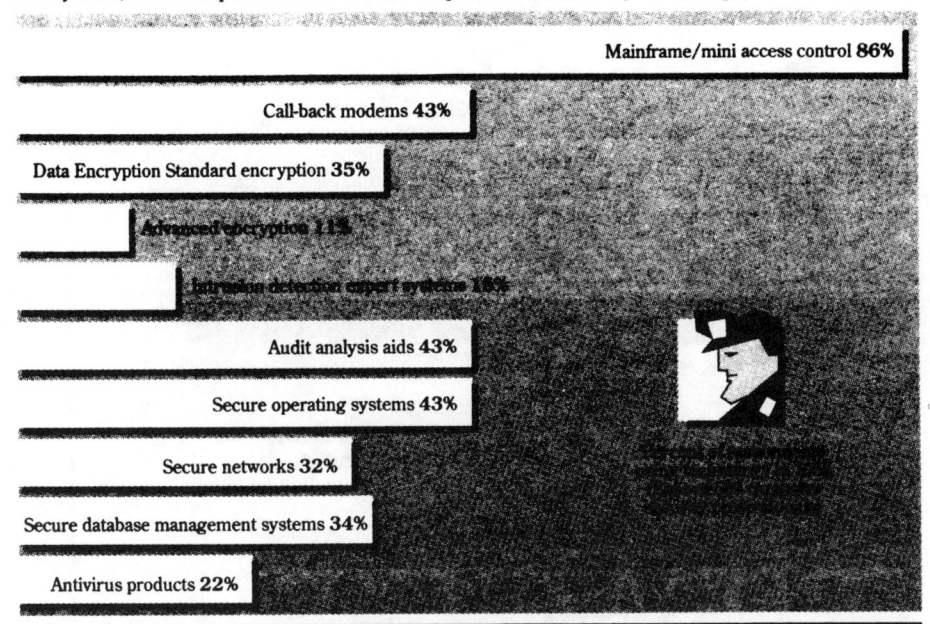

- Mainframe/mini access control **86%**
- Call-back modems **43%**
- Data Encryption Standard encryption **35%**
- Advanced encryption 11%
- Intrusion detection expert systems 16%
- Audit analysis aids **43%**
- Secure operating systems **43%**
- Secure networks **32%**
- Secure database management systems **34%**
- Antivirus products **22%**

SOURCE: NATIONAL CENTER FOR COMPUTER CRIME DATA AND RGC ASSOCIATES
CW CHART: TOM MONAHAN

framework within which vendors and customers can assess security offerings.

The standard also defines the security services and mechanisms within the OSI framework. Services are optional but implemented in a particular OSI layer if used.

Because the architecture was developed as an international standard, computer and communications vendors will begin to develop security features for their products and services based on this structured definition of services and mechanisms.

Thus, in coming days, it will be increasingly important for IS managers to understand security from the perspective of the ISO standard. Three concepts anchor the OSI network security architecture:

• **Security threat:** Any action that compromises the security of information owned by an organization.

• **Security service:** This is a communications service that enhances the security of information systems and an organization's information transfer.

• **Security mechanism:** A communications mechanism that is designed to detect, prevent or recover from a security threat.

Threats to network security can be categorized as passive and active (see chart on the following page). Passive threats include eavesdropping and monitoring transmissions to obtain information. Because they do not involve any alteration of data, passive threats are difficult to detect.

Such attacks can be prevented, however, so the emphasis should be on prevention.

Active threats involve some modification of data or the creation of a false stream. Preventing active attacks is very difficult because it requires continuous physical protection of all communications facilities and paths. A better goal is to quickly detect and recover from any disruption or delays caused by the attack.

Attacks can occur at any communications link: cable, microwave links or satellite channels. Active attackers need to gain physical control of a portion of the link so that they can insert and capture transmissions. A passive attacker needs only to observe transmissions.

Twisted-pair and co-axial cable can be attacked using either invasive taps or inductive devices that monitor electromagnetic emanation. Invasive taps allow both active and passive attacks, while inductive taps are useful for passive attacks. Neither type of tap is effective with optical fiber, which is one of the advantages of this medium. The fiber does not generate electromagnetic emanations and hence is not vulnerable to inductive taps. Physically breaking the cable seriously degrades signal quality and is therefore detectable.

Microwave and satellite transmissions can be intercepted with little risk to the attacker. This is especially true of satellite transmissions, which cover a broad geographic area. Active attacks on microwave and satellite are also possible, although this is more technically difficult and can be quite expensive.

Processors along the communications path are also subject to attacks. These might be attempts to modify hardware or software, gain access to processor memory or monitor electromagnetic emanations.

Solutions

By far, the most important automated tool for ensuring network and communications security is encryption. Encryption is a process that conceals meaning by changing intelligible messages into unintelligible messages. Encryption is accomplished by using a code or a cipher.

A code system employs a predefined table or dictionary to substitute a meaningless word or phrase for each message or part of a message. A cipher uses a computable algorithm that can translate any stream of message bits into an unintelligible cryptogram. Cipher techniques are more readily automated and thus are more popular in computer and network security facilities.

Conventional encryption is the process in which the original intelligible message, referred to as plaintext, is converted into apparently random nonsense, called ciphertext, using an algorithm and a key. The key is a relatively short bit string that controls the algorithm. The algorithm will produce a different output depending on the specific key being used at the time. Changing the key radically changes the output of the algorithm.

Once the ciphertext is produced, it is transmitted. Upon reception, the ciphertext can be transformed back to the original plaintext by using a decryption algorithm and the same key that was used for encryption. The encryption algorithm must be powerful enough so that it is impractical to decrypt a message on the basis of the ciphertext alone. In other words, the algorithm needn't be kept secret but the key must.

This feature makes the technique feasible for widespread use and has allowed manufacturers to develop low-cost chip implementations of data encryption algorithms. With the use of conventional encryption, the principal security problem is maintaining the secrecy of the key.

If encryption is used, managers need to decide what to encrypt and where the encryption gear should be located. In most cases, there are two fundamental alternatives: link encryption and end-to-end encryption.

With link encryption, each vulnerable communications link is equipped on both ends with an encryption device, securing all traffic over all communications links. However, the message is vulnerable at each switch. Users of a public packet-switching network have no control over node security.

With end-to-end encryption, this process is carried out at the two end systems. A source host or terminal encrypts the data, which is then transmitted in an unaltered state across the network. A destination terminal or host then decrypts the data by using a shared key. Although this approach would seem to secure the transmission against attacks on the network links or switches, there is still a weak spot. User data is secure but the traffic pattern is not, because packet headers are transmitted in the clear. To achieve greater security, both link and end-to-end encryption are needed.

When both forms of encryption are employed, the host encrypts the user-data portion of a packet using an end-to-end encryption key. The entire packets is then encrypted using a link encryption key. As the packet traverses the network, each switch decrypts the packet using a link encryption key. This permits reading of the header. It then encrypts the entire packet again for transmission, sending it to the next link. Now the entire packet is secure, except for the time that the packet is actually in the memory of a packet switch, at which time the packet header is in the clear.

For conventional encryption to work, the two parties to an exchange must have the same key, and that key must be protected from access by others. Frequent key changes limit the amount of data compromised if an attacker learns the key.

Public-key encryption

Securely distributing keys is a major difficulty of conventional encryption. A clever way around this requirement is public-key encryption.

For conventional schemes, encryption and decryption keys are the same. Public key encryption solves the distribution problem, because there are no keys to distribute. All participants have access to public keys, and private keys are generated locally by each participant and, therefore, need never be distributed. As long as a system contols its private key, its incoming communication is secure.

At any time, a system can change its private key and publish the companion public key to replace its old public key.

A main disadvantage of public-key encryption is that its algorithms are very complex. So, for comparable size and cost of hardware, the public-key scheme will provide much lower throughput.

One possible application of public-key encryption is to use it for the permanent key portion, with conventional encryption keys used for session keys. Because there are few control messages relative to the amount of user data traffic, the reduced throughput should not be a handicap.

Users concerned about security from traffic analysis can effectively use link encryption. In this approach, packet headers are encrypted, which reduces the opportunity for traffic analysis.

It is still possible, however, for an attacker to assess the network traffic volume and observe the amount of traffic entering and leaving each end system. An effective countermeasure to this attack is the use of traffic pad-

---

Potential network security threats
Prevention is the key to fighting passive threats; for active threats, quick detection and recovery are crucial

Passive threats:
Monitoring and/or recording data while data is being transmitted over a communications facility

- **Release of message contents**
  Attacker can read user data in messages.

- **Traffic analysis**
  Attacker can read user packet headers to determine location and identity of communicating hosts. Attacker can also observe length and frequency of messages.

Active threats:
Unauthorized use of a device attached to a communications facility to alter transmitting data or control signals or generate spurious data or control signals

- **Denial of message service**
  Attacker can destroy or delay most or all messages.

- **Masquerade**
  Attacker can pose as real host or switch and communicate with another host or switch to acquire data or services.

- **Message stream modification**
  Attacker can selectively modify, delete, delay, reorder and duplicate real messages. Attacker can also insert counterfeit messages.

SOURCE: COMP-COMM CONSULTING CW CHART: TOM MONAHAN

> ### On the safe side
>
> In addition to the mechanisms related to specific services, there are five referred to by the ISO as pervasive security mechanisms. These are not explicitly related to any service and are not assigned to any particular layer of the OSI model.
> • Trusted functionality. This technology can be used to extend the scope or effectiveness of other security mechanisms. Any functionality that directly provides, or provides access to, security mechanisms should be trustworthy.
> • Security labeling. This is used to indicate the classification level or sensitivity of the labeled data. A security label may also be additional data associated with the data transferred or may be implicit—that is, implied by the use of a specific key to encrypt data or implied by the context of the data such as the source or route.
> • Event detection. Security-relevant event detection includes the detection of apparent violations of security and may also include detection of "normal" events—for example, a successful access or log-on.
> • Security audit trail. This potentially permits detection and investigation of breaches of security by permitting a subsequent security audit.
>
> A security audit is an independent review and examination of system records and activities in order to test for adequacy of system control, ensure compliance with established policy and operational procedures, aid in damage assessment and recommend any indicated changes in controls, policy or procedures.
> • Security recovery. This category deals with requests from other mechanisms, such as event handling, and takes recovery actions as the result of applying a set of rules. These recovery actions may be immediate, temporary or long-term.
> —*William Stallings*

ding.

• Traffic padding. This is a function that generates a continuous stream of random data or ciphertext. This makes it impossible for an attacker to distinguish between true data flow and noise; therefore, it is impossible to deduce the amount of traffic.

• Message authentication. This is a procedure that lets communicating parties verify that received messages are authentic. This ensures that contents have not been altered and that the source is authentic.

A common method of message authentication involves the use of a message authentication code. Data plus the code are transmitted to the intended recipient.

The recipient performs the same calculation on the data, using the same secret key, to generate a new message authentication code. The received code is then compared with the calculated code.

Several algorithms can be used to generate the code. The National Bureau of Standards, in its publication, "DES Modes of Operation," recommends the use of the Data Encryption Standard (DES) algorithm. The DES algorithm is used to generate an encrypted version of the message, and the last number of bits of ciphertext are used as the code. A 16- or 32-bit code is typical.

The most common practical use of authentication has been for financial messages, such as payments. For example, the Society for Worldwide Interbank Financial Telecommunications uses an authentication function.

It is possible to perform authentication simply by the use of conventional encryption. If we assume that only the sender and receiver share a key, then only the genuine sender would be able to encrypt a message successfully for the receiver. Furthermore, if the message includes an error-detection code and a sequence number, the receiver is assured that no alterations have been made and that sequencing is proper.

Digital signature

Authentication protects two parties exchanging messages from any third party. However, it does not protect the two parties from each other. A solution to this problem is the digital signature.

The digital signature is analogous to a handwritten signature. It lets users verify the author, date and time of the signature and authenticate the contents at the time of the signature. The digital signature also can be verified by third parties to resolve disputes.

Administrative controls that boost the security of private keys can be employed with some success, but the problems can be circumvented using an arbitrated signature scheme.

While there are a variety of approaches, most signature systems operate as follows: Every signed message from a sender S to a receiver R goes first to an arbitrater A, who subjects the message and its signature to a number of tests to check its origin and content.

The message is then dated and sent to R with an indication that it has been verified to the satisfaction of the arbitrator. The presence of A solves the problem faced by direct signature schemes that S might disown the message.

The arbitrator plays a sensitive and crucial role in this sort of scheme, and all parties must have a great deal of trust that the arbitration mechanism is working properly.

Digital signature schemes provide authentication plus the ability to resolve disputes between the communicating parties. While authentication is becoming popular, digital signatures are still rare. The principal reason is that the scheme is more complex and, therefore, more costly. Digital signature schemes require administrative control mechanisms or procedures. In some circumstances, only pure authentication is required.

Definitive service

The ISO defines a security service as a function provided by communicating systems to enhance the security of the systems and the data transfers taking place. These services are broken down into five categories: confidentiality, integrity, authentication, access control and nonrepudiation.

A security mechanism is any software or hardware means of implementing a security service (see chart).

• Confidentiality. This category of service protects transmitted data from passive attacks. Several levels guard against the release of message contents. The broadest service protects all user data transmitted between two users over a period of time.

A key aspect is the protection of traffic flow from analysis. This tries to prevent an attacker from observing the source and destination, frequency,

Security services and mechanisms
Using OSI specs, vendors and customers can configure a set of services and mechanisms to their needs

Services	Encryption	Digital signature	Access control	Data integrity	Authentication exchange	Traffic padding	Routing control	Notarization
Confidentiality								
Selective field confidentiality	●	●	●	●	●	●	●	●
Connectionless confidentiality	●	●	●	●	●	●	●	●
Connection confidentiality	●	●	●	●	●	●	●	●
Traffic flow confidentiality	●	●	●	●	●	●	●	●
Integrity								
Selective field connectionless integrity	●	●	●	●	●	●	●	●
Connectionless integrity	●	●	●	●	●	●	●	●
Selective field connection integrity	●	●	●	●	●	●	●	●
Connection integrity with recovery	●	●	●	●	●	●	●	●
Connection integrity without recovery	●	●	●	●	●	●	●	●
Authentication								
Peer entity authentication	●	●	●	●	●	●	●	●
Data origin authentication	●	●	●	●	●	●	●	●
Access control	●	●	●	●	●	●	●	●

SOURCE: COMP-COMM CONSULTING   CW CHART: TOM MONAHAN

length or other characteristics of the traffic on a communications facility.

Another mechanism that may be relevant to confidentiality is routing control. For sensitive data, routes can be chosen that will use only physically secure networks or links. For example, a user may employ both a private network and public telecommunications networks to interconnect offices. If the private network is equipped with an encryption mechanism, then all sensitive data should be routed through the private network only.

• Integrity. This service assures that messages are received as sent, with no duplication, insertion, modification, replays or destruction. As with confidentiality, integrity can apply to a stream of messages, a single message or selected fields within a message.

Integrity of selective fields or individual messages can be provided by an error-detecting code, such as that used on data link control protocols. If any of the fields in a data unit are altered, then an error will be detected, just as if a bit error had occurred in transmission. Of course, the attacker might alter part of the message, recalculate the error-detection code and alter that as well. To prevent this maneuver, the error-detecting code or the entire message can be encrypted.

To protect the integrity of a sequence of data units (that is, protecting against misordering, losing or replaying of messages), sequence numbers can be used. As with error-detecting codes, sequence numbers are already incorporated into protocols such as High-Level Data Link Control, X.25 and the ISO transport protocol. Again, to protect the sequence number itself from modification, it may be encrypted.

A final technique that has relevance for integrity of a single message or fields within a single message is the digital signature mechanism. If the digital signature includes the encipherment of an error-detecting code, then the signature detects modification of the contents of the message.

• Authentication. This service is concerned with ensuring that a communication is authentic. In the case of a single message, such as a warning or alarm signal, the authentication service guarantees that the message is from the source that it claims to be from.

In ongoing interaction, such as the connection of a terminal to a host, two aspects are involved. First, at the time of connection initiation, the service ensures that the two entities are authentic; that is, that each is the entity it claims to be. Second, the service must ensure that the connection is not interfered with in such a way that a third party can masquerade as one of the two legitimate parties for the purposes of unauthorized transmission or reception.

Again, encryption is a key mechanism used for this service. If two parties and two parties alone share the information needed for mutual exchange of encrypted data, then no third party can claim a false identity. A more explicit technique is the digital signature technique. In effect, a sender must "sign" the message in such a way that the signature can be authenticated.

Other mechanisms relevant to authentication are the ISO's authentication exchange mechanisms. These include the use of passwords or other means of identifying a user and the exchange of acknowledgment signals. Also included in this category is the use of an encrypted message authentication code.

• Nonrepudiation. In network security, access control limits and controls the access to host systems and applications via communications links. To achieve this, each entity trying to gain access must first be identified, or authenticated, so that access rights can be tailored to the individual.

The nonrepudiation service prevents either sender or receiver from denying a transmitted message. The principal mechanism for this service is the digital signature, which involves the use of a private key applied to a portion of the data. To prevent the repudiation of the contents of a message, rather than the message itself, data integrity mechanisms, such as encrypting an error-detecting code, are used as part of the digital signature. Finally, third-party notarization may enhance the nonrepudiation service.

The reality of OSI Management

This is Part 1 of a two-part series examining Open Systems Interconnection Management.

**By Will Collins
and Kathryn Korostoff**
Special to Network World

Misconceptions about OSI Management have led to inaccurate conclusions about its current status and future potential.

OSI Management is simply a group of standards and definitions that vendors, committed to open systems, can use to ensure interoperability between their open systems and network management products.

Many of these standards and definitions are near completion, and three major components have already been accorded international standard or draft international standard status by the International Standards Organization (ISO). The management framework is an international standard, Common Management Information Protocol/Common Manage-

Collins is chairman of the ANSI/ASC/X3T5.4 OSI Management Committee, chartered with developing U.S. positions on Open Systems Interconnection Management protocols for the International Standards Organization. He is also a consulting engineer at Canton, Mass.-based Codex Corp. Korostoff is a market analysis manager at Codex.

ment Information Services (CMIP/CMIS) is a draft international standard, and the OSI Directory is an international standard.

Some misconceptions about the impact OSI Management will have on the future of network management also exist. Statements bandied about the industry, such as "Vendors won't be able to differentiate themselves" and "OSI Management won't be a reality until 1995," are based on misinformation.

Progress report

Confusion about OSI Management and the standards process has resulted in misconceptions about the progress that has been made thus far.

OSI Management is not a single standard. Rather, it is a set of standards currently consisting of 17 components, each of which is being evaluated within the standards process. Therefore, each component is at a different stage in the standard development cycle.

The parts of OSI Management are described and defined in six modular units, which are being developed by international standards committees. One of those committees is ISO/EIC JTC1/SC21/WG4, which is the International Organization for Standardization's international standards committee for OSI Management. Participating in that committee on behalf of the U.S. is ANSI/ASC/X3T5.4.

The six OSI Management modules from the ANSI/ASC/X3T5.4 committee are:

■ The framework module, which defines five Specific Management Functional Areas (SMFAs), introduces primary concepts such as managed objects and describes three methods of management information exchange within and between open systems.

■ The Common Management Information Services Element (CMISE) modules include CMIS, which defines a set of services used by management processes to act upon an agent process, and CMIP, which specifies an application-

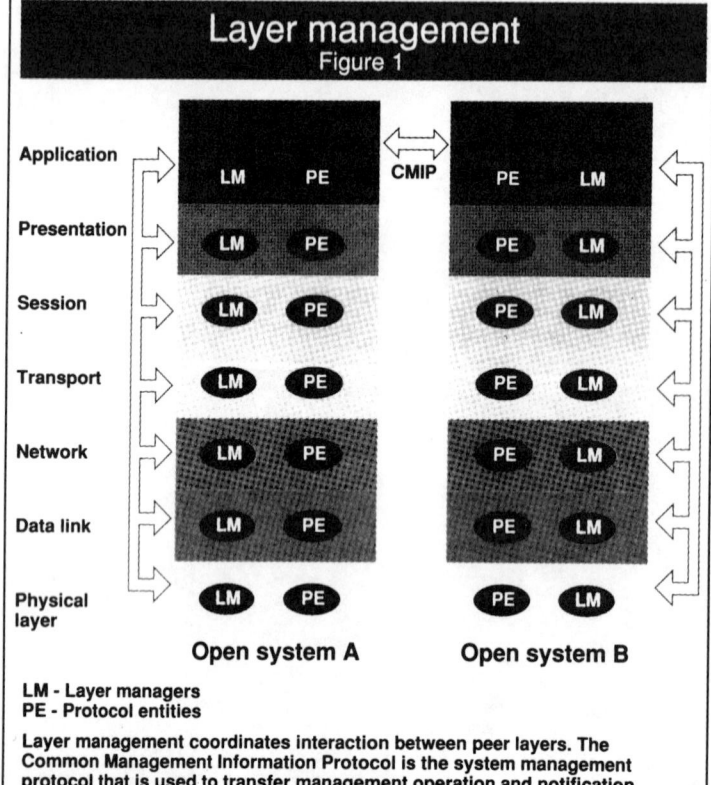

Layer management
Figure 1

	Open system A		Open system B	
Application	LM	PE	PE	LM
		CMIP		
Presentation	LM	PE	PE	LM
Session	LM	PE	PE	LM
Transport	LM	PE	PE	LM
Network	LM	PE	PE	LM
Data link	LM	PE	PE	LM
Physical layer	LM	PE	PE	LM

LM - Layer managers
PE - Protocol entities

Layer management coordinates interaction between peer layers. The Common Management Information Protocol is the system management protocol that is used to transfer management operation and notification instructions between the two open systems.

GRAPHIC BY SUSAN SLATER   SOURCE: CODEX CORP., CANTON, MASS.

Copyright © October 1989 by Network World, Inc., Framingham, MA 01701. Reprinted from *Network World*.

layer protocol for exchange of management information.

■ The Systems Management Overview (SMO), a document in which functional aspects describe the relationships between SMFAs and systems management functions. Each SMFA uses one or more systems management functions.

In the SMO, the section on communications aspects describes how interactions between managing and agent processes are realized through the exchange of management information. The section on organizational aspects describes how managing and agent processes interact, and the section on information aspects describes how to define managed objects.

■ The Structure of Management Information Module is a set of documents that provides principles for defining managed objects, and their attributes. These documents also define what operations (commands) can be used on managed objects and attributes.

■ Systems Management Functions, which describes a set of systems management functions that the five SMFAs use. The five SMFAs are: Configuration Management, Fault Management, Performance Management, Accounting Management and Security Management.

■ Functional Area Documents (FAD). Each SMFA has a FAD that provides details of its functions.

Although all parts of the OSI Management standards have not yet achieved international standard status, that does not mean they are far from it. A standard in the making goes through four stages — the working document, the draft proposal, the draft international standard and the international standard — and the process usually takes about two to three years. If a second draft proposal or draft international standard is not required, the time frame is easily under three years.

Figure 2 on this page illustrates the current status of OSI Management parts.

All ISO-approved standards are, however, based upon consensus. In a committee such as X3T5.4, which operates under ANSI but requires approval from the ISO for an international standard, reaching a decision by consensus is a formidable challenge.

Satisfying both the interests of U.S.-based organizations participating in ANSI and the various countries that the ISO represents often requires a great deal of compromise and time-consuming negotiation.

Most of the OSI Management components are at the draft proposal stage. While this may seem discour-

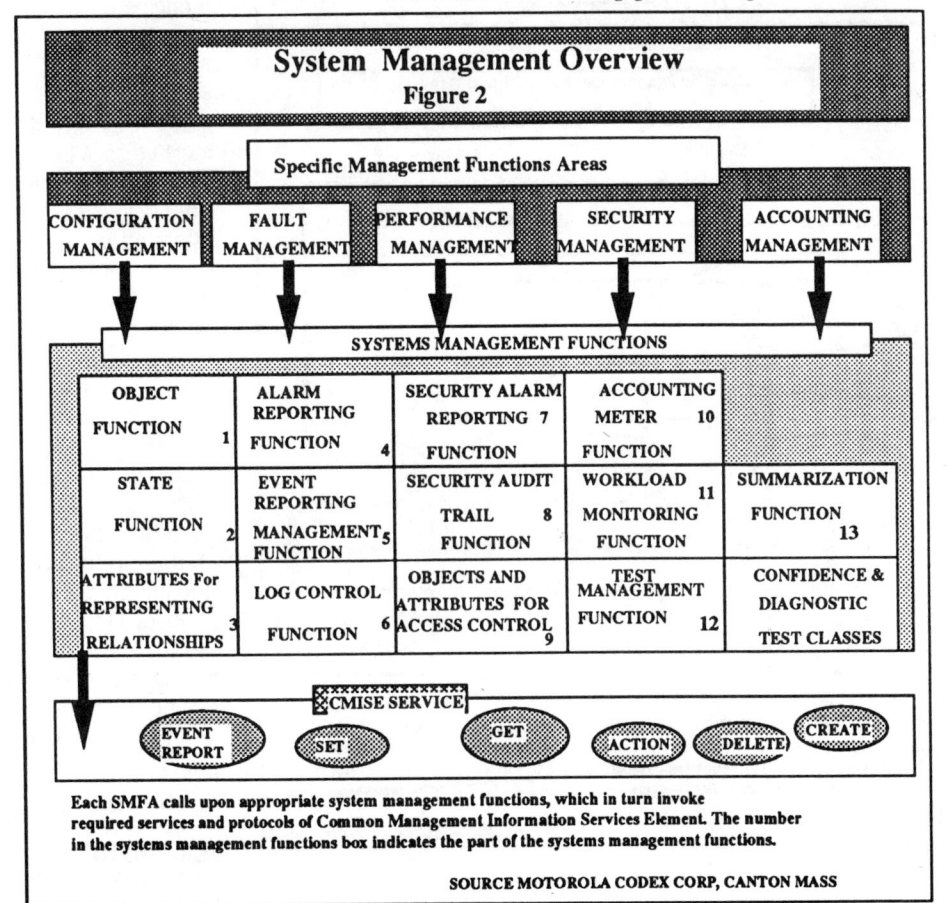

Standards status

Title	Status
OSI Management Framework	International Standard
Systems Management Overview	International Standard
Structure of Management Information	
Management Information Model	International Standard
Definition of Management Information	International Standard
Guidelines for Definition of Managed Object	International Standard
Generic Management Information	Committee Draft
Guidelines for Conformance Statement Proforma	Committee Draft
Common Management Information Services	International Standard
Common Management Information Protocol	International Standard
Systems Management Functions	
Object Management Function	International Standard
State Management Function	International Standard
Attributes for Representing Relationships	International Standard
Alarm Reporting Function	International Standard
Error Reporting Management Function	International Standard
Log Control Function	International Standard
Security Alarm Reporting Function	International Standard
Security Audit Trail Function	Draft International Standard
Object and Attributes for Access Control	Draft International Standard
Accounting Meter Function	Draft International Standard
Workload Monitoring Function	Draft International Standard
Test Management Function	Committee Draft

SOURCE: ANSI/ANSC X3T5.4

System Management Overview
Figure 2

Specific Management Functions Areas

CONFIGURATION MANAGEMENT | FAULT MANAGEMENT | PERFORMANCE MANAGEMENT | SECURITY MANAGEMENT | ACCOUNTING MANAGEMENT

SYSTEMS MANAGEMENT FUNCTIONS

OBJECT FUNCTION 1	ALARM REPORTING FUNCTION 4	SECURITY ALARM REPORTING FUNCTION 7	ACCOUNTING METER FUNCTION 10	
STATE FUNCTION 2	EVENT REPORTING MANAGEMENT FUNCTION 5	SECURITY AUDIT TRAIL FUNCTION 8	WORKLOAD MONITORING FUNCTION 11	SUMMARIZATION FUNCTION 13
ATTRIBUTES For REPRESENTING RELATIONSHIPS 3	LOG CONTROL FUNCTION 6	OBJECTS AND ATTRIBUTES FOR ACCESS CONTROL 9	TEST MANAGEMENT FUNCTION 12	CONFIDENCE & DIAGNOSTIC TEST CLASSES

CMISE SERVICE: EVENT REPORT, SET, GET, ACTION, DELETE, CREATE

Each SMFA calls upon appropriate system management functions, which in turn invoke required services and protocols of Common Management Information Services Element. The number in the systems management functions box indicates the part of the systems management functions.

SOURCE: MOTOROLA CODEX CORP, CANTON MASS

aging, the fact that the framework document has achieved international standard status is important. The framework is the OSI Management model. Because it has reached international standard status, it sets a precedent for the acceptance of the other components.

What OSI Management is

OSI Management is not a specification for network management systems. It provides specifications and definitions for applications that can be used in various products, including network management systems. No such product as an OSI network management system exists, nor does an OSI network management system standard.

OSI Management defines a subset of what performance measurement information should be captured and how it should be formatted for transfer between open systems. It does not define how vendors provide services such as performance measurement within their own network management systems.

Also, OSI Management does not require all vendors to offer the same management and control services. Thus, a vendor may choose to support configuration management and fault management as specified by OSI Management but may choose not to support performance measurement as specified by OSI.

In addition, OSI Management does not force vendors to provide identical user interfaces. Each vendor will still create its own graphical representations of equipment and network configurations, trouble ticket layouts and alarm notifications. Thus, just because a vendor announces support for OSI Management does not mean its critical alarms will change from red to yellow or its trouble tickets will be displayed in a new unrecognizable fashion.

OSI Management defines management operations and notifications as acting at the boundary of the managed object to which they relate. No corresponding internal systems interface is subject to standardization. Thus, it is possible to easily and inexpensively upgrade an existing network of modems to support OSI Management.

A common denominator

OSI Management provides a common language and the requisite protocol specifications that create a common denominator for participating vendors' products. Thus, two types of information are standardized: services and protocols used to transfer management information between open systems, and the syntax and semantics of the information transferred through OSI Management.

Much of the work of establishing OSI Management involves deciding what types of information open systems should share and creating definitions that OSI committee members can agree upon. The first task that had to be tackled was the creation of a framework that specifies what should be included in OSI Management.

The framework document of the OSI Management standards states that its purpose is "to provide a common basis for the coordinated development of management standards." The framework is not an implementation specification but a conceptual model.

OSI Management is concerned with identifying and defining the tools and services needed to monitor, control and coordinate interconnection activities among open systems. The conceptual model described by the framework can be divided into two parts: functional aspect definitions and model definition.

OSI Management currently defines five SMFAs: fault management, accounting management, configuration management, performance management and security management. Each SMFA is defined in detail in a set of FADs.

The framework as model

The framework document also introduces the concept of the managed object and its role in the OSI management model. A managed object is any resource that is subject to management within the open system environment.

For example, managed objects can be protocol entities, such as protocol machines; network connections, such as an X.25 connection; or communications equipment, such as modems.

In OSI management, a managed object is defined as having a set of characteristics. What are the object's attributes? What operations may be performed on the object's attributes? What information or notifications can the object send? What is the object's relationship to other objects in the open system? Thus, OSI management recognizes a resource within the open system as a managed object with specific types of characteristics.

As described in the OSI Management framework document, there are three types of management information exchange: layer management, systems management and management information in normal layer protocol.

Layer management refers to mechanisms that monitor and control objects that relate to a specific layer of

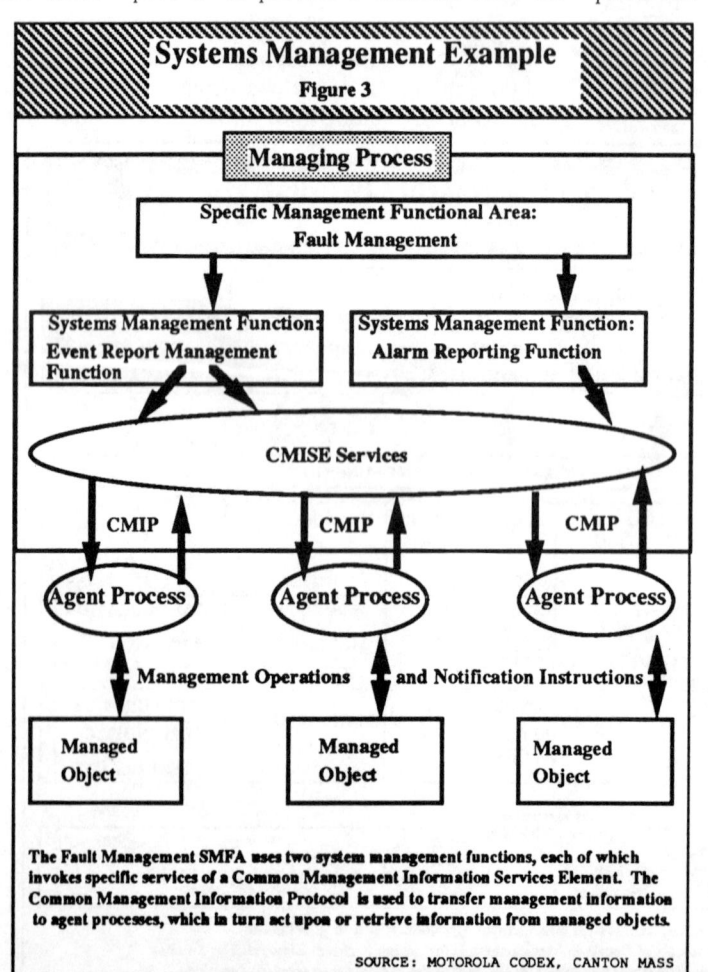

Systems Management Example
Figure 3

The Fault Management SMFA uses two system management functions, each of which invokes specific services of a Common Management Information Services Element. The Common Management Information Protocol is used to transfer management information to agent processes, which in turn act upon or retrieve information from managed objects.

SOURCE: MOTOROLA CODEX, CANTON MASS

the OSI model. This is referred to as (N)-layer management. Layer management coordinates interaction between peer layers and exists at each layer of the OSI reference model. Each layer also has protocol entities, which refer to the protocol standards developed for that layer (see Figure 1, page 1).

At each layer of the OSI model, layer management facilitates the coordination of OSI management functions and processes (referred to as agents and managers).

Systems management refers to mechanisms that monitor and coordinate managed objects through the use of application-layer systems management protocols. Systems management acts upon these objects to manage the resources that each object represents. OSI communications about systems management are realized through a systems management application entity (SMAE) (see "Summary of application layer services," this page).

One or more application service element (ASE) is called an SMAE. SMAEs define the services that can be provided by OSI Management applications.

SMAE management sends commands, responses and event reports to and from OSI systems. SMAE management services are provided by a set of four ASEs: systems management application service element, CMISE, remote operation service element and association control service element.

While the framework document introduces the role of SMAEs in the OSI Management model, their actual definitions are described in the systems management overview document.

Use of existing protocols

There are facilities embedded within existing protocols, and OSI Management can take advantage of both the facilities and the protocols. For example, the accounting information contained in an X.25 packet already exists in the X.25 protocol. The framework document recognizes the existence of such protocols as providing management information that can be used in OSI Management.

Much work has gone into the development of a detailed, conceptual model that all committee members agree on. It is important to understand that this is only a conceptual model and that there are no conformance requirements associated with the OSI Management framework.

The framework document has been approved as an international standard, setting an important foundation for further development of OSI Management.

CMISE

The CMISE document describes CMIS and CMIP. CMIS defines the services that are provided for realizing the systems management functions. There are three types of services: management association services, such as M-INITIALIZE, which allow CMISE service users to associate with one another; management notification services, such as M-EVENT-REPORT, which allow CMISE service users to report events to one another; and management operation services, such as M-GET, which allow CMISE service users to request management information from one another.

CMIP is a specification for a protocol used by application-layer entities to exchange management information. CMIP specifies protocols, such as transfer syntax, which can be used to provide the services defined in CMIS.

The CMISE module only introduces CMIS and CMIP and their roles in OSI Management. Actual definitions of the protocols are provided in the SMO document.

Network management systems that use OSI Management applications will be able to share information and recognize one another's commands since the services and protocols specified in CMIS and CMIP will be common. Thus, CMISE brings integrated network management within reach.

However, the CMISE module only introduces CMIS and CMIP and their roles in OSI Management; the SMO document provides actual definitions.

Systems management

The SMO document defines how the various parts of OSI Management work together to monitor, control and coordinate managed objects within the OSI environment. The SMO document is an important standard because it ensures a common approach to OSI systems management.

SMO currently defines four systems management standards. Functional aspects describe seven system management functions that support the five SMFAs: fault management, accounting management, configuration management, performance management and security management. Each SMFA is served by one or more systems management functions. Systems management functions use CMISE-defined services and protocols to manipulate managed objects (see Figure 2, page 2).

Thus, each SMFA calls upon appropriate systems management functions, which in turn invoke required CMISE services and protocols. The actual descriptions of the systems management functions are in the systems management function documents.

Management activities are realized

Summary of applications-layer services

A Systems Management Application Entity (SMAE) is made up of one or more Application Service Elements (ASE).

The Open Systems Interconnection management user has to implement OSI services at the application layer.

This is done through the use of SMAEs and ASEs, all of which reside within the application layer — Layer 7 of the OSI reference model.

Looking into Layer 7

ASEs have two components: a service component and a protocol component. For example, in the Common Management Information Service Element (CMISE), Common Management Information Services defines a set of services and Common Management Information Protocol defines protocol.

Currently, OSI management uses four ASEs:

■ Systems Management Application Service Element (SMASE), which includes the many system management functions that use CMISE services.

■ CMISE, which includes many common management information services and the specification for Common Management Information Protocol.

■ Remote Operation Service Element (ROSE), which includes a service component providing for remote OSI management operations. Includes the specification for remote operation protocol.

■ Association Control Service Element (ACSE), which includes a service component that provides association between peer SMAEs. Includes the specification for association control protocol.

SMASE, CMISE and ROSE all transfer information. ACSE is the ASE that establishes a connection, or association, among the peer SMAEs.

— *Will Collins*

through processes that manipulate managed objects. For the purpose of systems management, management processes are categorized as either managing processes or agent processes.

A managing process is responsible for one or more management activities and refers to a set of systems management functions and their corresponding CMISE services in a specific management application.

An agent process responds to managing processes by acting upon managed objects. Agent processes may also forward information or notifications about managed objects upon request by a managing process.

Communications aspects describe how underlying communications facilities support network management communications. Interactions between managing and agent processes are realized through the exchange of management information. This communications is accomplished using OSI protocols such as CMIP.

Figure 3 on page 3 is an example of how SMFAs, managing processes and agent processes fit into the model we have described so far. This example shows how one SMFA—in this case, fault management—uses two system management functions: Event Reporting Management Function and Alarm Reporting Function.

These systems management functions map to CMISE services and use CMIP to transfer management information to agent processes. The agent processes act upon or retrieve information from managed objects, illustrated by the two-way arrow between the agent process and managed object.

Information aspects describe the logical structure of management information, provide guidelines for the definition of objects and describe the classification of managed objects.

SMO introduces some definitions that are important throughout the OSI Management standard documentation:
- (N)-layer managed objects, a managed object specific to the (N)-layer.
- Agent process, a management process capable of performing operations on managed objects and issuing event reports on behalf of managed objects.
- Management process, an application process participating in systems management.
- Managing process, a management process capable of issuing operations and receiving responses and event reports from agent processes.

Management information

The Structure of Management Information (SMI) document provides principles for defining managed objects and their attributes. This document also defines which operations, or commands, can be used on managed objects and attributes.

Managed objects are "abstractions" of actual resources in an open system. Attributes describe an actual resource, providing the definition of a specific managed object. Attributes have specific values, which allow managing processes to act upon the managed objects. For example, a management process may be GET attribute value or SET attribute value.

The standardization of the definition and attributes of managed objects is critical to the realization of OSI Management applications in network management systems. If integrated network management systems are ever to become a reality, a common approach to defining network resources and their attributes must be accepted. For example, the ability to GET attribute value information from network resources, regardless of vendor make, is critical to integrated network management.

The current status of the four major components of OSI Management detailed in this article — the framework, CMISE, SMO and SMI — shows that X3T5.4 has made a great deal of progress in defining and describing OSI Management. The variety of processes and functions that X3T5.4 has defined will provide network management vendors and users with an unprecedented set of tools for managing open systems.

Current activities in OSI Management include:
- A National Institute of Standards and Technology Special Interest Group on OSI Management.
- The OSI Network Management Forum.
- The endorsement of OSI Management by major vendors, including AT&T and IBM.

In Part 2 of this series, we will discuss these current activities and other OSI Management issues of which network management users need to be aware.

Misconceptions vs. reality

Despite widespread misperception, the set of standards and specifications comprising OSI Management are healthy and rapidly approaching maturity.

Seven Systems Management Functions
Figure 1

1. Object Management Function
2. State Management Function
3. Attributes for Representing Relationships
4. Alarm Reporting Function
5. Event Reporting Management Function
6. Log Control Function
7. Security Alarm Reporting Function

SOURCE: ANSI/ANSC X3T5.4

Part 2 of a two-part series on Open Systems Interconnection Management.

OSI Management offers many potential benefits and raises many long-term strategic issues. Part 1 of this article examined the progress that has been made in the different areas of OSI Management.

Currently, the parts of OSI Management are described and defined in six modular units, which are being developed by international standards committees. One of these committees is ISO/EIC JTC1/SC21/WG4, which is the International Standards Organization's (ISO) international standards committee for OSI Management. Participating in that committee on behalf of the U.S. is ANSI/ASC/X3T5.4.

To understand the complexity and variety of functions being developed by the ISO committee, we must examine the two remaining areas: the Systems Management Functions (SMF) documents and the Functional Area Documents (FAD).

SMFs

SMFs carry out the management processes, or activities, specified by the various Specific Management Functional Areas (SMFA). Each FAD specifies which of the SMFs are used by the various SMFAs. For example, a state management SMF is used by the fault management and configuration management SMFAs.

Currently, thirteen SMF's are defined. Seven of the System Management Functions (SMFs) are discussed (Figure 1).

■ **Object management.** This uses OSI services, such as those specified in the Common Management Information Services (CMIS) standard, to perform actions on managed objects. These actions include creating, deleting and renaming managed objects. For example, the management function Object Management may invoke the CMIS service M-DELETE to delete a managed object from an open system.

Within the Object Management definitions, services are specified that allow reports about Object Management activities to be communicated to other open systems. For example, an attribute change event report service can be used to send an event report to another open system if an object's attributes change.

■ **State management.** This describes services that allow the OSI Management user to monitor the past state of managed objects and receive notices, or alarms, in response to changes in the state of managed objects.

The State Change Reporting service uses the general EVENT REPORT service to notify users of changes in the values of managed object state attributes.

■ **Attributes for representing relationships.** This describes a service that allows an end system in an agent role to report the changes in the values of managed object relationship attributes. This service uses the general EVENT REPORT service. Relationships among managed objects is a complicated issue.

In general, a relationship is a set of rules that describes how the operation of one managed object affects the operation of another managed object within an open system.

For example, two managed objects in an open system may have a relationship in which one is activated in the event that the other fails as a result of a fault management diagnostic.

Alarm reporting function. This allows various types of information to be reported and retrieved through the open system.

Descriptions of error types, probable causes and measures of severity are specified. This type of functionality will be essential in integrated network management scenarios where users have more than one network in place. For example, a single network management system's ability to access information about errors occurring in two open systems could be important in situations where a relationship exists between the two open systems.

Types of errors defined by this SMF are: communications failure, quality of service failure, processing failure, environment failure and equipment failure. Error reporting services for each type of error are defined in this SMF.

Probable cause information provided by this SMF would indicate the problem that results in an error.

For example, in the case of a communications failure, a probable cause might be a call establishment error.

Five severity parameters are defined: indeterminate, critical, major, minor and warning. In a network management application of this SMF, the ability to categorize alarms by severity helps the network manager decide quickly which alarms must be responded to immediately and which ones can wait.

This SMF uses the general EVENT REPORT service to report alarms.

■ **Event report management.** This describes services that allow the management system user to determine which event reports are to be sent where.

For example, this SMF could play a key role in network management systems scenarios by allowing the network manager to specify which information can be exchanged between Manager Processes and Agent Processes. Consider a scenario in which a user has one Manager Process that centralizes management of multiple separate Agent Processes (see Figure 2, page 7).

As the figure illustrates, the Management Service Control functions will allow the user to choose which types of event reports will be exchanged between the Manager Process and the individual Agent Process.

■ **Security alarm reporting function.** This describes the service provided to report security attacks, security service misoperation or other security-related events. This service uses the general EVENT REPORT service.

Log control. This service allows users to choose which event reports the system will log. The log control function also enables an external managing system user to change the criteria used for logging event reports.

The application of the log control function in a network management scenario is very important. The network manager wants the ability to specify which events should be logged, but the ability to add or delete event reports to be logged is also very important. For example, the user may want to log only critical event reports, but at a later date, perhaps the need to track all reports on a historical basis will become important.

These descriptions of the management functions detailed in the SMF documents verify that the X3T5.4 committee has made substantial progress toward providing a powerful set of OSI Management tools. The potential benefits of using these functions as applications in a network management system are obvious: The reality of integrated network management is within reach.

The accompanying chart shows the current status of the SMFs. While four of the seven SMFs are still draft proposals, their advancement to draft international standard status is expected by 1990 (see "Status of SMFs," this page).

FADs

The various functional areas are defined within the OSI Management Framework standard document. In addition, a FAD for each SMFA describes the

---

Status of SMFs

Title	Status
Object Management Function	International Standard
State Management Function	International Standard
Attributes for Representing Relationships	International Standard
Alarm Reporting Function	International Standard
Event Reporting Management Function	International Standard
Log Control Function	International Standard
Security Alarm Reporting Function	International Standard

OSI Management tasks that the functional area provides, the set of specific management functions that are necessary for the provision of the functional area and the procedures associated with the use of these functions.

■ **Configuration management.** This is a set of functions that can control and retrieve information from managed objects. These functions include the ability to define and name managed objects; the ability to create, delete and modify relationships among managed objects; the ability to change the operating state of a managed object, including creation and deletion; and the ability to receive and respond to requests for information about managed objects.

Configuration management's associated management functions are object management, state management and relationship management. It has working document status.

■ **Fault management.** This is a set of functions that detect, isolate and correct abnormal operations in the open systems environment. This includes accepting error notifications, tracing error sources, maintaining error logs and performing diagnostics.

Its associated management functions are management service control, confidence and diagnostic testing, and error reporting and information retrieval. Fault management has working document status.

■ **Performance measurement.** This is a set of functions that monitor the performance of an open system. These include a work load monitoring function, a response time tracking function and a measurement summarization function.

Work load monitoring recognizes potential resource overload situations, an important fault prevention function. Response time tracking reports response times and generates warnings in the event of excessive delays. Measurement summarization gathers statistics, over a period of time, about the performance of managed objects.

Performance measurement's associated management functions have not been specified yet; it has working document status.

■ **Security management.** This supports the application and control of security mechanisms in the open systems environment. For example, in a network management scenario, these functions allow users to create security mechanisms that monitor the network and report security-related events to an application.

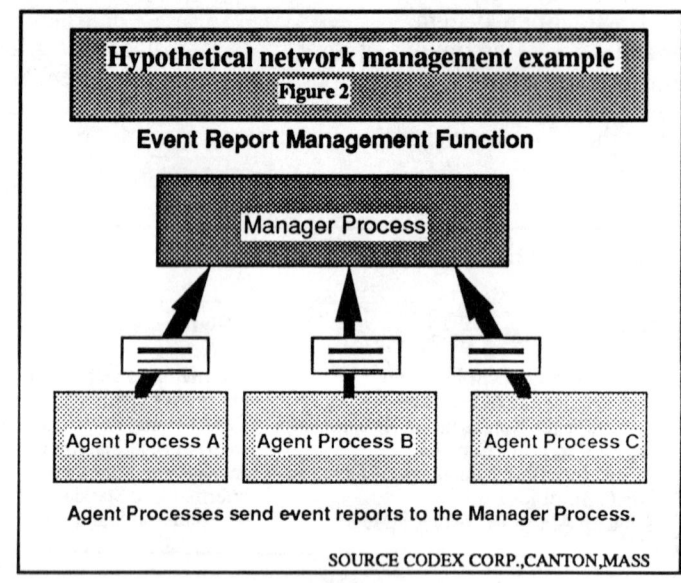

Security management has working document status. Its associated management functions have not been specified yet.

■ **Accounting management.** This provides functions that allow users to monitor their use of open systems and the costs associated with them.

This SMFA also allows network managers to monitor and store information about user accounts. These functions include the ability to set constraints.

For example, in a network management application of this SMFA, a network manager could impose time or expense constraints on users of specific network devices or facilities. It is not uncommon for network managers to want to track and sometimes limit expenses incurred from the use of network resources by specific individuals or departments. Accounting management's associated management functions have not been specified yet; it has working document status.

A great deal of industry activity surrounds OSI Management. The National Institute of Standards and Technology (NIST) has a special interest group following OSI Management. NIST's special interest group on network management serves as an implementors' advisory resource. NIST runs OSI implementors' workshops as a service to organizations interested in using OSI.

As part of its mission to assist users of OSI standards, the Network Management special interest group is working with the X3T5.4 Committee to support the standards development process. The special interest group is developing implementation agreements for OSI Management as part of its series of implementors' workshops. For example, the group is developing classes on OSI Management as part of its series of implementors' workshops.

Founded in September 1988, the OSI/Network Management (OSI/NM) Forum is a group of vendors working together to determine how they will actually use the OSI Management standards in their respective network management products. The group's goal is to ensure that the participating vendors develop compatible network management products based on OSI management standards.

The OSI/NM Forum counts among its 40-plus members key players such as AT&T, Hewlett-Packard Co. and Northern Telecom, Inc., but neither IBM nor Digital Equipment Corp. has joined. The forum's primary accomplishment to date has been the publication of two documents: the OSI/NM Forum Application Services document and the OSI/NM Forum Protocol Specification document. Forum members are using these documents to guide their development of network management products.

In addition to the vendors working toward OSI Management through the OSI/NM Forum, evidence abounds of vendor dedication to using OSI Management applications in their network management products. AT&T and IBM, the two vendors taking the strongest positions on integrated network management, have both stated their intentions to support OSI Management standards in their net management offerings.

AT&T's Unified Network Management Architecture offering has a Network Management Protocol (NMP) designed to be easily changed to the Common Management Information Protocol (CMIP). Thus, when CMIP becomes an international standard, AT&T will upgrade its systems from NMP to CMIP.

In September 1988, amongst a flurry of other OSI-related announcements, IBM

Hypothetical network management example
Figure 2
Event Report Management Function

Agent Processes send event reports to the Manager Process.
SOURCE CODEX CORP., CANTON, MASS

stated its intention to offer OSI Management support in NetView by mid-1990.

Figure 3 on this page illustrates vendor support of OSI Management as a standard for network management products.

Clearly, OSI Management has the potential to yield significant benefits for users interested in network management in general and integrated network management systems in particular. OSI Management provides a rich variety of functions which, if used in network management systems, will provide a powerful set of common services and functions.

For example, OSI Management-based network management products will be able to exchange information with and retrieve information from one another. Users will be able to decide and change which types of information will be exchanged or retrieved among network management systems.

Also, OSI Management-based network management products will be able to control and manage resources managed by other OSI Management systems. Users will be able to decide and change which commands may be invoked upon managed objects by remote network management systems.

Finally, users will expect to be able to enjoy the same level of functionality from all OSI-based network management products. Thus, vendors will be motivated to provide the full breadth of OSI Management applications in their OSI-based offerings.

OSI Management sets a precedent for the variety of functions network management systems should offer, even if the systems are not OSI Management-based. Thus, all suppliers of network management products will be motivated to develop a full range of functions to match those offered by OSI Management-based systems.

So, what strategic issues do users need to consider?

If integrated network management systems are part of your long-term planning, your short-term planning should include evaluation of vendors that plan to support OSI Management in their equipment and management systems. Do the vendors you are evaluating plan to support OSI Management?

And now that you are well versed in the functionality OSI Management can provide, you know what to look for in a network management product. So, when vendors make vague statements about OSI Management support, you can ask specific questions about which SMFAs they plan to support in their network management products.

Figure 4 on this page is a checklist of the five SMFAs. Under each SMFA, specific capabilities are identified. As you read the list, decide what level of importance the capability holds for you. With this list of prioritized capabilities in hand, you will be able to inform your network management suppliers of your OSI Management interests.

Vendor support of OSI Management applications
Figure 3

Vendor	OSI Network Management Forum member	ASC/X3T5.4 member	Product announcement
AT&T	Yes	Yes	Yes
Motorola Codex	Yes	Yes	Yes
Data General Corp.	Yes	Yes	Yes
Digital Equipment Corp.	Yes	Yes	Yes
Hewlett-Packard Co.	Yes	Yes	Yes
IBM	Yes	Yes	Yes
Northern Telecom, Inc.	Yes	Yes	Yes
Racal-Milgo	Yes	Yes	Yes
Unisys Corp.	Yes	Yes	Yes
Wang Laboratories, Inc.	No	Yes	Yes

Note: This is not a complete list of vendors supporting OSI Management applications for network management product development.

SOURCE CODEX CORP, CANTON, MASS

OSI Management checklist
Figure 4

OSI Management functions	Critical	Important	Somewhat Important	Not Important
Configuration management • Object management • State management • Attribute for representing relationships				
Fault management • Alarm reporting • Event report management • Log control • Test management				
Performance management • Workload monitoring • Summarization				
Security management • Security alarm reporting • Security audit trail • Object and attributes for access control				
Accounting management • Accounting meter				

SOURCE: CORDEX CORP, CANTON, MASS

The DARPA Internet Protocol Suite

Barry M. Leiner
Robert Cole
Jon Postel
David Mills

The suite of protocols supporting the DARPA internet system

The views represented in this paper are those of the authors and do not necessarily represent those of DARPA, DoD, or the U.S. Government. This research has been supported under a number of DARPA contracts.

THE MILITARY requirement for computer communications between heterogeneous computers on heterogeneous networks has driven the development of a standard suite of protocols to permit such communications to take place in a robust and flexible manner. These protocols support an architecture consisting of multiple packet switched networks interconnected by gateways. The DARPA experimental internet system consists of satellite, terrestrial, radio, and local networks, all interconnected through a system of gateways and a set of common protocols.

Introduction

The rapid proliferation of computers and other signal processing elements throughout the military, coupled with their need for reliable and efficient exchange of information, has driven the development of a number of computer networking technologies. The differences in both requirements and environments for these networks has resulted in different network designs. Furthermore, differences in requirements, coupled with changing technologies, has resulted in many different computer types being fielded. These different computers, although located on different networks, still have a requirement to communicate with each other.

Beginning with the ARPANET (the first packet-switched network) [1], the Defense Advanced Research Projects Agency (DARPA) has sponsored the development of a number of packet-switched networking technologies designed to provide robust and reliable computer communications. These networks have included the primarily land-line based ARPANET, packet radio networks [2,3], and satellite networks [4,5]. In addition, the use of other available technologies, such as local area networks and public data networks, has also been investigated.

As mentioned above, there is a significant need to be able to interconnect these various packet-switched networks so that computers on the various networks can communicate. Furthermore, this communication must be reliable and robust, making use of whatever communication facilities are available to accomplish end-to-end connectivity. To this end, DARPA initiated a program to investigate the issues in interconnection of different packet-switched networks. This effort has resulted in an architecture and set of protocols to accomplish this robust system of interconnected networks.

In this paper, the current status of the DARPA Experimental Internet System (the Internet for short) in terms of the architecture and set of protocols is described. The first section gives an overview of the Internet architecture, describing the key elements of the system, and their relation to each other. Following that, the set of protocols is described. Next, experiences in the test and development of the Internet are discussed. Finally, a summary and conclusions are given.

Throughout the reading of this paper, one should keep in mind that the Internet is still under development. Although a number of protocols have been standardized within the research community and are either currently Defense Department standards [4,5] or in the process of becoming standards, the Internet is constantly evolving with new functions and new protocols being developed to meet the ever-changing military requirements.

Architectural Overview

The DARPA Internet protocol suite is designed to support communication between heterogeneous hosts on heterogeneous

Reprinted from *IEEE Communications Magazine*, March 1985, pp. 29-34. Copyright © 1985 by The Institute of Electrical and Electronics Engineers, Inc. All rights reserved.

networks as shown in Fig. 1. A number of packet-switched networks are interconnected with gateways. Each of these networks are assumed to be designed separately in accordance with some specific requirements and environmental considerations (for example, radio line-of-sight and local cable networks). However, it is assumed that each network is capable of accepting a packet of information (data with appropriate network headers) and delivering it to a specified destination on that particular network. It is specifically not assumed that the network guarantees delivery of the packet. Specific networks may or may not have end-to-end reliability built into them.

Thus, two hosts connected to the same network are capable of sending packets of information between them. Should two hosts on different networks wish to communicate, the source host would send packets to the appropriate gateway, which then would route each packet through the system of gateways and networks until it reaches a gateway connected to the same network as the final host. At this point, the gateway sends the packet to the destination host.

The Internet can therefore be viewed as a set of hosts and gateways interconnected by networks. Each network can act as a link between the gateways and hosts residing on it, and a gateway looks like a typical host to any network. Packets are suitably routed between the hosts and gateways to use the correct networks to traverse the system from source to destination.

Taking this view, it is clear that the service required from each network is simply the ability to carry packets between attached hosts. Gateways attach to networks as hosts. Since mechanisms must be built into the system to provide end-to-end reliability even in the face of network failures (by, for example, routing packets through alternate networks), the only service required from the network is a datagram delivery service. This means that, given a packet with a destination address on the network, the network will attempt to deliver the packet to that destination.

The overall architecture can therefore be described as four layers. At the bottom layer, individual networks and mechanisms for connecting hosts to those networks are present. At the next layer, the Internet layer, are the mechanisms for connecting the various networks and gateways into a system capable of delivering packets from source to destination. At the next layer, end-to-end communication services are built in, including mechanisms such as end-to-end reliability and network control. Finally, at the upper layer, applications services are provided such as file transfer, virtual terminal, and mail.

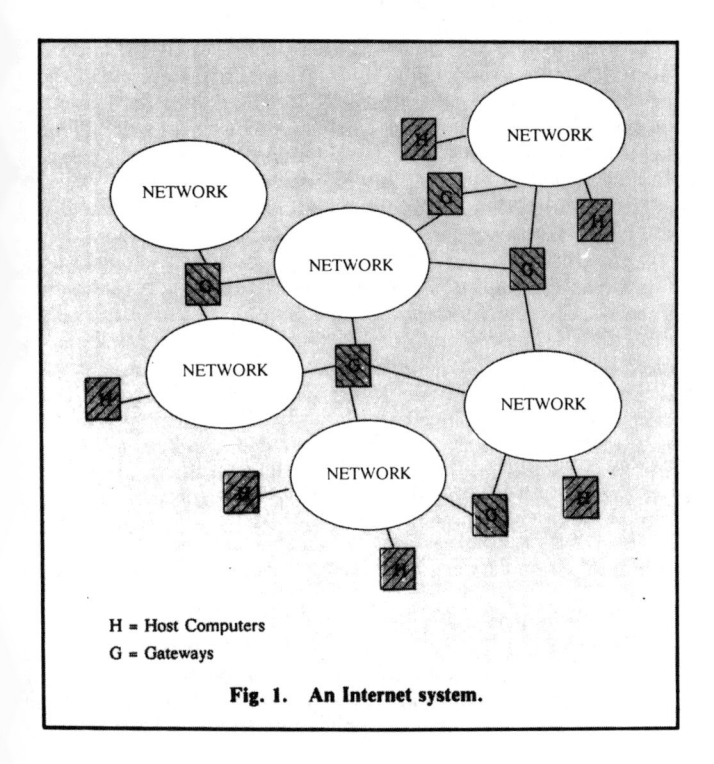

N = Network Protocols
I = Internet Protocol
S = Service Protocols
A = Application Protocols
H = Host computer
G = Gateway

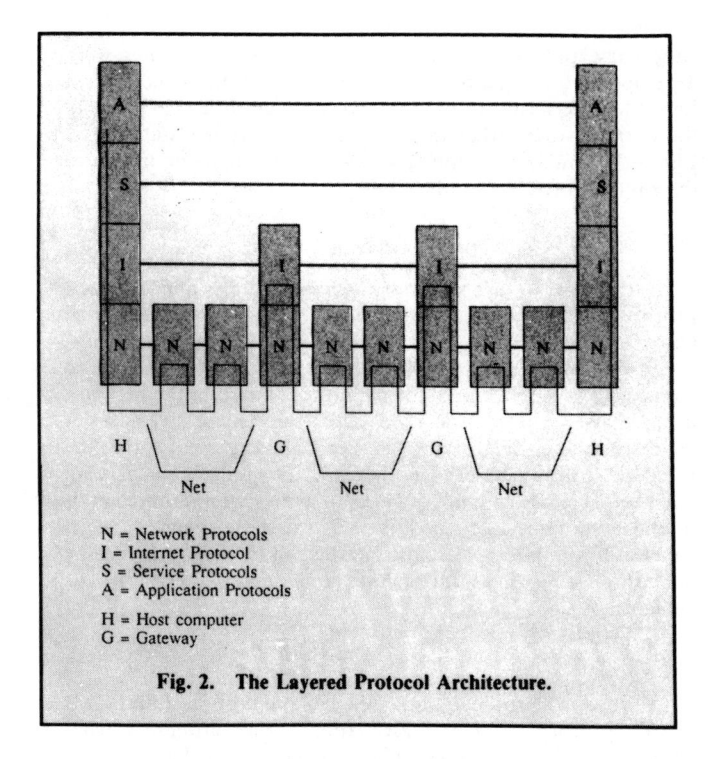

Fig. 2. The Layered Protocol Architecture.

To describe the Internet architecture, it is useful to trace a typical packet as it traverses the system from source host to destination host. Figure 2 shows the flow of a packet through the Internet. Data originates at an application layer and needs to be transported to the corresponding layer at the other end. Using the appropriate utility protocol and transport protocol, it packages the data into Internet packets. These packets are treated as data in the transmission through each of the individual networks, so that Internet packets move from host to gateway, from gateway to gateway, and from final gateway to destination host. In each case, they resemble a normal network packet on each network. The interface between the network, the hosts, and the gateways are defined by the individual networks; the hosts and gateways are responsible for packaging the Internet packets into network packets.

It should be noted that this approach, known as *encapsulation,* has some distinct advantages in the interconnection of networks. It is never necessary to build a "translation" device mapping one network protocol into another. The Internet layer provides a common language for communication between hosts and gateways, and can be treated as simple data by each network. This eliminates the "N × N" problem of building translating devices for each possible pair of networks, as it is only necessary to build the interface between the Internet layer and each individual network. Thus, hosts only need know about their local network and the Internet protocols.

The Internet Protocol Suite

To implement the above architecture, a set of protocols has been developed within the DARPA research community. These protocols have been developed with the above architecture in mind (namely a layered architecture with certain functionalities in the host-host protocols, and others in the gateways and networks). As additional functionalities have been required,

H = Host Computers
G = Gateways

Fig. 1. An Internet system.

either new protocols or modifications to existing ones were developed. It is anticipated that this will continue and, therefore, the description of the protocol suite given here represents the current state rather than a permanent set of "standards." Figure 3 shows the various protocols currently being used and their relation to one another.

Network Layer Protocols

At the lowest levels are the physical, link, and network protocols. These correspond to the network layer mentioned above, and provide the means for a host accessing the network. (Note that these normally describe the protocol for a host to connect to a network and not the protocol used in the network itself, that is between the switches of the network. This is of concern only to the network designer.) The key point is that the Internet accepts networks as they are, and utilizes them in an interconnected system of networks to achieve the required end-to-end communication capability. Thus, the primary areas of concern to the Internet are the interface to the network and the performance (such as throughput and delay) offered by the network.

Internet Protocol

The Internet Protocol [4,6] is the lynch pin of the Internet. It is this protocol that insulates applications programs from needing to know specifics about the networks. The Internet protocol (IP) unifies the available network services into a uniform Internet datagram service. The IP includes such functions as a global addressing structure, provision for type of service requests (to allow selection of appropriate network level services where required), and provision for fragmentation of packets and reassembly at the destination host, in the event that a packet's size is larger than the maximum packet size of the network through which the packet is about to traverse. The decision on what to put into IP and what to leave out was made on the basis of the question "Do gateways need to know it?". The key feature of IP is the Internet address, an address scheme independent of the addresses used in the particular networks used to create the Internet.

As can be seen from Fig. 2, the IP is used for communication between hosts and gateways, between gateways themselves, and between hosts on an end-to-end basis. It allows hosts to send packets through the Internet system, without regard to the network on which the destination host resides, by having the host send the packet to a gateway on the same network as the source host and letting the gateways take responsibility for determining how to deliver the packet to the final destination network (and thereby the destination host). The IP is critical to the proper operation of the Internet and the gateways in particular.

Service Protocols

The Internet protocol and layer provides an end-to-end datagram delivery service, permitting a host to inject a packet into the Internet and have it delivered with some degree of confidence to the desired destination. The customer application, however, typically requires a specific level of service. This may involve specification of reliability, error rate, and delay, or some combination of those characteristics. Rather than have each application develop its own end-to-end service protocols, it is desirable to have a number of standard services available upon which applications can build.

Currently, the DARPA experimental Internet system has two standard service protocols—the Transmission Control Protocol (TCP) [5] and the User Datagram Protocol (UDP) [8]. Other protocols are likely to be developed at this level.

In addition to end-to-end service protocols, there is a requirement for control of the Internet. An adjunct to the IP has been developed called the Internet Control Message Protocol (ICMP) [9] to serve this need.

Transmission Control Protocol

One of the prime uses for computer communication networks is the ability to reliably transmit and receive files and electronic mail. The characteristics of such use is the necessity to pass a fairly large amount of data (typically more than would fit into a single network packet) reliably and be able to reconstruct the data in sequence. To support such Internet services, the TCP was developed.

TCP provides an end-to-end reliable data stream service. It contains mechanisms to provide reliable transmission of data. These mechanisms include sequence numbers, checksums, timers, acknowledgments, and retransmission procedures. The intent of TCP is to allow the design of applications that can assume reliable, sequenced delivery of data.

User Datagram Protocol

Many applications do not require a reliable stream service. Sometimes, the basic datagram service of the Internet is sufficient for applications if enhanced by such services as multiplexing different addresses onto the same IP address and checksumming for data integrity. The UDP provides these services and permits individual datagrams to be sent between hosts. This supports applications requiring such a transaction-oriented service.

Internet Control Message Protocol

In systems as large and complex as the Internet, it is necessary to have monitoring and control capabilities, permitting hosts to interact with gateways, as well as both interacting with Internet monitoring and control centers. The ICMP provides the facility to carry out this control activity. It includes functions, such as redirect messages, to permit gateways to notify hosts that they should send packets to a different gateway (as well as error reporting).

Application Protocols

Clearly, the purpose of the Internet is to provide host-to-host and user-to-host computer communications service, thereby supporting the required applications. To accomplish this, the communicating hosts must agree on the protocol to be used for each application. A number of application protocols have been

Fig. 3. The Internet Protocol Suite.

agreed upon in the DARPA experimental Internet system, ranging from the very basic terminal access protocol, to permit timesharing over the Internet through the provision of such services as name servers and time servers.

Remote Terminal Protocol

TELNET [10] is the remote terminal access protocol in the DARPA protocol suite. TELNET allows the use of a terminal on one host with a program on another host. TELNET is based on three ideas: a network virtual terminal, negotiated options, and the symmetry of processes. TELNET is built on the services provided by TCP.

The network virtual terminal idea is used to define an imaginary terminal as the standard terminal. Then all real terminals are mapped by the TELNET implementations into or out of this imaginary standard. All the data traversing the Internet in TELNET applications is in terms of the imaginary standard terminal.

The negotiated options idea calls for a base level of capability as the default operation. Enhancements may be negotiated via the exchange of requests between the two hosts. One nice feature of this mechanism is that a request can be rejected without needing to know the semantics of the request.

The symmetry of processes suggests that the TELNET protocol should work the same both ways. That the protocol is mostly used for connecting terminals to remote programs should not drive the protocol to be too specialized. It should also work to link two terminals, or to support process-to-process communication.

File Transfer Protocol

The File Transfer Protocol (FTP) [11] is based on a model of files having a few attributes, and a mechanism of commands and replies. The command and reply mechanism is used to establish the parameters for a file transfer and then to actually invoke the transfer. Like TELNET, FTP runs over TCP and thus assumes the service level provided by TCP.

Mail Transfer Protocol

An important use of computer networks is the support of electronic mail. In fact, one could attribute the success of the DARPA packet-switching research to the availability of electronic mail facilities (first over the ARPANET and then over the Internet) to the researchers involved in the effort.

The Simple Mail Transfer Protocol (SMTP) [12] is similar to the FTP protocol in that it uses the same mechanism of commands and replies. The SMTP is simpler than the FTP, in that the data exchanged is restricted to just one of the many possible combination of attributes allowed under FTP. The main concerns in the SMTP protocol are the provision for negotiating the recipients of a message, and confirming that the receiving host has taken full responsibility for the message. Like FTP, SMTP is built on TCP services.

Other Application Protocols

To illustrate some of the other application protocols that are available as part of the Internet, we describe two simple applications—a time server and a name server.

The time server [13] provides a very simple service that returns the time of day whenever it receives a request. This service may be implemented either on TCP or UDP. On TCP, if a TCP connection is opened to the server, the server sends the time of day and closes the connection. On UDP, if the server received a datagram, the server sends back a datagram carrying the time of day.

In order that users not be required to know the address of each Internet host, and to facilitate the movement of hosts to different addresses as part of normal network operations, a host name server [14] is part of the Internet. The host name-to-address hookup service is a transaction style service implemented on UDP. It expects to receive datagrams containing the name of an Internet host (for example, USC-ISIF). When such a datagram arrives, it adds the Internet address to the information and sends back a datagram carrying all that information (for example, USC-ISIF = 10.2.0.52).

Gateway Protocols

As mentioned in the architectural overview, packets flow through the system through the use of gateways located between the networks. Thus, it is necessary that the gateways communicate with each other, both for passing data packets and for accomplishing the control of the Internet, as such control is fully distributed to the gateways.

Datagrams are exchanged between networks via gateways, each of which belongs to one of several Autonomous Systems (AS). The gateways of each AS operate an Interior Gateway Protocol (IGP) in order to exchange network reachability and routing information within the AS; however, each AS may operate a different IGP suited to its architecture and operating requirements. The Gateway-Gateway Protocol (GGP), used for some time in the present Internet system, is an example of an IGP. The Exterior Gateway Protocol (EGP) is operated between selected gateways in each AS in order to exchange network reachability and routing information. Each gateway, operating EGP or an IGP, maintains a database that selects the next gateway hop on the path to each destination network. Now there are over 65 in the Internet.

All gateways support the Internet Protocol (IP) and the Internet Control Message Protocol (ICMP), which are datagram protocols requiring only minimal state storage in the gateway itself. IP support includes fragmentation, for those networks that require it, along with several options including an explicit gateway routing override for special applications. ICMP support provides notification messages to the sender in cases of misrouted traffic, excessive flows, and special maintenance messages.

Summary of Experiences

It cannot be over-emphasized that the system described in this paper is not merely a set of standards, but rather has been in operation and used on a daily basis supporting research in networking, command, and control, and other areas of computer science for over a decade. Figure 4 shows a sample indicating the breadth and heterogeneity of the Internet. The system consists of land-line networks such as the ARPANET and X.25 public networks, several phases of packet radio networks, a number of local area networks, and two different satellite packet-switched networks. Currently, roughly 100 networks and 60 gateways, all interconnected into a unified system, provide the robust and reliable computer communications service required by both military and commercial users.

The Internet has been used to support a number of applications and experiments. Interestingly enough, due to its experimental nature, perhaps its most important use in the past decade has been the support of research into networking and other computer science areas. By permitting the easy and rapid exchange of information (through both electronic mail and file transfers), as well as permitting the distributed development of software, rapid progress in these fields has been encouraged and facilitated.

The Internet has also been used to explore the implications of advanced computer communications technologies on

Fig. 4. The DARPA Experimental Internet System.

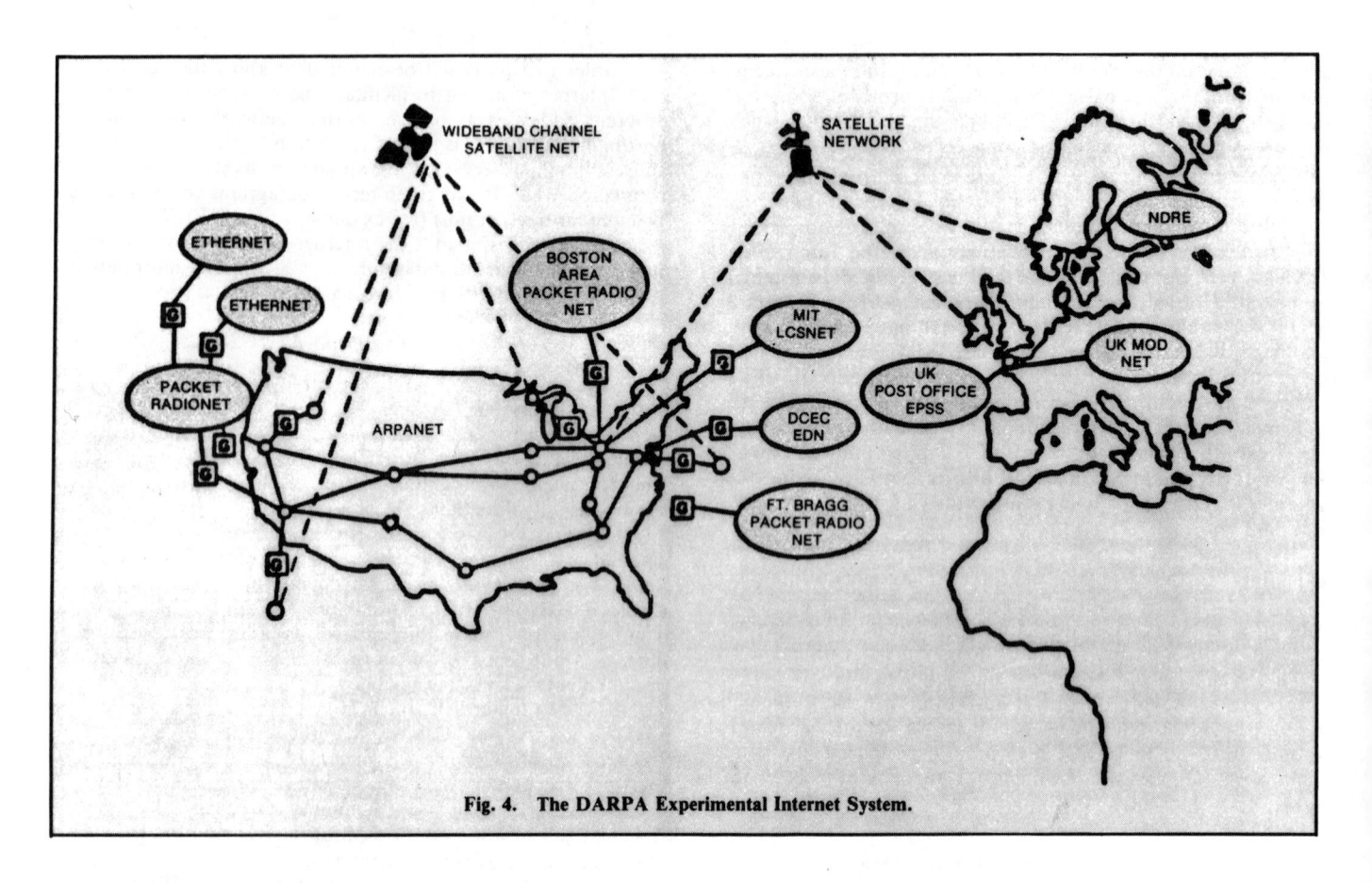

military concepts and doctrine. In cooperation with the U.S. Army, a testbed has been established at Ft. Bragg, NC, which is investigating the application of advanced communications and distributed processing technologies in the support of Army concepts in distributed command and control [15]. In cooperation with the Strategic Air Command (SAC), the Defense Communications Agency (DCA), and Rome Air Development Center (RADC) of the Air Force, a testbed has been established at Offutt AFB, NE, to investigate the use of the Internet technology to support strategic reconstitution efforts [15]. The Internet system provides the communications heart of a joint activity between the United States, United Kingdom, Germany, Norway, and Canada investigating command and control interoperability. In addition, a number of experiments have been carried out with the U.S. Navy using the Internet to demonstrate distributed command and control technologies. Clearly, none of these activities could have been performed with such effectiveness if it were not for the Internet system providing a unified and interoperable communication structure.

At present, the International Standards Organization (ISO) is discussing a proposal to use datagrams as the main mechanism for internetworking. The internetworking protocols will fit into a sublayer at the top of the network layer, just below the transport layer.

```
Transport layer
                  / internet sublayer
Network layer  <
                  \ network sublayer
```

ISO has adopted X.25 as their main network sublayer protocol, and has proposed their own protocol for the transport layer [16,17]. The DARPA TCP is functionally similar to the ISO proposal for a transport protocol and can be considered equivalent.

Two groups are currently using the TCP as a transport protocol, the IP as an Internet protocol, and X.25 as the network protocol in a manner which mirrors the ISO proposals. Both groups use the X.25 network as only one component of the path between the hosts, other networks include various local area networks and the other constituent networks of the DARPA Internet.

The CSNET group uses TELENET to provide connections between a number of hosts in computer science departments throughout the U.S. [18]. The second group is a number of European research sites, the main user being University College London (UCL).

UCL provides a relay service for mail and remote login that enables U.S. and UK research workers to access each others facilities [19]. A single international X.25 connection is used to connect hosts at UCL, in England, to various Internet hosts in the U.S. [20]. The primary protocols used on the international and U.S. sides are TCP and IP. These are carried on the international public X.25 services.

Another effective use of the Internet system has turned out to be the measurement of network performance. TCP and IP can be used in network and internetwork measurements in a particularly effective manner. The protocols give two advantages:

1) The same protocols can be used over a number of networks and therefore different types of networks. This can allow comparison of network media.
2) The datagram nature of the IP layer enables network saturation measurements, while the controlled TCP allows measurement of a more conventional nature.

By using a single system to carry out measurements on very different networks, the bias due to implementation can be eliminated (for instance, in a study to compare the response to overloading in two different satellite systems [21]).

The datagram based IP enables measurements to be made of the maximum throughput a network can provide to a user.

Then using the TCP protocol, it is possible to determine how much of that throughput can be utilized by an end user, and what techniques can be used to optimize the throughput [22].

Summary and Conclusions

An experimental system and set of protocols has been described that permits communications between heterogeneous host computers on heterogeneous networks. The Internet has evolved over the past 15 years and has resulted in a set of proven and tested protocols to support the military requirements for robust and reliable computer communications. As those requirements evolve through the development of both new technologies and new military concepts and doctrine, it is anticipated that the Internet system will also continue to evolve, developing new protocols and technologies to meet those ever-changing requirements.

Acknowledgments

The Internet system has evolved over the years through the dedication and hard work of a large number of researchers. Known as the Internet Research Group, it is their efforts that made the program a success. The authors would also like to thank the members of the Internet Configuration Control Board for their many helpful comments through the preparation of this paper. Finally, we would like to acknowledge Dr. Robert E. Kahn and Dr. Vinton G. Cerf for their vision and guidance in the carrying out of the Internet research activity.

References

[1] *DARPA: A History of the Arpanet: The First Decade*, Defense Advanced Research Projects Agency, (Defense Tech. Info. Center AD A1 15440), Apr. 1981.
[2] R. E. Kahn et al "Advances in packet radio technology." *Proc. IEEE* pp. 1468-1496, Nov. 1978.
[3] K. Klemba et al Packet Radio Network Executive Summary. DARPA, 1983.
[4] Defense Communications Agency. *MIL STD 1777: Internet Protocol*, 1983.
[5] Defense Communications Agency. *MIL STD 1778: Transmission Control Protocol*, 1983.
[6] V. G. Cerf and R. E. Kahn. "A protocol for packet network intercommunication," *IEEE Transactions on Communications COM-22*, May 1974.
[7] I. M. Jacobs, et al "General purpose satellite networks." *Proc. IEEE*, pp. 1448-1467, Nov. 1978.
[8] J. Postel, *User Datagram Protocol*, USC Information Sciences Institute, RFC-768, 1980.
[9] J. Postel, *Internet Control Message Protocol*, USC Information Sciences Institute, RFC-792, 1981.
[10] J. Postel and J. Reynolds, *Telnet Protocol Specification*, USC Information Sciences Institute, RFC-854, 1983.
[11] J. Postel, *File Transfer Protocol*, USC Information Sciences Institute, RFC-765, 1980.
[12] J. Postel, *Simple Mail Transfer Protocol*, USC Information Sciences Institute, RFC-821, 1982.
[13] J. Postel and K. Harrenstien, *Time Protocol*, USC Information Sciences Institute, RFC-868, 1983.
[14] P. Mockapetris. Domain Names—Concepts and Facilities. USC Information Sciences Institute, RFC-882, 1983.
[15] M. Frankel, "Advanced technology testbeds for distributed, survivable command, control and communications (C3)," *Proc. MILCOM82*, paper 10.2, 1982.
[16] H. Zimmerman. "OSI reference model—the ISO model of architecture for open systems interconnection," *IEEE Transactions on Communications*, pp. 425-432, Apr. 1980.
[17] ISO/TC97/SC16/WG6. "Transport protocol specification (N1169)," *Computer Communication Review*, Oct. 1982.
[18] D. Comer. "A computer science research network CSNET: a history and status report," *Communications ACM 26.10*, pp. 747-753, Oct. 1983.
[19] R. Braden and R. Cole, "Some problems in the Interconnection of Computer Networks," *Proc ICCC 1982*, pp. 969-974, Sept. 1982.
[20] R. H. Cole, "User experience and evaluation of international X.25 services," *Proc. Business Telecom Conf.*, Mar. 1984.
[21] P. Lloyd and R. Cole, "Transport protocol performance over concatenated local area and satellite networks," *Proc. Conf. Data Networks with Satellites*, Sept. 1982.
[22] P. Lloyd and R. Cole, "A comparative study of protocol performance on the UNIVERSE and SATNET satellite systems," *Proc. Conf on Satellite and Computer Communications*, pp. 353-368, Apr. 1983.
[23] L. Palmer et al "SATNET packet data transmission," *COMSAT Technical Review* pp. 395-404, Spring, 1982.

Barry M. Leiner is Assistant Director of the Information Processing Techniques Office at the Defense Advanced Research Projects Agency, where he is responsible for research and development into advanced command, control, and communications technologies. Dr. Leiner received the B.E. Degree in Electrical Engineering from Rensselaer Polytechnic Institute in 1967 and the M.S. and Ph.D. Degrees in Electrical Engineering from Stanford University in 1969 and 1973, respectively.

He was a systems engineer with GTE Sylvania from 1967 to 1973. From 1973 to 1976, he was on the faculty of Georgia Tech. Between 1976 and 1980 he was a Business Area Manager at Probe Systems. Since 1980, he has been with DARPA where he has concentrated on the development of distributed communications and processing technologies.

Dr. Leiner has published papers in a number of areas including rate-distortion theory, image compression, direction finding systems, and computer communication networks. He received the Barry M. Carlton Award (IEEE AES Paper of the Year) in 1980. Dr. Leiner is a Senior Member of the IEEE and a member of Eta Kappa Nu and Tau Beta Pi.

Robert Cole is a lecturer in the Department of Computer Science, University College London, where his current research interests are in network interconnection and the communications aspects of distributed computing. He has been involved in the DARPA Internet research program since 1979 and is currently a member of the Internet Activities Board. He is the author of a text book on computer communications.

Jon Postel is a project leader at USC Information Sciences Institute. He received his B.S. and M.S. degrees in Engineering and his Ph.D. in Computer Science from the University of California, Los Angeles. He has worked at the MITRE Corporation in McLean, Virginia, and at SRI International in Menlo Park, California.

At UCLA he was involved in the development of the ARPANET Network Measurement Center and the installation of the first host on the ARPANET. Since that time, he has participated in the development of many of the higher level protocols used in the ARPANET and the ARPA-Internet. His current research interests are the interconnection of computer networks, multimachine interprocess communication, and multimedia computer mail.

David L. Mills, Ph.D., is Director—Networks, with M/A-COM Government Systems Group, Telecommunications Division (LINKABIT), and is presently leading projects in packet-switching network development and internetworking research sponsored by the U.S. Defense Advanced Research Projects Agency (DARPA). He was formerly a Senior Research Scientist with Communications Satellite Corporation (COMSAT), working in the areas of packet-switching satellite and internetworking technologies. Before joining COMSAT, he was an Assistant Professor of Computer Science at the University of Maryland, where he was a principal investigator on several research projects in distributed computer networks and operating systems. Dr. Mills is a graduate of the University of Michigan and has held postdoctoral positions at the University of Edinburgh (Scotland) and the U.S. Defense Communications Agency. He has published and lectured extensively on data communications, computer networks, and operating systems, and has been a consultant to a number of corporations and government agencies.

THE DESIGN PHILOSOPHY OF THE DARPA INTERNET PROTOCOLS

David D. Clark

Massachusetts Institute of Technology
Laboratory for Computer Science
Cambridge, Ma. 02139

Abstract

The Internet protocol suite, TCP/IP, was first proposed fifteen years ago. It was developed by the Defense Advanced Research Projects Agency (DARPA), and has been used widely in military and commercial systems. While there have been papers and specifications that describe how the protocols work, it is sometimes difficult to deduce from these why the protocol is as it is. For example, the Internet protocol is based on a connectionless or datagram mode of service. The motivation for this has been greatly misunderstood. This paper attempts to capture some of the early reasoning which shaped the Internet protocols.

1. Introduction

For the last 15 years[1], the Advanced Research Projects Agency of the U.S. Department of Defense has been developing a suite of protocols for packet switched networking. These protocols, which include the Internet Protocol (IP), and the Transmission Control Protocol (TCP), are now U.S. Department of Defense standards for internetworking, and are in wide use in the commercial networking environment. The ideas developed in this effort have also influenced other protocol suites, most importantly the connectionless configuration of the ISO protocols[2,3,4].

While specific information on the DOD protocols is fairly generally available[5,6,7], it is sometimes difficult to determine the motivation and reasoning which led to the design.

In fact, the design philosophy has evolved considerably from the first proposal to the current standards. For example, the idea of the datagram, or connectionless service, does not receive particular emphasis in the first paper, but has come to be the defining characteristic of the protocol. Another example is the layering of the architecture into the IP and TCP layers. This seems basic to the design, but was also not a part of the original proposal. These changes in the Internet design arose through the repeated pattern of implementation and testing that occurred before the standards were set.

The Internet architecture is still evolving. Sometimes a new extension challenges one of the design principles, but in any case an understanding of the history of the design provides a necessary context for current design extensions. The connectionless configuration of ISO protocols has also been colored by the history of the Internet suite, so an understanding of the Internet design philosophy may be helpful to those working with ISO.

This paper catalogs one view of the original objectives of the Internet architecture, and discusses the relation between these goals and the important features of the protocols.

2. Fundamental Goal

The top level goal for the DARPA Internet Architecture was to develop an effective technique for multiplexed utilization of existing interconnected networks. Some elaboration is appropriate to make clear the meaning of that goal.

The components of the Internet were networks, which were to be interconnected to provide some larger service. The original goal was to connect together the original ARPANET[8] with the ARPA packet radio network[9,10], in order to give users on the packet radio network access to the large service machines on the ARPANET. At the
 it was assumed that there would be other sorts of

This work was supported in part by the Defense Advanced Research Projects Agency (DARPA) under Contract No. N00014-83-K-0125.

"The Design Philosophy of the DARPA Internet Protocols," by D. Clark from *SIGCOMM '88 Symposium on Communications Architectures & Protocols*, August 1988, pp. 106–114. Copyright © 1988 by the Association for Computing Machinery, Inc. Reprinted with permission.

networks to interconnect, although the local area network had not yet emerged.

An alternative to interconnecting existing networks would have been to design a unified system which incorporated a variety of different transmission media, a multi-media network. While this might have permitted a higher degree of integration, and thus better performance, it was felt that it was necessary to incorporate the then existing network architectures if Internet was to be useful in a practical sense. Further, networks represent administrative boundaries of control, and it was an ambition of this project to come to grips with the problem of integrating a number of separately administered entities into a common utility.

The technique selected for multiplexing was packet switching. An alternative such as circuit switching could have been considered, but the applications being supported, such as remote login, were naturally served by the packet switching paradigm, and the networks which were to be integrated together in this project were packet switching networks. So packet switching was accepted as a fundamental component of the Internet architecture.

The final aspect of this fundamental goal was the assumption of the particular technique for interconnecting these networks. Since the technique of store and forward packet switching, as demonstrated in the previous DARPA project, the ARPANET, was well understood, the top level assumption was that networks would be interconnected by a layer of Internet packet switches, which were called gateways.

From these assumptions comes the fundamental structure of the Internet: a packet switched communications facility in which a number of distinguishable networks are connected together using packet communications processors called gateways which implement a store and forward packet forwarding algorithm.

3. Second Level Goals

The top level goal stated in the previous section contains the word "effective," without offering any definition of what an effective interconnection must achieve. The following list summarizes a more detailed set of goals which were established for the Internet architecture.

1. Internet communication must continue despite loss of networks or gateways.
2. The Internet must support multiple types of communications service.
3. The Internet architecture must accommodate a variety of networks.
4. The Internet architecture must permit distributed management of its resources.
5. The Internet architecture must be cost effective.
6. The Internet architecture must permit host attachment with a low level of effort.
7. The resources used in the internet architecture must be accountable.

This set of goals might seem to be nothing more than a checklist of all the desirable network features. It is important to understand that these goals are in order of importance, and an entirely different network architecture would result if the order were changed. For example, since this network was designed to operate in a military context, which implied the possibility of a hostile environment, survivability was put as a first goal, and accountability as a last goal. During wartime, one is less concerned with detailed accounting of resources used than with mustering whatever resources are available and rapidly deploying them in an operational manner. While the architects of the Internet were mindful of accountability, the problem received very little attention during the early stages of the design, and is only now being considered. An architecture primarily for commercial deployment would clearly place these goals at the opposite end of the list.

Similarly, the goal that the architecture be cost effective is clearly on the list, but below certain other goals, such as distributed management, or support of a wide variety of networks. Other protocol suites, including some of the more popular commercial architectures, have been optimized to a particular kind of network, for example a long haul store and forward network built of medium speed telephone lines, and deliver a very cost effective solution in this context, in exchange for dealing somewhat poorly with other kinds of nets, such as local area nets.

The reader should consider carefully the above list of goals, and recognize that this is not a "motherhood" list, but a set of priorities which strongly colored the design decisions within the Internet architecture. The following sections discuss the relationship between this list and the features of the Internet.

4. Survivability in the Face of Failure

The most important goal on the list is that the Internet should continue to supply communications service, even though networks and gateways are failing. In particular, this goal was interpreted to mean that if two entities are communicating over the Internet, and some failure causes the Internet to be temporarily disrupted and reconfigured to reconstitute the service, then the entities communicating should be able to continue without having to reestablish or reset the high level state of their conversation. More concretely, at the service interface of the transport layer, this architecture provides no facility to communicate to the client of the transport service that the synchronization between the sender and the receiver may have been lost. It was an assumption in this architecture that synchronization would never be lost unless there was no physical path over which any sort of communication could be achieved. In other words, at the top of transport, there is only one failure, and it is total partition. The architecture was to mask completely any transient failure.

To achieve this goal, the state information which describes the on-going conversation must be protected. Specific examples of state information would be the number of packets transmitted, the number of packets acknowledged, or the number of outstanding flow control permissions. If the lower layers of the architecture lose this information, they will not be able to tell if data has been lost, and the application layer will have to cope with the loss of synchrony. This architecture insisted that this disruption not occur, which meant that the state information must be protected from loss.

In some network architectures, this state is stored in the intermediate packet switching nodes of the network. In this case, to protect the information from loss, it must replicated. Because of the distributed nature of the replication, algorithms to ensure robust replication are themselves difficult to build, and few networks with distributed state information provide any sort of protection against failure. The alternative, which this architecture chose, is to take this information and gather it at the endpoint of the net, at the entity which is utilizing the service of the network. I call this approach to reliability "fate-sharing." The fate-sharing model suggests that it is acceptable to lose the state information associated with an entity if, at the same time, the entity itself is lost. Specifically, information about transport level synchronization is stored in the host which is attached to the net and using its communication service.

There are two important advantages to fate-sharing over replication. First, fate-sharing protects against any number of intermediate failures, whereas replication can only protect against a certain number (less than the number of replicated copies). Second, fate-sharing is much easier to engineer than replication.

There are two consequences to the fate-sharing approach to survivability. First, the intermediate packet switching nodes, or gateways, must not have any essential state information about on-going connections. Instead, they are stateless packet switches, a class of network design sometimes called a "datagram" network. Secondly, rather more trust is placed in the host machine than in an architecture where the network ensures the reliable delivery of data. If the host resident algorithms that ensure the sequencing and acknowledgment of data fail, applications on that machine are prevented from operation.

Despite the the fact that survivability is the first goal in the list, it is still second to the top level goal of interconnection of existing networks. A more survivable technology might have resulted from a single multi-media network design. For example, the Internet makes very weak assumptions about the ability of a network to report that it has failed. Internet is thus forced to detect network failures using Internet level mechanisms, with the potential for a slower and less specific error detection.

5. Types of Service

The second goal of the Internet architecture is that it should support, at the transport service level, a variety of types of service. Different types of service are distinguished by differing requirements for such things as speed, latency and reliability. The traditional type of service is the bi-directional reliable delivery of data. This service, which is sometimes called a "virtual circuit" service, is appropriate for such applications as remote login or file transfer. It was the first service provided in the Internet architecture, using the Transmission Control Protocol (TCP)[11]. It was early recognized that even this service had multiple variants, because remote login required a service with low delay in delivery, but low requirements for bandwidth, while file transfer was less concerned with delay, but very concerned with high throughput. TCP attempted to provide both these types of service.

The initial concept of TCP was that it could be general enough to support any needed type of service. However, as the full range of needed services became clear, it seemed too difficult to build support for all of them into one protocol.

The first example of a service outside the range of TCP was support for XNET[12], the cross-Internet debugger. TCP did not seem a suitable transport for XNET for several reasons. First, a debugger protocol should not be reliable. This conclusion may seem odd, but under conditions of stress or failure (which may be exactly when a debugger is needed) asking for reliable communications may prevent any communications at all. It is much better to build a service which can deal with whatever gets through, rather than insisting that every byte sent be delivered in order. Second, if TCP is general enough to deal with a broad range of clients, it is presumably somewhat complex. Again, it seemed wrong to expect support for this complexity in a debugging environment, which may lack even basic services expected in an operating system (e.g. support for timers.) So XNET was designed to run directly on top of the datagram service provided by Internet.

Another service which did not fit TCP was real time delivery of digitized speech, which was needed to support the teleconferencing aspect of command and control applications. In real time digital speech, the primary requirement is not a reliable service, but a service which minimizes and smooths the delay in the delivery of packets. The application layer is digitizing the analog speech, packetizing the resulting bits, and sending them out across the network on a regular basis. They must arrive at the receiver at a regular basis in order to be converted back to the analog signal. If packets do not arrive when expected, it is impossible to reassemble the signal in real time. A surprising observation about the control of variation in delay is that the most serious source of delay in networks is the mechanism to provide reliable delivery. A typical reliable transport protocol responds to a missing packet by requesting a retransmission and delaying the delivery of any subsequent packets until the lost packet has been retransmitted. It then delivers that packet and all remaining ones in sequence. The delay while this occurs can be many times the round trip delivery time of the net, and may completely disrupt the speech reassembly algorithm. In contrast, it is very easy to cope with an occasional missing packet. The missing speech can simply be replaced by a short period of silence, which in most cases does not impair the intelligibility of the speech to the listening human. If it does, high level error correction can occur, and the listener can ask the speaker to repeat the damaged phrase.

It was thus decided, fairly early in the development of the Internet architecture, that more than one transport service would be required, and the architecture must be prepared to tolerate simultaneously transports which wish to constrain reliability, delay, or bandwidth, at a minimum.

This goal caused TCP and IP, which originally had been a single protocol in the architecture, to be separated into two layers. TCP provided one particular type of service, the reliable sequenced data stream, while IP attempted to provide a basic building block out of which a variety of types of service could be built. This building block was the datagram, which had also been adopted to support survivability. Since the reliability associated with the delivery of a datagram was not guaranteed, but "best effort," it was possible to build out of the datagram a service that was reliable (by acknowledging and retransmitting at a higher level), or a service which traded reliability for the primitive delay characteristics of the underlying network substrate. The User Datagram Protocol (UDP)[13] was created to provide a application-level interface to the basic datagram service of Internet.

The architecture did not wish to assume that the underlying networks themselves support multiple types of services, because this would violate the goal of using existing networks. Instead, the hope was that multiple types of service could be constructed out of the basic datagram building block using algorithms within the host and the gateway. For example, (although this is not done in most current implementations) it is possible to take datagrams which are associated with a controlled delay but unreliable service and place them at the head of the transmission queues unless their lifetime has expired, in which case they would be discarded; while packets associated with reliable streams would be placed at the back of the queues, but never discarded, no matter how long they had been in the net.

It proved more difficult than first hoped to provide multiple types of service without explicit support from the underlying networks. The most serious problem was that networks designed with one particular type of service in mind were not flexible enough to support other services. Most commonly, a network will have been designed under the assumption that it should deliver reliable service, and will inject delays as a part of producing reliable service, whether or not this reliability is desired. The interface behavior defined by X.25, for example, implies reliable delivery, and there is no way to turn this feature off. Therefore, although Internet operates successfully over X.25 networks it cannot deliver the desired variability of type service in that context. Other networks which have an intrinsic datagram service are much more flexible in the type of service they will permit, but these networks are much less common, especially in the long-haul context.

6. Varieties of Networks

It was very important for the success of the Internet architecture that it be able to incorporate and utilize a wide variety of network technologies, including military and commercial facilities. The Internet architecture has been very successful in meeting this goal; it is operated over a wide variety of networks, including long haul nets (the ARPANET itself and various X.25 networks), local area nets (Ethernet, ringnet, etc.), broadcast satellite nets (the DARPA Atlantic Satellite Network[14, 15] operating at 64 kilobits per second and the DARPA Experimental Wideband Satellite Net,[16] operating within the United States at 3 megabits per second), packet radio networks (the DARPA packet radio network, as well as an experimental British packet radio net and a network developed by amateur radio operators), a variety of serial links, ranging from 1200 bit per second asynchronous connections to T1 links, and a variety of other ad hoc facilities, including intercomputer busses and the transport service provided by the higher layers of other network suites, such as IBM's HASP.

The Internet architecture achieves this flexibility by making a minimum set of assumptions about the function which the net will provide. The basic assumption is that network can transport a packet or datagram. The packet must be of reasonable size, perhaps 100 bytes minimum, and should be delivered with reasonable but not perfect reliability. The network must have some suitable form of addressing if it is more than a point to point link.

There are a number of services which are explicitly not assumed from the network. These include reliable or sequenced delivery, network level broadcast or multicast, priority ranking of transmitted packet, support for multiple types of service, and internal knowledge of failures, speeds, or delays. If these services had been required, then in order to accommodate a network within the Internet, it would be necessary either that the network support these services directly, or that the network interface software provide enhancements to simulate these services at the endpoint of the network. It was felt that this was an undesirable approach, because these services would have to be re-engineered and reimplemented for every single network and every single host interface to every network. By engineering these services at the transport, for example reliable delivery via TCP, the engineering must be done only once, and the implementation must be done only once for each host. After that, the implementation of interface software for a new network is usually very simple.

7. Other Goals

The three goals discussed so far were those which had the most profound impact on the design on the architecture. The remaining goals, because they were lower in importance, were perhaps less effectively met, or not so completely engineered. The goal of permitting distributed management of the Internet has certainly been met in certain respects. For example, not all of the gateways in the Internet are implemented and managed by the same agency. There are several different management centers within the deployed Internet, each operating a subset of the gateways, and there is a two-tiered routing algorithm which permits gateways from different administrations to exchange routing tables, even though they do not completely trust each other, and a variety of private routing algorithms used among the gateways in a single administration. Similarly, the various organizations which manage the gateways are not necessarily the same organizations that manage the networks to which the gateways are attached.

On the other hand, some of the most significant problems with the Internet today relate to lack of sufficient tools for distributed management, especially in the area of routing. In the large internet being currently operated, routing decisions need to be constrained by policies for resource usage. Today this can be done only in a very limited way, which requires manual setting of tables. This is error-prone and at the same time not sufficiently powerful. The most important change in the Internet architecture over the next few years will probably be the development of a new generation of tools for management of resources in the context of multiple administrations.

It is clear that in certain circumstances, the Internet architecture does not produce as cost effective a utilization of expensive communication resources as a more tailored architecture would. The headers of Internet packets are fairly long (a typical header is 40 bytes), and if short packets are sent, this overhead is apparent. The worse case, of course, is the single character remote login packets, which carry 40 bytes of header and one byte of data. Actually, it is very difficult for any protocol suite to claim that these sorts of interchanges are carried out with reasonable efficiency. At the other extreme, large packets for file transfer, with perhaps 1,000 bytes of data, have an overhead for the header of only four percent.

Another possible source of inefficiency is retransmission of lost packets. Since Internet does not insist that lost packets be recovered at the network level, it may be necessary to retransmit a lost packet from one end of the Internet to the other. This means that the retransmitted packet may cross several intervening nets a second time, whereas recovery at the network level would not generate this repeat traffic. This is an example of the tradeoff resulting from the decision, discussed above, of providing services from the end-points. The network interface code is much simpler, but the overall efficiency is potentially less. However, if the retransmission rate is low enough (for example, 1%) then the incremental cost is tolerable. As a rough rule of thumb for networks incorporated into the architecture, a loss of one packet in a hundred is quite reasonable, but a loss of one packet in ten suggests that reliability enhancements be added to the network if that type of service is required.

The cost of attaching a host to the Internet is perhaps somewhat higher than in other architectures, because all of the mechanisms to provide the desired types of service, such as acknowledgments and retransmission strategies, must be implemented in the host rather than in the network. Initially, to programmers who were not familiar with protocol implementation, the effort of doing this seemed somewhat daunting. Implementors tried such things as moving the transport protocols to a front end processor, with the idea that the protocols would be implemented only once, rather than again for every type of host. However, this required the invention of a host to front end protocol which some thought almost as complicated to implement as the original transport protocol. As experience with protocols increases, the anxieties associated with implementing a protocol suite within the host seem to be decreasing, and implementations are now available for a wide variety of machines, including personal computers and other machines with very limited computing resources.

A related problem arising from the use of host-resident mechanisms is that poor implementation of the mechanism may hurt the network as well as the host. This problem was tolerated, because the initial experiments involved a limited number of host implementations which could be controlled. However, as the use of Internet has grown, this problem has occasionally surfaced in a serious way. In this respect, the goal of robustness, which led to the method of fate-sharing, which led to host-resident algorithms, contributes to a loss of robustness if the host mis-behaves.

The last goal was accountability. In fact, accounting was discussed in the first paper by Cerf and Kahn as an important function of the protocols and gateways. However, at the present time, the Internet architecture contains few tools for accounting for packet flows. This problem is only now being studied, as the scope of the architecture is being expanded to include non-military consumers who are seriously concerned with understanding and monitoring the usage of the resources within the internet.

8. Architecture and Implementation

The previous discussion clearly suggests that one of the goals of the Internet architecture was to provide wide flexibility in the service offered. Different transport protocols could be used to provide different types of service, and different networks could be incorporated. Put another way, the architecture tried very hard not to constrain the range of service which the Internet could be engineered to provide. This, in turn, means that to understand the service which can be offered by a particular implementation of an Internet, one must look not to the architecture, but to the actual engineering of the software within the particular hosts and gateways, and to the particular networks which have been incorporated. I will use the term "realization" to describe a particular set of networks, gateways and hosts which have been connected together in the context of the Internet architecture. Realizations can differ by orders of magnitude in the service which they offer. Realizations have been built out of 1200 bit per second phone lines, and out of networks only with speeds greater than 1 megabit per second. Clearly, the throughput expectations which one can have of these realizations differ by orders of magnitude. Similarly, some Internet realizations have delays measured in tens of milliseconds, where others have delays measured in seconds. Certain applications such as real time speech work fundamentally differently across these two realizations. Some Internets have been engineered so that there is great redundancy in the gateways and paths. These Internets are survivable, because resources exist which can be reconfigured after failure. Other Internet realizations, to reduce cost, have single points of connectivity through the realization, so that a failure may partition the Internet into two halves.

The Internet architecture tolerates this variety of realization by design. However, it leaves the designer of a particular realization with a great deal of engineering to do. One of the major struggles of this architectural development was to understand how to give guidance to the designer of a realization, guidance which would relate the engineering of the realization to the types of service which would result. For example, the designer must answer the following sort of question. What sort of bandwidths must be in the underlying networks, if the overall service is to deliver a throughput of a certain rate? Given a certain model of possible failures within this realization, what sorts of redundancy ought to be engineered into the realization?

Most of the known network design aids did not seem helpful in answering these sorts of questions. Protocol verifiers, for example, assist in confirming that protocols meet specifications. However, these tools almost never deal with performance issues, which are essential to the idea of the type of service. Instead, they deal with the much more restricted idea of logical correctness of the protocol with respect to specification. While tools to verify logical correctness are useful, both at the specification and implementation stage, they do not help with the severe problems that often arise related to performance. A typical implementation experience is that even after logical correctness has been demonstrated, design faults are discovered that may cause a performance degradation of an order of magnitude. Exploration of this problem has led to the conclusion that the difficulty usually arises, not in the protocol itself, but in the operating system on which the protocol runs. This being the case, it is difficult to address the problem within the context of the architectural specification. However, we still strongly feel the need to give the implementor guidance. We continue to struggle with this problem today.

The other class of design aid is the simulator, which takes a particular realization and explores the service which it can deliver under a variety of loadings. No one has yet attempted to construct a simulator which take into account the wide variability of the gateway implementation, the host implementation, and the network performance which one sees within possible Internet realizations. It is thus the case that the analysis of most Internet realizations is done on the back of an envelope. It is a comment on the goal structure of the Internet architecture that a back of the envelope analysis, if done by a sufficiently knowledgeable person, is usually sufficient. The designer of a particular Internet realization is usually less concerned with obtaining the last five percent possible in line utilization than knowing whether the desired type of service can be achieved at all given the resources at hand at the moment.

The relationship between architecture and performance is an extremely challenging one. The designers of the Internet architecture felt very strongly that it was a serious mistake to attend only to logical correctness and ignore the issue of performance. However, they experienced great difficulty in formalizing any aspect of performance constraint within the architecture. These difficulties arose both because the goal of the architecture was not to constrain performance, but to permit variability, and secondly (and perhaps more fundamentally), because there seemed to be no useful formal tools for describing performance.

This problem was particularly aggravating because the goal of the Internet project was to produce specification documents which were to become military standards. It is a well known problem with government contracting that one cannot expect a contractor to meet any criteria which is not a part of the procurement standard. If the Internet is concerned about performance, therefore, it was mandatory that performance requirements be put into the procurement specification. It was trivial to invent specifications which constrained the performance, for example to specify that the implementation must be capable of passing 1,000 packets a second. However, this sort of constraint could not be part of the architecture, and it was therefore up to the individual performing the procurement to recognize that these performance constraints must be added to the specification, and to specify them properly to achieve a realization which provides the required types of service. We do not have a good idea how to offer guidance in the architecture for the person performing this task.

9. Datagrams

The fundamental architectural feature of the Internet is the use of datagrams as the entity which is transported across the underlying networks. As this paper has suggested, there are several reasons why datagrams are important within the architecture. First, they eliminate the need for connection state within the intermediate switching nodes, which means that the Internet can be reconstituted after a failure without concern about state. Secondly, the datagram provides a basic building block out of which a variety of types of service can be implemented. In contrast to the virtual circuit, which usually implies a fixed type of service, the datagram provides a more elemental service which the endpoints can combine as appropriate to build the type of service needed. Third, the datagram represents the minimum network service assumption, which has permitted a wide variety of networks to be incorporated into various Internet realizations. The decision to use the datagram was an extremely successful one, which allowed the Internet to meet its most important goals very successfully.

There is a mistaken assumption often associated with datagrams, which is that the motivation for datagrams is the support of a higher level service which is essentially equivalent to the datagram. In other words, it has sometimes been suggested that the datagram is provided because the transport service which the application requires is a datagram service. In fact, this is seldom the case. While some applications in the Internet, such as simple queries of date servers or name servers, use an access method based on an unreliable datagram, most services within the Internet would like a more sophisticated transport model than simple datagram. Some services would like the reliability enhanced, some would like the delay smoothed and buffered, but almost all have some expectation more complex than a datagram. It is important to understand that the role of the datagram in this respect is as a building block, and not as a service in itself.

10. TCP

There were several interesting and controversial design decisions in the development of TCP, and TCP itself went through several major versions before it became a reasonably stable standard. Some of these design decisions, such as window management and the nature of the port address structure, are discussed in a series of implementation notes published as part of the TCP protocol handbook.[17, 18] But again the motivation for the decision is sometimes lacking. In this section, I attempt to capture some of the early reasoning that went into parts of TCP. This section is of necessity incomplete; a complete review of the history of TCP itself would require another paper of this length.

The original ARPANET host-to host protocol provided flow control based on both bytes and packets. This seemed overly complex, and the designers of TCP felt that only one form of regulation would be sufficient. The choice was to regulate the delivery of bytes, rather than packets. Flow control and acknowledgment in TCP is thus based on byte number rather than packet number. Indeed, in TCP there is no significance to the packetization of the data.

This decision was motivated by several considerations, some of which became irrelevant and others of which were more important that anticipated. One reason to acknowledge bytes was to permit the insertion of control information into the sequence space of the bytes, so that control as well as data could be acknowledged. That use of the sequence space was dropped, in favor of ad hoc techniques for dealing with each control message. While the original idea has appealing generality, it caused complexity in practice.

A second reason for the byte stream was to permit the TCP packet to be broken up into smaller packets if necessary in order to fit through a net with a small packet size. But this function was moved to the IP layer when IP was split from TCP, and IP was forced to invent a different method of fragmentation.

A third reason for acknowledging bytes rather than packets was to permit a number of small packets to be gathered together into one larger packet in the sending host if retransmission of the data was necessary. It was not clear if this advantage would be important; it turned out to be critical. Systems such as UNIX which have a internal communication model based on single character interactions often send many packets with one byte of data in them. (One might argue from a network perspective that this behavior is silly, but it was a reality, and a necessity for interactive remote login.) It was often observed that such a host could produce a flood of packets with one byte of data, which would arrive much faster than a slow host could process them. The result is lost packets and retransmission.

If the retransmission was of the original packets, the same problem would repeat on every retransmission, with a performance impact so intolerable as to prevent operation. But since the bytes were gathered into one packet for retransmission, the retransmission occurred in a much more effective way which permitted practical operation.

On the other hand, the acknowledgment of bytes could be seen as creating this problem in the first place. If the basis of flow control had been packets rather than bytes, then this flood might never have occurred. Control at the packet level has the effect, however, of providing a severe limit on the throughput if small packets are sent. If the receiving host specifies a number of packets to receive, without any knowledge of the number of bytes in each, the actual amount of data received could vary by a factor of 1000, depending on whether the sending host puts one or one thousand bytes in each packet.

In retrospect, the correct design decision may have been that if TCP is to provide effective support of a variety of services, both packets and bytes must be regulated, as was done in the original ARPANET protocols.

Another design decision related to the byte stream was the End-Of-Letter flag, or EOL. This has now vanished from the protocol, replaced by the Push flag, or PSH. The original idea of EOL was to break the byte stream into records. It was implemented by putting data from separate records into separate packets, which was not compatible with the idea of combining packets on retransmission. So the semantics of EOL was changed to a weaker form, meaning only that the data up to this point in the stream was one or more complete application-level elements, which should occasion a flush of any internal buffering in TCP or the network. By saying "one or more" rather than "exactly one", it became possible to combine several together and preserve the goal of compacting data in reassembly. But the weaker semantics meant that various applications had to invent an ad hoc mechanism for delimiting records on top of the data stream.

In this evolution of EOL semantics, there was a little known intermediate form, which generated great debate. Depending on the buffering strategy of the host, the byte stream model of TCP can cause great problems in one improbable case. Consider a host in which the incoming data is put in a sequence of fixed size buffers. A buffer is returned to the user either when it is full, or an EOL is received. Now consider the case of the arrival of an out-of-order packet which is so far out of order to lie beyond the current buffer. Now further consider that after receiving this out-of-order packet, a packet with an EOL causes the current buffer to be returned to the user only partially full. This particular sequence of actions has the effect of causing the out of order data in the next buffer to be in the wrong place, because of the empty bytes in the buffer returned to the user. Coping with this generated book-keeping problems in the host which seemed unnecessary.

To cope with this it was proposed that the EOL should "use up" all the sequence space up to the next value which was zero mod the buffer size. In other words, it was proposed that EOL should be a tool for mapping the byte stream to the buffer management of the host. This idea was not well received at the time, as it seemed much too ad hoc, and only one host seemed to have this problem.[2] In retrospect, it may have been the correct idea to incorporate into TCP some means of relating the sequence space and the buffer management algorithm of the host. At the time, the designers simply lacked the insight to see how that might be done in a sufficiently general manner.

11. Conclusion

In the context of its priorities, the Internet architecture has been very successful. The protocols are widely used in the commercial and military environment, and have spawned a number of similar architectures. At the same time, its success has made clear that in certain situations, the priorities of the designers do not match the needs of the actual users. More attention to such things as accounting, resource management and operation of regions with separate administrations are needed.

While the datagram has served very well in solving the most important goals of the Internet, it has not served so well when we attempt to address some of the goals which were further down the priority list. For example, the goals of resource management and accountability have proved difficult to achieve in the context of datagrams. As the previous section discussed, most datagrams are a part of some sequence of packets from source to destination, rather than isolated units at the application level. However, the gateway cannot directly see the existence of this sequence, because it is forced to deal with each packet in isolation. Therefore, resource management decisions or accounting must be done on each packet separately. Imposing the datagram model on the internet layer has deprived that layer of an important source of information which it could use in achieving these goals.

This suggests that there may be a better building block than the datagram for the next generation of architecture. The general characteristic of this building block is that it would identify a sequence of packets traveling from the source to the destination, without assuming any particular type of service with that service. I have used the word "flow" to characterize this building block. It would be necessary for the gateways to have flow state in order to remember the nature of the flows which are passing through them, but the state information would not be critical in maintaining the desired type of service associated with the flow. Instead, that type of service would be enforced by the end points, which would periodically send messages to ensure that the proper type of service was being associated with the flow. In this way, the state information associated with the flow could be lost in a crash without permanent disruption of the service features being used. I call this concept "soft state," and it may very well permit us to achieve our primary goals of survivability and flexibility, while at the same time doing a better job of dealing with the issue of resource management and accountability. Exploration of alternative building blocks constitute one of the current directions for research within the DARPA Internet Program.

---

[2] This use of EOL was properly called "Rubber EOL" but its detractors quickly called it "rubber baby buffer bumpers" in an attempt to ridicule the idea. Credit must go to the creator of the idea, Bill Plummer, for sticking to his guns in the face of detractors saying the above to him ten times fast.

12. Acknowledgments -- A Historical Perspective

It would be impossible to acknowledge all the contributors to the Internet project; there have literally been hundreds over the 15 years of development: designers, implementors, writers and critics. Indeed, an important topic, which probably deserves a paper in itself, is the process by which this project was managed. The participants came from universities, research laboratories and corporations, and they united (to some extent) to achieve this common goal.

The original vision for TCP came from Robert Kahn and Vinton Cerf, who saw very clearly, back in 1973, how a protocol with suitable features might be the glue that would pull together the various emerging network technologies. From their position at DARPA, they guided the project in its early days to the point where TCP and IP became standards for the DoD.

The author of this paper joined the project in the mid-70s, and took over architectural responsibility for TCP/IP in 1981. He would like to thank all those who have worked with him, and particularly those who took the time to reconstruct some of the lost history in this paper.

References

1. V. Cerf, and R. Kahn, "A Protocol for Packet Network Intercommunication", *IEEE Transactions on Communications*, Vol. Com-22, No. 5, May 1974, pp. 637-648.

2. ISO, "Transport Protocol Specification", Tech. report IS-8073, International Organization for Standardization, September 1984.

3. ISO, "Protocol for Providing the Connectionless-Mode Network Service", Tech. report DIS8473, International Organization for Standardization, 1986.

4. R. Callon, "Internetwork Protocol", *Proceedings of the IEEE*, Vol. 71, No. 12, December 1983, pp. 1388-1392.

5. Jonathan B. Postel, "Internetwork Protocol Approaches", *IEEE Transactions on Communications*, Vol. Com-28, No. 4, April 1980, pp. 605-611.

6. Jonathan B. Postel, Carl A. Sunshine, Danny Cohen, "The ARPA Internet Protocol", *Computer Networks 5*, Vol. 5, No. 4, July 1981, pp. 261-271.

7. Alan Sheltzer, Robert Hinden, and Mike Brescia, "Connecting Different Types of Networks with Gateways", *Data Communications*, August 1982.

8. J. McQuillan and D. Walden, "The ARPA Network Design Decisions", *Computer Networks*, Vol. 1, No. 5, August 1977, pp. 243-289.

9. R.E. Kahn, S.A. Gronemeyer, J. Burdifiel, E.V. Hoversten, "Advances in Packet Radio Technology", *Proceedings of the IEEE*, Vol. 66, No. 11, November 1978, pp. 1408-1496.

10. B.M. Leiner, D.L. Nelson, F.A. Tobagi, "Issues in Packet Radio Design", *Proceedings of the IEEE*, Vol. 75, No. 1, January 1987, pp. 6-20.

11. -, "Transmission Control Protocol RFC-793", *DDN Protocol Handbook*, Vol. 2, September 1981, pp. 2.179-2.198.

12. Jack Haverty, "XNET Formats for Internet Protocol Version 4 IEN 158", *DDN Protocol Handbook*, Vol. 2, October 1980, pp. 2-345 to 2-348.

13. Jonathan Postel, "User Datagram Protocol NIC-RFC-768", *DDN Protocol Handbook*, Vol. 2, August 1980, pp. 2.175-2.177.

14. I. Jacobs, R. Binder, and E. Hoversten, "General Purpose Packet Satellite Networks", *Proceedings of the IEEE*, Vol. 66, No. 11, November 1978, pp. 1448-1467.

15. C. Topolcic and J. Kaiser, "The SATNET Monitoring System", *Proceedings of the IEEE-MILCOM Boston, MA*, October 1985, pp. 26.1.1-26.1.9.

16. W.Edmond, S.Blumenthal, A.Echenique, S.Storch, T.Calderwood, and T.Rees, "The Butterfly Satellite IMP for the Wideband Packet Satellite Network", *Proceedings of the ACM SIGCOMM '86*, ACM, Stowe, Vt., August 1986, pp. 194-203.

17. David D. Clark, "Window and Acknowledgment Strategy in TCP NIC-RFC-813", *DDN Protocol Handbook*, Vol. 3, July 1982, pp. 3-5 to 3-26.

18. David D. Clark, "Name, Addresses, Ports, and Routes NIC-RFC-814", *DDN Protocol Handbook*, Vol. 3, July 1982, pp. 3-27 to 3-40.

Relationship of the Signaling System No. 7 Protocol Architecture to the OSI Reference Model

Nilo Mitra
Suzanne D. Usiskin

Signaling System No. 7 (SS7) is being implemented in telecommunications networks worldwide to provide signaling capabilities for a variety of telephony and Integrated Services Digital Network (ISDN) services. Since the late 1970s, the International Consultative Committee for Telephone and Telegraph (CCITT) has been developing the protocols that form the SS7 Recommendations. The evolution of SS7 has been guided by the stringent reliability and performance requirements of the public telephone networks. Even with the expected interconnection of SS7-based signaling networks worldwide during the 1990s, an SS7 network is still considered a "closed" system, as access to it is rigorously controlled, and SS7 network applications are expected to interoperate only with other SS7 network applications.

At approximately the same time as the beginning of work on SS7, the International Organization for Standardization (ISO) started work on an Open Systems Interconnection (OSI) framework for the data communications environment. OSI provides a reference model, which defines a framework or discipline for providing a communications infrastructure that may be used by any application in a distributed processing environment. It also specifies a set of common protocol standards, which provide uniform communications capabilities independent of the precise nature of the application. As the name OSI suggests, its aims are to allow any user with the communications capabilities provided by the ISO-standardized protocols to access the widest variety of applications.

Despite their inception at approximately the same time, OSI and SS7 did not significantly influence each other's models. Two different principles drove the development of OSI and SS7, principally because of the perceived differences between the data processing and telecommunications environments. In particular, the main requirement of the telecommunications environment is efficiency, while the data processing environment's main requirement is "openness." As a result, there was not great motivation to completely align the protocol architectures.

This article describes the relationships that currently exist between the SS7 and OSI architectures. The functions of each layer in the SS7 protocol stack, as well as the SS7 addressing mechanisms, are described to the extent necessary to show correspondences to those of OSI. In addition, this article highlights those areas where the two architectures do not align. If full alignment of the architectures is at some point undertaken, this article would be a starting point for such an activity.

The following section explains the criteria by which we judge alignment of SS7 with OSI standards. The section after that provides a brief overview of the SS7 protocol architecture and shows the correspondences (where possible) to the OSI Reference Model (RM) and standards. Next, the SS7 and OSI network layer services are compared. The next section describes the relationships between addressing mechanisms in SS7 and those of OSI as defined in ISO 7498-3. We then describe, in some detail, the relationships between the SS7 upper layers and the OSI transport, session, presentation, and application layers. The section following that describes the new work progressing in CCITT in defining the evolution of various SS7 application layer standards, where a conscious effort is being made to attempt to align with OSI standards. A glossary of terms and acronyms is given in the Appendix.

What It Means to Align with OSI

The OSI RM [1] is designed to provide a common communications infrastructure for all application processes in open systems. The key aspects of the OSI RM are layering, services, and protocols. Each layer of the RM is a collection of functions that provide layer services to its user, the layer above. These services allow access to the functions performed by that layer plus the cumulative effect of the services from underlying layers. Protocols are rules (syntactic and semantic) of communication by which peer layer entities communicate to cooperatively perform their layer service for the benefit of their users—the layer(s) above. To prevent the redefinition of services, common functions necessary for communications are assigned to and performed by specific layers. For instance, segmenting and reassembly of application data may be performed at the Network, Transport, or Session layers. This relieves the Presentation and Application layers and applications from handling length problems. The OSI RM provides a high-level description of the layer services, but the precise definitions of these and the protocols through which these are provided at each layer are specified by separate layer service and protocol standards.

In the following sections, the discussions of OSI alignment of (perhaps parts of) the SS7 protocol stack must be understood in the following ways. First, it is considered whether a layer service that is provided at some level in the SS7 protocol stack is aligned with that layer in the OSI RM where the same service is provided. The next point for consideration is whether the protocol exchange to provide such a layer service is also semantically identical. There are instances where a particular SS7 level and the corresponding OSI layer may ostensibly be providing the same layer service in terms of an identical abstract

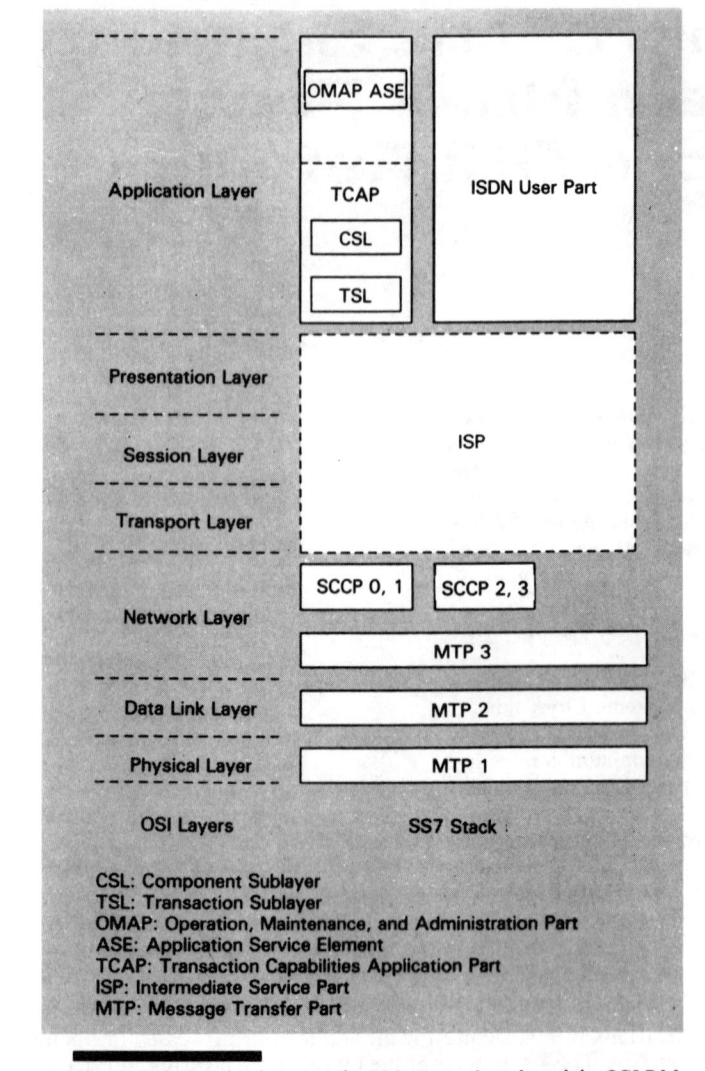

Fig. 1. Relationship between the SS7 protocol stack and the OSI RM.

service primitive interface. However, the semantics of the information conveyed in the protocol exchange may be quite different. A good example is the N-CONNECT primitive in Signaling Connection Control Part (SCCP) Recommendation Q.711 in SS7 and Recommendation X.213 in OSI. Despite the apparent alignment of the service primitives, the SS7 protocol cannot carry the OSI Network Address in its called party address. OSI experts would describe this as being OSI-incompatible, whereas the SS7 standard Recommendation Q.711 [2] actually states that it meets the OSI Network Service definition. In the following sections, this issue and many similar situations are pointed out.

An Overview of the SS7 Protocol Architecture

This section provides a very brief overview of the SS7 protocol architecture. More details on this topic may be found in [3]. A useful tutorial on SS7 is provided in [4]. The current protocol architecture of SS7 is shown in Figure 1. The left side of the figure shows the generally accepted correspondence to the various OSI layers.

The purpose of the SS7 network is to reliably convey critical signaling information between SS7 nodes, such as telephone exchanges and databases, related to call control and network management. To this end, the three levels of the Message Transfer Part (MTP) collectively provide a highly reliable and resilient connectionless message transport mechanism. Level 1 of the MTP defines the physical characteristics of the data links used in the signaling network. Level 2 of the MTP provides the functions and procedures for the reliable transfer of signaling information over a single data link. Level 3 of the MTP contains elaborate routing and signaling network management functions that permit in-sequence and nonduplicated connectionless message transfer even under adverse circumstances like signaling network congestion and failure. Level 4, the SCCP, enhances the services provided by the MTP to provide both connectionless (datagram) as well as connection-oriented (virtual circuit) message transport. It does this through four classes of service, two each for the connectionless and connection-oriented modes. It provides enhanced addressing capabilities for routing messages within the SS7 network and further distribution within a network node. One such addressing capability is a translation function that converts an address like a special telephone number—called a Global Title (GT)—into an address that the signaling network can use to route the message. (See "Relationship between OSI and SS7 Addressing" for more details.) The SCCP also provides management functions that broadcast the status of its "users" to other nodes in the network so that they may adapt their routing to the changing availability of these "users."

The Transaction Capabilities Application Part (TCAP) provides application layer formatting and procedures for real-time intensive query/response-type applications. An example of such an application is an exchange querying a database to verify the validity of a telephone calling card number being used to charge a phone call before allowing the call to be routed to its destination. TCAP is comprised of two sublayers, the Component Sublayer (CSL) and the Transaction Sublayer (TSL). The CSL of the CCITT Recommendations on TCAP is modeled after and aligned with the Remote Operations Service Element (ROSE) protocol [5]. (Actually, TCAP has one extension, described more fully below, thus making ROSE a subset of it.) The TSL of TCAP has no equivalent standard in OSI. This sublayer is designed to set up and terminate an end-to-end "association" or "connection" for application-protocol exchanges over the connectionless Network Service provided by SCCP Classes 0 and 1. For reasons of signaling efficiency, this "connection" establishment/release is unconfirmed and ROSE protocol data units are carried as user data in the connection establishment/release messages.

The Intermediate Service Part (ISP), which is undefined and therefore absent at present in the SS7 stack, is generally accepted as representing the collection of functions provided by the Transport, Session, and Presentation layers of the OSI RM should their services be found necessary by SS7 applications.

The Operations, Maintenance, and Administration Part (OMAP) is an example of a user of TCAP, i.e., a ROSE user Application Service Element (ASE) in OSI terms, and provides the SS7 network maintenance and management functions. It is modeled after the OSI management framework but, at present, its standards are confined to some SS7-specific Operation, Administration, and Maintenance (OA&M) functions such as the testing of valid MTP routing data through the MTP Routing Verification Test (MRVT) and circuit data through the Circuit Validation Test (CVT). The OMAP protocol is aligned with an early version of the OSI Common Management Information Protocol (CMIP), where OMAP has defined some of the same services and associated protocol.

The ISDN User Part (ISDN-UP) is a message-oriented, Application-layer protocol defined for providing call control, i.e., establishing, supervising, and releasing voice and data calls on an inter-office basis over circuit-switched connections between telephone exchanges that serve an ISDN. The ISDN-UP does not follow the modular structure of the OSI Application layer as defined in [6].

Comparison of the SS7 and OSI Network Layer Services

In OSI terms, the SCCP is like a convergence layer running over a connectionless subnetwork access protocol provided by the MTP. CCITT Recommendation Q.711 states that the combination of the MTP and the SCCP provide the OSI Network Service. MTP plus SCCP Classes 2 and 3 are described there as providing the connection-oriented Network Service defined in CCITT Recommendation X.213 [7]. However, this alignment is not complete for the following reasons.

While the abstract service primitive interfaces in Q.711 and X.213 are aligned, the semantics of the information conveyed is not. The SCCP called party address is designed to carry an SS7 network address, which is not the same as its OSI counterpart.

The OSI Connectionless Network Service (CLNS) is defined in [8]. MTP plus SCCP Classes 0 and 1 provide a connectionless Network Service via the N-UNITDATA service. Class 1 enhances the basic datagram service provided by SCCP class 0 by providing a sequenced delivery of a series of UNITDATA messages using a sequencing-guaranteed service provided by the MTP. There is no correspondence of this function to the OSI CLNS because an OSI connectionless service assumes that each protocol data unit could be transmitted and routed completely independently.

There is a functional similarity between the N-NOTICE indication primitive in SCCP Class 0 and 1 (which informs the SCCP user of an undelivered datagram) and the N-REPORT of the OSI CLNS; but once again, the semantics of the information carried (e.g., in the cause for message return) are different. Also, the connectionless SCCP does not provide the N-FACILITY request service of the OSI CLNS.

The connectionless SCCP also has a limitation of 254 octets on the length of the user data in the N-UNITDATA service.[1] This contrasts with the OSI connectionless service, which supports user data of 64,512 octets with the provision, in the protocol, of segmenting and reassembly of messages should the subnetwork(s) used not be capable of handling messages of this size.

Finally, the Quality Of Service (QOS) parameters requested in the two services are very different.

During the 1989-1992 study period of the CCITT Study Group XI, work is in progress to enhance the SCCP to carry the OSI Network Service Access Point (NSAP) address and provide a segmenting/reassembly capability in the SCCP connectionless protocol.

Relationship between OSI and SS7 Addressing

This section examines existing addressing information and concepts in SS7 and OSI. The first subsection describes the basic SS7 addressing information, provides a short review of OSI addressing principles, and describes the specific addressing scheme of the OSI Network layer. The next two subsections identify, respectively, the lower- and upper-layer addressing relationships.

Basic Definitions

The various addressing information elements present in an SS7 message, using the definitions given in Recommendation Q.700, are:

- *Point Code (PC)*: This addresses a node in the international SS7 network. It is used for internodal, intranetwork addressing in conjunction with the two-bit Network Indicator (NI) field of the Service Information Octet (SIO) defined below.
- *Service Information Octet (SIO)*: This contains a four-bit Service Indicator (SI) and a two-bit NI. The SI is used by a signaling point's distribution function to determine the "user" of the incoming message. The SI addresses "users" of the MTP. Examples of "users" are the SCCP and the ISDN-UP. The NI bits discriminate between international and national signaling messages.
- *Global Title (GT)*: This is addressing used by the SCCP, comprising dialed digits or another form of address, which is not recognized by the SS7 MTP level 3. Therefore, translation of this information to an SS7 network-routable address is necessary.
- *Subsystem Number (SSN)*: This is addressing information at the SCCP layer and identifies a subsystem accessed via the SCCP within a node and may be a User Part (e.g., ISDN-UP, SCCP management) or an Application Entity (AE) type containing the TCAP ASE.

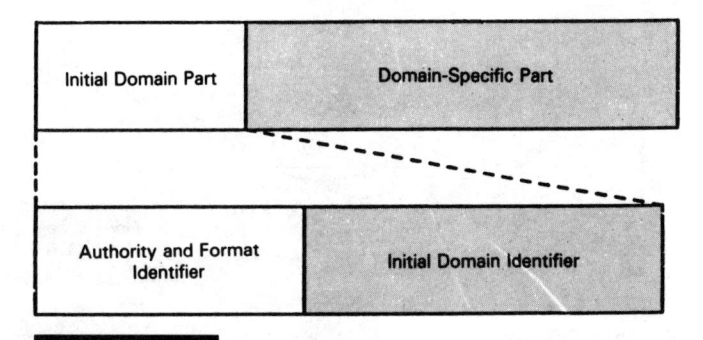

Fig. 2. OSI NSAP Address structure.

Next, the relevant definitions from OSI Naming and Addressing [9], which will help determine the necessary mapping of concepts and terminology, are provided.

In general, an (N)-Address is defined as a set of (N)-Service Access Points—(N)-SAPs—where (N) refers to any OSI layer and an SAP is the conceptual interface point through which a layer $(N+1)$ entity issues/receives service primitives to/from a layer (N) entity during an instance of communication. An (N)-SAP Address is used in the case when the (N)-Address identifies only one SAP. (N)-Addresses are used to identify sets of (N)-SAPs in order to locate $(N+1)$-entities.

Each (N)-SAP in the set identified by an (N)-Address is bound to an $(N+1)$-entity of the same type, i.e., each of these $(N+1)$ entities provides the same functions. Within an (N)-layer, an (N)-selector is that part of the (N)-Address used to identify an (N)-SAP, i.e., to address an $(N+1)$-entity once the end open system has been unambiguously identified. A locally chosen (N)-selector value would be known to communicating open systems through either directory look-up or advertisement, and exchanged as a part of the (N)-Protocol Addressing Information—(N)-PAI—during connection establishment.

When an actual connection is established between two peer $(N+1)$-entity invocations, each assigns a local (N)-Connection-Endpoint-Identifier $((N)$-CEI) to that particular instance of communication. Thereafter, the (N)-CEI is sufficient addressing information for the data transfer phase.

To summarize, an (N)-SAP locates a particular $(N+1)$-layer entity to be accessed during connection establishment. Within an (N)-SAP, after connection establishment, (N)-CEIs refer to particular instantiations of the $(N+1)$-entity, and is the only addressing information available during the data transfer phase.

Specifically, at the Network layer, a Network Address is in general a set of NSAPs, where each NSAP is structured as a part that identifies the network entity unambiguously in the open system environment, plus a locally specified "selector,"

---

[1] This is due to the deliberate choice of the size of an SS7 message to ensure that certain delay requirements are met.

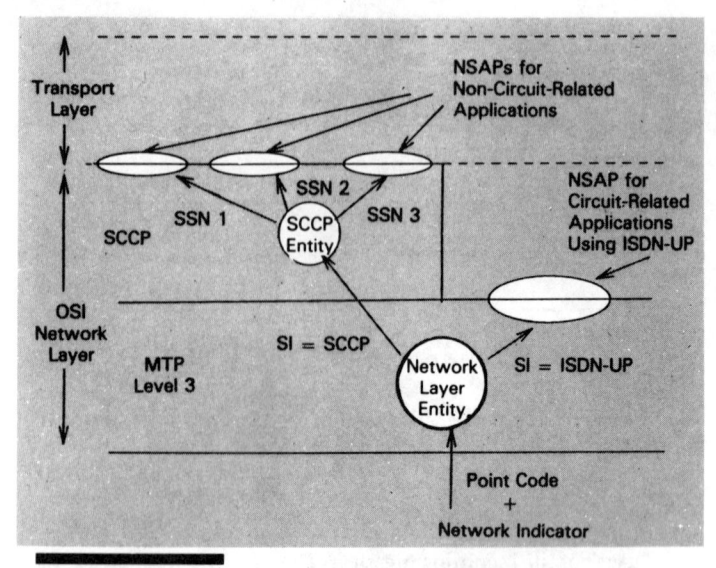

Fig. 3. Relationship of the SS7 PC, SIO, and SSN to the OSI NSAP.

which chooses a particular NSAP. Transport entities of the same type are bound to each NSAP within this Network Address and, in general, different types of Transport entities are bound to different Network Addresses. The most common sort of Network Address is an NSAP address, which is a Network Address consisting of only one NSAP. At connection establishment time, individual network connections between instances of peer Transport entities are assigned local network CEIs, which are then used as addressing information during the subsequent data transfer phase.

CCITT X.213 [7] has defined the structure and abstract syntax of an NSAP address, leaving the actual encodings to specific Network-layer protocol standards. This structure is shown in Figure 2. The format of the NSAP address is hierarchical in that the initial part of the address, the Initial Domain Part (IDP), unambiguously identifies an addressing domain, while the rest, the Domain-Specific Part (DSP), is allocated by the authority identified by that addressing domain. The IDP is further structured into two parts: the first part, the Authority and Format Identifier (AFI), names the addressing authority (e.g., ISO or CCITT) responsible for allocating values of the second part, the Initial Domain Identifier (IDI), as well as the abstract syntax (e.g., binary octets, decimal digits, or characters) of the DSP. The IDI identifies the network addressing domain and the network authority in that addressing domain responsible for allocating and ensuring unique values of the DSP.

Lower-Layer Addressing Relationships

The combination of SS7 PC, SIO, and SCCP SSN meets the criteria for providing the semantics of an OSI Network (NSAP) Address. It follows the hierarchical addressing structure defined for the OSI NSAP Address because CCITT defines the network addressing authorities, who in turn define the addresses within their subdomain. A part of the CCITT-specified SS7 PC, the 11-bit Signaling Area Network Code (SA/NC) field, together with the NI field in the SIO, serves the purpose of the OSI NSAP IDP because they identify the subdomain addressing authorities. Together with the remainder of the PC, which is domain-specific, an SS7 node can then be addressed in a "globally" unambiguous manner.

Within the Network layer at a node, there are a number of NSAP addresses with different types of upper-layer entities bound to these NSAPs. Once a node has been unambiguously identified by the PC and NI, local selectors administered within that node identify the possible NSAPs. In certain cases, the SI field is sufficient information to be able to locate these NSAPs. CCITT has standardized some of these SI fields. For instance, values have been assigned to those that directly access the AE of the call-processing application process. Also, another standardized SI locates an entity within the Network layer—that which provides the functions of the SCCP. In this case, a further piece of addressing information, the SCCP SSN, is the local "selector" to distinguish between the possible NSAPs at the Network/ISP layers' interface. CCITT has also standardized the values for a few SSNs to locate certain well defined and standardized upper-layer entities, e.g., those for the OMAP application; but it need not do so in general. Communications between application processes at different nodes is ensured by the proper maintenance and administration of network directory functions like routing tables and GT translation tables. These addressing relationships are illustrated in Figure 3.

The NSAPs that are of particular interest are those which provide the interface to the SCCP user for non-circuit-related signaling applications. When Network Connections (NCs) are set up between peer entities addressed through these NSAPs, they are identified by SCCP local reference numbers, which are, in the OSI Naming and Addressing terminology [9], network CEIs. Connectionless data transfer using the N-UNITDATA primitive also occurs through these NSAPs, although no CEIs are necessary for these instances of communication.

Upper-Layer Addressing Relationships

Earlier, it was stated that a type of $(N+1)$-entity is located by its binding to a particular (N)-SAP. According to OSI, the NSAPs that are addressed through SCCP SSNs would be used to locate a Transport entity. However, the absence of an explicit Transport-layer protocol in the SS7 protocol stack need not impede this comparison of addressing equivalences, as long as one compares functions provided by SS7 protocols with those provided at various OSI layers. Despite its specification in the Application layer, the TCAP TSL can be regarded as including a Transport-layer function because it is the first occurrence in the SS7 architecture of an end-to-end connection with its associated endpoint identifier, namely the Transaction Identifiers (TIDs); and it allows a mapping between an OSI Transport-layer function, which enables a Transport entity to multiplex a number of Transport Connections (TCs) over a single NC, and the possibility in SS7 of multiplexing a number of TCAP transactions over a single SCCP (class 2 or 3) logical connection.

From this point of view, in the SS7 architecture the TSL can be seen as fulfilling the role of a Transport entity, which is accessed by the NSAPs that are addressed by those SCCP SSNs selected for TC-based applications. Because there is no further addressing information in SS7, the Transport SAPs (TSAPs) have a one-to-one relation with the NSAP. At a TSAP, the locally assigned TCAP Transaction Identifiers (TIDs) then serve

Table I. Summary of SS7 and OSI Addressing Equivalences

OSI Term/Function	SS7 Equivalent
NSAP Address	{PC, SIO, SSN}
NSAP IDP	{NI, SA/NC portion of PC}
NSAP DSP	{Remainder of PC, SIO, SSN}
Network CEI	SCCP Local Reference Number
Transport SAP	SCCP SSN (by default)
Transport CEI	Local TCAP TID

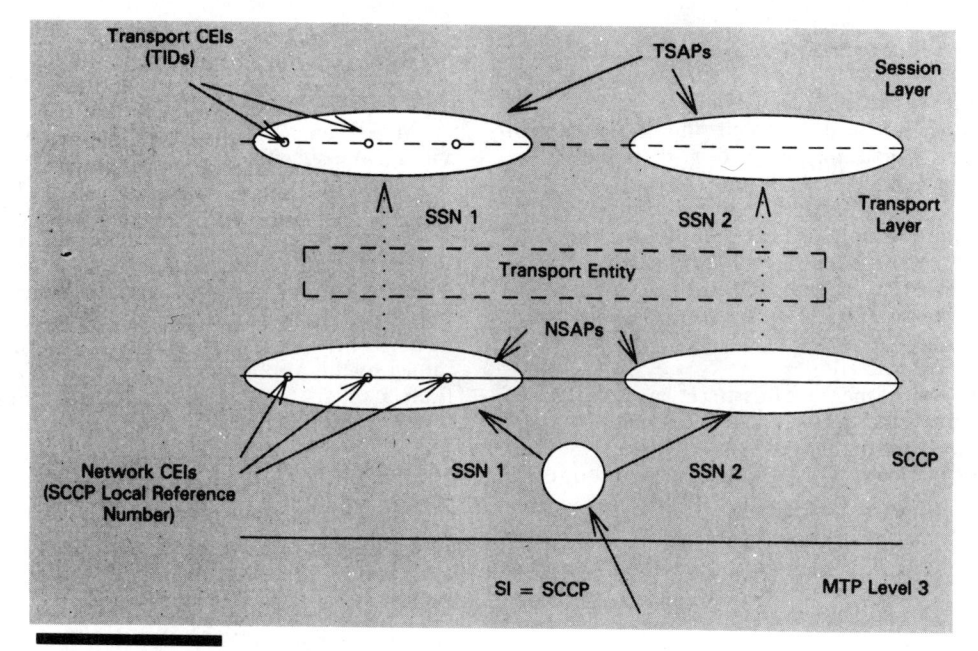

Fig. 4. Relationship of the SCCP SSN to the OSI TSAP.

as Transport CEIs. However, because of the function of multiplexing at the Network and Transport layer interface, the relation of the Network and Transport CEIs is not one-to-one. This view is illustrated in Figure 4.

A Session entity should normally be bound to each TSAP. However, because of the absence of Session- and Presentation-layer functions in SS7, the TSAPs have a one-to-one relationship to conceptually present Session SAPs (SSAPs) and Presentation SAPs (PSAPs). There is no protocol-addressing information in SS7 for these SAPs. A PSAP, which now has a one-to-one correspondence with a TSAP, then locates an AE type. This is in accordance with the current SS7 view given in [3, section 3.2.3.6.3], which states that "the AE is considered, in the connectionless mode, equivalent to an SCCP subsystem."

In addition to the one-to-one relationship of a TSAP with an SSAP and a PSAP, there is also a one-to-one relation between the CEIs within these SAPs. Thus, the TIDs are, by default, also Presentation CEIs. They identify Single Association Objects (SAOs) within an AE Invocation (AEI). Figure 5 summarizes all these relationships.

In the same way, the NSAP for ISDN-UP directly locates, because of the absence of intervening layers, distinct AE types belonging to the call processing application process(es). The Circuit Identification Code (CIC), which is present in every ISDN-UP message associated with the control of a circuit between two exchanges, serves as the CEI to distinguish different concurrent invocations of the call processing AE.

Summary of Addressing Equivalences Noted

Table I shows the relationships between SS7 and OSI addressing terminology and functions, explored and noted above.

Further Implications for SS7 Addressing

Some further points that may be noted are:

- In the connection-oriented environment, TIDs, which are currently defined as being Application-layer protocol elements, may also be considered as protocol addressing information for a lower layer, in particular the Transport layer.

- At present, the SCCP calling and called party address, which consist of a GT and SSN, are provided to the upper layer in the N-CONNECT and N-UNITDATA indication primitives. As the SSN is Network-layer addressing information (but also, by default, the TSAP), any further upper-layer addressing information can only be implied by the GT. The SCCP GT translation function, in which a GT is converted into an NSAP Address of a node, is simply the conversion of the generic name for a Network Address into an actual Network Address. This is unlike an OSI Application directory function, which converts an AE title into a more detailed Presentation Address of the form {PSAP, SSAP, TSAP, Network Address}. In other words, the SS7 GT currently is not providing an AE title, even though the GT is sent up to the upper layers in the N-UNITDATA and N-CONNECT indication primitives.

- In OSI, the Transport layer can multiplex data streams from many Session entities onto a single Network connection. At the receiving end, these streams can be separated through the use of Transport-layer address information. In SS7, the absence of any Transport-layer addressing information to distinguish among TSAPs prevents the complete multiplexing of TCs over a single NC. At present, as Figure 5 shows, only transactions between an SSN at one node and an SSN at a peer node can be multiplexed.

Relationship of SS7 Upper Layers with Layers 4–7 of OSI

Intermediate Service Part

The ISP, which is the collective name for layers 4, 5, and 6 of the SS7 protocol architecture, is currently absent. This means that none of the three layers contain any functionality with which to exchange protocol and offer services to higher layers.[2] Thus, the ISP is merely a place-holder for later inclusion of any appropriate protocols when the services of these

---

[2] Strictly speaking, SS7 TCAP does employ a Presentation-layer function which is the representation transformation of X.209-encoded Protocol Data Units (PDUs) into a single Abstract Syntax. SS7 has at present, due to the absence of a presentation protocol, only one Abstract Syntax and one Transfer Syntax, which must be understood *a priori* by both peers.

layers are found necessary for SS7 applications. Usually, the future protocols are thought to be the OSI Transport-, Session-, and Presentation-layer protocols.

The important item to note about the ISP's lack of functionality is that without any protocol at these layers, the corresponding layer connections are not available. In other words, the lack of layers 4, 5, and 6 implies that there are no means for requesting Transport, Session, or Presentation connections. Therefore, SS7 cannot offer an application association at the Application layer. Although in the TCAP recommendations there is mention of "associations," this is really assuming an implicit or "pseudo"-association, which is not a true OSI application association.[3]

Another implication of the three missing layers is the lack of addressing information that was already mentioned in the discussion of upper-layer addressing relationships. Thus, the concept of "nailed-up" selectors had to be used in order to relate selectors at these OSI layers with nonexistent selectors in SS7. Again, full OSI addressing is not possible without layers 4, 5, and 6.[4]

Application Layer Relationships

Key Concepts of the OSI Application Layer Structure

Some key concepts that are crucial for an understanding of the OSI Application Layer Structure (ALS) [6] are provided in this section.[5] Figure 6 shows the key elements of the architecture.

An Application Process (AP) represents all the resources required for the purpose of some information-processing activity. A distributed AP is of particular interest because the totality of its resources are provided by several disjoint instances that are in separate systems, either physical or logical. These separate instances communicate and cooperate with one another in a well defined manner. OSI application-layer protocols standardize the method of communication for the case when the disjoint instances of the AP are physically separated.

The part of an AP that is involved in the communications necessary for a specific distributed processing is the AE. The communications functions provided by the AE are modeled as being structured into some logically related sets, which are the ASEs. An ASE is an element that defines a function or set of related functions to help accomplish application communication. The definition of an ASE is split into a service definition and a protocol specification. The service defines, in an abstract way, how its functions may be used while the protocol specifies the information elements that will be communicated between the peers in the distributed processing. (Dividing the communication functions into such subsets as ASEs is useful if there is the possibility for the reuse of an ASE in other types of AEs for other instances of communications in different contexts. An example might be to separate the functions and necessary protocol for "authentication" from that of "number translation" into a separate ASE so that the authentication ASE may be used in a variety of applications.)

An AP can support several types of AEs. Each AE type provides some specific set of communications capabilities of the AP determined by the ASEs that comprise it together with all possible rules that govern their mutual interactions.

Any instance of communication for the purpose of distributed processing between peer AP instances (APIs) is modeled as the communications between AE instances over an application association. The actual procedures that will be or need to be performed during an instance of communication are determined by the Application Context (AC). While an AE type defines a set of functions used for communication, an actual instantiation might perform only a subset of these functions. The AC is used to state just which functions (e.g., ASEs) are needed for a particular instance of communication.

The initiating API provides the initiating AEI with an AC name, which enables the AEI to form an SAO. The SAO models the communications over the application association and consists of a particular choice of ASEs within that AE and an SACF, which specifies the rules for coordinating their mutual interaction. An application association is set up between the SAO in the initiating AE instance with an identical SAO in another AE instance using the services and protocol of the Association Control Service Element (ACSE), which is a mandatory ASE in every SAO. The AC name is a mandatory parameter in the ACSE protocol, to indicate to the receiving AE instance the appropriate AC.

ISDN User Part

The ISDN-UP is a message-based protocol at the SS7 application layer designed for the purpose of performing the signaling communication for controlling voice and data calls in the telephone network. The Initial Address Message (IAM) and the Address Complete Message (ACM) are very much like a generic OSI Connection Request and Connection Confirm message. (The Release—REL—and Release Complete—RLC—

---

[3]Having the OSI Association Control Service Element (ACSE) alone in the Application layer (as is sometimes proposed) will not change this situation, as an application association cannot be offered without a presentation connection (which needs a session connection, etc.).

[4]If, on the other hand, the ISP becomes aligned with the connectionless protocols of OSI, then the concerns about connections and selectors may go away. However, relating layer 7 becomes more complicated, as the Application Layer Structure (ALS) for a connectionless layer 7 in OSI is still being defined.

[5]Currently, work is going on in ISO on an extended ALS structure. Given that this work will not remove the validity of the current structure in ISO 9545 [6] and that for SS7 the new structure is too preliminary to be exploited, we have chosen to relate the SS7 Application layer to ISO 9545.

Table II. Mapping between ACSE /P-DATA Primitives and Existing TCAP Dialogue-Handling Primitives

ACSE Primitives	Equivalent TCAP Primitives
A-ASSOCIATE req/ind	TC-BEGIN req/ind
A-ASSOCIATE rsp/cnf (accept)	First TC-CONTINUE req/ind
A-ASSOCIATE rsp/cnf (refuse)	TC-END req/ind
A-RELEASE req/ind	Subsequent TC-CONTINUE req/ind
A-RELEASE rsp/cnf	TC-END req/ind (if request accepted) OR TC-CONTINUE req/ind (if request refused)
A-ABORT req/ind	TC-U-ABORT req/ind
A-ABORT ind	TC-P-ABORT ind
A-P-ABORT ind	No obvious mapping
P-DATA req/ind	Subsequent TC-CONTINUE req/ind
A-UNITDATA req/ind	TC-UNIDIRECTIONAL req/ind

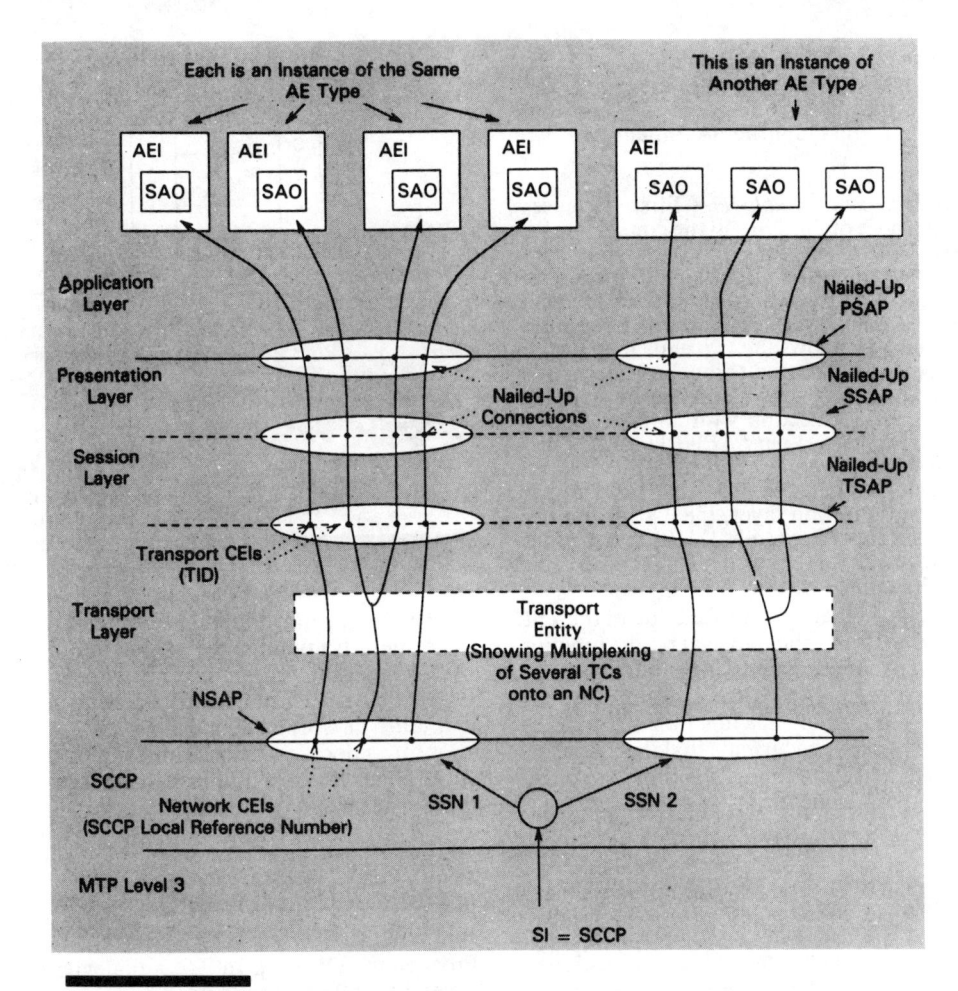

Fig. 5. Relationship of the SSN and local TIDs to AEIs.

messages that signal the release of a call resemble the OSI confirmed connection release messages.) Each message related to a call is identified by a link-by-link CEI that, conveniently, is also the identity of the circuit whose state these messages control. Other messages exchanged during the establishment and active phase of a call provide the ability to provide additional ISDN supplementary services.

The ISDN-UP protocol performs out-of-band signaling between peer call processing applications in two adjacent exchanges in the telephone network. This means that the protocol is used to control or provision some other resource, other than ones involved in the "association" being used, such as, for example, a physical-layer resource like a 64 kb/s circuit in a completely separate network over which two end users communicate. The OSI connection establishment procedure at any layer is for the purpose of establishing a communication path between the two peer entities at that layer to enable them to coordinate their control of resources at that layer for subsequent data transfer over that connection.

The ISDN-UP specifications, like all message-based protocols, have no analogy to any OSI application layer concepts, as there is no clear demarcation between the specifications of the AP specifications (e.g., dialed number translation for the purpose of determining the next exchange in the call path) from the specification of the communications protocol. This "monolithic" nature has led to considerable difficulties in expanding the protocol to meet the needs of new APs, which provide additional services that enhance the basic service of setting up a call between two users.

TC Application Layer

As shown in Figure 1, the TC Application layer is the TCAP and consists of the CSL and TSL. A typical example of a real-time application using TCAP is a number translation function, where a switch queries a remote directory (database) to perform, in real-time, the remote operation of converting an 800 number to a network-routable number.

• *Role of the Component Sublayer*—The CSL is modeled as consisting of two functional blocks: the Component Handler (CHA) and the Dialogue Handler (DHA).

The CHA is effectively the ROSE protocol machine defined in CCITT Recommendations X.219 and X.229. The ROSE Protocol Data Units (PDUs) are called "components" in TCAP. The protocol is completely aligned with X.229, except that it has one extension. This addition is a new PDU, Return Result Not Last, whose sole purpose is to carry segments of the result of a successfully completed operation whose length exceeds the connectionless SCCP user-data length limitation of 255 octets. The specifications for the CHA contain some purely local functions like timer supervision for executing a remote operation within an application-specified period.

The DHA generates no protocol but is concerned with concatenating (if necessary) ROSE PDUs that belong to a single end-to-end dialogue/transaction between two TCAP users in a single TSL message for transmission to the remote end. Thus, unlike the ROSE service, which maps to the underlying Presentation layer P-DATA service, the DHA provides the appropriate service interface to the TSL.

In OSI terms, the CHA is therefore the ROSE ASE (with the one extension described earlier), while local functions like timer supervision and concatenation of associated PDUs belonging to a dialogue can be seen as functions of the SACF. Together with any TC user ASE, which provides the type definitions of the application-specific remote operations and their expected responses, these constitute the SAO identified by a transaction.

• *Possible Roles of the Transaction Sublayer*—First, it is necessary to point out the purpose of the TSL. In the connectionless SS7 environment, the TSL provides the ability to group components (i.e., remote operation invocations and their associated responses) within the context of a "dialogue" (also called "TCAP transaction") between two AEIs. Even if no components are exchanged, the TSL allows the two ends to maintain and coordinate the state of a dialogue through messages like Begin, Continue, End, and Abort. This dialogue/transaction is a very "skinny" end-to-end connection with an implicit or *a priori* association between the two peer AEIs. The TIDs provided by each end serve as the end-to-end identification for each concurrent dialogue between two peer AEIs. As if to emphasize its place at the application layer, the TSL is defined using Abstract Syntax Notation One (ASN.1) [10] and encoded using the basic encoding rules (of the form Name, Length, and Value as specified in Recommendation X.209) [11].

However, it can be argued that the only function of the TSL that (by default) belongs to the Application layer is the function of blocking several Invoke components into units of some composite action, which requires that the individual operations be performed in a given order. The function of providing an end-to-end identifier to each concurrent "dialogue" appears to be similar to a Transport-layer connection, while the possibility of multiplexing many concurrent TCAP transactions over a single SCCP logical connection is akin to the OSI Transport entity function of multiplexing a number of TCs over a single NC for reasons of efficiency and cost. Therefore, the TSL can be said to provide a very "skinny" ISP function, with the closest relation to a Transport-layer function because it clearly has no Session- or Presentation-layer functions.[6]

In the connection-oriented OSI environment, however, remote operations or any other Application-layer protocol exchanges are performed assuming the existence of an underlying application association between the two AEIs. Such an application association is first established between two AEIs using the services of the ACSE defined in CCITT Recommendations X.217 and X.227, and provides a conversation "path" over which communication can take place. The ACSE is a mandatory ASE in every connection-oriented OSI Application protocol. The TCAP TSL "dialogue" also defines a communication "path," but does it over the connectionless environment. Thus, it appears that a "dialogue" provided by the TCAP TSL can also be related to an "application association" provided by ACSE. A high-level view of this equivalence is shown in Table II, where a mapping is provided between the ACSE service primitives [12] and the existing TCAP dialogue-handling primitives defined in Recommendation Q.771. (The mapping to the Presentation service P-DATA service primitive is also shown, as it is an integral part of the relationship.)

One point to note is the mapping between the Unidirectional message facility in TCAP (which supports a simple one-way data transfer facility) with the A-UNITDATA facility, which is currently being defined in the definition of connectionless OSI Application-layer protocols [13].

---

[6]The ANSI version of the TSL may even have a Session-layer function because of its concept of "permission to release" a transaction. However, the use of this feature over a connectionless Network Service has been found problematic. TCAP does provide a local Presentation-layer function, which is the transformation from the Transfer Syntax (X.209 encoding rules) to the Abstract Syntax (X.208) representation of the TCAP and TCAP user PDUs and vice versa.

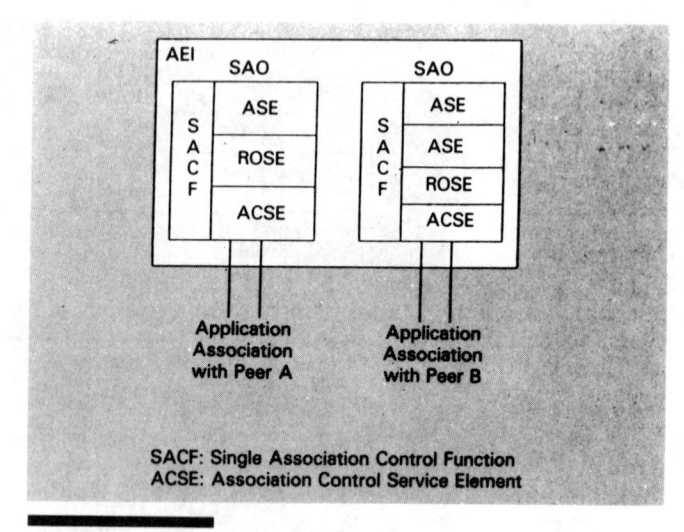

Fig. 6. OSI ALS.

However, a more speculative approach is to note that there are some extra functions that could be provided by the TCAP TSL, which differentiates it from the services provided by the ACSE. One such function appears to be the ability to group logical units of work (i.e., blocking remote operations) together over an underlying association/"dialogue." Another function is resiliency, the ability to retain "transaction" state information separate from the underlying "association" so that a transaction can survive the loss of its underlying association. Both of these functions are decidedly Application-layer functions.

The logical separation and resiliency of the TCAP transaction from the underlying "association" is a function that can be compared to the dialogue functional unit of OSI Transaction Processing (TP) [14]. In TP, a dialogue is a relationship between two TP users supported by a single application association; however, several dialogues may successively occur over an association (efficiency), and also, a single dialogue may span several application associations (resiliency). Within a dialogue, the TP service provides for the performance of units of work called "transactions." (Note that the latter have no correspondence to the TSL transactions.) The similarity we have noticed is only in the TP "dialogue" kernel, which supports the establishment/release of dialogue boundaries within which one may perform TP transactions.

Evolution of the SS7 Protocol Architecture

In the past few years, there has been a significant effort in CCITT Study Group XI, the body responsible for producing the ISDN signaling standards, to study OSI models and protocols to gauge their suitability for inclusion in the SS7 protocol stack. The first attempt at incorporating OSI protocols was made in the 1984–1988 study period, when the ROSE protocol was chosen as the basis of the TCAP protocol for those signaling applications based on the request/reply paradigm.

In the current study period, significant effort is underway to align the SS7 Application layer with the OSI ALS defined in ISO 9545. An attempt is being made to define a new signaling protocol at the Application layer called the ISDN Signaling Control Part (ISCP), which is expected to fulfill the future signaling needs of the ISDN and the emerging concepts of Intelligent Networks. In keeping with the modular "object-oriented" approach used in defining the OSI ALS, the ISCP will divide its communication capabilities into ASEs and define suitable ACs for the complex signaling requirements of multiparty and multimedia ISDN applications of the future.

However, it appears unlikely at this stage that the ISCP will require the services of the missing layers, the so-called ISP. The ISCP is being designed to sit directly on top of the OSI connectionless Network Service, which in SS7 will be the services of the connectionless SCCP, possibly enhanced. There are still no requirements for the missing Session and Transport layers. Should this direction continue, the use of the OSI ACSE for application association establishment and release would not be possible. There has been some very preliminary work in defining a so-called Signaling ACSE (SACSE), the purpose of which is to allow a mechanism to carry AC information, but tailored to meet the special efficiency requirements of signaling. These include the current capabilities of the TCAP TSL, which are the ability to support unconfirmed "association" establishment and termination, provide a capability for prearranged terminations, and allow ROSE (and possibly other) PDUs to be carried within the establishment PDU.

There has been considerable interest in the past few years in incorporating connectionless services at the upper layers of the OSI RM [15]. It has been found that there are a number of data applications that do not need the overhead of connection establishment/release and are naturally suited to operating in a connectionless mode. To this end, connectionless version of the Transport- [16], Session- [17], Presentation- [18], and Application-layer [13] protocols have been or are being defined. SS7 applications have not adopted or contributed to the development of these proposals on OSI connectionless upper-layer protocols. One reason is that SS7 TCAP applications are not truly connectionless applications but require, as described earlier, a very "skinny" and efficient end-to-end connection provided by the TSL on top of a connectionless Network Service.

Conclusions

This article has attempted to point out the similarities and dissimilarities between the OSI and SS7 architectures. Recent trends in telecommunications show that there are an increasing number of data applications that will play an important role in ISDN services. Thus, there has been a serious attempt to study the OSI model and protocols by SS7 experts. However, the incorporation of portions of OSI standards into the SS7 protocol architecture has been on an "as needed" basis. Such a method of assimilation will leave SS7 unaligned with OSI for a considerable time, unless steps are taken by both standards committees to actively seek a common ground that meets the needs of both the ISDN and data processing/communications environments.

One such attempt might be to study how one could include a certain minimal functionality for each of the layers currently missing in SS7, which would provide the needed OSI conformance but not introduce any excessive performance overhead for the ISDN signaling network.

Appendix

Glossary of Terms and Acronyms

AC:	Application Context
ACM:	Address Complete Message
ACSE:	Association Control Service Element
AE:	Application Entity
AEI:	Application Entity Invocation
AFI:	Authority and Format Identifier
ALS:	Application Layer Structure
AP:	Application Process
API:	Application Process Instance
ASE:	Application Service Element
ASN.1:	Abstract Syntax Notation One
CCITT:	International Consultative Committee for Telephone and Telegraph
CEI:	Connection Endpoint Identifier
CIC:	Circuit Identification Code
CHA:	Component Handler
CLNS:	Connectionless Network Service
CMIP:	Common Management Information Protocol
CSL:	Component Sublayer
DHA:	Dialogue Handler
DSP:	Domain-Specific Part
GT:	Global Title
IAM:	Initial Address Message
IDI:	Initial Domain Identifier
IDP:	Initial Domain Part
ISCP:	ISDN Signaling Control Part
ISDN:	Integrated Services Digital Network
ISDN-UP:	ISDN User Part
ISO:	International Organization for Standardization
ISP:	Intermediate Service Part
MRVT:	MTP Routing Verification Test
MTP:	Message Transfer Part
NC:	Network Connection
NI:	Network Indicator
NSAP:	Network Service Access Point
OA&M:	Operations, Administration, and Management
OMAP:	Operations Maintenance Administration Part
OSI:	Open Systems Interconnection
PC:	Point Code
PSAP:	Presentation Service Access Point
RM:	Reference Model
ROSE:	Remote Operations Service Element
SACF:	Single Association Control Function
SACSE:	Signaling ACSE
SA/NC:	Signaling Area Network Code
SAO:	Single Association Object
SCCP:	Signaling Connection Control Part
SI:	Service Indicator
SIO:	Service Information Octet
SSAP:	Session Service Access Point
SSN:	Subsystem Number
SS7:	Signaling System No. 7
TC:	Transport Connection
TCAP:	Transaction Capabilities Application Part
TID:	Transaction Identifier
TP:	Transaction Processing
TSAP:	Transport Service Access Point
TSL:	Transaction Sublayer

Acknowledgments

We thank Alex Wu, Bob Simms, Herb Bertine, Paul Bartoli, Jerry Peterson, Cherry Tom, Joe Alfred, Neil Lilly, Nick Di Iorio, and Janey Cheu for a careful reading of the manuscript and many helpful comments.

References

[1] CCITT Recommendation X.200, "Reference Model of Open Systems Interconnection for CCITT Applications," Fascicle VIII.4, 1989.
[2] CCITT Recommendation Q.711, "Functional Description of the Signaling Connection Control Part," Fascicle VI.7, 1989.
[3] CCITT Recommendation Q.700, "Introduction to Signaling System No. 7," Fascicle VI.7, 1989.
[4] A. Modarressi and R. Skoog, "Signaling System No.7: A Tutorial," IEEE Commun. Mag., July 1990.
[5] CCITT Recommendation X.219, "Remote Operations: Model, Notation and Service Definition," Fascicle VIII.4, and CCITT Recommendation X.229, "Remote Operations: Protocol Specifications," Fascicle VIII.5, 1989.
[6] ISO 9545, "Information Processing systems—Open Systems Interconnection—Application Layer Structure," 1989.

[7] CCITT Recommendation X.213, "Network Service Definition for Open Systems Interconnection for CCITT Applications," Fascicle VIII.4, 1989.
[8] Addendum 1 to ISO 8348, "Information Processing Systems—Data Communications—Network Service Definition. Addendum 1: Connectionless-Mode Transmission," 1987.
[9] ISO 7498-3, "Information Processing Systems—OSI Reference Model—Part 3: Naming and Addressing," 1989.
[10] CCITT Recommendation X.208, "Specification of Abstract Syntax Notation One," Fascicle VIII.4, 1989.
[11] Recommendation X.209, "Specification of Basic Encoding Rules for Abstract Syntax Notation One," Fascicle VIII.4, 1989.
[12] CCITT Recommendation X.217, "Association Control Service Element: Model and Service Definition," Fascicle VIII.4, 1989.
[13] Draft Addendum ISO 8649, "Information Processing Systems—Open Systems Interconnection—Service Definition for the Association Control Service Element. Addendum 2: Connectionless Mode ACSE Service," 1988, and Draft Proposal 10035, "Information Processing Systems—Open Systems Interconnection—Connectionless ACSE Protocol to Provide the Connectionless Mode ACSE Service," March 17, 1989.
[14] DIS 10026-1, "OSI Distributed Transaction Processing, Part 1: Model," DIS 10026-2, "OSI Distributed Transaction Processing, Part 2: Service Definition," and DIS 10026-3, "OSI Distributed Transaction Processing, Part 3: Protocol Specification."
[15] ISO/TC 97/SC 21/WG 6 N184, "Justification for Connectionless Services in the Upper Layers," June 27, 1986.
[16] ISO 8072/AD1, "Addendum to the Transport Service Definition Covering Connectionless-Mode Transmission," and ISO 8602, "Protocol for Providing the Connectionless-Mode Transport Service Utilizing the Connectionless-Mode Network Service or the Connection-Oriented Network Service."
[17] ISO 8326/AD1, "Addendum to the Session Service Definition Covering Connectionless-Mode Transmission," and ISO 9548, "Session Connectionless Protocol to Provide the Connectionless-Mode Session Service."
[18] ISO 8822/DAD1, "Draft Addendum 1 Covering Connectionless-Mode Presentation Service," and DIS 9576, "Connectionless Presentation Protocol to Provide the Connectionless-Mode Presentation Service."

Biography

Nilo Mitra received his Ph.D. in theoretical physics from Columbia University in 1983. Since then, he has been at AT&T Bell Laboratories, where he has been working on SS7 implementations and standards. He is currently a Rapporteur in CCITT Study Group XI for the group working on the SS7 TCAP protocol evolution.

Suzanne D. Usiskin received her B.S. from Cornell University and her M.S. from the University of Wisconsin, Madison, both in computer science. Since joining AT&T Bell Laboratories in 1986, she has worked on defining both SS7 and OSI standards. She is currently Supervisor of the Systems Architecture Standards Planning group.

Chapter 2
Physical and Data Link Protocols

Physical protocols

Most digital data processing devices possess limited data transmission capability. Typically, they generate only simple digital signals using two voltage levels to encode binary data. The distance across which they can transmit data is generally limited. Consequently, it is rare for such a device to attach directly to a long-distance transmission medium. The more common situation is depicted in Figure 2-1. The devices we are discussing, which include terminals and computers, are generically referred to as *data terminal equipment* (DTE). A DTE makes use of the transmission system through the mediation of *data circuit-terminating equipment* (DCE). An example of the latter is a modem used to connect digital devices to voice-grade lines.

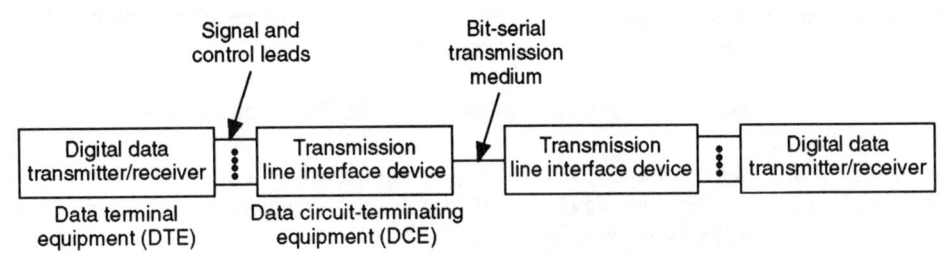

Figure 2-1. Generic interface to transmission medium.

On one side, the DCE is responsible for transmitting and receiving bits, one at a time, over a transmission medium. On the other side, the DCE must interact with the DTE. In general, this requires both data and control information to be exchanged. This is done over a set of wires referred to as *interchange circuits*. For this scheme to work, a high degree of cooperation is required. The two DCEs must understand each other. That is, the receiver of each must use the same encoding scheme as the transmitter of the other. In addition, each DTE-DCE pair must be designed to have complementary interfaces and must be able to interact effectively. To ease the burden on data processing equipment manufacturers and users, standards have been developed that specify the exact nature of the interface between the DTE and the DCE. In contemporary parlance, these standards are known as physical layer protocols.

Most but not all physical protocol standards employ the model depicted in Figure 2-1. More generally, a physical protocol refers to the interface through which a device transmits and receives data signals. For example, in the context of local networks, a physical protocol defines the interface between an attached device and the local network transmission medium; there is no model of DTE/DCE employed.

The interface has four important characteristics [BERT80]:

- Mechanical.
- Electrical.
- Functional.
- Procedural.

The *mechanical* characteristics pertain to the actual physical connection of the DTE and DCE. Typically, the signal and control leads are bundled into a cable with a terminator plug, male or female, at each end. The DTE and DCE must each present a plug of opposite gender at one end of the cable, to effect the physical connection. This is analogous to the situation for residential electrical power. Power is provided via a socket or wall outlet, and the device to be attached must have the appropriate plug (two-pronged, two-pronged polarized, or three-pronged).

The *electrical* characteristics have to do with the voltage levels and timing of voltage changes. Both the DTE and DCE must:

(1) Use the same coding scheme for representing data.
(2) Use the same voltage levels to mean the same thing.
(3) Use the same duration of signal elements.

These characteristics determine the data rates and distances that can be achieved.

Functional characteristics specify the functions that are performed by assigning meaning to the various interchange circuits. Functions can be classified into the broad categories of data, control, timing, and ground.

Procedural characteristics specify the sequence of events for transmitting data, based on the functional characteristics of the interface.

The most widely used physical protocol is RS-232-C. Although now considered obsolete this standard has survived because of the huge base of existing equipment that uses it. An improved interface is defined by a set of standards: RS-449, RS-422-A, and RS-423-A. This set of standards has achieved considerable acceptance. However, it too is being supplanted by standards that exploit the advances in electronic technology of recent years. Portions of both X.21 and the forthcoming ISDN standard are in this category.

Data link protocols

A physical interface or protocol provides only a raw bit stream service, which is subject to error. A data link protocol is used to manage the communication between two connected devices and to transform an unreliable transmission path into a reliable one. The key elements of a data link protocol are:

- *Frame synchronization:* Data are sent in blocks called frames. The beginning and end of each frame must be clearly identifiable.
- *Use of a variety of line configurations:* Devices may be connected by a point-to-point link or a multipoint link. Examples of the latter are (1) a multidrop line that connects multiple terminals to a single computer port, and (2) a local network.
- *Flow control:* The sending station must not send frames at a rate faster than the receiving station can absorb them.
- *Error control:* The bit errors introduced by the transmission system must be corrected.
- *Addressing:* On a multipoint line, the identity of the two stations involved in a transmission must be known.
- *Control and data on same link:* It is usually not desirable to have a separate communications path for control signals. Accordingly, the receiver must be able to distinguish control information from the data being transmitted.
- *Link management:* The initiation, maintenance, and termination of a sustained data exchange require a fair amount of coordination and cooperation among stations. Procedures for the management of this exchange are required.

With the use of a data link protocol, the next higher layer may assume virtually error-free transmission over the link. However, if communication is between two systems that are connected via a network, the connection will comprise a number of data links in tandem, each functioning independently. Thus the higher layers are not relieved of an error control responsibility.

The most widely used data link standard is HDLC and two very similar standards, LAP-B and ADCCP.

Summary

Perhaps the most widely used physical interface standard is RS-232. The most recent version of this standard, referred to as EIA-232-D, was issued in 1987 by the Electronic Industries Association. "Unraveling RS-232" provides a summary of this latest version; in addition, the paper examines the companion standard, EIA-530, which is a high-speed interface standard that uses the same physical connector as EIA-232-D.

EIA-232-D is typically used to connect individual devices such as terminals to modems or line drivers. A very different type of physical layer specification deals with the high-speed multiplexed digital transmission used in wide-area networking and in high-speed trunks of circuit-switched networks. "CCITT Standardization of Network Node Interface of Synchronous Digital Hierarchy" examines a family of specifications for interfaces in the tens- and hundreds- of megabits-per-second range.

The next paper, "A Tutorial on the IEEE 802 Local Network Standard," examines a standard that encompasses the physical and data link layers for local area networks. "IEEE 802.6 MAN" examines a related standard dealing with metropolitan area networks. Again, physical and data link layers are included.

The final paper, "Frame Relaying Service: An Overview," introduces an exciting new development known as frame relay. Lai examines this technology, introduced as part of ISDN, which is finding widespread application in a variety of networking architectures. In essence, frame relay provides a packet-switching capability that requires only the data link layer logic. Thus, this facility is more streamlined and efficient than X.25, which operates up to layer 3.

Unraveling RS-232

AN INTRODUCTION TO THE NEW EIA-232-D SPECIFICATION.

by Gary C. Kessler

The Electronic Industries Association (EIA) RS-232-C standard is the most commonly used asynchronous interface for data communications in North America. Every PC user has at least heard of the standard, which does everything from hooking modems to PCs and connecting terminals to mainframes to linking PCs together in low-cost "zero-slot" LANs.

Few users, though, really know how RS-232-C works — what all those pins are, what they do and how they do it. Even fewer are aware that there is actually a brand new version of the nearly 20-year-old standard. EIA-232-D — and its new companion standard, EIA-530 — offers a number of improvements over 232-C which promise to keep the standard alive for another 20 years. Here's a look at what the various standards are and how they work.

The RS-232 standard was first issued in 1962 and its third revision, RS-232-C, was issued in August, 1969. It describes the interface between data terminal equipment (DTE), like PCs and terminals, and data circuit-terminating equipment (DCE), like modems.

RS-232-C describes mostly electrical, rather than mechanical, characteristics. Among its specifications are:
- The maximum bit rate is 20,000 bits per second (bps).
- The maximum circuit capacitance is 2,500 picoFarads (pF). Since the EIA assumed a cable capacitance of 50 pF per foot, RS-232-C is often said to have a distance limitation of 50 feet. However, this 50-foot limit is not rigid — many RS-232-C devices work over longer distances.
- Polar signaling is utilized. That is, a voltage between +5 and +15 volts (V) indicates a 0 bit (for data) or the ON condition (for control). A voltage between -5 and -15 V signals a 1 bit or OFF condition.

Although the ubiquitous "D"-shaped, 25-pin subminiature connector (DB-25) became the market standard for RS-232-C interfaces, it was not specified in the RS-232-C standard. Many RS-232-C devices, in fact, use other connectors, such as the DB-9, or the RJ-11 or RJ-45 modular connectors (see "Alternatives to DB-25" sidebar).

The Next Generation

EIA-232-D (see Reference 1 at the end of the article) was introduced in January 1987. It is compatible with RS-232-C, specifies use of the DB-25 connector and defines three additional circuits for test operations. Table 1 lists

> **The EIA introduced the RS-449 standard in 1977 with the intention of replacing RS-232-C. But RS-232 is still around, while RS-449 is being replaced by EIA-530.**

the pin assignments, EIA circuit mnemonics and circuit names for the EIA-232-D interface. (CCITT Recommendation V.24 describes a standard similar to EIA-232-D that has widespread use throughout Europe. CCITT circuit designations are also included in Table 1. The EIA-232-D circuit descriptions below also apply to V.24).

The EIA-232-D circuits can be grouped into a number of categories based upon their functionality. This discussion will briefly describe all of the circuits; McNamara (reference 3) and Seyer (reference 4) provide in-depth explanations of the RS-232-C version.

The first set of circuits are for grounding. The Shield lead (pin 1) is for the connection of a shielded cable at the DTE side of the interface. Shielded cables are used for protection against things like electromagnetic interference (EMI). The Signal Ground lead (GND, pin 7) provides the ground reference for voltage measurements on the other leads (that is, the voltage on all other leads is measured with respect to the GND lead). Since there is a single reference circuit, EIA-232-D is an electrically unbalanced interface.

The second set of circuits are for data exchange. The Transmitted Data lead (TXD, pin 2) is used by the DTE to send data to the DCE. The Received Data lead (RXD, pin 3) is used by the DCE to transfer data to the DTE. The names of these leads suggests data exchange from the perspective of the DTE.

Note the four leads described so far provide the minimum subset of circuits for data communications. The Shield, GND, TXD and RXD leads will suffice for a full-duplex, asynchronous, dedicated connection.

Other communications environments can be supported by the nine control leads defined by EIA-232-D, six of which are used for asynchronous communication. Two of the control leads are used for half-duplex applications. When a half-duplex DTE is ready to send data and data is not being received on the RXD lead, the DTE will turn ON the Request to Send lead (RTS, pin 4). When the DCE has successfully seized the communications channel to the remote DCE, it turns ON the Clear to Send lead (CTS, pin 5). When the DTE detects the ON state of the CTS lead, it will start to transmit on the TXD lead.

Another two control leads are required for asynchronous, dedicated access. The DCE Ready lead (DCR, pin 6) allows the DCE to signal that it is ready and available for use (i.e., it is not in a diagnostic or test mode). The Received Line Signal Detector lead (RLSD, pin 8) allows the DCE to indicate that it is detecting a carrier signal from the remote DCE.

In half-duplex operation, the RLSD lead should be OFF when the DCE is transmitting and ON when the DCE is receiving; it will always be ON in full-duplex operation. The RLSD function may be called by different names on various test and communications equipment, including Carrier Detect (CD), Carrier On (CO) and Data Carrier Detected (DCD).

The final two asynchronous control leads apply to automatic answering (autoanswer) devices. Although the DCE actually answers an incoming call, it does so at the direction of the DTE. The normal ring cycle in the U.S. is two seconds ON (20 Hz signal) and four seconds OFF (quiet). The Ring Indicator lead (RI, pin 22) is turned ON by the DCE when it detects the ON phase of the ring cycle and turned OFF during the OFF phase. If the DTE wants the call to be accepted, it will turn ON the DTE Ready lead (DTR, pin 20). When the RI and DTR leads are both ON, the DCE will answer the incoming call.

Since the DTR lead is usually OFF when there is no call, the first ring causes the DCE to raise the RI lead momentarily, alerting the DTE to the incoming call. By the time the DTE turns ON the DTR lead, the RI lead is OFF! The DCE must wait for the next ON phase of the ring cycle before it can answer the call. This explains why a modem will typically answer a call on the second or third ring.

The next group of leads are for secondary circuits. Some EIA-232-D applications do not use the same bit rate in both directions. For example, a Bell 202 modem operates at 1,200 bps in one direction and 5 baud in the other. EIA-232-D supports the operation of these types of devices, since the primary and secondary circuits operate at different speeds.

The primary circuits always operate at the higher speed and the secondary circuits operate at the lower speed. The five secondary circuits are secondary RLSD (pin 12), secondary CTS (pin 13), secondary TXD (pin 14), secondary RXD (pin 16) and secondary RTS (pin 19).

EIA-232-D also supports *synchronous* communications and defines several circuits for that purpose. Three of the circuits are for control. The Signal Quality Detector lead (pin 21) is turned ON by the DCE to indicate that the quality of the incoming signal over the telephone line has deteriorated beyond some defined threshold. This control lead is *not* an error-detection lead; it only indicates that signal quality is poor.

Most high-speed modems support a number of transmission rates so that they can fall back to a lower speed if the telephone line becomes noisy. The Data Signal Rate Selector lead is used to change speeds, if necessary. Either the DTE or DCE will have the responsibility of selecting the speed. If the DCE controls this function, it will use pin 23; if the DTE controls this function, it will use either pin 12 or 23.

Three other synchronous circuits are for timing. Synchronous communication requires precise timing for data exchange between the DTE and DCE. The Transmitter Signal Element Timing lead provides timing for the TXD circuit (i.e., in the DTE-to-DCE direction). If the clock source is at the DTE, pin 24 is used; if the DCE is the clock source, pin 15 is used.

The Receiver Signal Element Timing circuit (pin 17) provides timing for the RXD lead (i.e., in the DCE-to-DTE direc-

TABLE 1: EIA-232-D (and V.24) Interchange Circuits

Pin	EIA Mnemonic (CCITT)	Circuit Name
1	—	Shield (see Note 1)
2	BA (103)	Transmitted Data
3	BB (104)	Received Data
4	CA (105)	Request to Send
5	CB (106)	Clear to Send
6	CC (107)	DCE Ready (see Note 2)
7	AB (102)	Signal Ground
8	CF (109)	Received Line Signal Detector
9	—	(Reserved for testing)
10	—	(Reserved for testing)
11	—	(Unassigned)
12	SCF/CI (122/112)	Secondary Received Line Signal Detector/Data Signal Rate Select (DCE source)
13	SCB (121)	Secondary Clear to Send
14	SBA (118)	Secondary Transmitted Data
15	DB (114)	Transmitter Signal Element Timing (DCE source)
16	SBB (119)	Secondary Received Data
17	DD (115)	Receiver Signal Element Timing (DCE source)
18	LL (141)	Local Loopback (see Note 3)
19	SCA (120)	Secondary Request to Send
20	CD (108.2)	DTE Ready (see Note 4)
21	RL/CG (140/110)	Remote Loopback (see Note 5)/Signal Quality Detector
22	CE (125)	Ring Indicator
23	CH/CI (111/112)	Data Signal Rate Select (DTE/DCE source)
24	DA (113)	Transmitter Signal Element Timing (DTE source)
25	TM (142)	Test Mode (see Note 3)

NOTES:

1. This circuit was Protective Ground (AA) in RS-232-C.
2. This circuit was Data Set Ready in RS-232-C.
3. This circuit was unassigned in RS-232-C.
4. This circuit was Data Terminal Ready in RS-232-C.
5. Remote Loopback (RL) was not included in RS-232-C.

tion); the DCE is always the clock source for this function. (Timing between the two DCEs is provided by the modulation scheme itself, which carries the clock information with the data).

Finally, EIA-232-D defines three circuits for testing that were not part of the RS-232-C standard. The DTE can enter Remote Loopback (RL, pin 21) or Local Loopback (LL, pin 18) mode by turning ON the desired lead. The DCE will respond by turning ON the Test Mode lead (TM, pin 25) and performing the appropriate test.

Null Modems

The EIA-232-D standard defines the interface between DTE and DCE. It often makes sense, however, to directly interconnect two DTEs. (For example, if a terminal and computer are in the same room, why invest in a telephone line and two modems?) An ordinary EIA-232-D cable will not work in this case because both DTEs will transmit on the TXD lead (pin 2) and both will expect input on the RXD lead (pin 3). A *null modem* is required for the DTE-DTE connection.

The topic of null modem cables (also called "modem eliminators") is beyond the scope of this article. In essence, though, null modems crisscross pins 2 and 3 (and some others) so that two DTE devices can communicate. McNamara, Seyer, and Sheridan (reference 5) go into greater depth on this important topic. There is no null modem standard in EIA-232-D, since that standard addresses only DTE-DCE interfaces.

As an aside, some devices can be configured to operate either like a DTE or DCE. Configuring a device as a DCE usually means that it will receive data on pin 2 and transmit data on pin 3. For example, many serial printers are configured as DCE so that they can be directly connected to DTE (e.g., a PC) with an ordinary EIA-232-D cable, obviating the need for a null modem.

Related EIA Standards

The EIA introduced the RS-449 standard in 1977 with the intention of replacing RS-232-C. RS-449 (or EIA-449) is a mechanical specification, defining a 37-pin interface (DB-37 connector) for primary circuits and a 9-pin interface (DB-9 connector) for secondary circuits.

EIA-449 uses two electrical standards. EIA-422-A is electrically balanced; it can operate at speeds up to 10M bits per second over distances up to 4,000 feet. EIA-423-A is electrically unbalanced; it can operate at speeds up to 100K bits per second over distances up to 4,000 feet. EIA-423-A can also operate in RS-232-C (or EIA-232-D) compatibility mode.

Despite the EIA's intentions, EIA-449 has not made the RS-232-C standard obsolete. This is partially due to the tremendous investment in DB-25 hardware. Also, a given product's surface area can hold fewer DB-37 connectors than DB-25 connectors, allowing fewer serial ports per square inch. Furthermore, EIA-449 added a number of additional circuits beyond RS-232-C, but little new practical functionality. Thus, the increased cost of the interface is not justified in many applications.

EIA-530

EIA-530 (reference 2) was introduced in March 1987 and is a high speed interface using the same 25-pin, DB-25 connector EIA-232-D uses. It is meant to replace EIA-449. Like EIA-449, EIA-530 uses the EIA-422-A and EIA-423-A electrical specifications.

ALTERNATIVES TO DB-25

Strictly speaking, the DB-25 connector is a requirement for an interface to meet the RS-232-D standard. But other connectors, like the DB-9 and the RJ-45, are frequently used nonetheless.

The "D"-shaped, 9-pin subminiature connector (DB-9), for example, is used on the IBM PC AT. The pinout for the DB-9 connector is given below (pin functions are from the IBM literature; names in parentheses are from EIA-232-D, if different):
1. Carrier Detect (Received Line Signal Detector)
2. Received Data
3. Transmitted Data
4. Data Terminal Ready (DTE Ready)
5. Signal Ground
6. Data Set Ready (DCE Ready)
7. Request to Send
8. Clear to Send
9. Ring Indicator

Another commonly used connector is the 8-pin modular telephone plug (RJ-45). The RJ-45 is used in some networking products, like AT&T's DATAKIT Virtual Circuit Switch. It also has applications when connecting devices using twisted pair telephone wire which may be already in place; in this case, an RJ-45/DB-25 adapter may be needed. RJ-45 connectors typically support the Transmitted Data, Received Data, Data Terminal Ready (DTE Ready), Data Set Ready (DCE Ready), Data Detect (Received Line Signal Detector), Request to Send, Clear to Send and Signal Ground circuits.

The DB-25 connector's 25 pins are rarely, if ever, all used. The standard defines several subsets for common applications and it is the use of these subsets that allows manufacturers to have connectors with fewer than 25 pins. There are definite advantages to these alternative connectors — wiring and assembly hassles are minimized, as is the amount of copper, insulation, plastic and gold/nickel plating that is wasted.

All EIA-232-D (RS-232-C) applications require the Transmitted Data, Received Data and Signal Ground leads. These three leads alone will allow full-duplex, asynchronous, dedicated communication between two devices. Addition of Request To Send and Clear To Send adds the ability to support half-duplex applications. Use of the DTE Ready, DCE Ready, Received Line Signal Detector and Ring Indicator leads supports additional applications, including switched (dial-up) communications.

I recently purchased an Epson LQ-850 printer and ran across yet another RS-232-C connector. The printer uses a standard 6-pin DIN connector and supports the following leads:
1. Transmitted Data
2. Data Terminal Ready (DTE Ready)
3. Received Data
4. (not connected)
5. Signal Ground
6. Frame Ground (Shield)

Note how few leads are supported. This small subset will work because this is only going to be used in a very specific application. Since PC-to-printer communication is typically full-duplex, Transmitted Data, Received Data and Signal Ground are sufficient leads for data exchange; Clear to Send and Request to Send are not necessary. Data Terminal Ready is used only to provide a flow control function. That is, the printer turns this lead OFF to indicate that it cannot receive more data and turns it ON when it can receive more data. (This implements the so-called XON/XOFF procedure).

— *Gary Kessler*

STANDARDS

TABLE 2: EIA-530 Interchange Circuits

Pin	Mnemonic	Circuit Name
1	—	Shield
2	BA	Transmitted Data (see Note A)
3	BB	Received Data (A)
4	CA	Request to Send (A)
5	CB	Clear to Send (A)
6	CC	DCE Ready (A)
7	AB	Signal Ground
8	CF	Received Line Signal Detector (A)
9	DD	Receiver Signal Element Timing (DCE source) (see Note B)
10	CF	Received Line Signal Detector (B)
11	DA	Transmit Signal Element Timing (DTE source) (B)
12	DB	Transmit Signal Element Timing (DCE source) (B)
13	CB	Clear to Send (B)
14	BA	Transmitted Data (B)
15	DB	Transmit Signal Element Timing (DCE source) (A)
16	BB	Received Data (B)
17	DD	Receiver Signal Element Timing (DCE source) (A)
18	LL	Local Loopback
19	CA	Request to Send (B)
20	CD	DTE Ready (A)
21	RL	Remote Loopback
22	CC	DCE Ready (B)
23	CD	DTE Ready (B)
24	DA	Transmit Signal Element Timing (DTE source) (A)
25	TM	Test Mode

Note:
A: Is one lead of the circuit.
B: Is the other lead of the circuit.

Table 2 lists the EIA-530 circuits, mnemonics and pin assignments. EIA-530 supports all of the EIA-232-D circuits except Ring Indicator, Signal Quality Detector, Data Signal Rate Selector and the five secondary circuits. The standard specifically warns users to take care not to accidentally interconnect an EIA-232-D device to an EIA-530 device, since some silicon devices may be damaged due to the different electrical characteristics of the two interfaces.

EIA-530 is electrically balanced. Rather than the voltage of a circuit being compared to ground (as in EIA-232-D), the voltage on the two leads of a circuit are compared to each other. If some interference occurs, both leads should be affected equally, increasing the chance of saving data.

Since EIA-449 devices are still out in the marketplace, the EIA has defined the interconnection between 37-pin EIA-449 devices and the 25-pin EIA-530 interface. ❏

Gary C. Kessler provides consulting and training services in the areas of data communications and computing. Electronic mail can be addressed to kumquat @ smcvax.bitnet or left on the LAN Magazine bulletin board.

REFERENCES

[1] *EIA-232-D: Interface Between Data Terminal Equipment and Data Circuit-Terminating Equipment Employing Serial Binary Data Interchange.* Washington, DC: EIA, 1987.

[2] *EIA-530: High Speed 25-Position Interface for Data Terminal Equipment and Data Circuit-Terminating Equipment.* Washington, DC: EIA, 1987.

[3] McNamara, J.E., *Technical Aspects of Data Communication (2nd ed.).* Bedford, MA, Digital Press, 1982.

[4] Seyer, M.D. *RS-232 Made Easy.* Englewood Cliffs, NJ, Prentice-Hall, 1984.

[5] Sheridan, W., *How to make and use null modem cables.* Data Communications, November, 1987.

CCITT Standardization of Network Node Interface of Synchronous Digital Hierarchy

Koichi Asatani
Keith R. Harrison
Ralph Ballart

THE INTEGRATED SERVICES DIGITAL NETWORK (ISDN) is evolving from the digital telephony network to provide new non-telephony services in addition to the existing telephony services. Network synchronization is essential for economical network operation that utilizes digital functions such as Time Division Multiplexing (TDM)-based crossconnecting, multiplexing, and switching. Current networks throughout the world are synchronized at most up to 6.3 Mb/s secondary level, because 1.5 Mb/s, 2 Mb/s, or 6.3 Mb/s synchronization was adopted taking into account the prevalence of 64 kb/s-based services and the available Large Scale Integration (LSI) technology.

However, because computer communication, office automation, and video communication have exhibited rapid rises in volume, there is a need for a network that has the capability of providing advanced broadband network services offering from 32 Mb/s up to 140 Mb/s of channel capacity economically. Recent progress in LSI, fiber optic, and software technologies makes it possible to satisfy this demand. From the network technology viewpoint, synchronizing networks at a higher level is one important objective. Some studies were undertaken, e.g., in Japan [1] and the United States [2], taking into account each national requirement. Meanwhile, due to the increasing demand for international interworking and broadband services, it has become more important to specify a worldwide universal Network Node Interface (NNI) for a new Synchronous Digital Hierarchy (SDH) [3], which is called Synchronous Optical Network (SONET) in North America. Based on technical experience and service requirements, a study on a new synchronous digital network was initiated in June 1986 in the International Consultative Committee for Telephone and Telegraph (CCITT) Study Group XVIII, and this resulted in specifications on the NNI as Recommendations G.707, G.708, and G.709 [4], approved in November 1988.

This article describes the main concepts and interfacing and multiplexing techniques for an NNI. Objectives and a historical survey of the NNI standardization are reviewed together with concepts, basic requirements, and features of the NNI. The nine-row-based frame structure and the Virtual Container (VC) concept, which are the main features of the NNI, are introduced. The multiplexing principle and method, the detailed frame structure and overhead, and mapping methods related to the NNI are described. Finally, applications of the NNI in the synchronous network and international interworking are presented. The future application of Asynchronous Transfer Mode (ATM) is also discussed.

Approach to the NNI

Current networks mostly employ synchronous working up to the primary level (1.5, 2 Mb/s), although occasional use of the secondary and tertiary hierarchical levels (6.312, 8.448, 44.736 Mb/s) may be found. A justification (asynchronous) scheme is used for higher levels. The advantage of a fully synchronous scheme is that it has the capability of accessing lower tributaries and channels directly on a multiplexed interface. Multiplexing and transmission costs are reduced because network synchronization permits higher transmission efficiency and direct multiplexing instead of step-by-step multiplexing from tributaries to a higher multiplexed interface. Furthermore, this feature allows advanced maintenance and operational features in networks because an Operations, Administration, and Maintenance (OA&M) channel can be identified directly on the interface. A high-speed synchronous network is also fundamental to the efficient and flexible carriage of broadband services such as high-speed computer communication and video distribution.

Recent progress in basic telecommunication techniques, such as LSI and fiber optic transmission and software, permits the economical development of higher-order synchronous digital networks.

The standardization of the basic characteristics of narrowband ISDN is almost achieved. One of the most important issues in the CCITT at the moment is Broadband ISDN (BISDN), and CCITT Study Group XVIII is currently wrestling with the technical problems that it presents. The issues of broadband channel specifications and broadband User-Network Interface (UNI) structures have been pursued with the highest priority. Proposed channel capacities have been based on the current network capabilities, and it was recognized that unified broadband channel capacity could not be easily obtained [5].

Reprinted from *IEEE Communications Magazine*, August 1990, pp. 15–20. Copyright © 1990 by The Institute of Electrical and Electronics Engineers, Inc. All rights reserved.

At the CCITT Study Group XVIII Brasilia ISDN Experts Meeting in February 1987, the United States and Canada proposed an NNI frame structure based on the SONET interface. The basic concept of SONET was to define a new synchronous interface based on a 50 Mb/s level together with bit interleaving to achieve a 150 Mb/s level interface. Meanwhile, NTT proposed the principle of a worldwide universal NNI of 150 Mb/s level byte structure and was supported by British Telecom (BT) and Sweden. The new synchronous multiplexing concept was also presented based on previous experience with such techniques.

At the CCITT Study Group XVIII Hamburg Meeting in July 1987, the United States and Canada proposed 150 Mb/s-level byte-interleaved multiplexing based on a 13-row-by-180-column frame, while NTT and BT proposed a 9-row-based frame structure for establishing a worldwide universal NNI. Eventually, two packages were produced [6]. One package consisted of the 9-row-by-270-column frame favored by the Conference of European Postal and Telecommunications administrations/European Telecommunications Standards Institute (CEPT/ETSI) countries and NTT. The other was the 13-row-by-180-column frame proposed by the United States and Canada. Both were byte-structured.

After the Hamburg Meeting, further meetings were held to seek a solution that would satisfy the requirements of all countries. In the Seoul ISDN Experts Meetings, this problem was resolved and a set of draft Recommendations [4] on NNI—G.707 (SDH bit rates), G.708 (NNI for the SDH), and G.709 (synchronous multiplexing structure)—were produced which were approved at the Melbourne meeting of the CCITT Plenary Assembly in 1988.

Basic Concepts for the NNI

Concept for Synchronous Digital Networks

The main features of a new synchronous digital network are the support of various signals, such as the B to H4 channels (64 kb/s to about 135 Mb/s), and the consequent establishment of an economical and flexible network together with an advanced OA&M capability. Some basic requirements for such future networks are the following:

- Handling capabilities for various signals, such as B to H4 (64 kb/s to around 135 Mb/s)
- Simple international interworking between digital hierarchies based on 1.5 Mb/s and 2 Mb/s
- Reducing the network node cost by the use of synchronous multiplexing and crossconnection
- Advanced maintenance and network operation capabilities
- Utilization of existing facilities to allow evolution from existing networks to those based on these new interfaces
- Easy accommodation of possible future services and technology, such as ATM
- Potential for flexible service rate provision

Some requirements for backward compatibility include 64 kb/s capability and an international interworking arrangement between 1.5 Mb/s- and 2 Mb/s-based networks; while requirements for forward compatibility include H4 (135 Mb/s) channel and ATM capabilities.

Basic Requirements for NNI

A transport network has two elementary functions: a transmission facility, for which there are various media (such as fiber-optic and radio) and a network node that performs terminating, crossconnecting, multiplexing, and switching. There are various types of nodes, such as 64 kb/s-based nodes, broadband nodes, simple nodes with just multiplexing, and nodes with full functionality. The NNI is the interface between the transmission facility and the network node. If a unique NNI can be specified for a combination of these various transmission facilities and network nodes, this NNI may have the appropriate flexibility and adaptability for future network evolution and will meet the basic requirements for digital synchronous networks. The basic requirements for an NNI that meets network needs are the following:

- Worldwide universal interface
- Unique interface for transmission, multiplexing, crossconnecting, and switching of various signals
- Enhanced OA&M capabilities
- Easy interworking with existing interfaces
- Easy ability to provide future services and technologies
- Applicability to all transmission media

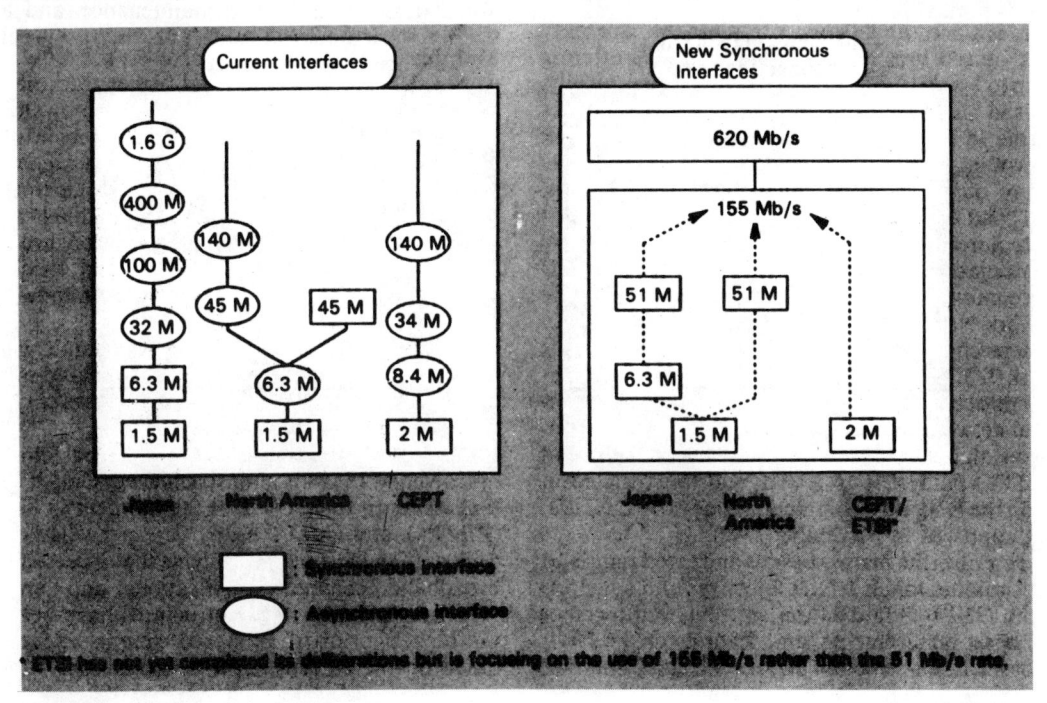

Fig. 1. Worldwide universal NNI.

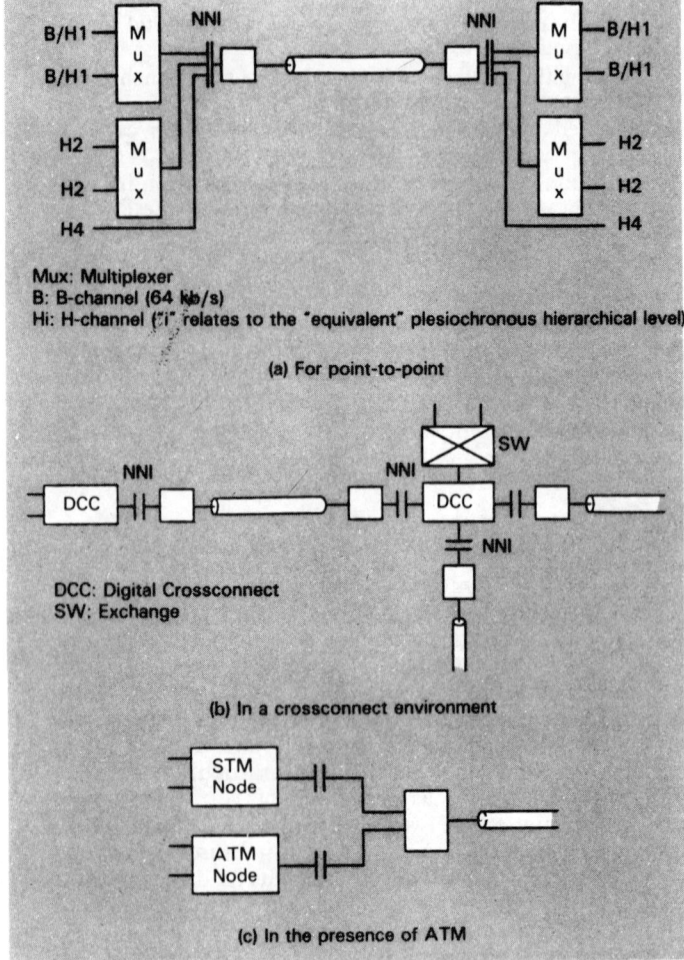

Fig. 2. NNI in various arrangements.

The Main Features of the NNI

The four most important features of an NNI that satisfy these basic requirements are described below.

Frame Structure

The key functions in a synchronous network are synchronous digital multiplexing, crossconnecting, and the digital switching of tributaries; the frame structure chosen should be applicable to all of these processes. A byte structure is adopted to provide direct access to tributaries. These functions are performed by writing and reading memory, so that it is preferable to map a tributary onto a frame in a periodic manner. Furthermore, it is desirable to distribute a tributary evenly throughout a single frame and to make good use of all the available bytes. This leads to a frame structure most conveniently depicted as a rectangle. The interface should also treat 1.5 Mb/s- and 2 Mb/s-based signals with equal ease for a worldwide universal interface. Hence, the 9-row structure forms the basis of a solution, because a 1.5 Mb/s tributary could be mapped as 27 bytes (i.e., 25 bytes for the tributary itself and 2 bytes for overhead), while 2 Mb/s tributary could be mapped as 36 bytes (32 bytes for the tributary and 4 bytes for overhead). In this way, a worldwide universal NNI was established and is shown in Figure 1.

Synchronous Multiplexing Method

The NNI employs a new concept, the VC [6]. This refers to a limited set of "payload structures," which have a specific size and structural relationship with each other and have the ability to carry several tributaries having different capacities and formats. This method makes it possible to multiplex, crossconnect, and switch various tributaries without knowledge of the tributaries or their contents. Furthermore, the VC "floats" within the NNI frame, so that VC frame alignment is not needed at a transit node. Hence, delay time at transit nodes should be minimized.

OA&M Capability

A layered approach is adopted corresponding to a digital section and path. The OA&M information is split into path and section layers and placed in the overhead of the VC and the Synchronous Transport Module (STM), respectively. The former is called Path Overhead (POH), while the latter is called Section Overhead (SOH). They are mainly used to transport supervisory and maintenance operation signals. In particular, a twelve-byte data communication channel and a one-byte user channel are defined in the SOH, and a one-byte user channel is specified in the POH. These embedded channels can be used for alarms, controls, and maintenance, and are based on a message-oriented protocol. This makes it possible to establish an advanced, flexible OA&M capability.

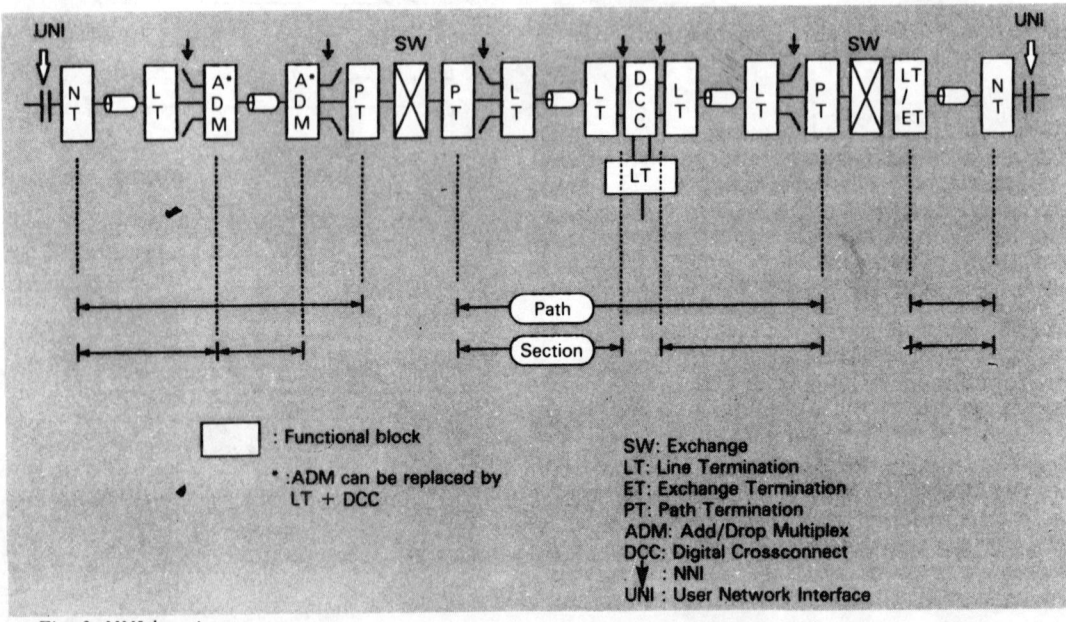

Fig. 3. NNI location.

Fig. 4. Multiplexing structure.

Network Evolution

The NNI can be applied to various types of network arrangements such as a trunk network, a local network, and a metropolitan network. Various combinations of nodes and transmission facilities may be achieved according to particular requirements, as shown in Figure 2.

The NNI and Synchronous Multiplexing

NNI Specifications

Network Configuration and NNI Location

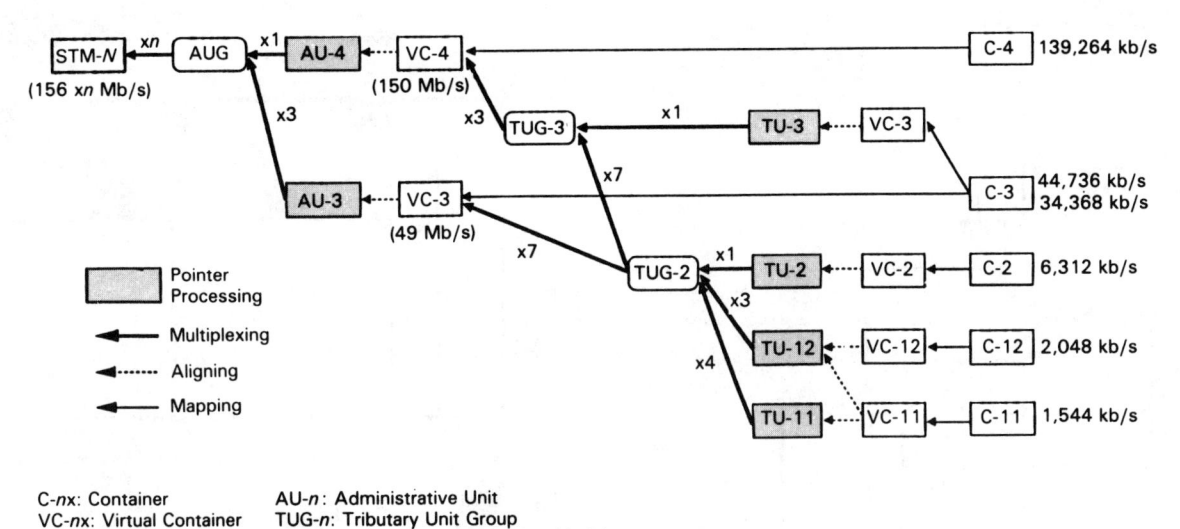

A typical example of network configuration and the location of the NNI are shown in Figure 3.

Multiplexing Principle and Elements

Multiplexing elements are defined according to the corresponding functional level and are classified into the following categories:

- A Container (C-nx; $n = 1-4$, $x = 1, 2$ where n relates to the "equivalent" plesiochronous hierarchical level, and x relates to the bit rate of the hierarchical level) is a defined unit for carrying tributaries.
- A VC (VC-n; $n = 1-4$) consists of a single container or an assembly of tributary units (tributary unit group) together with the POH. A VC is a unit that establishes paths in a network.
- A Tributary Unit (TU-nx; $n = 1-3$, $x = 1, 2$) consists of a VC together with a pointer, and an Administrative Unit (AU-n; $n = 3, 4$) also does. The pointer specifies the phase of the VC. Therefore, TUs and AUs contain sufficient information to enable crossconnecting and switching of the VC and its pointer to be undertaken.
- A Tributary Unit Group (TUG-n; $n = 2, 3$) is a national grouping of TUs formed by the multiplexing process (e.g., TUG-21 = 4 × TU-11 or 3 × TU-12).

A Synchronous Transport Module (STM-N; $N = 1, 4, 16$, etc.) is the basic building block for synchronous digital transmission. An STM-1 relates to a capacity of 155.52 Mb/s and comprises AU(s) together with the appropriate SOH. An STM-N is formed by synchronously interleaving N STM-1 signals on a one-byte basis and enables longer blocks of capacity to be formed by the use of concatenation (e.g., across 4 × STM-1).

The basic multiplexing principle is shown in Figure 4 and permits both direct and nested multiplexing. These two multiplexing methods are compatible (except for pointer processing), with direct multiplexing being more effective at handling the VC-1 to VC-3 process. On the other hand, nested multiplexing has the advantage that it can handle everything up to and including the VC-4.

Frame Structure

The STM-1 has a 9-row-by-270-column frame structure and is shown in Figure 5. The STM-N frame structure is formed by single-byte-interleaving N STM-1 signals.

Mapping Methods

The mapping of VC-4s and VC-3s into the STM-1 is shown in Figure 6. The VC "floats" in phase with respect to the AU

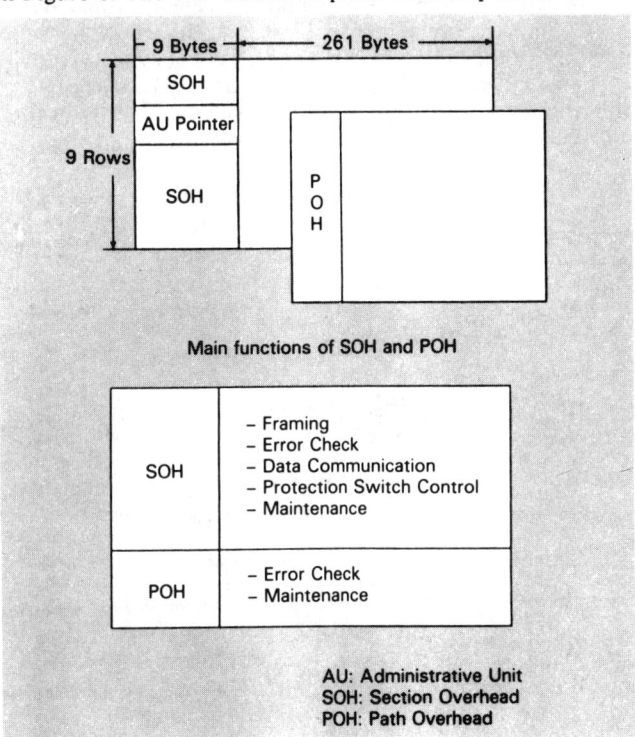

Fig. 5. STM-1 frame structure.

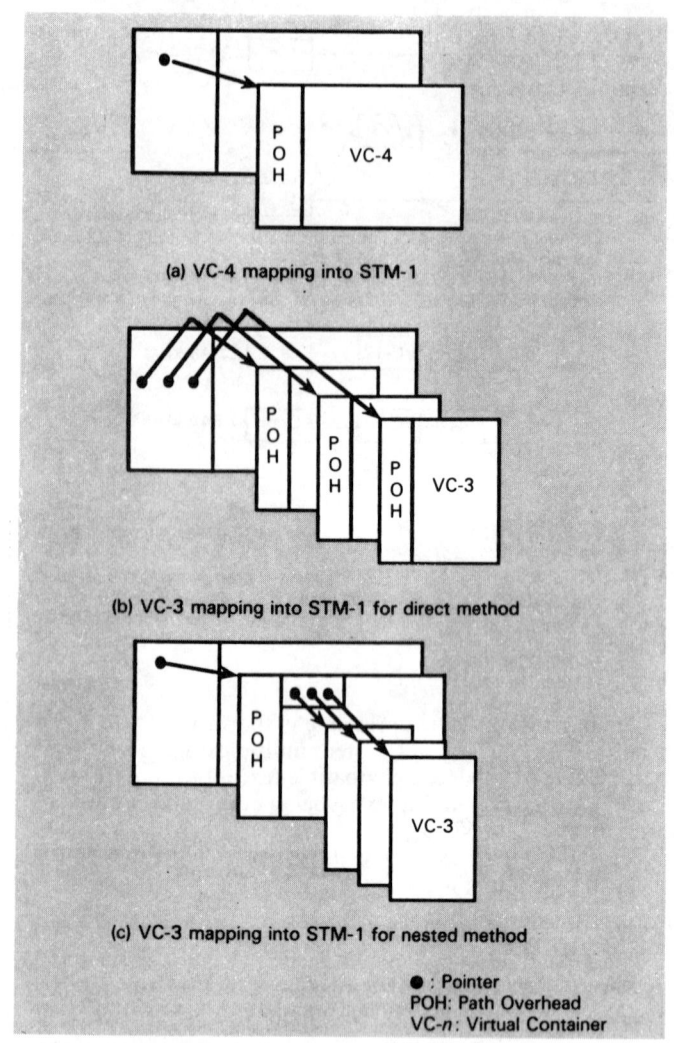

Fig. 6. Mapping method.

(shown by offset rectangles). The AU pointer value gives the offset in bytes between the pointer position and the first byte of the VC. Furthermore, if there is a frequency offset between the frame rate of the SOH and that of VC, frequency justification is possible by means of stuff bytes in the AU pointer. These pointer functions permit flexible and dynamic network operation, such as is required in today's environment.

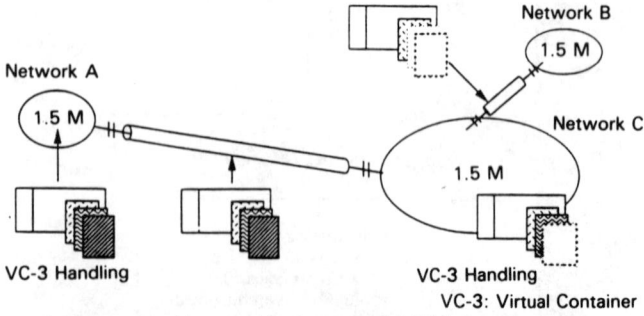

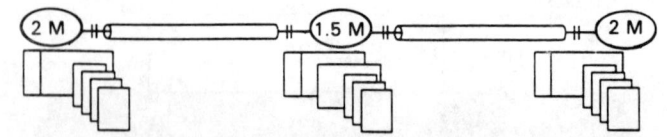

Fig. 7. Flexible handling for international interworking.

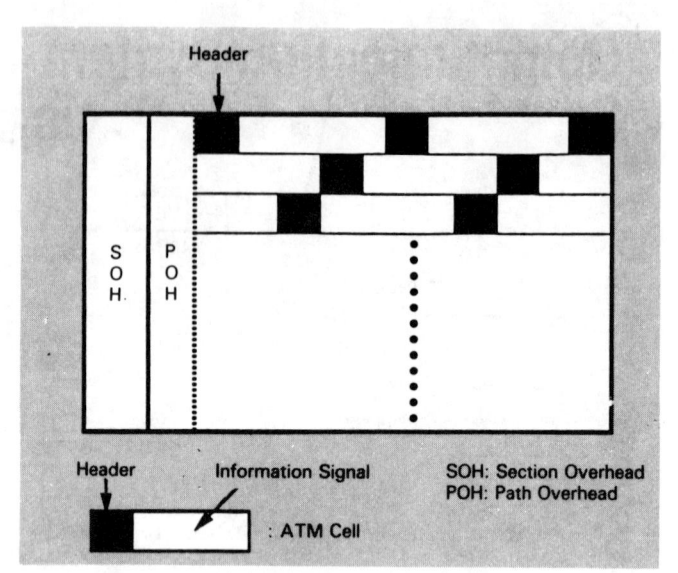

Fig. 8 NNI accommodating ATM.

Applications of the NNI

The main application is to evolve current plesiochronous-based networks toward synchronous networks that employ the NNI, as shown in Figure 2a.

Another important application is international interworking,. A worldwide universal NNI allows simple interworking arrangements because it employs a compatible multiplexing method for both 1.5 Mb/s- and 2 Mb/s-based tributaries. An appropriate VC type could be adopted according to the network requirements. For example, it is possible for VC-3 operation to be selected for national use and VC-4 operation to be adopted for international interworking, as shown in Figure 7a. This also would permit the interaction of 64 kb/s-based signals and broadband signals such as H4.

Another example is the interworking between 1.5 Mb/s-based and 2 Mb/s-based networks. There are several cases that depend on what types of VCs are employed in each network. A unique VC-4 or different types could be adopted. Figure 7b shows an example in which two 2 Mb/s-based networks interwork through a 1.5 Mb/s-based network. VC-4 operation has the advantage that it is compatible with all networks.

The NNI is also designed to meet future needs of BISDN. BISDN will use ATM techniques to carry all services in fixed length cells. Each cell is 53 bytes long and carries an explicit channel identifier in a 5-byte header. ATM cells will be carried at the BISDN NNI using the SDH STM-1 payload, as shown in Figure 8. The STM-4 signal can also carry a single payload of ATM cells by "concatenating" STM-1s together.

Using SDH transmission facilities to carry ATM cells allows a smooth transition to BISDN. In the early phases of BISDN, there will be relatively little broadband traffic. By mapping ATM cells into SDH signals, however, this traffic can be carried over an existing SDH network. BISDN can therefore evolve economically. This rationale has also been extended to the BISDN UNI, and the CCITT has defined a BISDN UNI based on SDH as Draft Recommendation I.432 [11].

Conclusion

The basic concepts of the NNI have been outlined, together with a discussion of the current situation regarding specifications and standardization. This NNI has been introduced in the context of worldwide application and should allow flexible, advanced yet simple network operation in Japan, the United States, and other countries [7–10], as well as facilitate potential evolutionary paths to new techniques, such as ATM, for

BISDN. CCITT is currently studying network application aspects of NNI to meet operational requirements for fully synchronous digital networks.

References

[1] H. Ueda and I. Tokizawa, "A Synchronous DS4 Multiplexer with Cross-Connect Function and its Impact on the Network," *IEEE GLOBECOM '85*, pp. 18.1.1–18.1.5, Dec. 1985.
[2] R. J. Boehm, Y. C. Ching, and R. C. Sherman, "SONET (Synchronous Optical Network)," *IEEE GLOBECOM '85*, pp. 46.8.1–46.8.8, Dec. 1985.
[3] K. Asatani, "Network Node Interface for New Synchronous Digital Network-Concepts and Standardization," *IEEE GLOBECOM '88*, pp. 4.5.1–4.5.7, Nov. 1988.
[4] CCITT Recommendation G.707, "Synchronous Digital Hierarchy Bit Rates," Recommendation G.708, "Network Node Interface for the Synchronous Digital Hierarchy," and Recommendation G.709, "Synchronous Multiplexing Structure," *Blue Book*, vol. 3, Fascicle 3.4, Nov. 1988.
[5] Y. Inoue, I. Tokizawa, and N. Terada, "Basic Considerations to Define Broadband Network Interfaces," *IEEE GLOBECOM '87*, pp. 13.2.1–13.2.5, Nov. 1987.
[6] CCITT Study Group XVIII, "Part B of the Report of the Hamburg Meeting," CCITT COMXVIII-R 44(B), Aug. 1987.
[7] K. Maki, H. Ueda, H. Tsuji, and H. Shirakawa, "Implementation and Application of Equipment with Network Node Interface," *IEEE GLOBECOM '88*, pp. 30.1.1–30.1.5, Nov. 1988.
[8] H. Ueda, H. Tsuji, and T. Tsuboi, "New Synchronous Digital Transmission System with Network Node Interface," *IEEE GLOBECOM '89*, pp. 42.4.1–42.4.5, Nov. 1989.
[9] R. Ballart and Y.C. Ching, "SONET: Now It's the Standard Optical Network," *IEEE Commun. Mag.*, vol. 27, no. 3, Mar. 1989.
[10] T. P. J. Flanagan, B. E. Allen, and G. C. Copley, "Application Benefits of Sonet Networking," *IEEE GLOBECOM '89*, pp. 30.3.1–30.3.5, Nov. 1989.
[11] CCITT Study Group XVIII, "Recommendations to Be Submitted at the Rules of No. 2," CCITT COMXVIII-R 22, Feb. 1990.

Biography

Koichi Asatani was born in Hiroshima, Japan, in 1946. He received his B.E., M.E.E., and D.E.E.E. degrees from Kyoto University in 1969, 1971, and 1974, respectively. He joined Nippon Telegraph and Telephone (NTT) Public Corporation in 1974. He has been engaged in Research and Development (R&D) on fiber optic transmission systems, including fiber optic subscriber loop systems, high-definition television transmission systems, ISDN, high-speed/broadband communication network, and R&D strategic planning on these technologies. He is currently Executive Manager of the Telecommunication Quality Laboratory, NTT Telecommunication Networks Laboratories, NTT Corporation.

Dr. Asatani is a member of the IEEE and the Institute of Electronics, Information, and Communication Engineers of Japan. He is Vice-Chairman of CCITT Study Group XVIII. He is a co-author of *Optical Communication Systems* and *ISDN User-Network Interface Protocol and Products* (both in Japanese).

Keith R. Harrison studied electrical engineering at Imperial College, London, where he obtained his first degree. After a brief spell at the Marconi Company, where he was working in the field of television, he joined British Telecom (then the U.K. Post Office). He subsequently obtained his Master's degree in telecommunications at Essex University. Until recently, he was responsible for the systems engineering aspects of optical transmission and digital transmission standards throughout BT. During the last few months, he has taken over responsibility for radio systems. He is Special Rapporteur of CCITT Study Group XVIII.

Ralph Ballart received his B.S. degree in physics from Polytechnic Institute of Brooklyn, in 1973, and his Ph.D. in physics from the University of Arizona in 1980. He is District Manager at Bellcore, Red Bank, New Jersey, with responsibility for the development of generic requirements for the switched DS1 service capability. His district is also active in the development of the SDH-based BISDN user network interface and the development of initial generic requirements for broadband transport equipment.

Dr. Ballart is a member of IEEE ComSoc. He is a regular attendee of CCITT Study Group XVIII.

A Tutorial on the IEEE 802 Local Network Standard

WILLIAM STALLINGS*

1.1 INTRODUCTION

The key to the development of the LAN market is the availability of a low cost interface. The cost of connecting requirement to a LAN must be much less than the cost of the equipment alone. This requirement, plus the complexity of the LAN protocols, dictates a VLSI solution. However, chip manufacturers will be reluctant to commit the necessary resources unless there is a high-volume market. A LAN standard would assure the needed volume and in addition would enable equipment from a variety of manufacturers to intercommunicate. This was the rationale of the IEEE Project 802 [1], a committee established by the IEEE Computer Society in February of 1980 to prepare local area network standards. The work of the committee has now come to fruition. Several portions of the standard are now working their way through national and international standards organizations, and the remainder of the standard will follow soon. The purpose of this paper is to provide a tutorial on the technical content of the standard.

1.1.1 An Architecture for Local Networks

The task of the IEEE 802 was to specify the means by which devices could communicate over a local area network. The committee characterized its work in this way [2]:

> A Local Network is a data communications system which allows a number of independent devices to communicate with each other. This Standard defines a set of interfaces and protocols for the Local Network.
>
> A Local Network is distinguished from other types of data networks in that the communication is usually confined to a moderate size geographic area such as a single office building, a warehouse, or a campus. The network can generally depend on a communications channel of moderate to high data rate which has a consistently low error rate. The network is generally owned and used by a single organization. This is in contrast to long distance networks which interconnect facilities in different parts of the country or are used as a public utility. The Local Network is also different from networks which interconnect devices on a desktop or components within a single piece of equipment.
>
> The objective of the Local Network Standard is to ensure compatibility between equipment made by different manufacturers such that data communications can take place between the devices with a minimum effort on the part of the equipment users or the builders of a system containing the equipment. To accomplish this, the Standard will provide specifications which establish common interfaces and protocols for local area data communications networks.

Two conclusions were quickly reached. First, the task of communication across the local network is complex, and therefore it needs to be broken up into more manageable subtasks. Second, no single technical approach will satisfy all requirements.

Reprinted with permission from *Local Area and Multiple Access Networks*, 1986, pp. 1–30.
©1986 by W.H. Freeman (Computer Science Press).

The first conclusion, reflected in a "local network reference model," is compared in Figure 1.1 to the better-known open systems interconnection (OSI) model. The model has three layers:

1. *Physical*. This layer is concerned with the nature of the transmission medium, and with the details of device attachment and electrical signaling.
2. *Medium access control*. A local network is characterized by a collection of devices all needing to share a single transmission medium. A means to control access is needed so that only one device attempts to transmit at a time.
3. *Logical link control*. This layer is concerned with establishing, maintaining, and terminating a logical link between devices.

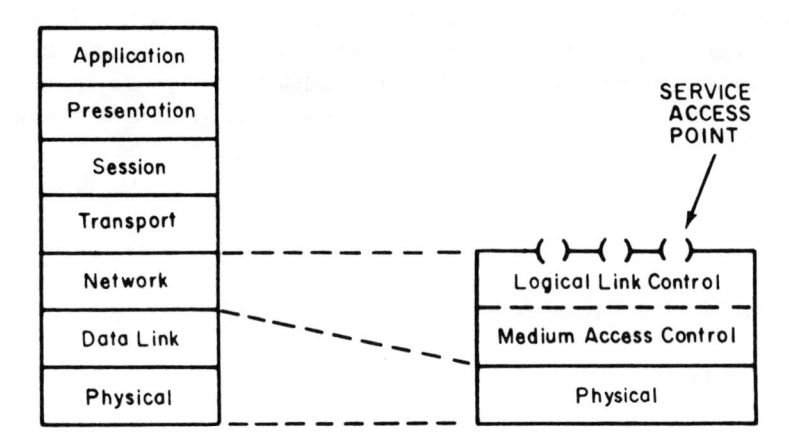

Figure 1.1 IEEE 802 Reference model.

The second conclusion was reluctantly reached when it became apparent that no single standard would satisfy all committee participants. There was support for both ring and bus topologies. Within the bus topology, there was support for two access methods (CSMA/CD and token bus) and two media (baseband and broadband). The response of the committee was to standardize all serious proposals rather than settling on just one. The result is depicted in Figure 1.2.

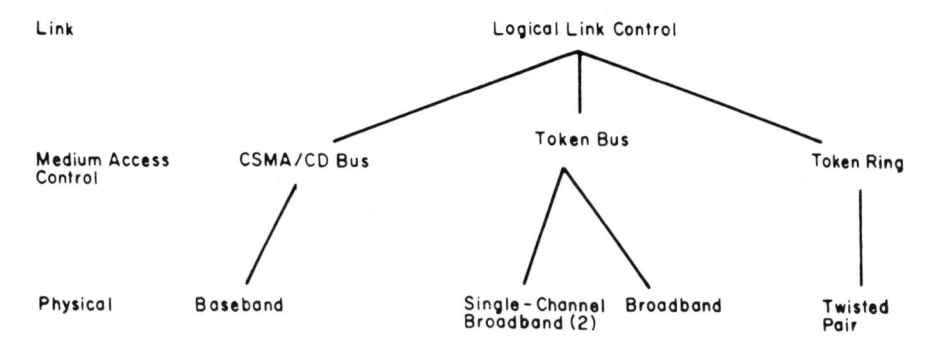

Figure 1.2 Structure of IEEE 802 local network standard.

1.1.2 Status

The work of the IEEE 802 committee is currently organized into the following subcommittees:

1. IEEE 802.1 Higher Layer Interface Standard (HILI).
2. IEEE 802.2 Logical Link Control Standard (LLC).
3. IEEE 802.3 CSMA/CD.
4. IEEE 802.4 Token Bus.

5. IEEE 802.5 Token Ring.
6. IEEE 802.6 Metropolitan Area Network (MAN).

The HILI subcommittee is working on a variety of related issues such as higher layer interfaces, internetworking, addressing, and network management.

Work has been completed on LLC, CSMA/DC, token bus, and token ring for an initial standard, and approved IEEE standards have been adopted for each [3-6]. Work on new options and features continues in each subcommittee.

The work on metropolitan area networks is just beginning to make progress. The subcommittee is attempting to develop a small number of reasonable alternatives for further study.

The acceptance of the IEEE 802 standards has been remarkably widespread. The National Bureau of Standards, which issues Federal Information Processing Standards (FIPS) for U.S. government procurements, has issued a FIPS for CSMA/CD and LLC [7]. The others will probably follow. The International Organization for Standardization (ISO) has decided to adopt the IEEE 802 documents in toto as a draft proposal. This is the first step in the development of international standards. The influential European Computer Manufacturers Association (ECMA), which had been actively drafting its own LAN standards, has now officially deferred to IEEE 802.

1.2 LOGICAL LINK CONTROL (LLC)

1.2.1 Overview

The link layer for LANs bears some resemblance to the more common link layers extant. Like all link layers, the LAN link layer is concerned with the transmission of a frame of data between two stations, with no intermediate switching nodes.

It differs from traditional link layers in three ways:

1. It must support the multiaccess nature of the link (this differs from multidrop in that there is no primary node).
2. It is relieved of some details of link access by the medium access control (MAC) layer.
3. It must provide some network layer (layer 3) functions.

Figure 1.3 will help clarify the requirements for the link layer. We consider two stations or systems that communicate via a LAN (bus or ring). Higher layers (the equivalent of transport and above) provide end-to-end services between the stations. Below the link layer, a medium access control (MAC) layer provides the necessary logic for gaining access to the network for frame transmission and reception.

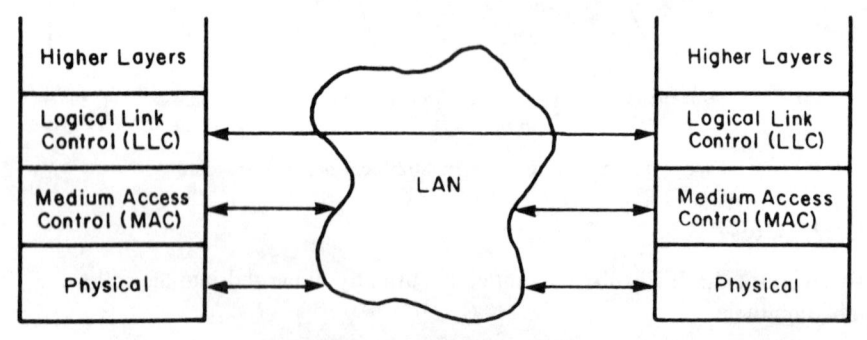

Figure 1.3 LAN communication architecture.

At a minimum, LLC should perform those functions normally associated with the link layer:

1. *Error control*. End-to-end error control and acknowledgement. The link layer should guarantee error-free transmission across the LAN.

2. *Flow control.* End-to-end flow control.
3. *Sequencing.* Frames are delivered in the order in which they are sent.

These functions can be provided in much the same way as for HDLC and other point-to-point link protocols—by the use of sequence numbers.

Because of the lack of intermediate switching nodes, a LAN does not require a separate network layer; rather, the essential layer-3 functions can be incorporated into layer 2:

1. *Datagram.* Some form of connectionless service is needed for efficient support of highly interactive traffic.
2. *Virtual circuit.* A connection-oriented service is also usually needed.
3. *Multiplexing.* Generally, a single physical link attaches a station to a LAN; it should be possible to provide data transfer with multiple end points over that link.

Because there is no need for routing, the above functions are easily provided. The datagram service simply requires the use of source and destination address fields. The station sending the datagram must designate the destination address, so that the frame is delivered properly. The source address must also be indicated so that the recipient knows where the frame came from.

Both the virtual circuit and multiplexing capabilities can be supported with the concept of the service access point (SAP). Figure 1.4 shows three stations attached to a LAN [8]. Each station has an address. Further, the link layer supports multiple SAPs, each with its own address. The link layer provides communication between SAPs. Assume that a process or application X in station A wishes to send a message to a process in station C. X may be a report generator program in minicomputer A. C may be a printer and a simple printer driver. X attaches itself to SAP 1 and requests a connection to station C, SAP 1 (station C may have only one SAP if it is a single printer). Station A's link layer then sends to the LAN a "connection-request" frame which includes the source address (A,1), the destination address (C,1), and some control bits indicating that this is a connection request. The LAN delivers this frame to C, which, if it is free, returns a "connection-accepted" frame. Henceforth, all data from X will be assembled into a frame by A's LLC, which includes source (A,1) and destination (C,1) addresses. Incoming frames addressed to (A,1) will be rejected unless they are from (C,1); these might be acknowledgment frames, for example. Similarly, station C's printer is declared busy and C will only accept frames from (A,1).

Thus, a connection-oriented service is provided. At the same time, process Y could attach to (A,2) and exchange data with (B,1). This is an example of multiplexing. In addition, various other processes in A could use (A,3) to send datagrams to various destinations.

One final function of the link layer should be included to take advantage of the multiple access nature of the LAN:

4. *Multicast, broadcast.* The link layer should provide a service of sending a message to multiple stations or all stations.

With these requirements in mind, we turn to the 802 specification.

1.2.2 IEEE 802 LLC Specification

The IEEE 802 Logical Link Control (LLC) is a good example of a LAN link control layer. It is well thought out, and offers a variety of services. This section summarizes the features of LLC.

The LLC can be specific in three parts:

1. The interface with the station, specifying the services that LLC (and hence the LAN) provides to the network subscriber.
2. The LLC protocol, specifying the LLC functions.
3. The interface with MAC, specifying the services that LLC requires to perform its function.

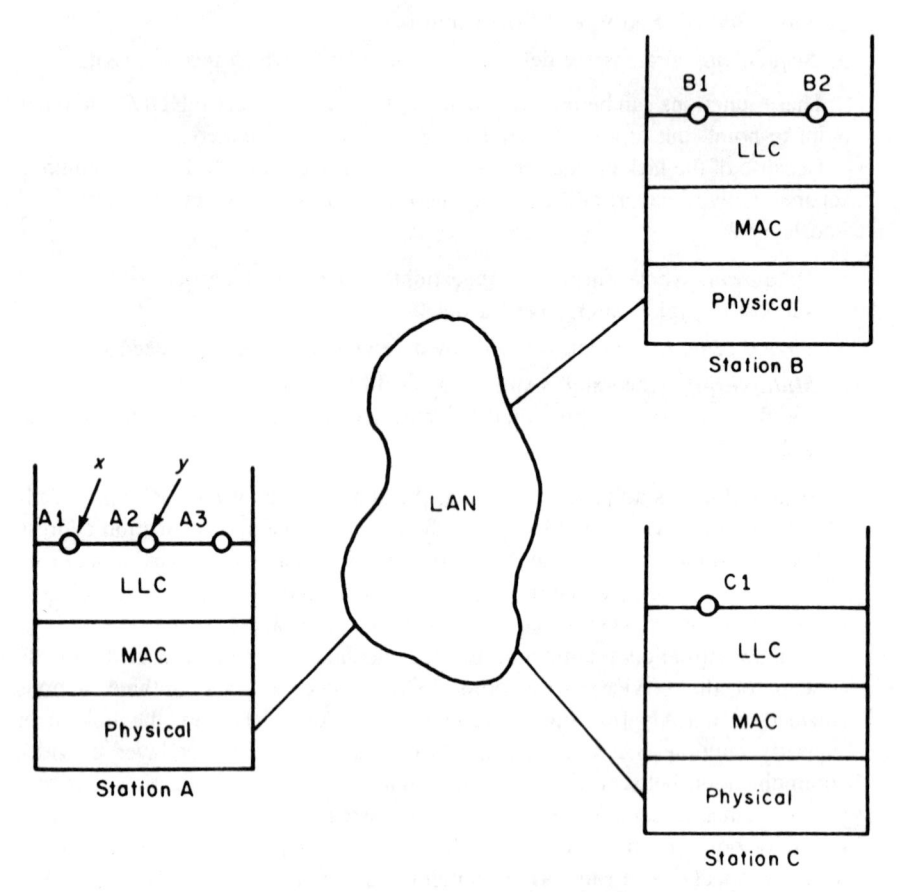

Figure 1.4 LAN link control scenario.

A variety of functions were mentioned in the previous section. Not all of these functions are needed in all environments. Accordingly, the 802.2 standard defines two types of data link control operation. The first is a connectionless operation which provides minimum service with minimum protocol complexity. This type is useful and efficient when higher layers (e.g., network, transport) provide error control, flow control, and sequencing functions. It is also useful when the guaranteed delivery of data is not required. The second type is a connection-oriented operation which provides the functions referred to above using a protocol similar to HDLC. These two types of operations are reflected in the specifications of both the LLC services and the LLC protocol.

LLC Services

The LLC standard specifies two alternative forms of service to higher-layer entitles: unacknowledged connectionless service and connection-oriented service. These services are defined by specifying the service primitives and parameters exchanged between an LLC entity and its users. These are listed in Table 1.1.

The Unacknowledged Connectionless Service is a datagram-style of service that simply allows for sending and receiving LLC frames, with no form of acknowledgment to assure delivery. It supports point-to-point, multipoint, and broadcast addressing, and multiplexing.

The Unacknowledged Connectionless Service provides for only two primitives across the interface between the next highest layer and LLC (not counting management service primitives). L-DATA.request is used to pass a frame to LLC for transmission. L-DATA.indication is used to pass a frame up from LLC upon reception. The local-address and remote-address parameters specify the local and remote LLC users, respectively. These parameters are logically equivalent to the

Table 1.1
LLC Primitives

Unacknowledged connectionless service
   L-DATA.request
   L-DATA.indication

Connection-oriented service
   L-DATA-CONNECT.request
   L-DATA-CONNECT.indication
   L-DATA-CONNECT.confirm
   L-CONNECT.request
   L-CONNECT.indication
   L-CONNECT.confirm
   L-DISCONNECT.request
   L-DISCONNECT.indication
   L-DISCONNECT.confirm
   L-RESET.request
   L-RESET.indication
   L-RESET.confirm
   L-CONNECTION-FLOWCONTROL.request
   L-CONNECTION-FLOWCONTROL.indication

LLC service access point (SAP) and the MAC address. This point is elaborated below. The l-sdu parameter specifies the LLC service data unit; this is the block of data exchanged between LLC and its user. The service-class parameter specifies the desired priority. This parameter is passed through the LLC entity to the MAC entity, which has the responsibility of implementing a priority mechanism. Token bus and token ring are capable of this, but the 802.3 CSMA/CD specification is not.

The Connection-Oriented Service provides a virtual-circuit-style connection between service access points. It provides a means by which a user can request or be notified of the establishment or termination of a data-link connection. It also provides flow control, sequencing, and error recovery. It supports point-to-point addressing and multiplexing.

The Connection-Oriented Service includes L-DATA-CONNECT.request and L-DATA-CONNECT.indication, with meanings analogous to those above, plus L-DATA-CONNECT.confirm, which conveys the result (acknowledged, failure) of the previous associated L-DATA-CONNECT.request via the status parameter. If the transfer was successful, this primitive indicates that the remote LLC entity received the l-sdu and positively acknowledged it via the LLC protocol.

The next six primitives listed in Table 1.1 are used to establish and subsequently tear down a logical connection between SAPs. The status parameter indicates whether or not the request was successful and, if not, the reason for failure. The reason parameter specifies the reason for an LLC-requested disconnection. The L-RESET primitives are used to reset a logical connection to an initial state. Sequence numbers are reset, and the connection is reinitialized.

The two flow control primitives regulate the flow of data across the SAP between LLC and the LLC user. The flow can be controlled in either direction. This is a local flow control mechanism which specifies the amount of data that may be passed across the SAP.

LLC Protocol

The LLC protocol is modeled after the HDLC balanced mode, and has similar formats and functions. These are summarized briefly in this section. The reader should be able to see how this protocol supports the LLC services defined above.

The LLC frame consists of four fields, as shown in Figure 1.5a. Unlike most link control formats, LLC requires both source and destination addresses to identify the two peer communicating entities. The source and destination are uniquely identified by a (node, SAP) pair. However, the node addresses are also used by MAC and are included in the outer MAC frame.

The format of the control field (Figure 1.5b) is identical to that of HDLC and the functioning is the same, with three exceptions:

1. LLC only makes use of the asynchronous balanced mode of operation, and does not employ HDLC's normal response mode or asynchronous response mode. This mode is used to support connection-oriented service. The set

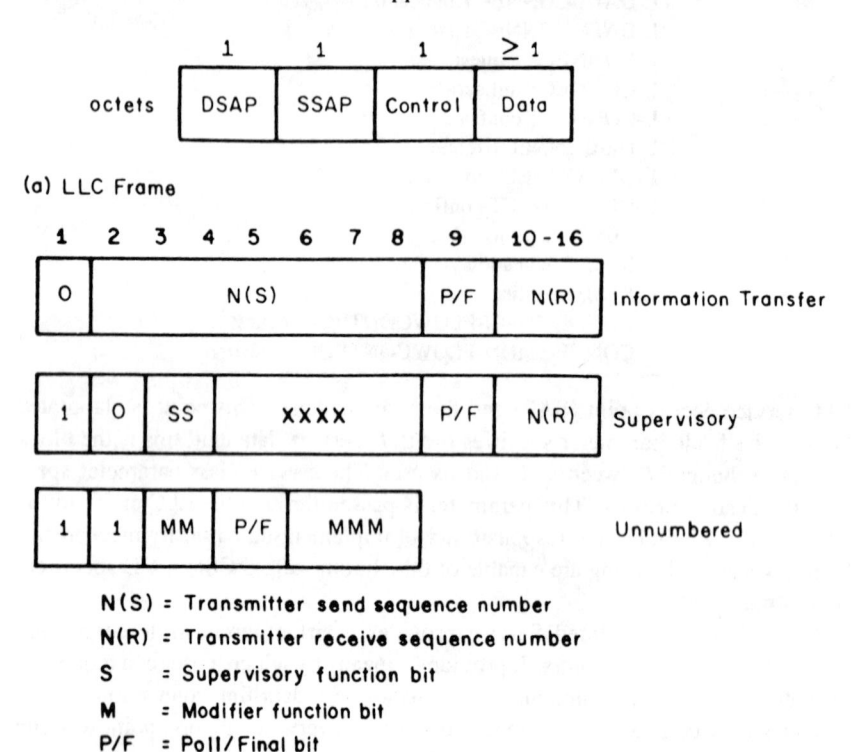

	1	1	1	≥ 1
octets	DSAP	SSAP	Control	Data

(a) LLC Frame

1	2 3 4 5 6 7 8	9	10-16	
0	N(S)	P/F	N(R)	Information Transfer

| 1 | 0 | SS | xxxx | P/F | N(R) | Supervisory |

| 1 | 1 | MM | P/F | MMM | Unnumbered |

N(S) = Transmitter send sequence number
N(R) = Transmitter receive sequence number
S   = Supervisory function bit
M   = Modifier function bit
P/F   = Poll/Final bit

(b) Control Field Formats.

Figure 1.5 Logical link control format.

asynchronous balanced mode (SABM) command is used to establish a connection, and disconnect (DISC) is used to terminate the connection.

2. LLC supports a connectionless (datagram) service by using the unnumbered information (UI) frame.
3. LLC permits multiplexing by the use of SAPs.

A brief summary follows.

As with HDLC, three frame formats are defined for LLC: information transfer, supervisory, and unnumbered. Their use depends on the type of operation employed. The types are Type 1 (connectionless) and Type 2 (connection-oriented).

With Type 1 Operation, protocol data units (PDUs) are exchanged between LLC entities without the need to establish a data link connection. There is no acknowledgment, flow control, or error control. This type of operation supports the Unacknowledged Connectionless Service.

Three unnumbered frame formats are used. The UI (unnumbered information) frame is used to send a connectionless data frame, containing data from an LLC user. The XID (exchange identification) frame is used to convey station class (Class I—only connectionless; Class II—connection-oriented and connectionless; plus window size). The TEST (test) frame is used to request a TEST frame in response, to test the LLC-to-LLC path.

With Type 2 Operation, a data link connection is established between two LLC entities prior to data exchange. This type of operation supports Connection-Oriented Service and uses all three frame formats.

The information transfer frames are used to send data (as opposed to control information). N(S) and N(R) are frame sequence numbers that support error control and flow control. A station sending a sequence of frames will number them, modulo 128, and place the number in N(S). N(R) is a piggybacked acknowledgment. It enables the sending station to indicate which number frame it expects to receive next. These numbers support flow control since, after sending 127 frames without an acknowledgment, a station can send no more. The numbers support error control, as explained below.

The supervisory frame is used for acknowledgment and flow control. The 2-bit SS field is used to indicate one of three commands: Receive Ready (RR), Receive Not Ready (RNR), and Reject (REJ). RR is used to acknowledge the last frame received by indicating in N(R) the next frame expected. This frame is used when there is no reverse traffic to carry a piggybacked acknowledgment. RNR acknowledges a frame, as with RR, but also asks the transmitting station to suspend transmission. When the receiving station is again ready, it sends a RR frame. REJ is used to indicate that the frame with number N(R) is rejected and that it and any subsequently transmitted frames must be sent again.

Unnumbered frames are used for control purposes in Type 2 Operation. The bit pattern defines one of the following commands:

1. SABME (set asynchronous balanced mode extended): Used by an LLC entity to request logical connection with another LLC entity.
2. DISC (disconnect): Used to terminate a logical connection; the sending station is announcing that it is suspending operations. Any outstanding unacknowledged I PDUs remain unacknowledged.

The foregoing frames are all commands, initiated by a station at will. The following frames are responses:

1. UA (unnumbered acknowledgment): Used to acknowledge SABME and DISC commands.
2. DM (disconnect mode): Used to respond to a frame in order to indicate that the station's LLC is logically disconnected.
3. FRMR (frame reject). Used to indicate that an improper frame has arrived—one that somehow violates the protocol.

The P/F bit is used to indicate that a response is requested to a command frame.

LLC-MAC Interface

The IEEE 802 LLC is intended to operate with any of the three MAC protocols (CSMA/CD, token bus, token ring). A single logical interface to any of the MAC layers is defined. The 802 standard does not define an explicit interface, but provides a "model." The basic primitives are:

1. MA-DATA.request. To request transfer of an LLC frame from local LLC to destination LLC. This includes information transfer, supervisory, and unnumbered frames.
2. MA-DATA.confirm. Response from local MAC layer to LLC's MA-DATA.request. It indicates the success or failure of the request, but has only *local* significance (i.e., it is not an end-to-end acknowledgment).
3. MA-DATA.indicate. To transfer incoming LLC frame from local MAC to local LLC.

1.3 CSMA/CD

1.3.1 Overview

The simplest form of medium access control adopted for IEEE 802 is carrier sense multiple access with collision detection (CSMA/CD). The original baseband version of this technique was developed and patented by Xerox [9] as part of its Ethernet local network [10,11]. The original broadband version was developed and patented by MITRE [12] as part of its MITREnet local network [13].

We begin by looking at a similar but simpler protocol known as Carrier Sense Multiple Access (CSMA). With this scheme, a station wishing to transmit first listens to the medium to determine if another transmission is in progress. If the medium is idle, the station may transmit. It may happen that two or more stations attempt to transmit at about the same time. If this happens, there will be a collision; the data from both transmissions will be garbled and not be received successfully. To account for this, a station waits a reasonable amount of time after transmitting for an acknowledgment. If there is no acknowledgment, the station assumes that a collision has occurred and retransmits.

With CSMA, an algorithm is needed to specify what a station should do if the medium is found to be busy. Three approaches are depicted in Figure 1.6. One algorithm is *non-persistent* CSMA. A station wishing to transmit listens to the medium and obeys the following rules:

1. If the medium is idle, transmit.
2. If the medium is busy, wait an amount of time drawn from a probability distribution (the retransmission delay) and repeat step 1.

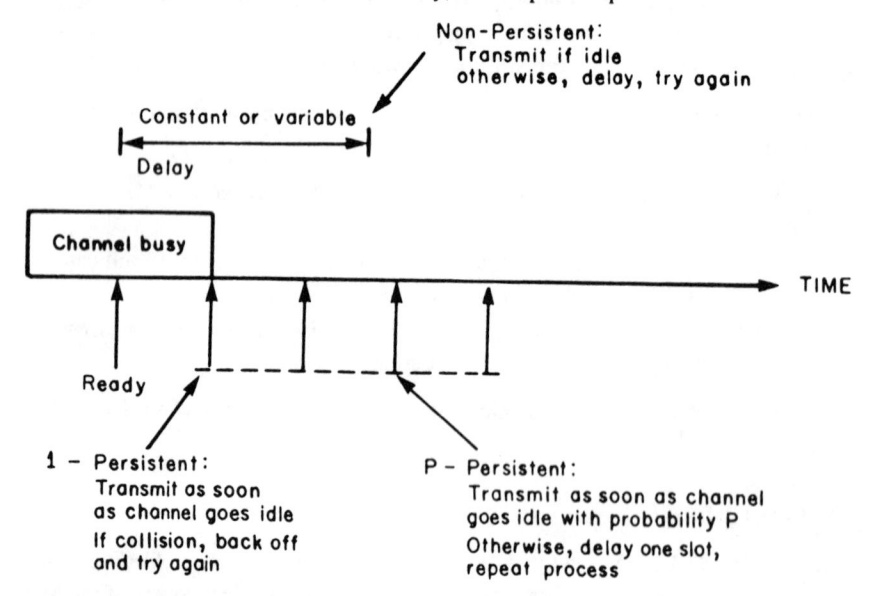

Figure 1.6 CSMA persistence and back-off.

The use of random retransmission times reduces the probability of collisions. The drawback is that even if several stations have a frame to send, there is likely to be some wasted idle time following a prior transmission.

To avoid channel idle time, the *1-persistent protocol* can be used. A station wishing to transmit listens to the medium and obeys the following rules:

1. If the medium is idle, transmit.
2. If the medium is busy, continue to listen until the channel is sensed idle, then transmit immediately.
3. If there is a collision (determined by a lack of acknowledgment), wait a random amount of time and repeat step 1.

Whereas non-persistent stations are deferential, 1-persistent stations are selfish. If two or more stations are waiting to transmit, a collision is guaranteed. Things only get sorted out after the collision.

A compromise that attempts to reduce collisions, like non-persistent, and to reduce idle time, like 1-persistent, is *p-persistent*. The rules are:

1. If the medium is idle, transmit with probability p, and delay one time unit with probability $(1-p)$. The time unit is typically equal to the maximum propagation delay.
2. If the medium is busy, continue to listen until the channel is idle and repeat step 1.
3. If transmission is delayed one time unit, repeat step 1.

CSMA has one glaring inefficiency. When two frames collide, the medium remains unusable for the duration of transmission of both damaged frames. For long frames, compared to propagation time, the amount of wasted bandwidth can be considerable. This waste can be reduced if a station continues to listen to the medium while it is transmitting. In that case, these rules can be added to the CSMA rules:

1. If a collision is detected during transmission, immediately cease transmitting the frame, and transmit a brief jamming signal to assure that all stations know that there has been a collision.
2. After transmitting the jamming signal, wait a random amount of time, then attempt to transmit again using CSMA.

Now the amount of wasted bandwidth is reduced to the time it takes to detect a collision. Question: How long does that take? Figure 1.7 illustrates the answer for a baseband system. Consider the worst case of two stations that are as far apart as possible. As can be seen, the amount of time it takes to detect a collision is twice the propagation delay. For broadband bus, the wait is even longer. Figure 1.8 shows a dual-cable system. This time, the worst case is two stations close together and as far as possible from the head end. In this case, the time required to detect a collision is four times the propagation delay from the station to the head end. The results would be the same for a midsplit system.

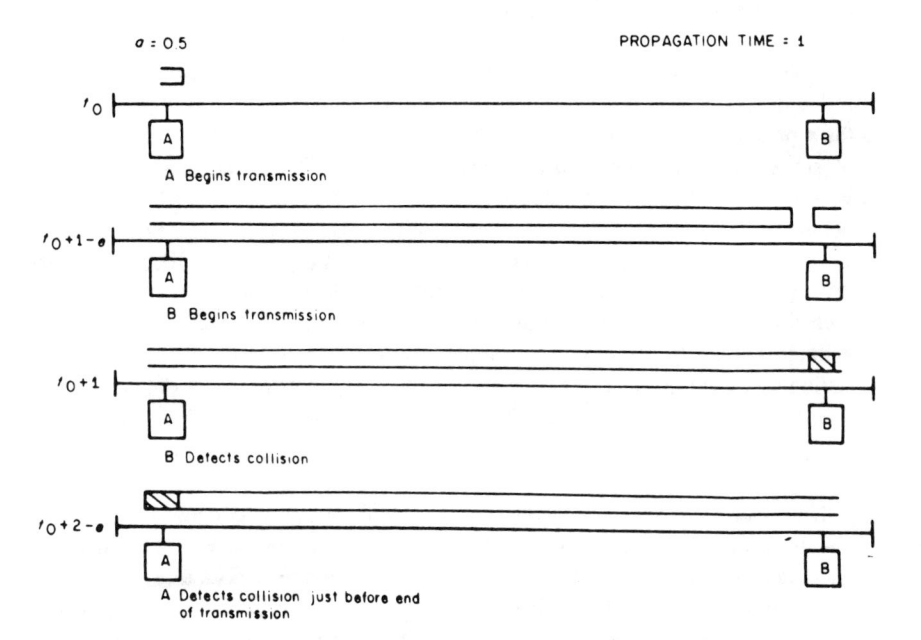

Figure 1.7 For baseband CSMA/CD, packet length should be at least twice the propagation delay.

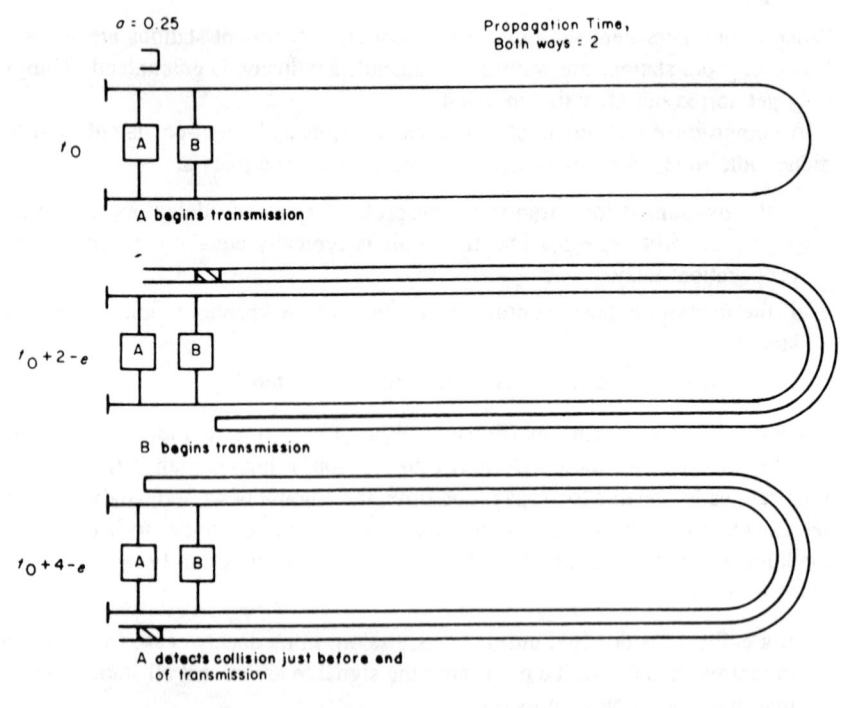

Figure 1.8 For broadband CSMA/CD, packet length should be at least quadruple the propagation delay.

Both figures indicate the use of frames long enough to allow CD prior to the end of transmission. In most systems that use CSMA/CD, it is required that all frames be at least this long. Otherwise, the performance of the system is the same as the less efficient CSMA protocol, since collisions are detected only after transmission is complete.

1.3.2 IEEE 802 CSMA/CD Specification

The IEEE 802 MAC specification follows the general outline described above. One detail worth mentioning is the persistence algorithm. You may be surprised to learn that the IEEE 802 standard specifies the 1-persistent algorithm.

Both non-persistent and p-persistent have performance problems. In the non-persistent case, capacity is wasted because the medium will generally remain idle following the end of a transmission even if there are stations waiting to send. In the p-persistent case, p must be set low enough to avoid instability, with the result of sometimes atrocious delays under light load. The 1-persistent algorithm, which, after all, means $p=1$, would seem to be even more unstable than p-persistent because of the greed of the stations. What saves the day is that the wasted time from collisions is mercifully short (if the frames are long relative to propagation delay); and with random back-off, the two stations involved in a collision are unlikely to collide on their next tries. To ensure that back-off maintains stability, 802 uses a technique known as binary exponential back-off. A station will attempt to transmit repeatedly in the face of repeated collisions, but after each collision, the mean value of the random delay is doubled. After some maximum number of unsuccessful attempts, the station gives up and reports an error.

The beauty of the 1-persistent algorithm with binary exponential back-off is that it is efficient over a wide range of loads. At low loads, 1-persistence guarantees that a station can seize the channel as soon as it goes idle, in contrast to the non- and p-persistent schemes. At high loads, it is at least as stable as the other techniques. However, one unfortunate effect of the back-off algorithm is that it has a last-in, first-out effect; stations with few or no collisions will have a chance to transmit before stations that have waited longer.

Figure 1.9 shows the MAC CSMA/CD frame structure. The individual fields are as follows:

1. *Preamble*. A 7-octet pattern used by the receiver to establish bit synchronization and then locate the first bit of the frame.
2. *Start frame delimiter (SFD)*. Indicates the start of a frame.
3. *Destination address (DA)*. Specifies the station(s) for which the frame is intended. It may be a unique physical address (one destination transceiver), a multicast-group address (a group of stations), or a global address (all stations on the local network). The choice of a 16- or 48-bit address is an implementation decision, and must be the same for all stations on a particular local network.
4. *Source address (SA)*. Specifies the station that sent the frame. The SA size must equal the DA size.
5. *Length*. Specifies the number of octets in the LLC data field.
6. *LLC data*. Field prepared at the LLC level.
7. *Pad*. A sequence of octets added to assure that the frame is long enough for proper CD operation. The minimum size is set as part of the physical layer specification.
8. *Frame check sequence (FCS)*. A 32-bit cyclic redundancy check value. Based on all fields, starting with destination address.

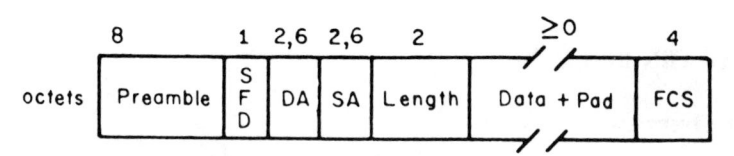

octets	8	1	2,6	2,6	2	≥ 0	4
	Preamble	SFD	DA	SA	Length	Data + Pad	FCS

Figure 1.9 CSMA/CD frame format.

1.3.3 CSMA/CD Physical Layer Specification

The physical layer specification calls for a baseband, 50-ohm coaxial cable. In this context, the term baseband refers to the use of digital signaling, as opposed to the use of a modem and analog signaling.

Digital signals are transmitted using Manchester encoding at a data rate of 10 Mbps. This is an encoding technique that assures at least one voltage transmission per bit time (see Appendix). A collision is detected if a larger-than-expected voltage swing is observed.

In addition to this specification, which is part of the current standard, the 802.3 committee is well on its way to adopting a number of additional physical layer specifications. These are summarized in Table 1.2.

To maintain adequate signal quality at 10 Mbit/s, the maximum length of a segment of cable is limited to 500 meters. To extend the length of the network, a repeater may be used. A repeater consists, in essence, of two transceivers joined together and connected to two different segments of coax cable. The repeater passes digital signals in both directions between the two segments, amplifying and regenerating the signals as they pass through. A repeater is transparent to the rest of the system; since it does no buffering, it in no sense isolates one segment from another. So, for example, if two stations on different segments attempt to transmit at the same time, their packets will interfere with each other (collide). To avoid multipath interference, only one path of segments and repeaters is allowed between any two stations.

Table 1.2
802.3 VARIATIONS

Version	Nodes per Segment	Relative Cost	Status	802.3 Compatibility
Basic Standard	100	High	Approved	
Cheapernet	30	⅓ to ⅕ of Basic	Close to Approval	Via Standard Repeater
Compatible Broadband	100	Much Cheaper Cabling	In Draft Form	Transceiver-Modem
Star-LAN	50	Similar to Cheapernet	Work Begun	Incompatible
Optimized Broadband	100s	Similar to Compatible Broadband	Awaiting Go-ahead	Incompatible
Inter-repeater Link	N/A	Unknown	Awaiting Go-ahead	Repeater

The maximum transmission path between any two stations consists of five segments joined by repeaters.

1.4 TOKEN BUS

1.4.1 Overview

Token bus is a relatively new technique for controlling access to a broadcast medium, inspired by the token ring technique discussed later.

For token bus, the stations on the bus or tree form a logical ring; that is, the stations are assigned logical positions in an ordered sequence, with the last member of the sequence followed by the first. Each station knows the identity of the stations preceding and following it. The physical ordering of the stations on the bus is irrelevant and independent of the logical ordering (Figure 1.10).

A control frame known as the *token* regulates the right of access. The token frame contains a destination address. The station receiving the token is granted control of the medium for a specified time. The station may transmit one or more frames and may poll stations and receive responses. When the station is done, or time has expired, it passes the token on to the next station in logical sequence. This station now has permission to transmit. Hence, steady-state operation consists of alternating data transfer and token transfer phases. In addition, non-token-using stations are allowed on the bus. These stations can only respond to polls or requests for acknowledgment.

This scheme requires considerable maintenance. The following functions, at a minimum, must be performed by one or more stations on the bus:

1. *Ring initialization*. When the network is started up, or after the logical ring has broken down, it must be reinitialized. A cooperative, decentralized algorithm is needed to sort out who goes first, who goes second, and so on.
2. *Addition to ring*. Periodically, nonparticipating stations must be granted the opportunity to insert themselves in the ring.
3. *Deletion from ring*. A station can voluntarily remove itself from the ring by splicing together its predecessor and successor.
4. *Recovery*. A number of errors can occur. These include duplicate address (two stations think it is their turn) and broken ring (no station thinks that it is its turn).

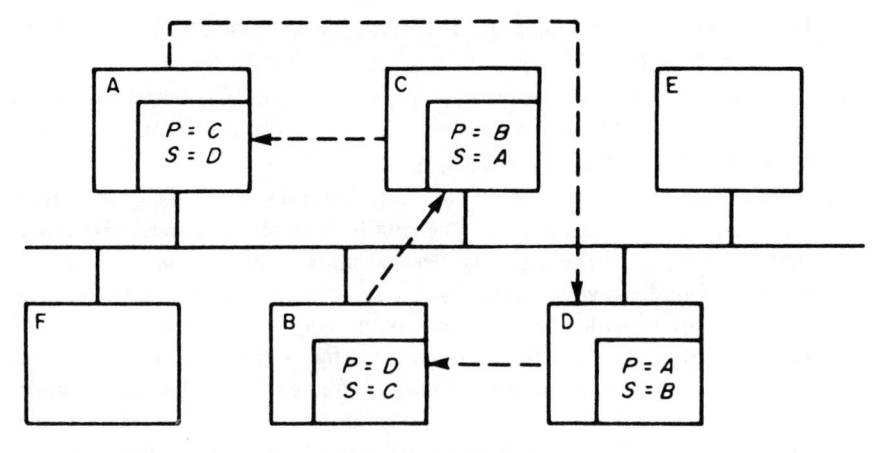

Figure 1.10 Token bus.

1.4.2 IEEE 802 Token Bus Specification

The IEEE 802 token bus protocol follows the general principles outlined above.

Figure 1.11 shows the MAC frame structure for token bus. The individual fields are as follows:

1. *Preamble.* A one or more byte pattern useds by receivers to establish bit synchronization and locate the first bit of the frame.
2. *Start delimiter (SD).* Indicates start of frame.
3. *Frame control (FC).* Indicates whether this is an LLC data frame. If not, bits in this field control operation of the token bus MAC protocol. An example is a token frame.
4. *Destination address (DA).* As with CSMA/CD.
5. *Source address (SA).* As with CSMA/CD.
6. *Data unit.* Field prepared by LLC, or used for MAC management signals.
7. *Frame check sequence (FCS).* As with CSMA/CD.
8. *End Delimiter (ED).* Indicates end of frame.

The details of the protocol can be grouped into the following categories, which will be considered in turn:

1. Addition of a node.
2. Deletion of a node.
3. Fault management by token holder.
4. Ring initialization.
5. Classes of service.

First, let us consider how *addition to node* is accomplished, using a controlled contention process called *response windows*. Each node in the ring has the responsibility of periodically granting an opportunity for new nodes to enter the

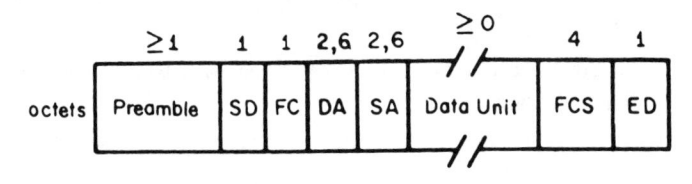

Figure 1.11 Token bus frame format.

ring. While holding the token, the node issues a *solicit-successor* frame, inviting nodes with an address between itself and the next node in logical sequence to demand entrance. The transmitting node then waits for one response window or slot time (equal to twice the end-to-end propagation delay of the medium). Three events can occur.

1. *No response*. Nobody wants in. The token holder transfers the token to its successor as usual.
2. *One response*. One node issues a *set-successor* frame. The token holder sets its successor node to be the requesting node and transmits the token to it. The requestor sets its linkages accordingly and proceeds.
3. *Multiple responses*. The token holder will detect a garbled response if more than one node demands entrance. The conflict is resolved by an address-based contention scheme. The token holder transmits a *resolve-contention* frame and waits four demand windows. Each demander can respond in one of these windows based on the first two bits of its address. If a demander hears anything before its window comes up, it refrains from demanding. If the token-holder receives a valid set-successor frame, it is in business. Otherwise, it tries again, and only those nodes that responded the first time are allowed to respond this time, based on the second pair of bits in their address. This process continues until a valid set-successor frame is received, no response is received, or a maximum retry count is reached. In the latter two cases, the token holder gives up and passes the token.

Deletion of a node is much simpler. If a node wishes to drop out, it waits until it receives the token, then sends a set-successor frame to its predecessor, instructing it to splice to its successor. If a node fails, it will not pick up the token when the token is passed to it, and this will be detected by the token sender, as explained below.

Fault management by the token holder covers a number of contingencies (Table 1.3). First, while holding the token, a node may hear a frame indicating that another node has the token. If so, it immediately drops the token by reverting

Table 1.3
Token Bus Error Handling

Condition	Action
Multiple Tokens	Defer
Unaccepted Token	Retry
Failed Station	"Who Follows" Process
Failed Receiver	Drop Out of Ring
No Token	Initialize After Timeout

to listener mode. In this way, the number of token holders drops immediately to one or zero, thus overcoming the multiple-token problem (which could be caused by two nodes having the same address). Upon completion of its turn, the token holder will issue a token frame to its successor. The successor should immediately issue a data or token frame. Therefore, after sending a token, the token issuer will listen for one slot time to make sure that its successor is active. This precipitates a sequence of events:

1. If the successor node is active, the token issuer will hear a valid frame and revert to listener mode.
2. If the issuer does not hear a valid frame, it reissues the token to the same successor one more time.
3. After two failures, the issuer assumes that its successor has failed and issues a *who-follows* frame, asking for the identity of the node that follows the nonresponding node. The issuer should get back a set-successor frame from the second node down the line. If so, the issuer adjusts its linkage and issues a token (back to step 1).
4. If the issuing node gets no response to its who-follows frame, it tries again.

5. If the who-follows tactic fails, the node issues a solicit-successor frame with the full address range (i.e. every node is invited to respond). If this process works, a two-node ring is established and life goes on.
6. If two attempts of step 5 fail, the node assumes that a catastrophe has occurred; perhaps the node's receiver has failed. In any case, the node ceases activity and listens to the bus.

Logical *ring initialization* occurs when one or more stations detect a lack of bus activity of duration longer than a time-out value: the token has been lost. This can result from a number of causes, such as the network has just been powered up, or a token-holding station fails. Once its time-out expires, a node will issue a *claim-token* frame. Contending claimants are resolved in a manner similar to the response-window process. Each claimant issues a claim-token frame padded by 0, 2, 4, or 6 slots based on the first two bits of its address. After transmisison, a claimant listens to the medium and if it hears anything, drops its claim. Otherwise, it tries again, using the second pair of its address bits. The process repeats. With each iteration, only those stations who transmitted the longest on the previous iteration try again, using successive pairs of address bits. When all address bits have been used, a node that succeeds on the last iteration considers itself the token holder. The ring can now be rebuilt by the response window process described previously.

As an option, a token bus system can include *classes of service* that provide a mechanism of prioritizing access to the bus. Four classes of service are defined, in descending order of priority: 6, 4, 2, 0. Any station may have data in one or more of these classes to send. The object is to allocate network bandwidth to the higher priority frames and only send lower priority frames when there is sufficient bandwidth. To explain, let us define the following variables:

1. THT = token holding time. The maximum time that a station can hold the token to transmit class 6 (synchronous) data.
2. TRT4 = token rotation time for class 4. The maximum time that a token can take to circulate and still permit class 4 transmission.
3. TRT2 = token rotation time for class 2: as above.
4. TRT0 = token rotation time for class 0: as above.

When a station receives the token, it can transmit classes of data according to the following rules (Figure 1.12).

1. It may transmit class 6 data for a time THT. Hence, for an *n*-station ring, during one circulation of the token, the maximum amount of time available for class 6 transmission is $n \times$ THT.
2. After transmitting class 6 data, or if there were no class 6 data to transmit, it may transmit class 4 data only if the amount of time for the last circulation of the token (including any class 6 data just sent) is less the TRT4.
3. The station may next send class 2 data only if the amount of time for the last circulation of the token (including any class 6 and 4 data just sent) is less than TRT2.
4. The station may next send class 0 data only if the amount of time for the last circulation of the token (including any class 6, 4, and 2 data just sent) is less than TRT0.

This scheme, within limits, gives preference to frames of higher priority. More definitively, it guarantees that class 6 data may have a certain portion of the bandwidth. Two cases are possible. If $n \times$ THT is greater than MAX[TRT4, TRT2, TRT0], the maximum possible token circulation time is $n \times$ THT, and class 6 data may occupy the entire cycle to the exclusion of other classes. If $n \times$ THT is less than MAX[TRT4, TRT2, TRT0], the maximum circulation time is MAX[TRT4, TRT2, TRT0], and class 6 data are guaranteed $n \times$ THT amount of that time.

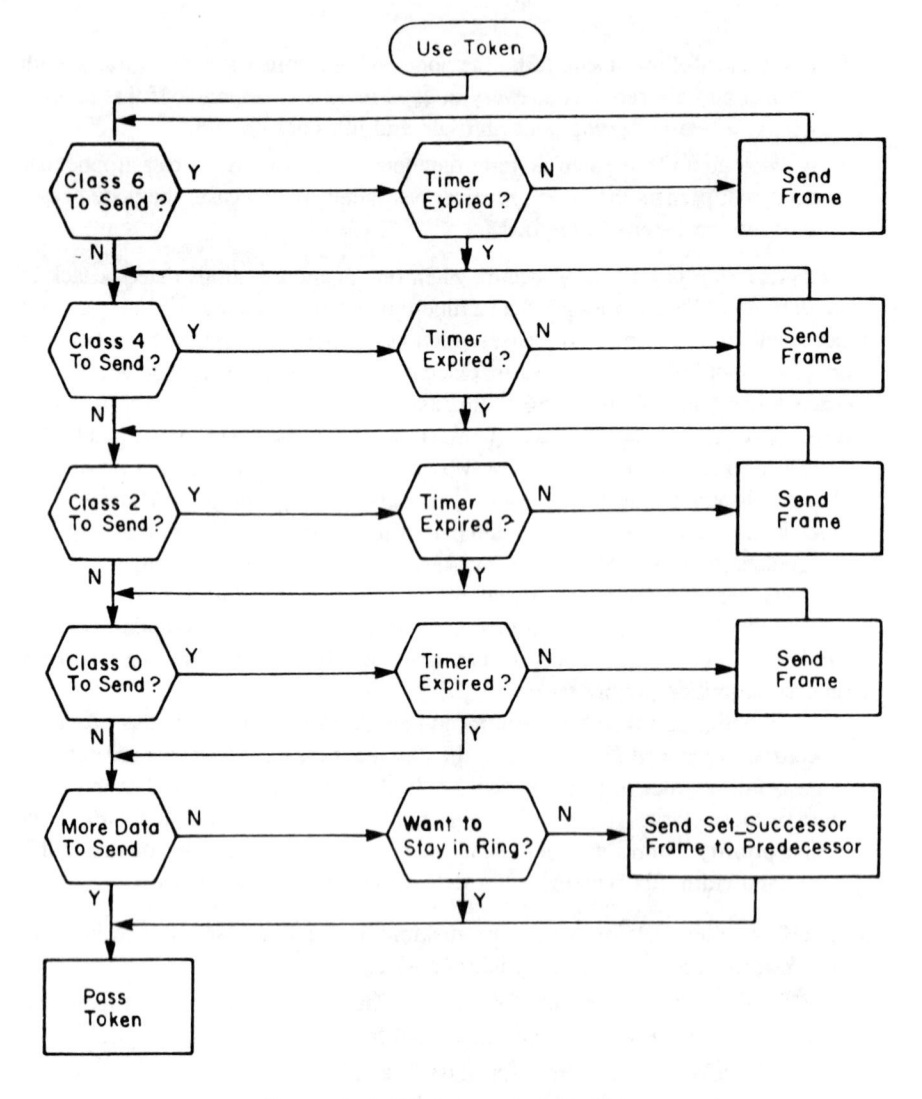

Figure 1.12 Token bus priority scheme.

1.4.3 Token Bus Physical Layer Specification

The 802.4 token bus standard specifies three alternative physical options. All three use 75-ohm CATV coaxial cable and analog (RF) signaling. Two of the medium specifications use "single-channel" broadband signaling. This means that analog signaling is used, but the transmitting modems do not have a tight bandwidth and therefore frequency-division multiplexing cannot be used. The single-channel systems are less expensive than full broadband and are intended to be cost-competitive with baseband.

The simplest and least expensive option uses a form of frequency-shift keying (FSK) and operates at 1 Mbps. The option is intended to provide a low-cost LAN that can be installed with flexible coaxial cable or semi-rigid cable. The system can use a variety of older cables already installed in buildings. The standard calls for the use of a single unbranched trunk cable with very short (<or = 36 cm) drop cables. Nondirectional taps are used so that a signal inserted onto the bus propagates in both directions. To achieve a tree topology and to achieve longer distances, repeaters are used, as in CSMA/CD baseband. Once a system is installed, it is intended that future changes will be limited to adding more drops on the existing cable and adding extensions to the end of the cable, but not significantly increasing the size of the network. The second option is also single-channel broadband, using FSK at either 5 or 10 Mbps. This system is more expensive and has a higher data rate than the first option, but is less expensive than a full-blown broadband system. When implemented with semi-rigid coaxial

cable, this system may be converted to broadband by making relatively simple hardware changes. Like the first option, this system uses non-directional taps so that inserted signals propagate in both directions. Splitters may be used to achieve a tree topology.

The final option is a full broadband system, which can carry multiple data channels, as well as video channels, simultaneously. Three data rates are provided: 1 Mbps, which occupies a 1.5-MHz channel; 5 Mbps, occupying a 6-MHz channel; and 10 Mbps, occupying a 12-MHz channel. Semi-rigid CATV cable is used as the trunk for a tree topology LAN. Directional taps are used and therefore signals propagate in only one direction. Thus, two data paths are required: one toward a headend (transmit), and one away from the headend (receive). Either dual cable or single cable technology can be used.

1.5 TOKEN RING

1.5.1 Overview

The token ring is the only medium access control protocol for rings specified by IEEE 802. The token ring technique was originally proposed in 1969 [14] and was referred to as the Newhall ring, after one of its developers. The version of token ring that has been adopted by IEEE 802 is an outgrowth of research and development at IBM [15,16]. The token ring technique is based on the use of a single token that circulates around the ring when all stations are idle (Figure 1.13). A station wishing to transmit must wait until it detects a token passing by. It then changes the token from "free token" to "busy token." The station then transmits a frame immediately following the busy token.

There is now no free token on the ring, so other stations wishing to transmit must wait. The frame on the ring will make a round trip and be purged by the transmitting station. The transmitting station will insert a new free token on the ring when both of the following conditions have been met:

1. The station has completed transmission of its frame.
2. The busy-token has returned to the station.

If the bit length of the ring is less than the frame length, the first condition implies the second. If not, a station could release a free token after it has finished transmitting but before it receives its own busy token; the second condition is not strictly necessary. In any case, the use of a token guarantees that only one station at a time may transmit.

When a transmitting station releases a new free token, the next station downstream with data to send will be able to seize the token and transmit.

Several implications of the token ring technique can be mentioned. Note that under lightly loaded conditions, there is some inefficiency since a station must wait for the token to come around before transmitting. However, under heavy loads, which is where it matters, the ring functions in a round-robin fashion, which is both efficient and fair. To see this, refer to Figure 1.13. Note that after station A transmits, it releases a token. The first station with an opportunity to transmit is D. If D transmits, it then releases a token and C has the next opportunity, and so on. Finally, the ring must be long enough to hold the token. If stations are temporarily bypassed, their delay may need to be supplied artificially.

1.5.2 IEEE 802 Token Ring Specification

The IEEE 802 token ring specification is a refinement of the scheme just outlined. The key elements are as follows:

1. *Single-token protocol.* A station that has completed transmission will not issue a new token until the busy token returns. This is not as efficient, for

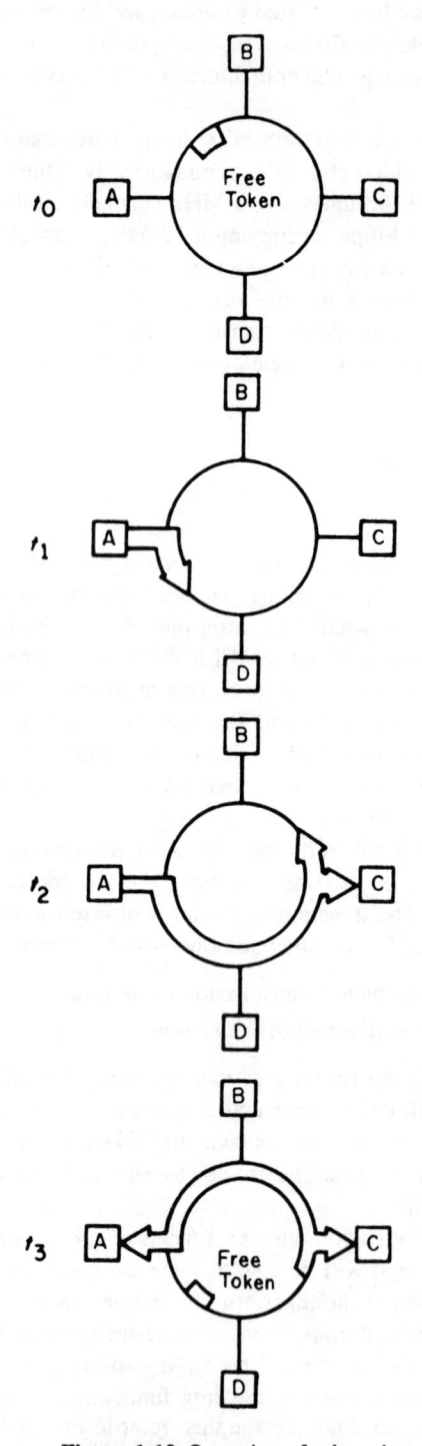

Figure 1.13 Operation of token ring.

small frames, as a multiple-token strategy of issuing a free token at the end of a frame. However, the single-token system simplifies priority and error-recovery functions.
2. *Priority bits*. These indicate the priority of a token and therefore which stations are allowed to use the token. In a multiple-priority scheme, priorities may be set by station or by message.
3. *Monitor bit*. It may be used if a central ring monitor is employed.
4. *Reservation indicators*. They may be used to allow stations with high priority messages to indicate in a frame that the next token be issued at the requested priority.

5. *Token-holding timer.* Started at the beginning of data transfer, it controls the length of time a station may occupy the medium before transmitting a token.
6. *Acknowledgment bits.* There are three: error detected (E), address recognized (A), and frame copied (C). These are reset to 0 by the transmitting station. Any station may set the E bit. Addressed stations may set the A and C bits.

Figure 1.14 shows the two frame formats for token ring. The individual fields are as follows:

1. *Starting delimiter (SD):* A unique 8-bit pattern used to start each frame.
2. *Access control (AC):* Has the format 'PPPTMRRR', where PPP and RRR are 3-bit priority and reservation variables, M is the monitor bit, and T indicates whether this is a token or data frame. In the case of a token frame, the only additional field is ED.
3. *Frame control (FC).* Indicates whether this is an LLC data frame. If not, bits in this field control operation of the token ring MAC protocol.
4. *Destination address (DA).* As in CSMA/CD and token bus.
5. *Source address (SA).* As in CSMA/CD and token bus.
6. *LLC.* As in CSMA/CD and token bus.
7. *FCS.* As in CSMA/CD and token bus.

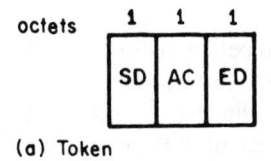

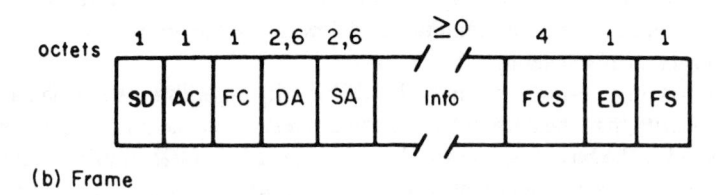

octets	1	1	1
	SD	AC	ED

(a) Token

octets	1	1	1	2,6	2,6	≥0	4	1	1
	SD	AC	FC	DA	SA	Info	FCS	ED	FS

(b) Frame

Figure 1.14 Token ring formats.

8. *Ending delimiter (ED).* Contains the error detection (E) bit and the intermediate frame (I) bit. The I bit is used to indicate that this is a frame other than the final one of a multiple frame transmission.
9. *Frame status (FS).* Contains the address recognized (A) and frame copied (C) bits.

Let us first consider the operation of the ring when only a single priority is used. In this case, the priority and reservation bits are not used. A station wishing to transmit waits until a free token goes by, as indicates by a token bit of 0 in the AC field. The station seizes the token by setting the token bit to 1. It then transmits one or more frames, continuing until either its output is exhausted or its token-holding timer expires. After the busy token returns, the station transmits a free token.

Stations in the receive mode listen to the ring. Each station can check passing frames for errors and set the E bit if an error is detected. If a station detects its own address, it sets the A bit to 1; it may also copy the frame, setting the C bit to 1. This allows the originating station to differentiate three conditions:

1. Station nonexistent/nonactive.
2. Station exists but frame not copied.
3. Frame copied.

The foregoing operation can be supplemented by a multiple-priority scheme. For example, bridges could be given higher priority than ordinary stations. The 802 specification provides three bits for eight levels of priority. For clarity, let us designate three values: P_m = priority of message to be transmitted by station; P_r = received priority; and R_r = received reservation. The scheme works as follows:

1. A station wishing to transmit must wait for a free token with $P_r \leq P_m$.
2. While waiting, a station may reserve a token at its priority level (P_m). If a busy token goes by, it may set the reservation field to its priority ($R_r \leftarrow P_m$) if the reservation field is less than its priority ($R_r < P_m$). If a free token goes by, it may set the reservation field to its priority ($R_r \leftarrow P_m$) if $R_r < P_m$ and $P_m < P_r$. This has the effect of preempting any lower-priority reservations.
3. When a station seizes a token, it sets the token bit to 1, the reservation field to 0, and leaves the priority field unchanged.
4. Following transmission, a station issues a new token with the priority set to the maximum of P_r, R_r, and P_m, and a reservation set to the maximum of R_r and P_m.

The effect of the above steps is to sort out competing claims and allow the waiting transmission of highest priority to seize the token as soon as possible. A moment's reflection reveals that, as is, the algorithm has a ratchet effect on priority, driving it to the highest used level and keeping it there. To avoid this, two stacks are maintained, one for reservations and one for priorities. In essence, each station is responsible for assuring that no token circulates indefinitely because its priority is too high. By remembering the priority of earlier transmissions, a station can detect this condition and downgrade the priority to a previous, lower priority or reservation.

We are now in a position to summarize the priority algorithm. A station having a higher priority than the current busy token can reserve the next free token for its priority level as the busy token passes by. When the current transmitting station is finished, it issues a free token at that higher priority. Stations of lower priority cannot seize the token, so it passes to the requesting station or an intermediate station of equal or higher priority with data to send.

The station that upgraded the priority level is responsible for downgrading it to its former level when all higher-priority stations are finished. When the station sees a free token at the higher priority, it can assume that there is no more higher-priority traffic waiting, and it downgrades the token before passing it on.

To overcome various error situations, such as no token circulating and persistent busy token, one station is designated as active token monitor. The monitor detects the lost-token condition by using a time-out greater than the time required for the longest frame to completely traverse the ring. To recover, the monitor purges the ring of any residual data and issues a free token. To detect a circulating busy token, the monitor sets the monitor bit to 1 on any passing busy token. If it sees a busy token with a bit already set, it knows that the transmitting station failed to purge its frame. The monitor changes the busy token to a free token.

Other stations on the ring have the role of passive monitor. Their primary job is to detect failure of the active monitor and assume that role. A contention-resolution algorithm is used to determine which station takes over.

1.5.3 Token Ring Physical Layer Specification

At the physical layer, IEEE 802 specifies a connection from a medium access unit (MAU) to a trunk coupling unit (TCU). The MAU contains the repeater and MAC logic. The specified connection consists of a shielded cable containing two

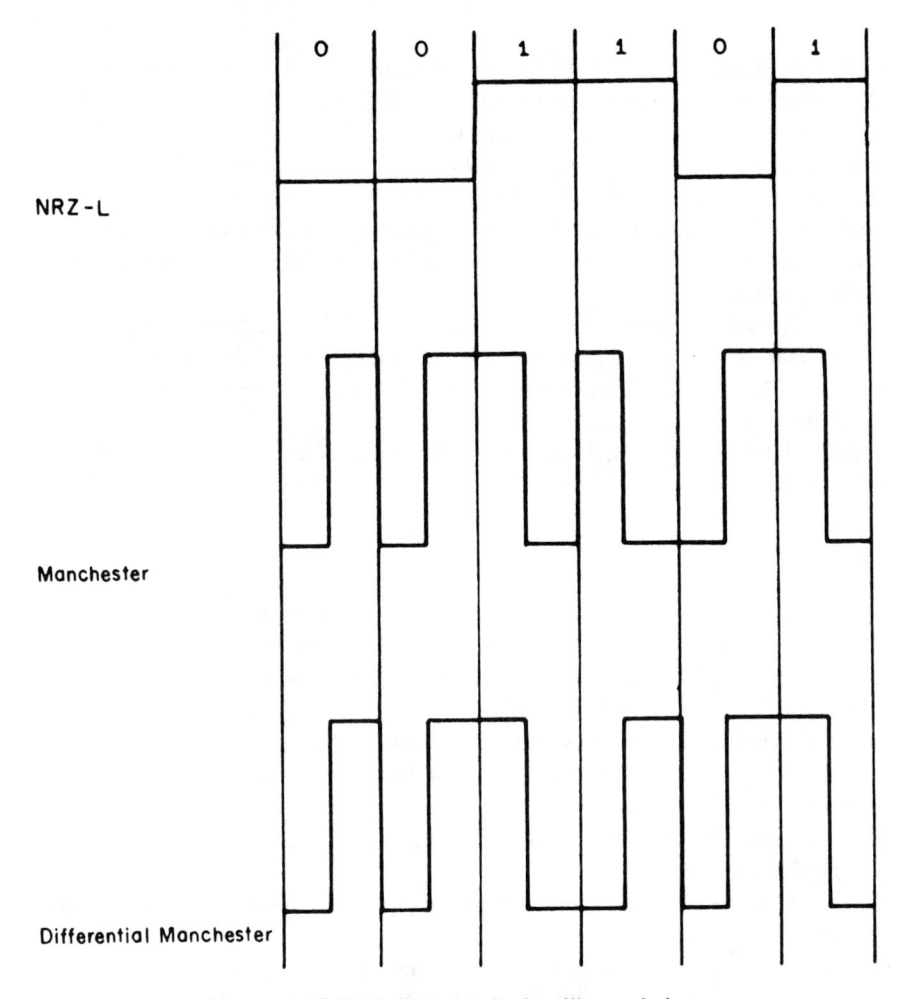

Figure 1.15 Digital(baseband) signalling techniques.

balanced 150-ohm twisted pairs. Data rates from 1 to 4 Mbps are allowed, using Differential Manchester Encoding.

Individual MAUs are connected into a ring by looping a trunk cable through the TCUs. The trunk cable is left unspecified by the standard, allowing the implementer to choose the optimum medium (twisted pair, coaxial cable, optical fiber). Implicitly, the standard requires that the trunk data rate match the data rate on the MAU-TCU link.

APPENDIX: DIGITAL SIGNALING TECHNIQUES [17,18]

The most common and easiest way to transmit digital signals is to use two different voltage levels for the two binary digits. For examle, the absence of voltage (which is also the absence of current) is often used to represent 0, while a constant positive voltage is used to represent 1. It is also common to use a negative voltage (Low) for 0 and a positive voltage (High) for 1. The latter technique is known as Non-Return to Zero (NRZ), illustrated in Figure 1.15a.

There are several disadvantages to NRZ transmission. It is difficult to determine where one bit ends and another begins. There needs to be some means of keeping the transmitter and receiver "clocked" or synchronized. Also, there is a direct-current (dc) component during each bit time which will accumulate if 1's or 0's predominate. Thus, alternating-current (ac) coupling, which uses a transformer and provides excellent electrical isolation between data communicating devices and their environment is not possible. Furthermore, the dc component can cause plating or other deterioration at attachment contracts.

An alternative coding scheme, which overcomes these disadvantages, is the Manchester code (Figure 1.15b). In the Manchester code, there is a transition at the middle of each bit period. The mid-bit transition serves as a clock and also as data: a high-to-low transition represents a 1, and a low-to-high transition represents a 0. A modified format, known as Differential Manchester (Figure 1.15c), is sometimes used. In this case, the mid-bit transition is used only to provide clocking. The encoding of a 0(1) is represented by the presence (absence) of a transition at the beginning of the bit period. In both cases, because the clock and data are included in a single serial data stream, the codes are known as self-clocking codes.

One other advantage of Differential Manchester is that the polarity of a signal is irrelevant: data is encoded as the presence or absence of a transition in either direction. This is helpful in a twisted-pair LAN since it prevents confusion as to the identify of the two wires in the pair.

Both Manchester and Differential Manchester schemes are used in the IEEE 802 standard.

REFERENCES

1. Clancy, G., et al. "The IEEE 802 Committee States its Case Concerning its Local Network Standards Efforts." *Data Communications*, April 1982.
2. IEEE Project 802. "Local Network Standards: Introduction." Draft C, May 17, 1982.
3. IEEE Standard 802.2-1985. *Logical Link Control*. 1985.
4. IEEE Standard 802.3-1985. *Carrier Sense Multiple Access with Collission Detection CSMA/CD*. 1985.
5. IEEE Standard 802.4-1985. *Token-Passing Bus Access Method and Physical Layer Specification*. 1985.
6. IEEE Standard 802.5-1985. *Token-Passing Ring Access Method and Physical Layer Specifications*. 1985.
7. National Bureau of Standards. Federal Information Processing Standard (FIPS) 107, Local Area Networks: Baseband Carrier Sense Multiple Access with Collision Detection Access Method and Physical Layer Specifications and Link Layer Protocol. 1985.
8. Stallings, W. *Local Networks: An Introduction*. New York: Macmillan, 1984.
9. Metcalfe, R.; Boggs, D.; Thacher, C.; and Lampon, B. "Multipoint Data Communication System with Collision Detection." U.S. Patent 4,063,220, 1977.
10. Metcalfe, R. and Boggs, D. "Ethernet: Distributed Packet Switching for Local Computer Networks." *Communications of the ACM*, July 1976.
11. Shoch, J.; Dala, Y.; and Redell, D. "Evolution of the Ethernet Local Computer Network." *Computer*, August 1982.
12. Hopkins, G. and Wagner, P. "Multiple Access Digital Communications System." U.S. Patent 4,210,780, 1980.
13. Hopkins, G. "Multimode Communications on the MITRENET." *Proceedings of the Local Area Communications Network Symposium*, May 1979.
14. Farmer, W. and Newhall, E. "An Experimental Distributed Switching System to Handle Bursty Computer Traffic." *Proceedings of the ACM Symposium on Problems in the Optimization of Data Communications*, 1969.
15. Strole, N. "A Local Communications Network Based on Interconnected Token-Access Rings: A Tutorial." *IBM Journal of Research and Development*, September 1983.
16. Dixon, R.; Strole, N.; and Markov, J. "A Token-Ring Network for Local Data Communications." *IBM Systems Journal*, No. 1, 1983.
17. Stallings, W. "Digital Signaling Techniques." *IEEE Communications Magazine*, December 1984.
18. Stallings, W. *Data and Computer Communications*, New York, Macmillan, 1985.

STANDARDS

IEEE 802.6 MAN

AN OVERVIEW OF THIS METROPOLITAN AREA NETWORK STANDARD

by Gary C. Kessler

LAN users increasingly want to build larger networks and/or interconnect their existing LANs. Networks that provide this type of backbone connection in a campus or metropolitan environment are called High-Speed Local Networks (HSLNs) or Metropolitan Area Networks (MANs). LANs will, in all likelihood, continue to dominate on-site data transport mechanisms in most corporate environments. The number of MAN implementations, then, should grow rapidly in the next decade.

LAN Magazine has had many articles on one of the most commonly employed MAN strategies so far; namely, ANSI's Fiber Distributed Data Interface (FDDI). FDDI does have some competition for MAN implementation, however, particularly the IEEE 802.6 MAN standard.

Metropolitan area networks (MANs) are designed to carry different types of communication traffic simultaneously, allowing more stations to communicate over longer distances and at greater speeds than LANs. MANs can act as digital backbone networks, providing an interconnection between homes, small businesses, and corporate LANs. By design, they will also accommodate the integration of voice, video, and data traffic. MAN media choices include optical fiber, CATV coaxial cable, and radio transmission.

The general characteristics of a MAN include:
- Very high data rates—typically in excess of 100 Mbps,
- Large geographic scope—from a few to several hundred kilometers,
- Many stations—theoretically any number, but practically limited to about 1,000, and
- Low error rate—less than one bit error every 10^9 bits.

The concept for metropolitan area networks clearly sprang from the LAN. However, LAN technology doesn't apply to MANs in large part due to the inherent inefficiencies in most LAN Medium Access Control (MAC) schemes. Contention schemes (e.g., Carrier Sense Multiple Access with Collision Detection, or CSMA/CD), for example, have idle time on the line because of collisions and/or backoff; token passing has idle time on the medium due to the required circulation of the token. These inefficiencies have a low impact on performance in the relatively small LAN. The larger geographical scope of the MAN magnifies the impact.

Evolution of MAN

The IEEE 802 standards generally deal with LANs operating at speeds between 1 and 20 Mbps, and include:
- IEEE 802.3—CSMA/CD, based upon Xerox, Intel, and DEC's Ethernet;
- IEEE 802.4—Token-passing Bus, based upon the General Motors' Manufacturing Automation Protocol (MAP); and
- IEEE 802.5—Token Ring, based upon IBM's Token Ring.

The many changes in the IEEE

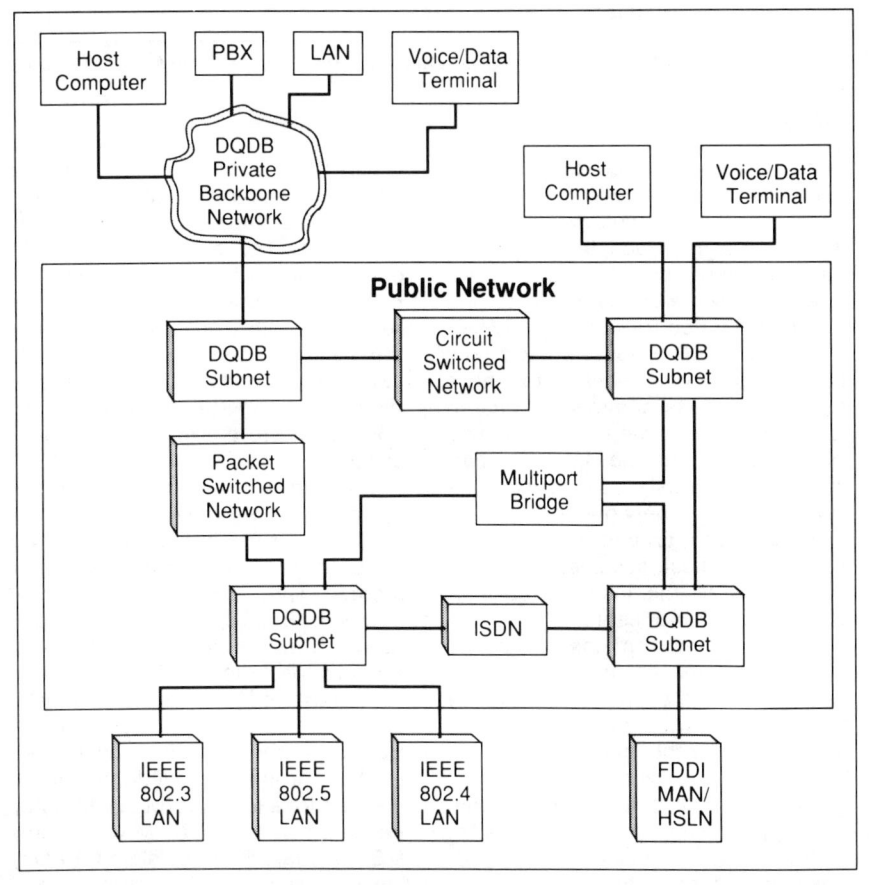

Figure 1 — *DQDB subnetworks provide data and telecommunications services within a metropolitan area which may exceed 50 km in diameter. Interconnected subnets form a MAN, and a MAN may be either a public or private network.*

STANDARDS

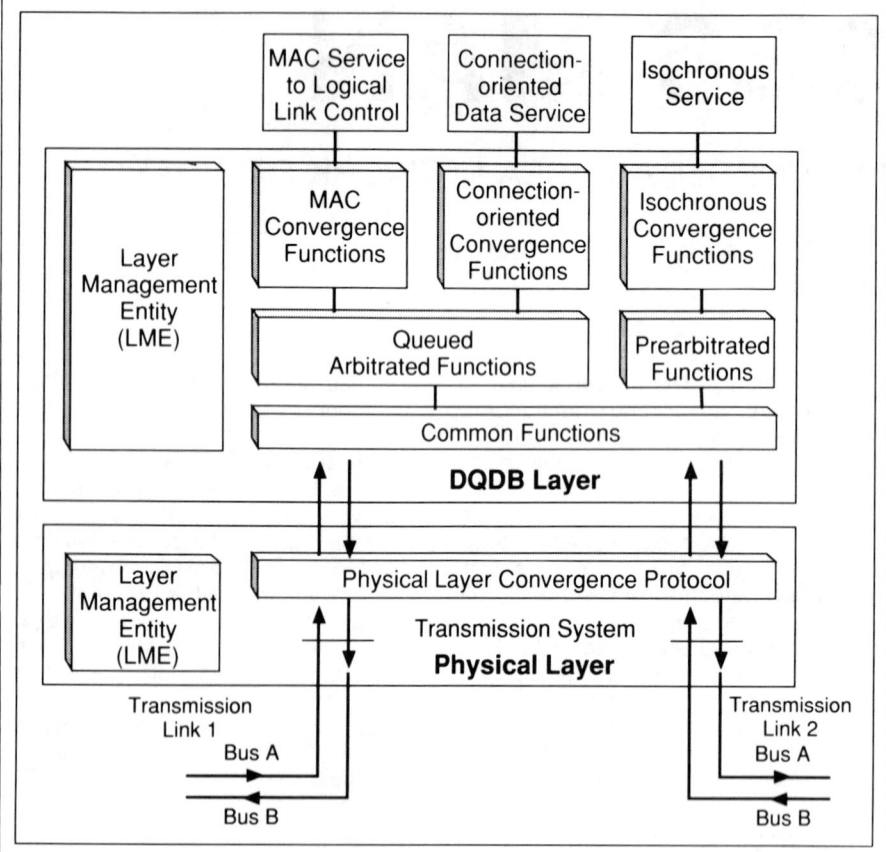

Figure 2 — The IEEE 802.6 standard describes the Physical Layer and the Distributed Queue Dual Bus Layer.

802.6 standard, since formation in 1981, mirror changes in the industry, economy, and technology. Unlike the 802.3—.5 committees, formed to create a standard around a specific MAC strategy, 802.6 was instructed to find the best solution for building a MAN.

Early 802.6 proposals used time division protocols similar to those found in satellite communications. In fact, MANs were seen originally as a way of providing the satellite communications industry with an economical, high-speed network for connections between ground stations and customers. These schemes were also well suited to the installed base of CATV (broadband) cable.

Data communications via satellite did not become as pervasive as expected, and the push by that industry to create MAN standards diminished significantly by the mid-1980s. Except for a few notable exceptions, the CATV industry has also shied away from carrying large amounts of data traffic. The committee rejected an early proposal based on radio networks because of the less-than-1-Mbps operating speed involved.

In late 1984, Burroughs led a group that proposed an optical fiber solution. Their proposal started as a 50-Mbps slotted ring, but later the speed was reduced to 43 Mbps for compatibility with digital carriers in use by the telephone industry. The speed required by this proposal, well above the 20-Mbps maximum of other 802 standards, led the IEEE to authorize the 802.6 committee to use any speed appropriate to the medium and MAC scheme.

Within two years, the Burroughs-led proposal was ready for the initial process that would lead to a formally adopted standard. After Burroughs merged with Sperry in late 1986, however, Burroughs ceased funding research in this area and the slotted ring proposal died.

Integrated Networks, a startup company comprising many former Burroughs people, came up with a new, related proposal called the Multiplexed Slot and Token (MST). Although based upon the FDDI MAC scheme, MST overlaid 64-Kbps slots for carrying time-sensitive data such as digitized voice. MST also offered a greater number of choices of operating speed and media than did FDDI. MST, however, never really gained wholehearted support of the committee.

During this same time frame (mid- to late-1986), Telecom Australia proposed a competing MAN strategy, called Queued Packet and Synchronous Exchange (QPSX). QPSX was a radical departure from FDDI (and MST): It uses a dual-bus topology rather than a ring; it supports a wide range of speeds and media; and it uses a very different MAC scheme. QPSX has received enthusiastic support, especially by AT&T, Bellcore, most of the regional Bell operating companies, other telephone companies, and several fiber by-pass operators. In 1987, it became clear that most of the committee preferred QPSX, and they dropped the MST proposal.

Telecom Australia formed a company called QPSX Communications to further develop QPSX technology. To avoid confusion between the standard and the company/product, the 802.6 committee renamed the QPSX proposal to Distributed Queue Dual Bus (DQDB).

The support of DQDB by the telephone industry is an important consideration. Since the divestiture of AT&T in 1984, the telephone companies have looked for ways to provide new services, especially data transport. Furthermore, initial public MAN service offerings will undoubtedly be made by the telephone companies since they possess both the facilities and the budgets.

DQDB Overview

The IEEE 802.6 standard describes DQDB subnetworks which can interconnect through bridges, routers, gateways, or other networks to form a MAN (See Figure 1.). As a public network, DQDB subnets can provide switching and routing for high-speed data, voice, and video applications, as well as the interconnection of private DQDB subnets and other private networks. A private DQDB network can interconnect host computers, terminals, LANs, PBXs, and videoconferencing services.

The IEEE will probably formally adopt the 802.6 standard by the end of 1990. It will then be forwarded to the International Organization for Standardization (ISO), as have IEEE 802.2-.5, for approval as ISO 8802-6.

DQDB Protocol Architecture

The 802.6 standard defines a high-speed network using the DQDB topology and a MAC scheme (See Figure 2.).

STANDARDS

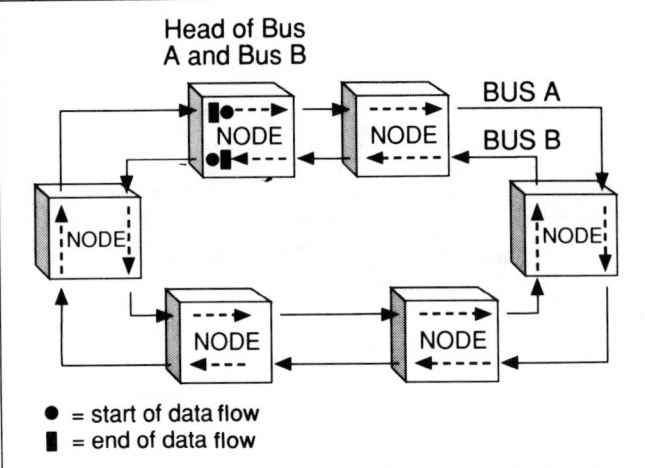

Figure 3 — *A looped dual bus differs from the regular dual bus in that one node acts as both head and end of the bus.*

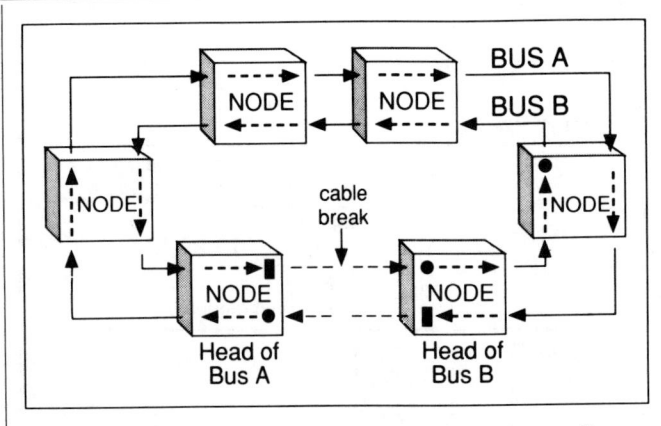

● = start of data flow
■ = end of data flow

Figure 4 — *When a cable break occurs, the network reconfigures itself so that the position of the nature break in the loop corresponds to the physical break in the cable. The reconfiguration procedure moves the head of bus functions to the adjacent nodes.*

Since the network utilizes a dual-bus topology, every station has two transmission links and two buses. Bus A and Bus B operate in opposite directions of transmission.

The 802.6 Physical Layer corresponds to the OSI Physical Layer and specifies how to use different underlying transmission media and speeds. The standard currently describes support for the following options:

- The North American telephone Digital Signaling level three (DS-3) rate of 44.736 Mbps (per ANSI standard);
- European digital telephone signaling level three and four rates of 34.368M and 139.264 Mbps (per CCITT standard); or
- The optical fiber Synchronous Digital Hierarchy (SDH) rate of 155.520 Mbps (per CCITT and ANSI Synchronous Optical Network, or SONET, standards).

The standard does not specify a maximum bus length nor a maximum number of stations; these characteristics depend on the transmission system used by the network.

The Physical Layer Convergence Protocol (PLCP), part of the Physical Layer, adapts the capabilities of the transmission system to provide the service expected by the DQDB Layer. The PLCP will be different for every transmission system, but it is this part of the Physical Layer that allows the wide range of media and speed options supported by the network.

The 802.6 DQDB Layer is equivalent to the MAC Sublayer of the 802.3—.5 LAN standards and roughly corresponds to the OSI Data Link Layer. It will provide support for higher layer services. At this time, the 802.6 standard specifies that the DQDB Layer is required to support:

- Connectionless (datagram) MAC service to the IEEE 802.2 Logical Link Control (LLC) sublayer, consistent with other IEEE 802 LANs;
- Connection-oriented (virtual circuit) data service for the transfer of bursty data, such as signaling or packetized voice; and
- Connection-oriented (virtual circuit) isochronous service; "isochronous" refers to the timing characteristic of an event or signal recurring at known, periodic intervals, such as conventional digitized voice or video.

The MAC, Connection-oriented, and Isochronous Convergence Functions enhance the access control functions of the DQDB Layer to meet the requirements of the higher layer service. Again, these convergence functions will be different for each type of higher layer service, but provide the DQDB protocol with enormous flexibility in terms of the services that can be supported.

The three types of higher layer services are supported by employing two access methods. The Queued Arbitrated access method supports those services that are not time-sensitive. A distributed queue access method allows users to request access to the medium as needed. This access method supports the connectionless MAC service and the connection-oriented data service.

The Pre-Arbitrated access method assigns specific octet positions within a transmission slot for use by different stations with time-sensitive applications. This access method supports isochronous connection-oriented services.

Finally, the Layer Management Entities (LME) provide network management functions for each layer, compatible with the network management procedures of IEEE 802.1.

DQDB Physical Topology

A DQDB network utilizes a dual-bus topology comprising two unidirectional buses and multiple nodes. The two buses, called Bus A and Bus B, support transmission in opposite directions, allowing full-duplex communication between any pair of nodes. A given node, however, must know which bus to use to communicate with another node.

Bus A and Bus B operate independently of each other. Since both buses are operational at all times, the effective capacity of the DQDB subnet is twice the capacity of a single bus.

The transmissions on each bus are formatted as fixed length entities called "slots." Nodes on the bus may write into slots according to the rules of the access protocol, discussed below. All slots originate at the head of the bus and terminate at the end of the bus.

Each node of the subnet comprises an Access Unit (AU) and the physical attachment of the AU to the two buses. The access unit performs the node's DQDB Layer functions and attaches to each bus with a single read-and-write connection.

A key feature of DQDB is that the operation of the bus is independent of the operation of the individual AUs. Therefore, access units may fail or be removed from the network without causing operational problems elsewhere in the network. The node at the head of the bus performs special "head of bus" functions such as regularly creating empty transmission slots into which the other nodes on the bus write.

111

STANDARDS

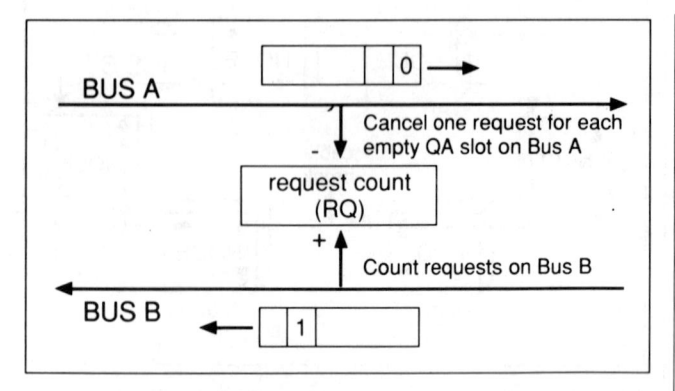

Figure 5 — *Each node tracks the number of slot requests that have been queued downstream on the forward bus by counting the number of bits set in the REQUEST (RQ) field of slots on the reverse bus. The above shows the RQ counter of a node not queued to send on Bus A.*

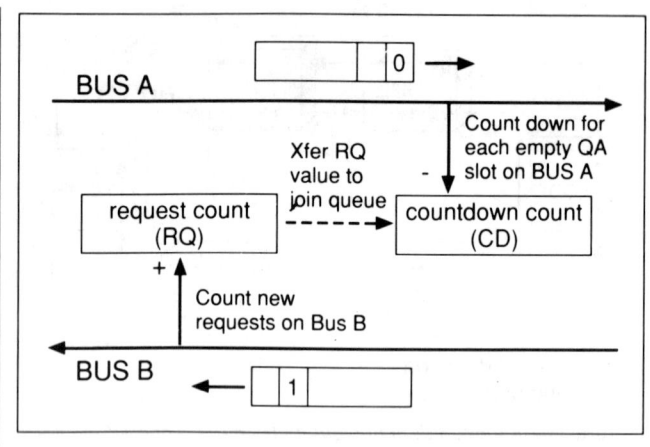

Figure 6 — *The Request (RQ) and countdown (CD) counters of a node queued to send on Bus A. Compare with Figure 5.*

Timing is another important consideration. Under normal conditions, the network has a single source for slot timing to ensure that all nodes transfer data at the same rate. This is essential to ensure the correct operation of the DQDB access scheme and see that the isochronous service won't have timing slips.

If connected to a public network with isochronous service, then an external source, usually the public network, must provide timing for the DQDB subnet. In other cases, a node within the DQDB network will suffice; typically the head of Bus A.

DQDB Fault Tolerance

Another important feature of DQDB is the ability of the network to heal itself in the case of bus failure. A special case of the dual bus topology, called a looped dual bus, may be employed in a DQDB network. This topology is a fault-tolerant implementation where one node acts as both head and end of the bus (See Figure 3.).

When a break occurs in the cable (due to mechanical failure, rodents chewing through the wire or what have you), the network automatically reconfigures itself so that the natural break in the network loop appears at the corresponding position of the physical break in the cable. The reconfiguration procedure, then, moves the head of bus functions to the nodes adjacent to the cable break (See Figure 4.).

If a node adjacent to the cable break does not support the head of bus functions, then the reconfiguration will be completed by the node nearest to the break that does support these functions. Whenever this happens, the node or nodes without the head of bus capability are effectively dropped off the network.

DQDB Access Control

DQDB networks must support a variety of services, as described earlier. Applications requiring isochronous service are time-sensitive; i.e., the application must be granted access to the medium on a regular, periodic basis. Isochronous service would be used, for example, for digitized voice applications. This application requires access to the medium on a regular basis and a guaranteed bandwidth of 64 Kbps. Time slots for isochronous service uses the Pre-Arbitrated (PA) access method, which reserves time on the medium for various time-sensitive applications.

Non-time-sensitive applications do not require medium access on a regular, periodic basis. This includes both the connectionless MAC and connection-oriented data services supported by DQDB. These applications need to have access to the medium only when they have data to send. Therefore, time on the medium is not reserved for specific applications but granted on an as-needed basis. The Queued Arbitrated (QA) access method is used for these services.

Queued Arbitrated Access Method

The QA access method is elegant and straightforward, but relatively complicated when compared to CSMA/CD and token passing (or even FDDI). The QA access method supports services that are usually bursty in nature; i.e., the bulk of the data transfer occurs in a relatively small amount of time. The unit of transmission is called a "QA slot," comprising a header and a fixed-length data field (called a "QA segment").

The operation of the access protocol depends upon two fields within the QA slot header. The BUSY bit indicates whether this slot is empty or not and the REQUEST field indicates whether a QA segment is being queued for transmission.

In short (leaving out a lot of detail), here is how the QA access protocol works. Recall that the DQDB network comprises two unidirectional buses. The terms "upstream" and "downstream" indicate the relative positions of two nodes on the bus. Node i is upstream of Node j if a slot arrives at Node i before it arrives at Node j; Node j, then, is downstream of Node i.

When Node i is ready to transmit to Node j, Node i must determine which bus to use. Let's assume that Node i will use Bus A. Node i, then, sets a bit in the REQUEST field of the next available slot on Bus B. In this way, all nodes downstream of Node i on Bus B will see the request and appropriately increment a counter. Note that all nodes downstream of Node i on Bus B are upstream of Node i on Bus A.

All nodes upstream of Node i on Bus A know how many prior requests are in the queue before them because of the counter that each maintains (although they do not know which nodes made requests). The counter tells each node how many requests are pending in the queue and, therefore, how many empty slots the node must let go by before it has a turn to access the medium. As empty slots pass each node, their counters are decremented. When its counter is zero, Node i may

STANDARDS

write data into an empty slot, which will travel downstream on Bus A to Node j.

The rest of this section will examine the QA access protocol in more detail. First, we must define two new terms, namely "forward" and "reverse" bus. Assume that Node i wishes to send a segment to Node j and will use Bus A. In this case, Bus A is the forward bus and Bus B is the reverse bus.

Recall that the header of every QA slot contains a BUSY bit and a REQUEST field. Requests to use the forward bus are placed in slots traveling on the reverse bus.

Each node tracks the number of slot requests that have been queued downstream on the forward bus by counting the number of bits set in the REQUEST field of slots on the reverse bus. This tells the node the length of the queue. Whenever an empty slot passes this node, it means that someone on the queue is being served. The request (RQ) counter, then, is incremented for every REQUEST passing on the reverse bus and decremented for every empty slot passing on the forward bus (Figure 5).

When a node wants to send a QA segment, it enters a "queued to send" state and invokes another counter called the countdown (CD) counter. When a node has a QA segment to send, it transfers the value of the RQ counter to the CD counter and resets the RQ counter to zero. The RQ counter now counts the number of new requests, and the CD counter tracks the node's position in the queue (See Figure 6). When the value of the CD counter is zero, the node is allowed to transmit its QA segment in the next empty QA slot. While waiting for the CD value to become zero, the RQ counter continues to count new requests. (Figures 7a—7h step through an example of the QA access protocol.)

DQDB supports multiple QA priorities on each bus. The REQUEST field of each slot contains four bits to provide a four-level priority scheme. The access procedures described here are essentially the same for the multiple priorities, where separate RQ and CD counters are maintained for each priority level (Refer to the standard for additional information.).

Pre-Arbitrated Access Method

The Pre-Arbitrated (PA) access scheme is designed for the transfer of isochronous service octets. Access to PA slots is very different than access to QA slots. PA slots, like QA slots, have a fixed length. Whereas a QA slot is wholly owned by a single node at a time, however, the different octets within a single PA slot may be used by different nodes.

The head of bus takes responsibility for sending a sufficient number of PA slots to ensure that all isochronous service users have adequate bandwidth available. When the head of bus generates a PA slot, it places a Virtual Channel Identifier (VCI) into the slot header. All nodes with an isochronous service examine the VCI in the passing PA slots. For each VCI value that the node must access, the node will maintain a table indicating which octet position(s) within the slot that it should use for reading and writing. Thus, the node will read from the appropriate octet positions within the slot and write to other positions within the slot. It ignores all other octets. If the PA slot contains a VCI that is not used by this node, the entire slot is ignored.

DQDB Transmission Formats

Compared to most other protocols, the DQDB frame format(s) are complicated since the DQDB network will split apart large messages. This section describes the basic concepts of the DQDB protocol data units.

DQDB receives data from higher protocol layers in the "MAC service data unit." The MAC service data unit is a message that will be sent from one node to another and may be from zero to 9,188 octets in length. The MAC service data unit is carried in the Information field of an Initial MAC Protocol Data Unit (PDU), or IMPDU. The IMPDU comprises four fields:
- Header—includes protocol information specific to the MAC layer, addresses, a protocol identifier, and a quality of service indication. 802.6 supports several address formats, including 16- and 48-bit addresses, like the other 802 MAC protocols, and 60-bit ISDN addresses. The header is 24 to 44 octets in length (in increments of four);
- Information—contains a MAC service data unit;
- PAD—additional octets to pad the length of the information field so that it is a multiple of four. The PAD is zero, one, two, or three octets in length; and
- Trailer—includes miscellaneous protocol information. The trailer is four octets in length.

An Initial MAC PDU is too large to be sent over the network as a single transmission entity. Therefore, it is split up into fixed-length blocks called "segmentation units," that are 44 octets in length. Nodes are responsible for fragmenting an IMPDU into segmentation units and reassembling segmentation units back into an IMPDU. An IMPDU may be between 28 and 9,236 octets in length, thus between one and 210 segmentation units will be required to transport a single IMPDU.

Each segmentation unit has a header and trailer associated with it, forming a 48-octet Derived MAC Protocol Data Unit, or DMPDU. The fields of a DMPDU are:
- DMPDU Header (DH)—contains two items of information. The first identifies this segmentation unit as the beginning, middle, or end of an IMPDU, or as a single segment IMPDU. The second item helps the receiving node reassemble the IMPDU;
- Segmentation Unit—If this is the final (or only) segment, some number of padding octets may be required; and
- DMPDU Trailer (DT)—comprises two subfields. The first subfield indicates the number of octets of the segmentation unit that contain IMPDU information. The second subfield is part of the error detection scheme and contains a cyclic redundancy check (CRC) remainder over the rest of the DMPDU.

Every DMPDU is carried in the 48-octet "segment payload" field of a QA segment. A PA segment is a collection of 48 octets for isochronous service users.

A segment has a four-octet segment header in addition to the segment payload field. Segment header information includes:
- A Virtual Channel Identifier (VCI)—used to identify the virtual channel to which the segment belongs;
- Payload Type—differentiates user data from other types of information, such as network signaling information;
- Segment Priority; and
- Header Check Sequence—provides for the detection of bit errors, and correction of single-bit errors, in the segment header.

Finally, the basic unit of transmission is the "slot." A 53-octet slot comprises a single-octet "access control field", followed by the 52-octet segment (a PA slot contains a PA segment and a QA slot contains a QA segment). The access control field includes:
- The BUSY bit—used to indicate whether the slot is empty or full (QA Slot only);

113

STANDARDS

TRANSMISSION UNDER THE QA ACCESS PROTOCOL

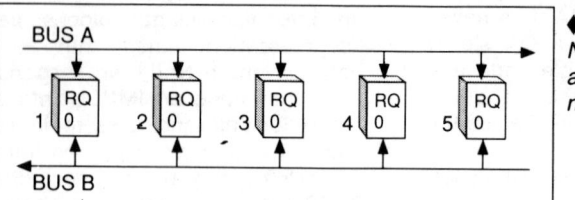

Figure 7a — In this example, the DQDB network has five nodes. Nodes 5, 2, and 3, in that order, will be queued to transmit on Bus A and then will do so. The first diagram shows the initial state of the network. All five nodes have a request (RQ) counter value of 0.

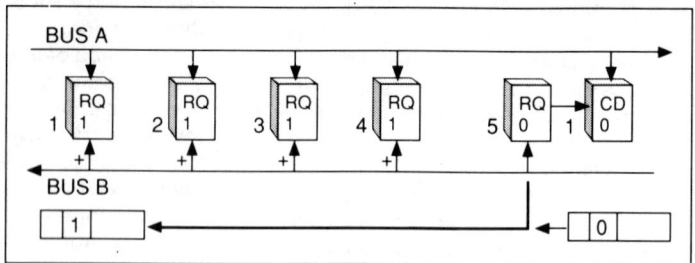

Figure 7b — Node 5 queues a request for Bus A. When Node 5 detects a QA Slot on Bus B with a free REQUEST bit (REQUEST = 0), Node 5 transfers its RQ counter value to the CD counter and sets the REQUEST bit in the QA slot. The RQ counter of all downstream nodes is incremented when they detect the QA Slot with the REQUEST bit set to 1.

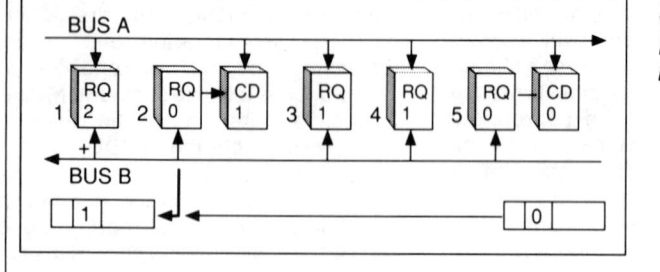

Figure 7c — Next, Node 2 queues a request for Bus A. Its RQ value is transferred to its CD counter, it sets a bit in the REQUEST field of a QA slot, and Node 1 (the only downstream node) increments its RQ value.

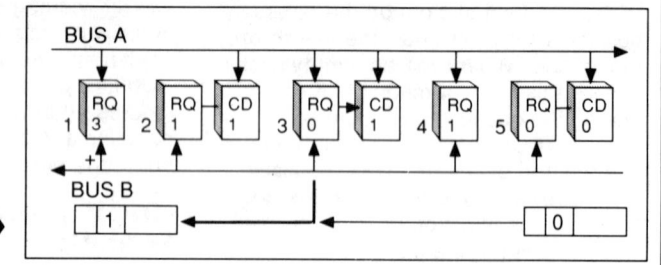

Figure 7d — Finally, Node 3 queues its request.

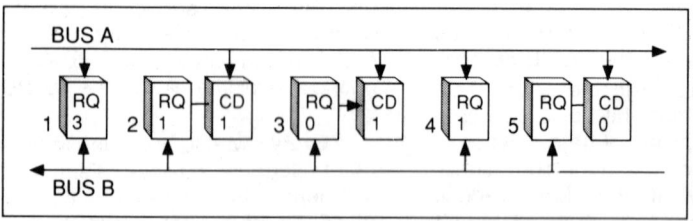

Figure 7e — At this point, Nodes 5, 2, and 3 have queued their requests to transmit on Bus A. We will now ignore what is happening on Bus B and examine how the nodes will transmit on Bus A.

Figure 7f — Node 5 gains access to Bus A. Node 5 knows that it can seize the empty QA slot (BUSY = 0) because its CD count is 0. It places its data into the slot and changes the BUSY bit to 1. Note that all upstream nodes decrement their RQ or CD counter by 1 when the empty slot goes by. After Node 5 transmits, its CD counter is no longer used.

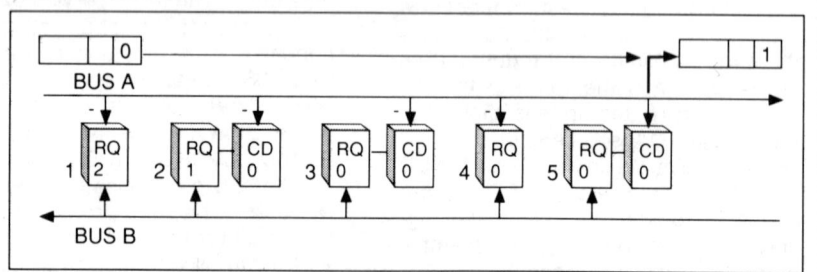

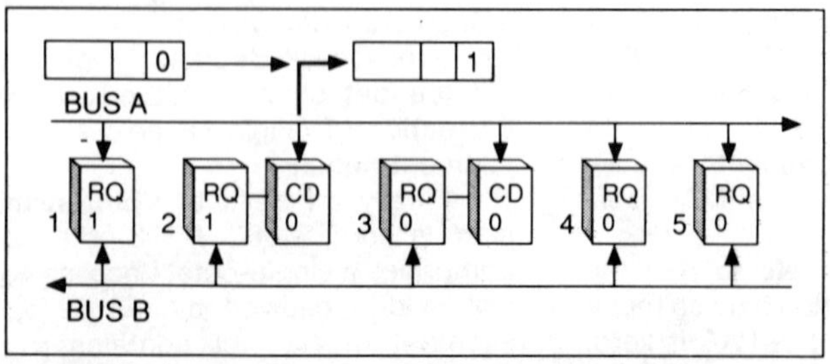

Figure 7g — The diagram at left shows that Node 2 is the next to gain access on Bus A. Since Node 2 has a CD value of 0 when it detects an empty QA slot, it changes the BUSY bit to 1 and places its data into the slot. Node 1, the only upstream node to see the empty slot, decrements its RQ value. After accessing the bus, Node 2's CD counter is no longer used.

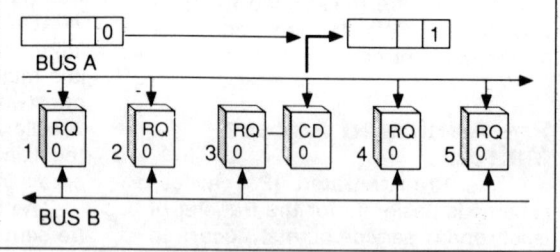

Figure 7h — Node 3 finally accesses Bus A. After Node 3 transmits, this example network returns to the initial state, as shown in Figure 5a. Although ignored in this example, the QA access control procedures for Bus B are identical to QA access on Bus A.

STANDARDS

- A Slot Type Indicator—specifies whether this is a PA slot or QA slot; and
- The REQUEST Field—comprising four bits so that nodes may request bus access in each of the four different priority levels.

Note that although a PA segment and QA segment have the same format, they are used differently by the network nodes. If an empty QA slot is seen at a node queued for access, that node can set the slot busy and write a QA segment into it. There is no concept, however, of an empty or full PA slot. When a node supporting isochronous service sees a PA slot, it examines the VCI. If the node must access the VCI supplied in the segment header, the node will read from and/or write to specified octets within the segment payload. Thus, many isochronous service users share the octets in the Segment Payload, and no one node owns a PA slot.

MAN's Future

Although QPSX Communications holds the patent rights for some inventions required for compliance with the standard, the company is producing products supporting the DQDB protocol and has agreed to grant licenses for its use. DQDB-based MANs are already being trialed, notably in Philadelphia (Bell of Pennsylvania) and Melbourne (Telecom Australia). Bell operating companies Switched Multi-megabit Data Service (SMDS) will probably offer initial public 802.6 networks for the U.S. in the early 1990s. Widespread use of this protocol will probably not appear until 1991 or '92.

Many sources view MANs as early implementations of Broadband ISDN (B-ISDN). In particular, DQDB is widely touted as providing many of the same services as an ISDN; namely, digital signaling, high rates of speed (well above the ISDN Primary Rate Interface speed of 1.544 or 2.048 Mbps), and the integration of voice, video, and data. The infrastructure that MANs provide may well become integral to the deployment of B-ISDN. (The term "broadband" comes from its telephony sense, i.e. any channel wider than 3.4 KHz, and not because it uses broadband cable. In fact, most B-ISDN networks will use fiber cabling.)

The DQDB has been designed to support the current digital hierarchies commonly used in the telephone industry, much like ISDN. Furthermore, DQDB will also operate with the synchronous digital hierarchy for optical fiber networks, which may also be the basis for B-ISDN's Asynchronous Transfer Mode. The ANSI T1S1.1 Task Group, one of the bodies responsible for U.S. ISDN standards, has recommended DQDB as the preferred multiplexing scheme for B-ISDN. In addition, the DQDB Slot Header format will probably be compatible with headers specified in the T1S1 B-ISDN standards. These facts place DQDB in an excellent position for a transition into ISDN. These comments are not meant to downplay the importance of FDDI. As LANs will remain an important communications strategy well into the ISDN era, private LAN internetworks and backbones will also be required. It is in this environment that FDDI will remain a very strong contender. ❏

Gary C. Kessler lives in Colchester, Vermont, and provides data communications and computer networking training and consulting services. Electronic mail can be sent to kumquat@smcvax.bitnet or left on the LAN Magazine BBS at (415) 267-7640.

FOR MORE INFORMATION
Standards may be obtained from the IEEE (Piscataway, N.J.) at (201) 981-0060. Drafts of IEEE 802 standards are available from Global Engineering (Irvine, Calif.) at (800) 854-7179 or Alpha Graphics (Phoenix, Ariz.) at (602) 863-0999.

FRAME RELAYING SERVICE: AN OVERVIEW

Wai Sum LAI [*]

Bell-Northern Research
P.O. Box 3511, Station C
Ottawa, Canada K1Y 4H7

ABSTRACT

Frame relaying is a new CCITT-recommended packet mode bearer service in ISDNs for data communications. Its major characteristics in terms of link layer multiplexing and out-of-band call control are summarized here.

The purpose of this overview is two-fold:

- to provide an introduction to frame relaying for the Panel on this service in the IEEE INFOCOM'89 Conference
- to serve as a foreword for the papers in this Panel that are devoted to the different aspects of frame relaying

1. PREAMBLE

Frame relaying is a new ISDN (Integrated Services Digital Network) packet mode bearer service for data communications at access speeds of up to 2 Mbit/s. A high level description of the architectural framework and service requirements of frame relaying is contained in the recently approved *Recommendation I.122*. This document was the result of an intensive investigation by Study Group XVIII of the CCITT (International Telegraph and Telephone Consultative Committee) during its 1985-88 Study Period.

In the U.S., frame relaying service has been a major focus of the T1S1.1 (formerly T1D1.1) Working Group in the T1 standards committee sponsored by the ECSA (Exchange Carriers Standards Association). This group has also actively participated in the CCITT work. It is expected that frame relaying will become an ANSI (American National Standards Institute) standard in the near future [T1S188a].

In Europe, ECMA (European Computer Manufacturers Association) published approximately one year ago a report on the application of frame relaying to private switching networks [ECMA87].

With such national and international activity in standardization, frame relaying has come of age. It is now time to take a snapshot of its status: to report on and review what has been done to bring the service closer to reality. This is the intent of the Panel on Frame Relaying Service in the IEEE INFOCOM'89 Conference.

In the next section, we will first set the scene for this Panel by discussing the two major characteristics of frame relaying service:

- link layer multiplexing
- out-of-band call control

Our description in this section is primarily from the perspective of a user-network access interface.

After this overview of the service concepts, we will present three topics of interest in Section 3:

- congestion control
- protocols
- application to LAN interconnection

Each one of these facets of frame relaying is to be covered in detail by a separate paper for the Panel [P1, P2, P3].

2. CHARACTERISTICS OF FRAME RELAYING

Presently, X.25 is a widely accepted and deployed data service in both public and private networks. Existing ISDN packet mode services, as defined in Recommendation X.31, are also X.25-based. This is because of the current utility of X.25 and the need to ensure compatibility with the already installed packet switched public data networks.

As is well known, X.25 is a network interface that has a 3-layer protocol architecture: packet layer (layer 3), link layer[1] (layer 2) and physical layer (layer 1). In view of the error performance of the transmission facilities currently available, the primary function of the link layer is to provide error recovery. It is in the packet layer that the statistical multiplexing of different logical channels or user data streams takes place.

While different packet types are used during the call control and data transfer phases of X.25 calls, the packets belonging to any given call all bear the same layer 3 logical channel number. This method of user-network signaling has been known as *inband signaling* since the signaling information is transmitted in the same logical channel as the user data.

So, packet layer multiplexing and inband signaling are two significant aspects of X.25. Frame relaying and X.25 are both ISDN packet mode bearer services. However, frame relaying differs from X.25 in that multiplexing is done in the link layer and out-of-band call control is being adopted. We now take a closer look at each one of these in turn, from the standpoint of a user-network access interface.

2.1 Link layer multiplexing

In X.25, it is effectively the packet layer that provides the switching function — link entities do not support multiplexing. With X.31 offering X.25-based services in an ISDN, this has been extended somewhat since the procedure used in the D-channel (LAPD, i.e., CCITT Recommendation Q.921/I.441) does allow for link layer multiplexing. However, the procedure in a bearer channel (LAPB) remains the same, i.e., without multiplexing. This situation is depicted in Figure 1.

---

[*] The author is now with AT&T Bell Laboratories, Holmdel, New Jersey 07733-1988.

[1] In OSI (Open Systems Interconnection) terms, layer 2 is called the *data link layer*. However, we will refer to it simply as the *link layer*.

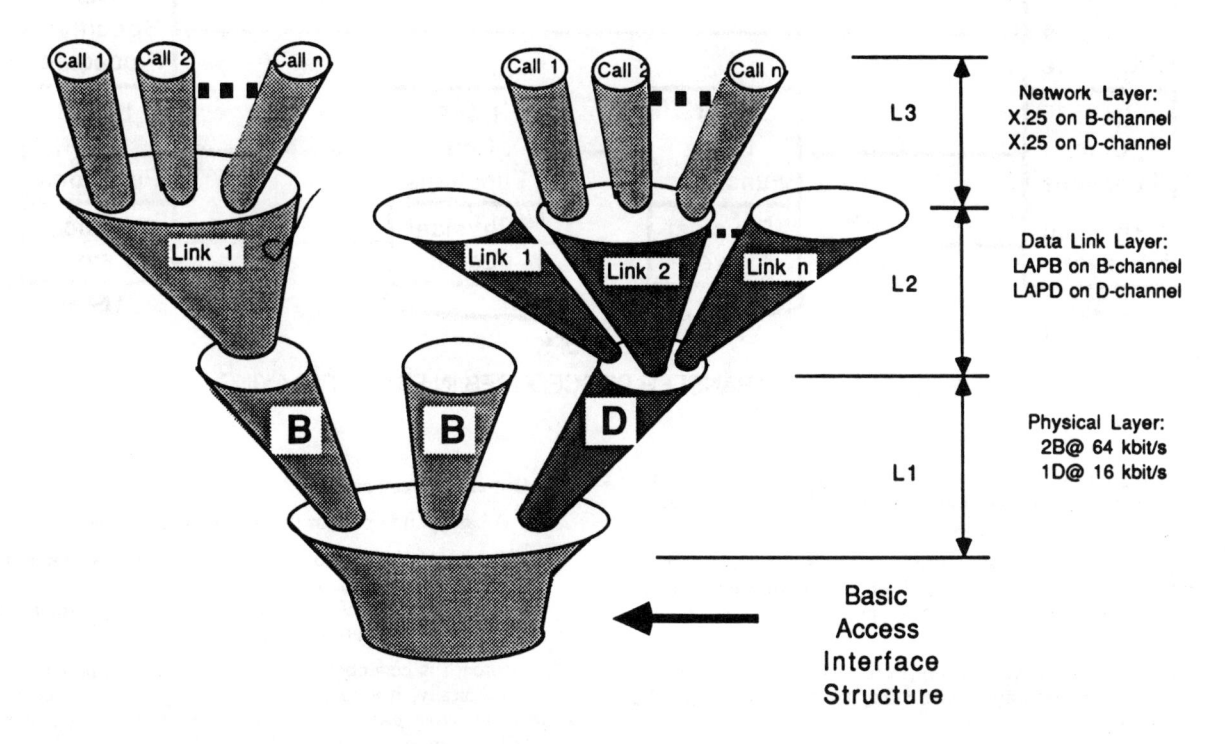

Figure 1. Packet layer multiplexing in X.25 and link layer multiplexing in the ISDN D-channel.

Frame relaying operates entirely within the link layer. Based on the multiplexing operation of LAPD, it statistically multiplexes different user data streams at this layer. Each user data stream is called a *data link connection* (DLC).

To identify the different DLCs in a physical channel, each DLC is assigned a *data link connection identifier* (DLCI) at the time when a frame relaying call is being established. Subsequently, during the data transfer phase, all the frames belonging to a frame relaying call carry the same DLCI in the link layer address field of each frame.

Since the DLCIs need to be unique only within the context of a physical channel either at the access or between two adjacent network nodes, global significance is not required. For details about the routing of frames based on the DLCI within a network, see the section on "Chained-link path routing" in [Lai88a].

With the use of link layer multiplexing, differentiation of multiple concurrent data flows on a common physical channel is done at the lowest possible layer in the data transfer protocols. The rationale for pushing the multiplexing function downwards in the protocol hierarchy is so that the advances in technology can be exploited.

Specifically, through the improvement in the error performance of transmission systems, the need for error recovery within a network is reduced or eliminated. At the same time, the increase in the capabilities of end-systems has resulted in a need for more flexibility in the network access protocol architecture.

To accommodate these trends for the migration of intelligence outwards to the network periphery, a network should provide only a common core set of functions that apply to all packet mode information flows. Any user could then add, upon these network functions, further functional blocks that are tailored to the particular end-to-end communications needs (Figure 2). In this way, the provision of redundant of duplicated functionality by a network would be avoided.

Such an approach is in harmony with the ISDN principle that, with a limited number of connection types and multi-purpose user-network interface arrangements, a wide range of services be provided.

Since such a network would offer its users with only a minimal common set of capabilities, the protocol functionality required at the user-network interface would be reduced. This would therefore demand less per-frame processing by a network. As a result, lower delay and higher throughput could be expected.

In frame relaying service, the network functions for data transfer that can be accessed by a user are called the *core functions of I.441*. They are, according to Recommendation I.122,

- frame delimiting, alignment, and transparency
- frame multiplexing/demultiplexing using the address field (i.e., DLCI)
- inspection of the frame to ensure that it consists of an integer number of octets prior to zero bit insertion or following zero bit extraction
- inspection of the frame to ensure that it is not too long or too short
- detection of transmission errors

Consistent with the spirit of minimal network service in the sense described above, it can be seen from this list of network functions that a network does not offer any flow control service to its users. Nor is there any correction of frame errors by a network: errored frames are simply discarded without notification to the

```
┌──────────┐                                                              ┌──────────┐
│   User   │                                                              │   User   │
│ Specified│──────────────────────────────────────────────────────────────│ Specified│
│ Procedure│                                                              │ Procedure│
├──────────┤    ┌──────────┐              ┌──────────┐                    ├──────────┤
│  I.441   │    │  I.441   │              │  I.441   │                    │  I.441   │
│   Core   │────│   Core   │──────────────│   Core   │────────────────────│   Core   │
│ Functions│    │ Functions│              │ Functions│                    │ Functions│
├──────────┤    ├──────────┤              ├──────────┤                    ├──────────┤
│ Physical │    │ Physical │              │ Physical │                    │ Physical │
│  Layer   │────│  Layer   │              │  Layer   │────────────────────│  Layer   │
└──────────┘    └──────────┘              └──────────┘                    └──────────┘
   USER         └──────────────NETWORK────────────────┘                      USER
```

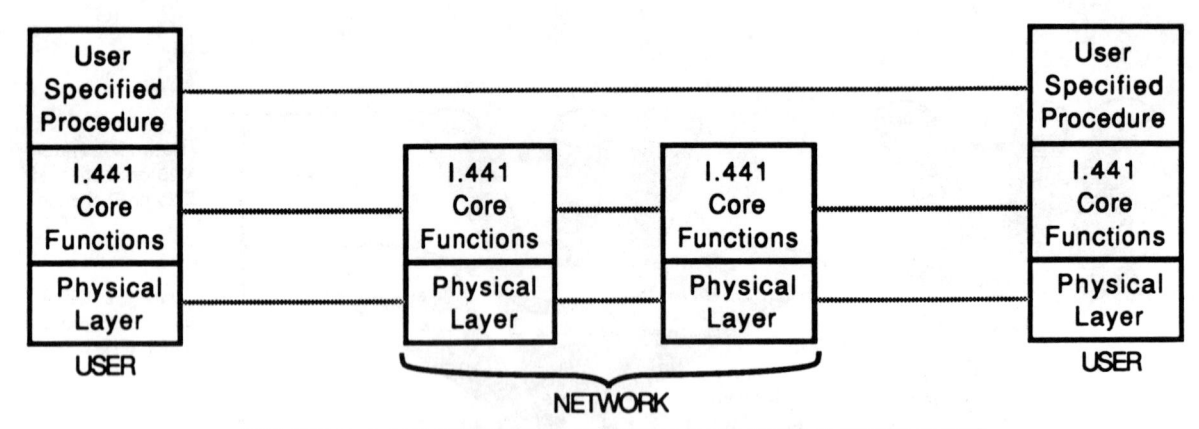

FIGURE 2. DATA TRANSFER PROCEDURES IN FRAME RELAYING

corresponding users. If so desired, flow control and/or error control are to be implemented as user functions above the core functions of I.441 on a user end-to-end basis.[2]

In this sense, user data transfer protocols are transparent to the network. As a result, minimal or no modification will be required of users on their data transfer protocols for connecting to the network.

Based on the above core functions, a network offers frame relaying as a connection-oriented link layer service with the following properties:

- preservation of the order of frame transfer from one edge of a network to the other
- non-duplication of frames
- a (very) small probability of frame loss

To conclude this discussion of link layer multiplexing, it is appropriate to add a historical remark on what's in a name, or why "frame relaying" is so called.

The elements of frame relaying were initially contained in a proposal called *LAPD-based packet mode service* [CCITT85]. This is because, as we mentioned earlier in this section, the support of multiple DLCs in the link layer utilizes the multiplexing operation based on the frame structure specified in LAPD. The use of LAPD means that the creation of a new protocol is not required.

Traditionally, data units in the link layer and packet layer of X.25 are called *frames* and *packets*, respectively. Hence, in X.25 packet layer multiplexing, *packets* are being *switched* since an X.25 network provides the full functions of the packet layer. Whereas in the link layer multiplexing of frame relaying, *frames* are being *relayed* since a frame relaying network provides only a core subset of the link layer functions.

Alas, as Mark Twain once noted, "names are not always what they seem"! With the introduction of frame relaying also as a packet mode bearer service (based on frame data units), packet mode services no longer count on packet data units only. The word "packet" in packet mode services is therefore used in a more generic (and classical) sense to mean that user data transfer is performed in a packetized manner.

---

2. Functions for flow control and error control usually form an intrinsic part of an HDLC-like elements of procedures such as LAPD, or LLC2 (Logical Link Control Type 2) of the IEEE 802 LANs. With users performing these functions end-to-end, there is lesser or no need for a network to do the same. (Note: While a network may not offer per-connection flow control, congestion control by a network is still required.)

2.2 Out-of-band call control

A basic philosophy for the provision of services in a ISDN is:

- the integration of control and signaling procedures for all telecommunications services
- the decoupling of user information transfer requirements from those of control information

This approach is commonly referred to as *out-of-band call control*. More technically, it is known as the principle of *separation of the control and user planes* in the ISDN protocol reference model (CCITT Recommendation I.320).

The concept of separate control and user planes (C-plane and U-plane) is used to distinguish interactions needed for the control and signaling functions from those needed to transfer user data. For example, procedures for call establishment and release belong to the C-plane, while user data transfer protocols are in the U-plane. In particular, the core functions of I.441 (Section 2.1) are part of the U-plane.

Some major benefits derivable from the separation of control from user data includes: simplification of user data paths within a network, sharing across all bearer services of functional units providing call control and supplementary services, accommodation of multi-media calls, etc. These are further discussed in [Lai88b].

Today, the above principle has been applied in ISDN, but only to the provision of circuit mode bearer services such as the "64 Kbit/s unrestricted" service for data transmission.

Current X.25-based packet mode services in ISDN do not follow this approach. According to Recommendation X.31, based on which these services are being offered, the complete packet layer of X.25 is used for both the call control and data transfer phases of a packet mode call. So, existing X.25 inband procedures continue to be employed for the establishment and release of virtual circuits. Stated differently, X.31 just encapsulates existing X.25 packet mode services in an ISDN envelope at the physical layer.

Since X.25 public data networks are now well established in many countries, X.31 packet mode services were developed for pragmatic reasons: to offer access to packet data services through an integrated physical interface while minimizing deployment and interworking difficulties. Indeed, with the X.25 packet layer procedures remaining intact, the number of modifications required to accommodate existing X.25 DTEs in an ISDN is minimized. In this way, a large population of packet switched data network users can easily migrate to ISDNs as these networks are deployed.

Frame relaying is a new ISDN packet mode bearer service that is based more fully on the principle of control separation.

According to Recommendation I.122, C-plane procedures can run separately from U-plane procedures in one of several ways:

- on a physically separate interface
- on another channel (time slot) within the same interface
- on a separate DLC within the same channel (e.g., the D-channel)

For example, the establishment and release of frame relaying calls in the C-plane can make use of Q.931 messages over the DLC in the D-channel that is dedicated for signaling[3] (Figure 3). After call establishment, the U-plane data transfer can take place over either a bearer channel such as a B-channel, or another DLC within the D-channel.

This contrasts with the X.31 packet mode services where, for a given X.25 call, both the call-related packets and data transfer packets use the same logical channel contained in a particular physical channel.

3. SOME ADDITIONAL ASPECTS OF FRAME RELAYING

Having briefly reviewed the salient features of frame relaying, we are now ready to diversify into different areas. In the following sections, we highlight the papers in the INFOCOM'89 Panel on Frame Relaying Service.

(Note: While originally planned to be part of this Panel, the subject of "interworking requirements" was excluded in the final program because of time limitation. More details on this topic can be found in [Lai88b, Lai89].)

3.1 Congestion control

With proper network dimensioning to prevent long-term congestion, short-term congestion can still occur in a frame relaying network as a result of traffic fluctuations or network failures. A network must therefore monitor the usage of its resources continually. At the onset of congestion and thereafter, a network must attempt to contain the effect of congestion, stave off unfair interference, and minimize performance degradation.

Besides network actions, users should also reduce their rate of sending frames when they perceive the impact of network congestion. One scheme is for a user to reduce its flow rate after it has sensed that it has to retransmit its frames. Since control is achieved implicitly through the user's own mechanisms such as reaction to a retransmission time-out or negative acknowledgement, this method has been referred to as *implicit congestion control*.

---

3. In LAPD terminology, this is the DLC with a SAPI value of 0. SAPI (service access point identifier) is an element of a DLCI.

When the user's end-to-end flow control is based on window rotations, the method of implicit control has also been called a *dynamic window algorithm*. Its characteristics are:

- no blocking of data flow under normal condition
- reduction to a smaller window size upon detection of possible network congestion
- progressive increase to the maximum window size upon congestion abatement

Paper [P1] presents some of the results of an investigation on the performance of this algorithm.

3.2 Protocols

As described in Section 2.2 and shown in Figure 3, functions for the access of frame relaying service are separated into control and user planes. Two corresponding sets of procedures are therefore required at the user-network interface.

The standardization of frame relaying access procedures has been actively pursued by Working Group T1S1.2 in the U.S. So far, two draft proposed ANSI standards have been developed: one for call control and signaling in the C-plane [T1S188b], and the other for data transfer in the U-plane [T1S188c].

The C-plane procedures [T1S188b] are based on an extension of Q.931 with special emphasis on the different types of information elements (such as throughput parameters) that are required to characterize a frame relaying connection. The U-plane procedure [T1S188c], based on the core functions of LAPD, specifies the frame format and address structures. The document [T1S188c] also includes a description of the dynamic window algorithm for congestion control.

In addition to these activities, there has also been a proposal in T1S1.2 to develop terminal adaption standards so as to allow connection of existing terminals to an ISDN that provides frame relaying service. For this purpose, it is particularly appropriate to extend CCITT Recommendation V.120, a recently approved terminal adaption standard for circuit-mode applications. It is expected that a similar specification for frame relaying application will share a vast majority of the text currently in V.120.

In the CCITT, Study Group XI has just begun work on the so-called *LAPD+* (Draft Recommendation Q.92x): extension of LAPD for non-D-channel applications. One of the stated objectives of this procedure is to "share the core aspects of the LAPD protocol as defined in Recommendation I.122 (1988)."

Paper [P2] illustrates with examples how Q.931 and Q.921 are adapted for use in frame relaying. It also shows that inter-nodal signaling within a private network can be based on Q.931 procedures with appropriate extensions.

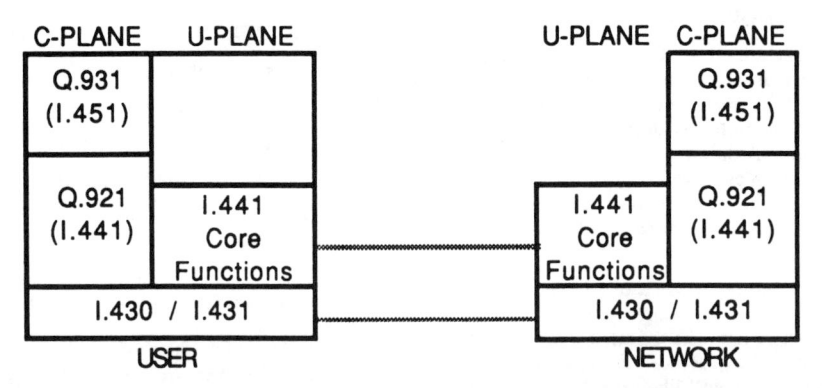

FIGURE 3. SEPARATION OF C-PLANE FROM U-PLANE AT THE USER-NETWORK INTERFACE FOR FRAME RELAYING.

3.3 Application to LAN interconnection

To extend the reach of local area networks (LANs), they can be interconnected together to form one large network. Interconnection can possibly be done at the physical layer (layer 1) by repeaters, the link layer (layer 2) by bridges, the network layer (layer 3) by routers, or even higher layers by gateways. A mixture of these technologies can potentially be used in an interconnected network.

While bridges are independent of higher layer protocols, routers or gateways usually require specific internetwork protocols to be used. Reference [Gerl88] contains several articles that deal with the comparison between bridges and routers. The general observation is that the choice between them depends on the networking environment.

As we discussed in Section 2.1, link layer multiplexing is inherent in the design of frame relaying. Our attention is therefore focused on the use of bridges for LAN interconnection.

For IEEE 802 LANs, the link layer consists of two sublayers with the logical link control (LLC) sublayer running above the medium access control (MAC) sublayer. The so-called *MAC bridges* [IEEE87] operate solely within the MAC sublayer and are not involved in the LLC protocols. They therefore provide a sort of "frame relaying" function within the MAC sublayer. In this light, a happy marriage of MAC bridges and ISDN frame relaying service can be anticipated.

In terms of geographic coverage, there are two methods of bridging: local and remote. Local bridges interconnect LANs directly. All the ports of a local bridge are attached to LANs. For a remote bridge, one or more of its ports interfaces to some wide area communications facility.

Since frame relaying is standardized as a data offering in public networks, our focus is further narrowed down to the remote bridging of LANs.

In paper [P3], the interconnection of remote bridges by different types of wide area transmission facilities are analyzed. These facilities include analog or digital private lines, circuit-switched services, ISDN circuit mode services, X.25 packet-switched services and frame relaying. It is shown that frame relaying, because of its simple access interface, relatively high access speed, and statistical multiplexing capability, is ideally suited to LAN interconnection.

[P3] also reports on their experience in interconnecting token ring LANs via a prototype frame relaying network. Their results further confirm the advantages of frame relaying.

4. CONCLUSIONS AND ACKNOWLEDGEMENTS

These are the topics that are covered in this INFOCOM'89 Panel. However, the whole story of frame relaying has not yet been told! To realistically offer frame relaying as a service to paying customers, work still needs to be done in such areas as OA&M (operations, administration and maintenance), performance specifications, and internetwork signaling procedures. It is hoped that this Panel will stimulate further advancement in these fronts, and more papers on this service in the INFOCOM conferences of coming years.

The progress of standardization depends to a large extent on contributions submitted by different companies and individuals in different countries. Together they have shaped what frame relaying is today. It has been a wonderful experience for me to participate in such a collective enterprise. I would like to acknowledge the many contributions from various sources, though they are too numerous to enumerate here.

The papers in this Panel were put together by the authors under very tight time constraints and when they had other commitments to meet. It has been a great pleasure working with these dedicated individuals and I thank them all.

I also appreciate the comments and reviews of my colleagues: James Doak, Ed Juskevicius, Jim Lamont, Bam Liem, Andy Nicholl, John O'Connell, Catherine Olinski and Cho-Lun Wong.

REFERENCES

[CCITT85] CCITT, "LAPD based packet mode — overview," Contribution No. D16/XVIII, London, U.K., 21-25 January 1985.

[ECMA87] ECMA (European Computer Manufacturers Association), "Packetized data transfer in private switching networks," Technical Report TR/43, December 1987.

[Gerl88] M. Gerla, L. Green and R. Rutledge (Editors), Special Issue on LAN Interconnection, *IEEE Network*, vol. 2, no. 1, January 1988.

[IEEE87] IEEE Computer Society, *MAC bridges*, Draft IEEE Standard 802.1: Part D, Revision D, December 1987.

[Lai88a] W.S. Lai, "Packet forwarding," *IEEE Communications Magazine*, vol. 26, no. 7, pp. 8-17, July 1988.

[Lai88b] W.S. Lai, "Packet mode services: from X.25 to frame relaying," to appear in *Computer Communications*.

[Lai89] W.S. Lai, "Network and nodal architectures for the interworking between frame relaying services," to appear in *ACM Computer Communication Review*.

[T1S188a] T1S1.1, "Frame relaying bearer service — architectural framework and service description," (Editor, N.T. Batis) T1S1.1/88-448R (T1S1/88-224), New Orleans, Louisiana, October 1988.

[T1S188b] T1S1.2, "DSS1 — Signaling specification for frame relay (Revision 6)," (Editor, R.J. Cherukuri) T1S1.2/88-440, McLean, Virginia, December 1988.

[T1S188c] T1S1.2, "DSS1 — Core aspects of frame protocol for use with frame relay bearer service (Revision 3)," (Editor, R.M. Amy) T1S1.2/88-441, McLean, Virginia, December 1988.

CITED CCITT RECOMMENDATIONS

[C0] I.122, "Framework for providing additional packet mode bearer services."

[C1] I.320, "ISDN protocol reference model."

[C2] I.441, also numbered as Q.921.

[C3] I.451, also numbered as Q.931.

[C4] I.462, also numbered as X.31.

[C5] I.465, also numbered as V.120.

[C6] Q.921, "ISDN user-network interface data link layer specification."

[C7] Q.92x, "A draft outline for an ISDN data link layer specification for non-D-channel applications."

[C8] Q.931, "ISDN user-network interface layer 3 specification."

[C9] X.25, "Interface between data terminal equipment (DTE) and data circuit-terminating equipment (DCE) for terminals operating in the packet mode on public data networks and connected to public data networks by dedicated circuits."

[C10] X.31, "Support of packet mode terminal equipment by an ISDN."

[C11] V.120, "Support of data terminal equipment with V-series type interfaces by an ISDN using statistical multiplexing."

PAPERS IN INFOCOM'89 PANEL ON FRAME RELAYING SERVICE
(Ottawa, Ontario, Canada, 24-27 April 1989)

[P0] W.S. Lai, "Frame relaying service: an overview."

[P1] K.J. Chen and K.M. Rege, "A comparative performance study of various congestion controls for ISDN frame-relay networks."

[P2] R.J. Cherukuri and J.H. Derby, "Frame relay — protocols and private network applications."

[P3] J. Lamont, M. Hui, and J. Doak, "LAN interconnection via frame relaying."

Chapter 3
Network Access Protocols

Overview

The *network layer* is designed to facilitate communication between systems across a communications network. It is at this layer that the concept of a protocol becomes a little fuzzy. This is illustrated in Figure 3-1, which shows two stations communicating via a packet-switched network, not via direct link. The stations have direct links to the network nodes. The layer 1 and 2 protocols are station-node protocols (local). Layers 4 through 7 are clearly protocols between entities in the two stations (remote). Layer 3 is a little bit of both. Layer 3 is a station-node protocol since it provides a means for the station to gain access to the network and use the services provided by the node to which it attaches. However, to exchange data between stations, there must be some coordination between the two station-node pairs. This gives the layer 3 protocol an "end-to-end" flavor.

The basic service of the network layer is to provide for the transparent transfer of data between transport entities. It relieves the transport layer of the need to know anything about the underlying communications medium. Thus, the layer 3 entity is responsible for invoking routing and relay functions through switched networks.

When a station attaches to a network, not only must a layer 3 protocol be used, but the physical and data link characteristics of the station-node link must be specified. Thus, it is convenient to consider a set of such protocols as a network access protocol. This, in fact, is the way in which most standards have been developed. That is, the standard specifies the protocols of layers 1 through 3 for network access.

The most widely known network access standard is X.25, which defines the protocols for accessing a packet-switched network. For circuit-switched networks, X.21 is common. Finally, standards are now being developed for the forthcoming Integrated Services Digital Network (ISDN).

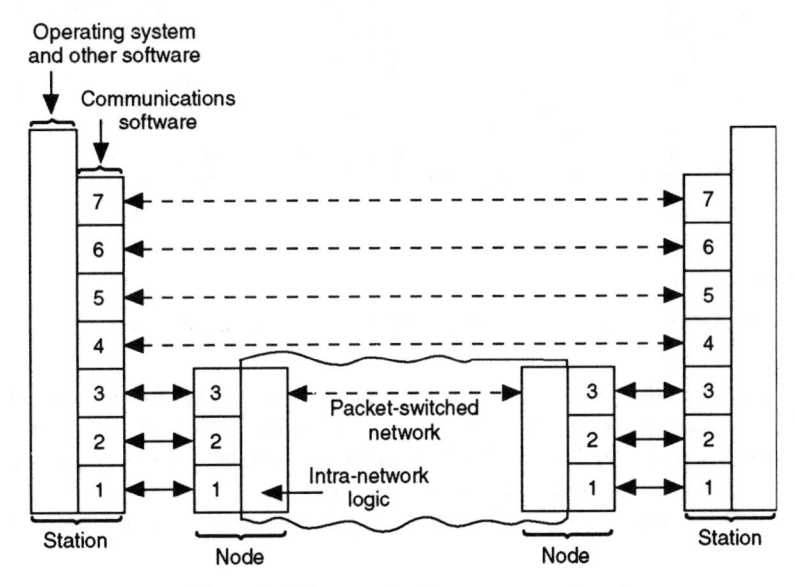

Figure 3-1. Communication across a network.

Circuit-switched network access

Let us consider what is required, in terms of functions, for two devices to communicate across a circuit-switched network, and relate that to the OSI model. There are two phases of operation that are of interest: the call establishment phase and the data transfer phase.

For the *data transfer phase*, a circuit-switched network provides a transparent data path between communicating stations. To the attached stations, it appears that they have a direct full-duplex link. They are free to use their own formats, protocols, and frame synchronization. This situation is depicted in Figure 3-2a. Each station is attached to a node of the communication network (example: a modem). The dashed line indicates the path of the data and the elements

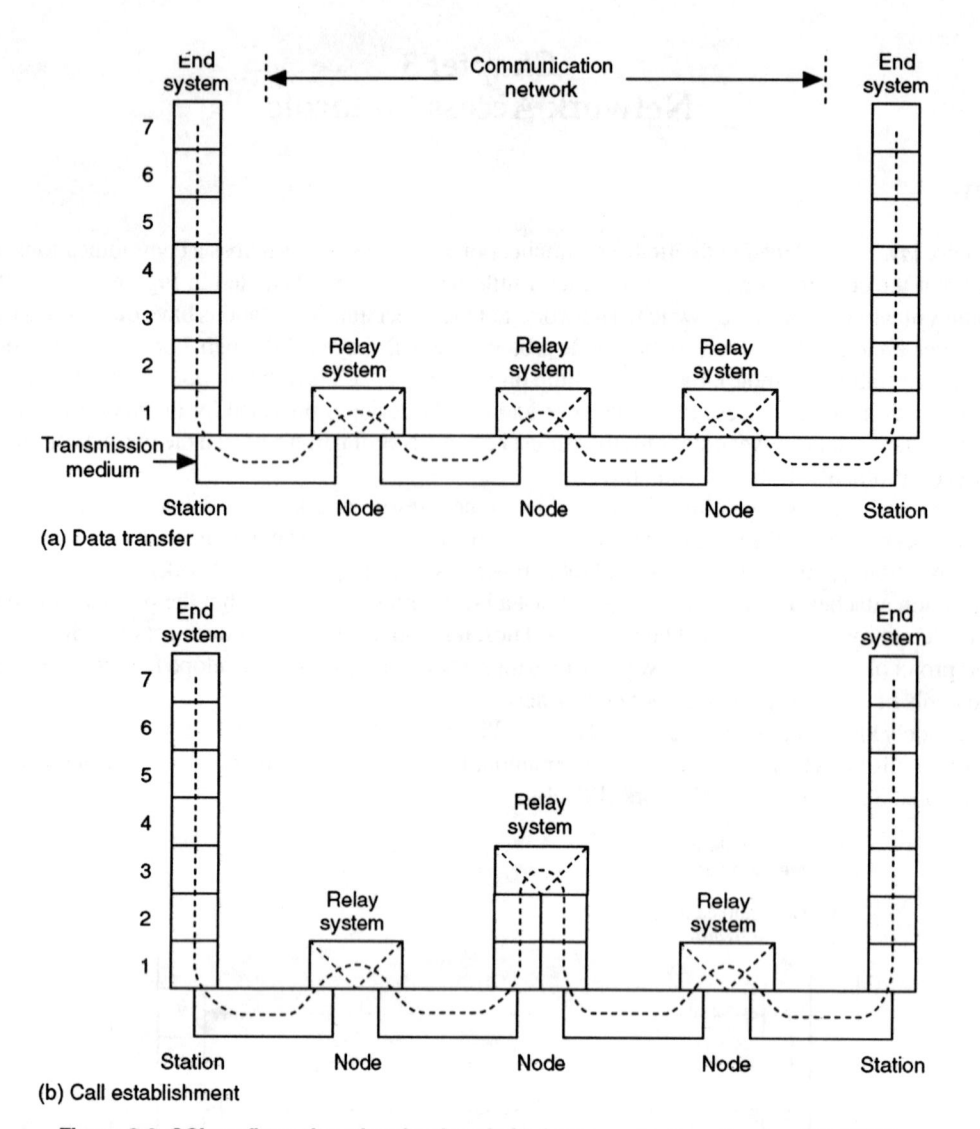

Figure 3-2. OSI configurations for circuit-switched communication. Source: [FOLT83]

through which it passes. Data from the source station pass through that node, one or more intermediate nodes, and finally through the node to which the destination station is connected. Because the connection is transparent, the protocol from station to node is just at the physical level. Each node acts as a relay, passing on data from input to output. The intermediate nodes perform a switching function but, again, simply relay the data transparently.

The *call establishment phase* is more complex. Both calling and called stations have a dialogue with an element of the network:

- *Calling station:* Sends a call request to the network identifying the called station; receives call progress signals from the network.
- *Called station:* Receives call request from network; sends call acceptance to network.

This dialogue is, in OSI terms, a layer 3 protocol. Figure 3-2b depicts this protocol as taking place between the station and some intermediate node which performs a network exchange function. This node can be considered to represent all of the switching nodes involved in setting up the connection. Note that this node still performs a relay function, but this now occurs at layer 3. Thus, two general types of functions are performed by the network:

- It relays call request and call accepted signals between stations.
- It has a dialogue with each station to establish the call.

Once the call is established, there is no need for an active network role, other than at the physical layer. Thus, the configuration of Figure 3-2a obtains. All protocols, down through layer 2, are end-to-end.

Packet-switched network access

Unlike a circuit-switched network, a packet-switched network is not transparent to attached stations, even during the data transfer phase. Stations must break up their data into packets. The station-node protocol must perform the following functions:

- Flow control.
- Error control.
- Multiplexing.

Flow control is needed in both directions. The network must protect itself from congestion, and to do this may need to limit the flow of packets from the attached stations. Similarly, a station needs to be able to control the rate at which the network delivers packets to it. These considerations did not apply in the case of circuit switching. The circuit-switched network provides a transparent path of constant data rate. The network allocates resources to maintain that data rate. The stations may use end-to-end flow control at the data link level to limit data flow.

Since station and node are exchanging control information as well as data, some form of *error control* is needed to assure that all of the control information is received properly.

Finally, most packet-switched networks provide a *multiplexing* service. With this service, a station can establish multiple virtual circuits with other stations at the same time.

Figure 3-3 depicts the protocol architecture implied by the above requirements. Each node, including intermediate nodes, performs functions up through layer 3. The papers reprinted in this section should help clarify this figure.

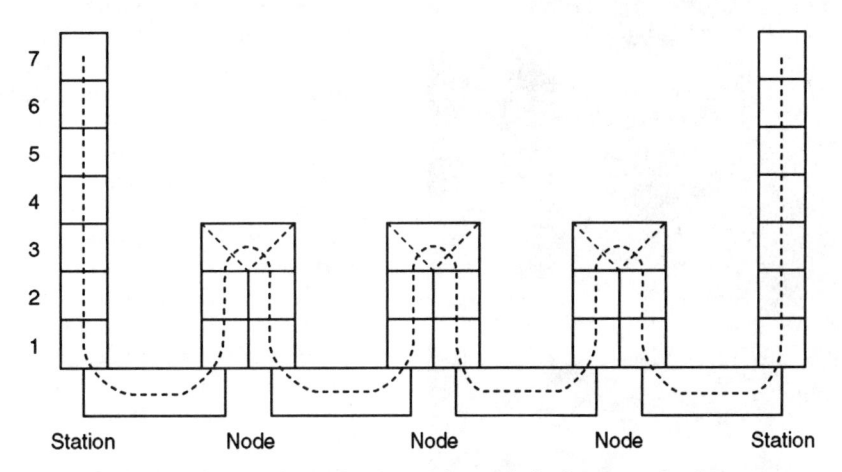

Figure 3-3. OSI configuration for packet-switched communication.

Summary

The X.25 standard for access to packet-switched networks is explored in "X.25: An Interface to Public Packet Networks."

"The Eternal Organization of the Network Layer: Concepts, Applications, and Issues," discusses the internal organization of the network layer. Unlike most of the other OSI layers, it will often be the case that the network layer will be implemented as two or more sublayers, to support internetworking or differences in network services.

"OSI Addressing Strategies," presents a survey of addressing principles used in the OSI reference model. Most of these addressing issues concern layer 3.

The final paper, "ISDN Protocols for Connection Control" looks at the layer 3 protocol, with supporting layer 1 and 2 protocols, used for common channel signaling at the ISDN user-network interface.

X.25: an Interface to Public Packet Networks

C. R. Dhas
V. K. Konangi

Communication networks based on the concept of packet switching offer an attractive alternative to circuit switching for data transmission. This article examines X.25 as an interface to public packet networks

Reprinted from *IEEE Communications Magazine*, September 1986, pages 18-25. Copyright © 1986 by The Institute of Electrical and Electronics Engineers, Inc.

With the dramatic reduction in the cost of processing power, communication networks based on the concept of packet switching offer an attractive alternative to circuit switching for data transmission. The bursty nature of data traffic leads to an inefficient utilization of the pre-allocated bandwidth under circuit switching technology. Packet switching, on the other hand, allocates transmission bandwidth dynamically, thereby allowing an efficient sharing of the transmission bandwidth among the many active users. In packet switching, data is sent using limited size blocks called *packets*. The information at the source end is divided into a number of packets and transmitted over the network to the destination where it is assembled to retrieve the original information. In addition, packet switching provides better connect time, reliability, economy, and flexibility [5]. This performance and cost effectiveness has lead to the development of a large number of packet switched networks around the world. In order to provide a public data communication service on a worldwide basis, standardized and compatible services are needed. The International Telephone and Telegraph Consultative Committee (CCITT) has formulated Recommendation X.25 which specifies the interface (protocol) to be followed by the user (subscribers) devices in accessing public packet switching networks [1]. The X.25 protocol is an internationally agreed upon Recommendation that specifies the details of the interactions between each user packet-mode device and the network node as shown in Fig. 1. The user packet-mode device and the network node are called Data Terminal Equipment (DTE) and Data Circuit-Terminating Equipment (DCE), respectively. The X.25 protocol is independent of the internal structure of the packet switching communication network Also, nonpacket switched services have to use packet assembly-disassembly (PAD) facilities. For example, the character-mode terminals connect to the network through PAD's which convert characters to packets. X.25 protocol is based on the concepts of layering, where each layer provides certain services to the next higher layer. This not only reduces the design complexities, but also shields each layer from the implementation details of the adjacent layers. CCITT Recommendation X.25 defines three levels of communications—physical, link, and packet. This article concentrates on the packet level and provides only a brief review of the physical and link levels.

Services for Packet-Mode Operation

The X.25 interface Recommendation provides access to two basic services that may be provided on public packet networks. The first is the switched virtual call (SVC) service. A switched virtual call is a temporary association between two DTE's and is initiated by a DTE sending a Call Request packet to the network. The second is the permanent virtual circuit (PVC)

---

*The views expressed are those of the authors and do not necessarily reflect the views of Telenet Communications

service. A virtual circuit (VC) is a bidirectional, transparent, flow-controlled path between a pair of logical or physical ports. A permanent virtual circuit is a permanent association between two DTE's. The permanent virtual circuit facility does not use a call establishment or clear procedures and in a sense it is similar to a point-to-point private line. In the SVC and PVC services the order of reception of packets at the destination is the same as the order of transmission of packets from the source.

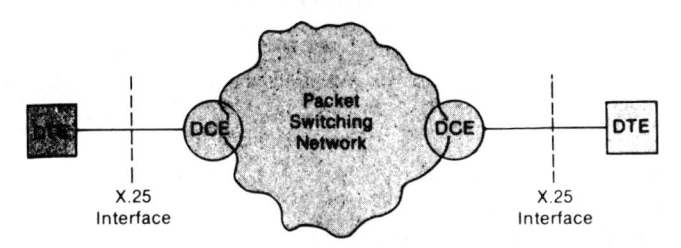

Fig. 1. X.25 Interface.

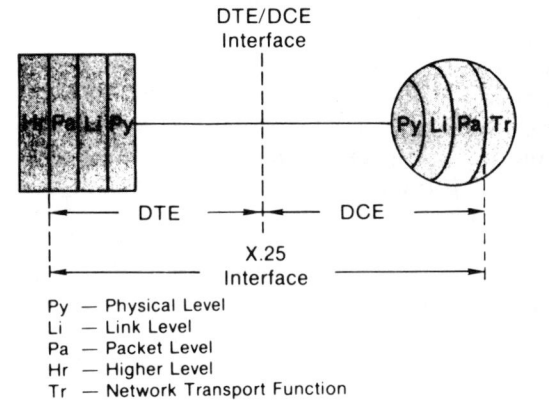

Fig. 2. Interface Block Diagram.

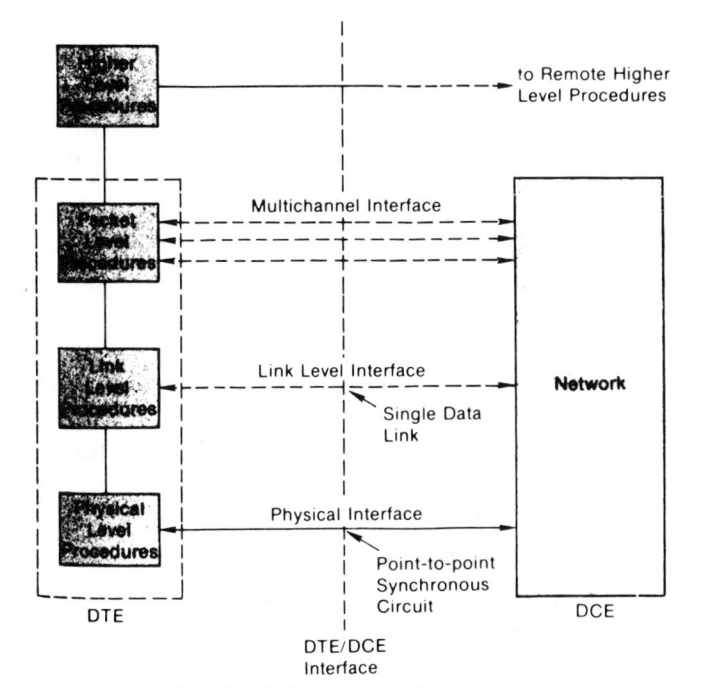

Py — Physical Level
Li — Link Level
Pa — Packet Level
Hr — Higher Level
Tr — Network Transport Function

Fig. 3. X.25 Interface Structure.

X.25 Interface Architecture

The X.25 interface between the DTE and DCE consists of three levels of protocols. These protocols give access to the services mentioned earlier. X.25 allows the multiplexing of connections between a DTE and a number of other DTE's on the network on the same physical circuit. The three levels of the X.25 interface are the physical level, the link level, and the packet level as shown in Figs. 2 and 3. All three levels of the interface are independent of each other, and the first two levels could be replaced by a functionally equivalent protocol. The packet level is unique to the X.25 interface and its replacement would result in a different interface [2].

The physical level specifies the use of a duplex, point-to-point synchronous circuit for the physical transmission path between the DTE and the network. Recommendation X.21 specifies the electrical and procedural characteristics for digital circuits [3]. These digital circuits have superior error characteristics. However, in order to make use of the existing analog circuits, Recommendation X.21 bis was defined. X.21 bis defines the electrical and procedural characteristics for the operation of analog lines for data transmission. The X.21 bis is compatible with the V.24 (RS-232C) physical interface between the DTE and the modem.

The link level is based on the International Standards Organization (ISO) High-level Data Link Control (HDLC) link level procedure [4]. The primary responsibility of the link level is to ensure the correct exchange of data between the DTE and the DCE. X.25 currently defines two protocols at the link level: Link Access Procedure (LAP) and Link Access Procedure Balanced (LAPB). LAPB is the preferred protocol and is compatible with the HDLC procedures. It differs from LAP in mode of operation and supervisory commands. In the LAPB protocol, each data frame carries a single packet across the X.25 interface. The most significant function of the link level is to provide an error free but a variable delay link between the DTE and the network.

The Packet Level

The packet level of the interface is the one which gives X.25 its character of a virtual circuit interface to a packet switched service. The packet level provides facilities to establish virtual circuits and to then send and receive data. Each virtual circuit may be flow controlled using a window mechanism. Recovery from errors at the interface can be effected using the reset,

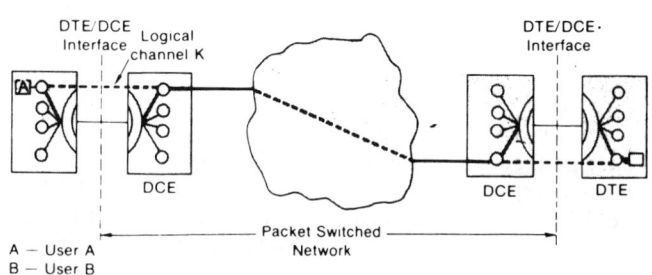

A — User A
B — User B

Fig. 4. Switched or Permanent Virtual Call Between Two Users.

clear, and restart procedures. Also, normal termination of a call closes the virtual circuits so that they can be used for other calls.

The packet level in the X.25 interface uses packet interleaved statistical multiplexing to establish concurrent virtual circuits over a single physical access circuit (Fig. 3) and consists of a number of logical channels each with a unique identifier. It is possible to have 16 groups of 256 channels each. The groups are identified using four bits and the channels by eight bits in each packet header. Every packet carries a logical channel number which identifies the packet as either a switched or a permanent virtual circuit for both directions of transmission. The range of logical channel numbers that can be used by a DTE is established at subscription time by agreement between the DTE and the network. In the 1984 version of X.25, the channel ranges may be dynamically changed using registration procedures. Also, it is possible to configure the packet level procedures to meet the needs of a specific environment using the optional facilities. These logical channel numbers are significant only at a particular DTE/DCE interface.

A DTE can have many switched and/or permanent virtual circuits active at the same time to other DTE's in the network. All packets associated with these calls share the same physical link and the link level error control procedures. Figure 4 shows the logical structure of an association using X.25.

TABLE I
PACKET TYPES

Call Request
Call Connected
Clear Request
Clear Confirm
Data
Interrupt
Interrupt Confirm
Receive Ready (RR)
Receive Not Ready (RNR)
Reject (REJ)
Reset Request
Reset Confirm
Restart Request
Restart Confirm

Packet Format

X.25 specifies a number of formats for the packets passed between the DTE and the DCE in order to establish, use, and clear virtual circuits. The general format of the packet is shown in Fig. 5. There are two types of packets: data packets and supervisory packets. The one-bit C/D field indicates whether a packet is a data packet or a supervisory packet. All packets carry a three octet common header field as in Fig. 5. The first field in the common header is called the general format identifier and consists of four bits. The first bit is referred to as the Q-bit or qualifier bit. The Q-bit may be set to 1 or 0 on data packets to give two levels of data transmission. X.25 does not specify how these two levels of data packets may be used. The second bit is called the data confirmation bit or D-bit and is used to request end-to-end or local acknowledgment from the network. The third and fourth bits distinguish between two possible window mechanisms for flow control. Table I shows a list of packet types that flow from the DTE to the DCE. There is a corresponding set of packet types from the DCE to the DTE. For more information on their structure, refer to [2].

Virtual Circuit Setup and Clearing

The virtual call setup is an end-to-end procedure [2,6]. The calling DTE selects a free logical channel and sends a Call Request packet to its local DCE. The Call Request packet may contain optional fields in addition to the three byte header fields and the called DTE address. One of the optional fields is the calling DTE address. Addresses are variable in length and each digit of the address is represented in binary coded decimal. A length field indicates the length of the variable address. The second optional field is the facilities field and it specifies special facilities required by this call such as reverse charging. Another optional field is used to carry user data up to a maximum of 16 octets.

The Call Request is transmitted through the packet switched network and the remote DCE then selects a logical channel to the called DTE and sends an Incoming Call packet. The Incoming Call packet has the same format as the Call Request packet. If the called DTE decides to accept the call, it returns a Call Accepted packet to the DCE. Once the Call Accepted information reaches the local DCE, it transmits a Call Connected packet to the calling DTE. This establishes a virtual call between the DTE's.

During the call setup process, there is a possibility for call collision taking place at the remote DTE. Call collision takes place when the remote DCE selects a logical channel to send the incoming call but in the meantime the called DTE selects the same logical channel to initiate a virtual call by sending a Call Request packet. If free logical channels are available, the incoming call can be transferred to a free channel and can also proceed with the outgoing call from the DTE on the collided channel. If the call collision persists, then the incoming call will be cancelled and a Clear Indication will be returned to the calling DTE with the clearing cause field indicating Number Busy. When a virtual call is established, a logical channel number is assigned to the call at the DTE/DCE

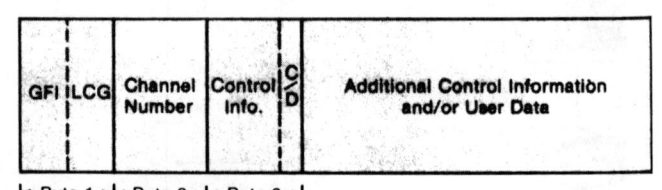

| GFI | LCG | Channel Number | Control Info. | C/D | Additional Control Information and/or User Data |

|←Byte 1→|←Byte 2→|←Byte 3→|

GFI — General Format Identifier
LCG — Logical Channel Group #
C/D — 0 for User Data Packet
    — 1 for Supervisory Packet

Fig. 5. X.25 Packet Format.

interfaces. The logical channel numbers assigned at each end are different and are assigned independently.

A virtual call cannot be established if the called DTE rejects an incoming call or if the attempt fails. In the event that the called DTE refuses to accept the call, it returns a Clear Request packet to the DCE instead of the Call Accepted packet. The called DTE may set the diagnostic code field in the Clear Request packet to signal to the calling DTE the reason for not establishing the call. After issuing a Clear Request, the called DTE cannot use that logical channel to set up a virtual call until it receives a Clear Confirmation packet from its DCE. At the calling end, the DCE sends a Clear Indication packet indicating the appropriate clearing cause and an octet of diagnostic information to the calling DTE. The calling DTE then returns a Clear Confirmation packet. If for some reason the network is not able to set up a virtual call, it sends a Clear Indication packet with the reason for clearing. Table II shows the Clearing Call progress signals.

Either DTE can terminate an established virtual call. Again, this is done by sending a Clear Request packet to the DCE. The receipt of the Clear Confirmation packet completes the clearing procedure and the released logical channel can be used for another call. Figure 6 shows the call establishment, data and call clear phases of a virtual call.

TABLE II
CLEARING CALL PROGRESS SIGNALS

DTE Originated
Number Busy
Out of Order
Remote Procedure Error
Reverse Charging Acceptance
 not Subscribed
Incompatible Destination
Fast Select Acceptance
 not Subscribed
Invalid Facility Request
Access Barred
Local Procedure Error
Network Congestion
Not Obtainable
Request Authorized Private
 Operating Agency (RPOA)
Out of Order

Data Transfer

The called DTE enters the data transfer phase as soon as it sends the Call Accepted packet to the DCE and it can start sending data packets on the established logical channel. Similarly, the calling DTE enters the data transfer phase after receiving the Call Connected packet. In the case of permanent virtual circuits, data packets can be sent at any time once the link is active. Figure 7 shows the data packet format. The first three bytes contain common header information. A 0 in the right-most field of the third byte identifies this packet as a data packet. The data field of the packet may be of any length up to a maximum. The packet length may be set to different values at each end of the virtual circuit. Recommendation X.25 requires all networks to support a maximum data field of 128 octets. The data qualifier bit, known as the Q-bit, in the general format identifier allows two different levels of data. The X.25 Recommendation does not specify how the two types may be used.

All the data packets on a given virtual circuit are numbered sequentially and, normally, a modulo 8 numbering scheme is used. The sequence numbers are placed in the third octet and coded in binary form. The send sequence number, P(S), is assigned a value of zero for the first data packet in either direction after the virtual circuit has been established. The maximum number of sequentially numbered data packets that a DTE or DCE may be authorized to transmit, without further authorization from the network or DTE, may never exceed seven for the modulo 8 numbering scheme. The actual maximum value, called the window size, is set at a constant value for each logical channel either at subscription time or at call setup time using an optional user facility. The default window size is two. A DTE defines two window sizes: the remote window size which specifies the number of data packets the DTE can transmit without authorization, and the local window size which specifies the number of data packets that the DTE is willing to receive before authorizing the transmission of more data packets. The send sequence number associated with the data packet on a virtual circuit allows both the DCE

Legend:
D — Data
D,P(R),P(S)
RR,P(R)
P(R) — Packet Receive Sequence Number
P(S) — Packet Send Sequence Number
RR — Receive Ready

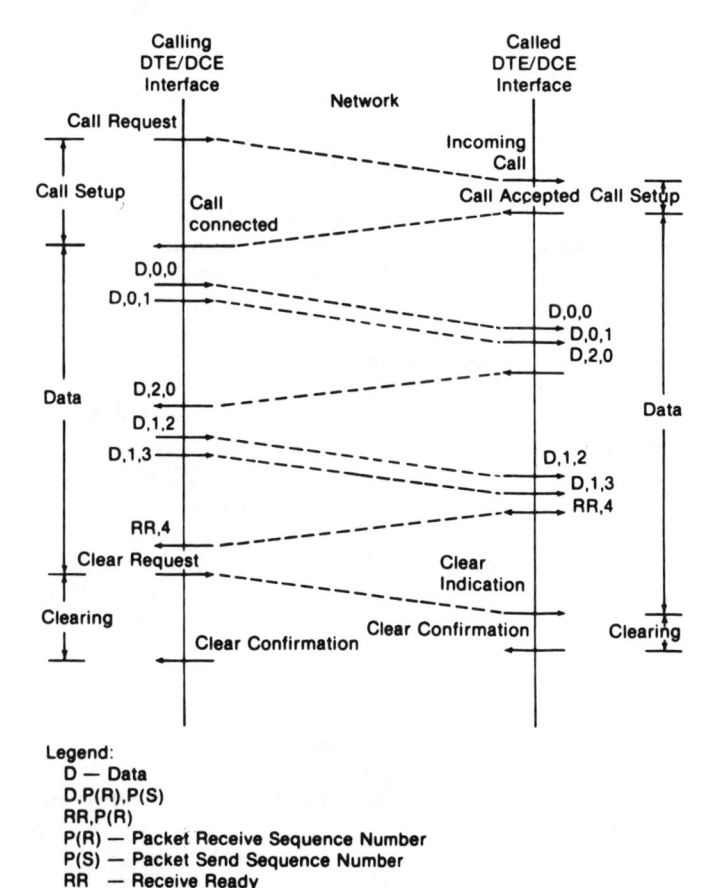

Fig. 6. Virtual Call Establishment, Data Transfer and Call Clear Phases; Window Size = 2.

| Q D 0 1 | Logical | Byte 1 |

Channel Number — Byte 2

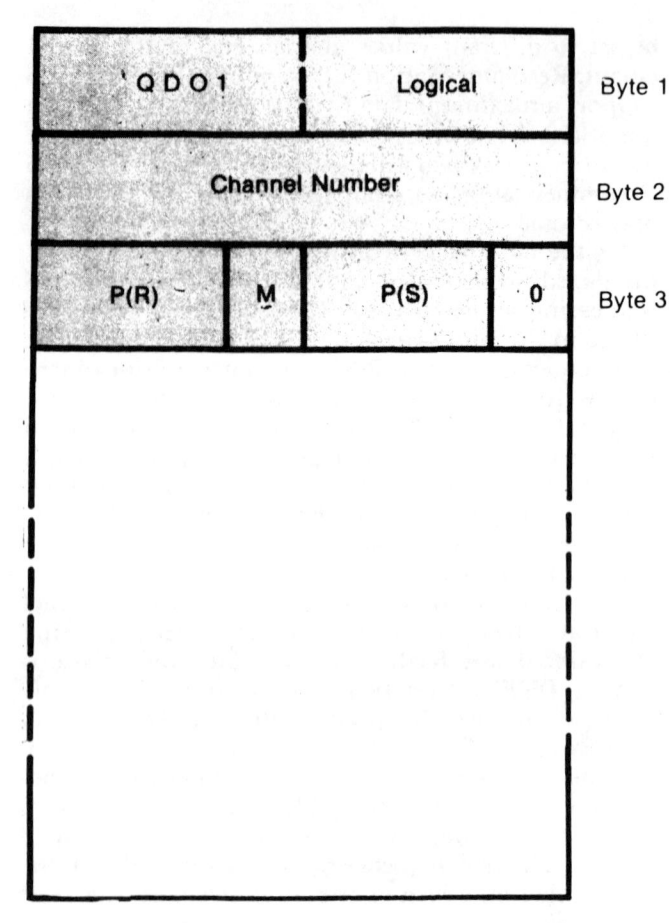

P(R) | M | P(S) | 0 — Byte 3

Q — Data Qualifier Bit
D — Delivery Confirmation Bit
M — More Data Bit
P(R) — Packet Receive Sequence Number
P(S) — Packet Send Sequence Number

Fig. 7. *Data Packet Format*

and the DTE to detect loss of data packets thereby maintaining the integrity of the data transfer. The send sequence number is also used to control the flow of data packets across the DTE/DCE interface.

In addition, each data packet also carries a packet receive sequence number, P(R), which is used to authorize the transmission of additional data packets. The number of packets allowed to be sent is equal to the window size. The authorization to transfer more data packets can be piggy-backed onto data packets flowing in the reverse direction. If there is no data flow in the reverse direction and if a DTE or DCE wishes to authorize the transmission of one or more data packets, it can send a Receive Ready (RR) control packet. If for any reason the DTE or DCE cannot accept data packets on a logical channel, it can transmit a Receive Not Ready (RNR) packet. A transition back to the normal data receive mode is achieved by forwarding an RR packet. The P(R) numbers transmitted across a virtual channel allows flow control of data packets thereby ensuring that the sending DTE does not transmit data at an average rate that is greater than the rate at which the receiving DTE can accept that data.

X.25 allows two communicating DTE's to select their own packet size for virtual circuit operation. Therefore, when different maximum packet sizes are used at each end of a virtual circuit, the number of data packets arriving at the destination DTE may be greater or smaller than the number originally sent by the source DTE. In general, a user data packet will not be combined with other preceding or succeeding packets. If the maximum packet size at the destination is less than that at the source, the network has to divide a packet into two or more packets. Now, two or more packets at the destination make up a packet at the source. In order that the true size of a packet may be indicated to the destination, the network uses the more data bit (M_bit) in Fig. 7 to define a logical sequence of packets. A packet with the more data bit off terminates the logical sequence of packets. The more data bit may be on only if the data packet is of the maximum length. The source DTE can also make use of the more data bit when the logical sequence of data cannot fit into one packet.

The general format identifier also has a D_bit for delivery confirmation purposes (see Fig. 7). The delivery confirmation bit (D_bit) permits dynamic selection of P(R) significance on a packet-by-packet basis by the transmitting DTE. When the D_bit is not used, the P(R) number has a local significance. This means that the window rotations at the local DTE/DCE interface are totally independent of window rotations at the remote DTE/DCE interface. Figure 8 illustrates the local P(R) significance.

When the delivery confirmation bit is set, the P(R) is used to convey delivery confirmation information and in this case P(R) has an end-to-end significance. Figure 9 shows the end-to-end P(R) significance. Here, the window rotation at the local DTE/DCE interface is not made until the window is rotated at the remote DTE and acknowledgment is received through the network.

X.25 uses a window mechanism to regulate the flow of data. The window size is a constant and is between one and seven for the modulo 8 numbering scheme. A DTE can transmit packets with sequence numbers

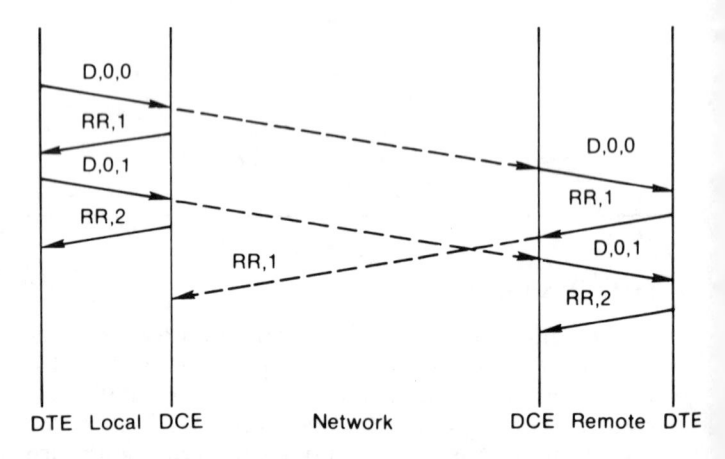

Legend:
D — Data
D,P(R), P(S)
RR,P(R)
P(R) — Packet Receive Sequence Number
P(S) — Packet Send Sequence Number
RR — Receive Ready

Fig. 8. *Local P(R) Significance.*

within the window only. Figure 6 shows data transfer using a window size of two. When a DTE starts transmitting data packets on a logical channel, the lower edge of the window is set to zero, and the send sequence number is zero for the first packet. If the window size is W, the DTE can transmit up to W packets before receiving an acknowledgment. The acknowledgment can be piggy-backed onto a data packet if there is data traffic in the reverse direction or a control packet can be used. In any event, when the receive sequence number P(R) from the receiver reaches the sender, the lower edge of the sender's window is set to P(R). Now, the sender can send packets numbered up to but not including P(R)+W. Therefore, as packets are transmitted and the acknowledgments returned, the lower and upper window edges rotate. A packet received with a P(S) outside the range between the upper and lower window edges is considered a procedural error and the DCE will initiate a reset procedure on that logical channel.

It is possible to use a modulo 128 packet numbering scheme by setting the third bit in the general format identifier. The larger window size of up to 127 is useful for links with large transmission delays. The packet formats the data and flow control have to be modified to allow seven bit fields for P(R) and P(S).

X.25 provides the capability to send out of band signalling as represented by an Interrupt packet. The Interrupt packet does not contain send and receive sequence numbers and it may be transmitted across the DTE/DCE interface even when packets are being flow controlled. Interrupt packets may contain up to 32 octets of user data and are delivered to the destination DTE even when it is not accepting data packets. An Interrupt packet is acknowledged by an Interrupt Confirmation packet. Only one unconfirmed Interrupt may be outstanding at a given time. Interrupt Confirmation has an end-to-end effect.

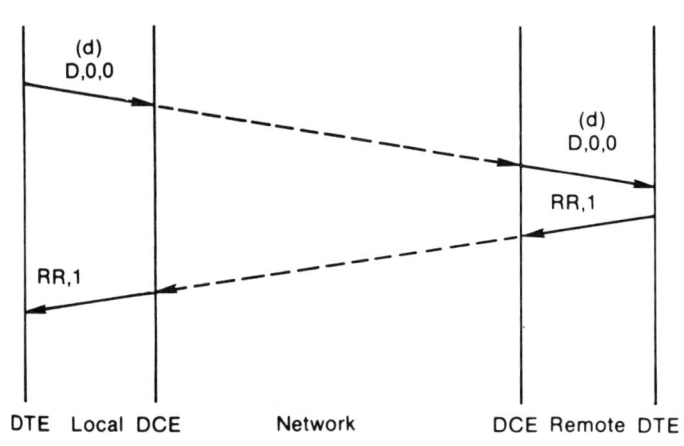

Legend:
D — Data
D,P(R),P(S)
RR,P(R)
(d) — Data Confirmation Bit (D-bit) Set
P(R) — Packet Receive Sequence Number
P(S) — Packet Send Sequence Number
RR — Receive Ready

Fig. 9. End-to-End P(R) Significance.

Error Recovery

The following set of principles were established to handle packet level errors at the X.25 interface. They are:

1) Procedural errors during call establishment and clearing are reported to the DTE by clearing the call;
2) Most procedural errors during the data transfer phase are reported to the DTE by resetting the virtual call;
3) A diagnostic field is included in the reset packet to provide additional information to the DTE;
4) Timers are essential for resolution of some deadlock conditions;
5) Some DTE procedural errors are a result of the DTE and the DCE not being aligned as to the subscription options provided at the interface; and
6) State tables define the action of the DCE on receiving various packet types in various states of the interface.

The diagnostic aids at the packet level include the definition of standard diagnostic codes and an optional diagnostic packet. The diagnostic packet is used by the DCE when restarting, resetting and clearing procedures are not appropriate. It requires no response from the DTE.

Two of the error recovery procedures, the reset and the restart, are presented below:

The reset procedure may be initiated either by the DTE or by the network when certain types of problems arise. The reset procedure does not clear a virtual circuit but simply reinitializes a permanent virtual circuit or a virtual circuit in the data phase. The reset procedure clears all the sequence numbers associated with a virtual circuit to zero and any data and interrupt packets in transit are discarded.

A DTE initiates a reset procedure by sending a Reset Request packet to its DCE. The reason for initiating a reset is encoded in the packet. Some of the reasons for the reset are remote procedure error, local procedure error, network congestion and PVC out of order. If the reset is initiated by the DCE, it sends a Reset Indication packet. The resetting procedure is completed when a Reset Confirmation packet is received by the DTE or DCE which intiated the reset. After the reset procedure, the virtual circuit is in the data transfer state. Figure 10 shows the resetting procedure.

The restart procedure permits recovery from major failures. The restart procedure is used to reinitialize all the logical channels at the DTE/DCE interface. A restart is equivalent to clearing all the switched virtual circuits and a resetting- of all logical channels for permanent virtual circuits. Therefore, the restart procedure will bring the DTE/DCE interface to the original state it was in when the service was initiated. The restart procedure may be initiated by either the DTE or the DCE.

The DTE initiates a restart by issuing a Restart Request packet to its local DCE. If the restart is initiated by the network, the DCE issues a Restart

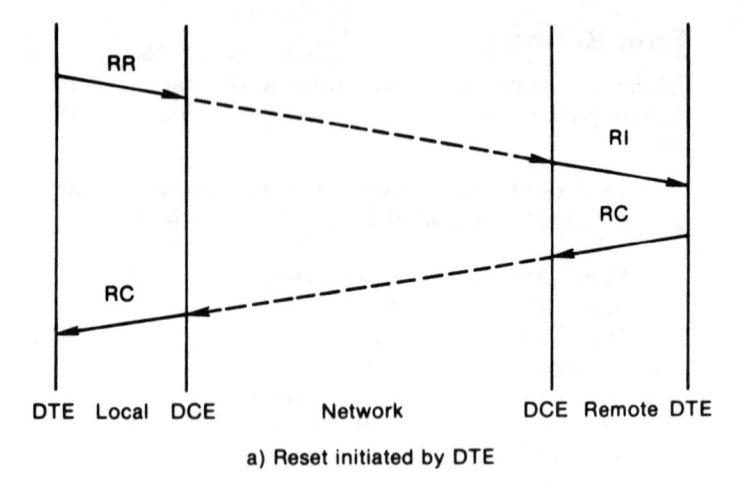

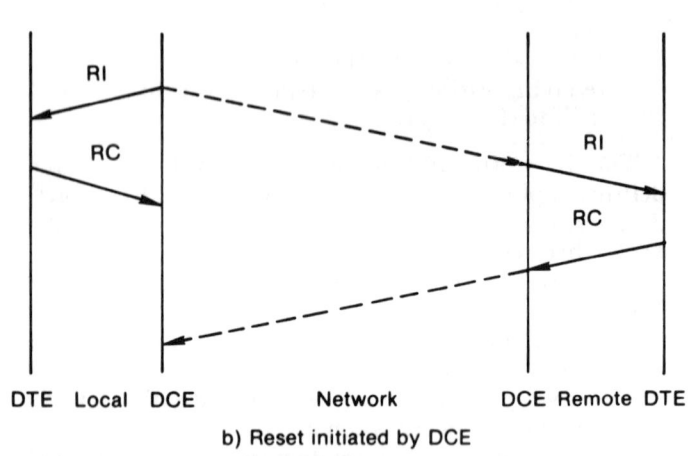

Fig. 10. Reset Procedure.

Legend:
RR — Reset Request Packet
RI — Reset Indication Packet
RC — Reset Confirmation Packet

Indication packet. A Restart Confirmation packet completes the restart procedure. The reset and restart actions can cause the loss of packets that have not been acknowledged at the DTE/DCE interface.

Optional User Facilities

X.25 provides a number of optional user facilities. An optional facility may be requested when setting up a virtual call by using the facilities field in the Call Request packet. Certain facilities can be requested by the calling DTE and subsequently negotiated by the remote DTE or DCE. Once the value of the facility has been established, it remains in effect until the call is cleared.

Recommendation X.25 defines two types of optional user facilities: essential and additional facilities. Essential facilities must be available on all public data networks whereas the additional facilities may be available on particular networks. A number of optional user facilities are presented below:

• *Closed user group:* This facility defines a subgroup of network users. Members of a closed user group are protected from unauthorized access and any call from a non-group member is refused by the network, thereby providing additional protection. A DTE may belong to more than one closed user group.

When setting up a virtual call, the calling DTE selects the closed user group by placing user facility parameters in the Call Request packet. This closed user group facility can be used to create a private subnet within a public data network.

• *Flow control parameter negotiation:* The flow control parameters are the packet length and the window size for each logical channel. All public data networks support a window size of two and a maximum data packet length of 128 octets at the packet level. Some DTE's may require a larger window size and/or packet length for higher throughput. In order to increase the packet or window size beyond the network default values, the calling DTE selects a packet/window size and this information is sent to the called DTE in the Call Request packet. The called DTE accepts the call if it can support the flow control parameters. Otherwise, it may reject by clearing the call or may negotiate. The one rule with negotiation is that the DTE must negotiate towards a packet size of 128 octets and a window size of 2. In some cases, the network may have to constrain the available parameter ranges in order to allow the call to be established.

• *Throughput class negotiation:* Throughput class is defined as the number of octets per second that can be transferred on a virtual circuit. This facility allows negotiation on a per call basis and the throughput classes are considered independently for each direction of data transmission. A throughput class is a function of the amount of network resources allocated. Due to the statistical sharing of transmission and switching resources, it is not possible to guarantee that the throughput class can be reached 100 percent of the time. Default values agreed upon between the DTE and the network correspond to the maximum throughput class which may be associated with any virtual circuit at the DTE/DCE interface.

• *One-way logical channel:* With this optional facility, the DTE is allowed to initiate calls but is prevented from accepting calls. Or, it is allowed to accept incoming calls but prevented from initiating outgoing calls.

• *Packet retransmission:* This facility allows a DTE to request retransmission of data packets that have not been acknowledged. To initiate the retransmission, the DTE sends a Reject packet to its local DCE. Only a DTE can send Reject packets.

• *Reverse charging:* Using this facility, the calling DTE indicates that the called DTE is to be charged for the call. If the called DTE is not designated to accept reverse charging, the network will clear the call.

• *Fast select:* The fast select facility allows up to 128 octets of user data to be appended to the Call Request, Incoming Call, Clear Request, and Clear Indication packets. Using this facility, one packet of data transfer needs only three packets to be transmitted. If the remote DTE did not subscribe to the fast select acceptance option, the network will block such calls to the DTE. The fast select facility becomes an essential facility in the 1984 version. A list of major revisions in the 1984 version of X.25 compared to 1980 version is given below [7]:

—Link Level
- Multilink procedures are defined to increase reliability and bandwidth. A level 3 packet can be transmitted over one or more links of the multilink group under the control of level 2.
- Extended sequence numbering (i.e., modulo 128 arithmetic), is introduced to allow transmission over satellite links.
- A new timer T_3 for the idle channel state is introduced.
- Miscellaneous changes in recovery actions to increase link efficiency.

—Packet Level
- Datagram feature deleted.
- The interrupt user data field in the interrupt packet is increased to 32 octets of data.
- Fast select is made essential for all networks to provide. Its definition is extended to allow user data during both call set-up and call clearing, regardless of when the call is cleared.
- Facility fields in call request, incoming call, call accepted, call connected, clear request, clear indication, and clear confirmation packets increased to 109 octets.
- A new essential facility, the transit delay selection and indication facility, permits the selection of the quality of service by negotiating the delay. Transit delay is expressed in terms of a 95 percent probability value.
- Facilities are added so that X.25 can be used to interconnect public and private packet switched networks: closed user group with outgoing access selection (so that a private network may screen the right of setting up or accepting a closed user group call) and called line address modification. In addition, the maximum number of closed user groups to which a DTE can belong is extended to 10,000 and the cause code number space for restart, clear, and reset packets is partitioned between public and private networks.
- Facilities are added for end-to-end DTE signaling: minimum throughput class negotiation, end-to-end transit delay negotiation, address extension, and expedited data negotiation (that is, the interrupt procedures).
- Registration procedures are added so that a user can dynamically modify, ascertain, invoke or revoke some of the subscription facilities applying to the interface.
- A mechanism is provided for explicitly selecting a sequence of transit networks during call set-up or per agreement for a period of time through expansion of the Recognized Private Operating Agency (RPOA) facility.
- Voice like features are added in the following facilities: hunt group, call redirection notification, charging information, local charging prevention, network user identification, called line address modification facility.
- Major enhancements in the packet level error handling procedures, cause codes and diagnostic codes were introduced.

Summary

Recommendation X.25 describes the interface between data terminal equipment (DTE) and data circuit-terminating equipment (DCE) for terminals operating in the packet-mode on public data networks. The Recommendation distinguishes three levels. The first is the physical level. The second level is the link level for which a subset of HDLC is defined. The third level is the packet level. This article presents a synergistic view of the virtual circuit-based packet-mode services that are accessible through the X.25 interface. A detailed description of virtual call setup, data transfer and call clearing is provided. The error recovery procedures and the optional user facilities are briefly narrated.

With the proliferation of public packet-switched networks, the use of these Recommendations will facilitate the connection of DTE's to a diversity of public networks. Progress in design and standardization of gateways between networks will lead to internetworking capabilities and eventually to international internetworking.

References

[1] Recommendation X.25, "Interface Between DTE and DCE for Terminals Operating in the Packet Mode on Public Data Networks," CCITT Fascicle VIII.3 (1984).
[2] D. W. Davies, D. L. A. Barber, W. L. Price, and C. M. Solomonides, *Computer Networks and their Protocols*, John Wiley & Sons, 1979.
[3] H. C. Folts, "Procedures for circuit-switched service in synchronous public data networks," *IEEE Trans. on Comm.*, vol. COM-28, no. 4, pp. 489–496, April 1980.
[4] ISO International Standard IS-7776, "Description of the 1984 X.25 LAPB-Compatible DTE Link Procedures." ISO, T697/SC6.
[5] L. G. Roberts, "The evolution of packet switching," *Proc. IEEE*, vol. 66, no. 11, pp. 1307–1313, Nov. 1978.
[6] A. Rybczynski, "X.25 interface and end-to-end virtual circuit service characteristics," *IEEE Trans. on Comm.*, vol. COM-28, no. 4, pp. 500–510, April 1980.
[7] M. H. Sherif, G. L. Hoover, and R. P. Wiederhold, "X.25 Conformance Testing—A Tutorial," *IEEE Communications Mag.*, vol. 24, no. 1, Jan. 1986.

C. R. Dhas is currently Director of Engineering Analysis Department at Telenet Communications Corporation, Reston, VA. He has worked on data flow architectures, distributed database, knowledge based systems, and protocol architectures. He is currently involved in design and analysis of packet switched networks, and network and capacity planning areas.

He received his Ph.D. in Computer Science from Iowa State University, Ames, IA in 1978 and an M.B.A. from Marymount College, VA in 1985.

Vijaya K. Konangi is an Associate Professor of Electrical Engineering at Cleveland State University. His research interests include computer communication networks, local area networks, and distributed systems. He received the B.E. and M.Sc. degrees from the University of Madras, India and the Ph.D. degree from Iowa State University. He is a Member of the IEEE and the ACM.

The Internal Organization of the OSI Network Layer: Concepts, Applications, and Issues

Christine Hemrick
U. S. Department of Commerce*

ABSTRACT ISO/TC97/SC6/WG2, which has responsibility within ISO for standards relating to the Network Layer of the OSI Reference Model, has developed and described a Network Layer "Internal Organization" (Document ISO/TC97/SC6/N3141). This Internal Organization was evolved through efforts to understand the ways in which "real" networks can be used to provide the "Network Service" within the context of OSI, in particular, in circumstances where different types of networks are interconnected and used in a concatenated manner for OSI communications. The Internal Organization of the Network Layer (IONL) developed within ISO defines terminology and concepts which provide a framework for identifying the other OSI Network Layer Standards needed to achieve useful Open Systems Interconnection. This paper describes the work on IONL, including the way it is reflected in the Network Layer protocol standards being developed, and some areas which have been identified for further study.

1. Introduction

Within the International Standards Organization (ISO), the task of developing international standards associated with the Network Layer of the Open Systems Interconnection (OSI) Reference Model [1], [2] is the responsibility of Technical Committee 97, Subcommittee 6, Working Group 2 (ISO/TC97/SC6/WG2). As part of this mandate, SC6/WG2 is currently engaged in a project (Project 97.6.32.3) to define and describe the "Internal Organization" of the OSI Network Layer (IONL) [20].

This paper reports the background and progress of SC6/WG2's effort on IONL, discusses its fundamental aspects, describes the emerging Network Layer protocol standards which demonstrate its application, and identifies some new and remaining issues that need to be further addressed.

2. Background and Progress of IONL Development

The purpose of the OSI Network Layer (NL) is to provide to the Transport Layer entities above it an end-to-end communications capability that is independent of any operational characteristics of the specific "real-world" transmission facilities used to support it. Thus, the NL, as well as the layers below it, must perform functions that deal with "real networks" and make use of them to provide a networking capability in the OSI context.

Organized efforts by SC6/WG2 to define these required NL functions and to specify the

---

Reprinted with permission from *Journal of Telecommunications Networks*, Fall 1984, pp. 15–22. ©1984 by W.H. Freeman (Computer Science Press).

way in which they should be performed were initially begun in June 1981. It was evident that the existence of many different types of "real" networks and of a diversity of views about how networks of different types should be interconnected for OSI made this task important and challenging. The problem was further complicated by the need to make the exploitation of existing networks efficient and cost-effective, and by the desire to limit the impact on already established international networking standards.

To promote progress in identifying the direction NL standardization should take, it was agreed that a clearly defined framework for discussing NL functions and protocols was required. The first attempt at creating such a framework resulted in the generation of the original version of the paper entitled "The Internal Organization of the Network Layer" (Document ISO/TC97/SC6/N2228, June 1981).

At subsequent SC6/WG2 meetings (February 1982, October 1982, September 1983, and April 1984), the description of the IONL has undergone significant evolution and change [4], [5], [6], [20]. The primary intent of the IONL, however, has remained the same—that is, to apply general architectural principles to define and describe the complexities of the OSI Network Layer, just as such techniques were previously used to develop the overall OSI Reference Model. The IONL document focuses mainly on concepts and principles; it describes types of protocols and different strategies that might be used and standardized for the "OSI" interconnection of real-world networks. The IONL does *not* specify particular services or protocols to which "real equipment" must conform. As a result, much of the contents of the "Internal Organization of the Network Layer" [20] may appear to many readers of the document to be extremely abstract and academic. Nevertheless, despite the fact that the description of the IONL cannot be classified as casual or uncomplicated reading, the development of the abstract IONL model has proved to be a valuable exercise for SC6/WG2, leading to better understanding of the possible alternatives for OSI NL standardization. This is demonstrated by the fact that SC6/WG2 has begun the progression of a number of NL protocol standards that are based upon and defined in terms of the concepts of the IONL. (Section 4 of this paper further describes these NL protocols being standardized).

At its meeting in April 1984, (in Zurich, Switzerland), SC6/WG2 determined that the document outlining the IONL should itself be progressed toward becoming an International Standard. WG2, therefore, agreed to ask the SC6 Secretariat to circulate a letter ballot asking the SC6 member bodies for permission to register and ballot SC6/N3141 as an ISO Draft Proposal.

3. Fundamentals of the IONL

The description of the IONL developed by SC6/WG2 begins by establishing a working vocabulary and a set of abstract concepts that model the "real-world" objects that must be dealt with. These concepts form the basis for identifying the possible methods by which the functions of the Network Layer may be implemented, and the corresponding NL protocols that may be developed and used for this purpose. From this basis, some specific strategies for achieving the interconnection of "real" networks can be prescribed.

3.1 Conceptual Models and Terminology.
In the early stages of SC6/WG2's study of the IONL, discussions about the use of "real-world" networks to provide an abstract OSI "Network Service" (within the framework of an abstract "Network Layer") were fraught with confusion, a fact largely attributable to the absence of a vocabulary of well-distinguished terms. In recognition of this difficulty, the development and use of a precise terminology, one which distinguishes "real-world" objects from the abstract models used in the definition of NL standards, has been an important element in the progression of the IONL. Although the vocabulary of the IONL, which is now in common use in SC6/WG2, is precisely defined, it is also complex and often subtle. In attempting to understand and utilize it, it is important not to forget the "real-world" versus "abstract" dichotomy that it is intended to clarify.

The "real-world" objects with which the IONL is primarily concerned are of three types:

(1) *Real subnetworks*—actually, the collection of equipment encountered and referred to in the "real world" as a "network"[1] (for example, a public data network, a local area network, etc.);

(2) *Real end systems*—the systems connected to "real subnetworks" for purposes of communicating with one another; and

(3) *Interworking units* ("IWU"'s)—pieces of equipment used to connect different "real subnetworks" together.

Each of these types of objects has a corresponding abstract representation which is used to denote those common properties of the objects that are relevant in an OSI context. "Real end systems" are abstracted as "end systems," while both "real subnetworks" and "interworking units" can be represented as "intermediate systems." The abstract terms "end system" and "intermediate systems," which are used here by SC6/WG2, refer to precisely the concepts that are described in the OSI Reference Model [1], [2].

In the Reference Model, an abstract "intermediate system" is an open system for which only the functionality of that system that belongs to the lower three layers of the OSI architecture (Network, Data Link, and Physical Layers) is of interest. Thus, the term can be applied to describing abstractly both "real subnetworks" and "interworking units" when they operate in an OSI context. In describing strategies for real-world interconnection, SC6/WG2 has found it useful in certain circumstances to be more specific when discussing the functionality of real subnetworks and interworking units, since there are cases where the distinction between the functionality of the two is significant. Therefore, SC6/WG2 has defined a "subnetwork" to be the specific abstract representation of a real subnetwork, and uses the term "relay system" as the specific representation of an interworking unit. The introduction of this terminology, although useful for SC6/WG2 purposes, is an example of terminology which is often confusing, since in some instances the distinct terms "subnetwork" and "relay system" are used, but in other instances in the IONL, real subnetworks, and interworking units are both still described using the more general term "intermediate system."

When the term "subnetwork" or "intermediate system" is used to describe a real subnetwork, it represents the functionality of the entire collection of equipment within the real subnetwork. When an interworking unit is physically independent of the real subnetworks which it interconnects, its functionality can be independently represented as a "relay system," in SC6/WG2 terms. However, there are also real-world situations where interworking functions are included as an integral part of, and physically indistinguishable from, a real subnetwork. In these cases, the abstract representation may identify the relay system (one intermediate system) functionality separately from the subnetwork (another intermediate system) functionality or may describe the entire collection of functions as a single subnetwork (a single intermediate system).

The terms "real subnetwork" and "subnetwork" may both be applied in a recursive fashion. That is, the term "real subnetwork" may be used to refer to a collection of "real subnetworks" which are interconnected in a manner such that they appear externally, to any system connected to them, as a single "real subnetwork." Similarly, the properties of a collection of "subnetworks" (which are abstract representations) may be functionally equivalent, from an external view, to those of a single "subnetwork." They may thus be described as such.

Table 1 summarizes the correspondence

---

[1] In 1981 SC6/WG2 began using the term "subnetwork" in its documents in place of the term "network" when referring to "the collection of physical equipment commonly called a 'network'" [7], [8]. This convention was introduced in an attempt to avoid misunderstandings about whether the "service provided by a network" must be equivalent to the "Network Service" defined for OSI [6], [7], [8]. In addition, use of the term "subnetwork" for a particular network emphasizes the global nature of the OSI "Network" Service which can, in some instances, represent the functionality provided by a number of individual subnetworks, utilized in a unified fashion.

**Table 1
Correspondence Between "Real World" Objects and Abstract Representations**

"Real world" object	Abstract representation
"real end system"	end system
"interworking unit"	intermediate system; relay system
"real subnetwork"	intermediate system; subnetwork

between "real world" objects and abstract concepts as used in the IONL. Figure 1 illustrates a graphical representation for these real objects and abstract entities.

The whole objective of the OSI Network Layer, of course, is to provide the (abstract) OSI Network Service. Two types of OSI Network Service have been defined, a connection-mode Service and a connectionless-mode Service [6], [7], [8]. Within either an "end system" or an "intermediate system," the collection of functions in that system that are defined to belong to the Network Layer is referred to as an "NL entity." It is the operation of NL entities acting in cooperation that provides the OSI Network Service.

Within the Network Layer for any particular "subnetwork," it is possible to define a corresponding abstract "subnetwork service" which represents the exploitation of that subnetwork's functions and capabilities. Such a subnetwork service may similarly be characterized as either a connection-mode or a connectionless-mode service, according to its properties. The abstract subnetwork service that a real subnetwork supports is defined to include functions performed by the end and/or intermediate systems that access and utilize

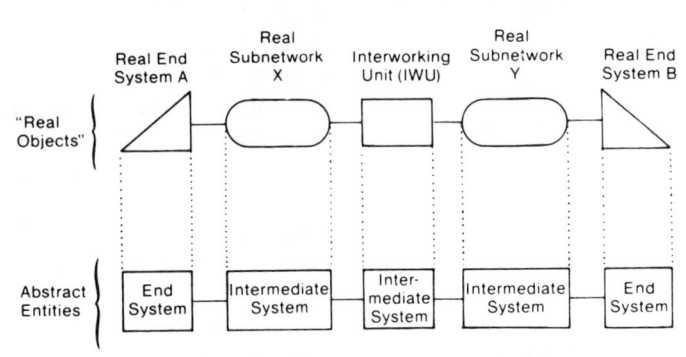

a) Real Subnetworks and Interworking Unit Represented as Separate Intermediate Systems

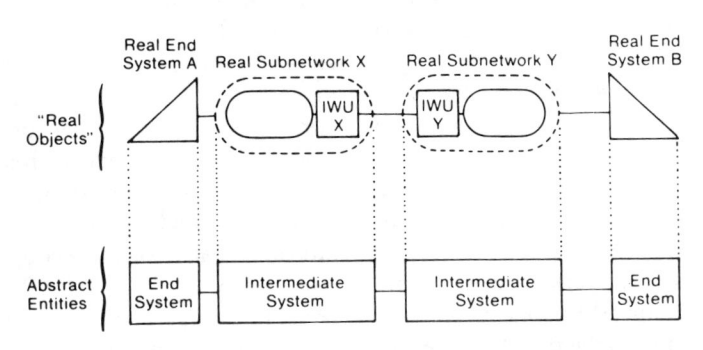

b) Interworking Units and Real Subnetworks Represented as Part of the Same Intermediate System

Figure 1. Graphical Representation of Real Objects and Abstract Entities.

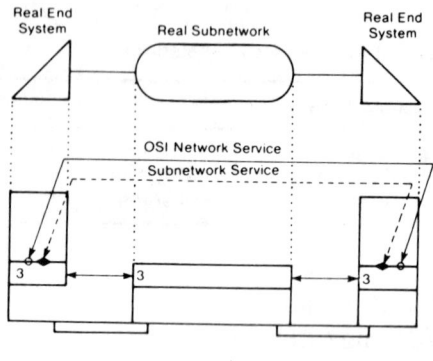

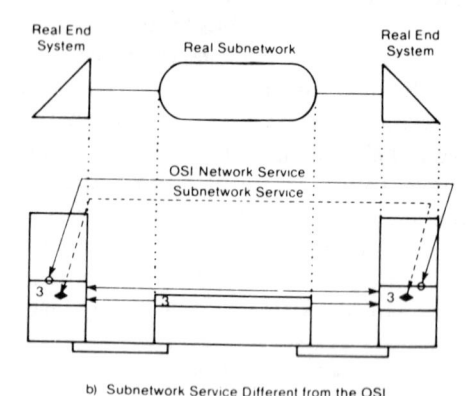

Figure 2. Possible Relationships Between Subnetwork Service and the OSI Network Service.

it. The resulting subnetwork service for any particular instance of communication may be exactly the same as the OSI Network Service, or it may be different from the OSI Network Service. (See Figure 2.) When the subnetwork service is exactly the same as the OSI Network Service, that subnetwork is said to "fully support the OSI Network Service."

A particular real subnetwork may be capable of supporting either a connection-mode subnetwork service, a connectionless-mode subnetwork service, or both. However, not all of the functions and capabilities of a real subnetwork will necessarily be reflected in the definition of its subnetwork service. Some subnetworks will be able to provide capabilities that are not defined to be a part of the OSI Network Layer and thus are outside the scope of consideration for the IONL.

3.2 Network Layer Functions and Protocols.

In most of the other layers of the OSI Reference Model, identifying the location of the layer's functions presents no difficulty, since only a single pair of entities, each in an end system, needs to be considered. When functions of the layer are performed by means of cooperation between such a pair of entities, a single protocol between the two will suffice.

Within the Network Layer, however, there may be in some circumstances NL entities existing in intermediate systems, in addition to those in the end systems. As a result, the distribution of functionality among these entities may be varied and complex. Consequently, too, there may be many possible choices concerning the design of protocols to support these functions. It is this possible variation in the functional distribution and protocol structure of the NL that the IONL seeks to model.

All of the functions of the NL are, of course, concerned with the provision of the OSI Network Service. One category of functions identified in the IONL, and referred to as the Relay and Routing functions, are performed individually by each NL entity. Relay and Routing functions are those that effect the switching of information through an entity, including determining the identity of the next NL entity to which the information is to be forwarded. Apart from the Relay and Routing functions, there are other types of NL functions that involve more than one NL entity acting in cooperation. Such functions require the operation of a protocol between the entities in order for the functions to be performed.

The *nature* of the functions which will be present in the NL will be determined to a large extent by the type of Network Service to be provided (connection-mode, or connectionless) and the particular subnetworks being utilized. There may still be choices that can be made, however, concerning the location and distribution of these functions. Among the functions that involve the cooperation of more than one NL entity, the IONL categorizes the possible choices according to the "role" that a protocol performs when realizing the function. The three categories of protocol roles which are defined for this purpose are:

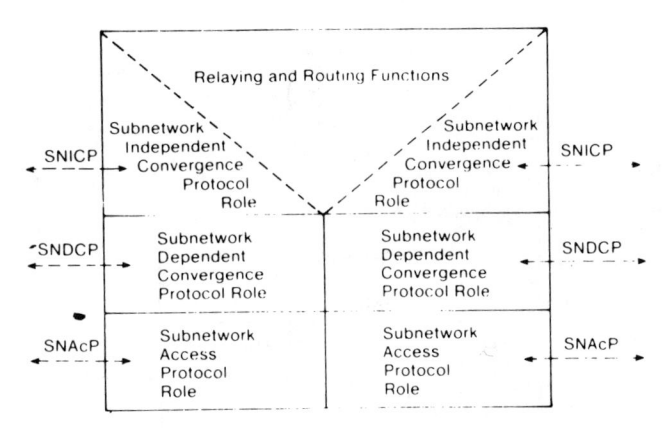

Figure 3. Network Layer Protocol Roles and Functions in an Intermediate System.

(1) Subnetwork access protocol (SNAcP) role;
(2) Subnetwork-dependent convergence protocol (SNDCP) role; and
(3) Subnetwork-independent convergence protocol (SNICP) role.

An illustration of an intermediate system operating with protocols performing these roles, as well as the necessary relay and routing functions appears in Figure 3.

A protocol fulfilling the subnetwork access role (SNAcP) is one that operates between an NL entity in a subnetwork and an entity outside the subnetwork (for example, a "DCE/DTE interface" protocol. The functions associated with a SNAcP are those that result in the provision of a subnetwork service. In cases where each subnetwork service provided is identical to the required OSI Network Service, there may be no need for additional cooperating functionality, or any protocols other than the SNAcP in the NL.

The two types of convergence roles, subnetwork dependent (SNDCP) and subnetwork independent (SNICP), both involve protocols that operate between NL entities which are outside a subnetwork. A convergence protocol operates over the top of a subnetwork service and utilizes it. An SNDCP is defined for, and requires beneath it, a particular type of subnetwork. An SNICP, on the other hand, is intended for use over a wide variety of different subnetwork types, and thus is defined to require a minimal subnetwork service underneath. The major distinction between SNDCP's and SNICP's then, is the choice between making the maximum use of the capabilities of a particular underlying subnetwork service (possibly leading to the definition of a different SNDCP for each subnetwork type), and maximizing the number of different subnetwork services over which the same convergence protocol can be utilized (at the possible expense of not utilizing available subnetwork capabilities).

In circumstances where convergence protocol is required in addition to SNAcP to provide the OSI Network Service, SNDCP may be used, SNICP may be used, or both types of protocol may be used in combination.

3.3 IONL Strategies for Interconnection. As is the case for most abstract models, the principal utility of the concepts of the IONL lies in their application to *realistic* problems that are of interest. ISO/TC97/SC6/N3141 describes a number of "generic" interconnection scenarios that attempt to illustrate how the IONL can be used in a practical context [20].

A simple scenario involves the interconnection of two end systems by a single subnetwork. If the subnetwork service available is equivalent to the OSI Network Service to be provided, then only a single NL protocol, operating in the SNAcP role, is required. (This might be the case, for example, of two end systems connected to an X.25, 1984 version, public data network. See Section 4.) If the

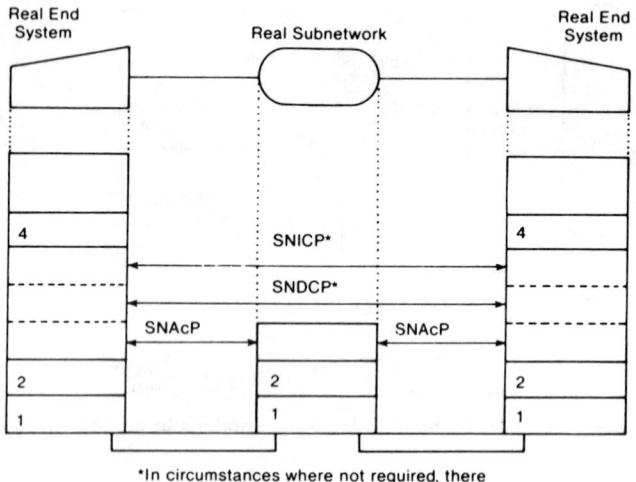

Figure 4. Interconnection of End Systems by a Single Subnetwork.

subnetwork service is not equivalent to the OSI Network Service, then the additional required cooperating entity functions may be performed by means of a protocol fulfilling a SNDCP or SNICP role (e.g., a connectionless local area network required to provide the connection-mode Network Service). IONL representations of these scenarios are shown in Figure 4.

Where the interconnection of multiple subnetworks is required, SC6/WG2 has identified two cases that represent different choices concerning how the necessary functions should be performed. The two cases are referred to as:

(1) "Hop-by-hop" enhancement over individual subnetworks; and
(2) Use of an internetworking protocol over multiple subnetworks.

In the case of "hop-by-hop" enhancement, the subnetwork service available from each subnetwork (e.g., each "hop") being utilized is enhanced individually, to the level of the OSI Network Service to be provided. The individual "enhanced services" are then concatenated by means of the Relay and Routing functions in the intermediate systems that connect the subnetworks. (See Figure 5.)

In some cases, when subnetwork service is equivalent to the OSI Network Service, no *enhancement* of the service will be required.

When enhancement is required, it will generally be done by means of an SNDCP. The functions required for each *enhancement* may include functions that mask some of the capabilities of a particular subnetwork service, as well as functions that provide additional capabilities.

An alternative approach to "hop-by-hop" enhancement is the use of an internetworking protocol over all the collection of subnetworks to be interconnected. Such an internetworking protocol is, by definition, an SNICP, designed to operate over some minimum service available from each of the subnetworks involved. (See Figure 6.) The Relay and Routing functions in the intermediate systems that connect the subnetworks act to convey the protocol information of the SNICP through the intermediate system. The OSI Network Service is thus provided in an end-to-end fashion, and may not necessarily be observable over any one particular subnetwork of the interconnected set of subnetworks for an instance of communications (for example, when an internetworking protocol is utilized over a series of interconnected LANs of the same or different types).

Even in the case where a subnetwork does not support the minimal subnetwork service required by a particular internetworking protocol, it is possible to use that internetworking protocol over the subnetwork. In such a case,

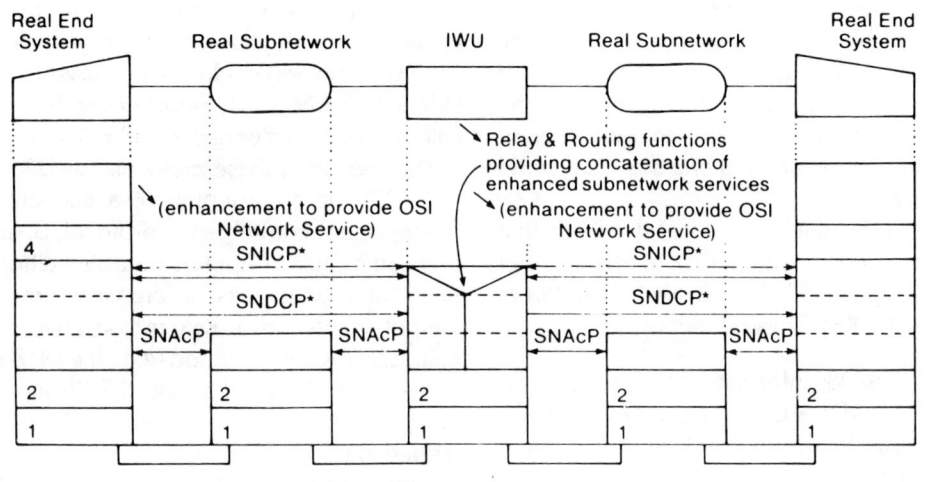

Figure 5. "Hop-by-Hop" Enhancement Over Individual Subnetworks.

an SNDCP is used over the deficient subnetwork (and below the SNICP) to provide the level of service that the SNICP requires.

In some internetworking circumstances, it may be possible and advantageous to employ the "hop-by-hop" enhancement and internetworking protocol methods in combination. As an example, an internetworking protocol could be used over some series of interconnected subnetworks, operating essentially as a "multi-hop" enhancement protocol to provide the OSI Network Service over that group of subnetworks. The "enhanced" subnetwork service could then be concatenated with another enhanced subnetwork service, or series of enhanced subnetwork services using the "hop-by-hop" enhancement methods.

4. IONL Application by NL Protocol Standards

While making progress in efforts to describe and document the IONL as an abstract

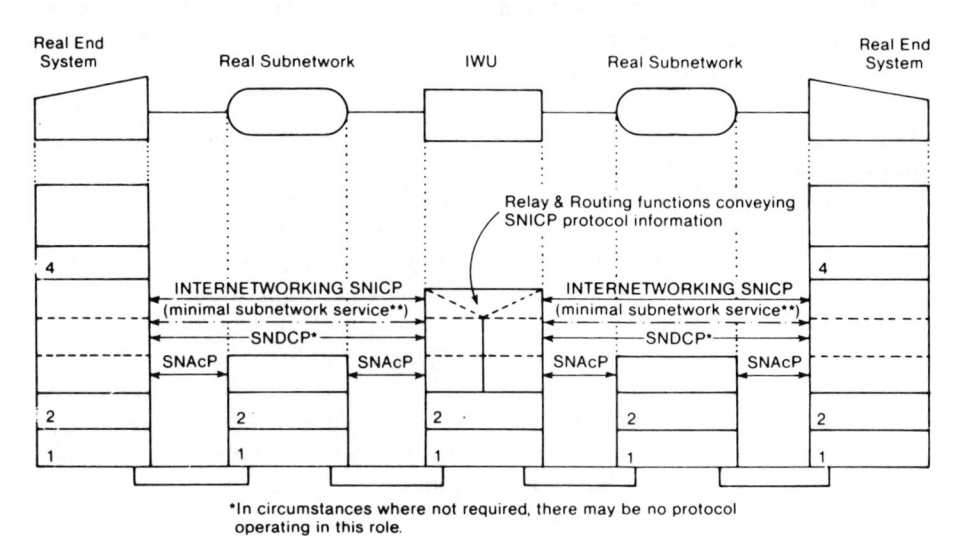

Figure 6. Use of an Internetworking Protocol Over Multiple Subnetworks.

model, SC6/WG2 has also been actively developing specific NL protocols that can be used to achieve actual interconnection of equipment. These protocols, which reflect the basic concepts of the IONL, do, in fact, demonstrate its application to practical, real-world problems.

There are three NL protocol standards that have progressed within ISO to the level of Draft Proposal (DP) or Draft International Standard (DIS). These standards are:

(1) DIS 8208, Information Processing Systems—Data Communications—X.25 Packet Level Protocol for Data Terminal Equipment;
(2) DP 8473, Information Processing Systems—Data Communications—Protocol for Providing the Connectionless Network Service; and
(3) DP 8472 (ISO/TC97/SC6/N2964), Information Processing Systems—Data Communications—X.25 (1980) Network Convergence Protocol.

The first protocol, specified in DIS 8208, is in IONL terms a subnetwork access protocol, SNAcP. DIS 8208 prescribes the procedures for use by an NL entity within an end system (an X.25 DTE) communicating with an NL entity of subnetwork (in this case, X.25, 1984 version, subnetwork). The operation of such a protocol results in the provision of the X.25 (1984) "subnetwork service" that is fully equivalent to the OSI Network Service (connection-mode). Thus, in the case of end systems interconnected by just a single X.25 (1984) subnetwork, the SNAcP specified in DIS 8208 would be the only protocol required in the NL to provide the OSI connection-mode Network Service. (i.e., in Figure 4, DIS 8208 would be used as the SNAcP, and the SNDCP and SNICP would be absent.) If an X.25 (1984) subnetwork is interconnected with another subnetwork of a different type by means of an intervening intermediate system (e.g., see Figure 5), the DIS 8208 protocol could be utilized by the end system and by the intermediate system attached to the X.25 subnetwork to provide the OSI Network Service over that subnetwork. The "hop-by-hop enhancement" method (with no further enhancement necessary in this case over the X.25 subnetwork) could then be used to provide the OSI Network Service over the entire collection of interconnected subnetworks.

The second of these protocols, specified in DP 8473, is an example of a subnetwork independent convergence protocol, SNICP, and can be used for interconnecting different types of subnetworks as prescribed by the "use of an internetworking protocol over multiple subnetworks" method (e.g., the DP 8473 protocol can be used as the SNICP as illustrated in Figure 6). The particular SNICP described in DP 8473 provides only the connectionless-mode OSI Network Service and requires a very minimal subnetwork service which is also defined to be of the connectionless-mode type. (One frequently mentioned application of DP 8473 is in the interconnection of connectionless LANs.) This SNICP can be used over a subnetwork service of greater functionality (either connectionless-mode or connection-mode) if appropriate convergence functions are provided.

The third of the protocol standards, the X.25 (1980) Network Convergence Protocol (DP xxxx) is a subnetwork-dependent convergence protocol, SNDCP. This SNDCP is defined for use between two NL entities which are outside of, but communicating over an X.25 subnetwork which conforms to the 1980 or earlier version of the X.25 Recommendation. Since X.25 subnetworks of this type do not fully support the OSI Network Service (connection-mode), this SNDCP can be used over such X.25 subnetworks to provide the OSI Network Service, or in an internetworking situation, to "enhance" a subnetwork of this type so that the "hop-by-hop enhancement" method of interconnection can be utilized. (e.g., as the SNDCP shown in Figures 4 and 5).

In addition to these three protocols, SC6/WG2 is studying other protocols for possible standardization. Two of the protocols being considered are SNDCP's proposed for use over X.21 circuit-switching subnetworks. One of the candidate SNDCP's is based on the Network Layer procedure for circuit-switching subnetworks in CCITT Recommendation

S.70. (Reference ISO/TC97/SC6/N2743—Annex 2 and N2908.) The other proposal is to utilize the protocol defined in DIS 8208 (X.25) as an SDNCP between NL entities operating over an X.21 subnetwork. (Reference ISO/TC97/SC6/N2981.)

As the need arises, it is expected that SC6/WG2 will develop other NL protocols and will continue to apply the IONL as a tool for defining the functional requirements of such protocols and their relationship to other NL protocols.

5. Issues for Further Study

One of the consequences of the progress achieved to date in defining the IONL is the identification of some additional issues and important areas which need further consideration. Some of the significant questions raised include how the functionality and operation of intermediate systems should be specified, how the internetworking strategy to be utilized in a specific configuration or subnetworks should be chosen (in particular, in cases where the subnetwork services available and the OSI Network Services type(s) to be provided include a mixture of connection-mode and connectionless-mode services), and what the relationship between the IONL and Network Layer management should be.

A number of proposals have been made for how the operation of intermediate systems (subnetworks and interworking units) should be specified when describing the "hop-by-hop" enhancement method of internetworking. Previous contributions (Reference ISO/TC97/SC6/N2731—Annex 10) have utilized service primitives corresponding to those of the OSI Network Service to describe how the subnetwork services on two sides of an interworking unit would be related to perform the concatenation of these services in an internetworking situation. Alternatively, it has been suggested that internetworking in this manner should be described in terms of "multi-entities" protocols established between the NL entities in the end and intermediate systems involved. (Reference ISO/TC97/SC6/N2871). An agreement upon the descriptive tools needed to specify this type of internetworking functionality satisfactorily would appear to require further study and discussions.

The definition of two types of OSI Network Service (connection-mode and connectionless-mode) and the existence of real subnetworks that support different types of subnetwork services (connection-mode and connectionless-mode) results in a large and complicated set of interconnection scenarios. These scenarios represent various combinations of the service types involved and the possible internetworking methods that could be used to connect them. Not all of the scenarios which it is possible to construct describe choices that are actually efficient, cost-effective interconnection strategies, and clearly, not all of them could or should be standardized. Additional study needs to be done to evaluate the possible internetworking choices and, where appropriate, to proceed with development of the necessary NL standards.

Finally, a necessary area of study that is extremely important but is currently not well-defined, involves the management aspects of the OSI Network Layer and their relationship to the IONL. Factors that should be considered in this context include the provision and management of multiple instances of communication via the OSI Network Service, the relationship of instances of providing the OSI Network Service to instances of providing a subnetwork service, the influence of the IONL on NL addressing structure and routing principles, and the provision and maintenance of Network Layer Quality of Service.

References

1. ISO 7498: "Information Processing Systems—Open Systems Interconnection—Basic Reference Model," January 1983.
2. CCITT Draft Recommendation X.200: "Reference Model of Open Systems Interconnection for CCITT Applications," March, 1984.
3. ISO/TC97/SC6/N2228: "The Internal Organization of the Network Layer," June 1981.
4. ISO/TC97/SC6/N2366: "The Internal Organization of the Network Layer," February 1982.
5. ISO/TC97/SC6/N2613: "The Internal Organization of the Network Layer," September 1982.
6. ISO/TC97/SC6/N2965: "Internal Organization of the Network Layer," October 1983.
7. ISO DIS 8348: "Information Processing Systems—Data Communications—Network Service Definition," November 1983.

8. CCITT Draft Recommendation X.213: "Network Service Definition of Open Systems Interconnection for CCITT Applications," March, 1984.

9. ISO/TC97/SC6/N2969: "Addendum to the Network Service Definition Covering Connectionless-Mode Transmission," September 1983.

10. ISODIS 8208: "Information Processing Systems—Data Communications—X.25 Packet Level Protocol for Data Terminal Equipment," September 1983.

11. ISO DP 8473: "Information Processing Systems—Data Communications—Protocol for Providing the Connectionless Network Service," September 1983.

12. ISO/TC97/SC6/N2964: "Information Processing Systems—Data Communications—X.25 (1980), Network Convergence Protocol," September 1983.

13. CCITT Recommendation X.25: "Interface Between Data Terminal Equipment (DTE) and Data Circuit Terminating Equipment (DCE) for Terminals Operating in the Packet Mode on Public Data Networks," Geneva, 1976 (amended 1980 and 1984).

14. CCITT Recommendation X.21: "Interface Between Data Terminal Equipment (DTE) and Data Circuit Terminating Equipment (DCE) for Synchronous Operation on Public Data Networks," Geneva, 1972 (amended 1976, 1980, and 1984).

15. CCITT Recommendation S.70: "Network Independent Basic Transport Service for Telematic Services," Geneva, 1980 (amended 1984).

16. ISO/TC97/SC6/N2743: "Provision of the OSI Network Service Using X.25 and X.21 (Using S70 Network Layer)," March 1983.

17. ISO/TC97/SC6/N2908: "Revision of N2743, Annex 2," September 1983.

18. ISO/TC97/SC6/N2981: "Use of X.25 over X.21 Networks," September 1983.

19. ISO/TC97/SC6/N2731: "Report of the ISO/TC97/SC6/WG2 Meeting, London, 14–18 March 1983," March 1983.

20. ISO/TC97/SC6/N3141: "Internal Organization of the Network Layer; April 1984," April 1984.

About the Author

Christine Hemrick received the B.S. degree in mathematics from North Carolina State University, Raleigh, in 1974. She has previously worked at the Research Triangle Institute in North Carolina from 1974 to 1976 and for Digital Equipment Corporation in Washington, D.C. from 1976 to 1979. While employed by Digital, she specialized in communications and real-time operating systems and was a Software Project Manager in the Government Projects Group. In 1979, she became a product engineer for GTE Telenet in Vienna, VA and began participating in international telecommunications standards activities. Upon its formation in 1981, she joined GTE Business Communications Systems as part of the Advanced Communications Planning Group. In 1983, Ms. Hemrick accepted a position with the National Telecommunications and Information Administration's Institute for Telecommunication Sciences. As a participant in CCITT, ISO, and ANSI, she has been an active contributor in a broad range of telecommunications standards efforts including work on Public Data Networks, Open System Interconnection (OSI), and Message Handling Systems (MHS). She has chaired the U.S. CCITT Working Party on Message Handling Systems and, since joining NTIA/ITS, has been responsible for coordinating U.S. participation in CCITT Study Group VII through the U.S. CCITT Study Group D.

OSI Addressing Strategies

Kai Jakobs
Technical University of Aachen, Informatik IV
Templergraben 64, 5100 Aachen, FRG
UUCP: ...seismo!unido!rwthinf!jakobs

Abstract

The paper presents a survey of addressing principles of the OSI/RM. Relevant OSI-specific terms and mechanisms are explained; the addressing capabilities of the seven layers are described.

1. Introduction

Recently, addressing has been realized as one of the most important and complicated issues in open systems communication. However, most attention has been paid to "tactical" (*how* to do it) problems like structure and length of the ISO Network Address. This paper, however, deals with addressing "strategies" (*what* to do).

In general, an address describes the location where a certain communication entity may be found. In order to guarantee clear identification, it has to be unambiguous throughout the whole network.

2. Addressing within OSI/RM

The OSI/RM [1] establishes a framework for the development of protocols and services for communication between open systems. It divides the complete communication tasks into seven hierarchical layers, from Physical Layer at the bottom up to Application Layer at the top.

The RM defines the term *"name"*. A name may be:

- a *title*, describing an entity which is neither a source nor a destination of data; e.g. a network-entity within a gateway.

- an *address*. An address always specifies an interface between two adjacent layers within one system. This interface is called *Service Access Point*, SAP.

- an *identificator* which defines any other object. This term is not considered in more detail within the RM, it might describe a DTE for example.

"OSI Addressing Strategies" ©1987, by K. Jacobs. Reprinted with author's permission.

Communication *between two open systems* is defined by a (horizontal) data transfer between entities in corresponding layers of the systems. (N)-layers communicate by using services provided by the (N-1)-layers.

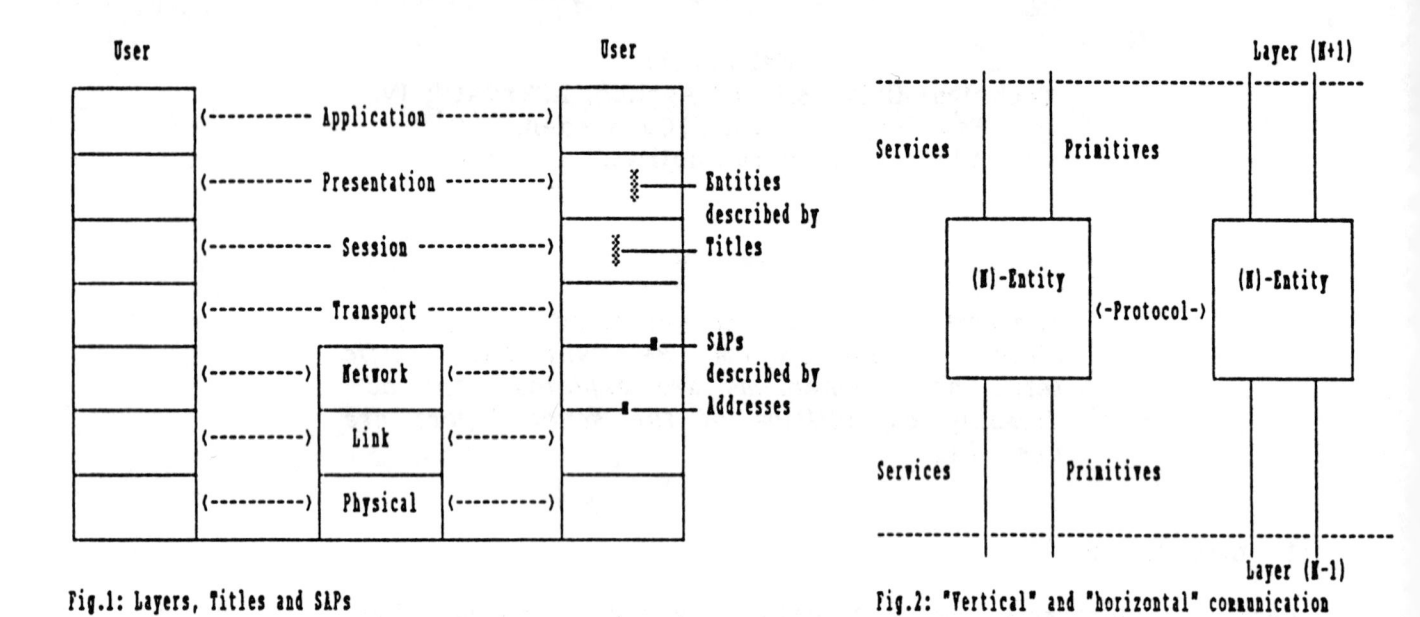

Fig.1: Layers, Titles and SAPs

Fig.2: "Vertical" and "horizontal" communication

Two adjacent layers *within the same system* communicate (vertically) via well-defined interfaces, the SAPs. This exchange of data uses so called *primitives*.

One primitive for example is the *Connection Request* (CR). By using this primitive, a (N+1)-entity indicates its wish to establish a (N)-connection with a remote (N+1)-entity. Inter alia, the CR conveys as parameters:

- the calling (N)-SAP address, i.e. the address that specifies the calling (N+1)-entity
- the called (N)-SAP address, specifying the remote (N+1)-entity

The (N)-entity maps these addresses onto (N-1)-SAP addresses and passes them to an appropriate (N-1)-entity.

Service Access Points and Connection Endpoint Identifiers

Besides the (N)-Service Access Points, the RM defines *(N)-Connection Endpoint Identifiers* (CEPIs). These two terms should not be mixed up:

- (N)-SAPs provide a means for identifying an entity

- (N)-CEPIs define the endpoint of a (N)-connection within one (N)-SAP. (N)-CEPIs are created locally by a (N)-entity at connection establishment time. Determination and maintenance of (N)-CEPIs is a local matter and not part of the (N)-layer protocol.

Using (N)-CEPIs, a (N+1)-entity distinguishes the (N)-connections accessible at that special SAP.

A (N)-CEPI is described consisting of two parts [2]:

- the (N)-address of the (N)-SAP
- the (N)-connection endpoint suffix, which is unambiguous within that SAP

The tuple (Transport-SAP-Address, T-Destination Reference), which maps onto a T-CEPI, might be regarded as an example.

3. Multiplexing

By definition, the use of CEPIs is required for multiplexing. The RM distinguishes between multiplexing

- within one (N+1)-<u>layer</u> (Fig. 3a)
  (N+1)-connections established by possibly several (N+1)-entities are mapped onto one (N)-connection.

- within one (N+1)-<u>entity</u> (Fig. 3b)
  (N+1)-connections established by one single entity within the (N+1)-layer are mapped onto one (N)-connection.

Depending on how multiplexing is realized within layer (N), a (N+1)-entity may be addressed via:

- one (N)-SAP between (N+1)-entity and (N)-layer (Fig 4a)
  there is only one address for the (N+1)-entity. The remote entity has to know this address. For the local entity having established several (N)-connections, each connection may be distinguished using the (N)-CEPIs determined by the supporting (N)-entity.

- many (N)-SAPs between (N+1)-entity and (N)-layer (Fig. 4b)
  now the (N+1)-entity may be accessed via several addresses (one address per SAP). The remote entity must have knowledge about at least one of these addresses.

The problem of multiplexing especially occurs at the Transport Layer:

ISO defines five classes of transport protocols with multiplexing-capability only in classes two, three and four. There are two alternatives for systems using transport protocols class zero or one:

- one Network-SAP per end-system
  the NSAP is attached exactly to one transport entity and there is no multiplexing capability within the Transport Layer. In other words, there is only one transport connection established at a time.

- several Network-SAPs per end-system
there may be as many transport connections as there are NSAPs. Each transport connection is mapped onto a different network connection. There is no need for multiplexing within the Transport Layer.

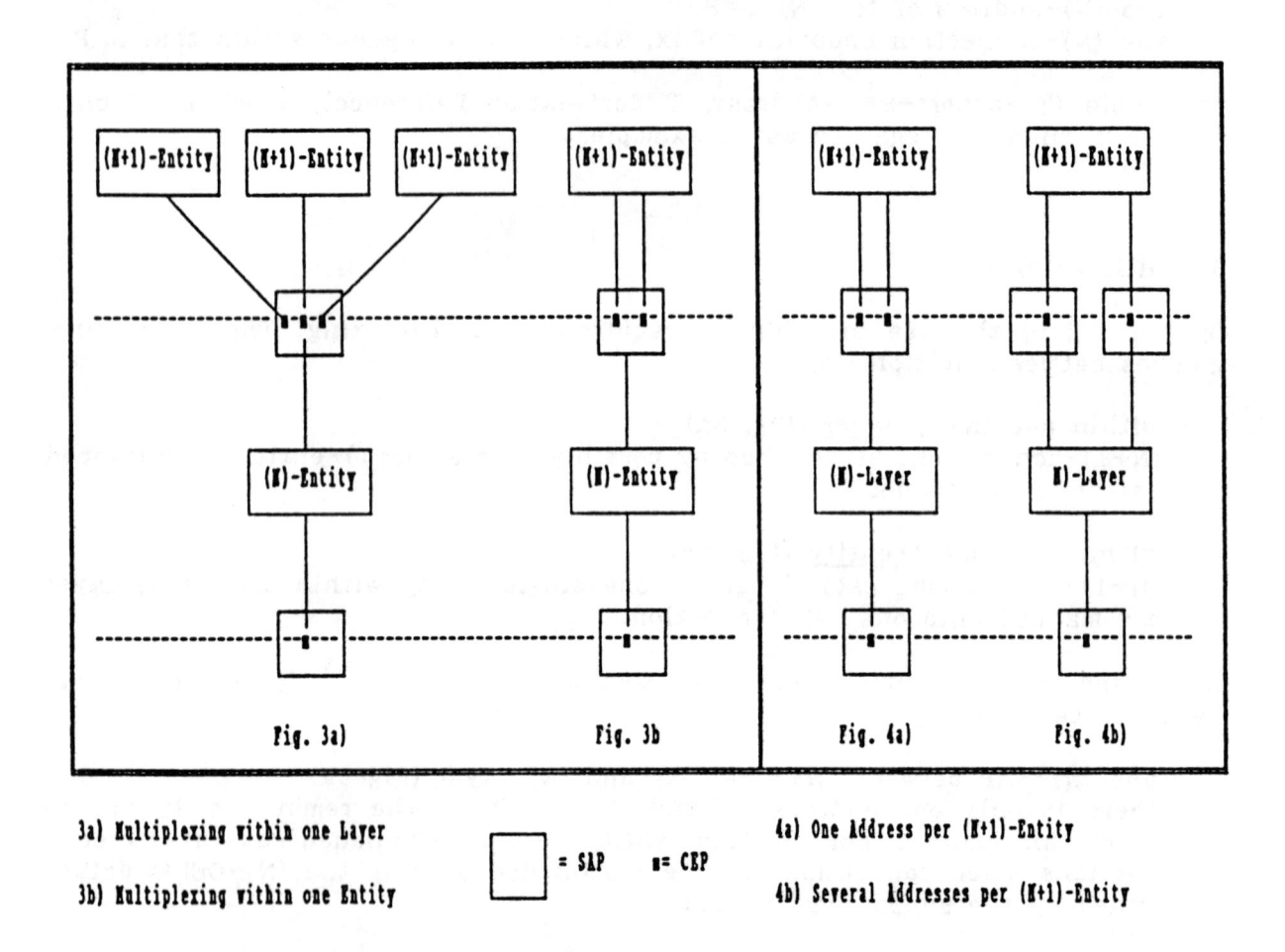

Fig. 3a) Fig. 3b) Fig. 4a) Fig. 4b)

3a) Multiplexing within one Layer

3b) Multiplexing within one Entity

☐ = SAP   ■ = CEP

4a) One Address per (N+1)-Entity

4b) Several Addresses per (N+1)-Entity

4. Addressing Capabilities within the layers

OSI demands an address to describe a SAP, i.e. the interface between two layers. The address of a (N)-SAP is constructed from the (N-1)-SAP address and a (N)-suffix.

Physical Layer and Link Layer

The RM requires no addressing capabilities within these layers (a problem may occur with Local Area Networks, for nearly all LANs provide an unambiguous Link Layer address). The Physical Layer, however, has to provide CEPIs in order to support several logical connections via asingle physical connection.

Network Layer

The Network Layer address implicitly describes the end-system. The RM requires global non-ambiguity.

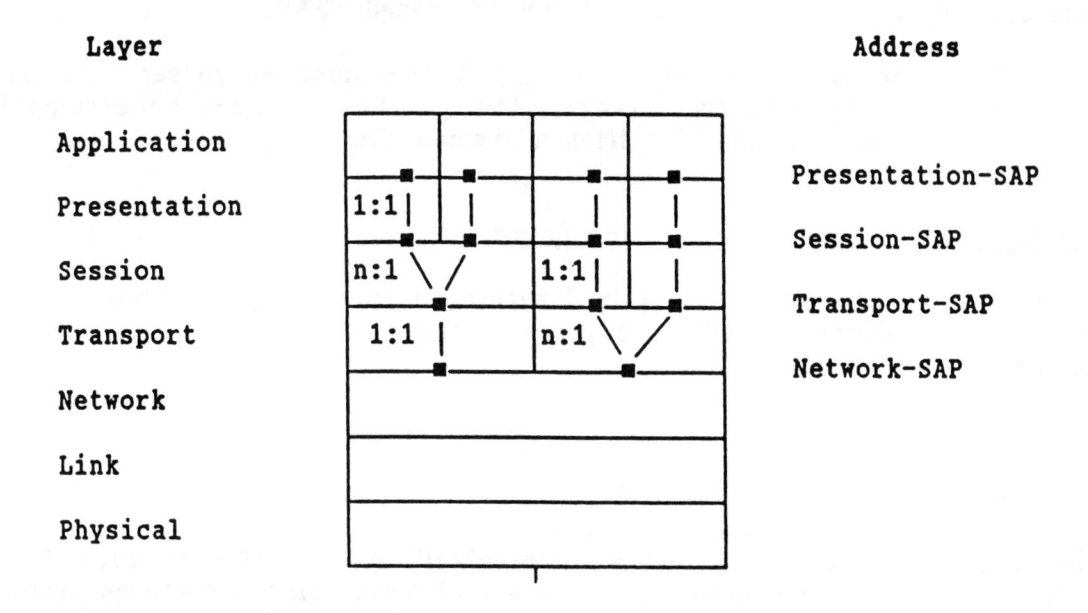

```
Layer                                                    Address

Application
                                                         Presentation-SAP
Presentation     1:1 |      |     |     |
                                                         Session-SAP
Session          n:1 \ /    1:1 | |     |
                                                         Transport-SAP
Transport        1:1 |      n:1 \ |     |
                                                         Network-SAP
Network

Link

Physical
```

Fig.6: Structure of the Application Process' Address
and some possible address-mappings

The Network Layer offers a subnetwork-independent service to the Transport Layer. In order to meet this complex task a subdivision into three sublayers 3a-3c has been defined by ISO [3]. The Network-SAP (NSAP) address is a 3c-address.

It might be useful to access several subnetworks via one common network-address (a gateway for many LANs for example). Therefore, mapping of subnetwork-specific 3a-addresses (Link Layer address in case of LANs) - which are not necessarily global unique - onto the NSAP-address is required.

There is no addressing capability within sublayer 3b, the Subnetwork Enhancement Layer.

Transport Layer and Session Layer

A many-to-one mapping occurs between TSAP address and NSAP address. An explicit transport address may be given at connection establishment time. If no address has been specified, a one-to-one mapping between network- and transport address is assumed [4].

In general, a transport address is constructed from network address plus a transport *selector* [5]. The selector specifies a transport entity that is attached to the addressed NSAP. The transport protocol does not specify the structure of the selector.

The transport entity analyzes the *Destination Reference* included in every Transport Protocol Data Unit (TPDU) and determines the corresponding transport connection within the scope of the addressed TSAP.

The RM demands a many-to-one mapping from session addresses onto transport addresses. In many systems, however, there is just a one-to-one mapping; i.e. the transport address also identifies a Session-SAP.

Presentation Layer and Application Layer

No addressing capability is required within the upper layers. Thus, the session address unambiguously defines a presentation entity as well as an application entity.

6. Summary

This paper pointed out the more "strategical" aspects of the addressing problem, i.e. the basic addressing principles and some related features provided by OSI/RM. Lenght and structure of the Network Layer Address – the more "tactical" aspects – have finally been standardized by CCITT.

References

[1]: ISO IS 7498
Open Systems Interconnection – Basic Reference Model, 1984

[2]: ISO/TC 97/SC 6/N 4052
Working Draft Addendum DAD3 to ISO 7498 on Naming and Addressing; 1986

[3]: ISO/TC 97/SC 6/N2727
Internal Organization of the Network Layer; 1983

[4]: ISO DIS 8073
Transport Protocol Specification, 1984

[5]: European Computer Manufacturer Association
ECMA TR/20: Layer 4 to 1 Addressing, 1984

ISDN Protocols for Connection Control

WENDY M. HARMAN AND CHERYL F. NEWMAN, MEMBER, IEEE

Abstract—The term Integrated Services Digital Network (ISDN) refers to the integration of various communication services that are transported over a single digital facility at the user–network interface. With ISDN, a user can have access to voice, circuit-switched data, or packet-switched data over one physical interface. ISDN provides communication control that allows users to request services while on a call, and to send and receive communication control messages independently of the voice, data, or video calls.

The ISDN concept has moved toward maturity over the past decade. The International Telegraph and Telephone Consultative Committee (CCITT), a technical standards organization of the United Nations, is responsible for establishing Recommendations that apply to aspects of international communication. The publication of the *Red Book* version of the ISDN Recommendations in 1985 instigated development of ISDN switches and the testing of ISDN with user trials. The ISDN Recommendations have been updated, are more complete, and include descriptions of many services. These updated ISDN Recommendations were published in the *Blue Book* version of the I-series Recommendations early in 1989.

The main focus of this paper is the description of the technical details of the ISDN access protocols for connection control. These protocols are the ISDN physical layer, link layer, and layer 3 which are documented in CCITT Recommendations I.430, I.441, and I.451, respectively.

This paper also describes other work that supports or enhances these protocols. In particular, coverage includes discussion of the ISDN protocol reference model and how it relates to the Open Systems Interconnection reference model, and a new CCITT Recommendation on service feature control on ISDN (Q.932). Possible uses of ISDN, possible evolution paths, and some outstanding issues related to ISDN are also described.

I. INTRODUCTION

THE term Integrated Services Digital Network (ISDN) refers to the integration of various communication services that are transported over a single digital facility at the user–network interface. With ISDN, a user can have access to voice, circuit-switched data, or packet-switched data over one physical interface. ISDN provides communication control that allows users to request services while on a call, and to send and receive communication control messages independently of the voice, data, or video calls.

The ISDN concept has moved toward maturity over the past decade. The International Telegraph and Telephone Consultative Committee (CCITT), a technical standards organization of the United Nations, is responsible for establishing Recommendations that apply to aspects of international communication. During the 1981–1984 CCITT study period, ISDN was first addressed in the international arena. The complete output of this work is in the I-series Recommendations of the *Red Book* [1]. The publication of the *Red Book* version of the ISDN Recommendations instigated development of ISDN switches and the testing of ISDN with user trials. The ISDN Recommendations have been updated and are more complete during the 1985–1988 CCITT Study period and include descriptions of many services. These updated ISDN Recommendations are in the *Blue Book* version of the I-series Recommendations published early in 1989.

Only the connection control protocols over access links to ISDN are addressed in this paper. The physical layer, the link layer, and "layer 3" are included. These protocol layers are defined to work at the S and T reference points which are logically defined by network termination functions (see Fig. 1). A T reference point occurs on the customer premises after the Network Termination 1 that provides the line termination, and optionally some multiplexing functions. The S reference point occurs on the customer premises after the optional Network Termination 2 that provides switching and multiplexing functions. The S and T reference points are generally called the "user–network interface."

This paper addresses the ISDN access protocols for connection control. Section II describes the ISDN protocol reference model and how it relates to the Open Systems Interconnection reference model. Technical details of the ISDN physical layer, link layer, and layer 3 protocols are addressed in Sections III, IV, and V. A new CCITT Recommendation on control of service features associated with connections (supplementary services) on ISDN (Recommendation Q.932) is summarized in Section VI. Possible uses of ISDN and possible evolution paths are described in Section VII, Section VIII discusses some outstanding issues related to ISDN, and Section IX briefly summarizes the paper.

II. ISDN PROTOCOL REFERENCE MODEL

The overall ISDN Generic Protocol Block architecture is shown in Fig. 2, representing three types of information with parallel protocol layering. The three types of information are control, user, and management, each of which is communicated independently of the others. The logical separation of the ISDN control information from user information through all layers stems from this ISDN protocol reference model. In contrast, the Open Systems Interconnection (OSI) model [2], [3] allows the separation of control from user information, but the OSI model does not *require* such a separation.

Manuscript received July 1, 1988; revised March 1, 1989.
The authors are with Bell Communications Research, Inc., Red Bank, NJ 07701.
IEEE Log Number 8929562.

Reprinted from *IEEE Journal on Selected Areas in Communications*, September 1989, pp. 1034–1042. ©1989 by The Institute of Electrical and Electronics Engineers, Inc. All rights reserved.

Fig. 1. S and T reference points.

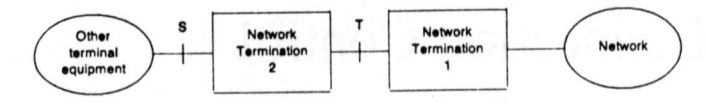

Network Termination 1: terminates the loop transmission, can perform other functions such as multiplexing
Network Termination 2 (optional): can perform functions such as switching and multiplexing

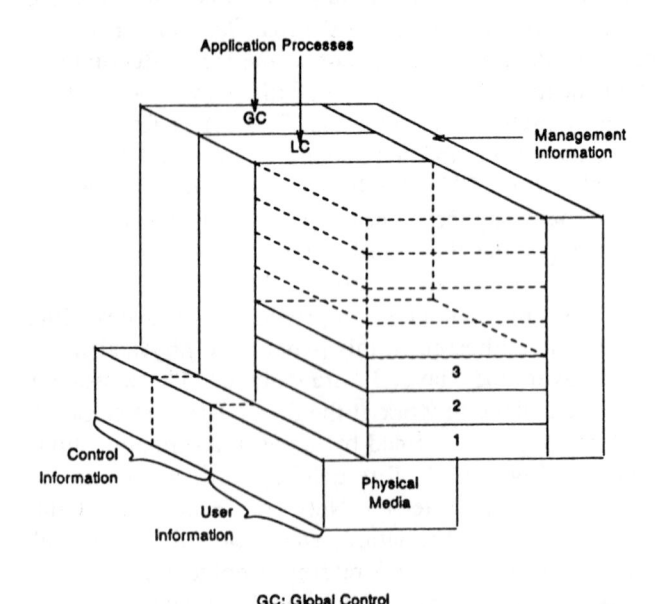

Fig. 2. Generic protocol block.

GC: Global Control
LC: Local Control

ISDN is designed to serve multiple applications, including voice, video, and data. Therefore, it is not practical for all layers to always provide functionality. While roughly modeled after OSI, the layers are explicitly not named. Adjacent layers within a type of information communicate using service primitives. However, if a layer is empty, the primitives are mapped directly onto primitives for the next nonempty layer.

In the *Blue Book* version of the ISDN protocol reference model (Recommendation I.320) [4], the concepts of local control and global control are introduced as refinements of the ISDN control information (see Fig. 2). Local control (LC) is control used between (logically) adjacent peer entities (within the same layer of protocol). Global control (GC) is used between two arbitrary peer entities where these entities are expected to be "remote" from each other. Coordination among all information types is accomplished using the management information type.

III. Physical Layer

ISDN currently has two physical layer interface specifications, the basic rate user-network interface and the primary rate user-network interface. In both interfaces, layer primitives are defined whose primary function is to activate and deactivate the physical layer, providing service to the link layer.

The basic rate interface physical layer is defined in Recommendation I.430 [4] as 192 kbits/s with well-defined framing.[1] The most common structure on the basic rate interface provides "$2B + D$," two 64 kbit/s information transport channels (called B channels) and one 16 kbit/s packetized control and information transport channel (called a D channel). At least two features in the basic rate interface are worthy of note with respect to higher layer protocols and services:

1) Customer premises multipoint configurations are supported ("Passive Bus") allowing contention for the use of the local (intrapremises) transmission facility.

2) D-channel signaling messages are given priority over other D-channel messages as a matter of policy governing the interactions between Layer 2 and Layer 1.

The primary rate interface physical layer is defined in Recommendation I.431 [4] as either 1544 kbits/s or 2048 kbits/s, each of which has well-defined framing. The most common structures on the primary rate access interface are "$23B + D$" and "$30B + D$," respectively, where the D channel is 64 kbits/s. On the primary rate interface, only point-to-point configurations of terminating equipment are supported, and no priority scheme exists on D-channel messaging.

IV. Link Layer

The purpose of the ISDN Link Access Procedure on the D channel (LAPD) is to provide the OSI layer 2 functionality of guaranteeing data integrity of information passed by layer 3 over the ISDN user-network interface. The general aspects of the ISDN user-network interface link layer are described in Recommendations I.440 (duplicated in Q.920) [5], including the layer services expected from the physical layer and provided to the network layer with the associated primitives. The link layer service is based on OSI's Data Link Layer Service [2], providing efficient and timely data transfer, link synchronization, error detection and correction, flow control, frame sequencing, and addressing for multiplexing.

Link layer procedures for LAPD are given in Recommendation I.441 (duplicated in Q.921) [5]. LAPD evolved from a basis in the Recommendation X.25 layer 2 protocol called LAPB [6]. In particular, the ISDN LAPD protocol supports multiple Layer 3 entities and multiple terminal equipments on one interface using octets of addressing via Data Link Connection Identifiers (DLCI's). DLCI's have two octets, the Service Access Point Identifier (SAPI) in the high-order octet, and the Terminal Endpoint Identifier (TEI) in the low-order octet. LAPD supports multiple frame operation with modulo 128 for point-to-point information transfer associated with most call control. Unacknowledged information procedures in LAPD handle broadcast information transfer for initial call setup to a passive bus from the network. Fig. 3 shows the

---
[1]Line format is not part of the user-network interface since line formats operate between Network Termination 1 and the Network (see Fig. 1).

Fig. 3. LAPD information frame structure.

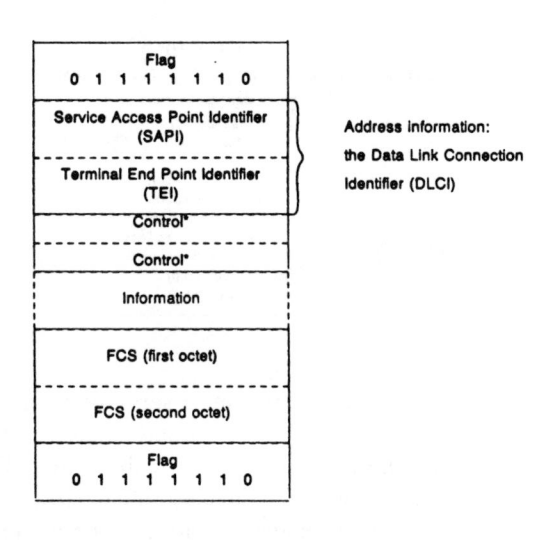

*Unacknowledged operation - one octet
Multiple frame operation - two octets for frames with sequence numbers
- one octet for frames without sequence numbers

LAPD information frame structure that carries the layer 3 protocol information in the Information octets.

Currently, there are four values of SAPI defined for use (all others are reserved):
- SAPI = 0: used for signaling,
- SAPI = 1: reserved for packet communications using I.451 (Q.931) call control procedures,
- SAPI = 16: used for packet communications conforming to X.25 level 3 procedures, and
- SAPI = 63: used for layer 2 management procedures.

Thus, in most implementations, for D-channel X.25 information transfer, X.25 layer 3 procedures are indicated at the data link layer by a SAPI value of 16. Those X.25 frames are routed based on recognition of this layer 2 SAPI to an X.25 packet handling function.

V. Layer 3

Recommendation I.450 (duplicated in Q.930) [7] describes general aspects of the ISDN layer 3 protocol.[2] This Recommendation explains the services expected from the data link layer by layer 3, and lists the peer functions of the layer 3, for example, network connection control and conveying user-to-network and network-to-user information.

The layer 3 protocol, specified in Recommendation I.451 (duplicated in Q.931) [7], is the key to ISDN call control. The layer 3 procedures deal with
- circuit-switched calls where the services are described in Recommendation I.231 [8] (type "C"),
- packet-switched calls based on Recommendation I.462 (X.31) [6][3] where the services are described in Recommendation I.232 [8] (type "P"), and

[2] Again, the ISDN protocols do not strictly adhere to OSI, so this protocol is not called a "network layer."
[3] Procedures described in I.462 (X.31) provide ISDN access control for calls providing X.25 service.

- user signaling connections, also known as user-to-user signaling not associated with a circuit-switched call (type "S"). No service descriptions are provided for these connections in the current I-series Recommendations.

In addition, link restart procedures for an entire DLCI have layer 3 messages and procedures defined (type "G" for global).

Messages for call control and their applicability by call type are listed in Table I.

Layer 3 messages are comprised of information elements. Fig. 4 shows the four information elements that appear in each layer 3 message in the same order: Protocol discriminator, Length of call reference value, Call reference value, and Message type information elements. In the general message structure, these common information elements have the following functions:

- *Protocol discriminator:* Distinguishes messages for ISDN user-network call control from other messages (for example, X.25).

- *Call reference value:* Identifies the call request or facility registration/cancellation request at the local user-network interface to which the particular message applies. The call reference does not have end-to-end significance across ISDN's. Two special cases are noteworthy. First is the case where the message has no third octet (that is, technically the message has no call reference octet), and the second octet (length of call reference value) is all zeros. This case is referred to as the all-zero (dummy) call reference value and is reserved for Q.932 supplementary service procedures which will be discussed in Section VI. The second case is the global call reference, used for link restart procedures, which has a meaningful second octet in a message (giving a nonzero call reference length), but the numerical value of the call reference itself is zero, triggering applicability of the message to all call references associated with the DLCI.

- *Message type:* Identifies the function of the message being sent. These are the messages listed in Table I.

Within this overall structure, some messages are pivotal in basic call control for computer communications: SETUP, CONNECT, DISCONNECT, and RELEASE.

Each of these messages will be described in Section V-A. Section V-B treats some of their key information elements, while Table II contains a brief summary of all the information elements associated directly with call control. Table III lists those information elements associated with control of features (supplementary services). Typical message sequences for 64 kbit/s unrestricted calling appear in Section V-C.

A. Message Contents

Message contents for certain key call control messages provide insight into the detail of the control a user can exert over an ISDN connection.

1) SETUP Message Contents: The SETUP message is sent by the calling user to the network and by the network to the called user to initiate call establishment for bearer

TABLE I

MESSAGES FOR CALL CONTROL

Message	Applicability C	P	S	G
Call establishment messages:				
ALERTING	yes	yes	yes	no
CALL PROCEEDING	yes	yes	yes	no
CONNECT	yes	yes	yes	no
CONNECT ACKNOWLEDGE	yes	yes	yes	no
PROGRESS	yes	yes	no	no
SETUP	yes	yes	yes	no
SETUP ACKNOWLEDGE	yes	no	yes	no
Call information phase messages:				
SUSPEND	yes	no	no	no
SUSPEND ACKNOWLEDGE	yes	no	no	no
SUSPEND REJECT	yes	no	no	no
RESUME	yes	no	no	no
RESUME ACKNOWLEDGE	yes	no	no	no
RESUME REJECT	yes	no	no	no
USER INFORMATION	yes	no	yes	no
Call clearing messages:				
DISCONNECT	yes	yes	no	no
RELEASE	yes	yes	yes	no
RELEASE COMPLETE	yes	yes	yes	no
RESTART	no	no	no	yes
RESTART ACKNOWLEDGE	no	no	no	yes
Miscellaneous messages:				
CONGESTION CONTROL	yes	no	yes	no
FACILITY	yes	no	no	no
INFORMATION	yes	no	yes	no
NOTIFY	yes	no	no	no
STATUS	yes	yes	yes	yes
STATUS INQUIRY	yes	yes	yes	no

C - circuit
P - packet
S - signaling
G - global reset

Protocol discriminator		
0 0 0 0	Length of call reference value (in octets)	
Call reference value		
0	Message type	
Other information elements as required		

Fig. 4. General message organization example.

TABLE II

SUMMARY OF INFORMATION ELEMENT USES

Information Element Identification	Use
Bearer capability	Transport specification
Call state	Error recovery
Called party number	Network destination addressing
Called party subaddress	Full destination addressing
Calling party number	Network source addressing
Calling party subaddress	Full source addressing
Cause	Reasons for a message and diagnostics
Channel identification	Specification controlled channel
Congestion level	Signaling service congestion indication
Display	Sending network-to-user ASCII information
End-to-end transit delay	End-to-end delay selection
High layer compatibility	End-to-end layer 4-7 descriptions
Information rate	Throughput class indication
Keypad facility	Sending user-to-network ASCII information
Low layer compatibility	End-to-end layer 1-3 descriptions
More data	Indication of blocks of end-to-end user information
Notification indicator	Unacknowledged network-to-user information
Packet layer binary parameters	Listing requested layer 3 parameter values
Packet layer window size	Window value
Packet size	Maximum packet size
Progress indicator	Interworking between networks
Redirecting number	Number from which call diversion occurs
Repeat indicator	Indication of prioritized, repeated information elements
Restart indicator	Identification of class of facility for restart
Segmented message	Indication of overall message too long for one frame
Sending complete	Indication of end of called party number
Signal	Triggering of special indications, such as tones
Transit delay selection and indication	Transit network delay selection
Transit network selection	Designation of desired transport networks
User-user	Transmission of user-to-user unrestricted information

TABLE III

SUPPLEMENTARY SERVICE CONTROL RELATED INFORMATION ELEMENTS

Call identity
Date/time
Facility
Feature activation
Feature indication
Invoke component
Network-specific facilities
Return error component
Return result component
Switchhook

services (fundamental transport services such as speech). As such, the message has information associated with the end-to-end establishment of a call (''global'' significance). Associated with that establishment, other information related to features (called ''supplementary services'' such as call waiting) may also be included. That information may, for example, be of local significance only.

Table IV summarizes the use of information elements in the SETUP message:

- information element name,
- direction in which the messages flow (network to user, user to network, or both),
- an indication of whether the information element is mandatory or optional, and
- indications of applicability [circuit-switched calling (*C*), I.462 (X.31)-based packet-switched calling (*P*), user signaling calling (*S*)].

The order of the information elements in Table IV is the order in which they would appear in an actual SETUP message. The rules for using the optional information elements are detailed in I.451 (Q.931).

2) CONNECT Message Contents: The CONNECT message is sent by the called user to the network and by the network to the calling user to indicate call acceptance for circuit-switched calls (type *C*) and for user signaling calls (type *S*). Thus, for these connections, CONNECT has global significance. For I.462 (X.31) packet-switched calls, CONNECT has only local significance, signifying acceptance of the access connection to the packet network. CONNECT messages, depending on the application, can have the following information elements in addition to the common header information elements (Fig. 4):

- Channel identification,
- Facility,
- Progress indicator,
- Display,
- Signal,
- Switchhook,
- Feature activation,
- Feature indication,
- Low layer compatibility,
- User-user.

3) DISCONNECT Message Contents: For circuit-switched calls, the DISCONNECT message is sent by the user to request the network to clear an end-to-end con-

TABLE IV
SETUP MESSAGE CONTENTS

Information Element	Direction	Usage	Applicability
Protocol discriminator	both	Mandatory	C,P,S
Call reference	both	Mandatory	C,P,S
Message type	both	Mandatory	C,P,S
Sending complete	both	Optional	C,S
Repeat indicator	both	Optional	C
Bearer capability	both	Mandatory	C,P,S
Channel identification	both	Optional	C,P,S
Facility	both	Optional	C
Progress indicator	both	Optional	C,P
Network specific facilities	both	Optional	C,S
Display	n→u	Optional	C,P,S
Keypad facility	u→n	Optional	C,S
Signal	n→u	Optional	C
Switchhook	u→n	Optional	C
Feature activation	u→n	Optional	C
Feature indication	n→u	Optional	C
Information rate	n→u	Optional	P
End-end transit delay	n→u	Optional	P
Transit delay selection and indication	n→u	Optional	P
Packet layer binary parameters	n→u	Optional	P
Packet layer window size	n→u	Optional	P
Packet size	n→u	Optional	P
Calling party number	both	Optional	C,P,S
Calling party subaddress	both	Optional	C,P,S
Called party number	both	Optional	C,P,S
Called party subaddress	both	Optional	C,P,S
Transit network selection	u→n	Optional	C,S
Redirecting number	n→u	Optional	P
Low layer compatibility	both	Optional	C,S
High layer compatibility	both	Optional	C,S
User-user	both	Optional	C,P,S

nection or is sent by the network to indicate that the end-to-end connection is cleared. For these connections, DISCONNECT has global significance. For I.462 (X.31)-based packet-switched calls, the DISCONNECT message has local significance only and is sent by the user to request the network to clear an access connection or is sent by the network to the user to indicate that the access connection has been cleared. The DISCONNECT message has no applicability in user signaling calls. DISCONNECT messages, depending on the application, can have the following information elements in addition to the common header information elements (Fig. 4):
- Cause,
- Facility,
- Progress indicator,
- Display,
- Signal,
- Feature indication,
- User-user.

4) RELEASE Message Contents: For all call types, the RELEASE message is sent by the user or the network to indicate that the receiving equipment should release the channel and prepare to release the call reference after sending a RELEASE COMPLETE message as a local RELEASE acknowledgment. For circuit-switched calls, the RELEASE message also indicates that the equipment sending the message has disconnected the channel, thus providing a local acknowledgment for the DISCONNECT message. For I.462 (X.31) packet-switched calls, when channel negotiation is used to establish the terminating channel to deliver the X.25 call, the RELEASE message is sent by the network to the user to indicate that the X.25 call itself has been delivered on either the *D* channel or an existing, active channel, and that the network intends to release the call reference used to negotiate the channel.

RELEASE messages, depending on the application, can have the following information elements in addition to the common header information elements (Fig. 4):
- Cause,
- Facility,
- Display,
- Signal,
- Feature indication,
- User-user.

B. Key Information Elements

The messages outlined above are constructed from information elements, some of which have functions that are intuitive from their names (see Tables II and III). Several are not so intuitive, including the Bearer capability information element used in the SETUP message (see Table IV), a backbone element in call control that will be described in detail. Several other important information elements will be discussed as well, namely, Calling and Called party number, Calling and Called party subaddress, Cause, Channel identification, High layer compatibility, User-user, and Information rate.

1) Bearer Capability Information Element: The Bearer capability informtaion element indicates a requested fundamental transport service, called a "bearer service" (I.231 and I.232) to be provided by the network. In addition, the Bearer capability information element contains detailed information on protocol options at each layer to construct the desired service. The network is expected to use[4] the bearer capability information, for example, in call routing. Fig. 5 lists the contents of the Bearer capability information element. The remainder of Section V-B1) describes the details of the Bearer capability information element, as shown in Fig. 5. The first two octets of the Bearer capability information element show some common aspects with all other information elements: the information element identifier and the length of the information element.

The third octet contains a coding standard indication. In addition, the third octet has the information transfer capability, stating that the associated call can be handled as one of the following: speech, 3.1 kHz audio, 7 kHz audio, unrestricted digital information, restricted digital information, or video. These transfer capabilities are frequently referred to as bearer services and are described in detail in Recommendations I.231 [8] and I.232 [8].

Octets 4, 4a, and 4b describe different aspects of the information transfer. Recognized transfer modes in octet 4 are circuit mode or packet mode. Also in octet 4, information transfer rates describe the bandwidth allocated to the circuit call (namely, 64 kbits/s, 2 × 64 kbits/s, 384

[4]This is in contrast to several other information elements whose contents the network effectively ignores.

Bearer capability Information element identifier					Octet 1
Length of the bearer capability contents					2
1 ext	coding standard	information transfer capability			3
0/1 ext	transfer mode	information transfer rate			4
0/1 ext	structure	configuration		establishment	4a
1 ext	symmetry	information transfer rate (destination → origination)			4b
0/1 ext	0	1	user information layer 1 protocol		5
0/1 ext	synch/ asynch	negot	user rate		5a V.110/V.120
0/1 ext	intermediate rate	NIC on Tx	NIC on Rx	Flow control on Tx	Flow control on Rx	0	5b V.110 only
0/1 ext	Hdr/ no Hdr	Multi frame support	Mode	LLI negot	As'nor/ As'nee	In/Out band negot	0	5b V.120 only
0/1 ext	number of stop bits	number of data bits	Parity		5c V.110/V.120
1 ext	duplex mode	modem type			5d V.110/V.120
1 ext	1	0	user information layer 2 protocol		6
1 ext	1	1	user information layer 3 protocol		7

Fig. 5. Bearer capability information element contents.

kbits/s, 1536 kbits/s, and 1920 kbits/s). For packet calls, information transfer rate is only a place holder. All octets *after* octet 4 are optional, with information supplied, as necessary, by defaults or by the user under circumstances detailed in I.451 (Q.931).

"Structure," contained in octet 4a, provides information on synchronization:
• explicit invocation of 8 kHz integrity, indicating the timing for framing;
• explicit invocation of service data unit integrity, indicating frame delimiting done by flags;
• default choice, governed by transfer mode choice:
  —for circuit mode: 8 kHz integrity;
  —for packet mode: service data unit integrity;
• explicit statement of unstructured.

Currently, the remainder of octet 4a and octet 4b only supports point-to-point configurations with on-demand establishment providing bidirectional symmetric transfer. Network implications for asymmetric and unidirectional traffic are for further study.

Octet 5 is used to indicate the coding rule followed for the information transfer capability (for example, Recommendation G.711 [9] for speech, Recommendation I.462 (X.31) for flag stuffing, Recommendation V.120 [10] for asynchronous rate adaption, Recommendation V.110 [10] for synchronous rate adaption, or non-CCITT standardized rate adaption). Rate adaption is the process by which user information streams encoded according to earlier (pre-ISDN) Recommendations become transferable on an ISDN channel. Multiple techniques have been standardized (in X.31 in [6], and in V.110 and V.120 both in [10]), with the choice depending on the type of application.

Octet 5a includes synchronous/asynchronous indicators that can be used for ambiguous coding indications, and negotiation indications that are used with the V.110 standard. Octet 5a also contains the user rate showing the base rate from which rate adaption occurs. Octet 5b deals with details of the chosen rate adaption technique and takes two forms, one used with V.110 (synchronous rate adaption) and the other used with V.120 (asynchronous rate adaption). For example, "NIC on Tx" is Network Independent Clock on Transmission, and "LLI negot" simply asks whether or not the default Logical Link Identifier will be used. Octets 5c and 5d contain, for both V.110 and V.120 use, number of stop bits, number of data bits, parity information, indication of half or full duplex, and modem type indication (based on network-specific support).

Octet 6 covers layer 2 use (I.441 (Q.921) or layer 2 of X.25). Similarly, octet 7 indicates layer 3 use, either I.451 (Q.931) or layer 3 of X.25.

2) Other Important Information Elements: Many other information elements gain importance in various contexts, including Calling/Called party number information elements, Calling/Called party subaddress information elements, Cause information element, Channel identification information element, High layer compatibility information element, User–user information element, and Information rate information element. Important aspects of each are discussed in this section. Information elements not discussed are not as important to understanding the fundamental functions of I.451 (Q.931).

Calling/Called party number information elements identify the subnetwork address of the origination and destination of the call. The most striking feature of these information elements is the inclusion of the numbering plan identification field, allowing indication of different numbering plans (for example, Recommendation X.121 [11] for Public Data Networks and E.164 [12] for the ISDN era).

Calling/Called party subaddress information elements include 20 octets for the subaddress. In addition, these information elements also have a *type* of subaddress indicator, allowing either Network Service Access Point (NSAP) (X.213 [2]) addresses or user-specified values (for example, four digit Private Branch Exchange extension number). Thus, subaddresses are defined by the users and can be used to address individual communicating end points (for example, specific terminals) or groups of end points (for example, sets of terminals).

The *Cause* information element provides the reason for generating the associated message and diagnostic information, and also the "location" of the cause originator. "Location" may be, for example, a local private network, a local public network, or somewhere unidentifiable beyond an interworking point. Cause information may be one of the 52 values (ranging from "normal call

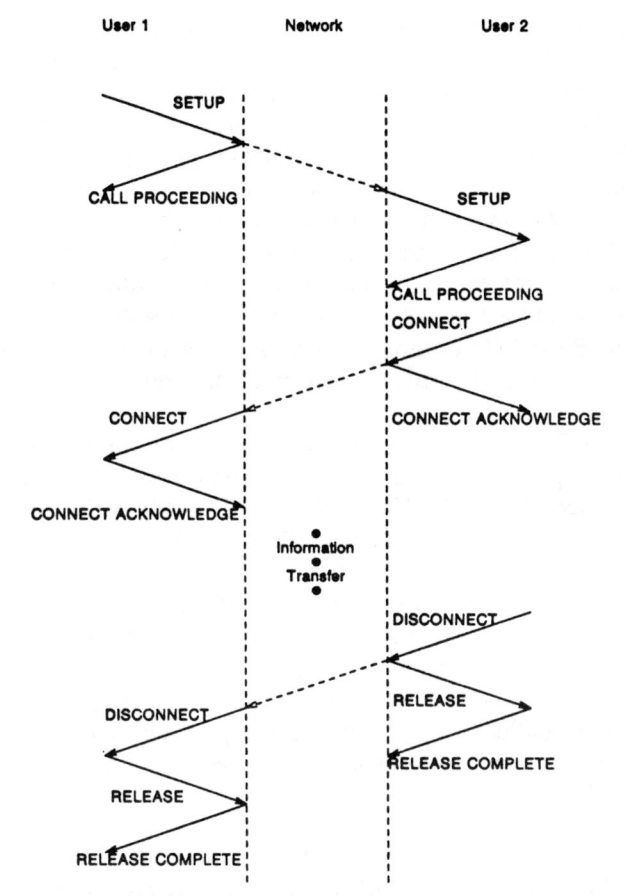

Fig. 6. Typical example message sequence for call control.

Most information elements dealing with I.462 (X.31) packet communications are used at the destination interface when negotiating the channel on which to terminate an incoming X.25 call. Some X.25 call request packet contents are mapped into I.451 (Q.931) information elements for inclusion in terminating SETUP message. One of those information elements is the *Information rate* information element, containing throughput class information.

C. Typical Message Sequences for Call Control

For circuit-switched, on-demand 64 kbit/s unrestricted service, Fig. 6 depicts a typical minimum call control message sequence with information transfer phase. In this figure, SETUP, CONNECT, DISCONNECT, and RELEASE messages have already been introduced. CALL PROCEEDING, CONNECT ACKNOWLEDGE, and RELEASE COMPLETE messages are local acknowledgments for those messages.

VI. SUPPLEMENTARY SERVICES CONTROL

Recommendation Q.932 [7] is a new Recommendation for the *Blue Book*, containing generic procedures for the control of ISDN supplementary services. Supplementary services provide additional capabilities to be used in conjunction with telecommunications services (in a Recommendation I.451 (Q.931) context, bearer capability). Supplementary services cannot be offered to a customer on a standalone basis. Desirable connection control-oriented supplementary services are hold and conferencing. Thus, the Q.932 procedures are carefully interleaved with those for I.451 (Q.931).

Q.932 identifies three major methods by which supplementary services may be controlled, namely,
- Keypad,
- Feature key management, and
- Functional.

The first two methods are classed as "stimulus," where individual keystrokes (Keypad) or button pressing (Feature key management) are used to trigger service operation. Such operation is seen to entail little more than, in effect, identifying the service request to the network. Terminals that operate essentially like today's voice telephones are envisioned to use these methods.

For service requests entailing more complicated invocation or activation or for terminals that have a means of supporting more than simple button pressing/keypad operation, "functional" methods are envisioned. For data applications, most interest focuses around these functional methods, which are currently least defined. The intention, as stated in Q.932, is to use a message, FACILITY, and a Facility information element to accomplish the service activation (desire for the service to start), invocation (service actually used), and deactivation. The functional methods are adapted from the OSI Remote Operations [2], [3].

clearing" to "protocol error, unspecified") from those specified in the I.451 (Q.931) code set or any others specified in standardized code sets.

The *Channel identification* information element allows identification of an information *channel* (for example, a B channel) whose connections are to be controlled by I.451 (Q.931) procedures on a separate D channel. The information channel may be in the same ISDN interface as the controlling D channel or in a separate interface. The information element contains a field for use in identifying a separate information channel interface, if needed. Channel choices may be either exclusive or negotiable as indicated in the information element.

The *High layer compatibility* information element supplies the type terminal that is on the user side of an S/T interface. The network transports this information transparently end-to-end. In particular, telematic terminals (defined by CCITT [13]–[16]) can be specified using this information element. Identified telematic terminals support telephony, facsimile (groups 2 and 3), facsimile (group 4), teletex, videotex, mixed mode communication (text and facsimile), message handling, and telex.

The *User-user* information element conveys up to 128 octets of information between ISDN end users. The network does not interpret contents of this information element. Presence of this information element helps support the OSI network service [2] across an ISDN.

Despite their inclusion in the *Blue Book*, the functional methods described in Q.932 are still evolving and will be studied further in the 1989-1992 CCITT study period.

VII. Uses and Evolution

Current uses for ISDN are built around the bearer services, which are themselves evolving, along with their control capabilities.

A. Uses

With ISDN, a user can have access to voice, circuit-switched data, packet-switched data, or video over one interface. The ISDN protocols for connection control and a variety of protocol supported applications have been tested and verified in several recent trials of ISDN.

The Bearer capability information element in I.451 (Q.931) was described in detail in Section V-B1) of this paper, including its use in selecting some of the standard bearer services [8]. Several standard ISDN bearer services currently support data communication applications in ISDN environments. The virtual call and permanent virtual circuit bearer services support X.25 packet-switched services via I.462 (X.31) interface control. 64 kbit/s unrestricted bearer services support circuit-switched, transparent transmission at 64 and 56 kbits/s. Support for transparent private lines has not been the subject of detailed service standards but has been emulated and tested in ISDN trials. The 3.1 kHz audio bearer service supports voice band data circuit-switched point-to-point calling.

User data applications that use these ISDN transport capabilities include: file transfer, billing applications, PC networking, simultaneous voice and data, remote computer access, high-speed facsimile, electronic mail, LAN interconnection via ISDN, and wide area networks. Voice applications using these transport capabilities include 7 kHz (high-quality) audio, encrypted voice, and "plain" voice.

In addition, the fact that the ISDN protocol reference model and the I.451 (Q.931) protocol implementation supports much of the OSI network service leads to other network capabilities that are very useful in data applications. In particular, ISDN calling number delivery and user-to-user signaling in conjunction with call control have many applications in data communications, including use in security screening. Furthermore, the ISDN user-to-user signaling supplementary services can also be used over the *D* channel in association with a circuit-switched call active on the *B* channel.

B. Evolution

To date, Recommendation I.451 (Q.931) control procedures have been developed to handle circuit-mode, point-to-point, on-demand, bidirectional symmetric calls for 64 kbit/s calls using *B*-channel access on either basic rate or primary rate interfaces. For packet mode, the current I.451 (Q.931) procedures primarily handle the establishment of local *B* channels accessing packet switches, supporting X.25 call control once the access has been established. Recommendation I.451 (Q.931) is approaching stability for control of these narrowband connections.

Thus, areas of extension to I.451 (Q.931), that are likely for standards activity in the 1989-1992 CCITT study period are in two major areas.

1) *H*0 (384 kbit/s) and *H*1 (1.536 Mbit/s and 1.920 Mbit/s) end-to-end circuit-mode, on-demand, bidirectional symmetric calls are to be defined further with primary rate access interfaces. Also, a use will be defined for *H*0 and *H*1 channels to access packet switches to carry some form of virtual call/permanent virtual circuit service.

2) Diverse needs of the data communications market have spurred exploratory work on additional packet bearer services during the 1985-1988 CCITT study period, leading to I.122 [8], a framework description for further work on some select packet bearer services. The proposed packet services all use I.451 (Q.931) call control over the local access. The differences between these packet services are in the data transfer phase of the services.

In addition, Recommendation Q.932 (or related Recommendations) will have explicit procedures to handle specific, key supplementary services such as hold and conferencing.

VIII. Issues

To date, work on ISDN protocols has been primarily devoted to connection establishment and ongoing control. Little work has been done on the issue of assuring that the terminal equipments connected to the ISDN will be able to communicate intelligibly. Particularly in the computer communication world, the variety of end systems and terminal equipment brings the need for intelligible interconnection to the forefront. Several ideas (such as directory numbers, subaddressing, and mandatory high-layer compatibility) have been proposed for helping to resolve the resultant problems; however, compatibility is still an open issue.

In addition, broadband applications will require a streamlined protocol for ordinary activities and will demand higher performance criteria. Such a broadband protocol may be a new development since it must be optimized for high-speed data of the sort envisioned for wide-area LAN interconnections and video transport. In broadband applications, multimedia, multipoint communications are likely to be common. Making such communications easy and simultaneously meeting on-demand performance criteria provides new requirements on a communications control protocol [17]. However, since existing applications are also likely to be used on broadband interfaces, many of the lessons learned from the development of ISDN may be of use in the specification of protocols for broadband.

IX. Summary

To date, work on ISDN connection control has developed a protocol architecture and a set of control protocols handling various types of circuit and packet calls. These are detailed in this paper. In addition, work has been done on a set of generic protocols for handling supplementary service control.

Future work for protocols dealing with direct extensions to those detailed in this paper will cover $H0$ and $H1$ channel control and additional packet bearer services.

Extensions to I.451 (Q.931)-based connection control per se are unlikely to handle terminal compatibility or broadband. Terminal compatibility for data uses will require stronger tie-ins with OSI, and broadband may require an entirely new protocol architecture. Both these issues are likely to be studied extensively by CCITT over the next four years.

References

[1] CCITT, *Red Book*, vol. III, fascicle III.5, "Integrated Services Digital Network (ISDN)," Recommendations of the I-series, Geneva, Switzerland, 1985.
[2] CCITT, *Blue Book*, vol. VIII, fascicle VIII.4, "Data communication networks: Open Systems Interconnection (OSI)—Model and notation, service definition," Recommendations X.200-X.219, Geneva, Switzerland, 1989.
[3] CCITT, *Blue Book*, vol. VIII, fascicle VIII.5, "Data communication networks: Open Systems Interconnection (OSI)—Protocol specification, conformance testing," Recommendations X.220-X.290, Geneva, Switzerland, 1989.
[4] CCITT, *Blue Book*, vol. III, fascicle III.8, "Integrated Services Digital Network (ISDN)—Overall network aspects and function, user-network interface," Recommendations I.310-I.470, Geneva, Switzerland, 1989.
[5] CCITT, *Blue Book*, vol. VI, fascicle VI.10, "Digital access signalling system, Network layer," Recommendations Q.920-Q.921, Geneva, Switzerland, 1989.
[6] CCITT, *Blue Book*, vol. VIII, fascicle VIII.2, "Data communication networks: Services and facilities interfaces," Recommendations X.2-X.32, Geneva, Switzerland, 1989.
[7] CCITT, *Blue Book*, vol. VI, fascicle VI.11, "Digital access signalling system, network layer, user-network management," Recommendations Q.930-Q.940, Geneva, Switzerland, 1989.
[8] CCITT, *Blue Book*, vol. III, fascicle III.7, "Integrated Services Digital Network (ISDN)—General characteristics and service aspects," Recommendations I.110-I.254, Geneva, Switzerland, 1989.
[9] CCITT, *Blue Book*, vol. III, fascicle III.4, "General aspects of digital transmission systems; Terminal equipments," Recommendations G.700-G.722, Geneva, Switzerland, 1989.
[10] CCITT, *Blue Book*, vol. VIII, fascicle VIII.1, "Data communication over the telephone network," Series V Recommendations, Geneva, Switzerland, 1989.
[11] CCITT, *Blue Book*, vol. VIII, fascicle VIII.3, "Data communication networks: Transmission, signalling and switching, network aspects, maintenance and administrative arrangements," Recommendations X.40-X.181, Geneva, Switzerland, 1989.
[12] CCITT, *Blue Book*, vol. II, fascicle II.2, "Telephone network and ISDN—Operation, numbering, routing, and mobile service," Recommendations E.100-E.300, Geneva, Switzerland, 1989.
[13] CCITT, *Blue Book*, vol. VII, fascicle VII.3, "Terminal equipment and protocols for telematic services," Recommendations T.0-T.63, Geneva, Switzerland, 1989.
[14] CCITT, *Blue Book*, vol. VII, fascicle VII.5, "Terminal equipment and protocols for telematic services," Recommendations T.65-T.101, T.150-T.390, Geneva, Switzerland, 1989.
[15] CCITT, *Blue Book*, vol. VII, fascicle VII.6, "Terminal equipment and protocols for telematic services," Recommendations T.400-T.418, Geneva, Switzerland, 1989.
[16] CCITT, *Blue Book*, vol. VII, fascicle VII.7, "Terminal equipment and protocols for telematic services," Recommendations T.431-T.564, Geneva, Switzerland, 1989.
[17] S. E. Minzer and D. R. Spears, "New directions in signaling for broadband ISDN," *IEEE Commun. Mag.*, vol. 27, Feb. 1989.

Wendy M. Harman received the B.S. degree in operations research and industrial engineering from Cornell University, Ithaca, NY, in 1982, and the M.S.E. degree in industrial and operations engineering from the University of Michigan, Ann Arbor, in 1983.

In October 1983 she joined Bell Laboratories, proceeding in January 1984 to Bellcore, where she is currently a member of the Technical Staff in the Intelligent Network Planning Division. Her work has included several areas of network planning functions, including work on X.25 packet protocols and Integrated Services Digital Network (ISDN) services and protocols. She has been an active participant in X.25 packet standards committees, and has also been a technical leader in ISDN standards committees, T1D1 in the United States and CCITT Study Group XVIII internationally. She has had experience in implementation of ISDN protocols on a system used to test integrated voice and data services. Currently, her primary interests are in the area of network architectures and implementation of services on Intelligent Networks.

Cheryl F. Newman (M'75) received the B.S., M.S., and Ph.D. degrees in electric engineering from Cornell University, Ithaca, NY, in 1970, 1972, and 1975, respectively.

In October 1974 she joined Bell Laboratories, proceeding in January 1984 to Bellcore, where she is currently a member of the Technical Staff in Integrated Services Planning. Her work has taken her into several areas of network planning functions, including transmission facility network planning, special services planning, and local switching network planning. Currently, her primary interests lie in the area of message handling, directory, and related services as they might be offered on an Integrated Services Digital Network (ISDN) with Intelligent Network elements. Other interests are in multimedia services on ISDN. As part of her work, since 1984, she has been participating in ISDN standards committees, T1S1 in the United States and CCITT Study Group XVIII internationally.

Chapter 4
Internetworking

Overview

Packet-switched and packet-broadcast networks grew out of a need to allow the computer user to have access to resources beyond those available in a single system. In a similar fashion, the resources of a single network are often inadequate to meet users' needs. Thus, in many environments, a number of networks are used. Because the networks involved exhibit so many differences, it is impractical in most cases to consider merging multiple networks into a single network. Rather, what is needed is the ability to interconnect various networks so that any two devices on any of the constituent networks can communicate.

Table 4-1 lists some commonly used terms relating to the interconnection of networks, or internetworking. An interconnected set of networks, from a user's point of view, may appear simply as a larger network. However, if each of the constituent networks retains its identity and special mechanisms are needed for communicating across multiple networks, then the entire configuration is often referred to as an *internet*, and each of the constituent networks as a *subnetwork*.

Table 4-1. Internetworking terms.

Communication network	A facility that provides a data transfer service among stations attached to the network.
Internet	A collection of communication networks interconnected by bridges, routers, and/or gateways.
Subnetwork	Refers to a constituent network of an internet. This avoids ambiguity since the entire internet, from a user's point of view, is a single network.
Interworking unit (IWU)	A device used to connect two subnetworks and permit communication between end systems attached to different subnetworks.
Bridge	An IWU used to connect two LANs that use identical LAN protocols. The bridge acts as an address filter, picking up packets from one LAN that are intended for a destination on another LAN, and passing those packets on. The bridge does not modify the contents of the packets and does not add anything to the packet. The bridge operates at layer 2 of the OSI model.
Router	A device used to connect two networks that may or may not be similar. The router employs an internet protocol present in each router and each host of the network. The router operates at layer 3 of the OSI model.

Each constituent subnetwork in an internet supports communication among the devices attached to that subnetwork. In addition, subnetworks are connected by devices referred to in the ISO documents as *interworking units* (IWUs)[1]. IWUs provide a communications path and perform the necessary relaying and routing functions so that data can be exchanged between devices attached to different subnetworks in the internet.

Two types of IWUs of particular interest are bridges and routers. The differences between them have to do with the types of protocols used for the internetworking logic. In essence, a bridge operates at layer 2 of the open systems interconnection (OSI) seven-layer architecture and acts as a relay of frames between like networks. A router operates at layer 3 of the OSI architecture and routes packets between potential networks. Both the bridge and the router assume that the same upper-layer protocols are in use.

Requirements

Although a variety of approaches have been taken to provide internetwork service, the overall requirements on the internetworking facility can be stated in general. These include:

(1) Provide a link between networks. At minimum, a physical and link control connection is needed.
(2) Provide for the routing and delivery of data between processes on different networks.
(3) Provide an accounting service that keeps track of the use of the various networks and gateways and maintains status information.
(4) Provide the services listed above in such a way as not to require modifications to the networking architecture of any of the constituent networks. This means that the internetworking facility must accommodate a number of differences among networks. These include:

> (a) *Different addressing schemes:* The networks may use different endpoint names and addresses and directory maintenance schemes. Some form of global network addressing plus a directory service must be provided.
> (b) *Different maximum packet size:* Packets from one network may have to be broken up into smaller pieces for another. This process is referred to as fragmentation.
> (c) *Different network access mechanisms:* The network access mechanism between station and network may be different for stations on different networks.
> (d) *Different timeouts:* Typically, a connection-oriented transport service will await an acknowledgment until a timeout expires, at which time it will retransmit its segment of data. In general, longer times are required for successful delivery across multiple networks. Internetwork timing procedures must allow successful transmission that avoids unnecessary retransmissions.
> (e) *Error recovery:* Intranetwork procedures may provide anything from no error recovery up to reliable end-to-end (within the network) service. The internetwork service should not depend on, nor suffer interference from, the individual network's error recovery capability.
> (f) *Status reporting:* Different networks report status and performance differently. Yet it must be possible for the internetworking facility to provide such information on internetworking activity to interested and authorized processes.
> (g) *Routing techniques:* Intranetwork routing may depend on fault detection and congestion control techniques peculiar to each network. The internetworking facility must be able to coordinate these to adaptively route data between stations on different networks.
> (h) *User-access control:* Each network will have its own user-access-control technique (authorization for use of the network). These must be invoked by the internetwork facility as needed. Further, a separate internetwork access control technique may be required.
> (i) *Connection, connectionless:* Individual networks may provide connection-oriented (e.g., virtual circuit) or connectionless (datagram) service. It may be desirable for the internetwork service not to depend on the nature of the connection service of the individual networks.

These points are worthy of further comment but are best pursued in the context of specific architectural approaches.

Architectural approaches

In describing the interworking function, two dimensions are important:

- The mode of operation (connection-mode or connectionless).
- The protocol architecture.

The mode of operation determines the protocol architecture. ISO has standardized two general approaches, as depicted in Figure 4-1.

Connection-mode operation

In the connection-mode operation, it is assumed that each subnetwork provides a connection-mode form of service. That is, it is possible to establish a logical network connection (e.g., virtual circuit) between any two DTEs attached to the same subnetwork. With this in mind, we can summarize the connection-mode approach as follows:

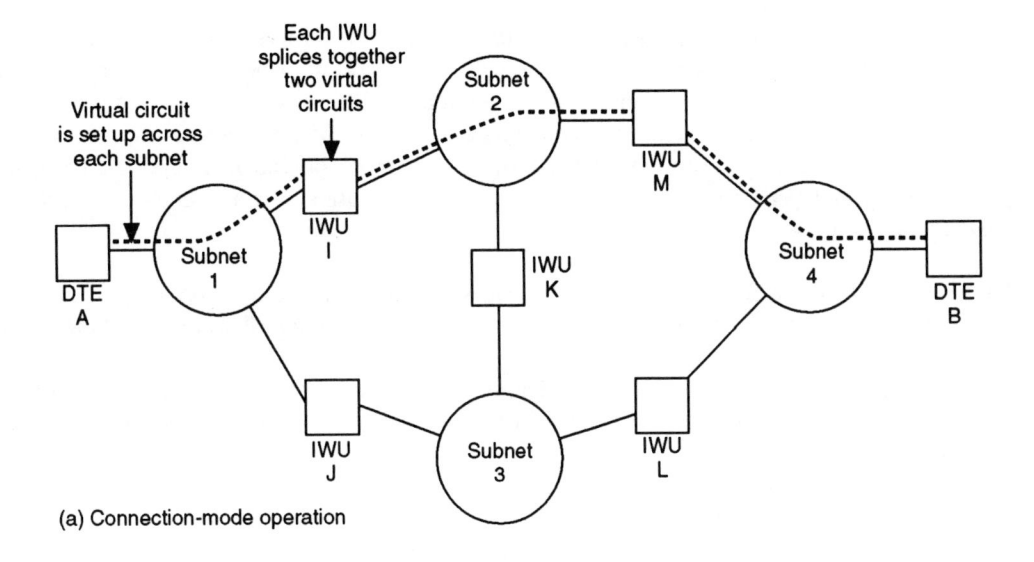

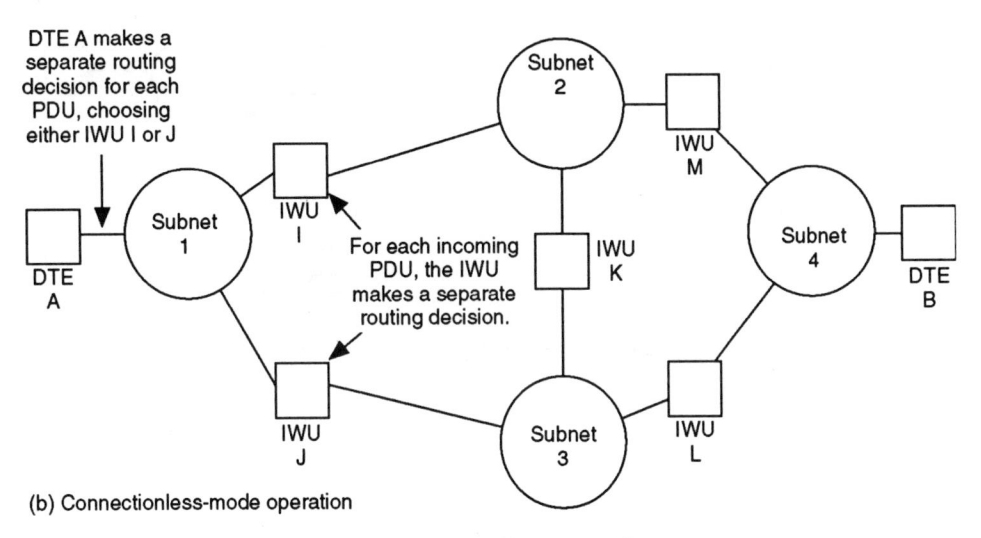

Figure 4-1. Internetworking approaches.

(1) Interworking units (IWUs) are used to connect two or more subnetworks; each IWU appears as a DTE to each of the subnetworks to which it is attached.
(2) When DTE A wishes to exchange data with DTE B, a logical connection is set up between them. This logical connection consists of the concatenation of a sequence of logical connections across subnetworks. The sequence is such that it forms a path from DTE A to DTE B.
(3) The individual subnetwork logical connections are spliced together by IWUs. For example, there is a logical connection from DTE A to IWU I across subnetwork 1, and another logical connection from IWU I to IWU M across subnetwork 2. Any traffic arriving at IWU I on the first logical connection is retransmitted on the second logical connection and vice versa.

Several additional points can be made about this form of operation. First, this approach is suited to providing support for a connection-oriented network access interface, such as X.25. From the point of view of network users in DTEs A and B, a logical network connection is established between them that provides all of the features of a logical connection across a single network.

The second point to be made is that this approach assumes that there is a connection-mode service available from each subnet and that these services are equivalent. Clearly, this may not always be the case. For example, an IEEE 802 or FDDI local area network provides a service defined by the logical link control (LLC). Two of the options with LLC provide only connectionless service. Therefore, in this case, the subnetwork service must be enhanced. An example of how this would be done is for the IWUs to implement X.25 on top of LLC across the LAN.

Figure 4-2(a) illustrates the protocol architecture for connection-mode operation. Access to all subnetworks, either inherently or by enhancement, is by means of the same network layer protocol. The interworking units operate at layer 3. As discussed previously, layer-3 IWUs are commonly referred to as routers. A connection-oriented router performs the following key functions:

- *Relaying:* Data units arriving from one subnetwork via the network layer protocol are relayed (retransmitted) on another subnetwork. Traffic is over logical connections that are spliced together at the routers.
- *Routing:* When an end-to-end logical connection, consisting of a sequence of logical connections, is to be set up, each router in the sequence must make a routing decision which determines the next hop in the sequence.

Thus, at layer 3, a relaying operation is performed. It is assumed that all of the end systems share common protocols at layer 4 (transport) and above for successful end-to-end communication.

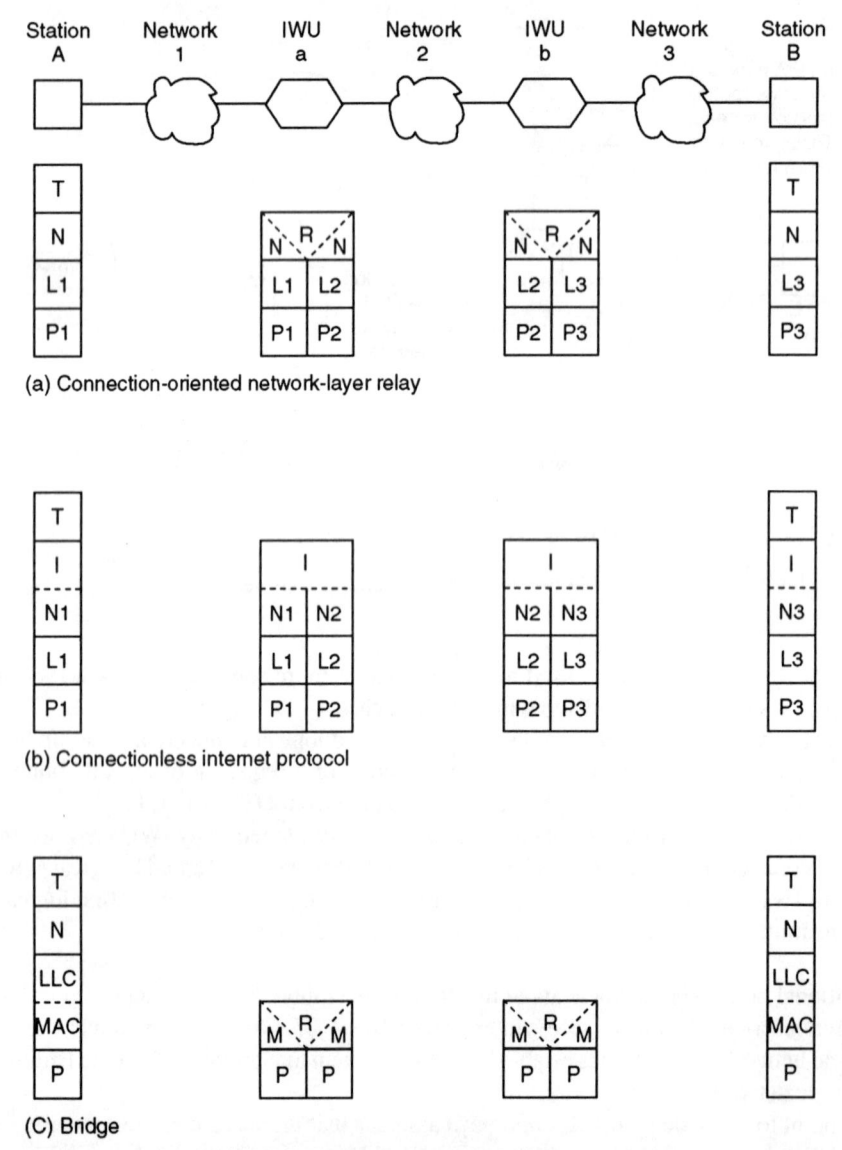

Figure 4-2. Internetwork architectures.

Connectionless-mode operation

Figure 4-1b illustrates the connectionless mode of operation. Whereas connection-mode operation corresponds to the virtual circuit mechanism of a packet-switching network, connectionless-mode operation corresponds to the datagram mechanism of a packet-switching network. Each network protocol data unit is treated independently and routed from source DTE to destination DTE through a series of routers and networks. For each data unit transmitted by A, A makes a decision as to which router should receive the data unit. The data unit hops across the internet from one router to the next until it reaches the destination subnetwork. At each router, a routing decision is made (independently for each data unit) concerning the next hop. Thus, different data units may travel different routes between source and destination DTE.

Figure 4-2b illustrates the protocol architecture for connectionless-mode operation. All DTEs and all routers share a common network layer protocol known generically as the internet protocol (IP). An internet protocol was initially developed for the DARPA internet project, and has been standardized by the U.S. Department of Defense. The ISO standard, ISO 8473, provides similar functionality. Below this internet protocol, there is needed a protocol to access the particular subnetwork. Thus, there are typically two protocols operating in each DTE and router at the network layer: an upper sublayer that provides the internetworking function, and a lower sublayer that provides subnetwork access.

Bridge approach

A third approach that is quite common is the use of a bridge. The bridge, also known as a MAC-level relay, uses a connectionless mode of operation (Figure 4-1b), but does so at a lower level than a router.

The protocol architecture for a bridge is illustrated in Figure 4-2c. In this case, the end systems share common transport and network protocols. In addition, it is assumed that all of the networks use the same protocols at the link layer. In the case of IEEE 802 and FDDI LANs, this means that all of the LANs share a common LLC protocol and a common MAC protocol. For example, all of the LANs are IEEE 802.3 using the unacknowledged connectionless form of LLC. In this case, MAC frames are relayed through bridges between the LANs.

Addressing

In order to transfer data from one DTE to another DTE, there must be some way of uniquely identifying the destination DTE. Thus, with each DTE, we must be able to associate a unique identifier, or address. This address will allow DTEs and IWUs to perform the routing function properly.

In the OSI environment, this unique address is equated to a network service access point (NSAP). An NSAP uniquely identifies a DTE within the internet. A DTE may have more than one NSAP, but each is unique to that particular system. We can refer to such an address as a *global internet address*. Frequently, this address is in the form of *(network, host)*, where the parameter *network* identifies a particular subnetwork and the parameter *host* identifies a particular DTE attached to that subnetwork.

Figure 4-3 suggests that another level of addressing may be needed. Each subnetwork must maintain a unique address for each DTE attached to that subnetwork. This allows the subnetwork to route data units through the subnetwork

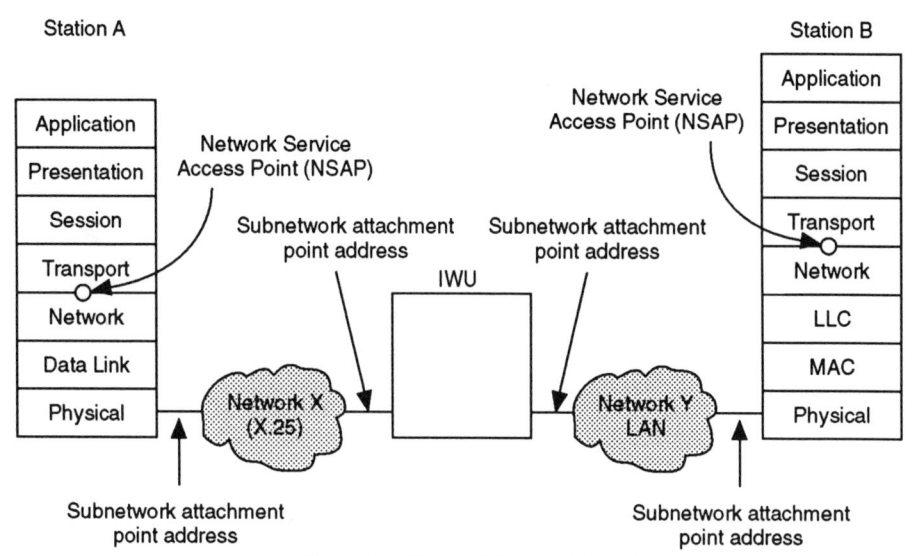

Figure 4-3. Network-layer addressing.

and deliver them to the intended DTE. We can refer to such an address as a *subnetwork attachment point address*.

It would appear convenient for the *host* parameter in the global address to be identical to the subnetwork attachment point address for that DTE. Unfortunately, this may not always be practical. Different networks use different addressing formats and different address lengths. Furthermore, a station may enjoy more than one attachment point into the same network. Accordingly, we must assume that the *host* parameter has global significance and the subnetwork attachment point address has significance only within a particular subnetwork. In this case, the internetworking facility must translate from the global address to the locally-significant address to route data units.

Summary

"Network Interconnection and Gateways" summarizes the major approaches to internetworking. The paper also examines key technical issues, such as addressing, routing, congestion control, and fragmentation and reassembly.

"Networking of Networks: Interworking According to OSI" expands on the concepts presented in this introduction, and looks at the connection-oriented and connectionless approaches to interconnection within the OSI model. Issues of protocols, relaying, addressing, and routing are discussed.

One of the most complex issues relating to internetworking is that of routing. "Design of Inter-Administrative Domain Routing Protocols" examines an important aspect of internetwork routing.

Finally, "Internetworking ISDN with LANs" examines one of the most important internetworking configurations, and describes a design approach.

[1]The term gateway is sometimes used to refer to an IWU or to a particular kind of IWU. Because of the lack of consistency in the use of this term, we will avoid it.

Network Interconnection and Gateways

CARL A. SUNSHINE

Abstract—As computer networks proliferate, the importance of interconnecting networks increases. Major technical issues that must be solved include selection of a protocol level at which to interconnect, addressing, routing, fragmentation, and congestion control. Often, a specialized *gateway* device is used to interconnect networks and implement any necessary internet protocols. Two leading alternatives have been developed by the DARPA Internet community (datagram internet protocol) and by the CCITT for public data networks (concatenation of virtual circuits). The new ISO standards encompass both approaches, but providing interoperability between them is still a problem.

I. INTRODUCTION

AS computer networks proliferate, the importance of interconnecting networks increases. The recent explosion in the numbers of personal computers is leading to even greater growth in the local area network (LAN) area. Interconnecting these diverse networks into an *internet* presents many technical problems, and may be pursued in many ways [9], [16], [31], [32], [37].

The term "network interconnection" has been used broadly to mean any technique which enables systems on one network to communicate with or make use of services of systems on another network. In this paper, we shall explore this full range of meanings, but we shall focus on the problem of providing general-purpose end-to-end communication at the network level in the protocol hierarchy, rather than the additional problems of integrating services at higher protocol levels.

Networks differ in geographic scope, type of using organization, types of services to be provided, and transmission technology. This leads to a variety of specific communication protocols and interfaces being used, at least at the lower levels, in different nets. There are good technical and marketing reasons for these different solutions, so diversity in network technologies is likely to persist. This suggests that for a network interconnection strategy to succeed, it must accommodate the autonomy and differences of individual networks to the greatest extent possible. We shall see to what extent this can be accomplished in what follows.

We first consider the major technical problems of network interconnection, including stepwise versus endpoint services, level of interconnection, addressing, routing, fragmentation, and congestion control, ending with a summary of functions performed by the "gateway" between networks. We next present several major current examples of internet systems, including the U.S. Department of Defense, Xerox Corporation, IBM, and public data networks. We finish with a review of standardization activity in ISO and likely future developments.

II. MAJOR TECHNICAL ISSUES

The technical problems of network interconnection have much in common with problems of designing an individual network. Indeed, a common viewpoint sees the individual networks as links, and the *gateways* as switching nodes interconnecting these "links" to form a "supernetwork." This leads to consideration of issues common to any switching system such as addressing, routing, congestion control, fragmentation, and multiplexing [16]. The following sections focus on the extra concerns that are important at the internet level in each of these areas, and on the extra issue of how to combine individual network services to provide end-to-end service.

A. Stepwise Versus Endpoint Services

A major question in designing network interconnection is whether services will be provided in a *stepwise* or *endpoint* fashion. For simplicity, consider connecting two networks. One approach is to take the existing service (say virtual circuits) in each system, and concatenate them, hoping that they are close enough to each other to provide an essentially equivalent end-to-end service. The alternative is to use a more basic service in each network (e.g., "datagrams"), and to provide the bulk of the virtual circuit service in the two endpoints, one on each network.

The stepwise approach has the virtue of providing service via existing mechanisms, without requiring any new implementation. However, it can only provide services end-to-end which are common to all subsystems. There may also be some variation in the "flavor" of service available, requiring a translation at intermediate points [17], [50].

Dealing with layer N service mismatches may often be done most simply by a translator at layer $N+1$, while a more complex but efficient approach requires dealing with the layer N protocols directly [48]. Padlipsky argues that functionality mismatches are nearly inevitable in any attempt to create such *translating gateways*, such that their resulting service limitations and/or greater complexity make them undesirable [42]. Another method for dealing with service mismatches is to add a *convergence sublayer* protocol to the side that is missing some service elements [48].

Manuscript received October 20, 1988; revised June 10, 1989.
The author was with the Unisys Corporation, Santa Monica, CA 90406. He is now with The Aerospace Corporation, El Segundo, CA 90009.
IEEE Log Number 8931245.

Reprinted from *IEEE Journal on Selected Areas in Communications*, January 1990, pp. 4–11. ©1990 by The Institute of Electrical and Electronics Engineers, Inc. All rights reserved.

The endpoint approach guarantees a full service with common attributes at both ends by requiring implementation of a common protocol in the two endpoint nodes. It makes use of simpler services on the individual networks along the way, and hence allows use of simpler gateways. There are fewer failure points since most errors along the path can be corrected by the endpoint mechanisms.

One common example of this tradeoff occurs at the transport level where a choice must be made on how to provide reliable end-to-end "virtual circuit" (VC) service (Fig. 1) [47]. The endpoint approach requires a common reliable transport protocol implemented in the end nodes, but makes use of simpler network service that need not be reliable or even connection oriented. The stepwise approach makes use of existing reliable VC service in each network, concatenating them to form an end-to-end VC. In this latter case, the gateways must function at the VC level, and any failure in the gateways would affect the end-to-end service.

B. Level of Interconnection

Another major question is at what level in the protocol hierarchy to interconnect networks. Alternatives exist all the way from the lowest (physical) level to the highest (application) level. As noted above, when different networks and protocols are involved, the interconnection involves a conversion process between the services provided for comparable functions in each network [17]. The complexity of this process and the quality of end-to-end services resulting are largely determined by the level of interconnection chosen. The following sections summarize the key features of each major alternative.

Physical Level: Interconnection devices operating at the physical level are generally called *repeaters*. They forward individual bits of the packet as they arrive, perhaps translating from one medium to another (e.g., baseband coaxial cable to optical fiber). The resulting interconnected system functions essentially as a single network at the data link level, and hence all subnets to be so connected must have identical data rates and link protocols. This approach is typically used to interconnect several physically separate segments of a LAN system, perhaps separated by a point-to-point link.

Link Level: Interconnection devices operating at the link level receive entire frames from one link, examine the link level protocol header, and possibly forward the frame onto another link [2], [3]. They are typically called *bridges* or, more specifically, *MAC bridges* (since they operate at the media access control level). As with repeaters, they may interconnect two or more local LAN segments or may interconnect remote segments over a long distance link. The major motivation for their use is to interconnect LAN segments with different MAC protocols or to increase network capacity by "filtering" incoming packets and forwarding only those whose link level destination is on another segment. MAC bridges transpar-

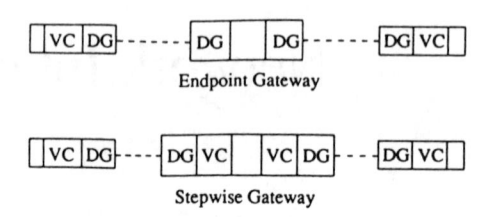

Fig. 1. Stepwise gateway is more complex than endpoint.

ently support systems with multiple network level protocols in use.

Network Level: Traditionally, interconnection at the network protocol level has been a wide area network (WAN) problem where different networks had independently developed different protocol mechanisms for the variety of network level functions such as routing, congestion control, error handling, and segmenting. If the network services are identical, then the problem becomes largely one of routing as with the X.25/X.75 approach in public data networks. When the network services differ, the complexity of protocols at the network level (e.g., X.25 versus ARPANET 1822) can make a translation approach difficult. There has been some success in one vendor emulating another vendor's network behavior (e.g., "SNA gateway").

An alternative gaining wide acceptance places a common *internet protocol* (IP) sublayer on top of the different network protocols. As we shall see below, this has particular benefits for supporting the sophisticated routing procedures needed for large internet systems, and devices operating at this level are often called IP gateways. If the networks to be interconnected provide connectionless service, the internet protocol can be particularly simple.

Choosing this level makes available the general-purpose services of the network level, and allows the gateway implementor to take advantage of what is normally a well-documented interface with many implementations. It allows each network to function autonomously with its own procedures internally, while requiring some standard "internet" procedures to be used on top of the normal network access for individual networks.

Transport Level: In the OSI architecture, the transport service is supposed to be an end-to-end service, so transport level gateways are, strictly speaking, a violation of the architecture. Nevertheless, they may be of practical benefit when common upper level protocols are in use, but different transport protocols are available. References [18] and [49] describe how to convert TCP and ISO TP4 to maximize end-to-end features. Onion and Rose [40] discuss a transport level gateway providing ISO TP0 service on top of X.25 connections on one side and TCP on the other side. Another situation where a pragmatic solution may be needed is to support interoperation between ISO protocol users employing TP Class 2 and TP Class 4 (see Section IV-D) [25], [49].

Higher Levels: No gateways functioning at session or presentation level have been developed to date, but many application level gateways have been implemented to support specific services found at the application level. This type of gateway is essentially a "Janus host" [42] that implements two (or more) full protocol suites. Common examples are interconnecting terminal concentrators or PAD's to provide an interactive terminal service [5] or electronic mail servers to form a mail forwarding service [10]. Where only a specific application service is wanted and the desired application services on each net match closely, this type of gateway may be easy to set up with existing equipment. However, the service provided is clearly not general purpose, and the limitations imposed by providing only those service elements common to the interconnected systems are often more irksome than anticipated [42].

C. Naming, Addressing, and Routing

To understand the problem of delivering data to the correct destination in an internet, a clear distinction must be drawn between names, addresses, and routes [34]. Although these concepts are applicable at each protocol level, we shall be primarily concerned with the network level where "hosts" or "end systems" and gateways are the relevant objects. A *name* serves to identify the host "logically," independent of its point(s) of attachment to the network(s). The same host may have several names to provide for convenient "nicknames" or aliases. An *address* identifies a point of attachment for purposes of delivering data to the host; since the same host may have multiple network interfaces, it may have multiple addresses. Finally, a *route* is the path taken from source to destination end system, and there are typically multiple routes available to the same destination.

The process of sending data to a destination generally involves first determining its address from its name using a directory service, and then determining the best route to that address. In large systems, this name lookup function is typically implemented in a distributed fashion, with a hierarchical name space where subdirectories are responsible for their portion of the name space [28], [44], as in the CCITT X.500 Recommendations.

1) Addressing: A method must be found for uniquely identifying all network interfaces in an internet system. One straightforward method is to employ relatively large addresses from the start, making sure each node receives a unique address (e.g., by incorporating the serial number as part of the address). This is the approach taken in the Xerox Network System using 48-bit addresses [13]. With an even larger address field, values can simply be assigned randomly, guaranteeing a sufficiently low probability of duplication (e.g., one billion nodes with 64-bit addresses implies a one in ten billion chance of duplication).

If existing networks with possibly overlapping addresses in use must be combined, several alternatives are possible. One is to merge one network into another, moving all its addresses to an unused range of addresses in the other network [Fig. 2(a)]. Of course, this is a major inconvenience for the moved addresses.

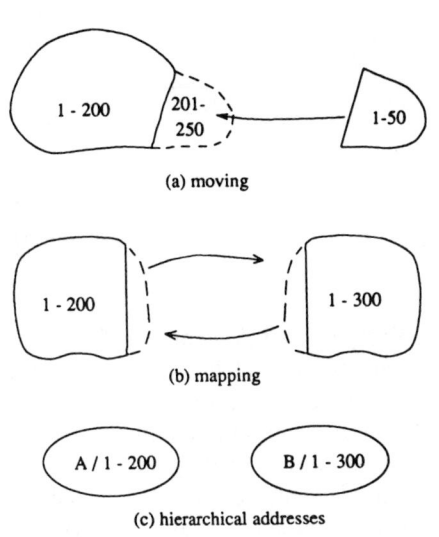

Fig. 2. Addressing alternatives.

Another strategy is to map unused addresses in each net to desired addresses in other nets [Fig. 2(b)], a technique called "proxy mapping" in [39] which was chosen by IBM to interconnect SNA networks [41]. It has the advantage of avoiding any changes to existing network addresses, but it requires sufficient unused addresses in each net for all external destinations, and leads to different addresses for the same node depending on what net it is referenced from. Hence, its major appeal is in situations where a limited number of networks and destinations is involved.

The most general strategy is to introduce a hierarchical address format where an explicit "network" prefix is added to existing "local" suffixes to form a complete address [Fig. 2(c)]. This network prefix may have routing significance and correspond to a "physical" network or it may have only administrative significance and correspond to an organizational domain. This is the approach used in the Federal Research Internet (see Section IV-A).

2) Routing: Once an addressing strategy is chosen, there is still the problem of routing or how to best reach each possible destination given its address. In the case that unused local addresses are mapped into external destinations, all packets to those destinations must be routed to a suitable gateway, which then does the address mapping as part of the forwarding process (Fig. 3).

With a flat internet address space (or one with only administrative significance to its hierarchy), gateways must maintain path information for all destinations individually, and hence have large routing tables. This approach is used in MAC bridges, which must maintain a list of all addresses "local" to each interface so they can filter out (not forward) received packets destined for those local addresses. For nonlocal packets to be forwarded, they must also implement a routing procedure that prevents duplication or flooding if there are multiple paths through the interconnected networks, and yet efficiently finds all destinations.

Considerable ingenuity has been devoted to this prob-

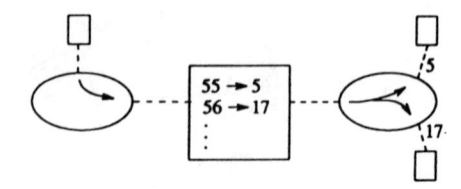

Fig. 3. Gateway intercepts and maps external addresses.

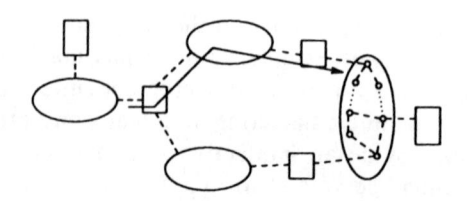

Fig. 4. Host unreachable due to partitioned net.

lem, particularly in the LAN context. One approach being adopted by the IEEE 802.1 committee is based on formation of a minimal spanning tree through the internet [2]. An alternative favored within the token ring LAN community uses source routing [15]. A third approach "discovers" and establishes an optimal route the first time each destination is contacted, and then sends subsequent packets over that route without requiring either source routing or routing calculations in the bridges [36]. All of these approaches depend on the broadcast capabilities of LAN's to send route finding packets efficiently, and hence the effective size of internets based on MAC level bridges is limited.

If a hierarchical address is used, as in internet protocols, then routing can be done in steps, first to the final network (ignoring the local suffix), and then within the final network to the local address. This reduces the size of routing tables at the cost of some loss in optimality. There may also be rare cases when a network becomes "partitioned" (divided into two or more portions that cannot communicate with each other internally), such that destinations erroneously appear unreachable in a strictly hierarchical routing procedure [35] (see Fig. 4).

Hybrid approaches have been used in other communication areas (e.g., telephone switching) to obtain the benefits of both hierarchical and flat routing. The majority of destinations are handled with a hierarchical procedure to reduce the size of routing tables, while high traffic or error recovery conditions can trigger the insertion of additional routes to specific individual destinations.

In any approach based on the use of routing tables by gateways, the tables must be built and updated to reflect changing traffic conditions. Accomplishing this task in large networks or internets with high reliability, efficiency, and timeliness has been a very challenging problem that has led to the development of many routing information exchange algorithms. Some examples such as the External Gateway Protocol (EGP) and the ISO End System to Intermediate System protocol are presented below.

Another design choice concerns the frequency of routing decisions. For maximum robustness, best route calculations may be performed every few seconds or minutes as in the Federal Research Internet [19]. Other systems choose to perform the best route determination process only for the initial packet to a destination. This route is then remembered in the routers (or the source in [15]), and subsequent packets to the same destination follow the same route. Often, this type of path setup is accompanied by an abbreviated addressing convention where only the first packet must carry full destination address, and subsequent packets carry only a shorter path identifier. Examples of this approach using hierarchical addressing include the Universe project [1] and CCITT X.75 (see Section IV-C), while examples using flat addressing include [2] and [36] mentioned above. Some mechanisms for timing out such routes or recovering from breaks in the path must also be provided.

Yet another approach employs flooding to avoid the need for intelligence in packet forwarders. Since flooding is expensive of network resources, this is typically used only for control purposes or for initially establishing a path that later packets to the same destination will follow [36]. Another way to avoid the need for intelligent routers is for the source to provide explicit path information in the packets it sends [15], [38].

A final complexity occurs when a node is *multihomed* (has multiple connections to the internet), and hence has multiple addresses. Normally, the routing system is designed to find an optimal route to a single destination address carried in the packet. To take full advantage of multihoming, either the source must select an optimal address in advance or the routing system must be enhanced to deal with multiple addresses in the packet (select the best of best routes) or even to accept a name for the destination, and perform the name to (multiple) address lookup function in the gateways along a path to the destination [35], [39].

D. Congestion Control

The problems of congestion control in an internet system are much like those of individual networks. Speed mismatches are likely to be more severe between LAN's and slower wide area networks (although recent advances in high-speed WAN service should reduce this). In some cases, the individual network procedures may be adequate (e.g., X.25 PDN's where buffering resources are typically reserved at VC establishment). In others, some form of explicit internet level control may be needed.

Questions have been raised about the ability of connectionless systems to provide effective congestion control. This is a particular concern when connectionless or "datagram" internet service is used to support higher level connection-oriented services. Several techniques have been proposed in this area, including input buffer limits, buffer classes, fair queueing [45], slow start [46], and choke packets [29]. Once the sender has determined that congestion has occurred (by receiving an explicit signal from a host or gateway or by timing out waiting for an acknowledgment), it must reduce its transmission rate for a while, and then try to increase it again. Various specific algorithms for this purpose have been proposed, and this is an active area of research [46].

E. Fragmentation and Reassembly

When networks with differing maximum packet size limits are interconnected, the need to fragment large packets for traversal through networks with smaller size limits must be considered. These fragments can be reassembled at the exit from the individual small packet network or allowed to propagate all the way to the final destination.

Mechanisms to support such fragmentation typically include some sort of additional sequencing information. The most general mechanisms allow further fragmentation of already created fragments, and proper reassembly of fragments from different (re)transmissions of the same data that may arrive out of order or have overlapping boundaries (e.g., DARPA IP [29]). The reassembly problem is simplified in networks providing connection-oriented services since fragments always arrive in order.

Although fragmentation was intended to add robustness to the internet system, recent results suggest that it can also cause problems [43]. In congested systems, fragments may be repeatedly lost, drastically reducing performance. Fragmentation can also cause many more total packets to be used than if the source host limited itself to sending the maximum packet size allowed on the path. Kent and Mogul [43] suggest several ways to reduce or avoid the need for fragmentation and these negative consequences.

III. IP Gateway Functions

The primary function of an internet gateway is to implement the network access protocols of the two (or more) networks it interconnects. This allows the gateway to receive packets from one network, reformat them, and forward them into the appropriate next network.

To determine the proper direction to forward the packet, the gateway must perform a routing function based on addressing information contained in the packet and in internal routing tables. These routing tables must be updated according to the routing procedures used in the internet system.

If a stepwise approach to providing services is being used, the gateway must terminate the protocol in one net and translate the functions required into appropriate form on the next network. Congestion control and fragmentation may also be needed in the gateway as discussed above. If performance monitoring or accounting functions are required, these must also be implemented in the gateway.

All of these functions may be performed in a dedicated machine. Alternatively, they may be split into separate gateway "halves" associated with each network, connected to each other by a communications link (Fig. 5).

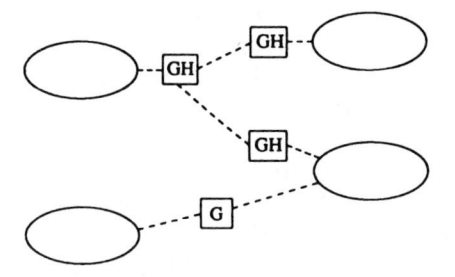

Fig. 5. Full gateways (G) and gateway halves (GH).

This allows the gateway functions to be merged with other network functions in an existing switching node owned and operated by each network authority. However, it adds the requirement of defining a standard procedure for use across the link between gateway halves. The CCITT X.75 Recommendation (see below) is an example of this approach.

IV. Current Practice

A. Federal Research Internet System

One of the first major internet systems was developed by the Defense Advanced Research Projects Agency (DARPA) in the U.S. [9], [19], [30], [31]. This system included the original ARPANET, packet radio nets, satellite networks, and various LAN's. The system is now split into separate systems for research users and for operational military users, and has been enlarged by inclusion of compatible networks run by other U.S. government agencies, most notably the National Science Foundation's NSFNET. Hence, it is now coming to be called the Federal Research Internet (FRI).

FRI networks are interconnected by gateways which implement a connectionless or datagram Internet Protocol (IP) [14], [29] to provide maximum robustness and routing flexibility. Dedicated gateway machines of the 16-bit minicomputer class were originally employed, but new 32-bit microprocessor based products are now coming into use. Most of the individual networks provide connectionless service, although there is a provision for running the IP over connection-oriented network services such as X.25 [11].

The major transport service is connection-oriented, implemented by a common protocol called TCP that must be present at the endpoints (not in gateways). The IP also supports other types of transport protocols including datagram and "stream" mode (for packetized voice).

Addressing in the FRI is hierarchical, with gateways designed to route to the network portion of the address first, and then the local portion once the correct net is reached. The address length is fixed at 32 bits, and as the internet has expanded, this fixed hierarchical structure has caused significant difficulties and led to the invention of a "subnetting" approach for large campuses. Host name to address lookup was initially supported by a single flat directory, but as the number of hosts grew, a hierarchical distributed directory service was adopted [44].

The IP provides for fragmentation at gateways, with

reassembly at the final destination so that individual fragments may follow different routes. Only the header is checksummed to allow delivery of packets with some data errors (higher level protocols may use their own checksums). A Time-To-Live field is also included to limit the maximum lifetime of packets in the system. Options are defined to allow inclusion of source routes, security markings, timestamps, etc.

There is a separate Internet Control Message Protocol (ICMP) used for signaling errors and diagnostic information. This includes destination unreachable, congestion control (choke packets), and redirect indications (giving a better route for a specific destination).

Internet routing information exchange was originally handled by a Gateway-to-Gateway protocol [19] that required interaction between all "neighboring" gateways. As the internet grew, a hierarchical scheme called the Exterior Gateway Protocol (EGP) [19] was developed to reduce the amount of routing traffic. In EGP, each "autonomous system" (typically a campus internet) elects one gateway to exchange routing data with a "neighbor" gateway in an adjacent autonomous system, and the systems then propagate the information to all their other gateways through an internal procedure. As currently defined, EGP requires all autonomous systems to use a single "core system" for interconnection with each other, rather than supporting a general mesh topology. Further extensions are under study.

B. Xerox

The original experimental Xerox internet system was developed about the same time as the DARPA system and shared many of its features, including hierarchical addressing and a connectionless internet layer [4], [9]. In addition to dedicated gateways, gateway halves were used to interconnect physically remote LAN segments via communication links. Fragmentation and reassembly were done on an individual network basis if needed. Because of the predominance of high speed, low error rate LAN's in the system, higher level protocols were somewhat simpler than in the DARPA system.

Sophisticated directory servers were included to convert names to addresses [28]. This directory service made use of the broadcast capabilities of the individual LAN's in the system to efficiently support distribution of its functions between user nodes, local servers, and centralized servers.

Several changes were then made to produce the current Xerox Network System (XNS) [12]. The major change was adoption of a large (48-bit) flat address to uniquely label each node ever manufactured, while an additional hierarchical network address was added to the internet packet format for routing purposes [13].

C. IBM

In 1983, IBM released an extension of their Systems Network Architecture (SNA) that supported the interconnection of SNA networks [41]. SNA defines a layered set of protocols similar to the OSI architecture, with routing provided by the path control layer [51]. Logical entities at the network layer, called *Network Addressable Units* (NAU), are identified by a hierarchical address specifying a subarea number and an element within that subarea. Initially, the address was 16 bits, but it has been expanded in recent releases to 46 bits. The basic communication service provided is a virtual circuit type of *session* between NAU's. Formation of sessions between user NAU's is facilitated by interaction with one or more *System Services Control Point (SSCP)* NAU's which provide a directory service translating names into NAU addresses, and help to determine the route for each session.

A major objective in supporting SNA network interconnection was to minimize the effects on existing individual SNA networks. Therefore, an address mapping approach was taken in which the gateways translate unused addresses in one SNA network into corresponding addresses in another SNA network [39]. The result is essentially a concatenation of sessions through individual nets, with the gateways terminating routing and flow control procedures in each net. The directories in each network's SSCP(s) are also extended to include names for remote NAU's that are to be made available. This allows an NAU in one net to have different names in each network from which it is accessible to avoid conflicts with existing local names, and makes the address mapping invisible to users.

Due to the relatively small address space initially available, provision for dynamic reuse of gateway addresses was desirable. When a session is requested, the directory in the SSCP for the calling node sends a message to the gateway to cause it to allocate a free NAU address for that application [52]. The gateway returns the address to the SSCP, which in turn informs the calling node of the destination alias address to use. When the session is finished, the SSCP tells the gateway to release the address.

D. Public Data Networks

In the late 1970's, the major public data networks developed the X.25 interface to provide connection-oriented service. By modifying this procedure slightly to make it more symmetric and adding some new utility functions, they were able to create the X.75 interface for use on the links between PDN's [7], [9], [31], [33].

To provide internetwork service to X.25 users, Recommendation X.121 defined the address fields in the X.25 Call Request packet to include a hierarchical network portion of three digits followed by a local portion of up to ten digits [8]. Each PDN was responsible for interpreting these addresses and routing calls to an appropriate internetwork link according to its own internal procedures. In the 1984 revision of X.25, address extension facility fields were added to the Call Request packet, providing a limited form of source routing. The PDN internet routes the call to a "private gateway" based on the X.121 address, and then the gateway can forward the packet based on the address extension field.

In PDN's, the gateway half approach is used, with

gateway functions typically performed by additional software in the existing network switching nodes. Virtual circuit network level service is provided by a stepwise concatenation of X.25-like links in each network (Fig. 6). This allows an easy (if conservative) method of resource allocation, and straightforward accounting and charging procedures. However, there is uncertainty about the end-to-end significance of some VC functions such as flow control and reset. End user service would be affected by the failure of any intermediate nodes performing VC functions.

Asynchronous terminal support is provided on top of these VC's in an endpoint fashion between the packet mode subscriber on one end and the PAD on the other (Recommendation X.29).

Unlike the previous two examples, PDN's employ a connection-oriented routing scheme whereby only the initial Call Request packet carries the full destination address and requires an optimal route decision in routing nodes. This first packet sets up a path entry in the routing nodes which is referenced by a short address in subsequent data packets, which are all sent over the same route. This reduces protocol overhead and processing time for data packets, at the expense of some robustness and optimality.

E. ISO

The International Standards Organization (ISO) has recently extended its OSI architecture to define three sublayers within the network layer [21]. The topmost layer corresponds to the internet protocol, and the middle layer is intended to adapt ("converge") specific network services to those required by the internet sublayer. One example would be use of a connectionless internet protocol over a connection oriented network, requiring a "connection management" intermediate layer protocol to set up and terminate connections as needed in order to send internet level datagrams [11], [24].

Various other combinations of link, network, and transport layer protocol types can be envisioned. The situation is complicated by the fact that most LAN's provide connectionless service, while most PDN's provide connection-oriented service. Interconnecting end users by means of both sorts of networks will require some "convergence" features, and the best strategy remains an open question.

One approach popular in Europe is to require all networks including LAN's to provide a connection-oriented service (e.g., see ISO standard 8881), and to use the TP Class 2 end-to-end. However, this may result in poor performance and inefficient use of the LAN's [26]. The alternative of assuming only connectionless service on all networks requires all end systems to implement and employ TP Class 4. This is popular in North America and is mandated by the U.S. Government OSI Profile (GOSIP) [27], but may be inefficient over connection-oriented networks. End systems taking the first approach will be unable to communicate with other systems taking the second approach unless some sort of transport level gateway as described in [25] is provided.

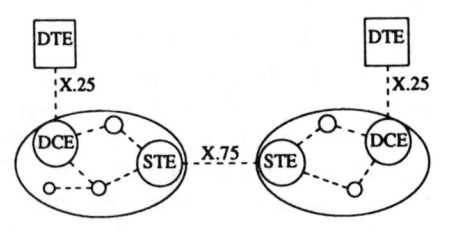

Fig. 6. Concatenated virtual circuits in PDN's.

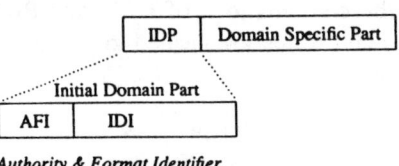

Fig. 7. ISO network service access point address.

ISO has defined an internet sublayer protocol [6], [20] much like the DARPA IP [24]. Although the format of the ISO IP packet header is different, most fields have a one-to-one correspondence with the DARPA IP. However, the ISO IP does not include a field for "upper layer protocol" (e.g., TCP or UDP) since this is viewed as part of the address information (see below). The ISO IP includes an error reporting capability, while the DARPA IP provides this through the separate ICMP protocol. The fragmentation (segmentation) fields are different, with the ISO IP including a field giving the total length of the original segment in each fragment to aid in assigning reassembly buffers.

The final major difference concerns the format of addresses at the network level, which is not part of the ISO IP itself, but covered in a separate document [22]. The ISO format is a variable length string that is intended to cover the requirements of both public and private, local and wide area networks for the foreseeable future. This involves a maximum of 16 octets of binary data, which could be alternately coded as 40 BCD digits. The first octet is an Authority/Format code meant to indicate what format the following data are in. Provision has been made to identify all the major current address formats as alternatives (X.121, F.69 (telex), E.163 (telephone), E.164 (ISDN), and ISO 6523). The address is assumed to be hierarchical with each "domain" responsible for defining the meaning of the suffix portion of the address under its control (Fig. 7).

The initial routing information exchange protocol defined by ISO is intended for *end systems* (hosts and workstations) to interact with *intermediate systems* (gateways and bridges). This ES-IS protocol [23] provides functions for end systems to announce and learn correspondence of network (IP) level addresses to MAC level addresses for nodes on the same network, and to learn the addresses of any gateways on their network which can serve as a path to other networks. The more difficult problem of IS-IS protocol is still under study.

V. CONCLUSIONS

The variety of individual network technologies is likely to continue increasing. Fortunately, by introducing standards at the internetwork level, it is possible to interconnect diverse networks while preserving their individual autonomy to a large degree. Truly universal addressing and routing schemes are now emerging from ISO work. The next few years should prove very interesting in determining the combinations of LAN and PDN protocols at the lower layers that are needed to provide good worldwide service.

REFERENCES

[1] C. Adams et al., "Protocol architecture of the UNIVERSE project," in *Proc. 6th Int. Conf. Comput. Commun.*, IEEE, 1982.
[2] F. Backes, "Transparent bridges for interconnection of IEEE 802 LANs," *IEEE Network*, vol. 2, pp. 5-9, Jan. 1988.
[3] E. Benhamou and J. Estrin, "Multilevel internetworking gateways: Architecture and applications," *IEEE Comput.*, pp. 27-34, Sept. 1983.
[4] D. Boggs et al., "PUP, An internetwork architecture," *IEEE Trans. Commun.*, vol. COM-28, Apr. 1980.
[5] R. Braden et al., "A distributed approach to the interconnection of heterogeneous computer networks," in *Proc. ACM SIGCOMM Symp.*, Mar. 1983.
[6] R. Callon, "Internetwork protocol," *Proc. IEEE*, vol. 71, pp. 1388-1393, Dec. 1983.
[7] CCITT, Recommendation X.75, "Terminal and transit call control procedures and data transfer system on international circuits between packet-switched data networks," *Red Book*, 1985.
[8] CCITT, Recommendation X.121, "International numbering plan for public data networks," *Red Book*, 1985.
[9] V. Cerf and P. Kirstein, "Issues in packet network interconnection," *Proc. IEEE*, vol. 66, pp. 1386-1408, Nov. 1978.
[10] D. Cohen, "Internet mail forwarding," in *Proc. IEEE COMPCON*, Feb. 1982, pp. 384-390.
[11] D. Comer and J. Korb, "CSNET protocol software: The IP-to-X.25 interface," in *Proc. ACM SIGCOMM Symp.*, Mar. 1983.
[12] Y. Dalal, "Use of multiple networks in Xerox' network system," in *Proc. IEEE COMPCON*, Feb. 1982, pp. 391-397.
[13] Y. Dalal and R. Printis, "48-bit Internet and Ethernet host numbers," in *Proc. 7th Data Commun. Symp.*, ACM/IEEE, Oct. 1981, pp. 240-245.
[14] U.S. Dep. Defense, "Internet protocol," MIL-STD-1777, 1983.
[15] R. Dixon and D. Pitt, "Addressing, bridging, and source routing," *IEEE Network*, vol. 2, pp. 25-32, Jan. 1988.
[16] M. Gien and H. Zimmermann, "Design principles for network interconnection," in *Proc. 6th Data Commun. Symp.*, ACM/IEEE, Nov. 1979.
[17] P. Green, Jr., "Protocol conversion," *IEEE Trans. Commun.*, vol. COM-34, pp. 257-268, Mar. 1986.
[18] I. Groenbaek, "Conversion between the TCP and ISO transport protocols as a method of achieving interoperability between data communications systems," *IEEE J. Select. Areas Commun.*, vol. SAC-4, pp. 288-296, Mar. 1986.
[19] R. Hinden, J. Haverty, and A. Sheltzer, "The DARPA internet: Interconnection of heterogeneous computer networks with gateways," *IEEE Comput.*, vol. 16, pp. 38-48, Sept. 1983.
[20] International Standards Organization (ISO), "Protocol for providing the connectionless network service," IS 8473, Mar. 1986.
[21] ISO, "Internal organization of the network layer," IS 8648, Feb. 1988.
[22] ISO, "Addendum to the network service definition covering network layer addressing, IS 8348 AD2, Nov. 1984.
[23] ISO, "End system to intermediate system routing information exchange protocol for use in conjunction with the protocol for the provision of the connectionless-mode network service," IS 9542.
[24] C. Kawa and G. Bochmann, "Hierarchical multi-network interconnection using public data networks," in *Proc. IEEE INFOCOM*, Mar. 1987, pp. 426-435.
[25] MAP/TOP Users Group, "Position paper on a solution for CONS/CLNS interworking," Oct. 1987.
[26] B. Meister, P. Janson, and L. Svobodova, "Connection-oriented versus connectionless protocols: A performance study," *IEEE Trans. Comput.*, vol. C-34, pp. 1164-1173, Dec. 1985.
[27] National Bureau of Standards, "Government open systems interconnection profile (GOSIP)," version 1.0, Oct. 1987.
[28] D. Oppen and Y. Dalal, "The clearinghouse: A decentralized agent for locating named objects in a distributed environment," *ACM Trans. Office Inform. Syst.*, vol. 1, pp. 230-253, 1983.
[29] J. Postel, C. Sunshine, and D. Cohen, "The ARPA internet protocol," *Comput. Networks*, vol. 5, pp. 261-271, July 1981.
[30] ——, "Recent developments in the DARPA internet program," in *Proc. 6th Int. Conf. Comput. Commun.*, Sept. 1982.
[31] J. Postel, "Internetwork protocol approaches," *IEEE Trans Commun.*, vol. COM-28, pp. 604-611, Apr. 1980.
[32] L. Pouzin, "A proposal for interconnecting packet switching networks," in *Proc. Eurocomp*, 1974.
[33] A. Rybczynski, J. Palframan, and A. Thomas, "Design of the Datapac X.75 internetworking capability," in *Proc. 5th Int. Conf. Comput. Commun.*, Oct. 1980, pp. 735-740.
[34] J. Shoch, "Internetwork naming, addressing, and routing," in *Proc. IEEE COMPCON*, Sept. 1978, pp. 72-79.
[35] C. Sunshine "Addressing problems in multinetwork systems," in *Proc. IEEE INFOCOM*, 1982, pp. 12-18.
[36] C. Sunshine et al., "Interconnection of broadband local area networks," in *Proc. 8th Data Commun. Symp.*, ACM/IEEE, 1983.
[37] ——, "Interconnection of computer networks," *Comput. Networks*, vol. 1, pp. 175-195, Jan. 1977.
[38] ——, "Source routing in computer networks," *ACM Comput. Commun. Rev.*, vol. 7, pp. 29-33, Jan. 1977.
[39] S. Zatti and P. Janson, "Internetwork naming, addressing, and directory systems: Towards a global OSI context," *Comput. Networks ISDN Syst.*, vol. 15, pp. 269-283, 1988.
[40] J. Onion and M. Rose, "ISO-TP0 bridge between TCP and X.25," ARPANET Request for Comment 1086, Dec. 1988.
[41] J. Benjamin et al., "Interconnecting SNA networks," *IBM Syst. J.*, vol. 22, pp. 344-366, 1983.
[42] M. Padlipsky, "Gateways, architectures, and heffalumps," in *The Elements of Networking Style*. Englewood Cliffs, NJ: Prentice-Hall, 1985.
[43] C. Kent and J. Mogul, "Fragmentation considered harmful," in *Proc. ACM SIGCOMM Symp.*, Aug. 1987, pp. 390-410.
[44] P. Mockapetris and K. Dunlap, "Development of the domain name system," in *Proc. ACM SIGCOMM Symp.*, Aug. 1988, pp. 123-133.
[45] J. Naigle, "On packet switches with infinite buffer storage," *IEEE Trans. Commun.*, vol. COM-35, pp. 435-438, Apr. 1987.
[46] V. Jacobson, "Congestion avoidance and control," in *Proc. ACM SIGCOMM Symp.*, Aug. 1988, pp. 314-329.
[47] V. DiCiccio, C. Sunshine, J. Field, and E. Manning, "Alternatives for interconnection of public packet switching data networks," in *Proc. 6th Data Commun. Symp.*, ACM/IEEE, Nov. 1979, pp. 120-125.
[48] G. Bochmann, "Principles of protocol conversion," Pub. 624, Dep. d'IRO, Univ. Montreal, Canada, May 1987.
[49] G. Bochmann and A. Jacques, "Gateways for the OSI transport service," in *Proc. IEEE INFOCOM*, 1987.
[50] S. Lam, "Protocol conversion," *IEEE Trans. Software Eng.*, vol. 14, pp. 353-362, Mar. 1988.
[51] D. Pozefsky, D. Pitt, and J. Gray, "IBM's systems network architecture," in *Computer Network Architectures and Protocols*, 2nd ed. C. Sunshine, Ed. New York: Plenum, 1989.
[52] IBM, *Systems Network Architecture Format and Protocol Reference Manual: SNA Network Interconnection*, SC30-3339, 1987.

Carl A. Sunshine received the B.A. degree in physics from the University of Chicago, Chicago, IL, in 1971 and the Ph.D. degree in computer science from Stanford University, Stanford, CA, in 1975.

While at Stanford, he helped develop the initial DoD TCP and IP internetworking protocols. He subsequently worked at the Rand Corporation, USC Information Sciences Institute, Sytek (now Hughes LAN Systems), and System Development Corporation (now Unisys). His work encompassed a range of topics including network protocol design, formal specification and verification, network management, and computer security. He is currently Director of the Computer Science Laboratory at The Aerospace Corporation, El Segundo, CA. He has published and lectured widely.

Dr. Sunshine is a member of the IEEE Computer Society, ACM, and IFIP Working Groups 6.1 and 6.6

Networking of Networks: Interworking According to OSI

FRED M. BURG AND NICOLA DI IORIO

Abstract—The availability of new technologies has resulted in a plethora of network types while the needs of new generation users have become more sophisticated. The most imminent users' need is the capability to communicate across heterogeneous networks both internal and external to administrative boundaries. Hence, the need of a formal plan for interworking the multitude of existing and emerging network types has been receiving considerable attention.

This paper describes the formal method of interworking networks in accordance with the overall Open Systems Interconnection (OSI) effort being pursued by both the International Organization for Standardization (ISO) and the International Telegraph and Telephone Consultative Committee (CCITT). After introducing the problem and defining the applicable OSI concepts, the basic architectural model for interworking and the resulting requirements on protocols, relaying, addressing, and routing are discussed.

I. INTRODUCTION

IN ITS infancy, data communications was limited in terms of its geographic scope and complexity—several terminals bound tightly to a host computer. Each vendor developed its own architecture (i.e., a complete set of rules) for realizing this. There was little motivation for a vendor to develop a common language for its hosts to talk to another vendor's terminals. As a result, the languages (more commonly called *protocols*) were expectedly different. Users of such equipment, as their own communications needs expanded, however, grew wary of proprietary protocols, thus providing the initial motivation for a common set of protocols.

Nevertheless, one could not expect an instantaneous transformation from islands of different data-communications protocols to one homogeneous environment. Work started almost ten years ago is just starting to bear fruit in providing a common model for data communications. That work, known as the Reference Model for Open Systems Interconnection (RM-OSI) [1], [2], provides the basis for development of common protocols as well as for interworking between heterogeneous environments.

The RM-OSI divides the communications problem into smaller tasks—seven smaller tasks (or *layers*) to be exact. While it is not our intent to provide a tutorial on the RM-OSI (there are enough of those; see, for example, [3]), we do need to observe an important division of responsibilities. In any communications architecture, a distinction can be made between functions used for moving information as opposed to those for processing information. In the RM-OSI, the bottom four layers (1-4) are responsible for the former set of functions, whereas the top three layers (5-7) are responsible for the latter. One method of attacking the interworking problem when considering two completely different architectures is to divide them along these lines (see, for example, [4]).

Our purpose here is to deal with interworking only with respect to Layers 1-4. As such, a critical element to be dealt with, in the scope of these layers, is the heterogeneity of networks across which information is to be moved. The earliest type of network used for data communications was the ubiquitous telephone network. From there, networking evolved to dedicated data networks—circuit-switched networks, packet-switched networks, and then local area networks (LAN's). As we look forward from today, we seem to have come full circle with the Integrated Services Digital Networks (ISDN's). Naturally, one cannot expect all terminals and hosts (collectively referred to as *end systems* hereafter) to migrate instantaneously to the latest technology. Even if we could, we would still have to overcome the administrative problems of maintaining autonomy and security while developing connectivity.

This paper looks at interworking from the perspective of the bottom four layers of the RM-OSI. We start out by approaching the problem in a heuristic and informal fashion in Section II. In Section III, we present the necessary background material using a rigorous set of tools as developed by the work on the RM-OSI. The discussion that then follows in Section IV further develops the concepts of interworking. Section V presents our conclusions and observations concerning ongoing work.

II. THE NEED FOR INTERWORKING

If *all* end systems (sources and sinks of data processed by applications) were connected to one network, users would perceive no need for interworking. For many reasons, such a case, of course, is not practical. What, then, are some of the areas of concern that need to be addressed when considering interworking?

Before we even attempt to identify these concerns, it is important to define *interworking*. Our approach starts by observing under what circumstances something out of the ordinary (i.e., interworking) is needed. Since we are concerned here with the movement of data, we will say that interworking, in an OSI sense, occurs when data need to

---

Manuscript received May 15, 1988; revised March 1, 1989.
The authors are with AT&T Bell Laboratories, Holmdel, NJ 07733.
IEEE Log Number 8929559.

be moved across two or more networks that differ in some fundamental way *as perceived by the users of those networks*. We will illustrate these concepts with some examples.

Let us start by considering two LAN's and the end systems attached to them. Suppose that two groups within a campus (such as the Administration Department and the Research Department) have installed "identical" LAN's (from a technology point of view) independently of each other. When a user on one LAN needs to send data to a user on the other, is there an interworking problem that needs to be solved? Probably yes, since the LAN's would be used in such a way that one LAN does not impose any constraints on the other. For example, the assignment of addresses used by the systems on one LAN may have been done without any concern for the address assignment of the other. When the two LAN's are physically connected, one must be concerned about uniqueness of addresses; clearly, the users now perceive a problem—if the union of the addresses assigned on the LAN's is not unique, data cannot be delivered correctly.

On the other hand, suppose a "communications planning" group on the campus had taken responsibility for installation and operation of both LAN's. While data flows may still have been localized at the beginning, users would not perceive any addressing problems when they finally need to send data to the other LAN.

The above example shows how interworking becomes necessary as a result of administrative procedures (or the lack of them). Even when the LAN technologies are exactly the same, there can still be problems. However, when the two networks share many characteristics, the burden of interworking is lessened. The more interesting challenges occur when the networks are quite different.

Consider end systems on a LAN and on an X.25 network that need to communicate with each other. Table I compares several characteristics of the two network types.

Clearly, there are more potential problems in this case than in the one above. For example, suppose an end system on the LAN needs to send data to an end system on the X.25 network. How should the LAN system identify the X.25-based system? In general, there may be several methods. Does it matter which one is chosen? Does one method have any limitations that make it feasible only under some conditions? Does it matter, when several LAN's are connected to the X.25 network, that a different selection is made in each case? What about the difference in packet sizes? Clearly, these and other questions need to be resolved before successful transfer of data from one end system to the other can occur.

III. Setting the Stage

As indicated above, the RM-OSI work provides a framework for development of common protocols as well as for interworking heterogeneous environments. With respect to the bottom four layers of the RM-OSI, the area of concern due to heterogeneity, of course, is the plethora of networking technologies that exist now and can be ex-

TABLE I
Some Characteristics of LAN's and X.25 Networks

Characteristic	X.25	LAN
Addressing	14 decimal digits	16 or 48 binary digits
Operational Speeds	Kbps	Mbps
Packet Sizes (octets)	128, 256, ...	1500+

pected to exist in the future. Given that Layer 4 (the Transport Layer) is end-to-end in nature (i.e., it operates only in the communicating end systems), then we can restrict our investigations to the interworking only as it relates to Layers 1–3 of the RM-OSI. We will restrict ourselves even further to considering interworking only as it relates to Layer 3 of the RM-OSI. Of course, these concepts are applicable to "bridging" at Layer 2; however, we have chosen to leave those aspects of interworking outside the scope of this paper.

A. Relay Functions

The growing need for connectivity to transfer data has all but ruled out direct connections between end systems and has given rise to environments where many systems can be connected in a more judicous way. This, of course, involves the use of "intermediaries." To facilitate communications between peers, one of the functions recognized by the RM-OSI is a *relay* function. This function, provided by systems acting in an "intermediary" (or "intermediate") fashion, can be viewed as a set of procedures by which a system forwards data from one system to another (i.e., the traditional "middle man" role).

B. Collections of Intermediate Systems

One can go a step further and group together a collection of intermediate systems. A grouping of such systems with common characteristics is, of course, referred to as a *network*. Common characteristics include such traits as ownership, language (i.e., protocols) used, cooperation for decision making, etc.; however, use of common technology is not a characteristic necessarily shared in a network. For reasons that will become clear in a moment, we will refer to this grouping as a *subnetwork* (which will be used hereafter) rather than a network. Formally, we define a subnetwork as a collection of intermediate systems and/or the transmission means for connecting them that forms an autonomous whole and that can be used to interconnect end systems for purposes of communication.

The above definition seems to imply that a subnetwork must contain at least one intermediate system, even though this was not explicitly stated. While that appeared to be the norm a decade ago, the concept of multisystem connectivity without the use of pairwise connections, but rather through a shared medium (e.g., a coax-based LAN) is not in concert with such an implication since there is no intermediate system. Therefore, we will refine our definition of a subnetwork such that it provides for multisystem connectivity through the use of zero or more intermediate systems and appropriate transmission media.

C. Role of Layer 3

When defining the functions needed to allow end systems to communicate, one must consider the functions related to accessing a subnetwork. The RM-OSI assigns the functions for accessing a subnetwork to Layers 1-3. Layer 1 is responsible for the mechanical, electrical, functional, and procedural means for bit transmission, whereas Layer 2 is responsible for detecting and/or correcting any errors that occur in Layer 1. Layer 3, also known as the Network Layer (note the upper case "N"), is concerned with the procedures for determining the end-to-end path over which data are to travel (i.e., *routing*) and actually conveying the data over that path (usually involving some form of *relaying*). Such paths may be simple or complex (or even nonexistent), depending on the location of the end systems needing to communicate. It should be clear now that the term "subnetwork" is used above to avoid confusion with the concept of the Network Layer. The former represents physical equipment, whereas the latter represents a logical set of procedures.

As indicated in Section II, it is impractical to expect all end systems to reside on the same subnetwork. Therefore, one must recognize that an end system may need to communicate with other end systems residing on a different subnetwork as well as with those on the same subnetwork. Nevertheless, the functions performed by the Network Layer must provide the necessary connectivity in either case.

D. OSI Network Service

The need for Network Layer functions to provide connectivity regardless of the location (same or different subnetworks) leads us to our next concept, that of the *OSI Network Service*.

The RM-OSI allocates to Layer 4 end-to-end functions; *end-to-end*, in this case, is independent of whether the path traversed between two communicating end systems spans one or more than one subnetwork. To provide for this independence (known as the RM-OSI principle of *Layer Independence*), it is necessary to decouple the idiosyncrasies arising from the various subnetwork technologies involved in an instance of communication from the set of capabilities provided by the Network Layer to the Transport Layer. This decoupling, in general, manifests itself in a *layer service definition*; in the case of the Network Layer/Transport Layer decoupling, we have the *OSI Network Service (NS) Definition*. We define the NS as the set of subnetwork-independent capabilities that are provided collectively by all of the procedures within and below the Network Layer (the *Network Service Provider*) and made available for use by the Transport Layer (the *Network Service User*). These capabilities are exercised through an abstract set of *primitives* that are part of the service definition. Fig. 1 depicts the Network Service concepts discussed here.

Two types of NS have been defined: a *connection-mode network service* [5], [6] (CONS), and a *connectionless-mode network service* [7] (CLNS).[1] The capabilities observed by the Transport Layer in the two cases are as described below.

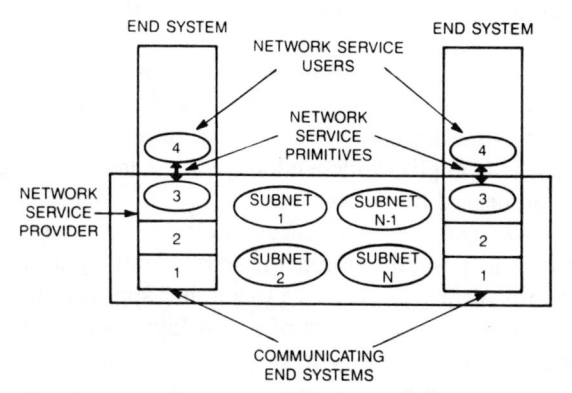

Fig. 1. Network Service concepts.

1) CONS provides for data transfer through a three-phase process: first, an association (i.e., a *Network Connection*) is established between the Transport Layer entities that need to communicate; data are then transferred; finally, the Network Connection is released. The distinguishing characteristics of the CONS is that data transfer is modeled as a first-in/first-out queue; that is, data are assumed to be transferred in sequence and without duplication (although not necessarily without loss). Associated with each phase are various parameters and subprocedures. For example, the identity of the remote end system is passed as a parameter from the Transport Layer to the Network Layer during the establishment phase. Furthermore, the Transport Layer has available to it the capability to reinitialize the Network Connection (i.e., "flush the pipe") on detection of an error during data transfer.

2) CLNS, in contrast to CONS, provides only a data-transfer capability to the Transport Layer. The distinguishing characteristics of the CLNS is that it gives no guarantees to the Transport Layer regarding the characteristics of the data transfer (i.e., there could be out-of-sequence delivery, duplication, and loss). Associated with this service are also several parameters; as expected, one of the necessary parameters is the identity of the remote end system to which the data are to be transferred.

A corollary associated with the general service-definition concept is that, in any given instance of communication, the service users observe exactly the same service, i.e., the same set of capabilities. This, in turn, facilitates the development of the protocol to be used by these higher layer entities.

E. Taxonomy of Interworking Terms

To provide a common basis for our subsequent discussion, we need to define several terms used when considering interworking. Terms such as *Relay*, *Gateway*, *Intermediate System (IS)*, *Interworking Unit (IWU)*, and

---
[1]Within ISO, both types of NS are recognized. Within CCITT, only CONS is recognized.

Router are often used interchangeably when discussing Layer 3 operation.

A *Relay* does not operate as a source or a sink of data, but maintains consistency of the semantics of the incoming and outgoing data streams. The term, when further unqualified, applies independently of the layer(s) of protocol processed by the system.

Gateway is reserved for cases where information is converted (and possibly stored for some time) by an application for further conveyance to another application. This implies the full processing of seven layers of communication functionality. It is most applicable to store-and-forward type of applications (e.g., electronic mail) or to conversion of totally different architectures (as described in the Introduction [4]). A gateway can be said to be an Application Layer Relay.

An *Intermediate System* (IS) is an abstract term used to identify the entities of the OSI environment which perform only the functions of the lower three layers of the RM-OSI. An Intermediate System may be a real subnetwork or it may be a unit used to interconnect one or more real subnetworks.

An *Interworking Unit* (IWU) is a real piece of equipment which behaves as an Intermediate System and is used to interconnect multiple subnetworks. An IWU is a relay system which performs its relaying function at the Network Layer.

A *Router* is a term applied to a type of IWU associated with Network Layer operation in which the IWU uses a protocol in common with end systems, independent of any subnetwork-specific protocol. The basic principle in applying this term is that the IWU only performs routing and no "relaying" of functionality from one subnetwork to the next (since the common protocol is independent of subnetworks). As such, this is somewhat misleading in that what is called a router may need, in practice, to perform relay functions, such as segmentation and reassembly to maintain the boundaries of Transport Layer data units.

For completeness, we also define two other terms pertaining to interworking (although they do not apply to Layer 3 operation).

A *bridge* is a relay that operates at Layer 2 within a LAN environment. More specifically, it operates as a relay with respect to the Layer 2 portion of the Medium Access Control (MAC) Sublayer of the IEEE 802 protocol architecture [8].

A *repeater* is a relay that operates at Layer 1 of the RM-OSI. Its purpose is to convey a transmission signal in environments where physical limitations would otherwise prevent its further propagation. For example, IEEE 802 LAN's have a limitation on the physical distance of a coaxial cable used for the medium. A repeater, also known as a medium extender, removes this limitation.

It should be noted that the above terms, except perhaps for the last one, should be viewed as logical descriptions of a system's functions, independent of its physical realization. It is possible to build a real system that operates in different modes, with respect to the above logical descriptions, depending on the instance of communication in which it participates. It is possible for a real system acting as a relay also to act, for a different instance of communication, as an end system.

IV. Interworking Elements

The previous section presented some of the concerns and basic concepts related to interworking. One of the fundamental concerns is the variety and number of subnetworks in existence. From these discussions, it should be clear that interworking must deal with the following first-order considerations:

1) the provision of a well-defined Network Service (either CONS or CLNS) to the Transport Layer to maintain independence from subnetwork types, topology, etc.;[2]

2) the specification of an address unique in the OSI environment that identifies an end system and, coupled with this, the *conveyance* of this information for the use by Intermediate Systems in reaching the destination;

3) the selection of the path to reach the destination; and

4) the heterogeneity of subnetworks traversed in going from source to sink.

When considering the above items, especially the last one, some important second-order concerns become apparent. These are

1) the protocol used for accessing each subnetwork on the source-to-sink path and, more importantly, the relationship of the abstraction of this protocol to the NS (which is in itself an abstract concept) to be provided to the Transport Layer;

2) the packet sizes allowed by the subnetworks traversed and, coupled with this, the maintenance of the boundaries of the data unit to be transferred at the request of the Transport Layer; and

3) the specification and maintenance of a set of *quality of service* characteristics (e.g., throughput, transit delay, etc.) so that all elements in the source-to-sink path can work cooperatively to fulfill the expectations of the Transport Layer.

From the point of view of layer independence and the decoupling of the Transport Layer from the Network Layer, the first of these second-order concerns can be viewed another way. That is, the provision of the chosen NS by protocols used within the Network Layer is of paramount importance; the actual protocols used, especially those for accessing a subnetwork (which are usually fixed by the subnetwork), are of secondary importance.

Given the range of the issues above, it would seem that it would be difficult, if not impossible, to accomplish interworking in an environment that is heterogeneous in even the slightest way. This is not quite true; by vigorous and creative attack, we will see that the task is not altogether impossible.

---

[2]It is outside the scope of this paper to discuss how an NS selection is made for a given instance of communication or to discuss the merits of the two NS's.

We have already discussed perhaps the most important element—a well-defined Network Service; this will not be discussed any further in this paper. The following subsections are divided into four broad areas that address all of the above remaining first- and second-order concerns, as follows:

1) the relationship between protocols used for accessing a subnetwork and the provision of the NS,
2) the abstract operation of an intermediate system and its role in relaying,
3) global identification, and
4) routing.

A. Layer 3 Protocols and the Network Service

The complexity of the Network Layer (NL), with respect to the real world objects it must deal with (i.e., the heterogeneous subnetworks[3]), led to a detailed modeling effort in the ISO, resulting in the Internal Organization of the Network Layer [9] (IONL). As depicted in Fig. 2, the IONL views the functionality needed for Network Layer operation as consisting of three components:

1) protocols, and their relationship to and provision of the NS;
2) relaying; and
3) routing.

This subsection will deal only with the relationship of the Layer 3 protocols to the NS and interworking, which is the main thrust of the IONL standard. The following subsections will deal with the other two components.

1) IONL Basic Concept: To understand the process of networking multiple subnetworks (i.e., interworking) together, in conformance to the OSI effort, it is necessary to understand the allowable interworking methods described in the IONL. According to the IONL, all methods for interworking must ensure that, for any given instance of communication, the NS observed by the two communicating users at the Network/Transport Layer boundary is the same. That is, for a given instance of communication, the communicating parties will either observe the OSI CONS or the OSI CLNS.

2) Partitioning of the Network Layer: The IONL concepts are built on the fundamental assumption that the functions required by the Network Layer (NL) in support of the OSI NS are not necessarily fulfilled by a single discrete protocol, but that, in fact, there are cases where several protocols collectively contribute to achieve the required service. In an effort to clarify this concept of a well-defined set of functions (i.e., the OSI NS) potentially partitioned among multiple protocols within the NL, the IONL specifies three roles in which an NL protocol may serve:

1) the role of the Subnetwork Independent Convergence Protocol (SNICP),
2) the role of the Subnetwork Dependent Convergence Protocol (SNDCP), and

[3] After all, life would be simpler if we had to deal only with a single subnetwork, a single subnetwork type, or isolated subnetworks from which no data ever left.

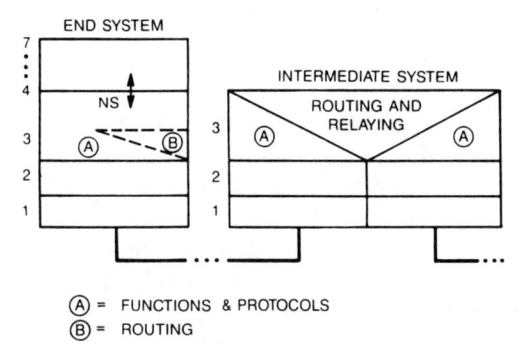

Fig. 2. Components of Network Layer functionality.

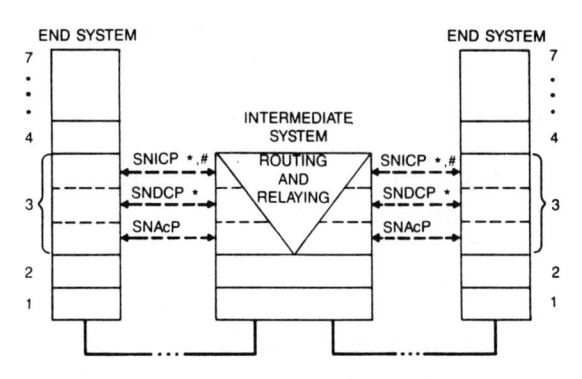

Fig. 3. Partitioning of the Network Layer.

3) the role of the Subnetwork Access Protocol (SNAcP).

Fig. 3 depicts the NL partitioning. There are two concepts that are particularly noteworthy. First, it is not necessary for the three roles to be fulfilled by three individual protocols. In fact, it is possible that a protocol acting in the SNAcP role may satisfy all the functions required to support the OSI NS; in this case, that protocol is considered to fulfill all three roles. Similarly, a protocol acting in the SNDCP role may fulfill all the functions required to support the OSI NS; in that case, that protocol is considered to be acting both in the SNDCP and SNICP roles. Second, it is possible that the fulfillment of a role may be achieved by implementing a set of functions only within the end systems, instead of having to implement a discrete protocol. Later on, some existing protocol examples will help clarify these concepts.

A protocol designed to act in the SNICP role supports all the elements of the OSI NS and assumes a strictly defined set of underlying service capabilities. As the name implies, its key distinguishing characteristic is that its underlying service assumptions need not be defined in accordance with the characteristics of a particular subnetwork.

Conversely, a protocol designed to act in the SNDCP role is, by definition, constrained to operate over the specific protocol used for accessing the subnetwork. Hence, the operations of a protocol acting in the SNDCP role are strictly defined by the underlying service characteristics provided by the SNAcP and by the service characteristics to be provided to the protocol acting in the SNICP role above, if any.

A protocol designed to act in the SNAcP role operates strictly according to the requirements of the specific subnetwork to be accessed. It provides a service which is specific to the protocols required to be used by the subnetwork in question; this resulting service may or may not need the intervention of other protocols in order to fulfill the requirements for the OSI NS.

3) Interworking Methods: Given the aforementioned three roles, the IONL describes three separate methods for interworking:

1) the interconnection of subnetworks whose respective SNAcP's support all the elements of the OSI NS method,
2) the hop-by-hop harmonization method, and
3) the internetworking protocol method.

The *interconnection of subnetworks whose respective SNAcP's support all the elements of the OSI NS* is, as expected, the simplest method of interworking. It addresses the case where the protocols used in the SNAcP roles of both subnetworks to be interworked inherently support all the elements of the OSI NS.

Fig. 4 depicts this simplest method of interworking. As shown, the 1984 version X.25 Packet Layer Protocol (PLP) can be used in both subnetworks to support all the elements of the OSI CONS without the need for additional augmentations [10], [11]. In this case, the X.25/PLP-1984 is a single protocol serving in all three roles in each subnetwork.

The *hop-by-hop harmonization* method describes the process of harmonizing the services observable across each subnetwork to be interworked such that each supports the same OSI NS—either the CONS or the CLNS.

In order to understand the harmonization concept, consider the case where at least one (although sometimes both) of the two subnetworks to be interworked does not support all the elements of the OSI NS chosen to be supported. That is, in one of the subnetworks, the protocol operating in the role of the SNAcP is somewhat "deficient." In this case, a protocol acting in the SNDCP role, a protocol acting in the SNICP role, or both may be required to enhance the "deficient" SNAcP such that it provides all the elements of the OSI NS chosen to be supported.

Some of the convergence functions/protocols needed to fulfill the SNDCP and/or SNICP roles, which complement existing protocols designed to act in the SNAcP role, have already been defined. Fig. 5 depicts the case where an SNDCP [10] is required to enhance the basic service provided by the 1980 version of the X.25 PLP, used in the left subnetwork, such that the full OSI CONS is provided.

The *Internetworking Protocol* method describes the process of utilizing a single protocol, operating in the

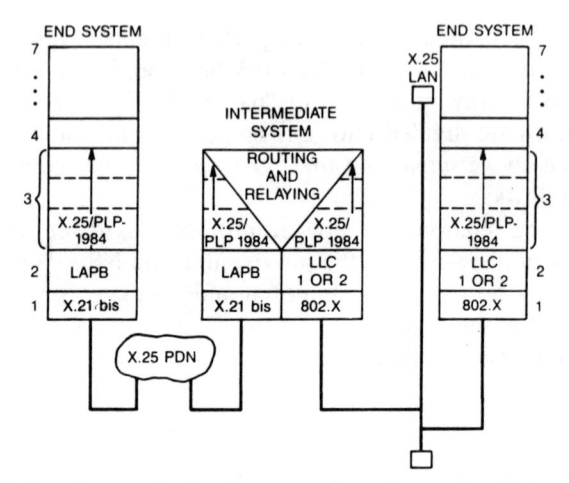

Fig. 4. Sample scenarios for interconnecting subnetworks which support all the elements of the OSI NS.

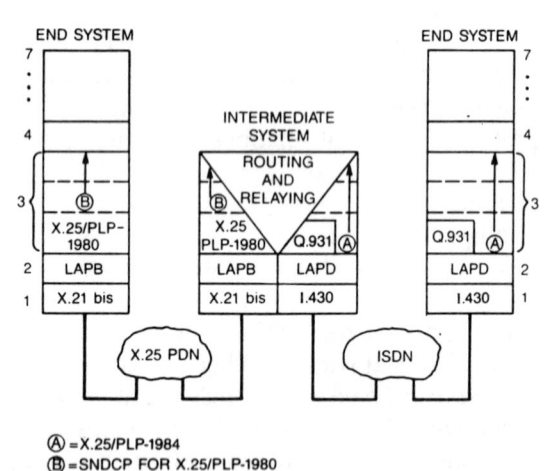

Fig. 5. Sample scenarios for hop-by-hop harmonization method.

SNICP role, across all the subnetworks involved such that the same OSI NS is provided. The basic assumption is that, wherever required, a function/protocol acting in the SNDCP role is defined such that the basic service provided by the subnetwork can be altered so as to be equivalent to the underlying service required by the SNICP. This approach to interworking is somewhat equivalent to the approach used in the well-known DoD Internet environment [12].

Fig. 6 shows a sample scenario depicting this approach to interworking. On the LAN side, an SNDCP [13] maps the underlying service provided by Logical Link Control (LLC) Type 1 procedures [14] to the underlying service required by the Protocol for Providing the Connectionless-Mode Network Service [13] (commonly known as CLNP[4]). On the PDN (Public Data Network) side, an

---

[4]The CLNP was originally called the "Connectionless Internetwork Protocol"; its name was changed in recognition of the fact that it applies to a single subnetwork and that it is not the only approach to providing interworking.

Fig. 6. Sample scenario for Internetwork Protocol method.

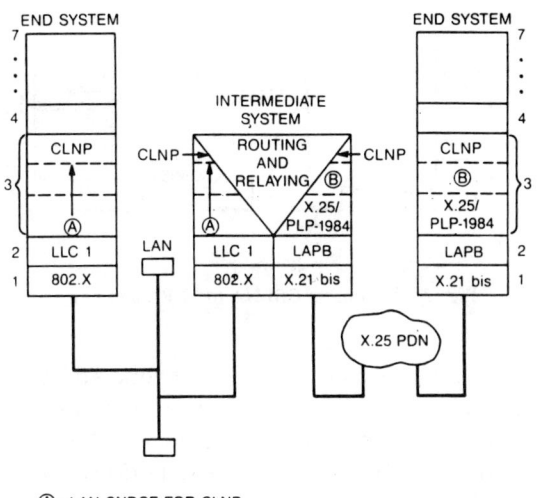

Ⓐ = LAN SNDCF FOR CLNP
Ⓑ = X.25 SNDCP FOR CLNP

SNDCP [13] is required to extract the underlying service required by the CLNP from the basic service provided by the X.25 PLP. In the latter case, it may be interesting to notice that the X.25/PLP being used in the SNAcP role may actually be a 1984 or later version which itself is fully capable of supporting the OSI CONS. However, since for this instance of communication it is assumed that the OSI NS to be supported is the CLNS, then the SNDCP is required.

Currently, the only Internetworking Protocol standardized is the CLNP; hence, this approach to interworking can only result in the provision of the OSI CLNS. Furthermore, the only methods applicable for the provision of the OSI CONS are the interconnection of subnetworks whose respective SNAcP's support all the methods of the OSI NS method and the hop-by-hop harmonization method. Similarly, since the CCITT supports only the OSI CONS, then it recognizes only the latter two methods [15].

4) More About the SNDCP Role: It may be worthwhile to say a little more about the SNDCP role. The purpose of the protocols/functions which act in the role of an SNDCP is to perform the work of the "middle man." That is, they perform the necessary steps to translate the subnetwork service provided by the SNAcP operating below it to the underlying service required by the SNICP operating above. Whether the SNDCP role is fulfilled by a distinct protocol (which exchanges protocol-control information) or a set of well-defined functions performed only within the end systems is dependent on the particular environment.

As previously mentioned, the only distinct protocol presently standardized to act in the SNICP role is the CLNP. The CLNP assumes a well-defined connectionless-mode underlying service. Hence, the SNDCP's are needed to extract this required service from whatever type of service is derived from the protocols used to access the subnetwork. The complexity of the protocols/functions acting in the SNDCP role varies based on the subnetwork.

For example, in looking at Fig. 6 again, a very trivial set of functions is defined to act in the role of the SNDCP on the LAN side. This is so since the service provided by the LLC Type 1 procedures is very similar to the underlying service required by the CLNP; the only real difference is in the meaning of the Priority Quality of Service.

Conversely, a more complex set of functions is defined to act in the role of the SNDCP on the PDN side. This is so since the underlying service required by the CLNP is connectionless, while the service provided by the X.25 subnetwork is connection-oriented; hence, the defined functions need to perform all the necessary steps concerning the setting up and clearing of connections for the transmission of datagrams, etc.

The above two SNDCP's consist of sets of functions performed only within the end systems. For the sake of completeness, notice that an example of a discrete protocol acting in the role of an SNDCP is the one required in the left subnetwork of Fig. 5 for the support of the OSI CONS. This protocol [10], although characterized as an SNDCP, actually fulfills both the SNDCP and SNICP roles.

B. Relaying

The key OSI concept of a well-defined NS made available to the Transport Layer entities of the communicating end system applies regardless of whether the end systems are on the same or different subnetworks. On the other hand, the fact that different protocols may be used within different subnetworks is *not* a concern. In fact, when crossing from one subnetwork to another, the IWU first determines the outgoing path (the routing function) and then applies the relaying functions to perform the mapping of the necessary information from the protocols used on one subnetwork to those used on the other. According to the RM-OSI, the fact that communication is relayed by a given layer is known neither to the layers above nor below the relaying layer.

From all that has been said so far, it should be clear that successful interworking can only occur by ensuring that the semantics of the incoming data are maintained unchanged across the IWU. This means that regardless of the method of interworking used, the relaying function performed by the IWU's must make sure that a minimum amount of well-defined control information is explicitly conveyed, by the NL protocol (or combination of protocols) used, across all subnetworks. This control information includes the unique OSI address of the communicating end systems, the boundaries of the Transport Layer's data, and, perhaps, the Quality of Service characteristics associated with an instance of communication. To this end, the ISO community has recognized the need for a formal specification of the functions internal to an

IWU. Effort is being dedicated to produce such a description to facilitate the implementation of IWU's [16].

There exist several documents dealing particularly with the relaying function performed when interconnecting multiple subnetworks. CCITT Recommendation X.75 [17] specifies the procedure for interworking X.25 PDN's, ISDN's (when providing packet-mode services), and X.25 PDN's to ISDN's. Additionally, ISO has standardized the definition of an IWU that describes the relaying operation when the X.25/PLP is used in both subnetworks [18], e.g., as depicted in Fig. 5. All of these specifications assume that the interworking methods being used are either *the interconnection of subnetworks whose respective SNAcP's support all the elements of the OSI NS* method or the *hop-by-hop harmonization* method; and the OSI NS to be supported is the CONS.

For the purpose of supporting the OSI CLNS, there is currently no explicit document describing the relaying function to be performed by the IWU's. In fact, since the same exact protocol is being used both by the end systems and all the traversed IWU's, then it is actually in the specification of the protocol itself that there is the differentiation made between the functions to be supported by the end systems and the functions to be supported by the IWU's.

C. Addressing

An essential ingredient for total connectivity/interoperability is the ability to uniquely identify every entity in the OSI environment. The notion of associating a unique string[5] to an entity such that it can be unambiguously identified is referred to as *addressing*.

In considering the traditional telephony environment, one may believe that the addressing problem is trivial since the telephone numbering system has guaranteed uniqueness for decades. However, the standalone telephony environment has traditionally be administered in a "centralized" fashion, i.e., the authority responsible for allocating and administering numbers has always operated in a singly rooted hierarchical fashion. Data environments, on the other hand, have developed independently from one another, under the control of different administrations, and without the control of a single authority. Hence, their addressing schemes are not only different from the telephony one, but are different and inconsistent among themselves. Consider, as examples, the 14-digit CCITT X.121 numbering plan for public data networks, the 15-digit CCITT E.164 numbering plan for ISDN's, the 48-bit IEEE MAC addressing plan, etc.

For the purpose of guaranteeing unambiguous and unique addressing within the OSI environment while avoiding the political implications of making the existing

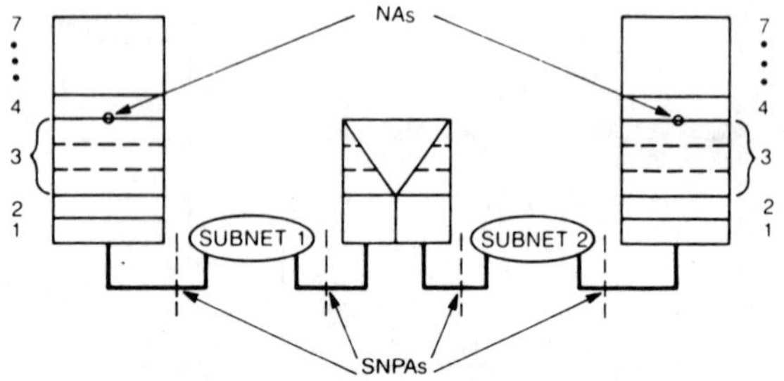

Fig. 7. Relation of OSI NA to SNPA address.

addressing plans obsolete, an OSI Network Address (NA) plan [6], [19] has been developed that specifies a common structure incorporating the existing plans. This plan succeeds by recursively allocating subauthorities for assigning OSI NA's while allowing end systems and individual subnetworks to retain their internal addresses. The relationship between the subnetwork addresses (known as *Subnetwork Point of Attachment*, or SNPA, addresses) and the OSI NA's is illustrated in Fig. 7. A key concept is that while the SNPA addresses identify the physical points at which end systems interface to the individual subnetworks, the OSI NA's identify the Transport Layer entities residing inside the end systems.

The OSI Network Address structure is shown in Fig. 8. The Initial Domain Part (IDP) consists of two subparts: the Authority and Format Identifier (AFI) and the Initial Domain Identifier (IDI). The IDP is always present. The Domain Specific Part (DSP) may or may not be present.

Presently, the first-level authorities identified by the OSI NA plan are the ISO and the CCITT, which are responsible for assigning the AFI's. In fact, the AFI represents the extra level of hierarchy introduced to group the existing numbering and organizational/geographical based plans under a single root.[6] The addressing authorities identified by the AFI include: the X.121 numbering plan for Public Data Networks [20], the E.164 numbering plan for ISDN's [21], the E.163 numbering plan for the Public Switched Telephone Network (PSTN) [22], the F.69 numbering plan for Telex Networks [23], the ISO-specified Data Country Code geographical plan [24], and the ISO-specified International Code Designator organizational plan [25]. The IDI, in turn, consists of an address from one of these plans, the particular plan being identified by the AFI.

The IDI may either specify an addressing subauthority or, in some cases, the actual subnetwork address of an end system. In the former case, the DSP must be present and its substructure is defined by the subauthority identified by the IDI; the ISO has not considered it necessary to standardize the DSP. In the latter case, the IDP may actually be considered the complete OSI NA without the need for the DSP.

---

[5]In networking contexts, the content of the string may be binary or decimal.

[6]At the root of the overall OSI Network Address hierarchy is ISO 8348/Addendum 2 and CCITT Recommendation X.213.

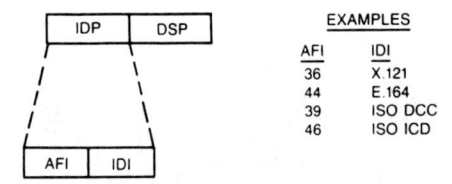

Fig. 8. OSI Network Address structure.

AFI	IDI
36	X.121
44	E.164
39	ISO DCC
46	ISO ICD

EXAMPLE 1: END SYSTEMS ON PUBLIC NETWORKS

INITIAL DOMAIN PART		DOMAIN SPECIFIC PART
AFI 36	IDI 31342019497525	DSP <NULL>

EXAMPLE 2: PRIVATE NETWORK UNDER ISO DCC FOR USA

AFI 39	IDI 840	DSP *000111 *0001 0001 F 4F 4F 4F 5F 401 FE <OI> <OSP>

*THESE ARE HEXADECIMAL DIGITS

Fig. 9. Samples of OSI NA schemes.

Fig. 9 shows two examples of OSI Network Addressing formats. Consider the case where an administration is in control of an X.25 PDN providing services only to end systems attached directly to it. Such an administration could choose to adopt an OSI NA scheme as shown in example 1 of Fig. 9 and, hence, allocate to its end systems NA's consisting of only the IDP (with a null DSP). Conversely, a U.S.-based private company may want to integrate itself within the OSI environment by adopting an NA scheme under the DCC plan of the U.S.[7] In this case, such a company would follow the procedures outlined by the American National Standards Institute [26] (ANSI) and ask the appropriate registration authority (designated by the ANSI) for an Organizational Identifier[8] (OI). Once assigned an OI, the company would proceed to define its own structure for the Organizational Specific Part (OSP) of the remaining DSP, and assign NA's to all the end systems within its domain. Example 2 of Fig. 9 shows what the NA scheme for such a company would look like.

D. OSI Routing

The capability of routing messages between communicating end systems across multiple subnetworks (i.e., herein referred to as *internetwork routing*) is a fundamental requirement of OSI interworking. Within the scope of OSI interworking, the process of internetwork routing is related to the process of routing within individual subnetworks (hereafter referred to as *intranetwork routing*[9]) in that the former assumes and relies upon the existence of the latter. This distinction will become clearer, hopefully, by describing the OSI internetwork routing approach.

1) Internetwork Routing Goals: The principal goals of the OSI internetwork routing scheme can be reduced to
1) global reachability,
2) subnetwork independence, and
3) acceptable performance.

Global reachability defines the basic capability of delivering messages between any combination of end systems participating in the OSI environment, regardless of the potentially different addressing conventions used in the traversed subnetworks (e.g., X.121 numbering, IEEE 802 addressing, etc.). Accordingly, part of the OSI effort has been to develop the addressing conventions outlined in the previous section.

Subnetwork independence implies that the core set of functions developed for internetwork routing can be implemented regardless of the inherent characteristics of specific underlying subnetworks. That is, the number and/or type of subnetworks (e.g., Broadcast LAN's, X.25 PDN's, ISDN's) that may have to be traversed when routing a message should not effect the core functions.

Acceptable performance implies some quantifiable levels of efficiency, reliability, and robustness that ensure an acceptable global routing process. Some of the key preconditions include: the ability for the scheme to converge towards a consistent view of the environment after a change has taken place, the ability to achieve convergence in a timely fashion (i.e., somewhat proportional to the diameter of the environment), the ability to fix partitions by discovering alternate paths, etc.

2) OSI Internetwork Routing Approach: Internetwork routing can be differentiated from intranetwork routing in that the latter performs the necessary functions to convey data units between entities attached to the same subnetwork, i.e., between SNPA addresses on the same subnetwork. Normally, the intranetwork routing process takes as input the destination SNPA address and makes all the appropriate routing decisions to reach it.

Internetwork routing is concerned with the broader task of conveying messages between entities attached to different subnetworks (i.e., the source-to-destination path traverses multiple subnetworks); as such, it augments the basic difficulties introduced by intranetwork routing. In the OSI context, it should be clear that internetwork routing is the process which operates on the globally unique OSI Network Address (NA). That is, the procedures that perform the internetwork routing take as input an OSI NA and are capable of deriving from it the SNPA address of the next "hop" en route to the final destination. The next "hop" may or may not be the final destination itself. Once the next "hop" SNPA is known, the intranetwork routing process of the subnetwork to be traversed apply at large.

---

[7] The DCC allocated to the U.S. is 840. Hence, 840 would be the IDI part of the NA's for the requesting company.

[8] The ANSI has specified the OI as a field within the DSP.

[9] From an OSI routing point of view, the concatenation of PDN's is considered as a single subnetwork, although each PDN may be under the control of a separate administration.

To solve the OSI internetwork routing problem, the following subtasks have been (and are still being) considered:

1) determining the extent to which the structure of the OSI addressing conventions can be exploited,

2) understanding and defining the *levels* of interaction that occur between the End Systems (ES's) and the Intermediate Systems (IS's), and

3) partitioning and allocating the routing functions among the ES's and the IS's.

A quick analysis of the possible types of OSI NA's shows that in some cases, their structure can be useful to facilitate the routing process in some complex environments, while in others, it cannot. For example, if an administration adopts an OSI Network Addressing scheme based on CCITT numbering plans, then its OSI addressing scheme is guaranteed to have a hierarchical structure and to be globally administered. But most important, its routing process is facilitated since the CCITT has already standardized on principles for establishing routes between public subnetworks across administrative and/or international boundaries. These principles [27] are based on bilateral agreement between the subnetworks involved and take into account delay, throughput, time of day, etc. Routes are preestablished and agreed upon in a static fashion. When setting up a call, a route connecting the two parties involved is chosen in a dynamic fashion from the available ones.

On the other hand, OSI NA's allocated under the ISO Data Country Code (DCC) or the ISO International Code Designator (ICD) do not have any formal hierarchy inherent in the IDP. Both the DCC and ICD plans are flat identifiers which do not provide any formally specified information concerning routing aspects. Consequently, the DSP of an OSI NA allocated under these schemes must be utilized to provide some amount of hierarchy.

Because of the variance in the structure of the various types of OSI NA's, the overall OSI internetwork routing architectural description has minimal (if any) dependence on the structure of OSI NA's. The standardized OSI routing architecture [28], [29] defines the basic elements of routing on an OSI NA, the interactions that ES's have with their immediately (one-hop) accessible IS's (ES-IS interactions), and the interactions that the IS's have among themselves (IS-IS interactions). The ES-IS and IS-IS interactions can be viewed as a hierarchical set of functions forming part of the overall routing framework. ES-IS interactions are considered to be the lowest level of interactions within the routing framework. The IS-IS interactions, which constitute the next two levels of interactions, are decomposed into intradomain IS-IS interactions and interdomain IS-IS interactions.

Intradomain IS-IS defines the interactions among IS's which belong to the same routing domain, while interdomain IS-IS defines the interactions among IS's belonging to different routing domains. A *routing domain* encompasses an environment consisting of one or more subnetworks under the control of a single administration and is defined by the routing procedures used by its IS's and the information operated on. That is, a set of IS's using the same set of routing procedures on the same kind of information and belonging to an environment under the control of a single administration are part of the same routing domain.

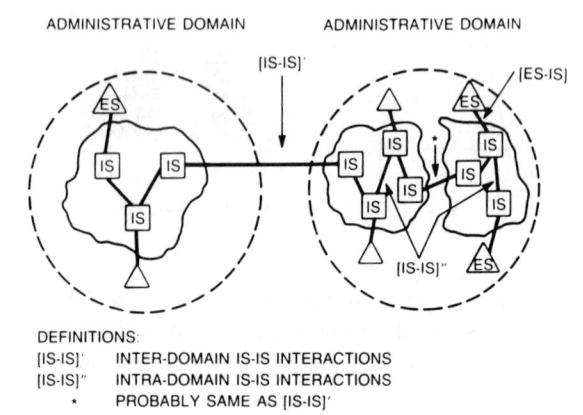

Fig. 10. Illustration of the routing hierarchy.

DEFINITIONS:
[IS-IS]' INTER-DOMAIN IS-IS INTERACTIONS
[IS-IS]" INTRA-DOMAIN IS-IS INTERACTIONS
• PROBABLY SAME AS [IS-IS]'

Interdomain IS-IS interactions, on the other hand, are applicable in two cases: when crossing administrative boundaries (i.e., the communicating IS's belong to different administrations or companies); or when a single administration controls multiple routing domains (i.e., the communicating IS's reside in routing domains that operate different routing procedures, although they are under the control of the same administration due to, for example, subnetworks from different vendors procured by a single administration).

Fig. 10 illustrates the proposed architectural partitioning of the internetwork routing problem. For both the ES-IS and IS-IS cases, the definition of interactions entails the specification of the type of information (e.g., addressing information) exchanged among each other, and the method, i.e., the protocol(s), by which this information is exchanged. For example, in the ES-IS interactions case, the ES's and the IS's periodically exchange messages with each other, establishing their existence and operational status. In essence, the ES's require only knowledge of the existence of at least one IS in order to route on a global basis, while the IS's, in addition to knowing about the ES's on its subnetwork, also gain knowledge of the reachability of ES's on other subnetworks via the information it exchanges with other IS's (IS-IS interactions). Hence, the basic internetwork routing concept on which ES's rely is to regard the OSI NA of the destination and, if the next-hop SNPA address is unknown, just forward the message to the SNPA address of an IS. The assumption is that since the IS has much more knowledge, it will know how to route the message or to which IS to redirect the message for further routing.

The ES-IS protocol for use in environments operating the CLNP protocol in environments with "inexpensive" broadcasting capabilities, such as IEEE 802-based

LAN's, has already been standardized [30]. A similar protocol for use in environments operating the X.25 PLP in support of the CONS per ISO 8878 is also being standardized [31]. The latter achieves equivalent functionality as the former without the assumption of inherent broadcasting capabilities, but with the aid of a central facility which performs the address resolution function (i.e., the Network Address-to-SNPA address mapping). The latter solution compromises some performance while gaining more subnetwork-type independence.

A number of IS-IS protocols exist both experimentally and in proprietary interworking solutions [32], [33]. The ISO is presently pursuing a solution to the intradomain IS-IS routing problem [34] that is based on the concepts of link-state routing [35], [36]. However, the standardization of an IS-IS routing protocol will likely take several years since not all the involved parties are eager to make their proprietary scheme obsolete.

The generation of a complete set of standards addressing the overall routing problem remains in itself a noble goal to pursue. However, it should be clear that interworking is not precluded by the lack of a standardized dynamic set of protocols to perform the functions. Clearly, every routing domain can use any proprietary scheme (static or dynamic based) for its internal distribution of information and resort to static exchange based on bilateral agreements when crossing administrative boundaries.

V. Conclusions

A significant amount of progress has been made concerning the interworking of subnetworks. Nevertheless, the existence of multiple OSI Network Services and of multiple methods for interconnection does not simplify the selection process. We are at a point where many of the critical tools are presently available for interworking according to OSI; however, there is still work to be done.

In the near future, we foresee more SNDCP's and SNICP's being developed to support subnetwork technologies not yet capable of providing the OSI NS inherently (e.g., Integrated Voice and Data LAN's, etc.). Certainly, the process of administering and/or allocating IDI's for the purpose of promoting the OSI NA scheme requires further refinements; therefore, it will continue to receive its due attention until fully resolved. The work begun on a formal description of the internal operation of the systems performing the relaying is likely to continue for a while. Similarly, the work on internetwork routing is likely to continue until the standardization of a complete suite of protocols is realized.

References

[1] Information processing systems—Open Systems Interconnection—Basic reference model," ISO 7498, 1984.
[2] CCITT Recommendation X.200, "Reference model of Open Systems Interconnection for CCITT applications."
[3] "Open Systems Interconnection reference model," OSI Data Transfer (published by Omnicom Inc.), Transmission 1, June 1982.
[4] W. P. Lidinsky, "An approach for interconnecting SNA and XNS networks," in Proc. 9th Data Commun. Symp., Sept. 1985.
[5] "Information processing systems—Data communications—Network service definition," ISO 8348, 1987.
[6] CCITT Recommendation X.213, "Network service definition for Open Systems Interconnection for CCITT applications."
[7] "Information processing systems—Data communications—Network service definition: Connectionless-mode transmission," ISO 8348/Addendum 1, 1987.
[8] IEEE Project 802, "Local and metropolitan area network standard—Overview, interworking, and system management," Draft IEEE Standard 802.1, July 1987.
[9] "Information processing systems—Data communications—Internal organization of the network layer," ISO 8648, 1986.
[10] "Information processing systems—Data communications—Use of X.25 to provide the OSI connection-mode network service," ISO 8878, 1987.
[11] CCITT Recommendation X.223, "Use of X.25 to provide the OSI connection-mode network service for CCITT applications."
[12] V. G. Cerf and E. Cain, "The DoD Internet architecture model," Comput. Networks, vol. 7, pp. 307-318, 1983.
[13] "Information processing systems—Data communications—Protocol for providing the connectionless-mode network service," ISO 8473, 1988.
[14] "Information Processing Systems—Data communications—Local area networks—Part 2: Logical link control," ISO 8802-2, 1987.
[15] CCITT Recommendation X.300, "General principles and arrangements for interworking between public data networks, and between public data networks and other public networks."
[16] "Information processing systems—Data communications—Definition of the relaying functions of the network layer intermediate system," ISO DP 10028, 1988.
[17] CCITT Recommendation X.75, "Packet-switched signaling system between public networks providing data transmission services."
[18] "Information processing systems—Data communications—Technical report (type 3): Operation of an X.25 to X.25 interworking unit (formerly ISO 8880/2 Annex A)," ISO TR 10029, 1988.
[19] "Information processing systems—Data communications—Network service definition: Network layer addressing," ISO 8348/Addendum 2, 1987.
[20] CCITT Recommendation X.121, "International numbering plan for public data networks."
[21] CCITT Recommendation E.164, "Numbering plan for the ISDN era."
[22] CCITT Recommendation E.163, "Numbering plan for the international telephone service."
[23] CCITT Recommendation F.69, "Plan for telex destination codes."
[24] "Codes for the representation of names of countries," ISO 3166, 1981.
[25] "Data Interchange—Structure for the identification of organizations," ISO 6523, 1984.
[26] "Proposal to ANSI for the operation of the ISO DCC network address assignment authority under the ISO 8348/Add. 2," ANSI X3S3.3/88-59, Mar. 1988.
[27] CCITT Recommendation X.110, "International principles and routing plan for public data networks."
[28] "Information processing systems—Data communications—routing architecture overview," ISO TR 9575, 1989.
[29] "Draft network layer routing architecture," ANSI X3S3.3/86-215R1, Feb. 1987.
[30] "Information processing systems—Data communications—End systems to intermediate systems routing exchange protocol for use in conjunction with the protocol for the provision of the connectionless-mode network service," ISO 9542, 1989.
[31] "Information processing systems—Data communications—End systems routing information exchange protocol for use in conjunction with ISO 8878," ISO/IEC DIS 10030, 1989.
[32] "Intermediate system to intermediate system routing exchange protocol," ANSI X3S3.3/87-150, Sept. 1987.
[33] "Intermediate system to intermediate system routing exchange protocol," ANSI X3S3.3/87-160R1, Sept. 1987.
[34] "Information processing systems—Data communications—An IS-IS intra-domain routing information exchange protocol," ISO/IEC JTC 1/SC 6/N4945, 1988.

[35] R. Perlman, "Fault-tolerant broadcast of routing information," *IEEE Commun. Mag.*, 1983.
[36] J. McQuillan *et al.*, "The new routing algorithm for the ARPANET," *IEEE Trans. Commun.*, May 1980.

Fred M. Burg received the B.S. degree in mathematics and the M.S. degree in operations research while on a teaching fellowship from the Polytechnic Institute of Brooklyn, Brooklyn, NY.

He is Supervisor for Networking Standards Planning at AT&T Bell Laboratories, which he joined in 1973. The scope of this work covers OSI Layers 2-4. He has been very active in CCITT and ISO on X.25 and other networking matters. In particular, he has worked on the application of X.25 to local area networks and to the general OSI environment. He is chair of several of the committees operating under ANSI, IEEE 802, and the NIST/OSI Workshop that deal with Network Layer protocols and interworking. He has also been active recently in defining the LAPM error-correcting protocol for use in V.42 modems and in heading an effort to demonstrate the operation of the OSI protocols over ISDN.

Nicola Di Iorio received the B.S. degree in computer science from the City College of New York, New York, NY, in 1981 and the M.S. degree in computer science from the Polytechnic Institute of New York, Brooklyn, NY, in 1982.

He is a member of the Technical Staff of the Networking Standards Planning Department at AT&T Bell Laboratories. He joined Bell Laboratories in 1985, coming in from GTE Communications Systems Division. At GTE, he was involved with various aspects of connectionless-mode data communications, with particular emphasis on security, TCP/IP, and Local Area Networks. Since joining Bell Laboratories, he has been primarily involved with data networking issues concerning the lower layers (Layers 4-2) of OSI. He is actively involved with the work on routing protocols in ANSI X3S3.3, in ISO (where he holds an Editorship), and ECMA; on CO/CL interworking solutions in ANSI X3S3.3, ISO and ECMA; and on X.25 matters in ISO and CCITT (where he holds an Editorship). Recently, he has also become active on matters concerning the relationship of the ISDN and OSI.

Design of Inter-Administrative Domain Routing Protocols

Lee Breslau   Deborah Estrin

Computer Science Department
University of Southern California
Los Angeles, California 90089-0782
breslau@usc.edu   estrin@usc.edu

Abstract

Policy Routing (PR) is a new area of development that attempts to incorporate policy related constraints on inter-Administrative Domain (AD) communication into the route computation and forwarding of inter-AD packets.

Proposals for inter-AD routing mechanisms are discussed in the context of a design space defined by three design parameters: location of routing decision (i.e., source or hop-by-hop), algorithm used (i.e., link state or distance vector), and expression of policy in topology or in link status. We conclude that an architecture based upon source routing, a link state algorithm, and policy information in the link state advertisements, is best able to support source-specific policies and special types of service. However, an architecture using a distance vector algorithm and hop-by-hop routing presents certain advantages when less policy control is needed. Development of a hybrid approach, combining features of both architectures, is the subject of ongoing research.

1 Introduction

Internetwork size has grown rapidly as a result of several factors: proliferation of the number of networked hosts, interconnection of technically heterogeneous local area and wide area networks, and finally, interconnection of autonomous Administrative Domains (ADs). An AD is a set of resources–hosts, networks, and gateways–that is governed by a single administrative authority. Interconnection across ADs comes about through interconnection of private networks, interconnection of commercial carriers in a competitive market, and division of an internet that has grown too large to manage.

Common approaches to network interconnection create a fully connected internet out of the constituent networks. In the case of AD interconnection this is undesirable for two reasons: scale and policy. As with other types of systems, manageability is a problem for very large internets. Naming, routing, fault isolation, and security are all functions that are more easily and efficiently realized in the context of multiple, smaller, semi-autonomous regions, than in the context of a single, large, undifferentiated region. This is particularly true when the regions represent areas in which significant locality exists, e.g., ADs.

By definition, an AD represents a region that is governed by a single authority.[14, 16] Consequently, when ADs interconnect, issues of policy arise at the boundary between neighboring administrative authorities, and transitively across all the administrative authorities in the collective internet. Network access control mechanisms have been designed for use in inter-AD gateways to control access to end-systems.[9, 21] When networks are used for transit purposes, as well as for access to end systems, network access control mechanisms are not adequate. Policy Routing (PR) is a new area of development that attempts to incorporate policy related constraints on inter-AD communication into the route computation and forwarding of inter-AD packets. Several architectures have been proposed to implement policy based, inter-AD, routing. [2, 5, 11, 17, 19, 20]

In this paper, we present a model of internets for which inter-AD routing protocols must be developed. These protocols must function in the presence of a large number of ADs, and they must make routing decisions in accordance with administrative policy. Design issues relevant to these routing protocols are described, and current proposals for inter-AD routing are discussed within the context of three design issues: location of

---

This research was funded in part by the National Science Foundation, Presidential Young Investigator Award, with matching funds from AT&T

routing decision (i.e., source or hop-by-hop), algorithm used (i.e., link state or distance vector), and expression of policy in topology or in link status. The ability of a particular architecture to support inter-AD routing depends on the types of policies that must be supported in a future internet. We conclude that an architecture based upon source routing, a link state algorithm and policy information in the link state advertisements, is needed to support some of the policy requirements of inter-AD routing, including policies based on source characteristics or special types of service. Such an architecture allows for flexible expression of source route selection criteria and transit policies, while limiting the computational burden on transit ADs and preventing routing loops. This approach can be used alone or in combination with hop-by-hop routing for more widely used, destination-based routes.

The remainder of the paper is organized as follows. Section 2 outlines the driving design requirements (i.e., model) for a PR architecture. Limitations of existing routing protocols are reviewed in Section 3. Design issues in inter-AD routing are presented in Section 4, and current proposals are discussed within the context of these design issues in Section 5. Section 6 concludes with a discussion of open research issues. An extended version of this paper can be found in [4].

2 Inter-AD Routing Model

Assumptions about inter-AD topology, scale and policies greatly influence the design of PR mechanisms. In this section we describe our model for the inter-AD environment.

2.1 Inter-AD Topology

The Research Internet has grown in a decentralized, evolutionary fashion. Many organizations connect to the Internet through bilateral arrangements with other organizations that already have Internet connectivity. The resulting topology is a mesh with varying degrees of connectivity at different places in the network. It now appears that the increasing availability of commercial high speed data services will lead to simpler and more hierarchical internet topologies. This hierarchical topology will consist of long haul backbone, regional, metropolitan, and campus networks. However, lateral links and other forms of bypass will persist at all levels of the hierarchy. Reasons for the persistence of these links include special technical requirement, economic incentives, and political/control incentives. For further justification see [4, 10].

The resulting topology is a hierarchy augmented with special purpose lateral links between some stub networks and between transit networks, as well as special purpose bypass links between stub networks and wide area backbone networks. Figure 1 shows an example internet with this kind of inter-AD connectivity. In this context *stub* network refers to an AD that is not used for transit by anyone outside of the AD. *Multi-homed* ADs are stub ADs that have more than one inter-AD connection but that wish to disallow any transit traffic. *Transit* network refers to an AD whose primary function is to provide transit services for many other ADs. Long haul backbone and regional networks are examples of transit networks. *Hybrid* (or limited-transit) networks are ADs that support access to end systems, as well as limited forms of transit to other ADs.

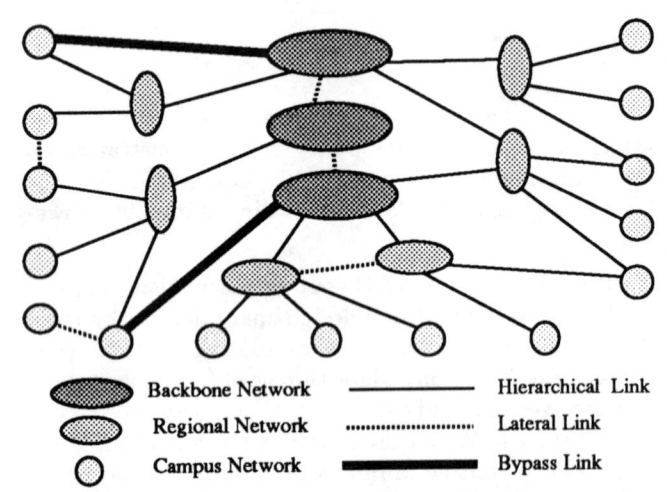

Figure 1: Example Internet Topology

In the context of a global internet we require mechanism that allow stub, transit *and* hybrid ADs to exert control over the use of their resources. Further, the assumptions about the inter-AD topology emphasize the need for algorithms that generate loop-free routes. Inter-AD routing protocols should work efficiently for the general hierarchical case, but they must accommodate lateral and bypass links in a graceful manner. It is acceptable for there to be some performance impact, but functionally, the integrity of the routing must be maintained in the presence on non-hierarchical structures. In return for the added complexity implied by this model, we will make some compensating assumptions about inter-AD dynamics.

2.2 Scale

We are interested in a general architecture to support the future world-wide internet of millions of networks spanning hundreds of thousands of ADs. Moreover, we are interested in the world of commercial carriers and other forms of private networks, as well as the Research Internet. Thus, the protocols should address the needs of a wide range of users.

For the sake of this evaluation we will assume that the global internet could grow to be on the order of 10^5 ADs. Many would be stub ADs but we would like an architecture that could work well for 10^4 transit ADs.[18]

In the context of this very large internetwork, it is desirable for inter-AD topology to change infrequently. Inter-AD topology changes when either an AD partitions, or the connection between two neighbor ADs fails. Since ADs are relatively large entities, it seems reasonable to make the assumption that intra-AD partitions will occur infrequently, as an AD is likely to be characterized by sufficient intra-AD network redundancy and a robust IGP. In other words, an AD must be configured to maintain relatively stable connectivity to the outside world if it is to get adequate service from the routing architecture. It is less practical to make such an assumption about inter-AD link redundancy. Consequently, the protocol must be somewhat adaptive to changes in inter-AD topology, since it is not desirable to rely on static routes.

2.3 Inter-AD Policies

We now consider the types of policies that ADs should be able to express and enforce and the implications for routing. The purpose of policy routing is to control use of network resources, not to act as end system access controls. Moreover, the security (i.e., assurance) of the control mechanisms is an orthogonal issue to the semantics of what kinds of controls can be expressed and enforced. Of course the level of assurance provided by the mechanisms will affect greatly the kind of policies that ADs express. For the sake of this paper we focus on the semantics of the kinds of policies we wish to express. Issues of security are addressed in [8].

As Clark points out in [5], the source of a packet as well as the carrier(s) of the packet should have the ability to express policy regarding its handling. We refer to policies of the carrier as transit policies and policies of the source as route selection criteria. Common source and transit policies may be based on such things as the source and destination of the traffic, the other ADs in the path, Type of Service (TOS), time of day, User Class Identifier, authentication and security requirements, and charging and accounting policies. For a more detailed discussion of these policy requirements, see [10].

Although the purpose of PR is to enlarge the range of policies that can be enforced in internets, not all conceivable policies must be supported in a PR architecture. In all of the PR proposals that we discuss it is critical to their operation and performance that the policies be *slow to change*. Moreover, specific policies adopted by participating ADs will affect the performance of the overall internet. ADs should adopt the least restrictive policies possible and should control access at the coarsest granularity possible to maximize connectivity and enhance performance.

The policies that must be supported imply that a transit AD might make different routing decisions depending on where the packet originated, where it is destined, the path that it has traversed, the TOS requested, and the user class of the originator. In particular, *source* ADs need to be able to express policies regarding packet handling, leading to different handling for different packet sources by transit ADs. Furthermore, *transit* ADs must be able to specify policies that depend on the identity of the source AD. As a consequence there is no single spanning tree that describes the best route to a destination for all sources in the internetwork. Determining "the best", and even the availability of a route, depends upon the source of the packet, as well as on other conditions. TOS routing is characterized by a similar but far more manageable issue, namely the existence of multiple spanning trees, one for each TOS. Because any particular TOS spanning tree applies equally to all sources the potential increase in overhead is not as radical as with PR. It is this aspect of policy routing that makes the problem more difficult, but at the same time an interesting area of research in routing protocols.

The remainder of the paper addresses routing protocol design for inter-Administrative Domain routing in more detail.

3 Limitations of Traditional Routing Protocols

Thus far we have described requirements for controlled flow of traffic across AD boundaries. Network access controls based on different kinds of gateway filters have been used to control the flow of traffic into and out of stub networks.[9, 21] These filters allow an AD to filter packets not meeting certain criteria. However, transit networks must advertise their filtering policies in order to prevent routing loops and dropped packets. It is not sufficient to discover a policy by having packets dropped until a higher level timeout occurs. Rather, policy restrictions must be incorporated into the route calculation and selection processes. In this section we describe how existing routing protocols lack the functionality required by inter-AD routing. We discuss both interior and exterior gateway protocols.

Interior gateway protocols (IGPs) are designed for use within a single AD. A new generation of these IGPs have been developed, among them are IGRP[15], OSPF[22], and DEC IS-IS[6]. Independent of whether they use a link state or distance vector algorithm[1], these

---

[1] See Section 4.3 for further discussion of link state and distance vector algorithms.

protocols have been refined to provide adaptive, shortest path routing with relatively low overhead (in terms of computation and information exchange) within regions of limited size.

All three of these IGPs provide support for TOS routing. IGRP, a distance vector protocol, uses a vector of metrics describing topological delay, bandwidth, channel occupancy, and reliability. The formula with which these individual metrics are combined into composite metrics can be adjusted to yield metrics suitable for different Types of Service. In OSPF and IS-IS, two link state protocols, link state updates can contain multiple metrics corresponding to different Types of Service, and the basic route computation is repeated for each TOS. These mechanisms support only a limited number of Types of Service; they are not scalable either to a large number of TOS or to source specific policies. As more sophisticated transport and internet protocols are developed to support more demanding TOSs, more will be demanded of IGPs to support TOS routing.

Exterior gateway protocols have been used to insulate regions of the internet from one another and thereby avoid the information and computational explosion that IGPs do not accommodate. Exterior gateway protocols support technical heterogeneity by allowing interconnection of regions that run different IGPs. One such protocol, EGP[25], was developed for the DARPA Internet to exchange reachability information across relatively autonomous collections of networks. EGP supports a very limited notion of policy. It allows ADs to define what portions of their connectivity database they will share, but it does not allow them to express TOS or finer grain restrictions on the use of those resources. EGP also allows an AD to manipulate the metrics assigned to different ADs as a means of favoring or disfavoring other transit ADs[2]. However, EGP does not allow the AD to explicitly advertise its policy information for incorporation into the routing decision of other ADs.

EGP allows ADs some autonomy in defining metrics, as described above. However, in order to maintain loop-free routing, EGP places a severe topology restriction on interconnected regions–there can be no cycles in the EGP graph. As noted in Section 2.1, this is an unreasonable restriction for a global internet. ADs require the flexibility to configure multiple inter-AD connections, and it is not feasible to monitor connectivity adequately to enforce the topology restrictions, even if they were acceptable.

Based on the inability of existing IGPs and EGPs to address the requirements of inter-AD routing, we consider the design of alternative architectures in the following sections.

4 General Design Issues for Inter-AD Routing Protocols

Four issues in particular affect the design of an inter-AD routing architecture. This discussion sets the stage for Section 5 where we step through the design space defined by these issues and evaluate three existing proposals for inter-AD routing.

4.1 Level of Abstraction

The first design issue effecting inter-AD routing is the level of abstraction at which inter-AD routing should be treated. Routing protocols operating inside a single AD exchange information about the status of individual gateways and networks. In inter-AD routing, however, it is advantageous to exchange information at the granularity of ADs, and to treat an inter-AD route as a sequence of ADs. This abstraction reduces the amount of information exchanged between ADs, as well as the frequency of these exchanges. Also, it allows ADs to hide internal details of their networks.

As with any abstraction or hierarchical routing, some optimality may be lost. Nonetheless the benefits of this abstraction far outweigh its costs. Therefore, throughout this paper, we consider an inter-AD route to be a sequence of ADs, and we ignore routing internal to administrative domains.

4.2 Policy in the Routing Architecture

Our model of the internet, presented in Section 2, requires that administrative domains be able to restrict or allow access to resources based on administrative policy. Therefore, policy must be reflected in the routing architecture.

One way to accomplish this is to embed policy in the internet topology. In this approach, relationships are defined between neighbor ADs so as to control the flow of routing information, and therefore data packets across inter-AD links. For example, a proposal discussed later (see Section 5.1.1) makes use of a partial ordering of nodes to constrain the flow of routing information. Effecting policy through such an ordering is problematic because it limits the combinations of policies expressible using a single partial ordering. Also, maintaining these inter-AD relationships may require the involvement of a central authority or excessive coordination among ADs. However, this method of expressing policy lends itself well to scaling, as it allows ADs to be grouped into a hierarchy without affecting

---

[2]See S. Brim, *IP Routing Between U.S. Government Agency Backbones and Other Networks*, December, 1989, available from the author.

the policies that are expressible.

A second approach to expressing policy in the routing architecture is to explicitly associate policy related information with routing exchanges between ADs. That is to say, link or path updates contain administrative constraints and service guarantees that apply to the resources they advertise. We refer to these constraints as *Policy Terms (PTs)*.[5]

4.3 Routing Algorithms

Routing algorithms used in computer networks can be classified as either distance vector or link state. For a general discussion of these algorithms see [7, 12, 13]. In Bellman-Ford distance vector algorithms, a node receives information about its neighbors' shortest path metrics to all destinations. The node calculates its shortest paths and distributes this information to its neighbors. Distance vector algorithms are relatively simple to implement, but they can converge slowly. In link state algorithms, each node floods the status of its adjacent links to all other nodes in the network. Each node computes its shortest paths to all destinations using this complete topological information. Link state algorithms are more complex to implement, but they do not exhibit the same convergence problems that distance vector algorithms do.

Traditional distance vector protocols hide information about paths, providing knowledge only about the first hop toward a destination. While this may be desirable in some environments, inter-AD policy routing is concerned with control of access to network resources based on administrative policy. Addressing such administrative policy may depend on more knowledge about an inter-AD path than is provided by distance vector algorithms. Link state algorithms, on the other hand, provide all nodes with global information. In an inter-AD environment, this can include information about policy constraints needed to make routing decisions consistent with administrative policy.

4.4 Location of Routing Decision

The final design issue we consider is the location of the routing decision. Source routing refers to a paradigm in which the source of traffic determines the route and includes this route in each packet. Under hop-by-hop routing, each routing entity makes an independent decision to determine the next hop towards the destination.

Under the hop-by-hop paradigm, all nodes must make consistent routing decisions based on consistent data in order to avoid routing loops. In an environment where routing decisions are made according to administrative policy, this implies that all ADs must be aware of all other ADs policies. Source routing, on the other hand, provides a simple mechanism for avoiding routing loops. Specifically, the source AD uses a loop-free route synthesis algorithm, and/or inspects a source route to guarantee that it contains no loops.

In hop-by-hop routing, a source AD is constrained by choices made at transit ADs. Specifically, when distance vector algorithms are used, a source AD can only choose from among those routes selected and advertised by its neighbors. Similarly, using link state algorithms, the source has no control over the routing decision made by transit ADs. Therefore, regardless of the algorithm used, valid routes that would be preferred by the source AD may not be available to it.

Applying hop-by-hop routing to inter-AD policy routing implies that the source AD must rely on other ADs to make routing decisions in accordance with its policies. In source routing, however, the source has control over the entire inter-AD path. Therefore, the dependence on other ADs to select paths consistent with the source's policies is reduced.

In an environment with source specific policies, hop-by-hop routing also places an increased burden on transit ADs. Each transit AD may have to compute many routes to a single destination, to be used by different packet sources. Source routing relieves transit ADs of this burden; since the source specifies the next-AD hop, independent route computations by transit ADs are not required for each packet source.

5 Routing Architecture Design Space and Proposed Mechanisms

In the previous section, we identified three areas in which alternative design decisions can be made when developing an inter-AD routing architecture. The various combinations of these decisions yield a design space with eight distinct points (see Table 1). In this section, we discuss the points in this design space, presenting actual proposals when they exist and identifying architectures that are impractical.

As listed in Table 1, we begin by discussing inter-AD routing architectures using a distance vector algorithm, hop-by-hop routing, and policy embedded in the topology. Successive design points are described by altering one aspect of the design at a time. That is, we then consider an architecture with distance vector and hop-by-hop routing, but with explicit policy terms used to express policy. Next, a link state algorithm is substituted for the distance vector algorithm, and the resulting architecture (link state, hop-by-hop, policy terms) is discussed. Finally, by using source routing instead of hop-by-hop routing, an architecture employing link state, source routing, and explicit policy terms is presented.

While the bulk of this section centers on the four design points mentioned in the previous paragraph, there are four other possible design points to be addressed. We conclude this section by briefly touching upon these remaining design points.

Decision Point

	Hop-By-Hop Routing	Source Routing	
DV	5.1 (ECMA)	5.5.2	Policy in Topology
LS	5.5.1	5.5.1	
DV	5.2 (IDRP)	5.5.2	Policy Terms
LS	5.3	5.4 (IDPR)	

Algorithm

Table 1
Design Space for Inter-AD Routing

5.1 Distance Vector, Hop-by-Hop Routing, with Policy Embedded in the Topology

The first point in the matrix of design possibilities represents architectures that employ a distance vector algorithm, use hop-by-hop routing, and express policy through topology. After outlining the features of such an architecture, a proposed protocol corresponding to this design is presented.

In this architecture, an AD exchanges routing table entries with its neighbors. An AD selects the "best" path from among those offered, and can then distribute its own routing table entries to its neighbors. Policy is reflected in the topology of the internet. That is to say, rather than explicitly including policy related information in routing updates, policy is reflected in implicit characteristics of links between neighbor ADs. For instance, in the proposal discussed below, a partial ordering is imposed on the topology, defining a relationship between neighbors.

An AD may opt not to distribute its routing table entries describing routes to other ADs. In this way, the AD acts only as a stub AD and will not carry transit traffic. Alternatively, the AD can advertise routes to a subset of destinations only, serving as a transit AD for traffic destined to this subset while refusing to carry traffic bound for other ADs.

The forementioned is an example of destination specific policies. Expression of source specific policy is more problematic in this architecture. If a partial ordering is imposed on ADs, distribution of routing table updates can be limited to only those ADs above or below an AD in the partial ordering. For instance, in the proposals discussed below, if an update is passed to a node lower in the partial order, this information can never be passed to a higher node. In this way, an AD can specify a policy with respect to a subset of sources.

This inter-AD routing architecture has several deficiencies. First, as with all distance vector algorithms, looping and speed of convergence must be addressed carefully. Second, using a single partial ordering to implement policy routing limits the specific policies that can be expressed by each AD. Third, as the route computation is distributed, ADs are constrained by decisions made elsewhere. The particular route selection made by a downstream AD may not adhere to a source ADs policy requirements, resulting in no available route when in fact a legal route exists (i.e., a route that is permitted by the policies of all transit ADs involved).

Now we turn our attention to a specific proposal for inter-AD routing that corresponds to the architecture described above. Attempts to deal with some of the problems identified with the architecture are evaluated.

5.1.1 ECMA

The National Institute of Standards and Technology (NIST) proposal, as submitted to ECMA[11][3], specifies a method for routing database distribution and for route computation based on the distance vector data. This proposal is designed for use in a topology containing cycles. The traditional looping and convergence problems are avoided through the use of a partial ordering of all clusters[4][5], or ADs. This partial ordering must be coordinated among ADs. Consequently, change in the partial ordering must be coordinated by an authority that manages the partial ordering for all ADs effected by the change. In addition, multiple routing databases can be used for different TOS.

The partial ordering of ADs prevents looping and convergence problems in the presence of an inter-AD topology containing cycles. Every inter-AD link is labeled as an up link or down link, depending upon the relationship between the neighboring ADs in the partial ordering. Data packets are marked as to the type

---
[3] A second protocol adhering to this architecture, Border Gateway Protocol (BGP), version 1, is not discussed here.[19]

[4] It has been proposed that the same physical group of AD resources may be replicated and represented as multiple logical clusters for the sake of reflecting policy in the topology, thus allowing a wider range of policies to coexist. However, logical replication requires that the replicated region be assigned multiple network addresses in order to determine which FIB (routing table) should be applied to a particular packet.

[5] A cluster is analogous to an AD. For consistency with the remainder of this paper, we use the term AD.

of links they have traversed. Once a packet traverses a down link, it cannot traverse another up link, thereby preventing loops. Routes described in distance vector updates are marked as to the types of links traversed to reach the destination, so that forwarding decisions that prevent loops can be made.

Changes in topology result in rapid convergence since the partial ordering suppresses looping. A topology change affects ADs close to the source of the change, and the effect weakens for those ADs farther away. The altered AD tells about a new link to all neighbors and they either reject it or pick it up in one computation. If the partial ordering is computed properly, and verified, the partial ordering and up-down rule prevent loops, and consequently prevent the count to infinity phenomenon common to other DV algorithms.

ECMA also has a mechanism for supporting TOS routing. Each AD can define multiple sets of Forwarding Information Bases (FIB) corresponding to multiple TOS indexes. An AD defines a separate metric for each TOS supported by at least one of its neighbors. If a particular neighbor does not advertise a particular TOS then the AD assigns an infinite metric to the neighbor for that TOS, and consequently the AD does not compute routes for that TOS through the neighbor.

As with distance vector protocols in general, ECMA supports information hiding, as well as the selection of one next hop over another. Similarly, destination specific filters can be applied to the distribution of routing updates in order to control the destinations to which transit traffic is carried. Source specific policies, however, are possible only to the extent that they can be reflected in the partial ordering of ADs. For instance, if an AD distributes a routing update over a down link, this information cannot be passed up the hierarchy by a subsequent AD. In this way the AD has some control over the eventual recipients of its routing updates, and hence the traffic sources for which it carries traffic.

We have two fundamental concerns with ECMA's suitability to inter-AD routing. The first is the limitations on policies expressible by the protocol. We have already mentioned problems associated with expressing source specific policies using the partial ordering. Also, ECMA is not well-suited to express finer grained policies based on such things as User Class Identifier. The TOS mechanism does not scale well with the number of possible packet classifications (e.g., UCI, TOS, source). Finally, policies of different ADs may not be mutually satisfiable. That is to say, there may not be a single partial ordering that simultaneously expresses the policies of all ADs.

The second, and related, concern regards scaling and the practicality of maintaining the global partial ordering. It is uncertain whether this scheme is workable for a large number of ADs that have varied, non-static policies. Establishing the global partial ordering requires both computation and negotiation either by a central authority or by a set of entities each with authority over a subset of the internetwork. First, the policies of all ADs must be collected. A computation is applied that attempts to accommodate all the policies in a single partial ordering. If unresolvable conflicts arise among policies, i.e., those that can not be accommodated in a single partial ordering, then the relevant authority must negotiate with the ADs involved to revise their policies in such a way that they can be accommodated in the single partial ordering. This scheme is intended to work for a near infinite number of ADs. However, when policy changes, the partial ordering may need to be recomputed and may require another round of negotiation with affected ADs. Therefore, whereas the scheme may be feasible for a very large internet with static policies it is not appropriate for an environment of variable policies as was described in Section 2.

In summary, the ECMA approach does incorporate policy routing within an architecture that uses hop-by-hop routing and DV route computation. However, the DV approach, by definition, implies that an AD advertise a single metric per-destination per-TOS to all of its neighbors. This metric is a function of the entire path from that AD to that destination. It allows the AD to hide information about its own path to the destination, and therefore it withholds information from its neighbors that possibly is relevant to the neighbors' policies. Moreover, the DV approach allows ECMA to support only transitive policy relationships. Policies that discriminate among traffic sources in a non-transitive manner are cumbersome, and sometimes impossible, to support in ECMA.

5.2 Distance Vector Hop-by-Hop Routing with Explicit Policy Terms

The discussion of the previous design revealed difficulties imposed on inter-AD policy routing by the use of topological restrictions to express policy. We next consider another design using distance vector, hop-by-hop routing. However, in this case, policy is expressed by explicitly including policy attributes in routing updates. Two proposed protocols that reflect this design, BGP version 2 and Inter-Domain Routing Protocol, are described.[1, 20]

In traditional distance vector protocols, routing exchanges include only a destination and a metric. In this section, we describe an architecture that includes additional information, related to the policy constraints of a path, thereby allowing more flexible expression of policy. For instance, a routing update may include a list of the source ADs that are permitted to use the route described in the routing update, and/or a list of all ADs traversed along the advertised route.

When an AD receives a routing update, the update specifies a destination and policy constraints associated with the route to that destination. The AD receiving the update must then determine whether it can use the route based upon these policy constraints. If so, the AD can apply its own policy filters to determine whether or not it wants to use the route. For instance, better (e.g. less constrained) routes to the same destination may already exist, so the new route may be rejected. If the route is accepted by the AD, it then determines whether to advertise this route to its neighbors, based on its own policies. If it chooses to advertise the route, additional policy constraints can be added to it before distributing the update to its neighbors.

Traditional protocols employing distance vector hop-by-hop routing only allow nodes to advertise a single route to each destination per-TOS in order to avoid looping. When routing decisions are based on administrative policy, it may be desirable to advertise multiple routes per destination, each with different policy attributes. In this case, a set of policy attributes can be treated much like a type of service in TOS routing. Thus, it is possible to advertise multiple routes, and still avoid looping, so long as each route and each packet can be identified with a unique set of policy attributes.

While this architecture is well suited to environments in which individual routes can be shared by many sources, it still suffers from problems inherent in hop-by-hop routing when source-specific policies are expressed or many TOSs are used. Transit ADs can use policy terms to compute and advertise routes with diverse policy requirements to their neighbors. However, if these policies are source specific, transit ADs might have to perform separate calculations for each possible source AD. This approach is analogous to maintaining multiple spanning trees. Moreover, in this hop-by-hop scheme, the source is dependent upon subsequent ADs to make routing decisions in accordance with the source's policy. Since source route-selection criteria are not advertised, there is no means for the source to assert its preference that particular routes be used or avoided. In summary, transit ADs may expend resources computing multiple routes per destination (many of which may never be used), and source ADs may be unable to use the routes they prefer.

5.2.1 Inter Domain Routing Protocol

Two protocols adhering to these design choices, Inter Domain Routing Protocol (IDRP) and BGP version 2, have been proposed. As the two protocols are very similar, we will focus the present discussion on IDRP, mentioning BGP only where it differs from IDRP.

IDRP attempts to solve the looping and convergence problems inherent in distance vector routing by including full AD path information in routing updates. Each routing update includes the set of ADs that must be traversed in order to reach the specified destination. In this way, routes that contain AD loops can be avoided.

IDRP updates also contain additional information relevant to policy constraints. For instance, these updates can specify what other ADs are allowed to receive the information described in the update. In this way, IDRP is able to express source specific policies.[6] The IDRP protocol also provides the structure for the addition of other types of policy related information in routing updates. For example, User Class Identifiers could also be included as policy attributes in routing updates.

Using the policy route attributes IDRP provides the framework for expressing more fine grained policy in routing decisions. However, because it uses hop-by-hop distance vector routing, it only allows a single route to each destination per-TOS to be advertised. As the policy attributes associated with routes become more fine grained, advertised routes will be applicable to fewer sources. This implies a need for multiple routes to be advertised for each destination in order to increase the probability that sources have acceptable routes available to them. This effectively replicates the routing table per forwarding entity for each TOS, UCI, source combination that might appear in a packet. Consequently, we claim that this approach does not scale well as policies become more fine grained, i.e., source or UCI specific policies.

5.3 Link State Hop-by-Hop Routing with Explicit Policy Terms

We now discuss another point in the design space by considering the use of a link state algorithm along with hop-by-hop routing and explicit policy terms in routing exchanges. Within the context of this discussion, nodes refer to ADs and links to inter-AD connections. In the design under consideration, link state updates can be augmented to include policy related attributes of the resources they advertise, such as restrictions placed on, or service guarantees provided by, their use. Such an approach was suggested in [24].

These link state updates will be flooded throughout the internet, giving each AD global knowledge of all links and their associated policy restrictions. This information permits each AD to compute routes satisfying any set of policy restrictions to all other ADs. Therefore, this architecture allows an AD to discover a valid route if one in fact exists. However, each AD along this

---

[6]The BGP protocol, as specified in [20] does not allow for the expression of such source specific policies, but we note that it would not be difficult to add this to the protocol.

route must repeat the same calculation to compute this route. In link state algorithms without policy routing, a node computes a single spanning tree for all possible destinations. This spanning tree is used to route packets regardless of their source. However, because we allow for the possibility of source specific policies, an AD potentially must compute a separate spanning tree for each potential source of traffic. Hence, the replicated nature of this computation may become an excessive burden for transit ADs. If each node does not compute and maintain multiple spanning trees, then limitations such as those described in the previous section exist.

Also, we note that as in the architecture outlined in the previous section, sources are dependent upon other ADs to make routing decisions that conform to their policy requirements. Even though the source has calculated an entire route that adheres to its policy, it still relies on other ADs to repeat and replicate this same computation. Further, in order to avoid loops, all ADs in the path must make the same decision as the source. This implies that all ADs in the path must be aware of policy related criteria used by the source to select from among multiple available routes. This problem, as well as the problem of computing multiple spanning trees, is addressed by the next design.

5.4 Link State Source Routing with Explicit Policy Terms

The final design that we consider in detail employs a link state algorithm with source routing and explicit policy terms. We begin with a general discussion of this design choice, and then present a specific proposal developed by D. Clark and the Internet Open Routing Working Group.[5, 17]

As with the previous design discussed, link state updates containing policy related information are flooded throughout the internet. Using complete knowledge concerning topology and policy, each node is able to discover routes (if they exist) to any destination with any combination of policy attributes.

However, in this architecture source routing is employed. That is, after the source calculates a route, it includes the entire route in the packet header so that subsequent ADs in the path need only examine the header to determine the next AD in the path; subsequent hops do not make an explicit routing decision. As stated previously, we consider an inter-AD route at the abstraction of a sequence of ADs. Thus the route calculated by the source, and included in the packet header, consists of a sequence of ADs. Intra-AD routes are a matter left to local concern. This approach attempts to balance the benefits of source control with adaptive routing capabilities of hop-by-hop routing.

This design affords important advantages. First, it grants the source control over the entire route. Therefore, the source can express and enforce any combination of its own policies, and it can keep these policies private from other ADs. Moreover, this control is achieved without requiring transit ADs to compute routes that adhere to the policies of all possible source ADs. A transit AD can concentrate on assuring that routes crossing it conform to its own policies, while leaving other ADs to enforce their own policies. Finally, source routing provides an efficient mechanism for assuring loop-free routes, independent of the network topology. Therefore, multiple paths to a single destination are feasible, without replicating entire routing tables.

We now turn to a review of a specific proposal that illustrates this design. In particular, we describe how policy is expressed, and how the overhead associated with source routing (e.g., increased header length) is minimized.

5.4.1 IDPR Architecture

The Internet Inter-Domain Policy Routing Working Group (IDPR) is developing a detailed architecture based on D. Clark's model for inter-AD routing, described in [5, 17].[7] IDPR represents a substantial departure from current routing protocols and is in the early stage of prototype development.

Routes are determined by the source at the level of abstraction of ADs. The path must traverse the ordered list of ADs but the physical nodes and links traversed between and across ADs may vary.

ADs advertise Policy Terms (PTs) that can express the types of policies described in Section 2.3. Specifically, PTs can associate path constraints, TOS, User Class, authentication requirements, and other global conditions with a path across an AD. Path constraints restrict access to the path based on source AD, destination AD, previous AD, or next AD in the path. An AD can use a Policy Term to traverse another AD only if it meets the conditions specified in the Policy Term. ADs also advertise their connectivity to other ADs.[8] A Route Server in each AD computes Policy Routes based on the advertised policy and topology information. Packets to a particular destination travel via the route specified in the Policy Route.

If a packet is traveling to a destination for which there is no currently valid policy route in use then the first packet sent must carry enough information in it to allow each AD on the path to validate the path as

---
[7]We will refer to the architecture as IDPR because where the two models differ we describe the IDPR variation. However, many of the general concepts were first described by Clark. We also leave out many of the protocol details described in [5, 17, 23].

[8]IDPR refers to the point of connection between ADs as virtual gateways. A virtual gateway may be comprised of multiple PGs in the interest of reliability and performance.

legal. The AD's border gateways, referred to as policy gateways (PGs), execute the validation for the AD. In effect, one can view the PGs as containing routing tables that are filled on demand. The combination of possible routes is so large that it is not practical to hold the entire set of possible routing choices. At the same time, the overhead of carrying and processing complete information for each packet is prohibitive. Thus, the first packet that travels to a destination under a certain set of conditions acts as a policy route setup packet. This packet carries the full policy route (list of ADs) and a Policy Term from each AD that the source AD believes will allow it to use this route. A policy gateway for each AD along the route checks the information and validates that the policy route is in accordance with the local policy terms of that AD. If it is, the setup information is cached and the setup packet is forwarded.

To avoid the latency of the Policy Route setup process and the header-length overhead of the source route in the Policy Route packet header, data packets that travel down an already-established policy route do not carry the same information as the Policy Route setup packet. Instead, a handle is assigned at the time that the Policy Route is set up and successive data packets use that handle. PGs use the handle ID as a key into the cache to allow for some per-packet validation (e.g., is it coming from the AD specified in the cached PT setup information). It is essential for the operation of this protocol that policy and topology change much more slowly than the time required for route setup.

This setup process has some similarities with a traditional virtual circuit model. However, there are no assumptions made about guaranteed and sequenced delivery. Packets may be delivered out of order by taking different routes within an AD. Sequencing and reliability are left to the transport layer to do as required by the application. Moreover, PRs may have a long lifetime and are not intended to correspond one to one with transport level sessions. Thus, a single policy route can support multiple pairs of hosts in the source and destination ADs.

This scheme allows for very general policies to be expressed by source and transit ADs. Sources are given control over route selection, and transit ADs can express a wide range of policies in the policy terms they advertise. However, route computation presents a significant concern.

Route computation complexity is a function of internet size, dynamics, and the granularity of the policies expressed by transit regions. Given that route computation is a computationally intensive task, it is not practical to recompute routes frequently. If policy terms are highly dynamic, PRs will frequently be out of date. Therefore, PTs should change slowly.

For similar reasons, policies should not be very granular. Although the protocol allows for host specific policies, the implication of such policies is many more PTs and an increase in the route synthesis overhead. The IDPR architecture is intended primarily for network resource control. It is not a replacement for end-system and network access controls for sensitive environments.[8]

Even with coarse grained policies that change slowly, route synthesis for the IDPR architecture presents a challenge. Precomputation of all policy routes in a large internet is computationally intractable, while on demand computation may introduce excessive latency at setup time. Consequently, a combination of precomputation and on-demand computation should be used. For example, precomputation could use heuristics to prune the search and limit it to commonly used routes. On-demand computation could then be used in those cases where a requested route was not discovered during the precomputation phase. Adapting route synthesis to an internet of global scale is the subject of ongoing research.

Finally, this architecture does not support the general aggregation of routing and forwarding information. For routes that are usable by many sources, route computation is replicated by all sources and state is replicated for each source in the transit nodes. Thus, while supporting special on demand routes better than the other schemes, there is some diminished efficiency for widely used routes.

5.5 Other Designs

The matrix of design possibilities that we presented contained eight elements. Thus far, we have reviewed four of these designs, for which proposals already exist or for which reasonable proposals could be developed. In this section we address the four remaining design possibilities, indicating why we have excluded them from more detailed coverage.

5.5.1 Link State and Policy in the Topology

Two of the designs neglected thus far include those using link state algorithms and topology to express policy. Link state algorithms depend upon flooding of link status to all nodes in a network. Policy routing based on topology, on the other hand, uses relationships among nodes to constrain the flow of routing information. For this reason, we see these two design choices as presenting no particular advantages over those schemes already described.

5.5.2 Distance Vector and Source Routing

The two remaining designs are those that include both distance vector algorithms and source routing. We do not view these choices as mutually incompatible. One could imagine, for instance, a protocol like BGP in which the source uses the full AD path information it receives in routing updates to create a source route. Such a protocol could address some of the deficiencies identified with distance vector, hop-by-hop designs. However, we opt against further discussion of such a protocol because there is little advantage in using source routing without also using a link state scheme. The power of source routing, in the context of inter-AD policy routing, is in giving the source control over the entire route. This goal cannot be realized fully without giving the source complete information for, and control of, the route computation itself–such as a link state algorithm provides.

6 Conclusion

We presented a model of internets for which inter-AD routing protocols must be developed. These protocols will be required to function in the presence of a large number of ADs, and they must make routing decisions that adhere to administrative policy. Existing protocols have either been designed for use inside a single administrative domain or they do not support a wide range of policies. Three current proposals for inter-AD routing mechanisms were discussed in the context of an eight element design space defined by routing algorithm, routing decision location, and policy definition. We concluded that an architecture including source routing and a link state algorithm with policy terms is best able to solve the long-term requirements of inter-AD routing, if source specific policies and source selection of routes is desired. This architecture allows flexible expression of source route selection criteria and transit policies, while limiting the computational burden on transit ADs and preventing routing loops. On the other hand, an architecture based on distance vector, hop-by-hop routing and explicit policy terms may support non-source-specific policies more efficiently. Consequently, development of a hybrid approach, that takes advantage of the strengths of each architecture, is the subject of continuing investigation.

In the context of these inter-AD routing architectures there remain many unanswered research questions, primarily related to scale. Two examples are database distribution strategies to provide the needed information for route computation while minimizing routing-data distribution overhead, and policy gateway state management and limitations. In addition, given any one of the routing architectures, it will be the job of local administrators to specify policies for their ADs. Given the interaction between local policies and the policies of other ADs, it will be possible to specify local policies that will result in unnecessarily poor service, both in terms of route computation overhead and the resulting inter-AD connectivity. Thus, it will be imperative for these administrators to have network management tools that can evaluate the impact of proposed policies on the service received from the routing architecture.

7 Acknowledgements

Members of the Open Routing Working Group have contributed to the ideas presented here. Yakov Rekhter provided many detailed comments and corrections to this and previous versions. Tassos Nakassis, Yakov Rekhter and Paul Tsuchiya provided many clarifications and explanations of the ECMA, BGP and IDRP proposals. Also, we appreciate Abhijit Khale, Martha Steenstrup, Gene Tsudik, Lixia Zhang, and the anonymous reviewers for their comments on previous drafts. This paper is a slightly revised version of [3].

References

[1] ANSI, *Intermediate System to Intermediate System Inter-domain Routeing Information Exchange Protocol*, **Document Number X3S3.3/90-132**, June 1990.

[2] H. Braun, *Models of Policy Routing*, **RFC 1104, SRI Network Information Center**, June 1989.

[3] L. Breslau and D. Estrin, *Design of Inter-Administrative Domain Routing Protocols*, **ACM Sigcomm**, 1990, pp 231-241.

[4] L. Breslau and D. Estrin, *Design and Evaluation of Inter-Domain Policy Routing Protocols*, **Internetworking: Research and Experience**, Vol. 2, No. 3, 1991.

[5] D. Clark, *Policy Routing in Internet Protocols*, **RFC 1102, SRI Network Information Center**, May 1989.

[6] Digital Equipment Corporation, *Intermediate System to Intermediate System Intra-Domain Routeing Exchange Protocol for Use in Conjunction with the Protocol for Providing the Connectionless-Mode Network Service*, October 1989.

[7] E. W. Dijkstra, *A Note on Two Problems in Connection with Graphs*, **Numerische Mathematik**, 1959, pp 269-271.

[8] D. Estrin and G. Tsudik, *Security Issues in Policy Routing*, **Proceedings of 1989 IEEE Symposium on Security and Privacy**, May 1989.

[9] D. Estrin, J. Mogul, G. Tsudik, *Visa Protocols for Controlling Inter-Organizational Datagram Flow*, **IEEE Journal on Selected Areas in Communications**, May 1989.

[10] D. Estrin, *Policy Requirements for Inter Administrative Domain Routing*, **RFC 1125, SRI Network Information Center**, November 1989.

[11] European Computer Manufacturers Association, *Inter-Domain Intermediate Systems Routing*, **Technical Report ECMA/TC32-TG10/89/56**, May 1989.

[12] L. R. Ford and D. R. Fulkerson. *Flows in Networks*, Princeton University Press 1962.

[13] J. J. Garcia-Luna-Aceves, *A Unified Approach to Loop-Free Routing Using Distance Vectors or Link States*, **ACM Sigcomm**, 1989.

[14] S. Hares, D. Katz, *Administrative Domains and Routing Domains, a Model for Routing in the Internet*, **RFC 1136, SRI Network Information Center**, December 1989.

[15] C. L. Hedrick *An Introduction to IGRP*, **Technical Report, The State University of New Jersey Center for Computers and Information Services**, October 1989.

[16] ISO, *OSI Routeing Framework*, **ISO/TF 9575**, 1989.

[17] M. Lepp and M. Steenstrup. *An Architecture for Inter-Domain Policy Routing* **DRAFT RFC**, January, 1990.

[18] M. Little, *Goals and Functional Requirements for Inter-Autonomous System Routing*, **RFC 1126, SRI Network Information Center**, October 1989.

[19] K. Lougheed and Y. Rekhter, *Border Gateway Protocol*, **RFC 1105, SRI Network Information Center**, June 1989.

[20] K. Lougheed and Y. Rekhter, *Border Gateway Protocol*, **RFC 1163, SRI Network Information Center**, June 1990.

[21] J. Mogul, *Simple and Flexible Datagram Access Controls for Unix-based Gateways*, **Proceedings of Summer 1989 USENIX Technical Conference**, August 1989.

[22] J. Moy, *The Open Shortest Path First (OSPF) Specification*, **RFC 1131, SRI Network Information Center**, October 1989.

[23] Open Routing Working Group, *Inter-Domain Policy Routing Protocol Specification and Usage: Version 1*, **DRAFT RFC**, April 1990.

[24] R. Perlman, *Incorporation of Service Classes into a Network Architecture*, **Proceedings of the Seventh Data Communications Symposium**, October 1981.

[25] E. Rosen, *Exterior Gateway Protocol (EGP)*, **RFC 827, SRI Network Information Center**, October 1982.

Internetworking ISDN with LANs

J. Tao   R. Martinez   C. Jiron   P. Afsharnejad

Computer Engineering Research Laboratory
Electrical and Computer Engineering Department
The University of Arizona
Tucson, AZ 85721

Abstract

This paper presents the outcomes of an ongoing research project, the design and implementation of ISDN gateway, to internetwork ISDN with LANs, and to extend network users' reachability. In the paper, the data communications scenario using the combination of ISDN and LAN technologies are explained; the design and implementation of an internetworking gateway between ISDN and Ethernet LAN are described. The data communications are realized between ISDN Work-Stations and Ethernet Work-Stations through ISDN, using TCP/IP protocol suite at the upper layers. The design is open to the adoption of new protocol standards. The project is funded by US West Advanced Technology, and the CCIT of University of Arizona.

1 Introduction

In recent years, the Integrated Services Digital Network (ISDN) technology has been growing steadily. The ISDN standards are evolving, the installation of ISDN service are rolling, and the co-existing of ISDN and LAN, WAN networks can be expected to appear soon as the results. In England, it is reported that the commercial ISDN services will be offered nation-wide in 1992. In the United States, the large amount of AT&T 5ESS switches installed can provide users with ISDN services subscriptions, and it will play an important role in promoting the non-destructive transition from current analog switch systems towards ISDN.

On the other hand, one of the well-recognized urgent problems regarding the expansion of ISDN service is the shortage of the kinds and the lack of availability of the ISDN Customer Premises Equipments (CPEs) to support user's ISDN service requirements. With this concern, it is the main objective of this research project to dress some important issues in solving some parts of this problem: interconnect the ISDN with LANs, to expand the ISDN services, and to extend the ISDN users' reachability.

In this project to internetwork ISDN with LANs, the characteristics of the ISDN data services are compared with that of the LANs technologies. The data communications scenario using the combination of the ISDN and LAN technologies are discussed. The internetworking gateway between ISDN and Ethernet LAN is designed and implemented. The data communications are realized between ISDN Work-Station and Ethernet Work-Station/Host, and between Ethernet Work-Stations through ISDN network. As the direct output of the project, prototype systems are demonstrated with one ISDN-to-Ethernet gateway system, one ISDN Work-station and one Ethernet Work-station, capable of coping with data communications through ISDN system. Current design is based on using the TCP/IP protocol suite and Ethernet at the LAN side, and both ISDN work-station and Ethernet work-station run TCP/IP and its upper layer application protocols. The design and implementation is open to the adoption of new protocol standards. Finally, the significance of the current and future research work in the area are commented.

2 The Rationale

The conversion from current analog telephone switch system to ISDN benefits both service providers and users. To the service providers, ISDN saves a considerable amount of equipment such as the analog multiplexers, etc. It also expands the variety and improves the quality of the network services. To the users, a single ISDN access can provide voice, packet and circuit switched data services simultaneously at moderate data rate. ISDN data terminal equipment, such as work station, FAX, viewdata, telemetry, slow scan TV, etc., can be directly hooked to the ISDN phone set to reach anywhere in the global ISDN network. Up to eight data terminal equipments can be served on a single ISDN line, as shown in figure 1. ISDN also provides potential for more new services in the future. Some of them can be realized with the combination of the ISDN and LAN technologies.

To explore the joint adventure of the ISDN and LAN technologies, the related characteristics of both technologies should be compared:

1. ISDN covers a global area, while each LAN covers a smaller local area;

2. ISDN provides circuit-switched, end-to-end connections within the single self-contained network, while LAN provides packet-switched data services either within single LAN or through multiple LANs interconnected by WANs;

3. ISDN provides data services in a moderate data rate, while LAN provides the service in a higher data rate;

4. To the user, ISDN provides the service in the connection-oriented manner at the Network Layer, while LAN such as TCP/IP network uses the connectionless datagram services at that layer;

5. In a typical case, ISDN transfers user data in B channels with very little protocol encapsulations, while more protocol processing is needed in LAN environment, some are essential such as Internet Protocol (IP) handling.

With these considerations, the interconnected networks of ISDN and LANs using the ISDN gateways can provide users with the superset services out of the services provided by the individual technologies:

1. With the easy access to the ISDN network, users can access any ISDN hosts or LAN hosts anywhere in the world;

2. From user's point of view, in the interconnected ISDN and LAN network, ISDN is just another network interconnected which covers wider geographic area;

3. The new network should be able to provide reasonable data transfer rate to the ISDN users;

4. The conversion between the connection-oriented (ISDN) and connectionless (ex, IP in LAN) services at the Network Layer is automatically handled by the ISDN gateway;

5. The ISDN hosts implementing LAN protocols such as TCP/IP can communicate with all other hosts in the new network with all kinds of upper layer services.

The data communication scenario with the ISDN gateway is shown in figure 1, in which ISDN work-stations can communicate with LAN work-stations through ISDN system and ISDN gateway, or LAN work-stations can communicate between different LANs interconnected by ISDN.

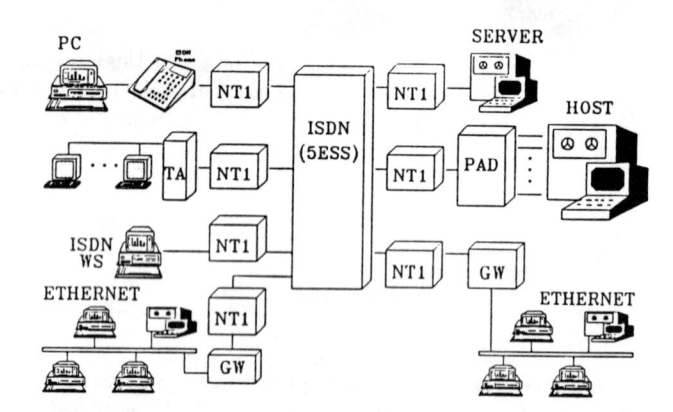

Figure 1: **Data Communication Scenario with ISDN Gateway**

3 ISDN Gateway Concerns

Since the first phase of the study is focused on the interconnection of ISDN and TCP/IP networks over Ethernet, following discussion will based on this assumption using Ethernet at lower layers, and TCP/IP protocol suite at the higher layers.

3.1 Internetworking Protocol Layer

Since the ISDN is viewed as another interconnected network, the overall system is designed to internetwork at the IP level. In terms of the functionality, the ISDN gateway will function as an IP gateway in the TCP/IP world, one of the stops in the IP packet routing path.

As ISDN gateway receives the IP packets from Ethernet, referring to figure 2, after the IP header checking, the forwarding IP address will be checked against the internal link control table to find which link to send the IP packet through. If the forwarding IP address is new, it will be translated into the ISDN address of the remote ISDN node or ISDN gateway (see section 3.2), and a new ISDN link should then be set up between (see section 3.3). Then the IP packet will be forwarded.

As ISDN gateway receives the IP packets from ISDN side, the packet control information is recorded, and the packet is forwarded onto the Ethernet. Even if the forwarding IP address is new to the internal link control table, the ISDN link is there before the packet being received. No link need to be established at the Ethernet side.

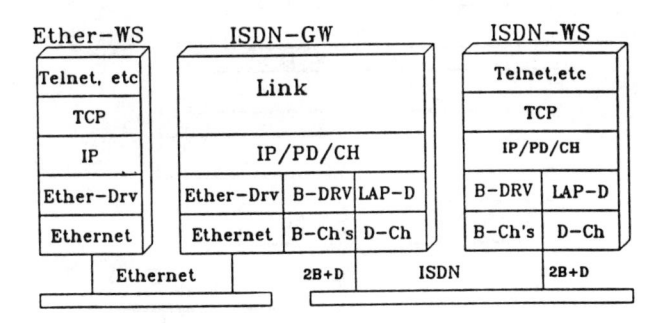

Figure 2: **Layered Protocol Interactions**

3.2 Gateway Address Translation

There is only one point-to-point link between two ISDN gateways interconnected through ISDN. In the IP packet received from local Ethernet, the IP address of the ISDN gateway at the other side of the link is indicated to the local ISDN gateway in the format of IP address, while it is actually an ISDN address. The translation scheme from the IP address to the ISDN address is needed inside the ISDN gateway so that the translation is done automatically in the gateway, without putting extra burden on the users.

The ISDN Gateway Address Resolution Protocol is under study to translate the IP address scheme into the ISDN address scheme, including the local ISDN addresses, long distance ISDN addresses, and international ISDN addresses.

3.3 Connectionless vs. Connection-Oriented

While IP packets travels inside the TCP/IP network, it is based on the connectionless datagram service which does not have any connection established for transferring the packets. On the other hand, ISDN is connection-oriented network, which means that before transferring any data, connection should be established between the source and destination of the link. The conversion between the connectionless and connection-oriented services should be performed inside the ISDN gateway. As an ISDN gateway receives a forwarding IP packet, it will check the IP address against those IP addresses inside the internal link control table. If it is found as a new IP address, the IP address will be translated into the ISDN address, and an ISDN call will be made to the ISDN gateway at the other side to set up the link. The ISDN link set up procedure is performed by the Call Handler submodule, based on the service calls provided by the LAP-D protocol, as indicated in figure 2. Then, the IP packets will be forwarded to the other side of the link.

The link should also be closely monitored by the ISDN gateway. As the connection closed by the upper layer protocols, the ISDN link should also be cut off. Basically, two kinds of connection monitoring methods are studied:

1. Having a partial TCP submodule implemented inside the gateway to sense the connection release; or

2. Having a watchdog timer to sense the stop of connection activities.

The TCP-sensor approach can terminate the connections in the least time delay, especially if the connection release is initiated from the Ethernet side, but the ISDN gateway system design will be less structured, and the approach introduces longer processing delay inside the ISDN gateway. The timer-sensor approach will wait a little longer after the TCP connection is actually closed, before being able to sense it. But the overall system performance can be improved by reducing one submodule. The timer-sensor approach is used in our design.

3.4 Packet- vs. Circuit- Switched

With packet-switched approach on B channels, X.25 and LAP-B protocol are used on packeting the user data. It can facilitate multiplexing operations of several actual connections over single ISDN link, but it dramatically reduces the gateway throughput which could be fatal to the gateway performance.

With circuit-switched approach on B channels, 64 Kbps of data rate can be achieved. User data is packetized using LAP-B or similar protocols. Much higher gateway throughput can be expected compared to the packet-switched approach. The circuit- switched approach is used in our design.

3.5 Extended Services on D Channel

To implement the ISDN Address Resolution Protocol (GARP) services, one new service may be needed though ISDN D channel. In order for a local ISDN-WS or an ISDN-GW to achieve the ISDN address translation information from remote ISDN gateway, a GARP_request packet may be sent from local ISDN-GW to the remote one, without the need to go through the whole call setup procedure to establish a permanent link. The remote ISDN-GW can send the GARP response in the same way. With this concern, X.25 is need to be implemented on D-channel. The problem is still under study.

4 ISDN Gateway Design

In this section, the software design and the hardware architecture of the ISDN gateway is explained, along with the design of the ISDN and Ethernet work-stations.

4.1 Top-Down System Design

In the ISDN gateway software design, top-down design and Bottom-up implementation and testing strategies are used. The software architectures and the protocol interactions are indicated in figure 2.

At the Application Layer in the ISDN and Ethernet work-stations, Telnet and File Transfer Protocol (FTP) are implemented for gateway performance testing and real application. The Transport Layer contains the TCP and the User Data Protocol (UDP). IP, Internet Control Message Protocol (ICMP), and Address Resolution Protocol (ARP) are implemented at the the Internet sublayer in both work-stations and ISDN gateway. Call Handler (CH) provides the ISDN call set up functions based on the underlying LAP-D services for the ISDN work-station and gateway. ISDN Gateway Address Resolution Protocol (GARP) is implemented along with the CH submodule to translate the IP address into the ISDN address. The Packet Driver (PD) module will provide the conversion between the connectionless and connection-oriented services, and some other services.

4.1.1 Control and Data Flows in ISDN-GW

The control and data flows in the ISDN-GW are depicted in Figure 3. It is basically the same as described in Figure 2, except the addition of the GARP module for the Gateway Address Resolution Protocol. One extra conceptual point which has to be explained here is that in terms of the peer-to-peer communications in the Network Layer in the TCP/IP protocol stack, the highest layer (sublayer) implemented in the ISDN gateway is IP, not the LINK or PD. The ISDN is considered, in this case, as one another subnet, and the PD is the interface between the IP and the subnet. But actually, the PD module performs the translation between the connection-oriented and the connectionless network services, and the LINK plays an important role in the individual circuit control and overall gateway control.

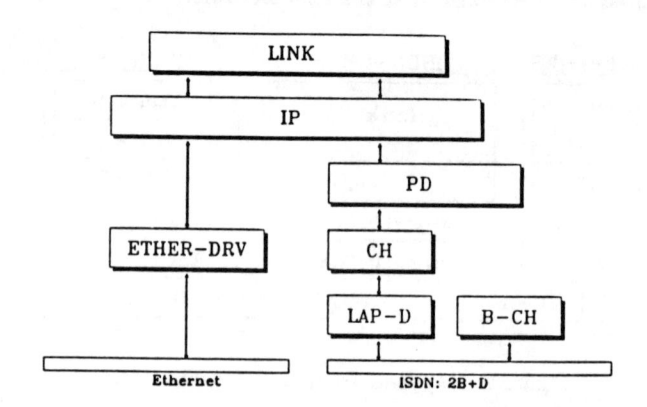

Figure 3: **Control and Data Flow in ISDN-GW**

4.1.2 Control and Data Flows in the ISDN-WS

The control and data flows in the ISDN-WS are shown in Figure 4. Besides the addition of the GARP module, an Packet Driver (PD) module is added between the IP and CH modules. The PD module functions are needed to interface between IP and CH: to translate between the Connectionless (IP) and Connection-Oriented (ISDN) network services, so that the services provided by the ISDN lower layers (layer 3 and 2) can be matched with the services required by the IP.

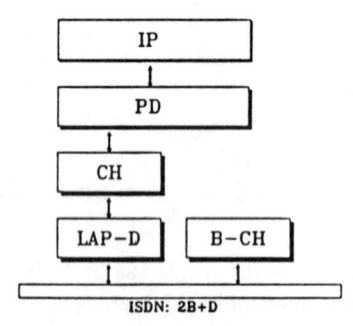

Figure 4: **Control and Data Flow in ISDN-WS and ETHER-WS**

4.1.3 ISDN Gateway Architecture and Module Layout

The ISDN gateway is designed and implemented using 80286- based AT-like systems, namely, Intel System 310s and 120s. The Application and Transport Layer modules in the work-stations and the link module in the ISDN gateway are running in the base systems, along with the Internet modules, Ethernet controller module, GARP module, performance monitoring module.

For the interface to the ISDN, an AdCOM2-I board from the Frontier Technology Corperation is used for each ISDN T interface. The board, the best suitable product could be found on the market at the time of search, contains the controller of two 64 Kbps synchronous data channels using RS-422 interface, which serves exactly two ISDN B channels. The on-board 80188 processor, 512 KB RAM, four PROM sockets are used to run the B and D channel buffer control modules, LAP-D module, Call Handler module, and link interface to the base system.

For the ISDN D channel, the RS-232C serial port on the base system is used at the 19.2 Kbps data rate, to match up the shortage of the AdCOM2 board. A D-Channel Trap submodule monitors the port, and transfer the data into the D-Channel buffer in the AdCOM2 board on time.

The link module in the base system also take the responsibility of communicating and controlling the AdCOM2-I board(s). The module is designed so that the expansion to multiple ISDN lines could be possible.

Figure 5 shows the base system architecture of the ISDN gateway, and figure 6 shows the subsystem architecture on the AdCOM2 board.

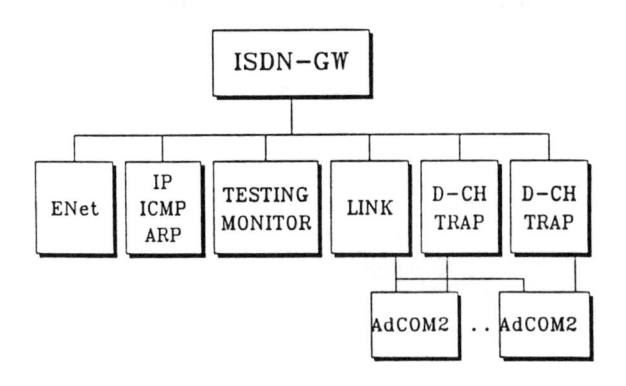

Figure 5: **Module Layout in ISDN-GW Base System**

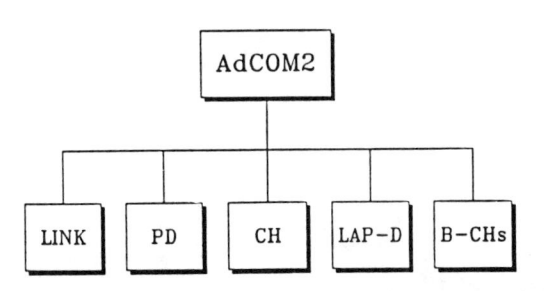

Figure 6: **Module Layout in AdCOM2-I Subsystem**

4.2 Bottom-up Module Implementation

Each protocol module inside the gateway and work-station is designed in the unified module form. In terms of the external view of each module structure from the upper layer, it basically provides the interfaces of the service function calls of the module, namely the Service Access Points (SAPs): n_OPEN, n_CLOSE, n_SEND, n_RCV, and n_STAT, in which "n" stands for the name of the module. Internally, each module contains the submodule to handle the SAP interfaces, the module entity for the peer-to-peer activity control, and the interfaces to the underlying layer or modules.

For the connection-oriented module, the open and close service calls provide the means to establish and close the connection. For the connectionless module, the open and close service calls provide the means for the administration module to initialize this module.

5 ISDN Gateway Development

In this section, issues related to the ISDN gateway implementation are briefly explained.

5.1 Development Environment

Figure 7 shows the ISDN-GW application environment. Since the ISDN service is not available at the time of the ISDN gateway implementation and testing, a development environment is set up using the Micro Vax II system to simulate the ISDN service line provided by the 5ESS switch system. The simulation package is provided by the US West Advanced Technology, to simulate the call set up, and some other ISDN functions. The DCT boards are used to multiplex two B channels and one D channel signal into one ISDN S/T interface line. As ISDN service will be available on UA campus when the installation of the 5ESS switch sys-

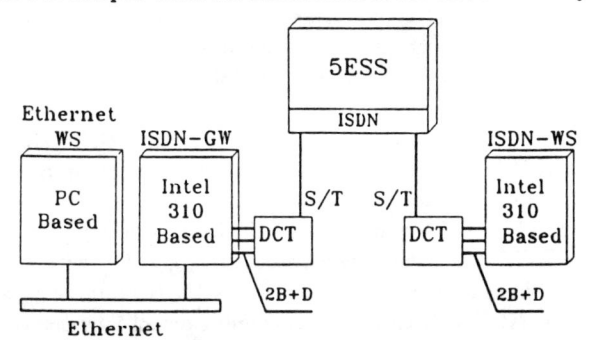

Figure 7: **ISDN Gateway Application Environment**

tem is completed, the ISDN gateway will be tested against the ISDN lines from 5ESS switch.

5.2 Monitoring Window

In the process of ISDN gateway development, an independent Monitor Window Module is designed and implemented. It provides the run-time switching capability between the packet mode to show the detail of the packet structures and the statistics mode to monitor the run-statistics; and the switching capability between different layers to be monitored. A data driven chained control structure of all monitored layers or modules should be fed into the Monitor Window Module to start the monitoring.

5.3 Resulting Prototype System

The resulting prototype systems developed in the first phase of this research project is shown in table 1. Those systems are demonstrated at the end of the project.

Table 1. Resulting Prototype Systems

PROTOCOLS \ SYS	ISDN GW	ISDN WS	ETHERNET WS
Telnet, FTP, SMTP		Yes	Yes
TCP, UDP		Yes	Yes
Link	Yes		
CH, IGWARP	Yes	Yes	
IP, ICMP, ARP	Yes	Yes	Yes
Ethernet	Yes		Yes
LAP-D, LAP-B	Yes	Yes	

6 Conclusion

In this research project, the ISDN gateway is designed and implemented to internetwork ISDN with Ethernet running TCP/IP protocol stack. During the process, prototyping ISDN and Ethernet work-stations are also built for the data communications through the ISDN system. We feel that it is an important project to us because that we accumulated the experience in dealing with both ISDN system and TCP/IP protocol stack, and that we also set up a development environment for the future research work in the area. In terms of the future work, the ISDN gateway performance will be further investigated, in connection with the studies in the area of the Broadband ISDN requirements and the Global Picture Archiving and Control Systems requirements specifications. The ISDN gateway design and implementation will also be considered to some other LANs using TCP/IP protocol stack, or to the networks using ISO standards.

References

[1] AT&T, "5ESS Switch: ISDN Basic Rate Interface Specification", 5D5-900-301, Issue 1.03, Sept. 1985

[2] AT&T Network Systems, "5ESS Switch: Integrated Services Digital Network - Terminal Equipment - Service Applications and Planning", 533-700-105, Issue 2, April 1989

[3] Berera, E., and P. Jardin, "Interconnection of LANs & PBXs in an ISDN environment", *Proceedings of the Conference ISDN 87*. London, UK. June 1987.

[4] Frontier Technologies Corp. , "AdCOM2-1 Plus User/Programming Manual", M-011-01-01, Release 1.1, Oct. 1988

[5] Heldman, Robert K. , "ISDN in the Information Marketplace", TAB BOOKS Inc. , 1988

[6] Knight, G., D. Deniz, and J. Fan, "Gateways to the ISDN", *Proceedings of the Conference ISDN 87*. London, UK. June 1987.

[7] Ronayne, John, "ISDN, the Story so far", *ISDN '88*, pp. 5-16

[8] Stallings, William, "ISDN: An Introduction", MacMillan Pub. , 1989

[9] US West Advanced Technology, "ISDN Swicth Simulator: 5ESS Version, User Guide", Release 001, Sept. 1988

Chapter 5
Transport and Session Protocols

Transport protocols

The transport protocol is the keystone of the whole concept of a computer-communications architecture. Lower-layer protocols are needed, to be sure, but they are less important pedagogically and to designers for a number of reasons. For one thing, lower-level protocols are better understood and, on the whole, less complex than transport protocols. Also, standards have settled out quite well for most kinds of layer 1 to 3 transmission facilities, and there is a large body of experience in their use.

Viewed from the other side, upper level protocols are also of lesser importance. The transport protocol provides the basic end-to-end service of transferring data between users. Any process or application can be programmed to directly access the transport services without going through session and presentation layers. Indeed, this is the normal mode of operation for DOD's transport protocols.

The purpose of a transport protocol is to provide a reliable mechanism for the exchange of data between processes in different systems. The transport protocol ensures that data units are delivered error-free, in sequence, with no losses or duplications. The transport layer may also be concerned with optimizing the use of network services and providing a requested quality of service to session entities. For example, the session entity might specify acceptable error rates, maximum delay, priority, and security. In effect, the transport layer serves as the user's liaison with the communications facility.

The size and complexity of a transport protocol depends on the type of service it can get from layer 3. For a reliable layer 3 with a virtual circuit capability, a minimal layer 4 is required. If layer 3 is unreliable and/or only supports datagrams, the layer 4 protocol should include extensive error detection and recovery. Accordingly, NBS has defined two versions of its Transport Protocol (TP): a relatively simple version for reliable networks and a more complex one for unreliable networks. The former is a subset of the latter. The more complex version is comparable in capability to another transport protocol standard, DOD's Transmission Control Protocol (TCP). ISO has gone even further and defined five classes of transport protocol, each oriented toward a different underlying protocol.

Session protocols

The essential purpose of a session protocol is to provide a user-oriented connection service. The transport protocol is responsible for creating and maintaining a connection between endpoints. A session protocol would provide a "user interface" by "adding value" to the basic connection service. Let us consider some of the value-added features. We can group them into the following categories:

- Session establishment and maintenance.
- Dialogue management.
- Recovery.

Session establishment and maintenance

The minimum service that a session protocol entity provides its users is the establishment, maintenance, and termination of sessions. When two users wish to establish a connection, their respective entities will create a session that is mapped onto a transport connection and will negotiate the parameters of the session (e.g., data unit size; see below for further examples).

Let us refer to the unit of data exchanged between a session user and a session protocol entity as a record. Then the entity accepts records from the user and transmits the data over a transport connection in a sequence of letters. The data are received on the other side and delivered to the user in proper order. The sending entity may, at its discretion, fragment records into multiple letters if the record size is too large. Alternatively, multiple records may be blocked into a single letter for efficiency of transmission. In any case, the receiving entity recovers the original records and passes these on to the receiving user.

The simplest relationship between sessions and transport connections is one to one. It might be desirable to multiplex multiple sessions onto a single transport connection. This reduces the processing burden and amount of state information required of the transport entity. However, caution must be observed. For example, a session supporting inquiry/response should not be multiplexed with a session supporting a file transfer, since the sending of the inquiry text may be significantly delayed when entering a long transport queue of text from the other session. Furthermore, if the receiving session entity is forced, for any reason, to stop receiving the file transfer text, the receiving queue may soon fill up. This will cause the source queue to fill up as well, and any text from the session multiplexed with the halted session may remain trapped in it.

A session might also be split between two transport connections. This could facilitate the transfer of expedited or interrupt data.

Dialogue management

The session entity may impose a structure on the interaction or dialogue between users. There are three possible modes of dialogue: two-way simultaneous, two-way alternate, and one-way.

The two-way simultaneous mode is a full-duplex type of operation. Both sides can simultaneously send data. Once this mode is agreed upon in the session negotiation phase, there is no specific dialogue management task required. This would probably be the most common mode of dialogue.

Similarly, the one-way mode requires no specific dialogue management mechanism once it is established. All user data flows in one direction only. An example of this is if data are to be sent to a temporarily inactive user, and are accepted by a "receiver server," whose only task is to accept data on behalf of other local users and store them. Note that the characteristic of being one-way is not absolute. There is a two-way dialogue required to establish the session. During data transfer, the receiving session entity may transmit acknowledgments and other control information. Furthermore, the receiving session user may need to send back some interrupt data. For example, the receiver may need to halt reception temporarily because of a local system problem.

The most complex of the three modes is two-way alternate. In this case, the two sides take turns sending the data. An example of the use of this mode is for inquiry/response applications. The session entity enforces the alternating interaction by informing each user when it is its turn. This is actually a three-step process:

- The user who has the turn informs its session entity when it has completed its turn.
- The sending session entity sends any outstanding data to the receiving entity, and then informs the receiving entity that the turn is being passed.
- The receiving entity passes up any outstanding data to its user, and then informs the user that it is its turn.

An economical means of accomplishing this process is to mark the data with a delimiter. Specifically, the sending user includes a delimiter in the last record of its turn. Let us call the sequence of records sent during one user's turn a *session interaction unit*. Then, on the last record of its turn, the user would include an end-of-interaction unit (I) delimiter. This delimiter is, in effect, a token that is passed to the other user.

With two-way alternate, the user is prevented from sending normal data unless it is its turn. However, a user may send interrupt data to demand the turn. As an example of the use of the demand-turn mechanism, consider a user who has requested data and is viewing them as they scroll onto a screen. The user may wish to abort the transmission once the first few lines have been viewed.

Recovery

Another potential feature of a session protocol is a recovery support service similar to the checkpoint/restart mechanisms used in file management.

This feature could be provided by defining a *session recovery unit,* which corresponds to the interval between checkpoints. Each user specifies the point at which a recovery unit ends, and the recovery units are numbered sequentially. To recover lost data (e.g., following a disk fault or a paper break on a printer), a user can issue a command to recover, using the recovery unit number to identify the point to which the session should be backed up.

Once a session has been backed up, some form of recovery will generally be attempted. This is a complex function, which would doubtless extend beyond the bounds of the session layer.

One fundamental point that needs to be mentioned is the degree of responsibility of the session protocol entities. When the session is backed up to the beginning of a session recovery unit, the session protocol entities may be requested to retransmit all records from that point forward. If so, the session entity must maintain a copy of each record. To avoid unbounded storage requirements, the user should periodically issue a release command, so that some prior session recovery units can be discarded. Alternatively, the session entity might only be required to remember the records of the current recovery unit.

On the other hand, the session entity may only be required to discard outstanding records and back up its recovery-unit counter to the point indicated, with the primary recovery responsibilities being handled at higher levels. In this case, there does not seem much point in having any recovery feature in the session layer. Indeed, NBS takes the position that recovery is inherently an application function and, based on the principle of functional separation of layers, should not be visible in the session layer.

Figure 5-1 indicates that a session recovery unit is made up of one or more records. However, there is no need for a defined relationship between session recovery units and session interaction units.

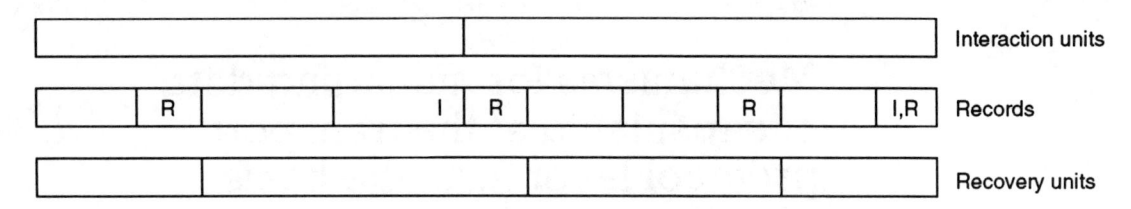

Figure 5-1. Session delimited data units.

Summary

"A Primer: Understanding Transport Protocols" provides a detailed discussion of transport protocol mechanisms, plus a summary of current standards. "Architectures, Features, and Implementation of High-Speed Transport Protocols" looks at a new generation of protocols designed to deal with the high data rates now becoming common on both local and wide-area networks. A high-speed, or lightweight, transport protocol combines and streamlines the functionality of traditional transport and internet protocols.

"Hints for the Interpretation of the ISO Session Layer" is a detailed discussion of this complex standard.

A primer: Understanding transport protocols

Mechanisms for managing data encapsulated at the transport protocol layer form the basis of communications architecture.

The transport protocol is the keystone of the whole concept of a computer communications architecture. Within the structure of a communications architecture, it is the transport protocol that provides a reliable mechanism for the exchange of data between processes in different computers. The protocol typically ensures that data is delivered error-free, in sequence, with no loss or duplication. The transport service relieves higher-level software of the burden of managing the intervening communications facility. Because the transport protocol provides for high-quality service, and because it may need to deal with a range of communications services, it can be the most complex of all communications protocols.

The transport layer shields applications from the details of the underlying communications service. This is depicted in Figure 1. Stations 1 and 2 each have one or more applications that wish to communicate. For each such application (for example, electronic mail) an application-oriented protocol is needed that coordinates the activities of the corresponding application modules and assures common syntax and semantics. The transport protocol in turn makes use of a network's services module, which provides access to the intervening communications network (for example, using X.25).

The basic service provided by a transport protocol is the transfer of data between two transport users, such as a session protocol or an application. Data is passed from a transport user to a transport protocol entity. This entity encapsulates that data into a transport protocol data unit (TPDU), which contains the user data plus control information, such as the destination address. Beyond this basic service, there are a number of other services offered to the transport user:

- *Connection type.* This provides for the logical connection between transport users. Connectionless service transmits each unit of data independently and generally does not guarantee delivery.
- *Grade of service.* Transport users can specify the grade of transmission service, such as acceptable error and loss levels, desired average and maximum delays and throughput, and priority.
- *Connection management.* With this connection-oriented service, transport entities are responsible for establishing, maintaining, and terminating logical connections between endpoints.
- *Expedited delivery.* This is an interrupt mechanism used to transfer occasional urgent data, such as a break character or alarm condition. The sending transport entity endeavors to have the transmission facility transfer the data as rapidly as possible; the receiving transport entity interrupts the user to signify receipt of urgent data.
- *Status reporting.* This service allows the transport user to receive information on the condition or attributes of a transport entity or connection.
- *Security.* The transport entity may be able to request security services from the transmission facility.

The complexity of a transport protocol depends upon the type of service it provides and the type of service it receives from the communications facility below it. Typically, a transport protocol provides a connection-oriented service. That is, a logical connection is established between two transport users. The transport protocol may guarantee the delivery of data over such a connection in the order in which it is sent with no losses or duplication.

The most difficult case for a transport protocol is that of an unreliable network service. There are two problems: TPDUs are occasionally lost; and TPDUs may arrive out of sequence due to variable transit delays. As we shall see, elaborate mechanisms are required to cope with these two interrelated network deficiencies. We shall also see that a discouraging pattern emerges. The combination of unreliability and nonsequencing creates problems with every mechanism. Generally, the solution to each problem raises new problems. While there are problems to be overcome for protocols at all levels, it seems that there are more difficulties with a reliable connection-oriented transport protocol than with any other sort of protocol.

The four key transport protocol mechanisms are:
- Ordered delivery
- Connection establishment
- Error control
- Flow control

Ordered delivery

If two entities are not directly connected, there is the possibility that TPDUs will not arrive in the order in which they were sent, because they may traverse different paths. In connection-oriented data transfer, it is generally required that the TPDU order be maintained. For example, if a file is transferred between two points, we would like to be assured that the data in the received file is in the same order as in the transmitted file, and not shuffled. If each TPDU is given a number, and numbers are assigned sequentially, then it is a logically simple task for the receiving entity to re-order received TPDUs on the basis of sequence number.

Thus, the header in the TPDU contains a sequence number field. The only hitch in this scheme is that sequence numbers repeat; when the maximum number is reached, the numbering sequence starts over again at zero. It is evident that the maximum sequence number must be greater than the maximum number of TPDUs that could be outstanding at any time.

Connection establishment

To provide connection-oriented service, any transfer of data between transport entities must begin with a connection-establishment procedure.

Connection establishment serves three main purposes:
- It allows each end to assure that the other exists.
- It allows negotiation of optional parameters (for example, TPDU size and grade of service).
- It triggers allocation of transport entity resources (for example, buffer space and entry in connection table).

Connection establishment is by mutual agreement and can be accomplished by a control TPDU (a TPDU that contains no user data, just control information). The side wishing to initiate a connection sends RFC X, which is a request for connection, and indicates that the requesting entity will begin issuing data TPDUs with sequence number X. The other transport entity accepts the connection by issuing an RFC Y, indicating that it

1. Shielded from details. *The transport protocol layer shields applications from the details of the underlying communications service. The two stations depicted here have applications that wish to communicate. Therefore, an applications protocol is needed that coordinates activities and assures common syntax and semantics.*

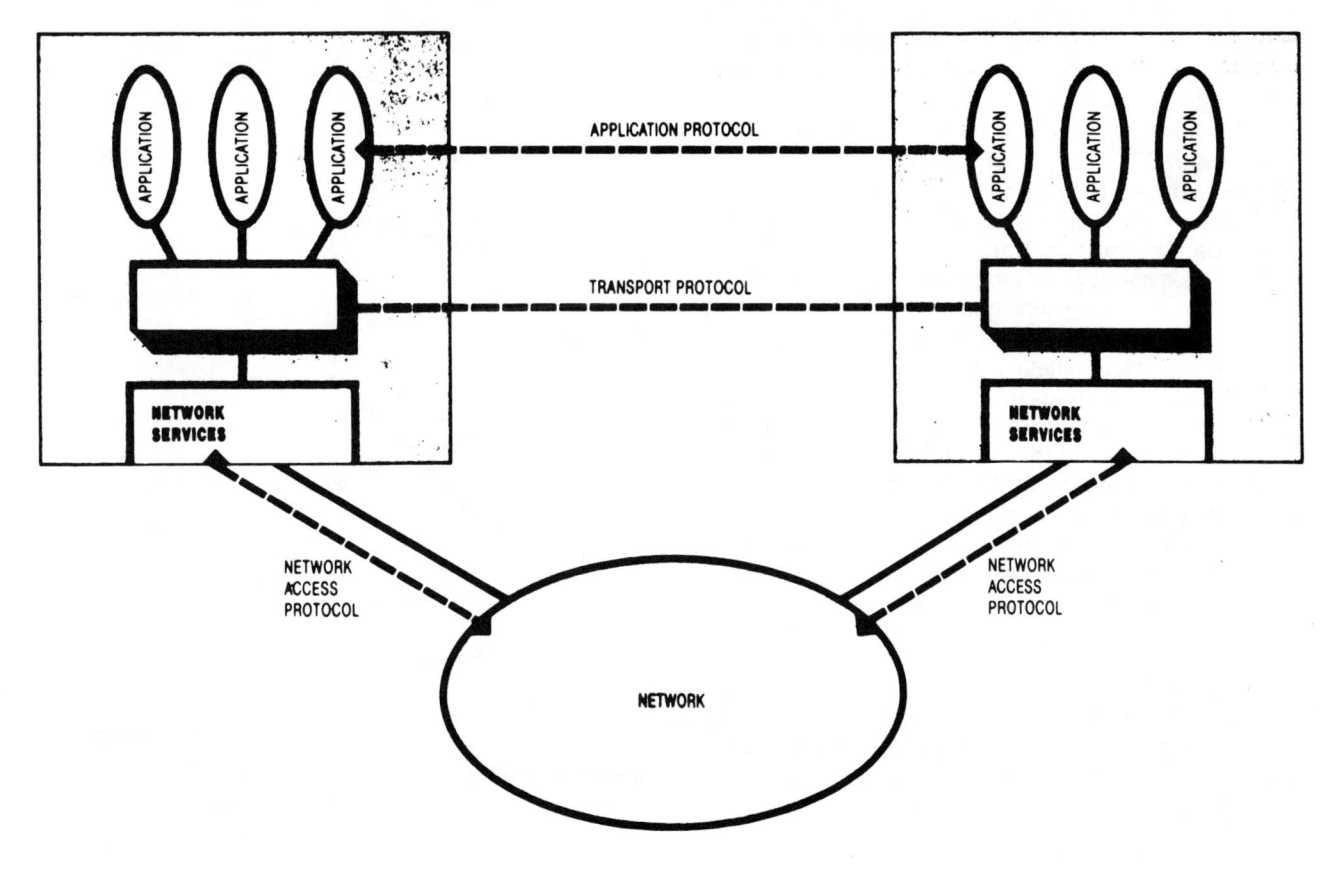

will send data TPDUs beginning with sequence number Y. Note that either side can initiate a connection, and if both sides initiate a connection at about the same time, it is established without confusion.

As with other protocol mechanisms, connection establishment must take into account the unreliability of the network service. Suppose that A issues an RFC to B. It expects to get an RFC back, confirming the connection. Two things can go wrong: A's RFC can be lost or B's answering RFC can be lost. Both cases can be handled by using a retransmit-RFC timer. After A issues an RFC, it will reissue the RFC when the timer expires.

This gives rise, potentially, to duplicate RFCs. However, if A's initial RFC is lost, there are no duplicates. If B's response is lost, then B may receive two RFCs from A. Further, if B's response is not lost, but simply delayed, A may get two responding RFCs. All of this means that A and B must simply ignore duplicate RFCs once a connection is established.

Now, consider that a duplicate RFC may survive past the termination of the connection. RFC X arrives at B after the connection is terminated. B assumes that this is a fresh request and responds with an RFC Y. Meanwhile, A has decided to open a new connection with B and sends RFC Z. B discards this as a duplicate. Subsequently, A initiates data transfer with a TPDU numbered Z. B rejects the TPDU as being out of sequence.

The way out of this problem is for each side to explicitly acknowledge the other's RFC and sequence number. The procedure is known as a three-way handshake. With this strategy, the transport entity hesitates during the connection opening to assure that any RFC that was sent has also been acknowledged before the connection is declared open. Plus, there is an additional control TPDU to reset (RST) the other side when a duplicate RFC is detected.

Figure 2 illustrates typical three-way handshake operations. An RFC is sent that includes the send sequence number. The responding RFC acknowledges that number and includes the sequence number for the other side. The initiating transport entity acknowledges the RFC acknowledgment in its first data TPDU. Next shown is a situation in which an old RFC X arrives at B after the close of the relevant connection. B assumes that this is a fresh request and responds with RFC Y, ACK X. When A receives this message, it realizes that it has not requested a connection and therefore sends a RST, ACK Y. Note that the ACK Y portion of the RST message is essential so that an old, duplicate RST does not abort a legitimate connection establishment. The final example shows a case in which an old RFC ACK arrives in the middle of a new connection establishment. Because of the use of sequence numbers in the acknowledgments, this event causes no mischief.

Error control

If the underlying communications facility is unreliable, the transport facility must cope with lost or damaged data TPDUs. For this purpose, a positive acknowledgment (ACK) scheme is used: the receiver must acknowledge each successfully received TPDU. For efficiency, we do not require one ACK per TPDU. Rather, a cumulative acknowledgment can be used. Thus, the receiver may receive TPDUs numbered 1, 2, and 3, but only send ACK 3 back. The sender interprets ACK 3 to mean that number 3 and all previous TPDUs have been successfully received.

Now, if a TPDU is lost in transit, no ACK will be sent. To cope with this situation, there must be a timer associated with each TPDU as it is sent. If the timer expires before the TPDU is acknowledged, the sender must retransmit.

So, the addition of a timer solves that problem. Next problem: At what value should the timer be set? If the value is too small, there will be many unnecessary retransmissions, wasting network capacity. If the value is too large, the protocol will be sluggish in responding to a lost TPDU. The timer should be set at a value slightly longer than the round-trip delay (send TPDU, receive ACK). Of course, this delay is variable even under constant network load. Worse, the statistics of the delay will vary with changing network conditions.

2. Three-way handshake. *Here are three examples showing connections initiated, accepted, acknowledged, or rejected before transmission begins.*

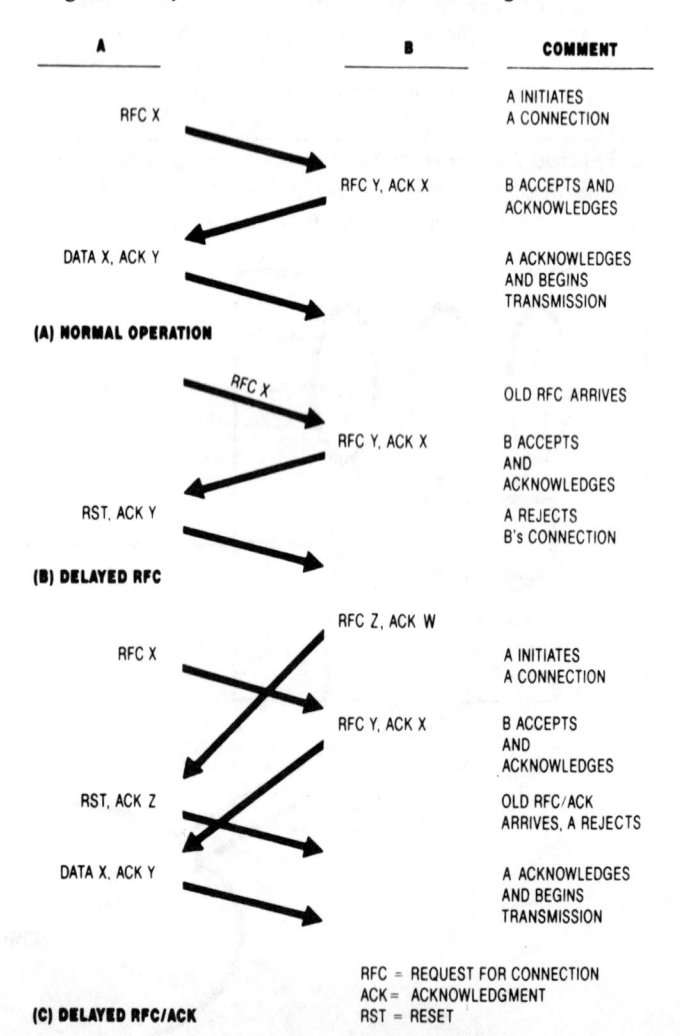

A	B	COMMENT
RFC X →		A INITIATES A CONNECTION
← RFC Y, ACK X		B ACCEPTS AND ACKNOWLEDGES
DATA X, ACK Y →		A ACKNOWLEDGES AND BEGINS TRANSMISSION

(A) NORMAL OPERATION

A	B	COMMENT
RFC X →		OLD RFC ARRIVES
← RFC Y, ACK X		B ACCEPTS AND ACKNOWLEDGES
RST, ACK Y →		A REJECTS B's CONNECTION

(B) DELAYED RFC

A	B	COMMENT
← RFC Z, ACK W		
RFC X →		A INITIATES A CONNECTION
← RFC Y, ACK X		B ACCEPTS AND ACKNOWLEDGES
RST, ACK Z →		OLD RFC/ACK ARRIVES, A REJECTS
DATA X, ACK Y →		A ACKNOWLEDGES AND BEGINS TRANSMISSION

(C) DELAYED RFC/ACK

RFC = REQUEST FOR CONNECTION
ACK = ACKNOWLEDGMENT
RST = RESET

Two strategies suggest themselves. A fixed timer value could be used, based on an understanding of the network's typical behavior. This solution suffers from an inability to respond to changing network conditions. If the value is set too high, the service will always be sluggish. If it is set too low, a positive feedback condition can develop, in which network congestion leads to more retransmissions, which increase congestion.

An adaptive scheme has its own problems. Suppose the transport entity keeps track of the time taken to acknowledge data TPDUs and sets its retransmission timer based on an average of the observed delays. This value cannot be trusted, for three reasons:
- The peer entity may not acknowledge a TPDU immediately. Recall that it has the privilege of cumulation acknowledgments.
- If a TPDU has been retransmitted, the sender cannot know whether the received ACK is a response to the initial transmission or a retransmission.
- Network conditions may change suddenly.

Each of these problems is cause for some further tweaking of the transport algorithm; but the problem admits no complete solution. There will always be some uncertainty concerning the best value for the retransmission timer.

If a TPDU is lost and then retransmitted, no confusion will result. If, however, an ACK is lost, one or more TPDUs will be retransmitted and, if they arrive successfully, they may be duplicates of previously received TPDUs. Thus, the sender must be able to recognize duplicates. The fact that each TPDU carries a sequence number helps, but, nevertheless, duplicate detection and handling are not easy. There are two cases:
- A duplicate is received prior to the close of the connection.
- A duplicate is received after the close of the connection.

Notice that we say "a" duplicate rather than "the" duplicate. From the sender's point of view, the retransmitted TPDU is the duplicate. However, the retransmitted TPDU may arrive before the original TPDU, in which case the receiver views the original TPDU as the duplicate. In any case, two tactics are needed to cope with a duplicate received prior to the close of a connection:
- The receiver must assume that its acknowledgment was lost and therefore must acknowledge the duplicate. Consequently, the sender must not get confused if it receives multiple ACKs to the same TPDU.
- The sequence number space must be long enough so as not to "cycle" in less than the maximum possible TPDU lifetime.

Figure 3 illustrates the reason for this latter requirement. In this example, the sequence space is of length 8. A transmits TPDUs 0, 1, and 2 and awaits acknowledgment. For some reason, TPDU 0 is excessively delayed. B has received 1 and 2, but 0 is delayed in transit. Thus, B does not send any ACKs. A times out and retransmits TPDU 0. When the duplicate TPDU 0 arrives, B acknowledges 0, 1, and 2. Meanwhile, A has timed out again and retransmits 1, which B acknowledges with another ACK 2. Things now seem to have sorted themselves out, and data transfer continues. When the sequence space is exhausted, A cycles back to sequence number 0 and continues. Alas, the old TPDU 0 makes a belated appearance and is accepted by B before the new TPDU 0 arrives.

It should be clear that the untimely emergence of the old TPDU would have caused no difficulty if the sequence numbers had not yet returned to 0. The problem is, how big must the sequence space be? This depends on, among other things, whether the network enforces a maximum packet lifetime and on the rate at which TPDUs are being transmitted. As we shall see, the standard transport protocols allow stupendous sequence spaces.

A more subtle problem is posed by TPDUs that continue to rattle around after a transport connection is closed. If a subsequent connection is opened between the same two transport entities, a TPDU from the old connection could arrive and be accepted on the new connection. Similarly, a delayed ACK can enter a new connection and cause problems.

There are a number of approaches to this particular problem. We mention two of the more promising. First, the sequence numbering scheme can be extended across connection lifetimes. This requires that a trans-

---

3. Exhausted. *When the sequence space is exhausted, A cycles back to the original TPDU 0, which is accepted by B before the duplicate TPDU 0 arrives.*

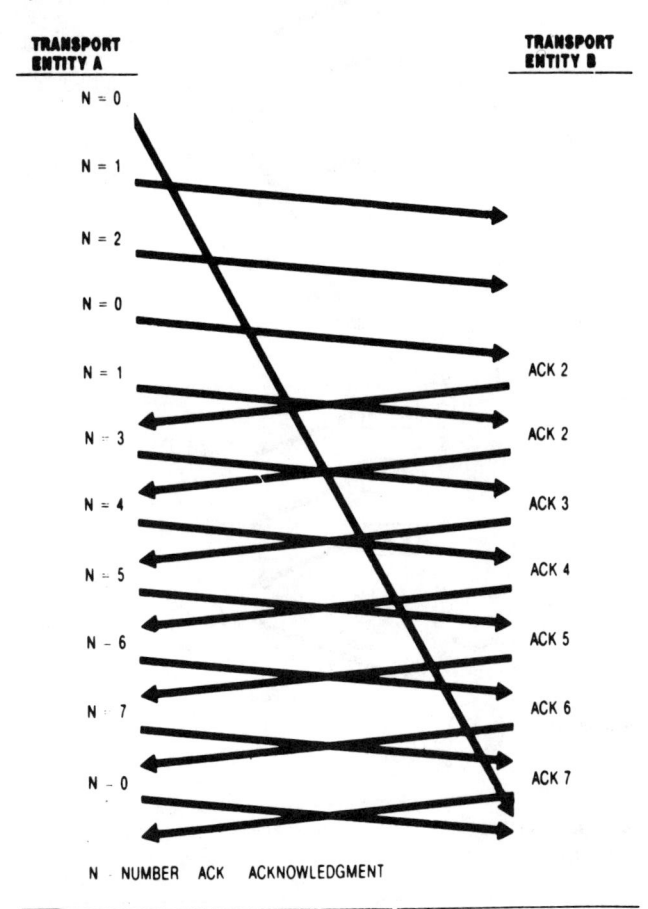

N — NUMBER   ACK — ACKNOWLEDGMENT

port entity remember the last sequence number that it used on transmission for each terminated connection. Then, when a new connection to a transport entity is attempted, the RFC contains the sequence number to be used to begin data transfer. Of course, this procedure is symmetric, with each side responsible for declaring the sequence number with which it will commence transmission.

The above procedures work fine unless a crash occurs. In that case, the transport entity will not remember what sequence number was used last. An alternative is simply to wait a sufficient amount of time between connections to assure that all old TPDUs are gone. Then, even if one side has experienced a crash, the other side can refuse a connection until the reconnection timer expires. This, of course, may cause undesirable delays.

Flow control

Flow control is the process of controlling the flow of data between two points. This seemingly simple concept leads to a rather complex mechanism at the transport layer, primarily for two reasons:
- Flow control at the transport layer involves the interaction of transport users, transport entities, and the network service.
- The transmission delay between transport entities is generally long compared with actual transmission time and, what is worse, is variable.

When a transport user wishes to transmit data, it sends that data to its transport entity. This triggers two events: the transport entity generates one or more TPDUs and passes these on to the network service. It also acknowledges to the user that it has accepted the data for transmission. At this point, the transport entity can exercise flow control across the user-transport interface by simply withholding its acknowledgment. The protocol entity is most likely to do this if the entity itself is being held up by a flow control exercised by either the network service or the target transport entity.

In any case, once the transport entity has accepted the data, it sends out a TPDU. Some time later, it receives an acknowledgment that the data has been received at the remote end. It then sends a confirmation to the sender.

At the receiving end a TPDU arrives at the transport entity. It unwraps the data and sends it on to the destination user. When the user accepts the data, it issues an acknowledgment. The user can exercise flow control over the transport entity by withholding its response.

Now, the target transport entity has two choices regarding acknowledgment back to the source transport entity. Either it can issue an acknowledgment as soon as it has correctly received the TPDU, or it can wait until it knows that its user has correctly received the data before acknowledging. The latter course is the safer. In this latter case, the acknowledgment is in fact a confirmation that the destination user received the data. In the former case, it merely confirms that the data made it through to the remote transport entity.

With the above discussion in mind, we can cite two reasons why one transport entity would want to restrain the rate of TPDU transmission over a connection from another transport entity:
- The user of the receiving transport entity cannot keep up with the flow of data.
- The receiving transport entity itself cannot keep up with the flow of TPDUs.

How do such problems manifest themselves? Presumably, a transport entity has a certain amount of buffer space. Incoming TPDUs are added to the buffer. Each buffered TPDU is processed by examining the transport header and the data sent to the user. Either of the two problems mentioned above will cause the buffer to fill up. Thus, the transport entity needs to take steps to stop or slow the flow of TPDUs to prevent buffer overflow. Due to the annoying time gap between sender and receiver, it is not always easy for the

4. Credit allocation. *In this example of a credit allocation protocol, data flows in one direction. Sending machine A is granted a credit allocation of 7.*

ACK = ACKNOWLEDGMENT
N = NUMBER
TPDU = TRANSPORT PROTOCOL DATA UNIT

ISO and DOD TPDU fields

ACKNOWLEDGMENT NUMBER (32 BITS)
A piggybacked acknowledgment.

ACKNOWLEDGE TIME
An estimate of the time taken by the entity to acknowledge a DT TPDU. This helps the other entity select a value for its retransmission timer.

ALTERNATIVE PROTOCOL CLASS
Specifies whether only the requested protocol class (2 or 4) is acceptable, or if both classes are acceptable.

CAUSE (8 BITS)
Reason for rejection of a TPDU.

CHECKSUM
For the ISO standard, the result of checksum algorithm for the entire TPDU. The checksum is used only for Class 4 and, within that class, it is mandatory for all CR TPDUs and for all other TPDUs when the checksum option is chosen.

CHECKSUM OPTION
For the ISO standard, it indicates whether checksum should be used.

CLASS (4 BITS)
Protocol Class 2 or 4.

CREDIT (CDT) (4 BITS)
Flow control credit allocation. Initial credit is granted in CR and CC, subsequent credit is granted in ACK. As an option, a 16-bit credit field is used with ACK and is appended after the TPDU-NR field.

DATA OFFSET (4 BITS)
Number of 32-bit words in the header.

DESTINATION PORT (16 BITS)
Identifies destination service access point.

EOT (1 BIT)
Used when a user letter has been fragmented into multiple TPDUs. It is set to 1 on the last TPDU.

FLAGS (6 BITS)
URG: Urgent pointer field significant
ACK: Acknowledgment field significant
PSH: Push function
RST: Reset the connection
SYN: Synchronize the sequence numbers
FIN: No more data from sender

FLOW CONTROL CONFIRMATION
Echoes parameter values in the last ACK TPDU received. It contains the values of the TPDU-NR, CDT, and sub-sequence number fields.

LENGTH INDICATOR (LI) (8 BITS)
Length of the header (fixed plus variable), excluding the LI field, in octets.

OPTION (4 BITS)
For the ISO standard, specifies normal (7-bit sequence number, 4-bit credit) or extended (31-bit sequence number, 16-bit credit) flow control fields.

OPTIONS (VARIABLE)
At present for the DOD standard, only one option is defined, one that specifies the maximum TPDU size that will be accepted.

PRIORITY
Priority of this connection.

REASON (8 BITS)
Reason for requesting a disconnect or rejecting a connection request.

RECEIVER TRANSPORT SUFFIX
Service access point that identifies the calling transport user.

REJECTED TPDU
The bit pattern of the rejected TPDU up to and including the octet that caused the rejections.

RESIDUAL ERROR RATE
Expresses the target and minimum rate of unreported user data loss.

SEQUENCE NUMBER (31 BITS)
Sequence number of the first data octet in this TPDU, except when SYN is present. If SYN is present, it is the initial sequence number (ISN), and the first data octet is ISN + 1.

SOURCE PORT (16 BITS)
Identifies source service access point.

SOURCE REFERENCE (16 BITS)
Reference used by the transport entity to give a unique identifier to the transport connection in its own networks.

SUB-SEQUENCE NUMBER
Number of the ACK that assures the sequentially correct processing of ACKs with the same TPDU-NR.

THROUGHPUT
Specifies the user's throughput requirements in octets per second. Four values are specified: the target and minimum acceptable throughput in both the calling-called direction and the called-calling direction.

TPDU CODE (4 BITS)
Type of TPDU:
- Connection request (CR)
- Connection confirm (CC)
- Disconnect request (DR)
- Disconnect confirm (DC)
- TPDU error (ER)
- Data (DT)
- Expedited data (ED)
- Acknowledgment (ACK)
- Expedited acknowledgment (EA)
- Reject (RJ)

TPDU SIZE
Maximum TPDU size in octets. The range of options is from 128 to 8,192 in powers of 2.

TRANSIT DELAY
Specifies the user's delay requirements in milliseconds. Four values are specified: the target and maximum-acceptable transit delay in both directions.

URGENT POINTER (16 BITS)
Points to the octet following the urgent data. This allows the receiver to know how much urgent data is coming.

VERSION NUMBER
Version of protocol to be followed. The current version is number 1.

WINDOW (16 BITS)
Flow control credit allocation, in octets.

transport entity to meet this requirement.

The most commonly used transport flow control technique is credit allocation, and it makes use of the fact that the TPDUs are numbered. At any time, the sender is allowed to transmit only a "window" of sequence numbers. Each time a TPDU is sent, the window is narrowed by 1. From time to time, the receiver will issue a credit, allowing the sender to widen the window by the granted amount. Credit allocation and acknowledgment are independent of each other. Thus a TPDU may be acknowledged without granting new credit and vice versa.

Credit allocation

Typically, the credit allocation scheme is tied to acknowledgments in the following way: to both acknowledge TPDUs and grant credit, a transport entity sends a control TPDU of the form (ACK N, CDT M), where ACK N acknowledges all data TPDUs through number N, and CDT M allows TPDUs numbers N + 1 through N + M to be transmitted. Figure 4 illustrates the protocol. For simplicity, we show a data flow in one direction only. In this example, TPDUs are numbered sequentially modulo 8. Initially, through the connection establishment process, the sending and receiving sequence numbers are synchronized, and A is granted a credit allocation of 7. A advances the trailing edge of its window each time that it transmits, and advances the leading edge only when it is granted credit.

This mechanism is quite powerful. Consider that the last control TPDU issued by B was (ACK N, CDT M). Then:
■ To increase or decrease credit to X when no additional TPDUs have arrived, B can issue one credit (ACK N, CDT X).
■ To acknowledge a new TPDU without increasing credit, B can issue (ACK N + 1, CDT M - 1).

In the credit allocation scheme, the receiver needs to adopt some policy concerning the amount of data it permits the sender to transmit. The conservation approach is to only allow new TPDUs up to the limit of available buffer space. If this policy were in effect in Figure 4, then the first credit message implies that B has five free buffer slots, and the second message implies that B has seven free slots.

A conservative flow control scheme may limit the throughput of the transport connection in long-delay situations. The receiver could potentially increase throughput by optimistically granting credit for space it does not have. For example, if a receiver's buffer is full but it anticipates that it can release space for two TPDUs within a round-trip propagation time, it could immediately send a credit of 2. If the receiver can keep up with the sender, then this scheme may increase throughput and do no harm. If the sender is faster than the receiver, however, some TPDUs may be discarded, necessitating a retransmission.

The credit allocation flow control mechanism is quite robust in the face of an unreliable network service. If an ACK/CDT TPDU is lost, little harm is done. Future acknowledgments will resynchronize the protocol. Further, if no new acknowledgments are forthcoming, the sender times out and retransmits a data TPDU, which triggers a new acknowledgment. However, it is still possible for deadlock to occur. Consider a situation in which B sends (ACK N, CDT M), temporarily closing the window. Subsequently, B sends (ACK N, CDT M), but this TPDU is lost. A is awaiting the opportunity to send data and B thinks that it has granted that opportunity. To overcome this problem, a window timer can be used. This timer is reset with each outgoing ACK/CDT TPDU. If the timer ever expires, the protocol entity is required to send an ACK/CDT TPDU, even if it duplicates a previous one. This breaks the deadlock and also assures the other end that the protocol entity is still alive.

An alternative is to provide acknowledgments to the ACK/CDT TPDU. With this mechanism in place, the window timer can have a quite large value without causing much difficulty.

ISO transport protocol standard

The International Organization for Standardization (ISO) has developed a family of transport protocol standards tailored to various levels of service and communications facilities. (For further reference on the ISO transport protocols, as well as on the similar Department of Defense transmission control protocol discussed below, see "ISO and DOD TPDU fields.") The ISO has defined three network types:
■ Type A: Network connection with acceptable residual error rate and acceptable rate of signaled failures.
■ Type B: Network connection with acceptable residual error rate but unacceptable rate of signaled failures.
■ Type C: Network connection with residual error rate not acceptable to the transport service user.

In this context, an error is defined as a lost or duplicated network protocol data unit. If the error is caught and corrected by the network service in a fashion that is transparent to the transport entity, then no damage is done. If the network service detects an error, cannot recover, and signals the transport entities, this is known as a signaled failure. An example would be the notification by X.25 that a reset has occurred. Finally, there are residual errors, that is, those which are not corrected and of which the transport entity is not notified.

In order to handle a variety of user service requirements and available network services, ISO has defined five classes of transport protocol:
■ Class 0: Simple
■ Class 1: Basic error recovery
■ Class 2: Multiplexing
■ Class 3: Error recovery and multiplexing
■ Class 4: Error detection and recovery

These classes are related to the three types of network service defined earlier, as follows: Classes 0 and 2 are used with Type A networks; Classes 1 and 3 are used with Type B networks; and Class 4 is used with Type C networks.

Class 0 was developed by CCITT (International Telephone and Telegraph Consultative Committee) and is oriented to Teletex, a text-transmission upgrade to Telex. It provides the simplest kind of transport con-

5. Fixed. Shown below are the fixed-header formats for the International Organization for Standardization transport protocol. Fixed headers are required in a TPDU. The fixed header contains the frequently occurring parameters. CC and CR use parameters from a variable header field in the connection establishment process.

CR:	LI	CR	CDT	—	SOURCE REFERENCE	OPTIONS	CLASS

CC:	LI	CC	CDT	DST REFERENCE	SOURCE REFERENCE	OPTIONS	CLASS

DR:	LI	DR	—	DST REFERENCE	SOURCE REFERENCE	REASON

DC:	LI	DC	—	DST REFERENCE	SOURCE REFERENCE

ER:	LI	ER	—	DST REFERENCE	CAUSE

DT:	LI	DT	—	DST REFERENCE	EOT	TPDU-NR

ED:	LI	ED	—	DST REFERENCE	EDTPDU-NR

AK:	LI	AK	CDT	DST REFERENCE	TPDU-NR

EA:	LI	EA	—	DST REFERENCE	EDTPDU-NR

RJ:	LI	RJ	CDT	DST REFERENCE	TPDU-NR

TPDU	TRANSPORT PROTOCOL DATA UNIT		EOT	END OF TRANSMISSION
EDTPDU	EXPEDITED DATA TRANSPORT PROTOCOL DATA UNIT		NR	NUMBER
CDT	CREDIT		EA	EXPEDITED ACKNOWLEDGMENT
CR	CONNECTION REQUEST		AK	ACKNOWLEDGMENT
CC	CONNECTION CONFIRM		ER	ERROR
DR	DISCONNECT REQUEST		RJ	REJECT
DC	DISCONNECT CONFIRM		LI	LENGTH INDICATOR
DST	DESTINATION		DT	DATA

nection. It is assumed that a Type A, connection-oriented network service is available. Transport connections are mapped one-to-one onto network connections (for example, an X.25 virtual circuit). No explicit ordering, or error control, is provided.

Class 1 was also developed by CCITT and is designed to run on an X.25 network and provide minimal error recovery. Its key difference from Class 0 is that TPDUs are numbered. This allows the protocol to resynchronize after an X.25 reset. When the network resets its virtual circuit, some TPDUs may be lost. Each transport entity informs the other of the number of the TPDU that it received last. In this way, the lost TPDUs may be retransmitted. Expedited data transfer is also provided.

Class 2 is an enhancement of Class 0 that still assumes a highly reliable network service. The key enhancement is the ability to multiplex multiple transport connections onto a single network connection. A corollary enhancement is the provision of explicit flow control, since a single network connection flow control mechanism does not allow individual flow control of

6. TCP header. *The transmission control protocol, whose header format is shown here, functions similarly to the International Organization for Standardization (ISO) Class 4 protocol. TCP uses only a single type of TPDU. One header performs all protocol mechanisms, and the TCP header is longer than ISO's.*

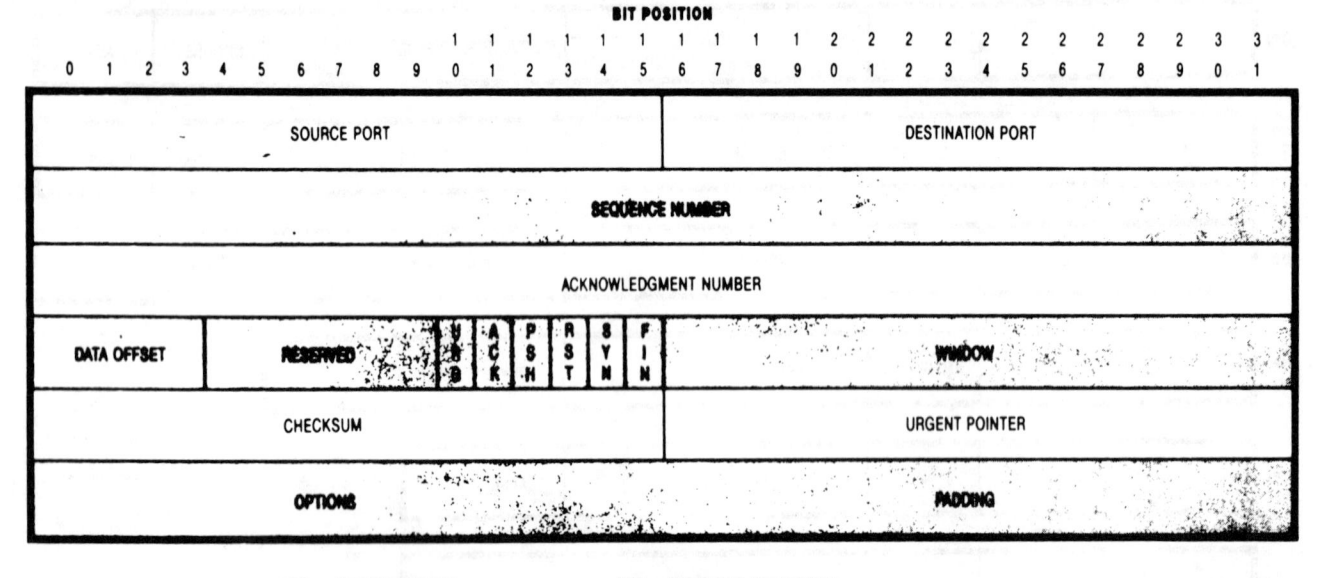

Bit position 0–15	Bit position 16–31
SOURCE PORT	DESTINATION PORT
SEQUENCE NUMBER	
ACKNOWLEDGMENT NUMBER	
DATA OFFSET / RESERVED / URG ACK PSH RST SYN FIN	WINDOW
CHECKSUM	URGENT POINTER
OPTIONS	PADDING

URG = URGENT POINTER
ACK = ACKNOWLEDGMENT
PSH = PUSH FUNCTION
RST = RESET THE CONNECTION
SYN = SYNCHRONIZE THE SEQUENCE NUMBERS
FIN = NO MORE DATA FROM SENDER

transport connections. A credit allocation scheme can be used.

Class 3 is basically the union of the Class 1 and 2 capabilities. It provides the multiplexing and flow control capabilities of Class 2. It also contains the resynchronization and reassignment capabilities needed to cope with failure-prone networks.

Class 4 assumes that the underlying network service is unreliable. Thus, most, if not all, of the mechanisms described in this article must be included.

The protocol makes use of 10 types of TPDUs:
- Connection request (CR)
- Connection confirm (CC)
- Disconnect request (DR)
- Disconnect confirm (DC)
- TPDU error (ER)
- Data (DT)
- Expedited data (ED)
- Acknowledgment (ACK)
- Expedited acknowledgment (EA)
- Reject (RJ)

Each TPDU consists of three parts: a fixed header, a variable header, and a data field. The latter two need not be present in a TPDU. The fixed header contains the frequently occurring parameters, as shown in Figure 5, and the variable header contains optional or infrequently occurring parameters. Each parameter field in the variable header consists of three subfields: a parameter code (8 bits), a parameter length (8 bits), and the parameter value (one or more octets). Most of the parameters are used by CC and CR in the connection establishment process.

The ISO transport protocols have only recently been approved as international standards. There are, consequently, comparatively few vendor-supported implementations. In contrast, the transport standard (MIL-STD-1778) from the Department of Defense (DOD), known as TCP, is well-established and implemented on a variety of machines.

TCP functions comparably to the ISO Class 4 protocol. It has, however, considerably more overhead bits. TCP uses only a single type of TPDU. The header is shown in Figure 6. Because one header must serve to perform all protocol mechanisms, it is rather large. Whereas the ISO fixed header is from five to seven octets long, the TCP header is a minimum of 20 octets.

Summary

ISO has been working away at its own protocol standard, which is now an international standard. It appears that the ISO standard will get early and widespread acceptance by computer vendors. As evidence of this, a number of vendors participated in a multivendor demonstration of the Class 4 protocol at this year's National Computer Conference. In addition, DOD has committed to eventually abandoning TCP in favor of the ISO Class 4.

The long-awaited arrival of standard transport protocols is welcome news for the customer and user. Customers can now begin the migration from proprietary protocols to the ISO standard. The widespread use of that standard is the key to open systems interconnection. ∎

William Stallings is a senior communications consultant at Honeywell Information Systems. This article is based on material in his book "Data and Computer Communications," published by Macmillan Inc.

Architectures, Features, and Implementation of High-Speed Transport Protocols

Thomas F. La Porta
Mischa Schwartz

As computer communications advance further into the era of lightwave networks, more strain is placed on data communication components. One component receiving much recent attention is the transport layer, the fourth layer of the Open Systems Interconnection (OSI) model, of communication protocols. There has been significant debate whether current transport protocols (e.g., Transmission Control Protocol (TCP) or International Standards Organization (ISO) TP4) can adequately handle the burden placed upon them by newly developing and futuristic high-speed networks. Alternatives such as the development of new transport protocols [1–4] or new protocol architectures have been proposed.

Lightwave networks currently being introduced (e.g., Fiber Distributed Data Interface—FDDI) supply much higher bandwidth to users than current networks. Future networks are expected to be able to supply users with gigabit capacity [5], which is several orders of magnitude above what current networks offer. The ability of current transport protocols to support these data rates has been questioned. In addition, lightwave networks will supply much more reliable service, with bit error rates as low as 10^{-9} compared to networks today with bit error rates of 10^{-4}. How transport protocols may take advantage of this improvement has also been examined.

The promise of these new networks has led to the planning and prototyping of true high-bandwidth applications. These applications place additional performance requirements on transport protocols.

This article presents the results of a literature survey of the characteristics of high-speed protocols, new protocol architectures, and implementation techniques for these protocols. We start with a general description of transport protocol services and follow with a small sample of gigabit applications that might utilize a high-speed network. The problems with current transport protocols and protocol architectures are then examined. General concepts for high-speed protocols and protocol architectures are then presented. Finally, specific design techniques suggested for high-speed protocols and the potential impacts of each are discussed.

Transport Protocol Responsibilities

The transport layer is the fourth layer in the ISO OSI 7-layer stack model of communication protocols. The transport layer operates directly above the network layer in the stack architecture and directly below the session layer (see Figure 1). Layers 2 and 3 operate within the communication network, supplying differing levels of flow control, error detection, and error correction, depending on the network. The layer 3 protocol is responsible for routing within the network.

The service provided by networks varies widely. At one extreme, a subnet might supply only datagram service, not guaranteeing delivery of packets, the order of packet arrival, or the prevention of duplicate packets arriving at an endpoint. At the other extreme, a network might supply reliable Virtual Circuit (VC) service, providing guaranteed, in-order, delivery of packets. Transport protocols should be able to operate in either environment.

The transport protocol is the first layer in the stack that operates on an end-to-end basis between the two communicating hosts. Usually implemented in software, typical transport protocols reside within a host, although they may also reside in a front-end processor.

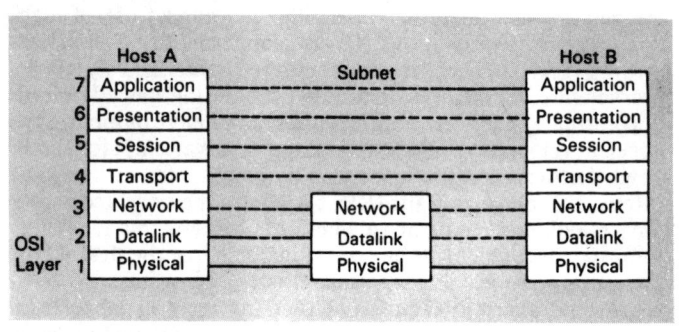

Fig. 1. ISO OSI 7 layer model.

The first responsibility of the transport layer is to manage the end-to-end connection between hosts. The transport layer must establish a connection between hosts and provide a method of ending connections.

The transport layer has several critical functions related to data transfer, all for providing reliable data delivery to the user (session layer). This includes detecting and correcting errored packets, usually through retransmission, delivering packets in order to higher layers, and providing a flow control mechanism for the system. Depending on the type of subnet being used by the transport service, the execution of these functions may or may not be trivial. For instance, operating over a datagram subnet with widely varying interpacket delays presents a challenge for expeditiously delivering ordered data to the user. Decisions must be made whether a packet is lost and must be retransmitted or if it has been delayed in the network.

Two popular transport protocols are TCP [6] and ISO TP4. A more complete description of the transport protocol responsibilities can be found in [7] [8].

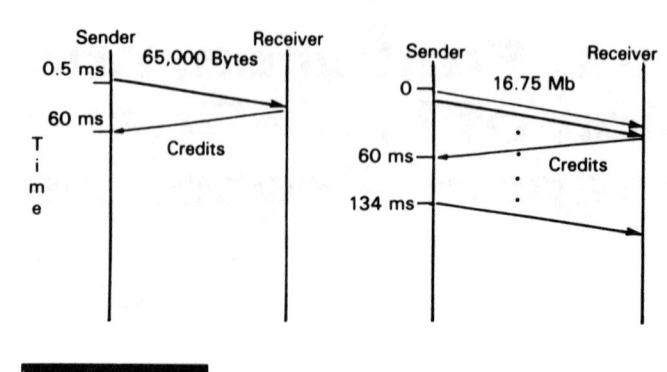

Fig. 2. Flow control example.

Gigabit Applications

Before debating the design of high-speed transport protocols, the need for gigabit per second service for an end user must be justified. This can be done by examining current potential gigabit applications. Several examples follow. These subsections are not meant to give a detailed description of the requirements of these applications, but a flavor of what is desired and may be accomplished with higher capacity delivered to the end user.

Distributed Processing

Distributed processing environments are becoming more popular as can be evidenced by the widespread use of high-performance workstations and interconnected Local Area Networks (LANs). They are commonly characterized by client-server interactions. As distributed processing has advanced, operating systems created for this type of environment have been developed [9]. These operating systems attempt to deliver high performance (low latency) to the end user for such tasks as Remote Procedure Calls (RPCs), remote memory access, remote look-ups, or database queries. The performance of the transport protocol will be critical in supplying the desired (or required) performance to the end-user application.

As the distributed processing environment expands from the LAN to the Metropolitan Area Network (MAN) or Wide Area Network (WAN) arenas, the performance of the transport protocol becomes even more critical.

The critical performance criterion for distributed processing applications is low delay. This suggests that time-consuming call setup procedures cannot be tolerated and perhaps datagram service best suits these needs. In addition, often a multicast or broadcast capability is needed, for example, to locate a resource on a network.

Full Motion Video

Full motion video, for use in video conferencing, may be possible with gigabit per second networks. Such an application will require extremely high bandwidth and put strict requirements on the magnitude and variance of network delay introduced before data is delivered to the end-application [10]. For this type of application, the required bandwidth must be available continuously over a long period of time, suggesting VC-type service. Also, data delayed over a certain period of time might be useless. Therefore, not retransmitting errored or lost packets might be a viable technique used to simplify the protocol processing.

Video-On-Demand

A similar video application using gigabit per second networks, is video on demand. For example, movies could be stored digitally at a central site, and broadcast to subscribers on an on-demand basis. Requirements for this application are similar to those for full motion video.

Computer Imaging

There are several desired and prototyped computer imaging applications that can only be implemented on gigabit per second networks. Examples are medical, seismic, and weather related systems [11]. For all of these examples, the data needed for a central computer to form full-motion images might be stored in several different networked computers [12]. The data would have to be acquired in real-time by the central computer (perhaps super-computer) and processed into an image that is transmitted to the end-device. The first part of the process, acquiring the data, is an example of a high-speed distributed system. The second part of the process, transmitting the image, requires high bandwidth. This application demands reliable, low-latency transport for gathering data, and high throughput for transmitting the image.

As is evidenced, the above applications all require high-speed (gigabit per second) networks, with varying emphasis on different aspects of performance. The desired latency, throughput, and error correction capabilities all vary. This points out the need for a flexible transport protocol, capable of transmitting and receiving data at very high speeds.

Problems with Old Transport Protocols/Implementations

The implementations of current transport protocols lead to performance limitations. Most implementations are tied heavily into host operating systems. The heavy usage of timers, interrupts, and memory read/writes, tax the main Central Processing Unit (CPU) and degrade the performance of the protocol. Functions such as buffer management, bus transfer time, and bus contention alone cause severe processing overhead for current protocol implementations [1] [13] [14]. Some of these problems may be solved with better implementations of existing protocols [14]. However, because of the design of current protocols, there are some limitations to the implementation improvements. The key design goal is to separate the protocol processing from the operating system as much as possible, and move implementations into Very Large-Scale Integration (VLSI) or several special purpose processors [13] [15].

Current transport protocols (e.g., TCP or OSI TP4) were designed with different restraints and requirements than are imposed by futuristic high-speed networks. Transmission speeds were typically on the order of 10 Mb/s for LANs, and 10–50 kb/s for WANs. Therefore, frame insertion time onto a communication link was often a primary source of delay, and hence, performance degradation. Meanwhile, available computing power was able to process and decode complex frame formats faster than the network could supply new data.

As network rates reach the 100 Mb/s–Gb/s range, it will be more difficult for processors to process packets in real-time, that is as fast as they arrive at the network interface. For example, a 1,024 byte frame arriving at a 56 kb/s interface will take 146 ms to be received from the network. This allows a processor 146 ms to process the previously received packet. The same frame arriving at a 1 Gb/s interface must be processed in approximately 8 μs. Failure to process packets in real-time will cause buffers at the receiver to fill and eventually lead to lost packets due to receiver overflow.

A characteristic of older transport protocols is that they were designed to minimize the number of bits transmitted to reduce insertion time, with the knowledge that incoming data could be processed at a high enough rate. This led to packet formats with bit-packed architectures, requiring extensive decoding. Packet fields often have variable sizes to reduce the number of unnecessary bits transmitted, and may change location within different packet types. These designs, while conserving bits, lead to slow packet processing when compared to the requirements of high-speed interfaces.

Due to the frame format, implementation restrictions arise for current protocols. Variable length fields, placement of checksums, etc., make it difficult to parallelize the processing of a single packet (i.e., process several fields simultaneously). It will also be difficult to implement these protocols in VLSI and remove their processing from the operating system of the host. It has been shown, however, that great performance gains can be achieved by processing many packets in parallel [16].

Another problem with the current protocols is packet field limitations. For example, the number of bits provided for windowing mechanisms must be increased to supply window sizes large enough to be effective at high-data rates. A cross continental link between New York and California might have a propagation delay of 30 ms. TCP [17] supplies 16 b for byte-based credit to transmit data. Therefore, TCP can have 65,000 unacknowledged bytes outstanding. At 1 Gb/s this amounts to 0.5 ms of transmission (see Figure 2). After sending this data, the transmitter must sit idle for approximately 60 ms waiting to get additional credits to transmit data from the receiver. Obviously, this yields unacceptable throughput performance. If the credit field were enlarged to 24 b, the transmitter could send for 134 ms, or about 134 Mb of data before exhausting its credit. This would be sufficient time to receive additional credit from the receiver.

The control algorithms supplied by current transport protocols will be strained by high-speed networks. For example, current protocols like TCP and ISO TP4 effectively use Go-back-N windowing schemes for error recovery. A message sent to request a retransmission of a lost packet will not cross the continent for 30 ms. During this time 3,750 1,000 byte frames may have been transmitted at 1 Gb/s that, when using a Go-back-N protocol, must be retransmitted (see Figure 3). This type of algorithm will severely degrade throughput and add unnecessary network congestion.

Finally, existing protocols may not be flexible enough for high-speed applications and networks. For example, TCP does not supply a mechanism for fast call setup or multicast transmission, two features attractive in distributed processing environments. For a protocol to be successful in a high-speed environment, it must be flexible enough to supply several grades of service to the user over varying network topologies [13].

General Concepts for High-Speed Protocols

The following present general concepts characterizing high-speed transport protocols.

Design Philosophies

The key change in the design philosophy of new high-speed protocols is to make the design "success oriented" [13] [15]. Current protocols were designed to be robust in the face of adverse network conditions. This added to their complexity and may prevent them from achieving gigabit rates. New protocols should be designed with the emphasis on streamlining the normal data transmission processing for maximum throughput. This is justified because future high-speed networks will offer extremely low-error rates.

The protocol designs often attempt to simplify receiver processing [18]. The simpler the receiver, the faster incoming packets can be processed, thus lowering the probability of the receiver dropping packets due to overflow. There are several mechanisms for simplifying the receiver, some of which add complexity to the transmitter. One example is to make the receiver a slave of the transmitter [18] [19]. In essence, the receiver issues no commands to the transmitter, other than to facilitate error recovery. Other design mechanisms simplifying the protocol receiver will be noted as presented in *High-Speed Transport Protocol Techniques*.

High-speed protocols should also be designed with expanded functionality to provide needed flexibility [13]. Increased flexibility within a single protocol will allow the protocol to be moved inside the network implementing active nodes and gateways within the network. This allows the network to supply several types of service to its users.

Architecture Philosophies

Much has been written about modifying the architecture of the current view of protocol stack implementation. The suggestions range from combining layers to implementing parallel layers.

For example, a suggested software implementation of Xpress Transfer Protocol (XTP) combines layers 3 and 4 into a single software data structure [3]. This reduces the amount of protocol processing overhead incurred, and simplifies the design. It also allows both layers to be part of network routers and gateways. This new "active" gateway can participate in error recovery and flow control at higher layers [15].

A proposal for a parallel protocol architecture is the Horizontal Oriented Protocol Structure (HOPS) [13]. HOPS proposes three layers. The Network Access Control layer operates below layer 3 of the ISO stack. The Communication Interface (CI) layer implements several parallel functions performing transport through presentation functions. The application layer is pure software. The parallel functions of the CI layer, including address lookup, sequence number verification, etc., map directly into parallel realization. The CI layer should be implemented to reduce its ties to the host operating system.

Both of these examples reduce protocol processing overhead, and reduce duplication of functionality at separate layers.

Implementation Philosophy

This section applies to both new protocols and future implementations of current protocols. Several articles point out that protocol processing accounts for less than 20% of all processing time in communication [14] [15]. The rest is expended managing timers, reading and writing data, and handling interrupts. One report states the TCP and ISO TP4 require 5–10 times the amount of processing as a new high-speed protocol, XTP [20]. A key goal is to implement protocols as separate from the host operating system as possible. This requires special network adapter boards with dedicated processors for communication and memory for storing data [21].

Some protocols have been designed with the ultimate goal of being implemented in VLSI, such as XTP, or with several special purpose processors working in parallel [1] [15].

High-Speed Transport Protocol Techniques

The following present common techniques used by transport protocols to fulfill transport responsibilities.

Connection Management

For short lived connections, typical of distributed processing applications, a fast connection setup is a necessity for achieving low latency. Therefore, the option of implicit connection setup is a desirable feature. This method is used in some new transport protocols like Versatile Message Transac-

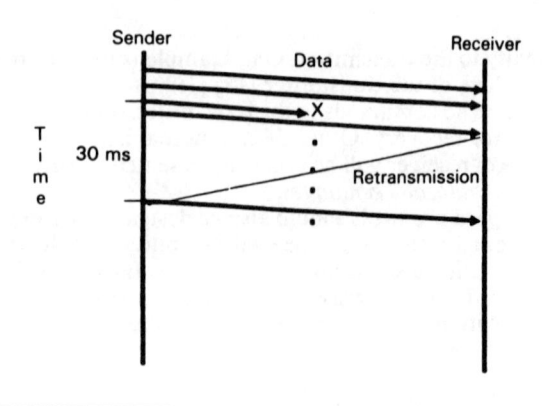

Fig. 3. Error correction example.

tion Protocol (VMTP) and XTP. This allows data to be transmitted to the user in a connection setup packet. Other data packets can immediately follow the first packet. This is useful in distributed processing applications, database queries, and requests for file downloads. The response to any of these requests would also contain data and simultaneously acknowledge the connection setup. Request-response transactions typical in client-server distributed environments contain short request packets and long response packets [22]. Provisions can be made, as in VMTP, to allow a short amount of user data to be contained in the header of a packet. This space is used for short requests and has been shown to supply excellent low-latency performance [22]. Implicit call setup does not only sharply decrease latency for short transactions, but increase throughput for even relatively large file transfers.

For example, a connection between New York and California may experience up to 30 ms of one-way propagation delay. If a 3-way handshake is used to establish a connection, the minimum amount of time for a short message to be delivered to the originator of the request is 2 round-trip times, or 120 ms. With implicit call setup, the minimum time is 60 ms. Consider the download of a single 1 Mbyte file over a single transport connection. The transmission time for this file at 1 Gb/s is approximately 8 ms. If a 3-way handshake is required to start the file transfer, the total transaction time is approximately 130 ms, reducing the effective throughput to 60 Mb/s. If implicit call setup is used, the transaction time is approximately halved, and effective throughput is approximately doubled (see Figure 4).

As the amount of data to be transferred grows larger, the difference between the two call setup methods becomes negligible. The options of a 2- or 3-way handshake upon connection establishment should also be available. These methods provide an easy mechanism for negotiating parameters used during the connection and may be required if the subnet, or portion of the subnet, does not provide reliable service. With implicit call setup, parameters must be negotiated during data transfer.

Transport protocols should support both VC and datagram communication. The first case is desirable for long-lived connections requiring dedicated bandwidth and relatively low-variance delay. The latter is desirable for short, bursty types of traffic, typical in distributed processing systems, or systems that acquire information updates frequently. In this case, delivery may not have to be as reliable, as new updated information will arrive shortly, even if the last sample is lost. Datagram service can be reliably implemented using implicit connection setup and treating datagram messages as short-lived VCs [2] [3].

Transport protocols should also support a provision for multicast transmission [23]. This is desirable for locating network resources or updating network configurations.

Connection tear down may also be done upon timeout (implicitly) or via a handshake mechanism (explicitly). The benefit of implicit tear down is the reduction in packet processing overhead. The disadvantage is the increased complexity of timers needed to release connections and ensure connection identifiers are not reused while still active [23].

The recommendation is for a protocol to allow the option of implicit or explicit connection establishment procedures to supply flexibility. Protocols should also support VC, datagram, and multicast operation. In order to reduce the timer management complexity, a known major contributor to processing overhead, explicit connection tear down should be implemented.

Data Transfer

Perhaps the most critical requirement of a high-speed protocol is its ability to sustain transmission and reception of data at the maximum allowable bandwidth. To do this, packets must be continuously transmitted. This requires that the transmission "window" always be open so that the transmitter does not have to sit idle, unnecessarily waiting for additional credits to send data. Therefore, end-to-end flow control techniques have a major impact on the effective throughput achievable by a transport protocol.

At the receiver, packets must be processed in real-time as they are received. This prevents receiver buffers from overflowing and dropping packets, thus lowering throughput. For example, for transmission at 1 Gb/s, 1,024 byte packets must be processed within approximately 8 μs. Items such as packet formats and error recovery techniques affect receiver performance.

Implementation of the "buffer layer" responsibilities also has a major impact on data performance. The "buffer layer" or "glue layer" can be viewed as the portion of the transport layer responsible for placing correctly received data in the appropriate format and location. This can include transport mechanisms for reordering out-of-sequence packets, and copying data to user memory.

Packet Organization

The structure of the packets of high-speed protocols is critical in simplifying the transport receiver. Typical high-speed protocols are designed to facilitate parallel decoding [15] [21]. To achieve this parallel processing capability, packet formats should be carefully designed. Some basic principles follow.

All fields within a packet should be in fixed places and of fixed length. The boundaries of the fields should fall on byte or word boundaries, even if this requires padding fields with null data. The additional insertion time for the "pad" data is negli-

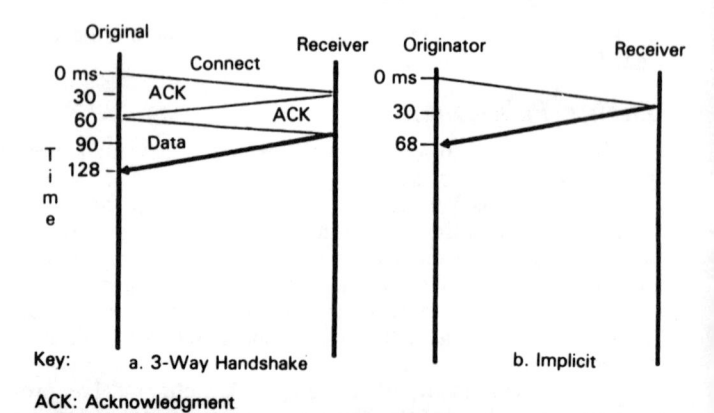

Key:
ACK: Acknowledgment

Fig. 4. Comparing 3-way handshake and implicit call setup.

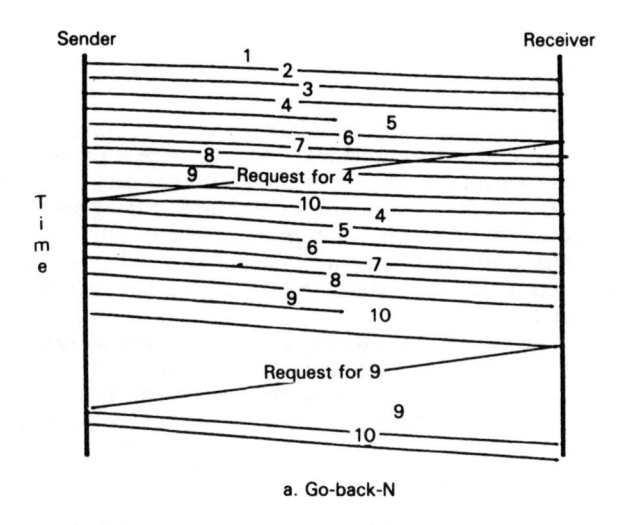

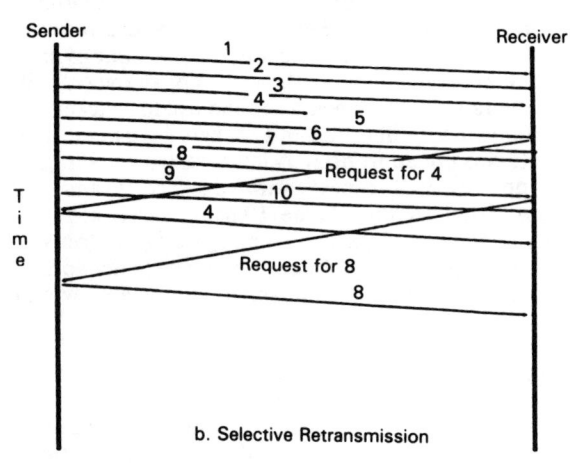

Fig. 5. Differences between go-back-N and selective retransmission.

gible, and major processing gains are made by following this guideline. This facilitates simpler and faster software implementations, and allows for development of hardware implementations. In addition, by placing header information fields in the proper order, parallel processing can be used [24]. For example, placing the addresses and transaction IDs first in a packet allows them to be processed first. They are used to locate the connection record containing the connection state information. As the sequence number is being received, it can be checked against the record for correctness. While this processing is ongoing, data being received is stored in a temporary register. Therefore, the data reception time is not wasted, but rather used for processing.

Because the addresses, sequence numbers, and transaction IDs are all checked in parallel, the amount of time needed to process a packet is approximately equal to the time taken to complete the longest task, not the sum of all the tasks [13]. It should be noted that the processing speed up, due to parallel processing of fields, is limited to the number of fields in a packet. Another method being researched at Columbia University considers processing several packets in parallel [16].

The trailer of each packet should contain two checksums—one for header integrity, and one for data integrity. By placing the checksums in the trailer, and choosing the correct algorithm, checksums can be computed as the bits of a packet are received. When the trailer arrives, the computed value is compared to the value being received; if they match, the data is valid and can be forwarded. Conversely, placing the checksum in the packet header requires waiting for an entire packet to be received before calculating the checksum.

The two checksums are used for multimedia applications. Different applications require different action to take place on the receipt of errored data. For example, in video and voice applications, retransmissions cannot be used due to delay constraints. Therefore, the first checksum is used to identify the connection and application, and the second is used as the application demands for data integrity.

The use of these guidelines facilitates transport protocol implementations in VLSI, using multiple special purpose processors, and utilizing parallel processing techniques.

Flow Control/Error Recovery

An important concept in the design of high-speed protocols is to separate flow control from error control as much as possible [1] [10]. The two functions are often lumped together using sequence number and windowing techniques. This is not effective because flow control and error recovery often have different goals in different types of networks. For example, when using a high-speed link with an appreciable propagation delay (30 ms), the flow control mechanism would prefer a large window to keep the pipeline full and maximize throughput. However, a large window size could severely slow down error recovery. If an entire large window must be retransmitted due to an errored packet, throughput of the system would degrade greatly.

- Flow Control—The transport layer is responsible for end-to-end flow control between two devices. The decision to invoke flow control is not made by the transport layer, but the mechanism through which flow control is asserted is supplied by the transport layer. A control mechanism for flow control will be based on buffer availability and information from the network. Certain applications, such as full-motion video require a fixed bandwidth and cannot be flow controlled. The area of flow control, and other control mechanisms such as access control, are major research areas. Here we present methods for implementing flow control.

The most efficient transmission, requiring the least amount of overhead, occurs when data is transmitted in large bursts [25]. The opposite occurs when windows are incorrectly used causing short bursts of data to be sent, separated by pauses, while the sender waits for permission to transmit again. An example of how this occurs using a credit-based flow control scheme follows. A sender has credit to transmit 10,000 bytes of data. The sender transmits 10,000 bytes of data and exhausts the allotted credit. At this time, the credit has not been increased by the receiver, so the transmitter sits idle. The receiver then gives the transmitter permission to transmit 100 bytes of data. The sender, having data queued for transmission, sends a single packet containing only 100 bytes of data and then awaits more credit. If this situation persists, referred to as lock-step transmission, a large amount of overhead is incurred while sending the file [26].

Algorithms should be designed to prevent lock-step from occurring. This can be done several ways. One method is to implement a credit scheme with a minimum credit size. If a credit of this minimum value cannot be allocated, no credit is given. A second method is to only allow transmission of defined block sizes. Therefore, if permission to transmit is granted by the receiver, this implies an entire block can be sent [25]. In this case, explicit crediting is not needed as it is implicit.

Usually the credit value, or permission to transmit a block, is determined by the receiver buffers available. It is desirable to allow a transmitter to send a maximum amount of data to fill the receiver buffers allocated to this sender. For example, if a user has 10 Mb of memory allotted to ten connections, it would allot 1 Mb to each connection. If the buffer for a certain connection was empty, the transmitter of that connection would have permission to send 1 Mb of data. This is done in XTP [3] (referred to as reservation mode) and other high-speed protocols. We will refer to this as a "maximized credit scheme." If the sender has more than this amount of data to send, it will send this amount in one blast, and wait for permission to send the remaining data.

To prevent the receiver from overflowing due to data arriving simultaneously from several connections, rate control is used [2–4]. Rate control can be implemented in two ways. A transmitter can be assigned a burst size and interval, or it can be assigned interpacket delay time. In the first case, the transmitter will send packets at its maximum rate until it has sent its allotted burst size. It will then wait the specified wait time determined by the burst interval before transmitting the next burst. The receiver can accommodate the maximum input data rate. Based on the number of active connections and available buffers, the receiver will assign burst size and intervals.

In the second case, the transmitter will send data as long as it has credit available and data to send, but will pause between each packet the time specified by the interpacket delay [27]. This allows for an even distribution of packet arrivals at the receiver. The receiver can accommodate a maximum rate, that must be shared among connections. The sharing algorithm determines the interpacket delay for each connection.

It is more difficult to implement interpacket delay algorithms because of the timers needed. However, the spreading of packet transmissions will help avoid packet overflow within the network and at the receiver. It has been shown that interpacket delay rate control greatly improves performance [22]. Implementing the burst time/burst duration algorithm is easier, but increases the probability of bursts of packets from several connections arriving at the receiver simultaneously. Often, both techniques are combined.

Implementing flow control by combining rate control with a maximized credit scheme achieves higher performance than using sliding window or standard credit mechanisms. In high-speed networks, windows may not be reactive enough to be effective flow control mechanisms. For example, for a New York to California link with a one-way propagation delay of 30 ms, closing a window or reducing credit takes 30 ms. In this time 3,750 packets of 1,000 bytes could have been transmitted. Using rate control will minimize the possibility of a receiver overflowing, and using a maximized credit scheme will eliminate the probability of a receiver exhausting buffer space with more data outstanding. This reduces the need to dynamically change flow control conditions.

End-to-end flow control settings need only be changed upon the establishment of additional connections. At this time the receiver reallocates the rate, and sends notification to the new connection and existing connections. This information should arrive at each destination at about the same time, which supplies adequate reactiveness.

The recommendation is to supply rate control and a maximized credit scheme. This will provide for more efficient use of processing and bandwidth, and will yield better performance than typical sliding window protocols.

- **Error Recovery**—Error recovery is typically accomplished by retransmitting undelivered or errored data. The retransmission can include an entire window of data, typical of Go-back-N window-type algorithms, or can include only the lost or errored data, called selective retransmission. The retransmission can be triggered by transmitter timeouts while waiting for acknowledgments, or receiver initiated negative acknowledgments. Depending on the implementation, the negative acknowledgments can be transmitted by the receipt of out-of-order packets or receiver timeouts.

Go-back-N vs. Selective Retransmission—Go-back-N algorithms are easy to implement, because once a packet is received in error or out-of-sequence, all other packets are discarded. This greatly simplifies the record keeping and buffer management for each connection. Selective retransmission schemes must continue to store data after out-of-order packets are received. This complicates the buffer management schemes.

Lightwave networks of the future should supply extremely low-error rate transmission, on the order of 10^{-9}. Therefore, most packet loss will be due to network overruns and receiver overruns [26]. While implementing a Go-back-N algorithm is fairly simple due to ease of managing buffers and storing connection state information, it does not solve the problem of receiver overruns.

For instance, consider a transmitter using a Go-back-N algorithm sending 10 packets to a host before receiving a response. The receiver loses the fourth packet due to an overrun. If the receiver realizes it is the victim of an overrun, it can reduce the rate of the transmitter, and ask for packet number 4. The transmitter will retransmit packets 4–10 at the new rate. If the rate was not appropriately lowered, packet 9 might be lost. The process will repeat with packets 9 and 10 being retransmitted. In this scheme, 19 packets were sent to successfully transmit all 10 packets (see Figure 5). Not only does this present a drop in throughput, but increases network load due to extra retransmissions that will aggravate a network congestion problem.

Using a selective retransmission approach, with the above example, the receiver would have lost every fourth packet, or packets 4 and 8. Therefore, the transmitter would have resent only packets 4 and 8 with a much lower likelihood of additional overrun since less packets had to be retransmitted. Therefore, the sequence would only require 12 packet transmissions, for a 30% increase in efficiency. Although more difficult to implement, the reduction in packets transmitted using selective retransmission can offer higher retained throughput under errored or congested conditions, and assist in alleviating network congestion. One study has shown that selective retransmission can provide approximately twice the bandwidth of Go-back-N algorithms under errored conditions [27]. Results also show that selective retransmission combined with rate control provides a high-performance method of communication between two devices of disparate capacity [22].

"Block acknowledgments" [28] can be used to help track out-of-order packets and missing packets. This entails including a number for the first and last packet being acknowledged in an acknowledgment packet. If a series of block acknowledgments are included in acknowledgment packets [3], as in XTP, sufficient, convenient tracking of missing packets can be done. For example, if packets 1, 2, and 3 arrive, 4 and 5 are missing, 6, 7, 8, and 9 arrive, 10 is missing, and 11 arrives, the acknowledgment would show 1,3;6,9;11,11. The transmitter may then react by transmitting the missing packets, or waiting for another acknowledgment to see if the packets were still in transit.

Error Notification—In order to simplify error recovery mechanisms, and reduce the number of unnecessary retransmissions, a receiver may not ask for a retransmission of a missing packet. Instead, the receiver might only acknowledge correct packets. The transmitter will timeout waiting for acknowledgments for the missing packets and retransmit them. Likewise, the receiver can wait for a specified time for each packet to arrive, and if it has not arrived within this time, it will send a request for retransmission of this packet.

Both of these schemes have potential shortcomings. Difficulty in setting timer values is well documented [25] [29]. If set too high, error recovery takes too long and performance suf-

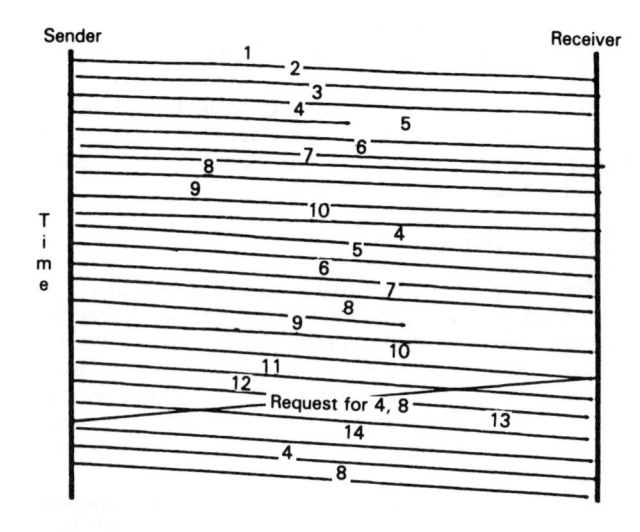

Fig. 6. Selective retransmission packet blocking.

fers. If set too low, spurious retransmissions can occur. Two improved techniques for error recovery, packet blocking, and periodic exchange of state information, have been proposed.

Packet Blocking—Packet "blocking" consists of grouping packets together in blocks or buffers [1] [3] [4]. A timer is set for the transmission or reception of an entire block. Due to statistical averaging properties, the variances of the single packet delays should approximately cancel each other out if there are enough packets in a block [29]. Therefore, it is easier to pick appropriate timer values. If the timer is at the transmitter, the transmitter sets the timer to wait for the acknowledgment of the block. If it does not receive this acknowledgment, it can either retransmit the entire block, or inquire as to the missing packets within the block and perform selective retransmission.

A possibly better scheme proposed at Massachusetts Institute of Technology (MIT) is to place the timer at the receiver [4] [29]. The receiver has knowledge of the size of each block in packets, and can be supplied a value for average packet delay, so that a timer value for the block can be set. When this timer expires, if the entire block has not yet been received, the receiver sends a request for retransmission for the missing packets.

When using a blocking technique, credits and windows can be calculated on either packets, blocks, or both. If done on blocks, selective retransmission can be done on a block basis, with missing blocks retransmitted in their entirety. This assists in simplifying receiver design by removing the need for action by the receiver upon the reception of an errored packet. Only one timer is needed, and must only be adjusted after each block time, not for each packet. This reduces the timer management processing.

In the case of bulk data transfer, relying solely on timers for the reception of a block of data is adequate, and simplifies the receiver and transmitter logic so that higher throughput may be achieved. However, for interactive applications where small amounts of data are transmitted, and latency is the key performance parameter, timer-based error control may be too slow. In this case, receivers should be allowed to generate requests for retransmission when errored and missing packets are detected.

Figure 6 shows the packet exchange of the previous selective retransmission example with packet blocking used. In this example, the block size is 10 packets and the transmitter has more than 10 packets to send. By using packet blocking and selective retransmission, high throughput is maintained, even under errored conditions.

Periodic State Exchange—An alternative error detection/correction method is to transmit complete state information frequently and periodically between the sender and receiver, regardless of the state of the protocol [1]. This eliminates almost all error recovery procedures, and reduces the error recovery timers that must be maintained. The receiver machine can then be almost wholly dedicated to processing incoming packets. A separate receiver machine can process state information and insert control packets into the output queue. This simplifies the transmitter and receiver design for data transmission by removing error recovery and state information responsibilities to a separate protocol machine.

The receiver control packets include information regarding flow control, buffer allocation, and what blocks have been received. The transmitter control packets include information regarding the last block transmitted and the last block acknowledged. If a control packet is lost, no additional steps need be taken, because within another period the complete state information will be exchanged again, containing any information lost in the previous control packets.

Bit maps in the control packets indicate what complete blocks were received successfully. After the transmission of a certain number of control packets following the final packet of a block, if the block has not yet been acknowledged it is retransmitted in its entirety. Therefore, this scheme uses selective retransmission on a per block basis, requiring blocks to be retransmitted in their entirety.

Drawbacks of this scheme include the timer management of sending control packets. However, these timers should be relatively easy to maintain compared to timers driven by error correction. Because selective retransmissions are used, data reordering must be performed at the receiver, and the transmitter must locate and resend lost data. If not implemented carefully, the buffer management overhead may be unacceptable. Advantages are the elimination of error recovery states from the main protocol engine, intensive calculation of control information in each packet, and the seriousness of the loss of a single control packet.

- Flow Control/Error Correction Summary—Transport protocols should separate flow control from error recovery procedures. The transport layer should supply both credit and rate control algorithms to the user. The credit should be allotted on the basis of maximum available buffer space, to maximize the duration of continuous data transmission and to increase efficiency and throughput. Error recovery should be implemented on a "block" basis to simplify and improve the accuracy of timer algorithms. Timers may be placed at the receiver if possible, as evidenced in the MIT NETBLT experiment [4], since the receiver can best judge interpacket delay when calculating timer values and contains the information regarding lost packets. The user should be allowed to generate immediate requests for retransmission in applications where low latency is of importance.

An interesting alternative scheme, as supported by the AT&T Bell Laboratories approach [1], would be to periodically exchange full state information between the transmitter and receiver.

Implementation/Buffer Management

Buffer management processing is critical to the operation and performance of any communication system, so much that the responsibilities are sometimes referred to as the buffer layer [14] or glue layer [15]. The buffer layer has been accused of being the main bottleneck in communication processing. While buffer management is more of an implementation issue than a protocol specification issue, certain protocols facilitate efficient methods for implementing buffer management responsibilities. The impact of buffer management on performance can be seen in a study [14] that states that TCP, if carefully implemented, and making certain assumptions about buffer management, can achieve a throughput of 800 Mb/s.

The major responsibilities of buffer management are writing data to a buffer as it is received, forwarding data to buffers for use by the transport user, and writing data to buffers for transmission. The buffer layer is also responsible for reordering out of sequence packets. One study [14] has shown that 50% of TCP processing time is used for network to memory copying. Bottlenecks result from read and write times, bus transfer time, and bus contention. The time spent by the host servicing interrupts to read data is also a bottleneck. These problems can be minimized with clever network adapter board designs, and advances in memory technology. This has been suggested by the VMTP architects [21]. Protocols that are designed to be implemented in hardware make it easier to design effective network adapter boards.

In addition, if packet blocking is used, the bus data transfer time and number of interrupts to the host will be reduced. For example, the host does not have to be interrupted by the arrival of each packet, but only once for every block of packets received.

State of the art network adapter designs contain on-board memory to supply temporary buffers. This helps reduce bus contention on the host by allowing processing of data to take place outside of the host. One attempt at a network adapter board design for VMTP [21] consists of five components:

- Network Access Controller (NAC)
- Pipeline
- On-board memory
- Host block copier
- On-board processor

The NAC is responsible for receiving data from the network and placing it in the pipeline. In the pipeline the packet is processed. Video-RAM (VRAM), which supplies serial and parallel access to store and retrieve data, is used as the memory component. Both the serial and parallel ports can be used simultaneously. Therefore, the pipeline can be placing data in the serial port of the VRAM, while the on-board processor manipulates the data within the VRAM. This eliminates bus and memory contention while processing the packet. However, analysis has shown that even with this design, 6% of the delay of a packet is due to network delay (assuming a lightly loaded medium size FDDI ring), 12% is due to processing on the Network Adaptor Board (NAB), and 88% is due to host processing [21]. The difficulty in removing protocol processing from host operating system dependencies is evident.

Functionality

A well designed transport protocol must be flexible enough to support various applications, and work over varying types of subnets. The idea of a protocol with a "menu" has been suggested [13]. By implementing a protocol with a menu, the protocol can be flexible enough to work within a subnet. Flexibility is essential to provide users the service required by their applications.

The transport protocol should give the user the option of choosing the grade-of-service needed for the application. This should include error correction/nonerror correction, and flow control/no flow control. The protocol should support both datagram and VC service. In addition, provisions for multicast transmissions should be included.

As high-speed networks are implemented, several older subnets will continue to be used. Therefore provisions for addressing compatibility with the more popular subnet protocol suites like TCP/Internet Program (IP) and ISO should be included.

Because of the varying subnets, different frame sizes on networks will be encountered. Therefore provisions for packet segmentation and reassembly should be included in transport level designs.

Conclusions

The ability to provide high bandwidth to high-speed network users depends heavily on protocol implementation. Implementations should be as separate from the host operating system as possible. Designs of new protocols can make these implementations easier and more efficient. It has been shown that it is be possible to apply some of these implementation techniques to existing protocols to supply high bandwidth to the user.

New protocol designs facilitate parallel processing, and real-time processing of packets at high rates. Some are targeted for implementation in VLSI or using special dedicated processors.

Besides implementation, new architectures for protocols have been explored, many emphasizing the reduction of protocol layers and parallel implementation. In addition these protocols should be flexible enough to support all applications, and provide users with selective functionality.

The following summarizes the best techniques for designing and implementing high-speed protocols:

- Design Philosophies—Success oriented, Simple receiver
- Architecture—Combine layers, Parallel functions
- Implementation—Separate from operating system, Attention to buffer layer
- Call Management—Implicit and explicit connection setup, Explicit connection tear down, Support datagram and VC operation, Support multicast
- Data Transfer—Fixed packet formats, Checksums in trailer, Separate error recovery from flow control, Flow control = Rate control + Maximized credit, Error recovery = blocking packets, Periodic state exchange, Selective retransmissions, Fewer timers
- Buffer Management—Special off-board processing
- Functionality—High flexibility

A follow-up article will examine several newly developed high-speed protocols and TCP in detail, and draw comparisons based on techniques presented in this article.

References

[1] A. N. Netravali, W. D. Roome, and K. Sabnani, "Design and Implementation of a High-Speed Transport Protocol," *IEEE Trans. on Commun.*, Nov. 1990.
[2] D. R. Cheriton, "VMTP: Versatile Message Transaction Protocol," *Protocol Specification RFC 1045*, Stanford University, Feb. 1988.
[3] "XTP Protocol Definition Revision 3.4," *Protocol Engines, Inc*, 1989.
[4] D. D. Clark, M. L. Lambert, and L. Zhang, "NETBLT: A Bulk Data Transfer Protocol," *RFC 998*, MIT, 1987.
[5] A. S. Acampora and M. J. Karol, "An Overview of Lightwave Packet Networks," *IEEE Computer Net.*, Jan. 1989.
[6] D. Comer, *Interconnecting with TCP/IP, Principles, Protocols, and Architecture*, Prentice-Hall, 1988.
[7] M. Schwartz, *Telecommunication Networks-Protocols, Modeling, and Analysis*, Addison-Wesley, 1988.
[8] A. S. Tannenbaum, *Computer Networks*, Prentice-Hall, 1981.
[9] D. R. Cheriton and W. Zwaenepoel, "The Distributed V Kernel and its Performance for Diskless Workstations," *Proc. of the Ninth ACM Symp. on Operating Systems Principle*, New Hampshire, Oct. 1983.
[10] L. Zhang, "High-Speed Protocol—Panel Discussion," *Proc. IEEE INFOCOMM*, San Francisco, 1990.
[11] "Gigabit Applications—Panel Discussion," *Proc. IEEE INFOCOMM*, San Francisco, 1990.

[12] Z. Haas and D. R. Cheriton, "A Case for Packet Switching in High-Performance Wide-Area Networks," *ACM SIGCOMM, Workshop: Frontiers In Computer Commun.*, 1987.

[13] Z. Haas, "A Communication Architecture for High-Speed Networking," *Proc. IEEE INFOCOMM*, San Francisco, 1990.

[14] D. D. Clark, V. Jacobson, J. Romkey, and H. Salwen, "An Analysis of TCP Processing Overhead," *IEEE Commun. Mag.*, June, 1989.

[15] G. Chesson, "XTP/PE Design Considerations," *Protocol Engines, Inc.*

[16] N. Jain, M. Schwartz, and T. R. Bashkow, "Transport Protocol Processing at Gb/s Rates," *Symp. SIGCOMM '90-Commun. Architectures & Protocols*, Philadelphia, PA, 1990.

[17] "Transmission Control Protocol-DARPA Internet Program Protocol Specification," *RFC 793*, September, 1981.

[18] G. Chesson, "Protocol Engine Design," *Protocol Engines, Inc.*

[19] A. G. Fraser and W. T. Marshall, "Data Transport in a Byte Stream Network," *IEEE J. on Sel. Areas in Commun.*, Sept. 1989.

[20] "NEWSFRONT: New LAN Protocol Promises Multigigabit Throughput," *Data Commun.*, Mar. 1989.

[21] H. Kanakia and D. R. Cheriton, "The VMP Network Adapter Board, High-Performance Network Communication for Multiprocessors," *Proc. ACM SIGCOMM Symp.: Commun., Architectures, and Protocols*, 1988.

[22] D. R. Cheriton and R. L. Williamson, "Network Measurement of the VMTP Request-Response Protocol in the V Distributed System," *ACM Sigmetrics Conf. on Measurement and Modeling of Computer Systems*, Alberta Canada, May, 1987.

[23] D. R. Cheriton, "VMTP: A Transport Protocol for the Next Generation of Communication Systems," *Proc. ACM SIGCOMM Symp.: Commun., Architectures, and Protocols*, Stowe, VT, 1986.

[24] G. Chesson, "The Protocol Engine Project," *Unix Review*, Sept. 1990.

[25] D. D. Clark, M. L. Lambert, and L. Zhang, "NETBLT: A High-Throughput Transport Protocol," *ACM SIGCOMM Workshop: Frontiers In Computer Net.*, 1987.

[26] V. Jacobson, "Congestion and Avoidance Control," *Proc.: ACM SIGCOMM Symp. on Commun., Architectures, and Protocols*, 1988.

[27] D. R. Cheriton and C. L. Williamson, "VMTP as the Transport Layer for High-Performance Distributed Systems," *IEEE Commun. Mag.*, June, 1989.

[28] G. Brown, M. Gouda, and R. Miller, "Block Acknowledgment: Redesigning the Window Protocol," *Proc.: ACM SIGCOMM Symp. on Commun. Architectures, and Protocols*, Austin, TX, 1989.

[29] L. Zhang, "Why TCP Timers Don't Work Well," *Proc.: ACM SIGCOMM Symp. on Commun., Architectures, and Protocols*, Stowe, VT, 1986.

Biography

Thomas F. La Porta received B.S. and M.S. degrees in Electrical Engineering from The Cooper Union, New York, NY, in 1986 and 1987 respectively. He is currently studying for a Ph.D. in Electrical Engineering at Columbia University, New York, NY

He joined AT&T Bell Laboratories in 1986. From 1986–1990 he worked in the Data Communications Planning Department in Holmdel, NJ, where he was involved with interoperability and performance analysis of various data communications protocols and systems. In 1991 he joined the Network Systems Research Department where he has been concentrating on high speed protocol design and performance.

Mischa Schwartz received the B.E.E. degree from Cooper Union, New York, N.Y. in 1947, the M.E.E. degree from the Polytechnic Institute of Brooklyn, N.Y. in 1949, and the Ph.D. degree in applied physics from Harvard University, Cambridge, MA in 1951.

From 1947 to 1952, he was a Project Engineer with Sperry Gyroscope Company and worked in the fields of statistical communication theory, radar detection, and radar design. From 1952 to 1974, he was Professor of Electrical Engineering at the Polytechnic Institute of Brooklyn and served as Head of the Electrical Engineering Department from 1961 to 1965. During the year 1965–66, he was an NSF Science Faculty Fellow at the Laboratoire de Physique, Paris, France. During the academic year 1973–74, he was a Visiting Professor at Columbia University, New York, N.Y. He joined that institution in September 1974 as Professor of Electrical Engineering and Computer Sciences. He is currently Charles Batchelor Professor of Electrical Engineering. For the 1980 calendar year, he was on leave as a Visiting Scientist with IBM Research. During 1986, he was on leave as a Resident Consultant with NYNEX Science and Technology.

Dr. Schwartz is a Fellow and former Director of the IEEE, former Chairman of the Information Theory Group, and past President of the Communications Society. He is author and coauthor of eight books on communications, signal processing, and computer communication networks, and has published extensively in the technical literature. He is on the editorial boards of *Networks* and *Computer Networks*.

Support of NFS grant #CDR-88-11111 is acknowledged.

HINTS FOR THE INTERPRETATION OF THE ISO SESSION LAYER

Fausto Caneschi

IBM European Networking Center

Tiergartenstrasse 15, D-6900 HEIDELBERG, West Germany

ABSTRACT:

This work originated from discussions on the interpretation of the ISO 8327 Session Protocol and the ISO 8326 Session Service. The author, who participated in the development of the above mentioned documents, discovered that many who attempted a thorough reading of them, either for implementing the Session layer or for a better understanding of the protocol, had a number of questions regarding the interpretation of the documents.

There are two principal reasons for these difficulties. First, the state table description of the protocol in Appendix A of ISO 8326 and ISO 8327 is not formal, and thus subject to different interpretations. Second, there are actions which are not explained in Appendix A, but rather are described in the text. This means that even after having solved all questions related to Appendix A, one cannot be sure that an implementation is in fact correct.

This paper is intended as an aid in interpreting the documents, and to correlate the plain text description to the state table description.

A number of persons contributed to the contents of this paper, and it is impossible to list them all. The author, however, wishes to mention the major discussions that had with Albert Fleischmann and Stefan Pappe during their implementation of the Heidelberg Session layer; Colin West of the Zuerich Lab when he was attempting to devise a testing strategy for the above mentioned implementation; and Marten van Sinderen of the Twente University and Giuseppe Scollo of the Catania University when using LOTOS to describe the ISO Session layer.

Wolfgang Effelsberg and Jim Staton of E.N.C., finally, deserve special thanks for their many valuable suggestions, both technical and structural, that they gave on the early versions of this document, which could now be titled "Hints for the interpretation of "Hints for the interpretation of the ISO Session Layer"".

"Hints for the Interpretation of the ISO Layer," ©1986 by F. Caneschi.
Reprinted with author's permission.

CONTENTS

1.0 Introduction 1

2.0 The Session Layer terminology 3
   2.1   **State Names** 3
   2.2   **Services and PDU's names** 4

3.0 The Session Layer variables 5

4.0 Problems in the Connection phase 7
   4.1   **Generalities** 7
   4.2   **Negotiation rules** 8
   4.3   **Initial Serial Number** 8
   4.4   **Please tokens** 9
   4.5   **Variables** 9
   4.6   **Timer** 10

5.0 Problems in the disconnection phase 11
   5.1   **Tokens** 11
   5.2   **Collisions** 11

6.0 Restrictions on the Use of Session Services 13

7.0 Loss of User Data 23

8.0 Problems with Serial numbers 25
   8.1   **Serial numbers assignment** 25
   8.2   **Serial numbers wrapping** 25

9.0 Protocol variables setting 27
   9.1   **Major synchronization and Activity End** 27
   9.2   **Resynchronization and Activity disruption** 28
   9.3   **Minor synchronization** 31
   9.4   **Activity Start** 33
   9.5   **Activity Resume** 35

10.0 Motivations for the Give Control service 37

11.0 Problems with Exceptions 39

12.0 Final remarks 41

Bibliography 43

FIGURES

Figure 1.	Protocol variables in the connection phase	10
Figure 2.	Release collision	11
Figure 3.	Protocol variables in the release phase	12
Figure 4.	Restrictions for CONNECT, ABORT, RELEASE and Token Management	14
Figure 5.	Restrictions for DATA, EXPEDITED, TYPED, CAPABILITY and Minor Sync	16
Figure 6.	Restrictions for Major Sync, Give Control and Activity End	18
Figure 7.	Restrictions for User Exceptions, Activity Start, Interrupt and Discard	20
Figure 8.	Conditions for Major synchronization or Activity end	27
Figure 9.	Protocol variables during Major synchronization or Activity end	28
Figure 10.	Conditions for Resynchronization and Activity Disruption	30
Figure 11.	Protocol variables during resynchronization and activity disruption	31
Figure 12.	Conditions for Minor synchronization	32
Figure 13.	Protocol variables during Minor synchronization	33
Figure 14.	Conditions for Activity Start	34
Figure 15.	Protocol variables during Activity Start	35
Figure 16.	Protocol variables during Activity Resume	36

1.0 INTRODUCTION

At IBM's European Networking Center in Heidelberg, an implementation of the ISO Session Layer was developed during 1985 in the Distributed Application Research department. The strategy adopted for that implementation was to derive the PASCAL code from a formal description of the ISO Session Layer ([ISO8326] and [ISO8327]) by means of an automated code-generator. This idea, which allows maintaining a limited amount of code for maintaining a rather complex software structure, is based on the assumption that what is written in the ISO text is, if not formal, at least easily formalizable. Unfortunately during this project many questions arose in interpreting the ISO documents. Some of these questions were solved only by consulting some 'gurus' who knew the spirit in which the standard was written. Others were discovered to be inconsistencies and even errors in the standard itself, which were unknown even to the most experienced gurus.

Further questions related to the ISO Session layer were being asked by the ISO group led by this document's author which is describing the Session service and protocol by means of LOTOS ([LOT1985] [LOTOS1985b] and [LOT1986]). Many questions were similar to the ones raised by the ENC, although new ones were also asked.

Time has produced a structured answer to all questions, and this document constitutes a record of both questions and answers. Thus, this document is not a tutorial on the ISO Session layer, but rather a collection of information on points which the author believes are of particular interest. As such, it can (and hopefully will) be enriched with more sections, if and when further questions arise and are answered.

It is assumed that the reader has a good knowledge of the ISO Session layer, and is interested in understanding why particular decisions have been made, or how certain mechanisms work.

The document is structured in the following way:

o   Each section is devoted to a specific issue of the Session layer, such as the connection phase, or the serial numbers handling, where doubts and/or misinterpretations arose.

o   Inside a section, only the peculiar aspects are described, i.e. those aspects that the author believes are difficult to interpret, or that have been misinterpreted at least once.

o   When an internal variable is set, or changed, the evolution of its values is shown on both sides of the connection.

By its nature the structure of this paper is flat; i.e. almost all of its body is at the same level, and a reader interested only in a particular issue can read only the related section, skipping all the rest.

However, it is highly recommended that the first two sections be read before all others, for they address issues of a general interest.

2.0 THE SESSION LAYER TERMINOLOGY

Although a major effort has been made to align the Session layer terminology with that used in other standards, there remain some terms which have a special meaning in the Session layer context.

A typical example is the word token, which means "exclusive right to perform a given function", but has a rather different meaning when used in different contexts (for example, Local Area Networks).

It is thus important that the first sections of the standard be read, as they are often skipped by the reader interested in the details. In particular, it is highly recommended that the reader review the 'Definitions' and 'Overview' sections, both of the service and of the protocol document. From these sections, one can understand the subtle differences between 'selecting' and 'proposing' a parameter, or among 'calling', 'sending' and 'requesting' SS-user. These terms (and others) are used with their peculiar 'Session' meaning throughout this paper.

The rationale behind some names is not, however, explained in the standard. This does not cause any technical harm, but sometimes gives the reader the uneasy feeling that 'there is something hidden behind it'. What follows gives some information on the origins of some of the terminology; it can be regarded as a short collection of curiosities, and the reader interested only in the technical aspects can skip it.

2.1 STATE NAMES

The ISO Session protocol is at the moment described by means of a finite-state automaton with 29 states. A Defect Report proposed the introduction of two new states, but has not been approved at the time this paper was written.

States have been given names which begin with the keyword 'STA', followed by a combination of numbers and, possibly, one letter. Why is that so? Why not numbering in a sequential manner all states? Why numbers get up to '22', but there is one state named STA713? What has happened to the other 691 missing states?

The original proposal, on which the current standard is based, was presented to ISO in 1981 and was based on the ECMA-75 standard. In the ECMA-75 document, almost all states were numbered in a sequential fashion (there were some minor exceptions). When the integration of the CCITT's T.62 protocol was decided, the "old" names were kept, mainly as an aid for the protocol designers in their synthesis work. New states were added in the appropriate places using old numbers, suffixed with a letter (A, B and even C). During the synthesis work, some errors were also corrected in the "old" protocol, and some enhancements were made as well. This led to the adoption of an increasing number of protocol variables, which allowed a more complete description of the events, as well as a decrease of the number of the states. For instance, some variables related to Resynchronization allowed the reduction of the Resynchronization states from 9 to 7.

The story of state 713 is a typical example. There was initially a number of states, collectively called "Data Transfer States", which differed in the definition and assignment of the tokens. The numbers assigned to these states ranged from 7 to 13 in the ECMA-75 standard. When, thanks to the introduction of variables and predicates which indicate the state of the tokens, those states collapsed into a single state, the initial name of that new state was 'STA7-13'. This allowed all people used to the old terminology to understand that STA7-13 meant the collection of states previously known as "Data Transfer States". The further abbreviations to 'STA7/13' (what is the meaning of that hyphen in STA7-13?), and finally to 'STA713' (why a slash in a state name?), which allows an automatic sorting of the state tables when they are in machine-readable form, with the "Data Transfer" state being always the last one, should now be obvious.

At this time, there are so many people who know the Session protocol states, that changing the state names would be traumatic.

2.2 SERVICES AND PDU'S NAMES

In general, a PDU is generated following a service primitive of the request or response type. In the former case, the PDU is given the service name, while in the latter one it is given the service name with the keyword 'ACK' (acknowledgment) as a qualifier. As an example, the PDU which is generated after an Activity End request is called ACTIVITY END SPDU (AE), and the PDU generated after an Activity End response is called ACTIVITY END ACK SPDU (AEA). Minor deviations from this rule (MAJOR SYNC POINT, instead of MAJOR SYNC, for instance) are unimportant.

There are some exceptions to this rule, namely:

o   Some services requests or responses provoke the generation of two PDU's. One PDU is named following the given rule (example: RESYNCHRONIZE SPDU); the other one is of the same type for all those services, and is called PREPARE (PR), with a qualifier enclosed in parentheses (example: PREPARE (RESYNCHRONIZE) SPDU) to indicate which is the event one should prepare.

o   The two PDU's which do not correspond to any service invocation, are ABORT ACCEPT and GIVE TOKEN ACK. In these cases, the protocol is confirmed, while the service is not. The different names reflect an attempt to give some semantics to the names.

o   There are two confirmed services to which three different SPDU's are related, namely:

   1. For the Connect service, there is a CONNECT SPDU corresponding to the service request, and an ACCEPT and a REFUSE SPDU for the service response. This is because of the possibility of giving a negative answer to a Connect, and of the need to differentiate between 'Yes' and 'No' in a strong way, for the strong semantics implied in a Connect operation.

   2. For the Release service, there is a FINISH SPDU corresponding to the service request, and a DISCONNECT and a NOT FINISHED SPDU for the service response. The same argument applies as in the Connect case, but with a further question: why FINISH SPDU and not RELEASE SPDU? The author must confess that the answer is lost in the mists of the past.

In conclusion, names should be used as such; that is, labels, with no particular rationale justifying one choice among other possible choices.

3.0 THE SESSION LAYER VARIABLES

As it has been mentioned in section "State Names" on page 3, a number of variables have been defined for the description of the Session protocol. These variables may assume predefined sets of values, and rules are given for updating variables. Major events related to updating variables are dealt with in "9.0 Protocol variables setting" on page 27.

The Session variables are called 'local variables', but this designation can cause confusion for those used to other environments. It is true that from a distributed operating system's point of view, those variables are local, as a copy of each is available in all communicating systems. But, if one considers the description of a layer in the Reference Model [ISO7498], there is no distinction between the communicating systems. They cooperate to create a functionality which, as seen from outside, is global. Inside a Session connection, which can be regarded as an instance of the Session layer, some variables are used, which can be seen from outside as single, atomic entities, and as such can be considered as global.

With this said, one can distinguish between:

Local variables: Those variables which have the same name on both sides of the session connection, but assume complementary values. These are:

1. Vtca, which is TRUE for the protocol machine which accepted the transport connection, and FALSE for the other protocol machine.

2. Vsc, which is TRUE for the protocol machine that can issue MINOR SYNC POINT ACK's, and FALSE for the other.

Furthermore, there is a Boolean function, SPMwinner, which is TRUE for the protocol machine that wins a resynchronization collision, and FALSE otherwise. This can also be regarded as a sort of local variable.

Global variables: These are all other defined variables. Their values are the same on both sides, and rules are given for maintaining consistency. The transient periods (when values are inconsistent) are clearly identified and all happens as a single variable for each sort existed in the overall Session. As seen from outside, in each session connection there is only one instance for each sort of these variables. The situation is like emulating a shared memory, which leads one to think in terms of global variables. Still, these variables are called local in the text of the standard.

As in many other issues regarding the Session, a word such as local, has been given a special meaning. Again, names in the Session layer should be considered as labels.

4.0 PROBLEMS IN THE CONNECTION PHASE

4.1 GENERALITIES

A CONNECT SPDU is sent as normal data on a Transport connection. The Transport connection may not exist at the time that a CONNECT request is issued by the SS-user. In this case it is created. The only options in creating a Transport connection are:

o   Transport Expedited, which is selected if either:

   1. The SS-user has requested "Extended control" as a QoS parameter

   2. The SS-user proposed the usage of the Expedited Functional Unit.

o   Transport QoS parameters. These are selected according to the corresponding Session QoS parameters. Nothing, however, is said about the case when the Transport connection is established, but has QoS different from that which the SS-user desires. This means that, according to implementation choices, the connection may be kept and used, or disconnected. Both choices are legal.

If there is an established Transport connection, on which no Session connection is active, the CONNECT SPDU may be sent over it, provided that:

1. The Transport Expedited flow is not available.

2. The side which issues the CONNECT SPDU is the same side which previously requested the Transport connection, and issued the CONNECT SPDU related to the previous session.

The first rule is to avoid "backwards penetration", that is the possibility that an SPDU belonging to a Session Connection arrives at one side which does not know yet that the previous connection has terminated. For example, after a RELEASE request, one could issue a new CONNECT, and then an ABORT request. If the Transport expedited flow is available, the ABORT would be sent over it, with the possibility of overtaking the CONNECT SPDU. Thus, on the remote side, the following sequence of PDUs would arrive:

1. FINISH

2. ABORT

3. CONNECT

which is not what the originator wanted.

The second rule is a drastic, yet effective, way to avoid collisions of CONNECT SPDU's, because it states the only side which is allowed to try to reuse a Transport connection.

4.2 NEGOTIATION RULES

Functional Units. In principle, the lists contained in the CONNECT and ACCEPT SPDU are independent, with the only constraint that if both Half Duplex and Full Duplex FUs are proposed in the CONNECT, then only one of them can be present in the ACCEPT. Apart from that, what is carried in the ACCEPT SPDU is just the list of requirements of the called Session user. The list of the FUs which will be used during the connection is computed on the called side after having sent the ACCEPT SPDU, and on the calling side after receiving it, by selecting only those FU's proposed on both sides (logical operation AND).

Segmenting The values contained in the ACCEPT SPDU are also independent of the corresponding values in the CONNECT. This means that the smaller values are used (if zero, no segmentation is performed), but any values may be carried in the ACCEPT. The negotiation rules also imply that the case when only one direction on the flow is subject to segmenting is allowed.

Serial Number As far as negotiation is concerned, the text does not say which serial number is chosen; the initiator's or the responder's. Looking at the state tables, it is clear that any value provided by the called user is chosen, regardless of the initiator's proposal. More about serial numbers in "Initial Serial Number" and in "8.0 Problems with Serial numbers" on page 25.

4.3 INITIAL SERIAL NUMBER

In the CONNECT SPDU, the Initial Serial Number parameter:

o   must be present if any of

   -   Minor Synch

   -   Major Synch

   -   Resynch

   Functional Units are proposed and Activity is not proposed.

o   cannot be present if Activity is proposed and none of Minor sync, Major synch or Resynch is proposed.

o   can be present if both Activity and any of Minor Synch, Major Synch or Resynch is proposed.

In the ACCEPT SPDU, the Initial Serial Number parameter:

o   must be present if any of:

   -   Minor Synch

   -   Major Synch

- Resynch

Functional Units are selected and Activity is not selected.

o   There are no rules for the remaining cases.

The rationale is that the CCITT Recommendation T.62 does not set any initial serial number, while the ECMA-75 standard does. When one tries to combine the two standards (Activity + Minor and/or Major synch or Resynch), the general understanding is that "Activity prevails".

4.4 PLEASE TOKENS

Due to the presence of the Token Item parameter in the ACCEPT SPDU, a Please Tokens indication can be generated, subsequent to the CONNECT confirmation (positive). This means that, in the presence of the Token Item parameter, an implementation is supposed to generate two service primitives, i.e. CONNECT confirm followed by PLEASE TOKENS indication on receipt of a single SPDU, i.e. ACCEPT.

This fact is not clear from the state table description, and although of marginal interest, could cause problems to imprudent implementers when trying to perform testing against a reference implementation.

4.5 VARIABLES

Figure 1 shows the setting of the protocol variables during the Connection phase.

Variable name	Value after sending (calling side)	Value after receiving (called side)	Value after responding (called side)	Value after receiving (calling side)
V(A)	Not defined	Not defined	Initial Serial Number if not Activity. If Activity, not defined.	Initial Serial Number if not Activity. If Activity, not defined.
V(M)	Not defined	Not defined	Initial Serial Number if not Activity. If Activity, not defined.	Initial Serial Number if not Activity. If Activity, not defined.
V(R)	Not defined	Not defined	0	0
Vsc	Not defined	Not defined	FALSE	FALSE
Vact	Not defined	Not defined	If Activity, set to FALSE, otherwise not defined	If Activity, set to FALSE, otherwise not defined
Vnextact	Not defined	Not defined	Not defined	Not defined
Vcoll	FALSE	Not defined	FALSE	FALSE
Vtca	FALSE	Not defined	TRUE	FALSE

Figure 1.   Protocol variables in the connection phase

4.6 TIMER

A timer, called TIM, is started by a protocol entity after having issued a REFUSE SPDU. At expiration of TIM, if no transport DISCONNECT indication has been received, the transport connection is disconnected (i.e., a DISCONNECT request must be generated). As the normal expected behaviour of an implementation is to issue a DISCONNECT after having received a REFUSE, one could be tempted to set TIM to infinite (which is a legal value), or, in other words, avoid using a timer. This might cause a deadlock in the case of release collision, as explained in "Collisions" on page 11, because the same timer TIM is used in both cases.

5.0 PROBLEMS IN THE DISCONNECTION PHASE

5.1 TOKENS

To prevent collision cases, only the owner of ALL available tokens may issue a FINISH SPDU, as a consequence of a RELEASE request. This includes the case when the release token has not been defined. If no tokens have been defined for the session, RELEASE collision may happen.

5.2 COLLISIONS

If no tokens are defined, a sequence as in Figure 2 may occur.

```
    RELEASE.request --->     |        |<---RELEASE.request
                             |        |
    RELEASE.indication <---  |        |--->RELEASE.indication

        A collision is detected (Vcoll is set to TRUE)
        State is STA 16 (wait for T_DISCONNECT)
        The timer TIM is started

                             |        |
    RELEASE.response --->    |        |<---RELEASE.response
                             |        |
```

The receipt of a DN SPDU in STA16 does not provoke any event. The SPDU is discarded. User data are lost.

Due to the timer, a disconnection will be performed anyway.

Figure 2. Release collision

The problem is that user data contained in a RELEASE response, which may be of great interest for the Application protocol, may be lost due to the collision. A solution has been proposed, but not balloted yet.

This gives an answer to the question of using or not the timer TIM, that has been raised in "Timer" on page 10: the timer TIM should be used. However, if one does not want to be bothered with timer interrupts, a possibility is to set TIM to a suitably large value, although not infinite. The efficiency of the disconnection phase will be decreased in the case of Release collision, but one should not expect great efficiency in any collision case.

Figure 3 on page 12 shows the setting of the only one relevant protocol variable during the Release phase in the case of a RELEASE collision.

Variable name	Value before	Value after sending (requestor side)	Value after receiving (acceptor side)	Value after responding (acceptor side)	Value after receiving (requestor side)
Vcoll	FALSE	FALSE	If an FN PDU is received in state 3 (wait for DN SPDU), set to TRUE	unchanged	If an FN PDU is received in state 3 (wait for DN SPDU), set to TRUE

Figure 3. Protocol variables in the release phase

6.0 RESTRICTIONS ON THE USE OF SESSION SERVICES

The tables contained in Figure 4 on page 14, Figure 5 on page 16, Figure 6 on page 18, and Figure 7 on page 20 show the restrictions which apply on the use of session services after some certain events occurred at the service boundary. It may happen that, after a certain event happened at the service boundary, a user issues one permitted primitive which brings further restrictions. This is not indicated in the tables, for two main reasons:

1. Any other different representation of restrictions would have caused multidimensional arrays to be drawn, which would have complicated the description.

2. In practice, after a certain event only those primitives which imply a wider set of restrictions are valid, so that one can avoid remembering the history of the events, at least as far as restrictions are concerned.

Events which do not imply restrictions are not indicated in the tables. This is to keep the tables' size as compact as possible.

The tables should be read in the following way:

o   Look for the service to be invoked: it will be the name of a column which appears in only one table.

o   In the column representing the service, any valid intersection (marked by a capital X) with a row shows that the service may be invoked after the event represented in the row happened.

If the intersection is empty, this means that the service cannot be invoked.

If the event you look for is not represented in a row of a table (rows are the same for each table), the service can always be invoked after the event described in the column happened.

Finally, the tables only represent those restrictions which apply in any case: thus, a certain service, even if allowed after a specific event according to the tables, may in fact be forbidden due to token assignment, or the like.

After this event	The following primitives may be invoked						
	SCONreq	SCONrsp	SRELreq	SRELrsp	SUABreq	SGTreq	SPTreq
SCONreq					X		
SCONind					X		
SRELreq					X		
SRELind				X	X		X
SRELrsp					X		
SRELcnf					X		X
SUABreq	X						
SUABind	X						
SCDreq					X		
SCDind					X		X
SSYNMreq					X	X	
SSYNMind			X		X	X	X
SRSYNreq					X		
SRSYNind					X		
SCGreq					X		
SUERreq					X		
SUERind					X	X	
SPERind					X	X	
SACTSreq			X	X	X	X	X
SACTSind			X	X	X	X	X
SACTRreq			X	X	X	X	X
SACTRind			X	X	X	X	X
SACTIreq					X		

Figure 4 (Part 1 of 2). Restrictions for CONNECT, ABORT, RELEASE and Token Management

After this event	The following primitives may be invoked						
	SCONreq	SCONrsp	SRELreq	SRELrsp	SUABreq	SGTreq	SPTreq
SACTIind					X		
SACTDreq					X		
SACTDind					X		
SACTEreq					X	X	
SACTEind					X	X	X

Figure 4 (Part 2 of 2). Restrictions for CONNECT, ABORT, RELEASE and Token Management

After this event	The following primitives may be invoked						
	SDTreq	SEXreq	STDreq	SCDreq	SCDrsp	SSYNmreq	SSYNmrsp
SCONreq							
SCONind							
SRELreq							
SRELind	X	X	X				X
SRELrsp							
SRELcnf							
SUABreq							
SUABind							
SCDreq							
SCDind					X		
SSYNMreq							
SSYNMind	X	X	X				X
SRSYNreq							
SRSYNind							
SCGreq	X	X	X				
SUERreq							
SUERind							
SPERind							
SACTSreq	X	X	X	X	X	X	X
SACTSind	X	X	X	X	X	X	X
SACTRreq	X	X	X	X	X	X	X
SACTRind	X	X	X	X	X	X	X
SACTIreq							

Figure 5 (Part 1 of 2). Restrictions for DATA, EXPEDITED, TYPED, CAPABILITY and Minor Sync

After this event	The following primitives may be invoked						
	SDTreq	SEXreq	STDreq	SCDreq	SCDrsp	SSYNmreq	SSYNmrsp
SACTIind							
SACTDreq							
SACTDind							
SACTEreq							
SACTEind	X	X	X				X

Figure 5 (Part 2 of 2). Restrictions for DATA, EXPEDITED, TYPED, CAPABILITY and Minor Sync

After this event	The following primitives may be invoked							
	SSYNMreq	SSYNMrsp	SRSYNreq	SRSYNrsp	SCGreq	SACTEreq	SACTErsp
SCONreq							
SCONind							
SRELreq							
SRELind			X				
SRELrsp							
SUABreq							
SUABind							
SCDreq							
SCDind							
SSYNMreq			X				
SSYNMind		X	X				
SRSYNreq							
SRSYNind			X	X			
SCGreq							
SUERreq							
SUERind			X				
SPERind			X				
SACTSreq	X		X		X	X	
SACTSind	X		X		X	X	
SACTRreq	X		X		X	X	
SACTRind	X		X		X	X	
SACTIreq							
SACTIind							

Figure 6 (Part 1 of 2). Restrictions for Major Sync, Give Control and Activity End

After this event	The following primitives may be invoked						
	SSYNMreq	SSYNMrsp	SRSYNreq	SRSYNrsp	SCGreq	SACTEreq	SACTErsp
SACTDreq							
SACTDind							
SACTEreq							
SACTEind		X				X	

Figure 6 (Part 2 of 2). Restrictions for Major Sync, Give Control and Activity End

After this event	The following primitives may be invoked					
	SUERreq	SACTSreq	SACTDreq	SACTDrsp	SACTIreq	SACTIrsp
SCONreq						
SCONind						
SRELreq						
SRELind	X					
SRELrsp						
SRELcnf	X					
SUABreq						
SUABind						
SCDreq						
SCDind						
SSYNMreq			X		X	
SSYNMind	X					
SRSYNreq						
SRSYNind			X		X	
SCGreq						
SUERreq						
SUERind			X		X	
SPERind			X		X	
SACTSreq	X	X	X		X	
SACTSind	X	X	X		X	
SACTRreq	X	X	X		X	
SACTRind	X	X	X			X
SACTIreq						

Figure 7 (Part 1 of 2). Restrictions for User Exceptions, Activity Start, Interrupt and Discard

After this event	The following primitives may be invoked					
	SUERreq	SACTSreq	SACTDreq	SACTDrsp	SACTIreq	SACTIrsp
SACTIind						X
SACTDreq						
SACTDind			X			
SACTEreq			X		X	
SACTEind	X					

Figure 7 (Part 2 of 2). Restrictions for User Exceptions, Activity Start, Interrupt and Discard

7.0 LOSS OF USER DATA

In principle, the Session protocol relies upon the Transport Service, which by definition is reliable. However, there are some situations in which user data can be lost. These are:

1. During Abort.

    If Transport Expedited has been selected, the ABORT SPDU is sent over that flow, so that it can overtake data sent before in the normal data flow. Data arriving after the receipt of Abort will be discarded, and not passed to the user. This situation can be avoided by means of suitable implementation choices, although some choices could jeopardize the Abort mechanism. In any case, it is impossible to determine that all data sent after the last confirmed service and before the Abort have been successfully delivered before the Abort itself is received.

2. During Resynchronization

    The same argument as in the case of Abort applies, with the only difference that the connection remains active after Resync.

3. In the case of Release collision.

    This case has already been discussed in "Collisions" on page 11, but is mentioned here for completeness. It is distinct from the other cases, in that the lost data is that which is contained in the user data parameter of the DISCONNECT SPDU.

The rules which apply to the serial number in the Connect phase have already been dealt with in "Initial Serial Number" on page 8. In this section, the emphasis is on the Data Transfer phase.

8.1 SERIAL NUMBERS ASSIGNMENT

When issuing a synchronization point the user does not provide the serial number, as it might be interpreted erroneously when reading the text of the Session Service. In fact, that parameter is marked as MANDATORY in the primitive description. The meaning of that Mandatory in this case is that the Service provider is required to inform its user of the value which has been given by the provider itself, and not the other way round.

This can be concluded from the text of the Session protocol, which states (for example in Clause 7.18.1, page 57) that the value of the serial number in the PDU is taken from the current value of the internal variable V(M).

There is another pitfall: if one looks at the State Tables in ANNEX A, which, in case of doubt, take precedence over the informal text, no mention is made from where the value of the serial number is taken. This means that a straightforward implementation of the Session Layer, as in the case when code is automatically generated from the state tables, will probably either:

o   Produce an incorrect PDU, not setting the serial number

o   Expect the serial number from the user.

8.2 SERIAL NUMBERS WRAPPING

The space assigned to serial numbers in PDU's is finite, and limited to a figure not exceeding 999999. What happens when the serial number reaches that value? The question is not of marginal importance, for any legal value can be given in the Connect request. This means that wrapping can happen after a few synchronization points have been issued.

The standard says that "It is the responsibility of the SS-user to ensure that the number assigned by the SS-provider in a synchronization point request does not exceed 999998" (this is not a typo: the last number is '8').

The fact that the predicates which control the setting of the protocol variables use the well-known symbols of "greater than" or "less than", which have a precise mathematical meaning, and the warning stated in the above mentioned sentence, should provide a clue for understanding the serial number mechanism.

Serial numbers do not wrap. When the next available serial number is 999999, it is not possible to discern the ordering in which synchronization points have been issued. Setting the value of V(M) to 999999 (which is possible at Connect or

Resynchronization time) will not harm the numbering mechanism, because as soon as a synch point is issued, the value corresponding to the next one will be 0, which is just fine.

This aspect is a bug in the definition of the standard, and it has not yet been fixed: people who developed the Session are aware of it, but had not enough time to produce a more efficient solution apart from giving the responsibility to the SS-user. A safe solution is thus that the SS-user, as soon as the serial number reaches the magic figure of 999998, issues a Resynchronize (set or abandon) request, and thus cause a new setting of the synchronization points counter (i.e. V(M)).

This does not solve the problem, as it leaves the solution to the SS-user's behaviour. A better solution will probably not be forthcoming in the immediate future.

9.0 PROTOCOL VARIABLES SETTING

The protocol variables, which are defined during the connection phase (see "4.0 Problems in the Connection phase" on page 7), can be modified or even re-defined following certain SS-user service primitives or the arrival of certain SPDUs.

The sections which follow describe in detail what happens to those variables when some relevant event happens. The relationship between the synchronization variables and the serial number (indicated by sn) are shown when relevant. The term "response PDU", a term which is misleading, is used in some tables to indicate the PDU generated by the session protocol machine following a response-type service.

Most information is taken from Table 42 of ISO 8327, on page 132.

9.1 MAJOR SYNCHRONIZATION AND ACTIVITY END

The conditions which have to be applied to verify that a Major Sync or Activity end request or response, or the related PDUs, are valid are shown in Figure 8. Those are only related to variables or PDU parameter values. General restrictions due to previous service interface events can be found in "6.0 Restrictions on the Use of Session Services" on page 13.

The operations on variables are shown in Figure 9 on page 28.

```
+------------------+------------------+------------------+------------------+
| Invoking     the | Accepting    the | Invoking     the | Accepting    the |
| service request  | request          | response         | response         |
|                  | generated PDU    |                  | generated PDU    |
|                  |                  |                  |                  |
|------------------+------------------+------------------+------------------|
| None             | sn = V(M)        | sn = V(M) - 1    | sn = V(M) - 1    |
+------------------+------------------+------------------+------------------+
```

Figure 8. Conditions for Major synchronization or Activity end

Variable name	Value after sending PDU (requestor side)	Value after receiving PDU (acceptor side)	Value after responding (acceptor side)	Value after receiving response PDU (requestor side)
V(A)	If Vsc = TRUE set to V(M); otherwise unchanged	If Vsc = TRUE unchanged; otherwise set to V(M)	V(M)	V(M)
V(M)	V(M) + 1	V(M) + 1	unchanged	unchanged
V(R)	unchanged	unchanged	V(M)	V(M)
Vnextact	TRUE if Major Sync FALSE if Activity End	TRUE if Major Sync FALSE if Activity End	unchanged	unchanged
Vact	unchanged	unchanged	Vnextact	Vnextact
Vsc	FALSE	unchanged	unchanged	unchanged

Figure 9. Protocol variables during Major synchronization or Activity end

9.2 RESYNCHRONIZATION AND ACTIVITY DISRUPTION

The conditions which must be applied to verify that a Resync, Activity Interrupt or Activity Discard (henceforth called Activity disruption) request or response, or the related PDUs, are valid are shown in Figure 10. Those are only related to variables or PDU parameter values. General restrictions due to previous service interface events can be found in "6.0 Restrictions on the Use of Session Services" on page 13.

The operations on variables are shown in Figure 11 on page 31.

In the tables, the same abbreviations used in the standard are used, which are also repeated here.

a   stands for "Resynchronize abandon"

r   stands for "Resynchronize restart"

s   stands for "Resynchronize set"

int   stands for "Activity interrupt"

dsc   stands for "Activity discard"

There is a peculiarity in the use of the variables Vrsp and Vrspnb which is worth mentioning. As explained in the standard, Vrsp is used during Resynchronization or Activity disruption to keep track of the type of event that is happening; i.e., a, r, s, dsc or int. This variable has been introduced because Resynchronization can collide with another Resynchronization or an Activity disruption, and the standard defines rules for handling collision cases.

Vrspnb carries that serial number which is transferred by means of the Resynchronize PDU's. This variable is also used to resolve collisions.

The problem is that, as the two session users can disagree during Resynchronization on the Resynchronization type or on the proposed serial number, collisions may occur in a recursive manner. This means that an implementation should maintain two Vrsp's and two Vrspnb's, one which carries the incoming (from the local SS-user or from the remote SS-user) value, and the other one that carries the "old" value, which has to be kept until a comparison has been made with the new one and the collision rules have been applied. This also implies that the session protocol, at least in this particular case, has been described keeping in mind a sequential structure. One who implements this protocol in a parallel fashion should pay particular attention to the handling of these (and all other) session variables.

Invoking the service request	Accepting the request generated PDU	Invoking the response	Accepting the response generated PDU
a none	a sn =< 999999	a sn = V(M)	a sn >= V(M)
r V(R) =< sn =< V(M)	r V(R) =< sn =< V(M)	r sn as in RS SPDU	r sn as in RS SPDU
s sn =< 9999999	s sn =< 9999999	s sn =< 9999999	s sn =< 9999999
int Vact = TRUE	int Vact = TRUE	int none	
dsc Vact = TRUE	dsc Vact = TRUE	dsc none	

Figure 10. Conditions for Resynchronization and Activity Disruption

Variable name	Value after sending PDU (requestor side)	Value after receiving PDU (acceptor side)	Value after responding (acceptor side)	Value after receiving response PDU (requestor side)
V(A)	unchanged	unchanged	sn	sn
V(M)	unchanged	If type = a MAX(sn,V(M)); otherwise unchanged	sn	sn
V(R)	unchanged	unchanged	a 0 r unchanged s 0	a 0 r unchanged s 0
Vact	unchanged	unchanged	FALSE	FALSE
Vrsp	a, r, s, dsc or int according to the type of Resynchronization or Activity disruption	a, r, s, dsc or int according to the type of Resynchronization or Activity disruption	no	no
Vrspnb	sn	sn	unchanged	unchanged

Figure 11. Protocol variables during resynchronization and activity disruption

9.3 MINOR SYNCHRONIZATION

The conditions that must be applied to verify that a Minor sync request or response, or the related PDUs, are valid are shown in Figure 12. Those are only related to variables or PDU parameter values. General restrictions due to previous service interface events can be found in "6.0 Restrictions on the Use of Session Services" on page 13.

The operations on variables are shown in Figure 13 on page 33.

```
+-----------------------------------------------------------------------+
| Invoking     the | Accepting    the | Invoking     the | Accepting    the |
| service request  | request          | response         | response         |
|                  | generated PDU    |                  | generated PDU    |
|                  |                  |                  |                  |
|------------------+------------------+------------------+------------------|
| none             | sn = V(M)        | Vsc = TRUE and   | Vsc = FALSE and  |
|                  |                  | V(A)  =<  sn  <  | V(A)  =<  sn  <  |
|                  |                  | V(M)             | V(M)             |
|                  |                  | sn cannot  be =  | sn cannot  be =  |
|                  |                  | V(M)  -   1  if  | V(M)  -   1  if  |
|                  |                  | Major  sync  or  | Major  sync  or  |
|                  |                  | Activity    end  | Activity    end  |
|                  |                  | outstanding      | outstanding      |
+-----------------------------------------------------------------------+
```

Figure 12. Conditions for Minor synchronization

Variable name	Value after sending PDU (requestor side)	Value after receiving PDU (acceptor side)	Value after responding (acceptor side)	Value after receiving response PDU (requestor side)
V(A)	If Vsc=TRUE, set to V(M); otherwise unchanged	If Vsc=TRUE, unchanged; otherwise set to V(M)	sn+1	sn+1
V(M)	V(M)+1	V(M)+1	unchanged	unchanged
Vsc	FALSE	TRUE	unchanged	unchanged

Figure 13. Protocol variables during Minor synchronization

9.4 ACTIVITY START

The conditions that must be applied to verify that an Activity Start request or the related PDU, is valid are shown in Figure 14. Those are only related to variables or PDU parameter values. General restrictions due to previous service interface events can be found in "6.0 Restrictions on the Use of Session Services" on page 13.

The operations on variables are shown in Figure 15 on page 35.

```
+----------------------------------+
| Invoking     the | Accepting  the |
| service request | request         |
|                 | generated PDU   |
|                 |                 |
|-----------------+-----------------|
| Vact = FALSE    | Vact = FALSE    |
+----------------------------------+
```

Note: Activity Start is a non-confirmed service and only one Protocol Data Unit is involved.

Figure 14. Conditions for Activity Start

Variable name	Value after sending PDU (requestor side)	Value after receiving PDU (acceptor side)
V(A)	1	1
V(M)	1	1
V(R)	1	1
Vact	TRUE	TRUE

Note: Activity Start is a non-confirmed service and only one Protocol Data Unit is involved.

Figure 15. Protocol variables during Activity Start

9.5 ACTIVITY RESUME

The conditions that must be applied to verify that an Activity Resume request or the related PDU, is valid are the same as for an Activity Start, and are shown in Figure 14 on page 34. Those are only related to variables or PDU parameter values. General restrictions due to previous service interface events can be found in "6.0 Restrictions on the Use of Session Services" on page 13.

The operations on variables are shown in Figure 16 on page 36.

Variable name	Value after sending PDU (requestor side)	Value after receiving PDU (acceptor side)
V(A)	sn + 1	sn + 1
V(M)	1	1
V(R)	1	1
Vact	TRUE	TRUE

Note: Activity Resume is a non-confirmed service and only one Protocol Data Unit is involved.

Figure 16. Protocol variables during Activity Resume

10.0 MOTIVATIONS FOR THE GIVE CONTROL SERVICE

The Give Control service allows one user of the Session Service to pass all defined and owned tokens to the other user.

There are two characteristics of this service which can cause questions to a reader of the ISO Session layer documents. These characteristics are not such that an implementer can be misled, and are only reported here as curiosities.

First of all, why a service that can do the same thing another service can do? The Give Tokens service, if the token item parameter is so set, can pass all tokens at once.

The reason derives from the integration of the CCITT T.62 protocol into the ISO one. In T.62 there is no concept of tokens, but rather a concept of control. Moreover, during the transmission of a document (inside an Activity), the control stays on one side and is not exchanged. Thinking in TELETEX terms, you can receive a TELETEX document only after you have finished sending another document (if you are sending). As a consequence, after Activity End, or Discard or Interrupt, and before the next Activity Start, a user (the TELETEX entity) can pass all rights to send to the other partner to allow it to start an Activity and send a document.

In the first synthesis work, only a few services were allowed "between activities", and the Give Token was not among them. This explains the need for a different mapping of the Give Token PDU from the CDCC (Command Document Change Control) of T.62, which was reserved for this new service, with slightly different semantics.

A second question is: "Why is the Give Control a non-confirmed service, while it is performed by means of a couple of PDUs?"

Again, the response comes from T.62. First of all, it is worth reminding the reader here that the T.62 Recommendation only describes a protocol, and not a service. Secondly, any T.62 PDU has a corresponding ACK PDU, that is, the T.62 protocol is a confirmed one. On the other hand, introducing a confirmed Give_tokens-like service would not have been useful, and possibly even confusing for the Session users, as the generally accepted semantics of a Give tokens (or similar service) indication is that of a signal of something which does not need any answer.

11.0 PROBLEMS WITH EXCEPTIONS

Almost all questions related to Exceptions (the Provider_Exception and the User-Generated_Exception) are derived from the fact that the Exception protocol has been introduced when the standard was fairly stable. There were two reasons for doing that. The first reason was the need of mapping a T.62 PDU not yet taken into account, i.e. the RDPBN (Response Document Page Boundary Negative). In a second time, a new service (the User-Generated_Exception) was introduced.

The big problem was one of altering a stable, but delicate, equilibrium. The results were that:

1. A number of restrictions were imposed over a service which, like Abort or Resynchronization, by its nature must be unrestricted to be useful.

2. There are some situations in which sending the Exception Report SPDU may cause deadlocks. This happens typically when some state is entered, in which PDUs are discarded and no action is taken (STA05A, STA05B, STA05C, STA06, STA15C and STA16). A means of avoiding this deadlock could be the introduction of a timer bound to the SS-user response, which has been judged an unsatisfactory solution by the ISO Session group. There is currently no other solution to the problem.

12.0 FINAL REMARKS

During the writing of this paper, which originated as a one-page list of the restrictions on the use of the session services, several sections were added which were not initially foreseen. Other sections have been written in a completely different way from their initial. This is to say not only that there are more things to be cleared than the author initially thought, but also that explaining a complicated text sometimes creates text at the same level of complication. The author thus strongly recommends any person interested in the ISO Session layer to read carefully the ISO documents, and to try to find the answers to questions in the text itself. It is not an easy job, but, by an old Italian adage, "the Devil is never as ugly as they paint him".

BIBLIOGRAPHY

[ISO7498] ISO7498, Information Processing Systems - Open Systems Interconnection - Basic Reference Model

[ISO8326] ISO8326, Information Processing Systems - Open Systems Interconnection - Basic Connection Oriented Session Service Description.

[ISO8327] ISO8327, Information Processing Systems - Open Systems Interconnection - Basic Connection Oriented Session Protocol Specification.

[LOT1985] ISO DP8807, Information Processing Systems - Open Systems Interconnection - LOTOS - A formal Description Technique Based on the Temporal Ordering of Observational Behaviour.

[LOT1985b] H. Brinksma: "A tutorial on LOTOS", proceedings 5th IFIP wg 6.1 workshop on protocol specification, testing, and verification, North-Holland, Amsterdam, 1985.

[LOT1986] T. Bolognesi, R. De Nicola: "A tutorial on LOTOS" to be published.

Chapter 6
Presentation and Application Protocols

Presentation protocols

The *presentation layer* is concerned with the syntax of the data exchanged between application entities. Its purpose is to resolve differences in format and data representation. The presentation layer defines the syntax used between application entities and provides for the selection and subsequent modification of the representation to be used.

Examples of presentation protocols are teletext and videotex, encryption, and virtual terminal protocol. A virtual terminal protocol converts between specific terminal characteristics and a generic or virtual model used by application programs.

Application protocols

The *application layer* provides a means for application processes to access the OSI environment. This layer contains management functions and generally useful mechanisms to support distributed applications. Examples of protocols at this level are virtual file protocol and job transfer and manipulation protocol.

Summary

"Components of OSI: The Presentation Layer" provides a survey of the concepts embodied in the ISO standards for the session layer.

"ASN.1 and ROS: The Impact of X.400 on OSI" looks at two supporting elements of X.400 that have become key components of OSI. ASN.1 (Abstract Syntax Notation One) is a language for describing the syntax of information. ROS (Remote Operations) is a language for describing application-level interactions between open systems.

"File Transfer Protocols" examines the ISO standard for file transfer, known as File Transfer, Access, and Management (FTAM). "The Development of Office Document Architecture (ODA)" provides an overview of the developing standards for ODA.

"X.400 MHS: First Steps Towards an EDI Communication Standard" provides an overview of two key information exchange standards: X.400 is an electronic mail standard issued in 1984, with a major revision in 1988; EDI (electronic data interchange) is a developing set of standards for the exchange of a wide variety of business forms.

With the increasing emphasis on multimedia, multicasting, and groupware for cooperative information processing, there has been increasing activity to define a model of open distributed processing. The final two papers introduce this topic. "Telecommunication Services and Distributed Applications" discusses some key standardization efforts for distributed applications; it profiles and compares two concepts: distributed processing in ISO and CCITT, and intelligent networks in CCITT. "Distributed Multimedia Information Handling and Processing" discusses the requirements for distributed handling of multimedia information, especially the communication aspects, taking appropriate standards into consideration.

Components of OSI: The Presentation Layer

by David Chappell

Introduction The presentation layer, layer six in the OSI architecture, plays an important role in solving the problem of open networking. Although actually quite simple, this layer's function is often misunderstood. This is due in part to the layer's somewhat misleading name: "presentation" seems to imply that this layer must be responsible for determining how data is "presented" to a human user, e.g., on a terminal screen. In fact, this is not the case (how data is actually shown on a terminal screen is left to each local system in the OSI architecture). A better name for this layer might have been the "representation" layer, since this more accurately describes its function. This function can be stated very simply: the presentation layer is responsible for determining how all data exchanged by its users (i.e., by application entities) will be represented while in transit across the network.

Concepts The need for the presentation layer stems from the heterogeneous computing environment for which OSI is intended. Because different computer systems represent information in different ways, some common representation must be agreed upon before that information can be exchanged. For example, IBM 370 series computers represent characters using EBCDIC, while most other computers use ASCII. To transfer a file of characters from an IBM 370 to an ASCII system, a common representation must be used during the actual transfer. This representation may be EBCDIC, ASCII, or something else. Similarly, integers, floating point values, and other kinds of information may be stored internally in a variety of ways. Some common format must be agreed to before this information can be exchanged. It is the job of the presentation layer to provide a mechanism for reaching this agreement.

Translation If information is represented differently on two communicating systems, one or both must translate from the local form into and out of the standard representation agreed to for communication. In an actual implementation, this may be done by the same software which implements the presentation layer protocol or by software implementing an application layer protocol or both. Where this translation takes place within a computer system is not visible to the outside world (as long as it *does* occur somewhere). It is therefore a local issue and is not subject to standardization.

The presentation layer service and protocol are specified in ISO 8822 and ISO 8823, respectively. Technically identical text is also published as the 1988 CCITT Recommendations X.216 and X.226.

Translating characters from ASCII into EBCDIC may seem like a relatively simple problem. The presentation layer, while providing a means to solve this problem, also allows for solving the more general problem of mapping between differing representations of a much broader range of information. Toward this end, the presentation standards define several abstractions to aid in the solution.

Types and values In thinking about the presentation layer's problem, it is useful to ask: what aspects of the transferred information are preserved? Clearly it is not the actual bits, as they may be changed, e.g., from ASCII to EBCDIC. What is always preserved, however, is the *type* and *value* of the information transferred.

Reprinted with permission from *ConneXions*, Vol. 3, No. 11, November 1989.

17

In the context of OSI's presentation layer, a type may be defined (very informally) as a collection of values distinguished for some reason. Common examples of types includes characters, integers, and floating point (or real) numbers. Every possible value may be considered to be of some type. The value 1, for instance, may be of type "integer," while the value 'A' is of type "character." When information is transferred from one system to another, its representation may change, but its type and its value must be preserved.

Grouping types and values

The example types mentioned so far are all relatively simple. If we admit more complex types into our purview, the problem becomes more difficult. Record types, for example, may be constructed by combining several other types into a single structure. Types of this sort are supported by most high level programming languages. By combining existing types in various ways, a potentially infinite group of types may be created.

Abstract syntaxes

Before two application entities may exchange any information, their supporting presentation entities must reach agreement on how values of all possible types of this exchanged information will be represented. Ideally, every presentation entity would be able to understand and represent all values of every possible type. Because the set of possible types is infinite, however, this is not possible. Instead, types which will be used for a particular instance of communication are grouped into one or more *abstract syntaxes*.

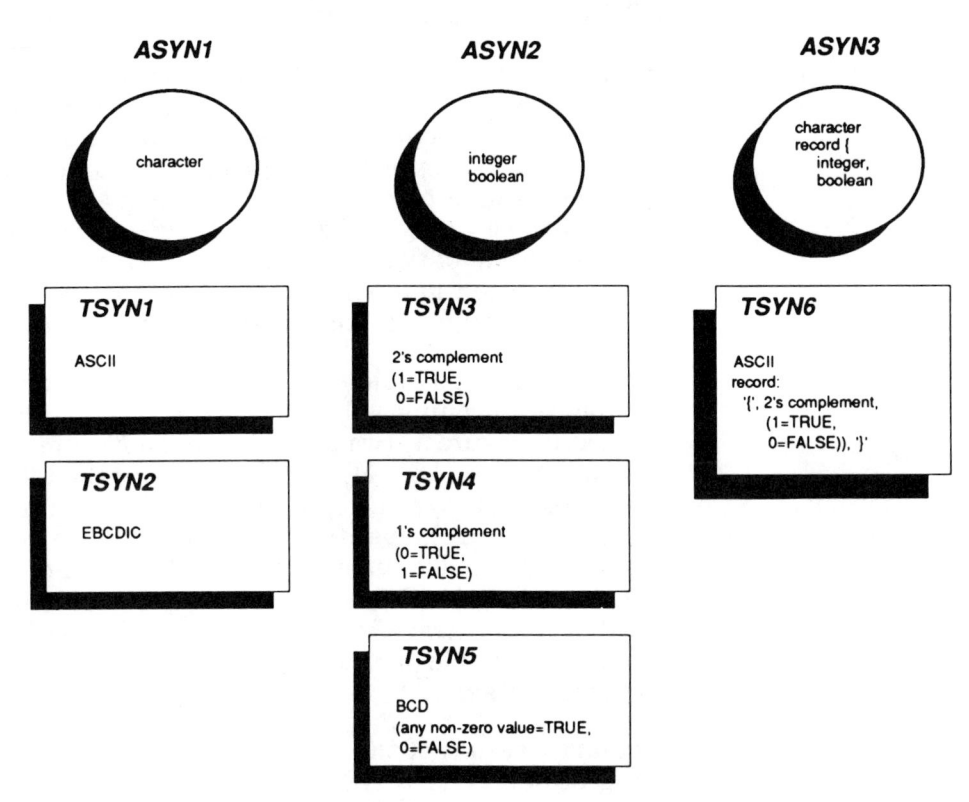

```
       ASYN1              ASYN2                ASYN3

     ( character )      ( integer          ( character
                          boolean )           record {
                                               integer,
                                               boolean )

   TSYN1              TSYN3                TSYN6
   ASCII              2's complement       ASCII
                      (1=TRUE,             record:
                      0=FALSE)              '[', 2's complement,
                                              (1=TRUE,
                                              0=FALSE)), ']'

   TSYN2              TSYN4
   EBCDIC             1's complement
                      (0=TRUE,
                      1=FALSE)

                      TSYN5
                      BCD
                      (any non-zero value=TRUE,
                      0=FALSE)
```

Figure 1: Abstract and Transfer syntaxes

An abstract syntax can be informally thought of as a named group of types. The actual definition, given in ISO 8822, is "the specification of application layer data or application-protocol-control-information by using notation rules which are independent of the encoding technique used to represent them."

The Presentation Layer *(continued)*

As this more formal definition suggests, an abstract syntax merely defines its constituent types—it does not specify how to represent values of those types.

Examples of abstract syntaxes

An abstract syntax may be very simple or very complex. For instance, the abstract syntax called ASYN1, shown at the upper left of Figure 1, contains only the single type "character." The next example, ASYN2, is more complex, containing the types "integer" and "boolean," while the third example, ASYN3, is still more complex, including "character" and a record type containing "integer" and "boolean" elements. (The names assigned to abstract syntaxes are not really character strings; for the moment, however, this simplification is made.)

Note that the same type may occur in more than one abstract syntax—"character," for example, appears in both ASYN1 and ASYN3. Note also that how types are grouped into abstract syntaxes is somewhat arbitrary. We could have combined, say, ASYN1 and ASYN2 into a single abstract syntax, one containing the types "character," "integer," and "boolean." How types are grouped into abstract syntaxes depends on the application at hand. One final point: each type shown in Figure 1 is specified quite informally. In most OSI abstract syntaxes defined so far, the types are specified in a formal language called *Abstract Syntax Notation One* (ASN.1). ASN.1 will be further described in a future issue of *ConneXions*.

Transfer syntaxes

While describing the types to be used by the application entities is useful, it is not enough. As indicated earlier, the primary responsibility of the presentation layer is to determine how values of those types are to be represented during communication. This is achieved by agreeing on a *transfer syntax* for each abstract syntax. A transfer syntax can be thought of as a set of rules for encoding values of some specified group of types, i.e., of some abstract syntax. The term is also sometimes used to describe the actual bit-level representation which results from applying those rules to a particular value.

It is generally possible to define several different transfer syntaxes capable of encoding values of the types contained in any abstract syntax. In Figure 1, two possible transfer syntaxes are shown for the abstract syntax ASYN1. The first, here called TSYN1 (although, as with abstract syntaxes, transfer syntax names are not really character strings), specifies that values of the single type in ASYN1 should be encoded using ASCII. The second possibility, TSYN2, specifies that ASYN1's character values should be encoded using EBCDIC. For a transfer syntax to be usable with an abstract syntax, it must be capable of encoding the values of all types contained in the abstract syntax.

Similarly, values of the types contained in ASYN2 could be encoded using either TSYN3, TSYN4, or TSYN5. For ASYN3, only a single transfer syntax, called TSYN6, is given. Note that, once again, how the encoding rules are grouped together into transfer syntaxes is somewhat arbitrary. While TSYN1 and TSYN2 obviously could not be combined, since they contain two choices for encoding values of a single type, it would be perfectly reasonable to combine TSYN1, TSYN3, and TSYN6 into a single transfer syntax called, say, TSYN99. This new transfer syntax could then be used with any or all of the abstract syntaxes ASYN1, ASYN2, or ASYN3.

Presentation contexts   For each abstract syntax which an application entity wishes to use, exactly one transfer syntax must be selected. (This selection occurs during establishment of the presentation connection, as will be seen later in this article). Each negotiated abstract syntax/transfer syntax pair is called a *presentation context*. All data transferred between two users of the presentation layer (i.e., between two application entities) is contained within some presentation context. The set of presentation contexts which is available at any given time on a presentation connection is known as the *defined context set* (DCS).

Typically, the DCS will contain at least two presentation contexts. For some application layer protocols, or for combinations of those protocols, the DCS may become much larger. To see why this is so, we need to look beyond the simplistic examples of abstract syntaxes given earlier to more realistic examples. One very common example of an abstract syntax is the set of PDUs defined by an application layer protocol. Recall that *all* data exchanged between two presentation users must be part of some presentation context, and thus must be described with an abstract syntax. Perhaps the most important data exchanged by application entities are the PDUs which comprise a particular application protocol, such as FTAM. Each PDU in a particular protocol can be thought of as a value of some type, analogous to a record or structure. The set of all PDUs in some particular application layer protocol, then, comprises a group of types, and thus an abstract syntax. A transfer syntax must be selected for this abstract syntax, and so a presentation context is created.

A second example of an abstract syntax is one describing the data transferred by application entities. Again using FTAM as an example: the contents of every file accessed or transferred by FTAM must be described with an abstract syntax. If the file contains just characters, for example, the abstract syntax ASYN1 from Figure 1 might be used. Since each abstract syntax requires a transfer syntax, each accessed file could potentially have a different presentation context. In any case, distinct presentation contexts are required for the FTAM PDUs and the file's contents.

In some cases, it may not be possible to accurately determine which presentation context is in effect. A *default context* may be defined for these situations. This default may either be negotiated during connection establishment or may by agreed upon *a priori*.

Context management   The initial contents of the DCS are agreed upon during establishment of the presentation connection. In some cases, however, the presentation users may not know all the abstract syntaxes they will need at the time the connection is established. Two users of the FTAM protocol, for example, must agree on an abstract syntax for each file to be transferred or accessed. But they might not learn a file's abstract syntax until the file is opened, which occurs *after* the presentation connection is established. To allow for this possibility, the presentation layer provides *context management*.

The service provided is just what it sounds like: the presentation users can manage, i.e., add to and delete from, the current DCS. Either user can give the presentation layer a new abstract syntax and request it to negotiate a transfer syntax capable of representing that abstract syntax's types.

The Presentation Layer *(continued)*

In other words, either user can request the creation of a new presentation context. Similarly, either user can request the deletion of an existing presentation context from the DCS.

The presentation protocol

The service provided by the presentation layer to its users is quite simple: they are allowed to establish a presentation connection, transfer data across it, and release that connection. Optionally, they may modify the defined context set through context management.

One other group of services is also provided by the presentation layer. These provide a direct pass-through of the session layer's services, allowing an application entity to access those services. This aesthetically unappealing but necessary function occurs because, although the presentation entity is the direct user of all session services, it is not intelligent enough to know how and when to use them. Instead, the application entity (or sometimes the application process itself) must decide when the protocol tools provided by the session layer are used. Because the OSI architecture doesn't allow skipping layers, the presentation service definition contains these pass-through services, allowing application layer access to session services without (technically) violating OSI's strict layering rules.

Establishing connections

Before any information exchange may take place, both systems must agree on which abstract and transfer syntaxes are to be used. This agreement is reached during the establishment of the presentation connection.

Connection initiator

When one application entity wishes to communicate with another, it must first establish a presentation connection between the two systems. To do this, it issues a P-CONNECT request primitive to its supporting presentation entity (see Figure 2). Among the various parameters associated with this primitive is the list of abstract syntax names which it wishes to use on this connection. Only the names of predefined abstract syntaxes may be passed; it is not possible to define a new abstract syntax dynamically.

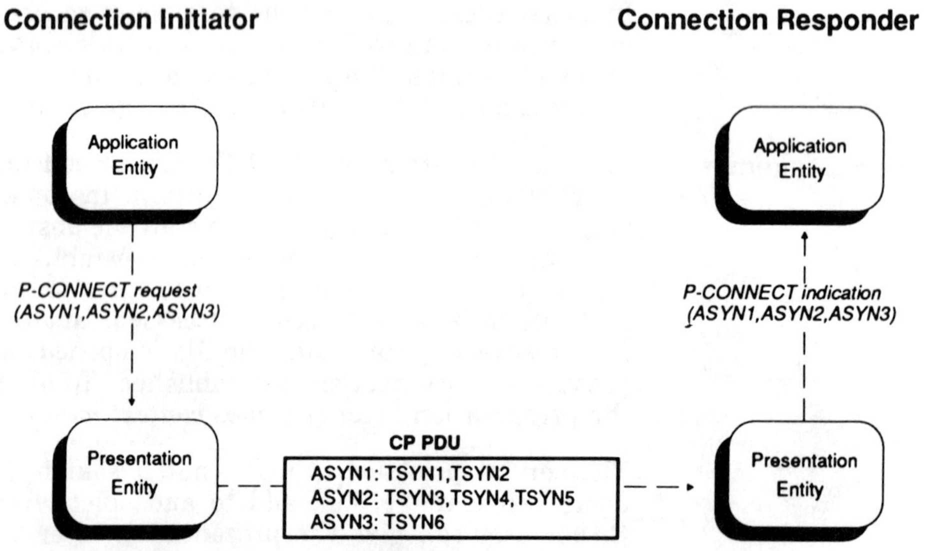

Figure 2: Establishing a presentation connection

An application entity could, for example, issue a P-CONNECT request indicating the abstract syntaxes ASYN1, ASYN2, and ASYN3.

The supporting presentation entity which receives this P-CONNECT request must determine which transfer syntaxes it can use to represent information from each of the specified abstract syntaxes. It then sends a CP PDU to its peer presentation entity indicating both the requested abstract syntaxes and the transfer syntaxes it is willing to support for each abstract syntax. (Any necessary lower layer connections must also be established before this PDU is sent.) For instance, transfer syntaxes TSYN1 and TSYN2 may be listed for ASYN1, TSYN3, TSYN4, and TSYN5 for ASYN2, and TSYN6 for ASYN3.

(An important note: this is an architectural description. Although the protocol exchanges must remain unchanged, an implementor is free to implement the presentation/application layer interface any way he or she chooses. In fact, a real implementation isn't even required to contain a neat software interface between the two layers.)

Connection responder   Upon receipt of a CP PDU, the responding presentation entity must issue a P-CONNECT indication primitive to the application entity above (also shown in Figure 2). It includes among the parameters of this primitive the names of the abstract syntaxes contained in the CP PDU. The responding application entity then responds with a P-CONNECT response primitive (see Figure 3), again containing the names of the abstract syntaxes it is willing to use. These abstract syntax names must include all or a subset of those found on the P-CONNECT indication. Note once again that only *names* are used for both abstract and transfer syntaxes; no mechanism currently exists for describing new syntaxes during connection establishment.

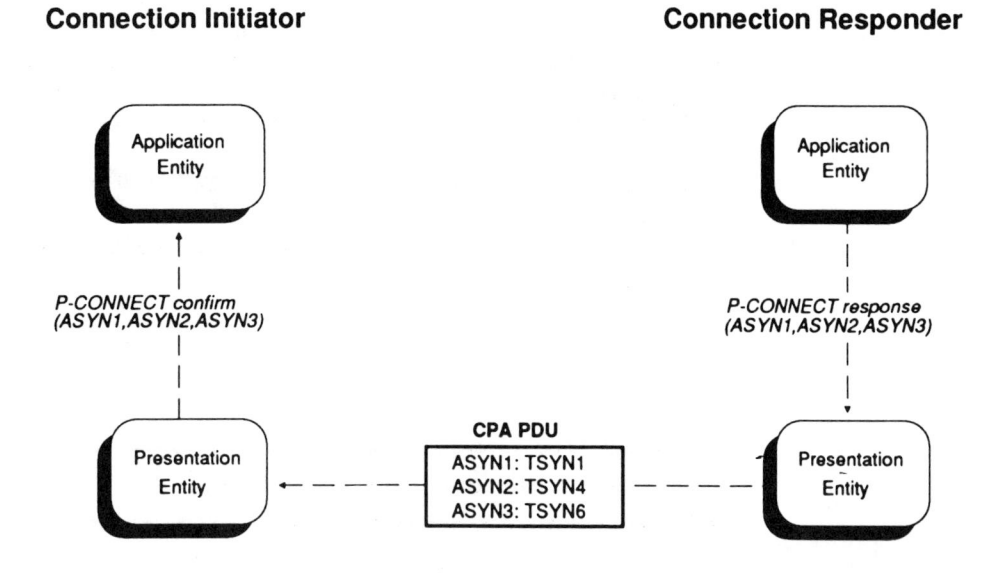

Figure 3: Establishing a presentation connection (continued)

The Presentation Layer *(continued)*

The responding presentation entity, after receiving the P-CONNECT response accepting the presentation connection, must build and send a CPA PDU. On this PDU it indicates which of the proposed transfer syntaxes it has chosen for each selected abstract syntax. For example, the responding presentation entity may choose TSYN1 for ASYN1, TSYN4 for ASYN2, and TSYN6 for ASYN3.

The initiating presentation entity must accept these choices. It also, upon receipt of the CPA PDU, indicates the chosen abstract syntaxes as parameters on the final primitive in this sequence, P-CONNECT confirm, which is given to the initiating application entity. Once this exchange is complete, several things have been accomplished:

- A presentation connection has been established;

- The application entities have negotiated which abstract syntaxes they wish to use, i.e., they have agreed on the types of data they will exchange during this communication;

- The presentation entities have negotiated a representation, a transfer syntax, for each abstract syntax selected by the application entities.

Transferring data

All data transferred in presentation PDUs is always encoded using the agreed transfer syntax for the data's presentation context. In general, each unit of information to be transferred is considered a presentation data value (PDV). The type of this value must appear in at least one of the abstract syntaxes available in the defined context set. PDVs are then grouped into PDV-lists, each containing one or more PDVs from the same presentation context (and thus the same abstract syntax), encoded according to that context's transfer syntax. Each encoded PDV-list begins with a presentation context identifier (PCI), a unique integer value assigned to each presentation context during connection establishment. The PCI allows the receiver to identify this data's presentation context and thus correctly decode the incoming information. A single instance of presentation user data may contain several encoded PDV-lists, and thereby convey information in several different presentation contexts at once.

A simplified diagram of this appears in Figure 4. Two encoded PDV-lists are shown, each with its own presentation context identifier (PCI) and encoded presentation data values.

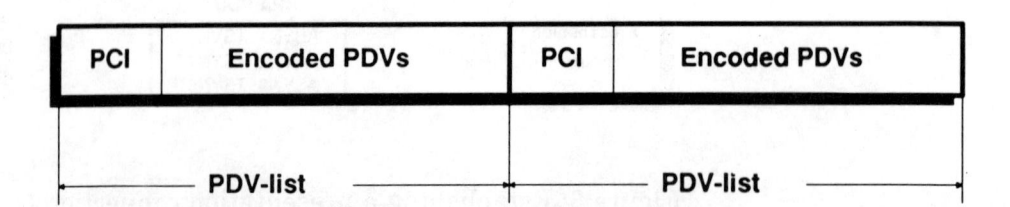

PCI	Encoded PDVs	PCI	Encoded PDVs
← PDV-list →	← PDV-list →

Figure 4: Presentation user data

Releasing connections The presentation protocol provides three ways to release a connection: orderly release, user abort, and provider abort. If a presentation user wishes to ensure that no data is lost during connection release, that user will choose the orderly release option. In some cases, however, the presentation user may not care whether any data is lost, wishing instead just to end the communication. In this situation, that user may issue a user abort service, abruptly ending the presentation connection and possibly losing some of the data currently in transit. Finally, one or both of the presentation entities may detect some anomaly or error in communication. If this occurs, the provider of the presentation service (i.e., the presentation entities themselves) will indicate to their users that a provider abort has occurred and the presentation connection is gone.

Conclusion The OSI presentation protocol itself is very straightforward, with none of the complex timers, flow control mechanisms, and retransmission schemes found in the lower layers. The concepts embodied in the layer's operation, however, are not so simple, and neither is the construction of software to implement this protocol and the associated encoding/decoding functions. And yet, by freeing application layer protocols from concern with the representation of transferred information, the presentation layer is nevertheless an important piece in the structure of OSI.

Copyright © 1989 by David Chappell. All rights reserved. Used with permission.

DAVID CHAPPELL has been active in the design and implementation of OSI protocols for the past several years as a software engineer with NCR Corporation and Cray Research. He has also been an active participant in the NIST OSI Workshops, and currently chairs the Workshop's Upper Layers Special Interest Group. David holds an M.S. in computer science from the University of Wisconsin, and now spends most of his time writing, consulting, and teaching about OSI and related topics.

Host Requirements RFCs have arrived!

The long awaited Host Requirements RFCs are now available from the Network Information Center in the online library at NIC.DDN.MIL.

RFC 1122: Requirements for Internet Hosts—Communication Layers. This RFC is an official specification for the Internet community. It incorporates by reference, amends, corrects, and supplements the primary protocol standards documents relating to hosts.

RFC 1123: Requirements for Internet Hosts—Application and Support. This RFC is an official specification for the Internet community. It incorporates by reference, amends, corrects, and supplements the primary protocol standards documents relating to hosts. Distribution of these documents is unlimited.

Getting RFCs RFCs can be obtained by anonymous FTP from NIC.DDN.MIL, with the pathname RFC:RFCnnnn.TXT (where "nnnn" refers to the number of the RFC). The NIC also provides an automatic mail service for those sites which cannot use FTP. Address the request to SERVICE@NIC.DDN.MIL and in the subject field of the message indicate the RFC number, as in "Subject: RFC 1122."

ASN.1 and ROS: The Impact of X.400 on OSI

JAMES E. WHITE, MEMBER, IEEE

Abstract—The X.400 standards are universally accepted worldwide as the basis for interconnecting electronic mail systems. Additionally, the two major supporting elements of X.400, Abstract Syntax Notation One (ASN.1) and Remote Operations (ROS), have profoundly affected the course of OSI in general. This paper describes these two technologies. It also briefly recounts their history, summarizes their impact upon OSI to date, and speculates on their future importance.

I. INTRODUCTION

IN 1981, a number of office equipment vendors, computer manufacturers, and value-added telecommunication service providers began work on what was to become a comprehensive set of technical specifications for interconnecting electronic mail systems. They did this work under the auspices of the Consultative Committee for International Telegraphy and Telephony (CCITT), the standards-making body for the world's Postal, Telegraph, and Telephone administrations (the PTT's). In 1984, the CCITT approved the results of this work as a series of eight documents called the X.400-series Recommendations (X.400 for short). During the years 1985-1988, X.400 was functionally extended, editorially rewritten, and in 1988, reissued jointly with the International Standards Organization (ISO), the other major international standards body in the field and the source of much of the work on Open Systems Interconnection (OSI).

Since its introduction in 1984, X.400 has gained virtually universal acceptance throughout the electronic mail industry. Even more importantly in some respects, X.400 has had a profound effect upon the course of OSI generally. This effect is due to the widespread acceptance, in virtually all other realms of OSI standardization, of two major supporting elements of the X.400 architecture. The first is Abstract Syntax Notation One (ASN.1), the other Remote Operations (ROS).

ASN.1 and ROS, and their impact upon OSI, are the subjects of this paper. Section II describes the former, Section III the latter. The final section of the paper, Section IV, briefly recounts their history, summarizes their impact upon OSI to date, and speculates on their future importance.

II. ABSTRACT SYNTAX NOTATION ONE

Abstract Syntax Notation One (ASN.1) is best understood as the data declaration portion of a high-level computer programming language (HLL) such as C or Pascal. Its purpose, among those of any HLL, is to elevate the description of complex data structures to a level of abstraction unachievable by less powerful or less formal means [e.g., the graphical depiction of data structures as individual bits or bytes (octets)]. The data definition capabilities of a typical HLL are used to define the data structures, e.g., to be maintained as local or global variables or to be passed as parameters of a procedure. ASN.1, on the other hand, is used primarily to define the data structures two open systems exchange to effect a particular information processing task (e.g., the relay between systems of an electronic message). In the vernacular of OSI, such data structures are called *application protocol data units* (APDU's). Thus, ASN.1 is an HLL for the specification of application protocols.

A typical HLL treats the octet-level representation of data structures as an internal design issue. Whether integers are stored in twos or ones complement form, e.g., is usually unimportant and unknown to the programmer. Indeed, the fact that the HLL hides such details from him is among the reasons he selects an HLL over assembly or machine language. Furthermore, an HLL implemented on several hardware engines may represent a particular data structure in different ways on those various machines.

An HLL for the specification of application protocols must meet somewhat different requirements. While insulating the application protocol designer (like the programmer) from representational details is among them, those details cannot vary from one implementation of the language to another because they represent the basis for communication between diverse machines. ASN.1, therefore, is supplemented by standard rules for representing data structures as sequences of octets.

Among the most fundamental concepts of ASN.1 (as of many HLL's) are those of type and value. A *value* is a particular data structure or information item (e.g., the integer 409). A *type* is a set or class of one or more values (e.g., all integers). A *subtype* is a type that is a subset of another type (e.g., just the integers 208, 209, and 409). The ASN.1 specifications define a number of *built-in types*. They also define a number of tools with which the ASN.1 user can define other, *constructed types*. These tools are of two kinds, type and subtype constructors. A *type constructor* is a tool for defining a type that encompasses values beyond those of any or any one other type. A *subtype constructor* is a tool for defining a type that encompasses only a subset of the values of another, parent type.

Note: The terms "built-in type," "constructed type," and "subtype constructor" do not appear in the ASN.1

Manuscript received May 15, 1988; revised March 1, 1989.
The author is with RAPPORT Communication, Palo Alto, CA 94306.
IEEE Log Number 8929564.

Reprinted from *IEEE Journal on Selected Areas in Communications*, September 1989, pp. 1060–1072. ©1989 by The Institute of Electrical and Electronics Engineers, Inc. All rights reserved.

specifications, although the concepts they denote do. The term "type constructor," on the other hand, is used, but not as precisely as might be desired. In particular, the distinction between a type constructor and the types defined by means of it is not always upheld.

The following sections overview ASN.1. They begin by describing the built-in types and the type and subtype constructors from which other types can be developed. They continue by describing the rules for representing values as sequences of octets, taking up as a preliminary the related subject of tagging, and by touching upon the ASN.1 notation itself. They conclude by discussing two aspects of ASN.1 of unique importance, Object identifiers and macros. Throughout, the term *user* denotes a person who employs the notation in protocol design.

A. Built-in Types

The built-in types of ASN.1 are listed in Table I and described below. As the table shows, each type falls into one of two categories, depending upon the method of its definition. The *simple* built-in types are notationally integral to ASN.1, while the *useful* built-in types are defined by means of type constructors.

Several built-in-types have logical, numerical, or temporal values. The *Boolean* type comprises two values, *true* and *false*. The *Integer* type comprises the integers. The user can name one or more integer values for notational purposes. The *Real* type comprises a subset of the real numbers, along with plus and minus infinity. The *Time* type comprises points in time. Each value is a date and time, the latter expressed as local time, Greenwich Mean time, or both. The range of dates the type encompasses and the precision with which times can be expressed are limited by other international standards upon which ASN.1 depends for this type's definition. There are actually two Time types—*Generalized* and *Universal Time*—which differ in these various respects.

Several built-in types have variable-length strings as their values. The *Bit String* type comprises the ordered sequences of zero or more bits. The user can name one or more bits for notational purposes. The *Octet String* type comprises the ordered sequences of zero or more octets. The *Character String* type comprises the ordered sequences of zero or more characters. There are actually several Character String types—*General, Graphic, IA5, Numeric, Printable, Teletex, Videotex,* and *Visible String*—which limit their values to different character sets.

Several built-in types enable the worldwide identification of both standard and user-defined information object classes (e.g., the contents of all messages exchangeable in a particular application, e.g., Interpersonal Messaging). The *Object Identifier* type comprises the globally unambiguous and unique names of those classes (see Section II-G). The *Object Descriptor* type comprises the classes' textual descriptions, which are not necessarily unambiguous. The *External* type comprises the instances of the classes (e.g., a particular interpersonal message),

TABLE I
ASN.1 BUILT-IN TYPES

Simple Types	Useful Types
Any	External
Bit String	Object Descriptor
Boolean	Time
Character String	
Integer	
Null	
Object Identifier	
Octet String	
Real	

each accompanied by the Object Identifier and Object Descriptor (if any) assigned to its class.

The *Null* built-in type comprises a single value, *null*. In practice, it sometimes appears among the alternative types of a Choice or the optional element or member types of a Sequence or Set, respectively (see Section II-B). In every case, *null* conveys information by its very presence.

The *Any* built-in type comprises the values of another, *subject* type which the user does not immediately specify and which may vary from one instance of communication to another. If Any is among the element or member types of a Sequence or Set, respectively, the user may designate another of those types, which must be Integer or Object Identifier and not optional, as identifying by its value the subject type.

B. Type Constructors

The type constructors of ASN.1 are listed in Table II and described below.

The *Enumerated* type constructor enables the user to define a type comprising one or more previously undefined values, which he names (for notational purposes) and numbers (for encoding purposes).

The *Choice* type constructor enables the user to define a type that is the set union of one or more specified *alternative* types with distinct tags (see Section II-D). ASN.1 provides notation (which it somewhat misleadingly calls *Selection* type notation) for referring to a particular alternative type.

Two type constructors enable the user to define a type whose values are *ordered* collections of values, in one case homogeneous, in the other possibly heterogeneous. Using the *Sequence Of* type constructor, the user specifies a single, *element* type, and each collection comprises any number of values of that type. The user may attach significance to the order of those values. Using the *Sequence* type constructor, the user specifies an ordered set of zero or more (n) element types which need not all be distinct. Notation is provided for including among the element types of one Sequence type those of another. In the simplest case, the number of values in each collection is n, and the ith value is of the ith type, for i in $[1, n]$. In more complex cases, the user declares one or more types *optional*, and those types need not be represented among the values. One or several consecutive types may be designated optional if and only if their tags and that of the next type, if any, are distinct. The user can associate a default

TABLE II
ASN.1 TYPE CONSTRUCTORS

Choice
Enumerated
Sequence
Sequence Of
Set
Set Of
Tagged

TABLE III
ASN.1 SUBTYPE CONSTRUCTORS

Contained Subtype
Inner Subtyping
Permitted Alphabet
Single Value
Size Constraint
Value Range

value, serving both notational and encoding purposes, with an optional element type.

Two type constructors enable the user to define a type whose values are *unordered* collections of values, in one case homogeneous, in the other possibly heterogeneous. Using the *Set Of* type constructor, the user specifies a single, *member* type, and each collection comprises any number of values of that type. The user may not attach significance to the order of those values. Using the *Set* type constructor, the user specifies zero or more (n) member types with distinct tags. Notation is provided for including among the member types of one Set type those of another. In the simplest case, the number of values in each collection is n, and each type is represented exactly once among them. In more complex cases, the user declares one or more types *optional*, and those types need not be represented among the values. The user can associate a default value, serving both notational and encoding purposes, with an optional member type.

The *Tagged* type constructor enables the user to define a type that differs from a specified *subject* type only by virtue of its tag. The user specifies the tag and the mode of tagging (see Section II-D).

C. Subtype Constructors

The subtype constructors are listed in Table III and described below. A subtype is actually defined by one or more *subtype specifications*, each comprising one or more subtype constructors. Each of the latter nominates values of the parent type for inclusion in the subtype. A subtype specification nominates for inclusion the set union of the values nominated by its subtype constructors. The subtype comprises the set intersection of the values nominated by the subtype specifications.

Several subtype constructors are provided. The *Single Value* constructor nominates a single, specified value. The *Contained Subtype* constructor nominates a specified subtype. Provided the parent type is Integer or Real, the *Value Range* constructor nominates the values in a specified open, partially open, or closed interval. Notation is provided for symbolically designating as one of the two end points of the interval either the smallest or largest value of the parent type. Provided the parent type is Character String, the *Permitted Alphabet* constructor nominates the values formed using only specified characters, which the user designates by identifying a subtype of the type comprising the Character String values one character in length. Provided the parent type is Bit, Octet, or Character String, or a Sequence Of or Set Of type, the *Size Constraint* constructor nominates values constrained to specified lengths, which the user designates by identifying a subtype of the type comprising the nonnegative Integer values. The unit of length is understood to be the bit, octet, character, or element or member value, depending upon the parent type. The *Inner Subtyping* constructor has several variants, each applicable to one or more parent types. If the parent type is a Sequence Of or Set Of type, it nominates the type derived from the parent type by constraining its element or member type, respectively, is a specified subtype. If the parent type is a Sequence or Set type, it nominates the type derived from the parent type by constraining each of one or more specified element or member types, respectively, to a specified subtype, to be present or absent if optional, or both. If the parent type is a Choice type, it nominates the type derived from the parent type by constraining to a specified subtype, or excluding entirely, each of one or more specified alternative types.

D. Tagging

Associated with each ASN.1 type, whether defined by the user or ASN.1, is a descriptor called a *tag* (in the case of the Any and Choice types, a set of tags) that uniquely but not necessarily unambiguously identifies that type. The encoding rules for each type require the incorporation of its tag in the encoding of each of its values. To the extent that they are unambiguous, therefore, tags provide a basis for distinguishing at run-time values of one type from values of another. ASN.1 assigns tags to the built-in types and to the types defined by means of type constructors (other than Tagged). It also provides a tool, the Tagged type constructor, with which a user can assign, to any or all of the types he defines, tags that both uniquely and unambiguously identify those types throughout any of several domains of his choosing.

A tag has two parts, its class and number. A tag's *class*, of which four are defined, determines the domain or scope of its *number*, which is a nonnegative integer. *Universal* tags are assigned within the ASN.1 specifications themselves. A distinct tag is assigned to each built-in type except Any (which inherits the tags of its possible subject types), to the Enumerated types collectively, to the Sequence Of and Sequence types collectively, and to the Set Of and Set types collectively. (A Choice type inherits the tags of its alternative types.) Users assign tags of the other classes to the types they define using the Tagged type constructor. *Application* tags vary in meaning from one module (see Section II-F) to another, *private* tags from one assigning organization to another, and *context-specific* tags from one arbitrarily defined context to another, typically that formed by the alternative, element, or member types of a Choice, Sequence, or Set type, respectively.

Using the Tagged type constructor, one can select from among two *modes* of tagging, *explicit* and *implicit*, which determine whether a value's encoding retains or discards, respectively, the subject type's tag.

E. Basic Encoding Rules

The *basic encoding rules* (BER) provide a means for representing any value of any type as a sequence of octets. In principle, other, alternative encoding rules could be defined but this has not been done.

Encoding rules serve several purposes. First and foremost, they define a *transfer syntax* for values, allowing them to be communicated between open systems. Second, they provide a basis for defining computations upon values, computations of the kind required, e.g., for the generation and verification of digital signatures. For encoding rules to adequately serve this second purpose, they must prescribe a single encoding for every value, i.e., the encodings must be unique. Because the BER do not yield unique encodings, both the Message Handling and Directory Recommendations impose (the same) additional encoding constraints in the context of the provision of various security services which they define and standardize. The constraints effectively define a normalized or canonical encoding of every value. (For historical reasons alone, these canonical encodings are presently defined in joint CCITT-ISO standards for directories, but are more properly a part of ASN.1 itself.)

The basic encoding of every value has three and possibly four parts, the identifier, length, contents, and end-of-contents octets. The *identifier* octets encode the value's tag and thus its type, and signal which of two possible forms the contents octets take. The *length* octets indicate how the final octet of the encoding is located. The *contents* octets encode the value itself so that it can be distinguished from other values of the same type. The *end-of-contents* octets, if present as required by one form of the length octets, mark the end of the encoding.

The identifier octets, depicted in Fig. 1, take either of two forms, short and long. The *short* form comprises a single octet that encodes tag numbers from zero to 30. The *long* form comprises two or more octets that encode tag numbers 31 and greater, without limitation. All types ASN.1 defines, and virtually all types defined in practice using the Tagged type constructor, employ the short form.

The length octets, depicted in Fig. 2, take either of three forms, short, long, and indefinite. The *short* form comprises a single octet that encodes the number of contents octets, provided that that number is from zero to 127. The *long* form comprises two or more octets that encode the number of contents octets, whatever that number (without practical limitation and including numbers from zero to 127). The *indefinite* form comprises a single, fixed octet that signals the presence in the encoding of the end-of-contents octets. This last form may be employed only in connection with the constructed form of the contents octets (see below).

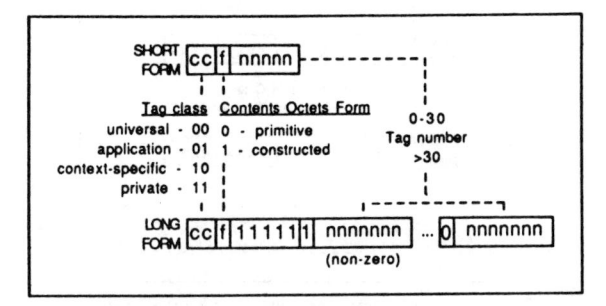

Fig. 1. Identifier octets as prescribed by the BER.

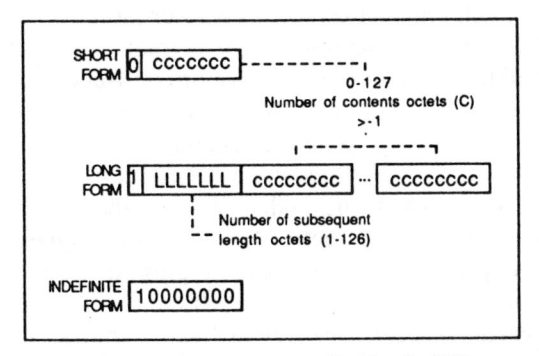

Fig. 2. Length octets as prescribed by the BER.

The contents octets, depicted in Fig. 3, take either of two forms, primitive and constructed. The *primitive* form comprises zero or more octets whose meaning depends upon the type of the encoded value. The *constructed* form comprises the encodings of zero or more other values whose meaning depends upon the type of the encoded value. (In the case of a Sequence type, e.g., each value is of one of its element types.) The constructed form thus makes the definition of encodings, in general, recursive.

For some types, the BER define only primitive or constructed forms of the contents octets. The Boolean, Integer, Real, Object Identifier, Null, and Enumerated types have only primitive forms; the Sequence Of, Sequence, Set Of, Set, and External types have only constructed forms.

For other types, the BER define both primitive and constructed forms of the contents octets. This is so for the Bit String type. In the latter case, those octets are the encodings of zero or more Bit String values, each representing a segment of the overall bit string. Each segment except possibly the last comprises a multiple (possibly zero) of eight bits. The Bit String value representing a segment may itself be encoded using either the primitive or constructed form of the contents octets, i.e., a segment may itself be segmented, recursively. Segment boundaries are an artifact of the encoding and have no semantics.

The BER also define both primitive and constructed forms of the contents octets for the Octet String type (as well as the Time, Character String, and Object Descriptor types, all of whose values are strings). In the latter case, those octets are the encodings of zero or more Octet String values, each representing a segment of the overall octet

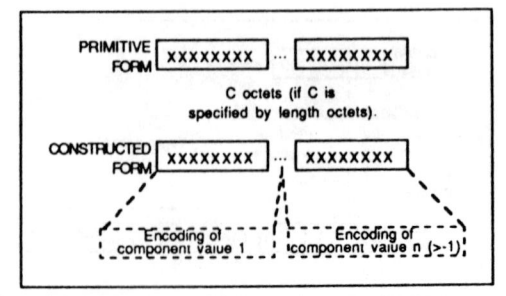

Fig. 3. Contents octets as prescribed by the BER.

Fig. 4. End-of-contents octets (when present) as prescribed by the BER.

```
ExtensionField ::= SEQUENCE {
    type        [0] ExtensionType,
    criticality [1] Criticality DEFAULT {},
    value       [2] ANY DEFINED BY type DEFAULT NULL NULL }

ExtensionType ::= INTEGER (0..ub-extension-types)

Criticality ::= BIT STRING {
    for-submission (0),
    for-transfer   (1),
    for-delivery   (2) }
    (SIZE (0..ub-bit-options))

ub-extension-types INTEGER ::= 256
ub-bit-options INTEGER ::= 16
```

Listing 1. Examples of the ASN.1 definition of types and values.

string. Each segment comprises zero or more octets. The Octet String value representing a segment may itself be encoded using either the primitive or constructed form of the contents octets, i.e., a segment may itself be segmented, recursively. Segment boundaries, here again, are an artifact of the encoding and have no semantics.

The BER also define both primitive and constructed forms of the contents octets for the Tagged types. The choice depends upon the mode of tagging and possibly the value of the subject type selected. If the mode is explicit, the contents octets are constructed and comprise the (entire) encoding of the selected value. If the mode is implicit, the contents octets are primitive or constructed, depending upon the subject type, and are (only) the contents octets of the value's encoding.

When present the end-of-contents octets, depicted in Fig. 4, comprise two zero octets which may be interpreted as the encoding of a value of a fictitious type with the universal tag whose value is zero (which is not otherwise assigned) and whose contents octets are zero in number and of the primitive form.

A value of the Any type is encoded as dictated by its subject type, a value of a Choice type as dictated by the selected alternative type.

F. Notation

A detailed exposition of the ASN.1 notation is beyond the scope of this paper. Briefly, however, it enables the user to reference all built-in types and all of their values; reference all types (and all of their values) constructable with the type and subtype constructors; assign names to types and values, built-in or constructed; employ such names in constructed types; assemble such assignments into named collections called *modules* (modules are named by Object Identifier values); make certain type and value names but not others accessible to modules other than those that define them (a result achieved in two steps called *exporting* and *importing*); annotate a module by means of textual insertions called *comments*; and specify the default tagging mode for a module. The notation also allows its own extension (see Section II-H).

An example of the use of the notation to define both types and values is found in Listing 1. Three types are assigned the names **ExtensionField, ExtensionType,** and **Criticality**, respectively. Two values are assigned the names **ub-extension-types** and **ub-bit-options**, respectively. Collectively, these assignments define the structure of a field of the electronic envelope employed in X.400's P1 protocol.

The type named **ExtensionField** is a Sequence type having three member types which are assigned the names **type, criticality,** and **value**, respectively. The first identifies the service that the field requests and is mandatory. The second indicates whether that service is critical to the message's submission, transfer, delivery, or a combination of these transmittal steps; it is optional and has a default value signifying that the service is completely non-critical. The third parameterizes the service request as necessary; it, too, is optional and has as its default value the (one) value of type Null. All three element types are Tagged types to which the context-specific tags numbered zero, one, and two, respectively, are assigned. Their subject types are that named **ExtensionType**, that named **Criticality**, and Any, respectively. The subject type to which the Any type is bound in a particular instance of communication is identified by the value of the element type named **type**.

The type named **ExtensionType** is that subtype of Integer comprising the integers in the closed interval beginning with zero and ending with the value named **ub-extension-types**.

The type named **Criticality** is that subtype of Bit String comprising values whose lengths in bits are in the closed interval beginning with zero and ending with the Integer value named **ub-bit-options**. The first three bits of the bit string (numbered zero, one, and two), those with meaning in the present version of P1, are assigned names reflecting their purpose, namely, **for-submission, for-transfer**, and **for-delivery**. Setting one of these bits to one signifies that the requested service is critical for the corresponding transmittal step.

Each of the two named values, **ub-extension-types** and **ub-bit-options**, is of type Integer. They determine the precise upper bounds imposed upon, respectively, the Integer that identifies the service requested and the length of the Bit String that documents criticality.

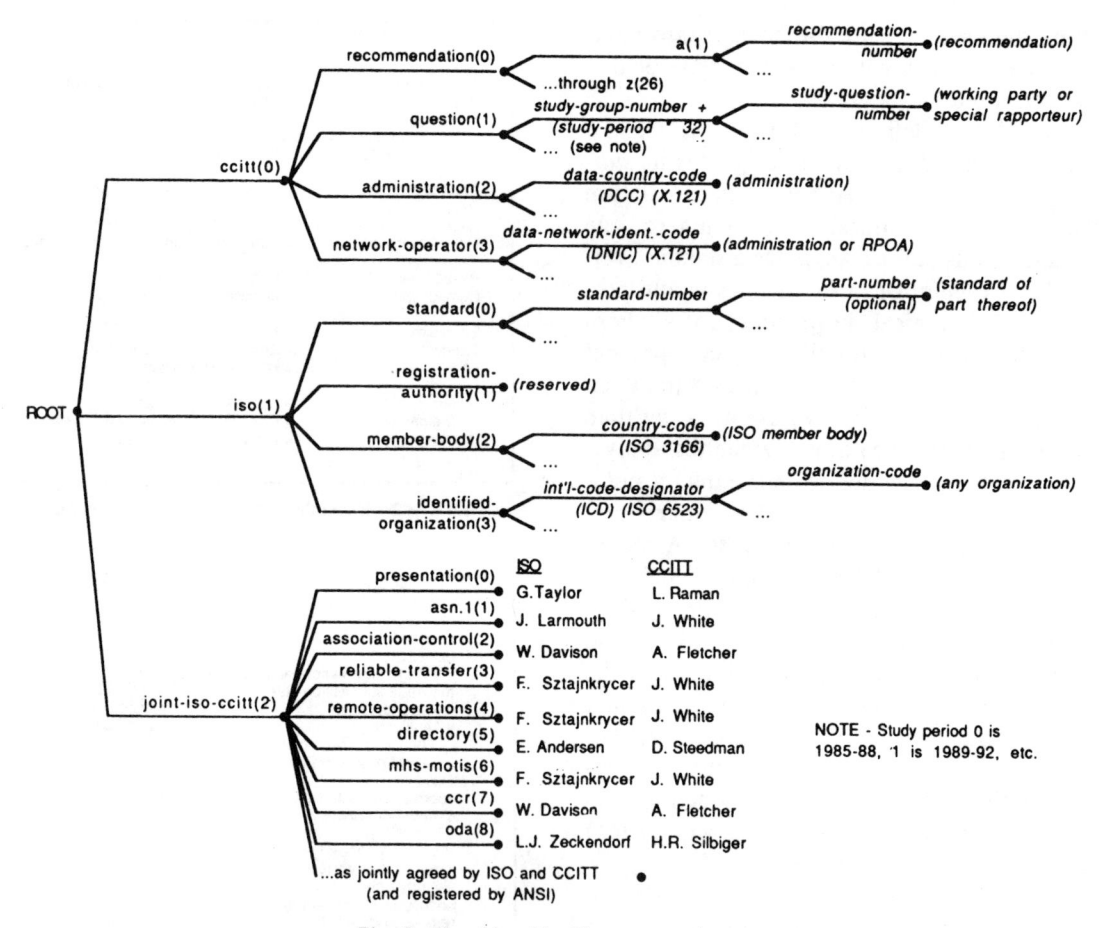

Fig. 5. The object identifier tree near its root.

Note: Rather than refer directly to the type named **ExtensionType**, the type named **ExtensionField**—as actually defined in X.400—invokes a macro (see Section II-H) that provides nonstandard notation for that type.

G. Object Identifiers

As mentioned in Section II-A, the ASN.1 specifications define a type that comprises the globally unambiguous and unique names of classes of information object. This type, Object Identifier, is defined by means of an administrative hierarchy called the *object identifier tree*. Each vertex of the tree denotes a class of information object, an administrative authority, or both (the latter being rare in practice). In typical practice, leaf vertices represent classes, interior vertices authorities. Initially a leaf, each administrative authority can create new growth beneath it by defining vertices subordinate to its own. An integer labels each arc of the tree, and each vertex can be considered to be named by the ordered set of integers that identifies the oriented path from the root to that vertex. The Object Identifier type comprises the names of all of the tree's vertices except the root and its immediately subordinate vertices (including, strictly speaking, the vertices that represent only administrative authorities).

The root of the object identifier tree represents the ASN.1 specifications themselves. ASN.1 defines three subordinate vertices, one representing CCITT alone, another ISO alone, and a third CCITT and ISO jointly. CCITT has defined additional nodes subordinate to its own, ISO has done likewise, and the two international standards bodies together have defined vertices subordinate to their joint vertex for the areas of standardization in which they collaborate. The object identifier tree that has resulted from this process to date is shown in Fig. 5. For each arc, the figure indicates either its integer label and an equivalent mneumonic serving notational purposes or a description of the manner in which the integer label is determined. For each leaf vertex, the figure identifies the naming authority it represents. From the figure one can discern, e.g., that any CCITT Recommendation or ISO International Standard can assign Object Identifier values, further extending the tree. More significantly, any organization whatsoever—a manufacturer, e.g.—can obtain a place in the tree by way of the ISO branch, thereby acquiring the ability to assign Object Identifier values itself.

The phase "class of information object" is intended to be very broadly construed. It encompasses, e.g., classes with single members, j.e., individual information objects.

H. Macros

ASN.1 permits its own extension. It does so by enabling a user to define alternative, nonstandard notation for referencing a particular type, its values, or both. Once he has done this, the user may use the nonstandard notation wherever the standard notation for that type or one of its values is permitted.

Users extend ASN.1 by defining and using *macros*. To define a macro, one assigns it a name, designates its *subject* type, and specifies in detail the nonstandard notation desired for that type and its values. To use a macro, one employs the notation thus defined anyplace a standard reference to the subject type or one of its values would otherwise be required. It is typical, in practice, for a macro to define nonstandard notation for the subject type, but not for its values. It is further typical for a user to attach semantics to a macro and, therefore, to use it, rather than the standard notation, only when those semantics apply.

In a macro definition, a user defines nonstandard notation for a type and its values using Backus–Naur Form (BNF), extended specifically for this purpose. A macro definition comprises two main BNF productions and zero or more supporting productions. The first main production has the phrase "TYPE NOTATION" as its left-hand side and defines the nonstandard type notation, with the exception of its first token, which is the macro's name. The second main production has the phrase "VALUE NOTATION" as its left-hand side and defines the nonstandard value notation. The supporting productions define any nonterminals used in the main (or supporting) productions and not built into the BNF.

Two extensions to BNF enable other ASN.1 types and values to be used in a macro definition. First, the user may embed one or more type or value assignments at any point in the BNF. Second, he may employ either or both of two ASN.1-specific nonterminals. The first stands for a reference, standard or otherwise, to any ASN.1 type, the second for a reference, standard or otherwise, to any value of a specified type. The macro definition may assign a name to the particular type or value that is referenced in a particular use of the macro (the use under scrutiny).

The association between a name and a type or value is made at the point in the parse of the nonstandard type or value notation at which the assignment is embedded or the type or value reference recognized. For this purpose, the parse of the type notation is considered to immediately precede each parse of the value notation. The associations made during the former, therefore, are in effect at the onset of the latter. A macro definition can redefine a name, and all associations are strictly local to the macro definition and have no effect outside of it.

Exactly once during the parse of each instance of the nonstandard value notation, the distinguished name "VALUE" must be associated with a value. It is the type of this value that is the macro's subject type. (In its most general form, a macro definition can nominate each of several types as the subject type. In such a situation, the subject type is the Choice type whose alternative types are the types nominated, if their tags are distinct, and the Any type otherwise.)

In addition to the capabilities of Section II-F, the ASN.1 notation enables the user to include the definition of a ma-

```
OPERATION MACRO ::=
BEGIN

TYPE NOTATION        ::= Argument Result Errors LinkedOperations
VALUE NOTATION       ::= value (VALUE
    CHOICE {
        localValue  INTEGER,
        globalValue OBJECT IDENTIFIER } )

Argument             ::= "ARGUMENT" NamedType | empty
Result               ::= "RESULT" ResultType | empty
Errors               ::= "ERRORS" "{" ErrorNames "}" | empty
LinkedOperations     ::= "LINKED" "{" LinkedOperationNames "}" | empty

ResultType           ::= NamedType | empty
NamedType            ::= identifier type | type

ErrorNames           ::= ErrorList | empty
ErrorList            ::= Error | ErrorList "," Error
Error                ::= value (ERROR) | type

LinkedOperationNames ::= OperationList | empty
OperationList        ::= Operation | OperationList "," Operation
Operation            ::= value (OPERATION) | type

END
```
Listing 2. Example of the ASN.1 definition of macros.

```
message-submission OPERATION
    ARGUMENT SEQUENCE {
        envelope                    MessageSubmissionEnvelope,
        content                     Content }
    RESULT SET {
        message-submission-identifier  MessageSubmissionIdentifier,
        message-submission-time        [0] MessageSubmissionTime,
        content-identifier             ContentIdentifier OPTIONAL,
        extensions                     [1] EXTENSIONS CHOSEN FROM {
            originating-MTA-certificate,
            proof-of-submission } DEFAULT {} }
    ERRORS {
        submission-control-violated,
        element-of-service-not-subscribed,
        originator-invalid,
        recipient-improperly-specified,
        inconsistent-request,
        security-error,
        unsupported-critical-function,
        remote-bind-error }
    ::= 3
```
Listing 3. Example of the ROS definition of operations.

cro in a module, assign another name to a macro, use as described above the nonstandard type and value notation that a macro defines, and export and import the names (and thereby the definitions) of certain macros but not others.

An example of the definition of a macro occupies Listing 2, an example of the use of that macro Listing 3. Named OPERATION, this macro is one member of an important family of macros defined in the Remote Operations standards (see Section III). (Another member of the family is the ERROR macro, cited in the example.) The macro's subject type is the Choice type whose alternative types are Integer and Object Identifier. Each use of the macro's nonstandard type notation defines a class of procedures or operations that one open system might perform at another's request. Each use of the macro's nonstandard value notation designates an instance of that class, namely, the particular operation identified by the specified Integer or Object Identifier value. A class of operation is determined by the calling sequence of its members.

The two main productions of the macro definition define no nonstandard value notation, but complex nonstandard type notation. The purpose of the latter is to formalize and standardize the specification of the calling sequences of operations. From the first main production, one might correctly infer that specifying the calling sequence of the operations in any class involves specifying four aspects of those operations: their arguments and results, the errors they report, and any operations—so-called linked operations—that performing systems may request of requesting systems during the operations' performance.

The supporting productions (rearranged for this paper for increased readability) define the notation for specifying the four aspects of the calling sequence of operations in a class. The **Argument**, **Result**, **Errors**, and **LinkedOperations** productions indicate that each aspect's specification is optional and that its presence is signaled by the keyword "ARGUMENT," "RESULT," "ERRORS," or "LINKED" as appropriate. The **NamedType** production indicates that an operation's argument or result is a value of a specified and optionally named type, the **ResultType** production that the result's type need not be stated. The **ErrorNames**, **ErrorList**, and **Error** productions indicate that an operation may report errors chosen from among zero or more classes of error, each denoted by a type (the ERROR macro's subject type), and individual errors, each denoted by a value of that type. The **LinkedOperationNames**, **OperationList**, and **Operation** productions indicate that an operation may be linked to operations chosen from among zero or more classes of operation, each denoted by a type (the **OPERATION** macro's subject type), and individual operations, each denoted by a value of that type.

III. REMOTE OPERATIONS

Remote Operations (ROS) is best understood as the procedure declaration portion of a high-level language. Its purpose is to elevate the description of complex interactions between open systems to a level of abstraction unachievable by less powerful or less formal means (e.g., diagrams or prose). The procedure declaration capabilities of a typical HLL are used to define, e.g., how software modules interact. ROS, on the other hand, is used primarily to define how OSI *application entities* (*entities*, for short) interact to effect a particular information processing task (e.g., the submission of an electronic message). Like ASN.1, therefore, ROS is an HLL for the specification of application protocols. ROS is particularly suited to interactive protocols involving the exchange of requests and replies. However, it can support arbitrary protocols because it admits replyless requests as a degenerate case.

A typical HLL treats the physical realization of procedure calls and returns as an internal design issue. Exactly how control is passed from one procedure to another is usually unimportant and unknown to the programmer. Indeed, the fact that the HLL hides such details from him is among the reasons he selects an HLL over assembly or machine language. Furthermore, an HLL implemented on several hardware engines may realize procedure calls and returns in different ways on those various machines.

An HLL for the specification of interactive application protocols must meet somewhat different requirements. While insulating the application protocol designer (like the programmer) from low-level details is among them, those details cannot vary from one implementation of the language to another because they represent the basis for communication between diverse machines. ROS, therefore, is supplemented by standard rules, themselves an application protocol, governing system interaction.

The fundamental concepts of ROS are those of remote operation and remote error. A remote operation is a task that one open system can ask another to carry out, a remote error an exceptional condition that can prematurely terminate such a task. The concept of remote operation is thus a generalization of the concept of procedure. In the case of a remote operation, however, the "caller" and "callee" reside in different computers. Thus, e.g., the former can continue to execute while awaiting the latter's reply. Remote operations are like processes in this regard.

The following sections overview ROS. They begin by more fully presenting the ROS paradigm, which leads to the concept of types of remote operation or remote error. They continue by describing the ROS notation for application protocol specification. They conclude by describing how protocols specified using that notation are realized. Throughout, the term *user* denotes an application protocol designer, i.e., a person who employs the ROS notation in protocol design.

A. Paradigm

ROS is based upon a simple communication paradigm. A *remote operation* is a task that one entity can request another carry out even though the two entities are in different open systems. In a particular instance of communication, the entity that makes the request is called the *invoker* and is said to *invoke* the remote operation to which the request refers. The entity of which the request is made is called the *performer* and is said to *perform* the remote operation. If the performer cannot complete the task requested of it, the remote operation is said to have *failed* because of a *remote error*; otherwise, the remote operation is said to have *succeeded*. The distinction between success and failure is called the remote operation's *outcome*. The performer may acknowledge the remote operation's performance in reply to the invoker's request. Doing so is called *reporting* the remote operation's outcome. Depending upon the remote operation, the performer reports its outcome only if success, only if failure, in either case, or in neither. A remote operation is said to be *confirmed* if both success and failure are reported, *conditionally confirmed* if one but not both outcomes are reported, and *unconfirmed* if neither outcome is reported.

When a request or reply is conveyed between invoker and performer, information qualifying the request or reply may accompany it. A single ASN.1 value, the remote operation's *argument*, may accompany the request. A single value, its *result*, may accompany the reply if the outcome is success. A single value, the remote error's *parameter*, may accompany the reply if the outcome is failure. The ASN.1 types of the argument and result depend upon the remote operation, that of the parameter upon the remote error. As the above might seem to imply, the ROS notation brings the ASN.1 notation to bear upon the tasks of defining the arguments and results of remote operations and the parameters of remote errors.

Two entities perform remote operations at one another's request in the context of an ongoing *association* between them. The task of establishing or terminating an association is itself a remote operation, but one of a special nature. A remote operation whose successful performance establishes an association between its invoker and performer is called a *bind operation*, a remote error encountered during its performance a *bind error*. A remote operation whose performance, successful or not, terminates an established association is called an *unbind operation*, a remote error encountered during its performance an *unbind error*. A remote operation serving neither purpose is called simply an *operation*, a remote error encountered during its performance simply an *error*. An operation can be invoked or performed only in an established association.

A typical operation is performed without the invoker's assistance. During the performance of an occasional operation, however, the invoker may have to ask the invoker to itself perform other operations. An operation in whose performance the invoker may be involved in this way is called a *parent operation*, the one or more operations each of which may but need not be invoked during its performance *child operations*, and the parent and child operations collectively *linked operations*. A child may be the parent in another set of linked operations, recursively.

In a particular instance of communication, the entity that invokes a bind operation is called the *initiator* of the resulting association, the entity that performs the bind operation the *responder*. Only the initiator can invoke the unbind operation that terminates the association. During the association and depending upon the application protocol that governs it, either the initiator, the responder, or both may invoke operations to be performed by the other. Linked operations, e.g., require the last of these three classes of association.

B. Remote Operation and Error Types

The ROS specifications enable users to define different types of remote operation or remote error. Each type is characterized by the constraints the user imposes upon the use and behavior of the remote operations or remote errors the type encompasses.

To define a type of remote operation, one declares whether instances of the type are bind operations, unbind operations, or operations; if the latter, whether they are parent operations; if so, their one or more child operations; whether instances require an argument; if so, its ASN.1 type; whether their success is reported; if so, whether a result is returned; if so, its ASN.1 type; whether their failure is reported; and if so, the one or more remote errors that may cause failure.

To define a type of remote error, one declares whether instances of the type are bind errors, unbind errors, or errors; whether a parameter accompanies their report; and, if so, its ASN.1 type.

The ROS specifications limit the types of bind and unbind operations, and bind and unbind errors, that users can define. A result or parameter necessarily accompanies a report of the outcome of any such operation. Furthermore, no such operation may be subject to more than one bind or unbind error, nor may it be a parent or child operation.

C. Notation

The ROS specifications provide formal notation for referencing types of remote operation or remote error, specific operations and errors, groups of functionally related operations, and entire application protocols. The notation is provided by means of six ASN.1 macros (see Section II-H) which the ROS specifications define: BIND, UNBIND, OPERATION, ERROR, APPLICATION-SERVICE-ELEMENT, and APPLICATION-CONTEXT. Each macro defines nonstandard type and value notation for its subject type. All six are briefly described below. The OPERATION macro is detailed in Section II-H above, and its definition occupies Listing 2.

The *BIND* or *UNBIND* macro enables a user to simultaneously reference a type of bind or unbind operation and the type of the bind or unbind error, if any, characteristic of such bind or unbind operations. This is accomplished using the macro's type notation as shown in Listing 4. The macro's value notation serves a more esoteric purpose beyond the paper's scope. (The macro's subject type is a Choice type whose alternative types are the type of the bind or unbind operation's argument, the type of its result, and the type of the parameter of the bind or unbind error, if any, all context-specifically tagged.)

The *OPERATION* or *ERROR* macro enables a user to reference either a type of operation or error, or the identifier of a particular operation or error, irrespective of its type. As illustrated in Listings 3 and 5, the former is done using the macro's type notation, the latter using its value notation. The macro's subject type is a Choice type whose alternative types are Integer and Object Identifier. An Integer value unambiguously identifies a particular operation or error in a suitably small domain; an Object Identifier value does so globally.

The *APPLICATION-SERVICE-ELEMENT* macro enables a user to reference either a group of functionally related operations (e.g., those for message submission, or those for message delivery) or the identifier of such a group. As illustrated in Listing 6, the former is done using the macro's type notation, the latter using its value notation. The macro's subject type is Object Identifier. A value of that type uniquely and unambiguously identifies a functional group. Using the type notation, the user identifies each operation in the group and specifies which of the two entities in an association may invoke it. (Child operations are identified implicitly, the types of the parent operations

```
MTSBind ::= BIND
  ARGUMENT SET {
    initiator-name        ObjectName,
    messages-waiting      [1] EXPLICIT MessagesWaiting OPTIONAL,
    initiator-credentials [2] InitiatorCredentials,
    security-context      [3] SecurityContext OPTIONAL }
  RESULT SET {
    responder-name        ObjectName,
    messages-waiting      [1] EXPLICIT MessagesWaiting OPTIONAL,
    responder-credentials [2] ResponderCredentials }
  BIND-ERROR INTEGER {
    busy (0),
    authentication-error (2),
    unacceptable-dialogue-mode (3),
    unacceptable-security-context (4) } (0..ub-integer-options)

MTSUnbind ::= UNBIND
```

Listing 4. Examples of the ROS definition of bind and unbind operations and errors.

```
recipient-improperly-specified ERROR
  PARAMETER
    improperly-specified-recipients
      SEQUENCE SIZE (1..ub-recipients) OF
        ORAddressAndOptionalDirectoryName
  ::= 3
```

Listing 5. Example of the ROS definition of errors.

```
mSSE APPLICATION-SERVICE-ELEMENT
  CONSUMER INVOKES {
    message-submission,
    probe-submission,
    cancel-deferred-delivery }
  SUPPLIER INVOKES {
    submission-control }
  ::= id-ase-msse
```

Listing 6. Example of the ROS definition of application service elements.

```
mts-access APPLICATION-CONTEXT
  APPLICATION SERVICE ELEMENTS {aCSE }
  BIND MTSBind
  UNBIND MTSUnbind
  REMOTE OPERATIONS {rOSE }
  INITIATOR CONSUMER OF {MSSE, mDSE, mASE }
  ABSTRACT SYNTAXES {
    id-as-acse, id-as-msse, id-as-mdse, id-as-mase, id-as-mts }
  ::= id-ac-mts-access
```

Listing 7. Example of the ROS definition of application contexts.

identifying them explicitly.) In this regard, the relationship between the entities may be either *symmetric*, in which case all operations may be invoked by either entity, or *asymmetric*, in which case each particular operation may be invoked by either one entity designated the *consumer*, the other entity, designated the *supplier*, or both.

The *APPLICATION-CONTEXT* macro enables a user to reference either an application protocol or the identifier of such a protocol. As shown in Listing 7, the former is done using the macro's type notation, the latter using its value notation. The macro's subject type is Object Identifier. A value of that type uniquely and unambiguously identifies an application protocol. Using the type notation, the user identifies, principally, the groups whose operations may be invoked in an association governed by the protocol, the type of the bind operation used to establish such an association, and the type of the unbind operation used to terminate it. (The remote errors that may be reported are identified implicitly, the types of the remote operations identifying them explicitly.) For each group of operations requiring the initiator and responder to be asymmetrically related, the user indicates which is the supplier and thus which is the consumer.

In practice, a user "declares" an application protocol via a collection of ASN.1 type and value assignments. Each of the former employs the nonstandard type notation defined by one of the six ROS macros, each of the latter both the nonstandard type and value notation defined by such a macro. One type of assignment uses the BIND macro to specify the type of the bind operation via which associations governed by the protocol are established.

Another uses the UNBIND macro to specify the type of the unbind operation via which such associations are terminated. Some value assignments use the OPERATION macro to specify the types and identifiers of the operations that may be invoked during an association. Others use the ERROR macro to specify the types and identifiers of the errors that may be reported during an association. Still others use the APPLICATION-SERVICE-ELEMENT macro to identify the groups among which the operations are divided. A final value assignment uses the APPLICATION-CONTEXT macro to identify the application protocol itself. (The OPERATION macro permits the *type* of a child operation or error to be specified instead of its identifier. When this option is exercised, the value assignment that identifies the child operation or error must specify that type.)

Every application protocol, of course, has aspects beyond those formally declared as described above, e.g., the semantics of the remote operations it comprises. Furthermore, and in particular, an application protocol must specify whether each confirmed operation is synchronous or asynchronous, at what priorities requests, replies, and rejection notices are to be conveyed between the two entities, and whether exactly-once, at-most-once, or neither semantics is to be guaranteed. All of these things are specified in prose. The concepts of synchrony, priority, rejection notice, and semantics are introduced in Section III-E below.

Note: In the terminology of OSI, an application protocol is called an *application context* (AC), a functional unit such as one of the groups of operations mentioned above an *application service element* (ASE). It is from these terms that the two ROS macros described above derive their names. The declaration of a protocol also involves the identification of any other, supporting ASE's involved in its definition, e.g., the Association Control Service Element (ACSE), via which bind and unbind operations and errors are realized (see Section III-D), and the Remote Operations Service Element (ROSE), by means of which operations and errors are realized (see Section III-E). The declaration of an application protocol also involves the identification of the *abstract syntaxes* the protocol employs. This latter concept is beyond the scope of this paper.

D. Realization of Bind and Unbind Operations.

The invocation of bind and unbind operations and the reporting of their outcomes are accomplished via a functional unit of an open system called the *Association Control Service Element* (ACSE) (alternatively, by another functional unit, the Reliable Transfer Service Element (RTSE), but this is beyond the scope of the paper). An ACSE is colocated with each of the two entities in an association. Residing within the application layer and communicating with one another using the services of lower layers, the two ACSE's establish, release, and possibly abort the *application association* that underlies the ROS association between the two entities they serve. Bind and unbind operations are realized by means of two ACSE-provided services, A-ASSOCIATE and A-RELEASE. The BIND and UNBIND macros are said to be *mapped onto* these services.

A bind operation is invoked by means of the *A-ASSOCIATE* service whose function, in general, is to establish an application association between two entities at the instigation of one, allowing the other to either accept or decline the proposition. In either case, the service also enables the two entities to exchange *user information*. As used by ROS, the service conveys the bind operation's argument, if any, from the initiator to the responder. In the other direction, it conveys either the bind operation's result or the bind error's parameter, depending upon whether the bind operation succeeds, in which case the association is accepted, or fails, in which case it is declined.

An unbind operation is invoked by means of the *A-RELEASE* service whose function, in general, is to terminate an application association between two entities at the request of one, allowing the other to declare the termination complete or incomplete. In either case, this service, too, enables the two entities to exchange user information. As used by ROS, the service conveys the unbind operation's argument, if any, from the initiator to the responder. In the other direction, it conveys either the unbind operation's result or the unbind error's parameter, depending upon whether the bind operation succeeds, in which case termination is declared complete, or fails, in which case it is declared incomplete.

E. Realization of Operations

The invocation of operations and the reporting of their outcomes are accomplished via a functional unit of an open system called the *Remote Operations Service Element* (ROSE). A ROSE is colocated with each of the two entities in an association. Residing within the application layer and communicating with one another using the services of lower layers (alternatively, by the RTSE, but again this is beyond the paper's scope), the two ROSE's carry requests for and replies to operations between the entities they serve. They do so by providing five services to those entities. The first four, RO-INVOKE, RO-RESULT, RO-ERROR, and RO-REJECT-U, convey requests, replies, and rejection notices (see below) from one entity to the other and are initiated by them. The fifth service, RO-REJECT-P, aborts the provision of any of the first four services and is initiated by a ROSE when circumstances require it. The OPERATION and ERROR macros are said to be *mapped onto* these services.

A *rejection notice* (the term is coined for this paper) conveys from one ROSE to the other the inability or unwillingness of the former, or the entity it serves, to act upon a request or reply it received from the latter. Throughout the remainder of this paper, requests, replies, and rejection notices are referred to collectively as *messages*. A request or reply can be rejected if it violates the application protocol governing the association, e.g., by referencing an operation the protocol excludes, referencing an included operation or error in a way inconsistent with its type, or violating the request–reply discipline in a more fundamental way (e.g., by citing an unassigned invoke ID; see below). A prospective performer also can reject a request for lack of resources or if it initiated the association and wishes to terminate it.

Messages are scheduled for transfer between ROSE's on the basis of integer values called their *priorities*. (The lower the value, the higher the priority.) Each entity attaches a priority to each message whose conveyance it initiates. A reply's priority normally exceeds that of the request that provoked it. When several messages await transfer, a ROSE first transfers the one of highest priority. If several are of that priority, it transfers them first come, first served. If the association is *two-way alternate* (i.e., half duplex), rather than *two-way simultaneous* (i.e., full duplex), the priority of the message it must transfer next determines whether one ROSE requests the turn from the other.

So that its ROSE can optimally manage the turn if the association is two-way alternate, an entity must specify the *class* of each operation it invokes. Five classes of operation are defined on the basis of their outcome reporting characteristics and whether they preclude performers from performing other operations concurrently. Operations that impose the latter restriction are said to be *synchronous*, others *asynchronous*. One entity can perform several asynchronous operations concurrently. Class 1 comprises the synchronous operations, class 2 the confirmed asynchronous operations, class 3 the conditionally confirmed operations whose failure is reported, class 4 the conditionally confirmed operations whose success is reported, and class 5 the unconfirmed operations.

Messages are distinguished from and correlated with one another by means of integer values called *invoke ID*'s. An invoker assigns an invoke ID to each request it issues. A performer includes that same invoke ID in any reply or rejection notice it issues in response to the request. The invoke ID thus distinguishes the request from other requests, e.g., for the concurrent performance of other operations. It also enables replies, rejection notices, and requests for the performance of child operations to be correlated with the requests that provoked them.

The two ROSE's provide the following services collaboratively. The *RO-INVOKE* service enables one entity to request that the other perform an operation. The request comprises a newly assigned invoke ID; the identifier of the operation being invoked; the operation's argument, if any; and, if the operation is a child operation, the invoke

ID of the request for the parent operation. The service also conveys from the invoker to its ROSE the operation's class and the request's priority. The *RO-RESULT* service enables one entity to report to the other the success of a previously invoked operation. The reply comprises the request's invoke ID and, if the operation returns a result, both the identifier of the operation and that result. The service also conveys from the performer to its ROSE the reply's priority. The *RO-ERROR* service enables one entity to report to the other the failure of a previously invoked operation. The reply comprises the request's invoke ID, the identifier of the error being reported, and the error's parameter, if any. The service also conveys from the performer to its ROSE the reply's priority. The *RO-REJECT-U* service enables one entity to convey a rejection notice to the other. The notice comprises the invoke ID borne by the request or reply being rejected and the reason for its rejection. The service also conveys from the first entity to its ROSE the notice's priority. The *RO-REJECT-P* service enables a ROSE to abort the provision of another service requested by the entity it serves. There are two possible causes, loss of the underlying application association, and rejection by the other ROSE of the message to have been conveyed on the grounds that it was malformed. In the former case, the service returns to the originating entity the unconveyed message. In the latter case, it returns the reason given for rejection of the message and, if available, the invoke ID borne by it.

To provide the five services above, one ROSE interacts with the other in accordance with an application protocol which the ROS specifications provide for that purpose. The protocol employs APDU's of four kinds, all of which are defined using ASN.1. An *Invoke* (ROIV) APDU embodies a request, a *Result* (RORS) APDU a report of success, an *Error* (ROER) APDU a report of failure, and a *Reject* (APDU) a rejection notice. APDU's of all four kinds are conveyed between ROSE's by means of the *P-DATA* service the presentation layer provides (alternatively, by the RT-TRANSFER service of the RTSE, again beyond the scope of this paper).

An invoker may, but need not, reuse the invoke ID it assigns to a request once it is certain that the performer will not subsequently issue a message that refers to that request. At such a time, the request is said to be *silent* (a term coined for this paper). Any operation is silent if and when the invoker receives a reply to or rejection notice concerning its request. An unconfirmed or conditionally confirmed operation is silent if and when the performer notifies the invoker of its completion by other means (e.g., by invoking or replying to another operation designed for that purpose); failing that, such an operation may be considered silent after a reasonably long period of time.

A precept of the Remote Operations paradigm as so far described is that invoking a remote operation (in a manner consistent with its type and with the application protocol in force) causes that operation to be performed *exactly once*. However, because not all operations are confirmed, and because the unbind operation, as actually realized (see Section III-D), may cause messages to be lost, the initiator cannot, in general, terminate its association with the responder without leaving one or both entities in doubt about whether certain messages were received and thus about whether certain invoked operations were actually performed. Thus, the precept is not, so far, fully realized in practice.

An application protocol may incorporate additional rules, identified below, that ensure that invoked operations are performed exactly once. Alternatively, an application protocol may incorporate a subset of those rules, also identified below, that provides a lesser but sometimes still useful guarantee, namely, that invoked operations are performed *at most* once. A third possible guarantee, namely, that invoked operations are performed *at least* once, while sometimes useful (e.g., for idempotent operations), is not addressed by the ROS specifications. Failing its adoption of these additional rules or the identified subset thereof, an application protocol is subject, in principle, to the unpredictability described above and must take this fact into account in its design. (The cost of providing either the exactly-once or the at-most-once guarantee in the face of either unconfirmed or conditionally confirmed operations calls into question the utility of such operations. The ROS specifications, therefore, advise against their general use.)

To provide the at-most-once guarantee, an application protocol incorporates three additional rules. First, a performer must reply to or reject each confirmed operation in the association in which the request was made. Second, if the protocol comprises only confirmed operations, an invoker must assign a distinct invoke ID to every request it issues during the association. Otherwise, an invoker must assign a distinct invoke ID to every request it makes of the performer, irrespective of the association in which that request is made, and a performer must detect a violation of this rule, decline to honor the offending request, and issue a rejection notice explaining why. Third, the initiator must not invoke the unbind operation until all confirmed operations it invoked are silent or while it is performing or has yet to perform an invoked operation. If performing an operation, it must await the operation's completion and reply as necessary to the request. If yet to perform an operation, it must reject the responder's request.

To provide the exactly-once guarantee for confirmed operations, the above rules are sufficient. To provide it for other operations, an application protocol must require an invoker of such an operation to elicit a rejection notice from the performer by rerequesting the operation. An operation is said to be *rerequested* (the term is coined for this paper) if the invoker sends a second (or subsequent) request for its performance to ensure that the first request reached the performer, rather than to cause the operation to be performed a second time. A rerequest bears the invoke ID of the original request.

Invoking the unbind operation has the following consequences, even when the above rules are followed. Any messages (necessarily requests or rejection notices) the responder may subsequently send are lost. The responder may forcibly abort any operation it is performing and may reject any invoked operation it has yet to perform. From the initiator's perspective, the outcome of each of these operations (necessarily unconfirmed or conditionally confirmed) is indeterminate. An application protocol must avoid or take these consequences into account.

IV. History and Conclusions

Both ASN.1 and ROS arose from work by the author, first at SRI International [1]–[2] and later at Xerox Corporation [3], in an area of computer communication that has come to be called *remote procedure calling* [4]. In the context of X.400, ASN.1 was developed and introduced as a means of concisely and precisely specifying X.400's P1 protocol for message transfer and its P2 message format for interpersonal messaging. ROS was introduced as a means of specifying X.400's P3 protocol for message submission and delivery. Within CCITT, the initial proposal for ASN.1 incorporated two additional types, Operation and Error, which were removed from the final proposal when they proved controversial. The ASN.1 macro facility was then developed and introduced so that formal notation for the specification of operations and errors could be defined outside of the ASN.1 specifications, namely, in the specifications for ROS. The Object Identifier type was introduced (much later) to solve the entire class of problems typified by that of allowing an arbitrary organization to define and globally name its own message format.

From the outset, ASN.1 and ROS were designed and documented with an eye toward their use in applications other than message handling. When CCITT approved its original specification in 1984, ASN.1 had already been used in the specification of document interchange format standards, an area of work now known by the names Office Document Architecture (ODA) and Office Document Interchange Formats (ODIF). During the years 1985–1988, the original ASN.1 and ROS specifications of CCITT [5]–[6] were rewritten and, in 1988, reissued as joint CCITT–ISO standards [7]–[10]. At the time of this writing (May 1988), virtually every OSI application layer protocol developed or under development internationally employs ASN.1 for its specification, and ASN.1 compilers, run-time environments, and software utilities are available in the marketplace. In 1988, both CCITT and ISO, in joint standards on the subject, adopted ROS as the basis for the specification and implementation of protocols for accessing and constructing distributed directory systems. This and other uses of ROS internationally suggest that it also will become a fixture of OSI. ROS runtime environments are already available commercially.

The impact of ASN.1 and ROS on OSI has been profound. Their principal achievement has been to elevate the task of OSI application protocol specification to a level of abstraction, embodied in the notation they define, at which formal techniques can be applied, e.g., to the tasks of protocol verification, implementation, and conformance testing. They also effectively grant OSI applications independence from OSI itself, thus making feasible a next-generation realization of the seven-layer model should the advance of technology make that necessary or desirable.

Acknowledgment

ASN.1 and ROS were codesigned by D. Steedman, formerly of Bell-Northern Research, Canada, and now with PSC International, Scotland. The 1988 text of the ASN.1 specifications and their acceptance within ISO are due to J. Larmouth of the University of Salford, England. The 1988 text of the ROS specifications, much of their technical content, and the acceptance of ROS within ISO are due to L. Temme of Siemens, Germany.

References

[1] J. E. White, "A high-level framework for network-based resource sharing," in *AFIPS Conf. Proc., Nat. Comput. Conf.*, 1976, pp. 561–570.
[2] ——, "Elements of a distributed programming system," *Comput. Languages*, vol. 2, pp. 117–134, 1977.
[3] "Courier: The remote procedure call protocol," Xerox System Integration Standard, XSIS 038112, Xerox Corp., Dec. 1981.
[4] B. J. Nelson, "Remote procedure call," CSL-81-9, Xerox Corp., Palo Alto Res. Cen., May 1981.
[5] Recommendation X.409, "Message handling systems: Presentation transfer syntax and notation," in *CCITT Red Book*, fascicle VIII.7, Int. Telecommun. Union, Oct. 1984, pp. 62–93.
[6] Recommendation X.410, "Message handling systems: Remote operations and reliable transfer server," in *CCITT Red Book*, fascicle VII, Int. Telecommun. Union, Oct. 1984, pp. 93–126.
[7] Recommendation X.208, "Specification of abstract syntax notation one (ASN.1)," in *CCITT Blue Book*, submitted for publication, 1988. Also to be published by ISO as ISO 8824.
[8] Recommendation X.209, "Specification of basic encoding rules for abstract syntax notation one (ASN.1)," in *CCITT Blue Book*, submitted for publication, 1988. Also to be published by ISO as ISO 8825.
[9] Recommendation X.219, "Remote operations: Model, notation and service definition," in *CCITT Blue Book*, submitted for publication, 1988. Also to be published by ISO as ISO 9072-1.
[10] Recommendation X.229, "Remote operations: Protocol specification," in *CCITT Blue Book*, submitted for publication, 1988. Also to be published by ISO as ISO 9072-2.

James E. White (M'77) received the B.S. degree in electrical engineering from the University of California, Santa Barbara, in 1969, and the M.S. degree in computer engineering from Stanford University, Stanford, CA, in 1980.

He is cofounder and Vice President of RAPPORT Communication, Inc., a Palo Alto-based firm that provides to users and suppliers strategic consulting concerning the technical, marketing, regulatory, and other aspects of messaging. Prior to forming RAPPORT, he was Director of Messaging Architecture at Telenet. He also designed and implemented distributed messaging and other network communication systems while associated with 3Com, Xerox, SRI International, and UCSB. From 1985 to 1988 he led the international standardization of ASN.1, ROS, and X.400 as CCITT Special Rapporteur in those areas.

File Transfer Protocols

PETER F. LININGTON

Abstract—File transfer protocols are essential for the management and dissemination of shared information within a wide variety of distributed systems. The ISO standard for File Transfer, Access, and Management is the result of an assessment of the mechanisms used in a number of previous file transfer protocols. The approach taken by earlier protocols and the design decisions resulting from them are discussed. This process involves consideration of many issues, including filestore resource modeling, control structures, negotiation, access, concurrency, and recovery mechanisms. The resultant ISO protocol provides a range of facilities for different styles of application, covering both simple transfer and access to shared information. Work is in progress to add further file management facilities to the basic protocol. The FTAM standard has a wide scope, and the commonest styles of use are being codified in a series of functional standards; it is primarily these functions which are being implemented initially by industry.

I. INTRODUCTION

THE concept of a file transfer protocol is almost as old as data communication itself. However, recent years have seen a convergence and refinement of approach, culminating in the publication of an international standard for file transfer, access, and management (FTAM) [1]. FTAM is an OSI protocol, and like all OSI standards, it aims to allow communication between dissimilar systems, taking into account the differences of file types, formats, and filing operations found in a heterogeneous set of systems. Modern file transfer protocols can be characterized by their use of an explicit model of the file resources they manipulate, and by a systematic approach to the transformation of the file contents conveyed, based on knowledge of the type of the material communicated.

This paper begins by giving a brief review of the history of file transfer protocols and the development of the concepts on which they rely. References are made to the seminal protocol descriptions, although not to all subsequent updates of the protocols concerned. The paper then outlines the modeling of filestores and file structures which form the basis for the meaning of the protocol exchanges. The concept of a document type is then introduced to bring together the many and various aspects which characterize the definition of a particular class of information.

File transfer is a major application area for the OSI communication architecture. The use made of supporting services, particularly the presentation service, is explained. The main sequence of events taking place during file transfer is then outlined.

Manuscript received May 13, 1988; revised March 5, 1989.
The author is with the Computing Laboratory, University of Kent, Canterbury, Kent CT2 7NF, England.
IEEE Log Number 8928988.

Various more detailed protocol design choices are then described, including organization of the flow of control, negotiation, concurrency control, access control, and error recovery.

Finally, current activities to extend the international standard and identify common functional styles of usage are reviewed and the current situation summarized.

II. SOME NOTABLE FILE TRANSFER PROTOCOLS

Before examining the technical elements of a file transfer protocol, it is worth introducing some of the prominent protocol designs which have affected thinking over the last 15 years. But first, what is a file transfer protocol? It is a protocol which allows the specification of a file and its properties, as a prelude to the communication of part or all of the file's contents. Information about the file of interest is exchanged by reference to an explicit model of the filestore which is specified as part of the protocol. The lack of a fully specified file semantics excludes from the current survey such useful but more limited utilities as Kermit [2], which require a substantial awareness of the nature of the target system.

During the early and mid-1970's, a number of groups were involved in the development of file transfer protocols for newly developed computer networks. One of the first of these was the Arpanet file transfer protocol [3], which was first widely circulated in 1973. Unlike most later protocols, this design separated control and bulk data transfer onto separate connections.

In the UK, work had also started shortly after this on a network-independent protocol design, initially for use with the EPSS network. It was first published in 1975 [4], although substantially revised before implementation [5], [6] and again after some initial operational experience [7]. This protocol, which became known as the Blue Book, has been widely used for the exchange of scientific data both within and outside the UK, and has become one of the most widespread open protocols for use over public networks.

At the same time, Gien working at INRIA developed a protocol proposal [8], [9] which, although not widely taken up, contributed significantly to the understanding of dialog structures and the management of control. In Germany, the group working at HMI designed a protocol for their regional network with well-developed features for access to hierarchically structured files [10], [11]. The protocol developed by the European Centre for Medium Range Weather Forecasts [12] included analysis of the timing requirements to maintain quality of service. At the end of this initial period of protocol development, the Autodin II file transfer protocol [13] brought together a number of the ideas in the protocols mentioned above into a single specification.

The above list of highlights has concentrated on attempts to define protocols for file transfer between heterogeneous systems. There were, of course, also many vendor specific protocols. Of these, perhaps the most significant in terms of its structure and facilities was the Digital Equipment DAP protocol [14], the structure of which foreshadowed a number of the later developments in the standards arena.

From 1978 onwards, work on the OSI Reference Model and its associated family of standards was in progress. File transfer was identified from the start as a necessary application protocol, but initial progress was slow, partly because of the parallel development of the applications, their supporting services and protocols, and the application layer structure itself. In many areas, the file transfer application became a test case to determine the effectiveness of the evolving architecture. Throughout this period, file transfer protocol designs continued to appear, being progressively more strongly influenced by the work with ISO.

In 1980, NBS sponsored first a study of the features required of a file transfer protocol [15], and then an outline service and protocol proposal based on the OSI architecture as it then was [16], [17]. At about the same time, the Norwegian networking project Uninett developed a file management protocol based on the OSI structure [18]. Although soon overtaken by changes within ISO, these were the first serious attempts to extract a separate presentation function.

By 1982, work by the computer manufacturers within ECMA had produced a complete file transfer protocol [19], [20] which was submitted as input to the standards process. This work was quite closely aligned with the activity within ISO, although many of the concepts of the presentation layer were still not stable.

During the mid-1980's, the development of FTAM progressed through the formal stages of ballot as an international standard, and a number of groups began to track the drafts and perform trial implementations. Perhaps the most notable of these efforts formed part of the MAP/TOP initiative, with work being focused via the agreements of the NBS Implementor's Workshops [21]. These demonstrated the soundness of the developing standard on a wide range of machines.

Finally, the International Standard for FTAM, ISO 8571, was itself completed at the start of 1988. For a technical overview of the stages in its development, see, for example, [22]-[24]. The remainder of this paper examines a number of the technical choices it embodies.

III. THE DESCRIPTION OF FILES AND FILESTORES
A. The Virtual Filestore

In order that a communication protocol can provide an interface to a system which maintains files, the information encoded in the protocol requests and responses must be interpreted as statements about the stored files. This interpretation depends on the establishment of an abstract model of the storage system and its properties. The model needs to cover the way files are named, the meaning of their properties, and the types of information they may contain [25].

The model defined in FTAM is known as the virtual filestore. It is based on the definition of a set of file attributes which are pieces of information capturing the essential properties of the file. For example, single attributes express historical information such as the time of creation or identity of last accessor of the file. Other attributes reflect properties of the file contents such as the type of information stored or the file size. The model also describes sufficient information about the users accessing the file service to support the definition of constraints on use of the files, such as access controls. The idea of a separate filestore model was first developed in detail in the Blue Book file transfer protocol in the mid-1970's, but has now been widely adopted.

A schema outlining the major components in the FTAM filestore model is given in Fig. 1. It shows that a filestore can contain any number of files, each of which has some contents; the file and its contents are described by a set of attributes. The model also describes the relevant properties of the set of connected users and the state of their activities in a similar style.

Ideally, a system design should use a single model for each general resource. Unfortunately, this is seldom the case. The comparison of file models can identify potential implementation problems in integrating, for example, the way files are manipulated by the command language and the communication subsystems.

B. File Structures

The process of file transfer concentrates on the contents of the file. In real systems, there are very many types of file and file structure, varying from the simple text file to the complex, indexed, record-oriented file. It is therefore an essential part of a file transfer protocol to categorize and describe these structures.

The FTAM standard uses a hierarchical model, based on the earlier work at HMI in Germany, to provide a unifying description of the many possible types of file. The file is considered to be a tree, each subtree of which can potentially be accessed independently; a subtree is called a file access data unit (FADU). The nodes of the tree may each carry identifiers and may have file data units (DU's) associated with them. An example of such a tree is given in Fig. 2.

Note that the structure needed is the structure on which the protocol operates—its access structure. There will, in general, be an even richer structure of references within the file data to support the meaning of the information stored, and this structure can be any directed graph; however, its form is not of concern in the operation of the protocol.

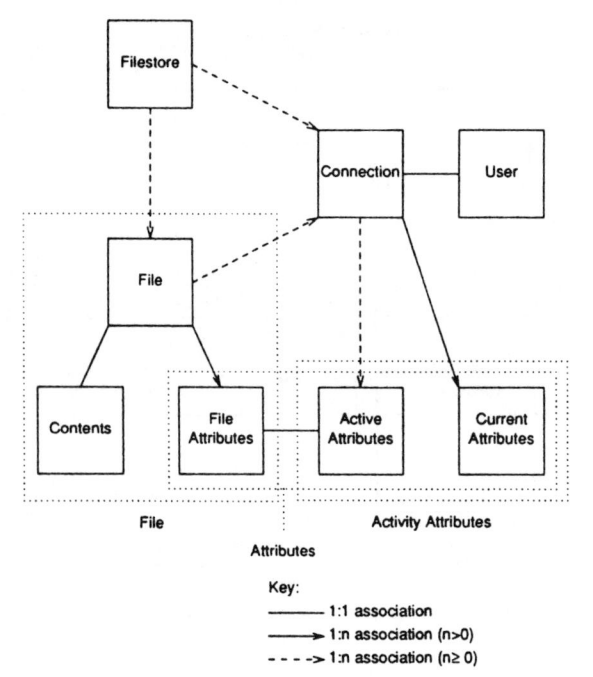

Fig. 1. The virtual filestore schema.

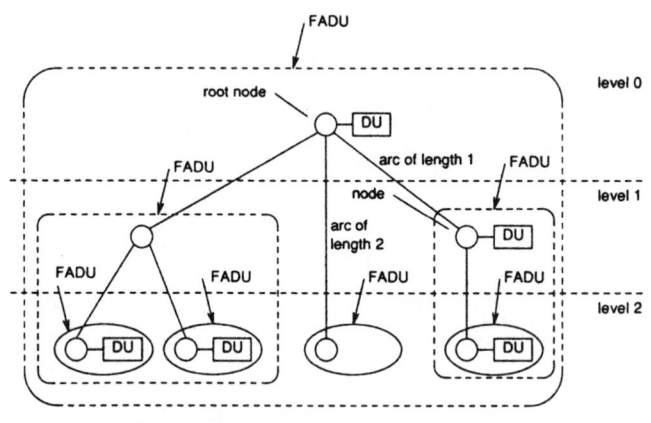

Fig. 2. An example of a file access structure.

A hierarchical model was chosen for the access structure because it is sufficiently general and includes most of the commonly used file structures as special cases; the unstructured file is a trivial tree with only a root node, that flat file of records is a tree with only a single level below the root, and so on. In order to capture the static and dynamic restrictions for the common cases, a series of seven constraint sets are introduced into the standard which each express a well-known style of use.

C. Document Types and File Contents

Although the file transfer protocol operates by transferring the values of abstract data types (see the discussion of the role of the presentation service below), a real system requires much more information about both encoding and interpretation to be able to support a particular type of file contents. This information characterizes the file type, but does not form part of the file transfer protocol, which can manipulate a wide range of file types. It is therefore defined by registration of a document type, allowing the introduction of new types to fulfil new user requirements.

The specification of a document type details the abstract and transfer syntaxes needed, the rules for mapping the file contents onto data values, and the meaning to be associated with these data values. For example, a printable file will need to be interpreted after transfer according to a particular set of formatting rules. It also includes the definition of how the document may be manipulated by the protocol operations for access to individual file access data units.

The FTAM standard itself includes a few common document types to satisfy basic requirements for text or binary file transfer. Further document types will be defined and registered in the future by standards bodies, user organizations, or suppliers.

IV. THE FILE TRANSFER PROTOCOL ARCHITECTURE

A. Position Within the OSI Architecture

After an initial period of uncertainty as to the role and division of function between the upper layers of the OSI architecture, the various user-oriented protocols such as FTAM and the Virtual Terminal Protocol were eventually positioned entirely within the application layer. They are now seen as building blocks, called application service elements, each contributing to the function of OSI applications. As a result of this structure, FTAM is able to exploit other application layer services, such as the general-purpose mechanisms for association control and concurrency control, as required by the overall user requirements.

Like all application protocols, the file transfer protocol is an abstract statement of the information to be communicated, depending on the services of the supporting layers to give substance to the communication. In particular, it draws upon the presentation layer for data representation and the session layer for synchronization and resynchronization.

Some aspects of the file transfer specification are difficult to express entirely within the OSI architecture. This is inevitable because the architecture is an architecture for communication, and is unable to express constraints which persist after the communication is complete, such as the constraints which characterize the storage of files after transfer. Current work within ISO on the creation of a reference model of open distributed systems can be expected to make good such deficiencies in the architectural description.

B. Using the Presentation Service

The main purposes of the OSI presentation layer are to provide tools for the communication of type information relating to the data values transferred and to support the negotiation of suitable representations for these data items. By doing so, the presentation protocol allows the communicating systems to manage local format conversions without loss of significant information and to support communication between systems with different data representations. Exchange of information is possible as long as the systems share a uniform view of a set of abstract data elements that characterize the dialog.

For file transfer, the main interest is in providing for the transmission of data from as wide a range of types of file as possible. The contents of a file can be characterized by their abstract syntax and by a sufficient view of the semantics to be associated with them. The way this process is managed has been described in [26], and Fig. 3 summarizes the steps in transmission.

The file is divided into a number of meaningful data elements, such as lines of text or fields in a record, which are transferred by the presentation service as presentation data values (PDV's); the boundaries of these presentation data values are preserved by the mechanisms providing the presentation service. They become the atomic units of data to the file service; lower layer transmission mechanisms may segment and reassemble these units during, for example, the recovery from errors in the network layer, but they may not be subdivided above the presentation service. This indivisibility is a direct consequence of the delegation to the presentation layer of the management of encoding and transformation, which may, in extreme cases, reorder information within the representation of a data value. Any application protocol control information, such as a checkpoint request, must be placed at the boundaries between data values.

In addition to the management of the representation of the file data, the presentation layer also provides transparency by distinguishing between file contents and file transfer protocol control information. The separation is achieved by establishing distinct presentation contexts for control and data, ensuring a logical distinction even where the data value encodings might otherwise be ambiguous.

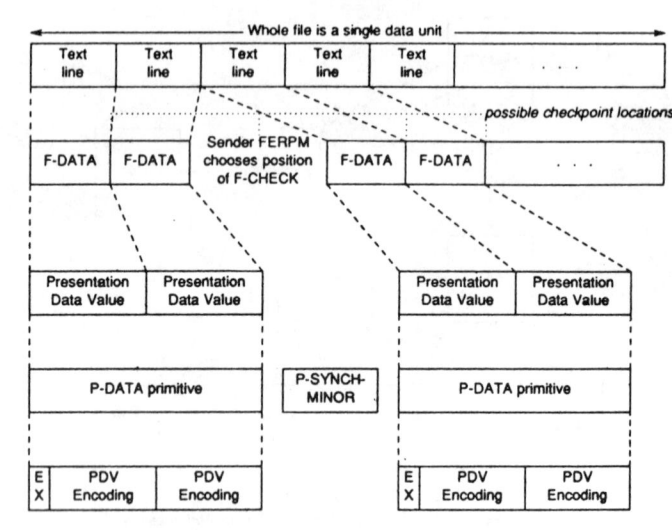

Fig. 3. Transmission of an unstructured text file.

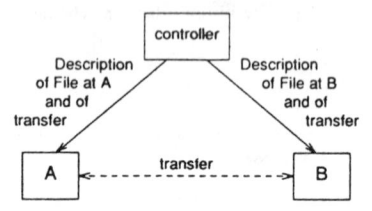

Fig. 4. Logical flows of information in file transfer.

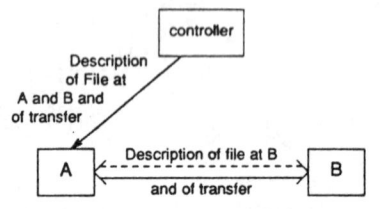

Fig. 5. Actual flows of information in FTAM.

C. Control Structures

Turning now to the organization of information flow in the protocol, a basic distinction can be made between the file data to be transferred and the control information specifying where it comes from and where it goes to. One can identify three players in the activity: a controller, which wishes the transfer to happen and specifies it, a source or sender of data, and a sink or receiver of data. The controller can be located with the source or the sink or it may be quite separate. A decision has to be made as to whether the controller communicates with both source and sink, directly mirroring the logical flow (Fig. 4) or delegates responsibility to one of them (Fig. 5). The delegation implies a level of trust, but can simplify synchronization and control.

Of the early file transfer protocols, the Arpanet file transfer protocol is notable in having chosen to separate control from the bulk data transfer, while all the other proposals, including FTAM, chose to delegate control to one of the parties involved in the transfer, although the choice of delegation to sender or receiver has generally been left open to the eventual user.

D. Sequence of Events in the FTAM Protocol

The main functions to be performed during a file transfer are the initialization of communication between the initiator and responder involved in the activity, the selection of the file and of any data transfer options, the data transfer itself, deselection of the file, and termination of the communication. These form the steps in establishing, using, and releasing a series of nested regimes, in which different pieces of shared information are built up. These regimes allow for the efficient combination of related parts of the user's activity. For example, once communication has been established, a number of files may be accessed. Once a file has been selected, a number of data transfers may be performed to and from different parts of it.

The situation is complicated somewhat by the need to manage the filed information, examining or changing at-

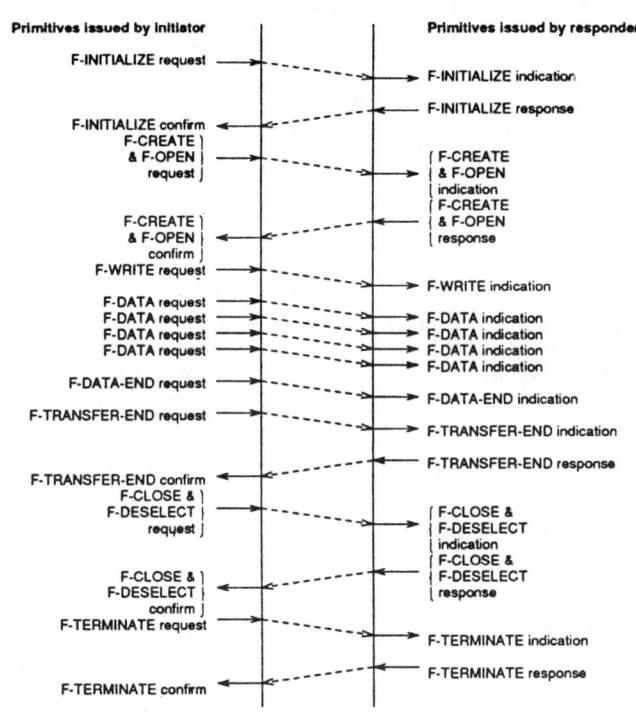

Fig. 6. Sending a file to a remote system.

tributes, or to access the same information in different ways, first reading it, and then updating selected parts. To allow for a variety of different uses, the control information is grouped into a number of distinct primitives. For simple transfer, these are normally concatenated as fields within a single protocol message, but in the more complicated cases, they can be sent separately, allowing, for example, a file to remain selected while its attributes are changed or preparation is made for a different style of transfer by closing and reopening it. The protocol therefore provides a toolkit from which either simple file transfer or more complex file access operations can be constructed.

This ability to vary the exact sequence of activity is itself optional, and communication with simple systems is assisted by making the simpler one-stage operations mandatory for even the more complex systems, which may, when necessary, wish to be able to break up the preferred grouping of control information.

Once the file is opened, the protocol for data transfer consists of an initial command which specifies the direction and content of the transfer, followed by the transfer itself, and completed by an exchange of terminating acknowledgments before the file is closed. This final exchange of messages, in combination with the error recovery procedures defined in the standard, suffices to ensure that requested transfers are performed once and only once.

The full sequence of events in transferring a file from one system to another is indicated in Fig. 6

V. Mechanisms Within the File Transfer Protocol

A. Negotiation Mechanisms

Because of the physical separation between networked systems and the wide range of system types, there has been interest in the provision of negotiation mechanisms which search for a good fit between system capabilities or file properties.

Of the early protocols, the Blue Book protocol contained the richest negotiation mechanisms. It allowed the selection of files by attribute values, supporting not only exact matching, but also inequalities and exclusions. Thus, a user could, for example, specify all files of greater than a certain age except those with a certain name extension.

In retrospect, however, the full power of these mechanisms has seldom been used, and they are difficult to implement. The basic FTAM standard is therefore restricted to selection of functions by simple reduction, in which the initiator offers a set of options and the responder picks exactly one. Files are selected by name only. The extensions now under development (see below) will introduce the option of more complex operations to negotiate the use of groups of files.

B. Concurrency Control

The objective of a concurrency control mechanism is to ensure that an initiator has a consistent view of the file by restricting shared access. Such mechanisms are designed to provide a way for a user to perform a coordinated series of actions without interference from concurrent accesses.

Concurrency control is provided solely to control the correct parallel execution of multiple tasks. Its effects must be distinguished from those of access control, which provides security mechanisms.

Individual filestore actions are expected to be implemented in such a way that any single action, such as a read or a write data transfer, appears atomic and serializable. This means that although the sequence of actions on a set of associations is not, in general, predictable, actions on one association are seen from other associations only when they are complete.

Two levels of concurrency control are provided in FTAM. The outer level controls access to the whole file, while the inner level can be used to allow separate control of the access to individual file access data units. The outer, or file, level can be applied when the file is selected or created and released when the file is deselected or deleted. It can also be modified for the duration of the file open regime if, for example, the file is first to be read and then reopened for updating.

File concurrency is applied separately to each type of action which can be performed on the virtual filestore, in one of the following categories:
1) *not required:* the initiator will not perform the operation—others may,
2) *shared:* the initiator can perform the operation—so can others,
3) *exclusive:* the initiator can perform the operation—others cannot,
4) *no access:* no one may perform the action.

Thus, for example, a distributed application may specify shared read access, and no access to other actions, to ensure the integrity of the data it reads. However, if all users requested shared read and exclusive write for the whole file, only one user at a time could access the file because of the updating restriction, and this would defeat concurrency.

To allow a finer level of granularity, the second type of control, file access data unit (FADU) locking, is introduced. If the FADU locking is requested, concurrency controls specified at the time the file is opened are not applied immediately (although any concurrency control requested at file selection remains in force). Instead, the control requested is applied for the duration of each file access action requested. Thus, for example, a request to read a FADU might bring into effect for the duration of the read action a shared concurrency control requested when the file was opened.

In addition, individual file access data units can have a lock applied for some period within the file open regime, bounded by a pair of file access actions which are suitably marked in the protocol.

C. Access Control

The access control mechanisms provided by FTAM are based on the concept of an access control list. Each of the entries in this list gives a set of actions and concurrency constraints, and a set of tests which an initiator needs to satisfy before these filestore actions can be performed; the actions are allowed if the conditions given by any one of the entries in the list are satisfied. Thus, a list might contain entries, each allowing a number of named initiators to read a file, and a separate entry allowing any entity quoting a particular password to read from and write to it.

In addition to the actions given in the entry, allowed concurrency control combinations can also be included. If they are not included, the performance of concurrency control is determined locally by the filestore.

As explained above, the concurrency control on access to a file is at a finer level than a simple yes or no; this is reflected by a similar finer level of access control. For example, an initiator may be allowed to request shared read access to a file and be given the ability to specify no access for anybody to the delete action for the duration of the read, even if the delete action is not itself accessible with either shared or exclusive access.

In establishing the FTAM regime and the file selection and open regimes, values are established for various activity attributes corresponding to the possible items in the list. In particular, the initiator asks to perform a certain set of actions by setting the current access request activity attribute when establishing a file selection regime. Before allowing the requested actions, the responding entity scans the access control list to determine if the activity attribute values match any of the entries. If a match for the set of actions is found and the associated tests are satisfied, the actions can be performed; if no match is found, the request is rejected.

D. Error Recovery

The aim of the error recovery procedures specified in FTAM is to provide an uninterrupted file service to the external file service users, correcting errors by exchanges between the protocol machines without the user being

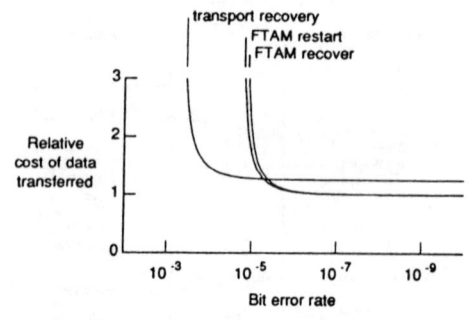

Fig. 7. Comparative costs of three different recovery mechanisms, showing the advantage of low transmission overhead on even moderately reliable networks.

made aware that anything out of the ordinary has happened.

FTAM provides two styles of error recovery, both of which depend on the marking of checkpoints within the data transferred (although in simple cases, only the start of the transfer needs to be marked). One, called Restart, allows for resynchronization to a checkpoint following discovery of an error which did not interrupt the supporting communication. The other, called Recover, allows for an activity to be resumed following a more complete failure.

Since errors may destroy the supporting communication or one of the end systems may fail and be restarted, the high-level association between the communicating applications must be maintained by both systems holding matching records of the transfer, called dockets. The error recovery protocol reconstructs the supporting connections and the state of the data transfer prior to the failure, based on the information held in the dockets, and the communication then continues.

The file service user gives the file error recovery protocol machine the information necessary for it to select the mechanisms needed from those just outlined by means of statements of its quality of service requirements.

The choice of which error recovery mechanism to use or whether to rely on the inherent mechanisms in the supporting layers will depend on the expected probability of the various kinds of error and the susceptibility of the application to them. In general, low error rates favor mechanisms with low normal overhead, even at the cost of more expensive recovery. Fig. 7 shows the expected relative costs, in terms of data segments transferred, of the two FTAM mechanisms when using a spacing of 10K bytes between checkpoints and, for comparison purposes, that of the ISO class 4 transport protocol error recovery mechanism with 256 byte protocol data units. Of the two FTAM mechanisms, recovery is to be preferred because it also has the advantage of coping with end system failures.

VI. Future Work on FTAM

A. Filestore Management

In practice, users of distributed systems are concerned not with single files, but with organized collections of files. A protocol for manipulating files should therefore be able to take account of this structure. However, the choice of an organizational style has a much stronger relationship to the supporting operating system than is necessary to identify a single file by name. Attempts to standardize filestore structure and organization progressed slowly within ISO, and a decision was taken to produce a basic file transfer standard first, and then return to augment it with further filestore management facilities.

This second stage is now well underway, and work is focusing on the creation of a filestore model to provide a common meaning for operations on groups of files. This model will allow the organization of files into a multilevel directory structure in which attributes can be associated with the various directories. The naming structure is not, however, restricted to be a simple hierarchy since references can be made to a file from more than one directory.

Operations on the file directories allow their contents or properties to be listed. The access to files or directories can be restricted by access control based on the path through the naming structure via which the object is reached.

A generalization of file selection will allow groups of files to be identified in terms of their attributes. Once a group of files has been identified, its members can be accessed one after another, so that operations can be performed selectively on some or all of the members of the whole group.

B. Overlapped Access

Another area of extension currently being developed in the standards bodies allows for more efficient random access to structured files. In the basic protocol, individual file access data units can be accessed one after another, but data transfer may only be in progress in one direction at a time, and the completion of each data transfer must be confirmed before the next is requested. These restrictions simplify error recovery, but can limit the efficiency of applications where a series of small file access data units have to be read and possibly updated.

The overlapped access extension allows read or write transfer requests to be queued by the initiator, data transfer being performed whenever the supporting communication path is available, possibly in both directions at the same time. Confirmations of checkpoints and of completion of the individual transfers may be interleaved with the file data since they are distinguished by their context via the presentation service. In this way, a pipelined application may keep the communication path fully occupied.

VII. Supporting the FTAM Standard

A. Functional Standardization

The OSI protocol standards support a wide range of styles of use. If simple interworking is to be achieved, it is important that there is agreement on certain basic styles. This has lead to efforts to define subsidiary functional standards, first on a regional basis, and then internationally.

The European standards forum, CEN/CENELEC has established functional standards for simple file transfer, and is working on drafts for transfer and access to files with a flat structure. Work in support of transfer and access for more general structured files is scheduled. This program of work, now taken over by the European Workshop for Open Standards (EWOS), parallels the activities of the NBS Implementors' Workshop in the U.S.; both are feeding their results into the international discussions.

The publication of a functional standard for simple file transfer has helped to concentrate the efforts of manufacturers on a common basic set of functions.

B. Testing and Conformance

The successful use of a protocol depends not only on the protocol definition, but also on the production of clear statements of conformance and on the ready availability of facilities for testing the correctness of implementations. Test houses for the FTAM protocol have already been established in both Europe and America.

To support the needs of conformance testing, ISO is producing a further part of the FTAM standard providing a pro forma on which implementors can state the exact capabilities of their implementations [27]. Work has also been started on the standardization of agreed test suite for the protocol [28].

VIII. Conclusions

The final text of the FTAM standard was approved technically in March 1988 and is now in the process of publication. The addenda on filestore management and overlapped access are expected to be sufficiently stable to begin formal processing as draft standards in 1989.

The production of these standards represents one of the milestones in the establishment of OSI, and the introduction of file transfer products by the major computer suppliers will greatly facilitate the open exchange of information between systems. Several of the major computer suppliers have already announced FTAM products, and many more are known to be under development. In the public domain, the ISODE [29] implementation for use with the UNIX™ operating system is being used by a growing community of users.

The standardization of file transfer protocols is the result of ten years of effort by many people, and builds upon underlying research and initial development by many others over a longer period. The rapid expansion of open file transfer services can now be expected as a result of their efforts.

References

[1] ISO 8571, "Information processing systems—Open systems interconnection—File transfer, access and management," Mar. 1988. "Part 1: General introduction" "Part 2: Virtual filestore definition," "Part 3: File service definition," "Part 4: File protocol specification."
[2] F. Da Cruz, *Kermit, A File Transfer Protocol*. Digital Press, 1987.

™UNIX is a trademark of AT&T Bell Laboratories in the U.S. and other countries.

[3] N. J. Neigus, "File transfer protocol for the ARPA network," in *ARPA Protocol Handbook*, E. Feinler and J. Postel, Eds., Apr. 1976.
[4] "EPSS. A basic file transfer protocol," EPSS Liaison Group, HLP/cp(75)3, June 1975.
[5] "NIFTP, The network independent file transfer protocol," UK High Level Protocol Group, Dec. 1977.
[6] D. Rayner and A. W. Jones, "UK network independent file transfer protocol," in *Kommunikation in verteilten systemen*. Berlin: Springer-Verlag, 1979, pp. 110-120.
[7] "NIFTP, The network independent file transfer protocol (revised)," File Transfer Protocol Implementors Group, Feb. 1981.
[8] M. Gien, "Proposal for a standard file transfer protocol," EIN INRIA/77/4, May 1977.
[9] ——, "A file transfer protocol (FTP)," in *Computer Network Protocols*, A. Danthine, Ed. Belgium: Univ. Liege, 1978, pp. D5-1-D5-7.
[10] R. Popescu-Zeletin and B. Butscher, "Specification of the remote data access system in the HMInet," Hahn Meitner Institut fur Kernforschung, HMI B279, Berlin, Oct. 1978.
[11] R. Popescu-Zeletin, B. Butscher, L. Henckel, W. Heinze, G. Maiss, and K. Jacobsen, "The virtual file system," Hahn Meitner Institut fur Kernforschung, HMI B333, Berlin, Oct. 1980.
[12] P. Quoilin, "The ECMWF file transfer protocol," European Centre for Medium Range Weather Forecasts, Nov. 1979.
[13] H. C. Forsdick, "Autodin II file transfer protocol," BBN Rep. 4246, Feb. 1980.
[14] "DECNET: Data access protocol (DAP)," Digital Equipment Corp., July 1975.
[15] S. E. Clopper, "Features of the file transfer protocol (FTP) and the data presentation protocol (DPP)," NBS Rep. ICST/HLNP 80-6, Sept. 1980.
[16] S. E. Clopper and J. E. Swanson, "Service specification of the file transfer protocol (FTP) and the data presentation protocol (DPP)," NBS Rep. ICST/HLNP 80-9, Oct. 1980.
[17] J. E. Swanson and S. E. Clopper, "Specification of the file transfer protocol," NBS Rep. ICST/HNLP 81-4, Dec. 1981.
[18] D. Belsnes, O. Braaten, A. Engdal, W. Jensen, E. Lillevold, and A. Loraas, "Uninett file management system, The Uninett file management system," Uninett Rep. 10, July 1980.
[19] "ECMA 85, Virtual file protocol," Sept. 1982.
[20] P. Bucciarelli, A. Poublan, J. Schumacher, and W. Thiele, "The ECMA file transfer protocol—An overview," in *Proc. ICCC'82*, Sept. 1982, pp. 859-864.
[21] P. Amaranth and P. Bucciarelli, "File transfer specification," presented at the NBS LAN Workshop, Nov. 1984.
[22] P. F. Linington, "File transfer protocols," in *Network Architectures*, Pergamon Infotech State of the Art Rep., Feb. 1982.
[23] D. Lewan and H. G. Long, "The OSI file service," *Proc. IEEE*, vol. 71, pp. 1414-1419, Dec. 1983.
[24] I. E. Baker, "File transfer, access and management: FTAM ISO 8571," in *Proc. Open Syst. '87*, Online Publ., Mar. 1987, pp. 159-172.
[25] P. F. Linington, "The virtual filestore concept," *Comput. Networks*, vol. 8, no. 1, p. 13, 1984.
[26] O. K. Thomsen, "Value added file transfer in OSI," in *Proc. INDC '88*, Sept. 1988.
[27] DIS 8571-5, "Information processing systems—Open systems interconnection—File transfer, access and management—Part 5: Protocol implementation conformance statement proforma," Feb. 1989.
[28] DP 10170-1, "Information processing systems—Open systems interconnection—Conformance test suite for the FTAM protocol—Part 1: Test suite structure and test purposes," Feb. 1989.
[29] M. Rose and D. E. Cass, "The ISO development environment at NRTC: User's manual," NRTC Tech. Paper 702, Sept. 1986.

Peter F. Linington joined the Computer Laboratory at Cambridge University, England, after a period of research at the Cavendish Laboratory. He has been involved in computer communication since the mid-1970's; he has worked on the UK Coloured Book interim standards and participated in international work on Open Systems Interconnection from its inception, being Rapporteur for FTAM until 1984. In 1979 he was a member of the UK Department of Industry's Data Communication Protocols Unit. In 1982 he became coordinator of the UNIVERSE project, an experiment with broadcast satellite interconnection of local area networks. In 1983 he became Head of the Joint Network Team and the Network Executive, responsible for network coordination and operation of the JANET network for the UK Academic Community. He was one of those involved in the establishment of the European networking association RARE, and was its first President from 1986 to 1988. In 1987 he became the Professor of Computer Communication in the University of Kent, Canterbury. His current research interests cover a range of topics in networks and distributed systems, including distributed multimedia systems exploiting video information. Within ISO, he is currently involved in the standardization of a Reference Model for Open Distributed Processing.

Open Systems Data Transfer

advising on Open Systems Interconnection standards, technology, and products

ISSN 0741-286X

Transmission #48 — October 1990

The Development of Office Document Architecture (ODA)

By William McDonald

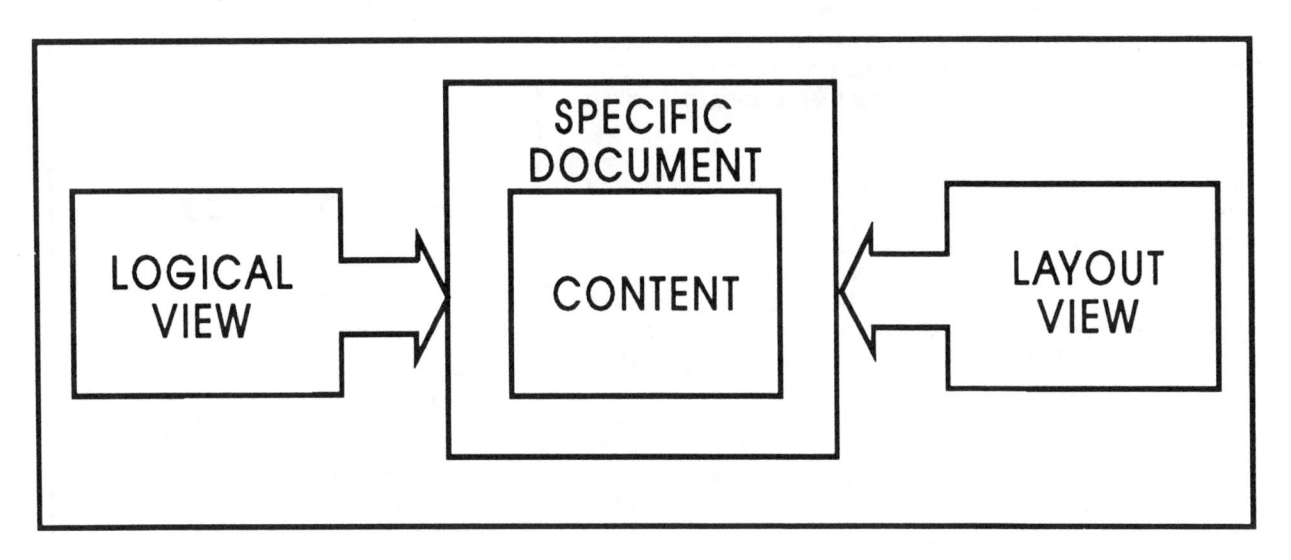

Figure 1: Two Views of a Document

Since the first rudimentary word processors began to create documents in the early 1960s, the problem of exchanging these documents between different systems has been recognized. At first, this was done by physically interchanging magnetic tapes or magnetic cards. Some early attempts at adding communication features to word processors met with limited success, and in any case, it was only possible to exchange simple documents between like word processors using the same media or communications protocol.

As years passed and more word processors began to appear, it became necessary to provide conversion packages to change documents from one word processor format to another. Eventually, the number of conversion packages required, and the number of formats they needed to support, became very large. The problems were further compounded by more advanced word processors and other text systems that made possible the use of pictures composed of raster or vector graphic images along with the conventional character text. These problems would not have a general solution until the late 1980s.

Reprinted with permission from *Open Systems Data Transfer*, October 1990, pp. 1–8.

The beginning of standardization efforts

In 1981, the International Organization for Standardization (ISO) formed a new subcommittee, SC18. This subcommittee, now known as Text and Office Systems, was assigned the task of solving the problems caused by the proliferation of word processing formats. Fortunately, the standardization of a communications protocol was already under development. The Open Systems Interconnection (OSI) standards would make it possible for computer systems from different manufacturers to communicate with each other. The only remaining problem was with the document itself. It would be necessary to develop standard rules to specify the structure of the document, its elements, and the electronic representation of the document. This chore was assigned by SC18 to its Working Group 3 (WG3 - Document Architecture).

SC18/WG3 had its first meeting in February 1982. The European Computer Manufacturers Association (ECMA) had just begun work on a document architecture standard, and brought its work to the ISO group. ECMA continued to develop its standard in parallel with the ISO standard and worked to maintain compatibility between the two; indeed, they were essentially the same standard. Sensibly enough, both ISO and ECMA decided to call their standards "Office Document Architecture" (ODA).

Strong technical leadership in the development of ODA came from ECMA and its representatives. However, before one assumes that ODA is a European standard, it should be pointed out that North American representatives were there from the beginning. In fact, some of the important features of ODA originated on the west side of the Atlantic. Japan was also represented from the beginning and was later joined by Korea, making ODA a truly international standard.

One of the first actions of WG3 was to define two different forms of representation of a document. The "formatted" form of representation would provide for the presentation of a document as intended by the originator. That is, the recipient would be able to print or display the document in much the same way as it was done by the document originator. The "processable" form would provide for further processing (*e.g.*, revision or formatting) by the recipient. Certain constraints on both of these processes could be specified by the originator. It was then decided to allow these two forms to be combined into a *third* form called "formatted processable." This form would contain all of the necessary layout information to image the document as well as the information needed to revise and reformat it.

Document structures

When WG3 began to examine the elements and constraints necessary to implement these three document forms, an-

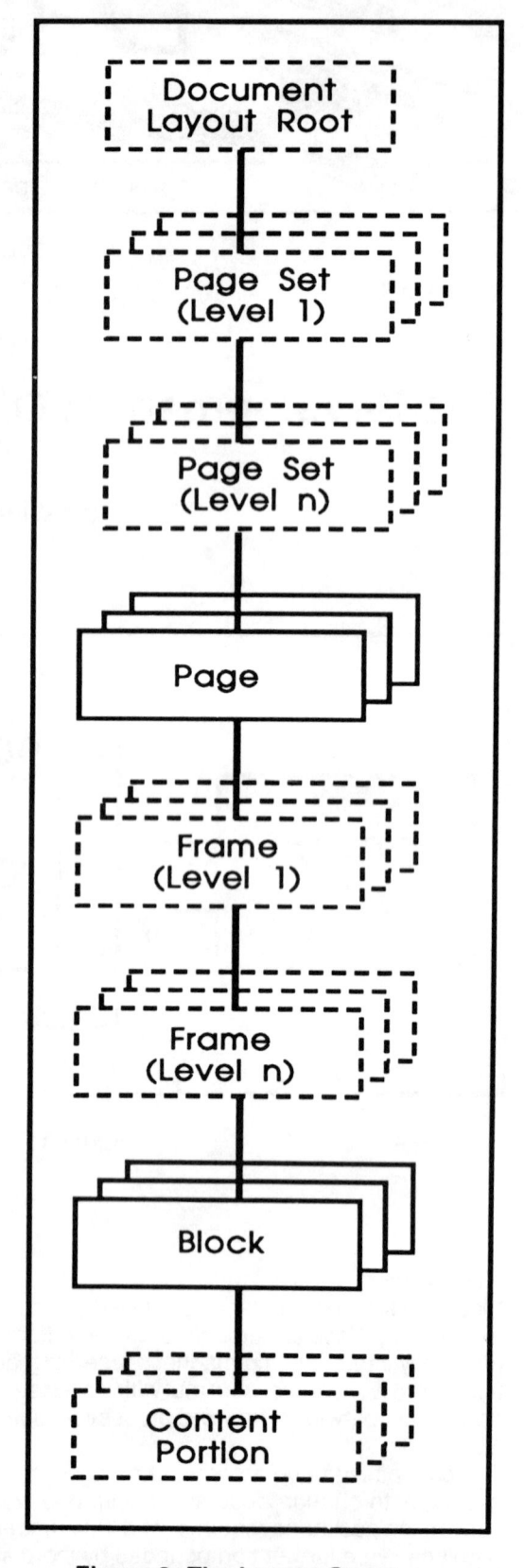

Figure 2: The Layout Structure

other concept began to emerge. As illustrated in **Figure 1**, a document can be viewed in terms of its layout components or its logical components. A *formatted-form* document would consist only of layout components. These layout components would describe how the content of the document is laid out on pages. This would be all that was required to view the document. A *processable-form* document would consist primarily of logical components. These logical components would describe the content of the document in terms that are meaningful to the user, *e.g.*, chapters, sections, paragraphs, headers, footnotes, figures, and captions. A document containing both layout and logical components would be called a "formatted processable document."

The formatted-form document (*i.e.*, the layout view) defines the relationship between the content elements in a document in terms of their presentation on media. This is accomplished by a hierarchical layout structure that decomposes the document into layout objects (illustrated in **Figure 2**). A document may consist of "page set" objects, where each page set contains pages with similar characteristics: "table of contents" pages, for example. Each page can be further subdivided into rectangular areas called "frames." The position and dimensions of the frames may be fixed by the document designer or may be allowed to vary to adapt themselves to the content information that they will contain. Frames may contain other frames or may serve only as a container for laying out the content portions, such as pictures, paragraphs, headers, and so on. As each content portion is laid out, a rectangle is constructed around it. This rectangle forms the basic layout object called a "block."

The processable-form document (the logical view) defines the relationship between the content portions in a manner defined by the application, such as chapters, paragraphs, footnotes, pictures, and so forth. This is also a hierarchical structure, as illustrated in **Figure 3** with the basic logical object containing the content portion.

Many of the objects present in a specific logical or layout structure have similar characteristics. For example, all paragraphs in this *Open Systems Data Transfer* have identical attributes. Many pages in a document may have a similar layout including column layout, headers, footers, etc. This led to the concept of "object classes," which specify those characteristics common to all objects that belong to the class. Taken collectively, these object classes form the generic structures. There can be both a generic layout structure and a generic logical structure. The detailed structures that are unique to a specific document are termed specific structures.

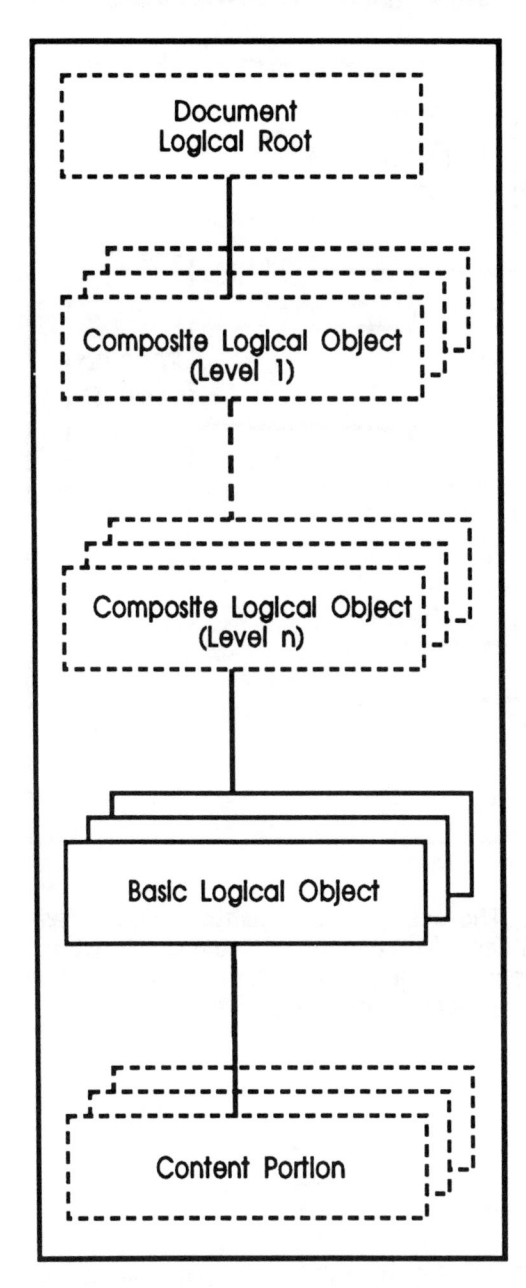

Figure 3: The Logical Structure

In 1984, WG3 began work to define a document processing model. The original purpose was simply to show the relationships of these three document forms. As time went on, however, this model became more significant. As shown in **Figure 4**, the model contains an editing process, a layout process, and an imaging process. From the beginning there were many caveats placed on the description of the processes. It is clearly stated that it is not intended to standardize implementation. The processes are only described to clarify the semantics of the attributes included in the document description.

An important feature of this model is the reference layout process. The input to the process is a processable-

Open Systems Data Transfer - October 1990

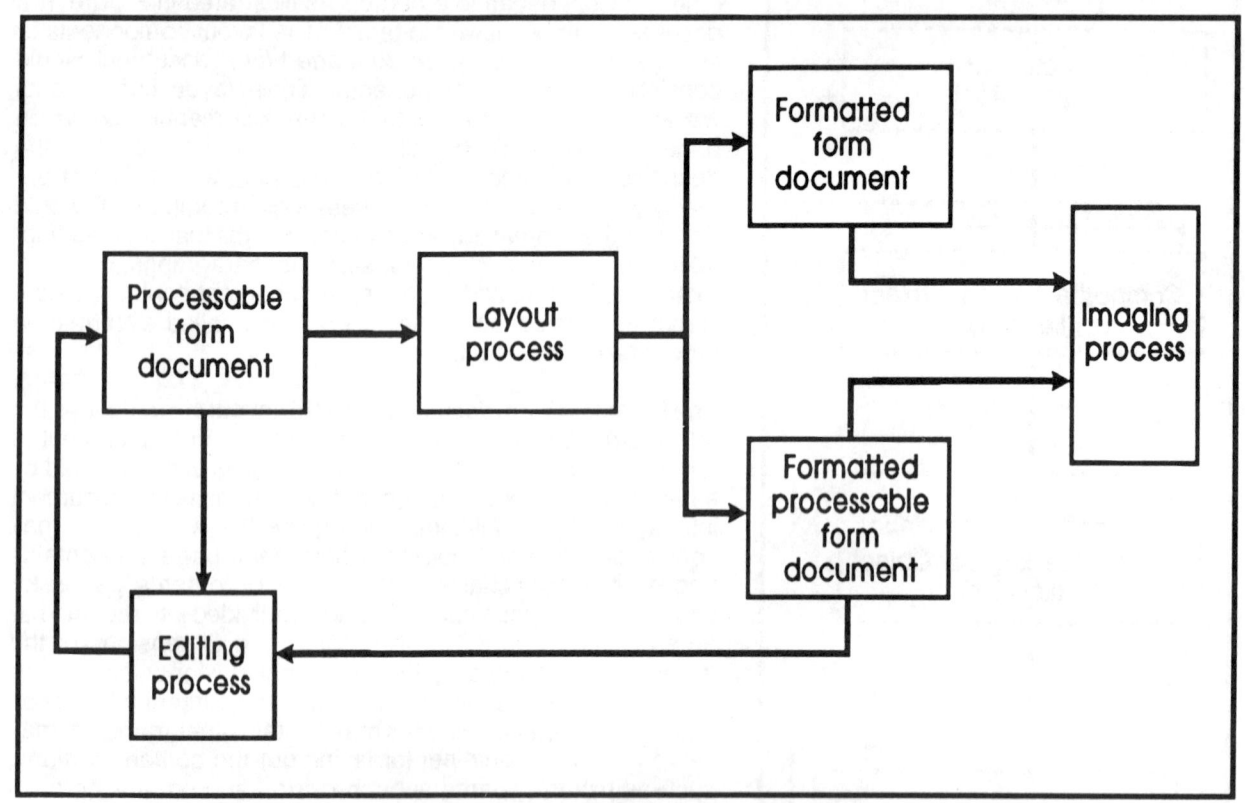

Figure 4: The Document Processing Model

form document which is completely defined by the standard. The output is a formatted or formatted-processable-form document also completely defined by the standard. The attributes necessary to instruct the layout process are defined in terms of the referenced layout process itself. An implementation does not have to duplicate this reference process, but must produce results that are consistent with it.

Styles

From almost the beginning of ODA development, it was intended that a processable-form document should be able to be interchanged along with sufficient information to allow the recipient to lay out the document as intended by the originator. This would produce a formatted or formatted-processable document corresponding to the original processable document. The document could then be imaged by the recipient, using a little more information supplied by the originator, to produce a copy similar to the original document. Defining the information necessary to instruct the recipient to accomplish these things properly and unambiguously was a major undertaking.

It was not until October 1985 that the concept of "styles" was added to the ODA draft text. This concept recognizes that the logical and layout structures should contain only the description of the structures along with the content. The information needed to control processes would be contained in another set of constituents called "styles." That is, the attributes necessary to lay out a processable form document or to image a formatted-form document would be contained in styles referenced from the components in the structures.

This separation between document structures and the processes to be performed on them has many advantages. The structure and content of a document can be changed without regard to the effect on layout and imaging. Conversely, changes can be made in how the document is presented without affecting the document itself. In fact, by changing the styles and generic layout structure, a completely new layout can be achieved for the same document: for example, using this concept, a draft document can be changed to final-form layout very easily.

Content architecture

Most of the early work on ODA related to document structures as described above. It was obvious, however, that some structuring of the information within content portions was necessary: for example, to specify certain text to be underlined or to specify the number of pels per line in a raster graphics picture. The use of other international standards was assumed to be the answer to this problem. The question of how to use these other standards along with the ODA standard led to another important new concept of two levels or tiers of architecture.

What was originally called the "upper tier" is now called "document architecture." This specifies the structure of the document as a whole without regard to the content types used in the document. The layout structure and logical structure are parts of the document architecture. When we define pages, frames, chapters, and so on, we are not really concerned with the content type that they will contain.

The other tier is "content architectures." This includes the rules for structuring information contained in content portions. There are three standardized content architectures in ODA: *Character Content Architecture*, based on ISO 2022 and related character set standards; *Geometric Graphics Content Architecture*, based on ISO 8632; and *Raster Graphics Content Architecture*, which uses coding specified in CCITT Recommendations T.4 and T.6.

Many of the text processor formats that preceded ODA used a different approach. These were developed when character text was the only content type used. Other content types were added later by defining exception conditions. The ODA structure, however, defines a document architecture independent of content type, along with separate architectures for each content type, including character text.

As with any new approach, problems soon developed. It was noted, for example, that *form feed* codes in the content architecture would define page boundaries. This was intended to be done by the layout object page in the document architecture. There were many similar problems. Clearly, rules were needed. The constraints placed on the document architecture and the content architectures were developed along with relationships to be maintained between them. This set of rules and relationships became the "Architecture Interface."

Fortunately, this interface was defined before much work had been done on content architectures, so they could be defined to meet the requirements of the interface. An important objective of the interface was to make it general enough that it could be used for any content type — *including* those not yet envisioned. This interface was put into place in September, 1984. At that time, a reorganization was taking place in SC18. SC18/WG5 picked up the responsibility for developing content architectures for ODA, with SC18/WG3 continuing with the document architecture. This meant that this work not only provided an important architectural interface, but an organizational interface as well.

Document profile

The ODA constituents described above belong to the "document body." Another constituent, the "document profile," is a set of attributes that provide information useful for processing the document as a whole. The document profile provides information concerning the content of the document body, such as the type of structures and content architectures used. This will allow the recipient to determine quickly whether or not he/she can process or image the document. The document profile also contains document management information such as title, subject, author, creation date, and other data which may be used by the recipient for applications such as filing and retrieval.

Document representation

Along with the definition of the architecture, WG3 began very early to develop the means for representing the document in interchange. This would involve a syntax to express the constituents defined by the architecture as well as the actual coding. Although a "type-length-value" syntax was assumed, not much progress was made until some work in CCITT SG VII was investigated. This was the Abstract Syntax Notation One (ASN.1) of Recommendation X.409 and ISO 8824, along with the basic encoding rules of ISO 8825. An application of ASN.1 was developed consisting of interchange data elements corresponding to the constituents in ODA. This representation is called Office Document Interchange Format (ODIF).

An alternative representation was proposed early in the development of ODA, and actual development work began in 1984. This is a clear text representation using an application of the Standard Generalized Markup Language (SGML) of ISO 8879. SGML is a descriptive language that was designed for the purpose of representing document structure. It was therefore well-suited to represent the constituents of ODA. It has the added advantage of providing a gateway to the many systems already using SGML in other applications. This representation is called Office Document Language (ODL). Because both of these representations refer to the same constituents, there is a simple one-to-one mapping between them.

CCITT enters the picture

In 1983, SC18/WG3 formed a close liaison with CCITT SG VIII (Terminal Equipments for Telematic Services). In this CCITT study period, there was a question relating to adding "mixed-mode" capability to Teletex and another to add some text capability to facsimile. These questions had been combined and were being addressed by one rapporteur group. It appeared that these requirements could be met by use of the ODA formatted-form document. The CCITT group agreed, but faced with a deadline: the study period was to close in early 1984.

Therefore, WG3 concentrated on the layout structure definitions and worked frantically with the CCITT group to meet the schedule. The result of all of this was CCITT Recommendation T.73, *Document Interchange Protocol for the Telematic Services*. This was published in the 1984 "Red Book." WG3 experts assured the CCITT group that T.73 would remain a proper subset of ODA as the standard was further developed. Although this caused a few problems in the next few years, the commitment was kept.

The three ODA standards

ECMA published its ODA standard, ECMA-101, in 1985. At the time, it was consistent with the ISO version. ISO continued to further develop ODA with help from ECMA representatives.

In the 1985-1988 study period, CCITT developed a complete version of ODA. Except for procedural terminology, the text in the CCITT version was kept identical to corresponding parts of the ISO ODA. This was done by using the same document editors and a large joint membership.

However, there were two differences in these two versions of ODA. CCITT defined a Videotex interworking feature that was not in the ISO version: videotex is standardized in CCITT but not in ISO. The CCITT version does not include the SGML representation, ODL: SGML is standardized in ISO but not in CCITT. The only other difference was in the name. The CCITT T.410 series of Recommendations, *Open Document Architecture and Interchange Format*, was published in the 1988 "Blue Book."

From a technical standpoint, the ISO version of ODA was essentially completed in November 1987. This allowed the CCITT to meet its early 1988 date with identical text. ISO 8613, *Office Document Architecture (ODA) and Interchange Format*, was published in 1989.

ECMA-101 was revised to contain text identical to that in ISO 8613 and CCITT T.410. It is a true subset, and contains neither Videotex nor ODL. ECMA followed the CCITT, using the name *Open Document Architecture (ODA) and Interchange Format*. At the recent SC18 Plenary, a resolution was passed to change the name on ISO 8613 to *Open Document Architecture*.

Document application profiles

ODA provides for a wide range of capabilities and options. Subsets of these can be created by defining a "Document Application Profile" (DAP). The 1988 CCITT blue book contains four DAPs for telematic services. Additionally, user and manufacturer groups, along with the CCITT, are developing three hierarchically-related DAPs for interchange of documents ranging from simple text to very complex multi-content-type documents.

In North America, the National Institute of Standards and Technology (NIST) hosts an ODA Special Interest Group as part of its Workshop for Implementors of OSI (NIST-OIW). This work forms the basis for a proposed Federal Information Processing Standard (FIPS) and is included in version 2.0 of the U.S. Government Open Systems Interconnection Profile (GOSIP). Similar DAP development is being done by the European Workshop on Open Systems, the Asia-Oceania Workshop, and CCITT SG VIII. These groups have established an informal group called PAGODA (Profile Alignment Group of ODA) to produce a core set of internationally-aligned DAPs. At least two of these are expected to be proposed as Draft International Standardized Profiles (DISPs) by the end of 1990.

Extensions

Before the ODA standard was complete, a number of additional capabilities were already defined and some development work had begun. This first group of extensions included color, styles improvements, streams improvements, alternate representation of content, security, tiled raster graphics, and DAP proforma and notation. Because these are being progressed jointly with the CCITT, the schedule is dictated by the September 1990 SG VIII Plenary. All were expected to be completed by that time.

SC18/WG3, SC18/WG5, and SG VIII WP4 are jointly beginning work on a number of new extensions to ODA. A Special Working Group (SWG) on Data in Documents has been formed and one meeting has been held. This group will develop extensions related to improvements in formula, spreadsheets, business graphics, and other uses of data in ODA documents. Another SWG will concentrate on extensions to enhance document processing. This will involve expanding the document processing model to extend the applications of ODA. These will allow the use of ODA in such areas as remote editing, distributed applications, external references, temporal relationships, and hypermedia.

Current status

The 1980s were busy and interesting years as ISO, CCITT, and ECMA worked together to develop a world-wide standard for document interchange. ODA makes possible the interchange of multimedia documents between systems of different manufacturers in an open systems environment. In view of the tremendous potential of the ODA extensions, the 1990s may be even more fun!

References

1. *Information Processing: Text and Office Systems; Office Document Architecture (ODA) and Interchange Format*; ISO 8613, Parts 1-8 (1989).

2. *Open Document Architecture and Interchange Format*; CCITT T.410 series of recommendations (1988).

3. *Document Interchange Protocol for the Telematic Services*; CCITT Recommendation T.73 (1984).

4. *Office Document Architecture*; ECMA-101 (1985).

5. *Open Document Architecture (ODA) and Interchange Format*; ECMA-101, 2nd edition (1988).

6. *Information Processing Systems - Open Systems Interconnection - Specification of Abstract SyntaxNotation One (ASN.1)*; ISO 8824 (1987).

7. *Information Processing Systems - Open Systems Interconnection - Basic Encoding Rules for AbstractSyntax Notation One (ASN.1)*; ISO 8825 (1987).

8. *Information Processing Systems - Text and Office Systems - Standard Generalized Markup Language*; ISO 8879 (1987).

X.400 MHS: First Steps Towards an EDI Communication Standard

Guy Genilloud
Laboratoire d'informatique technique (LIT)
EPFL - EL Ecublens
CH-1015 Lausanne
Switzerland

email: genilloud@litsun.epfl.ch (EARN/BITNET)

Abstract

Electronic Data Interchange (EDI) is an increasingly important application of computer communications. Until recently, EDI has developed independently of the communications technology and related standards. EDI users coped with this situation by setting up bilateral communications agreements or by using the services of Value Added Data Services centres, which provided protocol conversion. The introduction of X.400 MHS based systems and services is slowly modifying the general attitude towards EDI communications. For the first time, a CCITT rapporteur group is drafting a recommendation for EDI communications within the context of X.400 MHS. More importantly, there already exist official guidelines, both in the U.S.A. and in Europe, which explain how to take advantage of X.400 MHS systems today.

The purpose of this paper is to comment upon these first approaches to an EDI communication standard. For this reason, and because we expect only a few readers to be familiar with both EDI and X.400 MHS, we begin with introductions to both subjects.

Keywords: Data communications, Computer communications, Standardization, Electronic mail, EDI, X.400 MHS, MOTIS.

1 Introduction

This may not be apparent to everyone familiar with both acronyms, but OSI and EDI have some fundamental goals in common : both intend to facilitate the exchange of meaningful information between application processes. OSI, standing for Open Systems Interconnection, is a well defined model created by ISO, the International Standards Organization, to serve as a framework for the definition of communication services and protocols: it defines a stack of seven layers from the physical layer at the bottom to the application layer at the top. Users see only the services offered by the application layer, whose purpose is to serve as a window between correspondent application processes that are using the OSI to exchange meaningful information [9]. EDI, standing for Electronic Data Interchange, is an increasingly important three letter acronym for which it is difficult to find a good definition. Some people see in it a new way to do business, while others think of it as a new information technology. For the scope of this paper, we will limit ourselves to saying that EDI is essentially concerned with the exchange of meaningful information between application processes. This statement should not be controversial. Another point that is not controversial is that EDI has a lot to do with standards: in particular, there are standards dedicated to it, such as ISO EDIFACT [10] or ANSI X12 [1]. However, EDI is not and probably should not be limited to these standards.

Until now EDI and OSI standards have been developed independently with the consequence that there is now some overlapping and inconsistencies between them. Proponents of EDI or OSI standards are starting to debate about whether this situation is normal and tolerable, or whether standards will have to be aligned in the future [17, 18]. The solution to such an argument may well depend on the nature and requirements of the various EDI applications that are emerging.

"X.400 MHS: First Steps Toward an EDI Communication Standard,"
©1990 by G. Genilloud. Reprinted with author's permission.

Until this issue is resolved, users who wish to use OSI standard protocols for transporting EDI messages need to find ad-hoc methods to do so. This may not be technically difficult, but it is not convenient for users to be isolated. There is an imperative need for coordination between the users themselves as well as between the users and the software manufacturers. The NIST (National Institute for Standards and Technology, previously known as the National Bureau of Standards) in the U.S.A. and the CEC (Commission of the European Communities) in Europe have established guidelines which describe how to take advantage of new public or private networks, known as X.400 MHS (Message Handling Systems), to transport EDI messages [8, 13].

These guidelines have been established for the short term; they are therefore very simple and indeed fairly short. Also, both guidelines are intended for systems currently available, i.e. for systems based on the 1984 version of the X.400 series of recommendations. On the other hand, perhaps because EDI is perceived differently in the U.S.A than in Europe, they recommend two radically different approaches for using X.400 MHS. Fortunately, care has been taken to make them compatible through a simple gateway.

On the longer term, EDI users will benefit from a better adapted, more powerful, communication solution. A CCITT rapporteur group is currently drafting a recommendation that will indicate how to support EDI communications within the context of X.400.

2 Electronic Data Interchange

Companies normally exchange documents such as purchase orders, invoices, customs declarations, and technical specifications, by physical mail. When these documents are processed by computers at both ends, it is more logical to transfer them electronically (fig. 1).

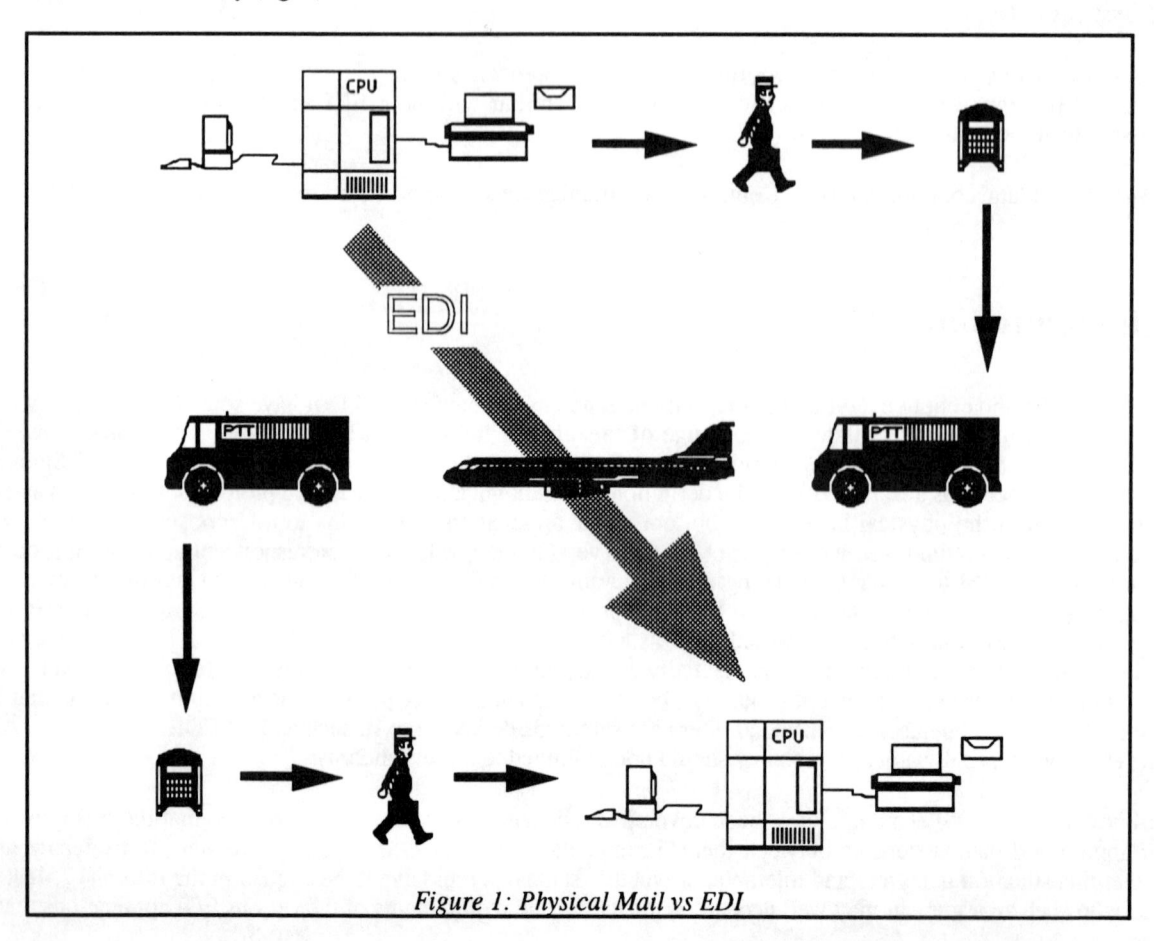

Figure 1: Physical Mail vs EDI

The costs created when using paper documents, which can be identified as paper handling costs, typing costs, and costs caused by typing errors, can be minimized by transmitting data electronically. This represents significant savings: a survey ordered by the United Nations Organization has evaluated paper related costs to represent 7% of the price of shipped merchandise (up to 200 paper documents need to be produced during the exporting/importing of one set of goods). Note that we do not mention mailing costs, as they are comparatively insignificant: cost reductions are to be made directly on the company premises, not on the communication channels.

In fact, the advantages of exchanging data electronically go well beyond these simple cost reductions. Physical mail and data reentry are characterised by long and unpredictable delays for the transmission which prevent companies from organizing their business in a much more effective manner. When these delays can be reduced to hours or minutes (in general, it is perfectly acceptable for documents to be delivered overnight, as long as there is no uncertainty about this delay), companies can make a better use of human, material, and capital resources.

It is of this kind of application that most people think when they say "EDI", although they certainly realize that EDI covers several more aspects than just this one. Nevertheless, it is precisely this aspect of EDI that is most compatible with X.400 communication mechanisms. For the scope of this paper, we call it *asynchronous EDI*, or simply *EDI*, and we define it to be the asynchronous exchange, from computer to computer, of inter-company business documents and information.

3 Fundamental Difficulties of Using EDI

There are several good reasons that companies may have for starting to use EDI. Sometimes, companies hope that this will result in an increased competitiveness (a recent study suggests however that this advantage, if it exists, will only be temporary [3]). More often, they want to use EDI for specific applications where savings are guaranteed to be significant. Yet, companies may also be forced into EDI, because their clients demand it, or because their competitors start using EDI and are successful with it. In any case, companies hesitate because switching to EDI is not an easy process.

3.1 Data Structures and Formats

It is difficult to exchange meaningful data between EDI application processes. One of the most fundamental reasons is that the processes we call EDI applications in this article (a consistent naming scheme or reference model is lacking for EDI) are in fact business management programs that have been developed for a specific purpose, without consideration for standards or other applications. These applications are therefore all different from one another. Moreover, the data formats and structures that they use are quite particular, and generally not suitable for communications.

Without a reference basis, it is very difficult for different companies to agree on something more than the kind of data that need to be exchanged. So companies look for appropriate standards, such as EDIFACT (Electronic Data Interchange For Administration, Commerce, and Transport[1]), for suggestions concerning data elements and data structures [10, 11, 19, 20, 21]. Then, they use special programs, called EDI translators, to reformat their own data accordingly.

However, standards are still undergoing development and are sometimes difficult to interpret correctly. They cannot be implemented overnight, even when using translators. These are not magic programs; they can be difficult to use or have major limitations in what they can do. Changes to an EDI application to make it standard compatible cannot

---

[1] EDIFACT designates, in fact, a set of standards that are currently being developed by UNECE (United Nations, Economic Commission for Europe) in cooperation with ANSI X12; it covers: the syntax rules (ISO #9735), the data elements and their formats (EDED: EDIFACT Data Element Directory, *in development*), the message components (EDSD: EDIFACT Data Segment Directory, *in development*), and the messages (EDMD: EDIFACT Data Messages Directory, *in development*).

generally be limited to the translator; it is often necessary to write a special translation module to complement the translator, or to make significant changes in the application. Also, trading partners who are using different translators may discover that there are incompatibilities between them; care must be taken to ensure that no truncation of data or similar problems occur.

3.2 Applicability of Standard Messages

A more fundamental problem is that the data to be exchanged are very dependent on the nature of the business in which the companies are involved, and even on the administrative methods used by these companies.

Therefore, it is impossible for standards to describe messages that are treatable (i.e. not overly complex), and that meet all the business, administrative, and operative requirements of all companies. Universal standards can only provide a framework that helps corporate groups and individual companies design EDI messages. For example, EDIFACT messages, at least those which are called UNSMs (United Nations Standard Messages), are supersets of messages used in practice; they contain all possible pieces of information that may be required in almost any business scenario. Users must compare them with their business requirements in order to derive their own messages which might be, but are not necessarily, proper subsets of the UNSMs. Finding an agreement on a UNSM subset that will be functional, sufficient, and well understood, is not easy.

3.3 Legal Considerations

Using EDI instead of paper changes the legal context in which transactions take place. In fact, this new context is not clear at all, and it can be quite different from one country to another. In France, for example, only paper documents have a legal value. Other countries are more flexible, as they accept telex or computer data as legal evidence, provided some security provisions have been respected. Things naturally get worse when EDI is done over national borders. Also, computer and network security, as it is implemented today, is too weak to have a strong and definitive legal significance.

Companies tend therefore to use EDI only with partners that they can trust, after signing a specific contract with them. NORDIPRO, the Trade Facilitation Committee of the Nordic Countries, has published the UNCID rules (the Uniform Rules of Conduct for Interchange of Trade Data by Teletransmission [14]) which can serve as a reference to establish this EDI contract.

3.4 Communication Aspects of EDI

EDI standards are designed to be totally independent of the communication technology, whether it is based on open (OSI) or proprietary solutions; today, even tapes or telex are being used. EDI standard messages are self-contained, including all the necessary service elements, such as address indications, message number, password, etc.. Coding is based almost exclusively (EDIFACT level B syntax) or totally (level A syntax) on printable characters. It has been said, quite correctly, that OSI standards are intended to enable systems to interwork, while (current) EDI standards are intended to enable data to be interchanged without interworking [18].

In most cases, EDI communication is essentially a bulk transfer of printable character files. This does not sound complicated, but it is more easily said than done. Trading partners have to find communication methods which are effective, reliable, practical, and reusable for other purposes. This may be difficult or easy, depending on particular cases, but it is always an annoying problem for the users because it is generally not within the scope of their business.

The first users of EDI (a few large companies and national administrations) were happy to exchange very large amounts of data with only a few partners, making use of one of two simple methods: the physical transfer of magnetic tapes (or punched cards) or the use of leased lines. Nowadays, these methods are inadequate: the timeliness of communications has become more important; the size of the data to be exchanged has varied; and companies cooperate with more trading partners than before.

Using existing data communication networks, such as X.25 networks, is a good idea, and in effect, users take advantage of them whenever they are available at an acceptable cost. However, this is only part of the solution. Data communication networks solve communication problems which are confined to the lower layers of the OSI model (up to layer 3 or 4). To allow different application programs running on different, heterogeneous, computers to exchange data, it is necessary to define and to implement protocols up to the application layer. Also, communication may need to take place over not only one, but several networks which do not necessarily run the same low level protocols. Therefore, there is a need for higher level protocols to cope with all these differences and associated difficulties.

Another problem, that has already appeared to be quite significant, is that most communication protocols, and in particular all low level protocols, are *synchronous*, i.e. both computers, sender and recipient, must be available at the same time for communication to take place. A sender may need several attempts to establish a session with a recipient computer, simply because this computer is overloaded by other requests, or is disconnected for backups and maintenance. For the sender, this communication approach is more cumbersome than using mail, and can be costly over long distances.

Today, in order to solve their communication problems, trading partners have to analyze their particular requirements and capabilities. After comparing the various possible solutions, they select one that is acceptable for them both.

3.5 Bilateral Agreements

Message design, resolution of legal requirements, communication means, and even message coding, are activities that can be handled essentially on a case by case basis. Companies are therefore very selective about how and where they start to use EDI: at first, they choose to use EDI with a small number of trading partners which account for a large percent of their commercial exchanges. They sign a document with them, generally called a bilateral EDI agreement, which covers all the questions mentioned above. Often, companies group themselves into sectorial associations and try to agree on a multilateral EDI agreement: such a document may lower or eliminate the need for further bilateral agreements.

As companies try to use EDI with more and more partners, sometimes outside of their main sectorial domain, they will be able to do so faster and more smoothly if they can reuse the same software and hardware equipment used with their other EDI partners. This is difficult to achieve because business requirements, practices, and methods vary from one sectorial domain to another, or from one country to another. However, there are no fundamental reasons that prevent companies from using the same coding techniques and the same communication methods for asynchronous EDI.

4 Favoured Communication Methods for EDI

In this paper, we intend to discuss how and why X.400 MHS can be used for *asynchronous* EDI. We present short term solutions which have a long term perspective. Nevertheless, today there is a widely accepted approach to EDI communications which is likely to remain important in the future: it consists in using VADS (Value Added Data Services) centres. We will first describe this well known approach in order to compare the use of X.400 MHS with it.

X.400 MHS and the VADS are clearly in competition with one another, but they are not incompatible. In fact, it is very likely that they will be integrated in the future. How well this will be done, however, is an important question that remains to be answered.

4.1 Value Added Data Services

Several companies, generally known as VADS (Value Added Data Services) companies, are taking advantage of their large computer centres to offer several services to EDI users, to help them cope with most EDI communication problems. Basic services are the renting of mailboxes and the conversion of protocols, this latter service being almost implicit. In fact, VADS simply give access to mailboxes through several communication protocols.

With VADS, EDI communication between partners becomes asynchronous. The sender simply establishes a connection to the VADS centre, which is always available, and submits messages which will be distributed by the VADS system to the addressees' mailboxes. Recipients can check and read the contents of their mailbox whenever they want, or if they request it, they can be notified of any mail that they receive. VADS centres offer other additional services, such as reports on the status of expedited messages, logging, auditing, some security services, as well as the translation of syntaxes and formats of EDI messages.

The VADS role is even more important than it might appear at first glance. When using the services of a VADS company, a company sending an EDI message (e.g. an invoice or a purchase order) is confident that its message will be received and stored in its recipient's mailbox; it will then be the responsibility of the recipient company to read the contents of its mailbox. It is impossible, for example, for a recipient company to temporarily refuse to receive an invoice or an order by refusing communications or even shutting down a computer. When establishing their EDI bilateral agreement, trading partners can agree to consider the VADS company as a trusted third party, thereby simplifying some legal questions.

VADS companies solve the communication problems of their clients as long as communication is limited to within their system. So far, they have been reluctant to communicate with other competitive VADS systems, and even more with companies which are not clients of any VADS centre. Even if they agree in principle to do so, VADS companies find it difficult to establish tariffs that are both consistent and acceptable to their clients. Also, there are some services that are difficult to implement when more than one VADS center is involved in the communication: for example, the status indication (retrieved, not retrieved, etc.) of messages.

Until recently, VADS companies did not have to interconnect their systems, because EDI was confined to sectorial domains or national borders. This is no longer true, because EDI domain is enlarging constantly.

Moreover, another challenge that VADS companies must face today is the emergence of new universal standards in messages and communications (OSI, X.400). These standards, provided they are well accepted by EDI users, can lower the need of services that VADS companies currently offer. On the other hand, VADS companies may benefit from these standards, with solutions to technical problems, and with a new range of services to be offered. In any case, there will be an increase in the EDI traffic, and VADS companies could attract some of it.

4.2 The X.400 Message Handling System

It is well known and quite understandable that computer manufacturers are reluctant to implement and to support communication products that give a direct advantage to a competitor. They prefer to implement their own solutions or they choose to implement communication systems which are based on standard protocols, preferably those developed by the International Standards Organization (ISO). Users themselves have discovered that, if they intend not to be restricted in their choice of new computer equipment, they have to commit themselves to using standard protocols. For inter-company communications, this is even a necessity since communication takes place between all possible kinds of computers.

In 1984, ISO and CCITT introduced a universally applicable, logical communications structure which is now known as the Open Systems Interconnection (OSI, [9]). OSI is now serving as reference for the development of new communication protocols and services. At the same time, ISO and CCITT standardized a first version of a service situated at the application layer (the top level of the OSI structure)[1]. This service, which is today essentially known under its CCITT appellation X.400 MHS (Message Handling System), or simply X.400, is based on a store-and-forward communication system [4]. In other words, X.400 can be seen as an *asynchronous* communication system. It is therefore of great interest to EDI users. Another advantage of X.400 is that it is specified up to the application layer: it is therefore relatively easy to design a simple interface between the X.400 software and the EDI application processes.

X.400 MHS was developed primarily for the purpose of supporting electronic mail and related services, but its design was made open to supporting other applications. Recognizing the growing importance of EDI, CCITT is currently working on an EDI extension to the X.400 series of recommendations [15, 16]. Products and services based on this

---

[1] X.400 has been updated in 1988. However, systems and services conformant to this new version will not replace current ones before several years from now.

new recommendation are expected to be available within a few years. However, EDI users do not have to wait until then; current X.400 products can be adapted to provide a reasonably good support to EDI communications.

4.2.1 Architecture

Figure 2 shows the architecture of the X.400 MHS. The most important component of X.400 is the MTS (Message Transfer System), which provides the store-and-forward communication. The MTS conveys a message submitted by one user, the originator, and subsequently delivers it to one or more users, the message's recipients. The MTS is a distributed system; it is composed of several MTAs (Message Transfer Agents) which cooperate among themselves using an application layer protocol that is known as P1.

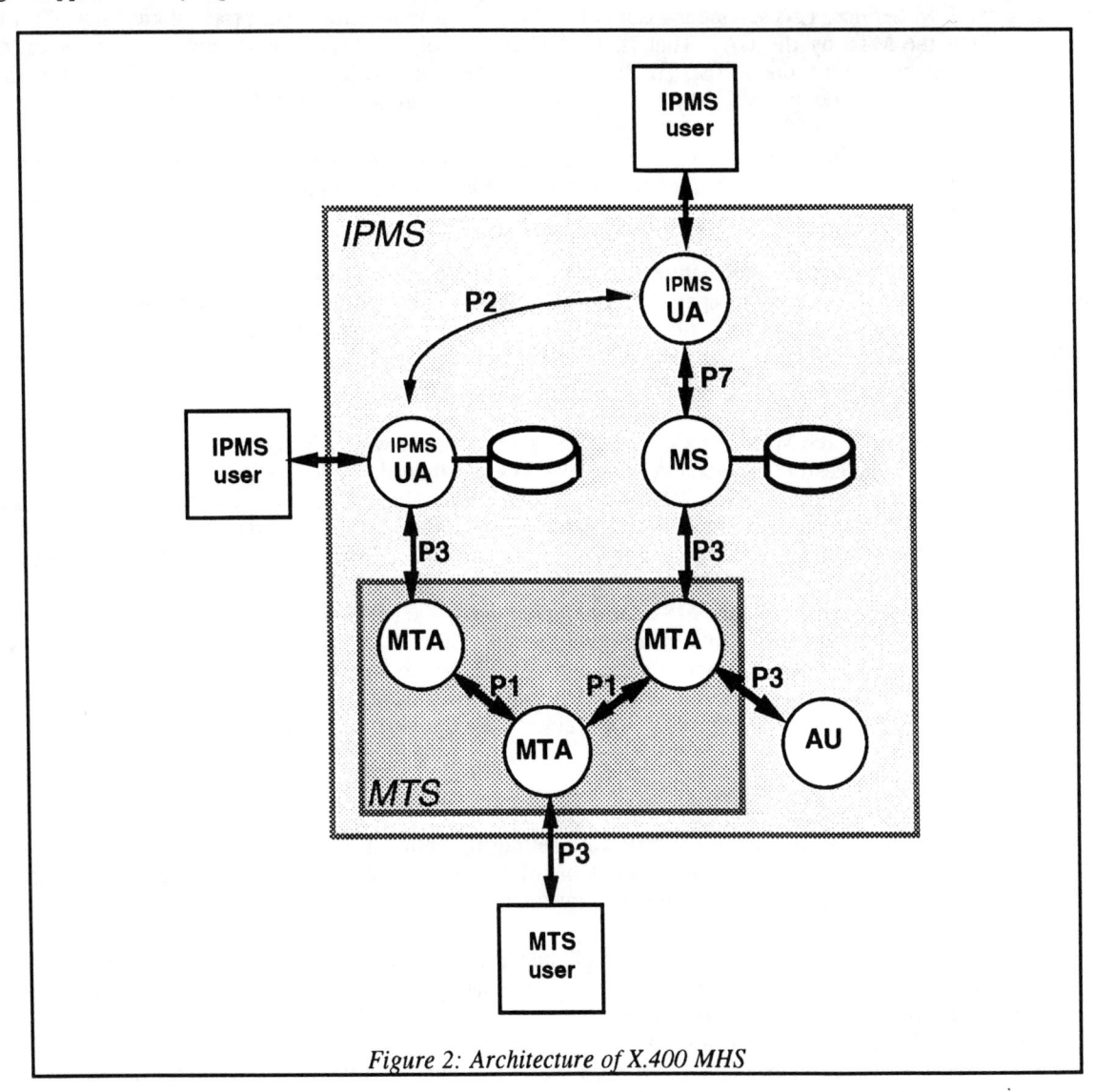

Figure 2: Architecture of X.400 MHS

An MTA is often linked to some other entities, the MTS users. An MTS user and its MTA can be located in different systems. In this case, the MTS user and the MTA interwork through a standard application layer protocol called P3. In the case where they are collocated, they interwork through a proprietary interface, based on the P3 protocol. Neither ISO nor CCITT standardize interfaces inside a system.

According to the 1984 version of the X.400 recommendations, MTS users are only AUs (Access Units) and UAs (User Agents). AUs are simply gateways to other communication systems, including telex, teletex, facsimile, and physical delivery. Like all gateways, AUs are extremely useful but provide limited functionality. Although they can potentially be used for EDI, AUs are not covered in this paper.

UAs are application processes that interact with the MTS to submit or receive messages on behalf of a single user. UAs are normally grouped into classes that are capable of offering a particular series of services. They interwork with one another through the MTS, using an application layer protocol specific to their class. The way a UA offers its services to its user is not specified in the X.400 standards. Actually, UAs may even provide other services than those which are standardized; for example, they can provide some mechanism to store and retrieve messages locally. In a UA implementation, it may be difficult to separate the code that implements the standard from the code that provides supplementary local functionality.

Until now, only one class of UAs has been standardized by ISO and CCITT, the class of IPM UAs (InterPersonal Messaging UAs). IPM UAs assist users in communicating with other IPM users, achieving a service that is globally referenced as the IPM Service. This service is essentially based on an application layer protocol known as P2, which is performed over the MTS by the UAs. That is, IPM UAs always insert structured data conforming to P2 in messages that they submit to the MTS. To differentiate these messages from all other X.400 messages, communications exchanged among IPM UAs (user messages and notifications) are called IP-messages.

According to X.400-1984, storage and retrieval of messages was always a local matter. There was no specification nor provision in the standard for something analog to a mailbox. However, it was clear that most UAs would provide such a functionality.

There are many situations where the architecture of X.400-1984 is appropriate (for example when a document storage and retrieval server already exists in an open system). However, there are other cases, particularly where PCs are involved, where this architecture is not suitable. This is mainly due to the fact that a UA must be continually available to receive incoming messages. To remove this constraint, ISO and CCITT have included the concept of the MS (Message-Store) in the 1988 version of X.400.

Inserted (optionally) between the MTS and a UA, the MS is a new entity which fits quite nicely in the MHS model, so well in fact that it can be easily incorporated in an 1984 system. Indeed, the MS is linked to the MTS via the P3 protocol, as are the independent UAs. The MS acts as a server for a single UA, with which it is linked by a new protocol, called P7. This protocol is never initiated by the MS. So, the UA which is its client can be switched off when it is not used. Moreover, P7 provides quite a few more services than P3 (namely selective message retrieval).

As the reader may already have noticed, the MS concept makes the X.400 MHS standards more confusing. This is due to the fact that a UA, which is an MS client, is not quite the same thing as an independent UA, although both kinds of UAs may provide the same functionality to an end-user. To get around this problem, the reader may find it useful to consider that an MS is always present (either the MS exists by itself, or it is included in the UA). Of course, a single UA may provide much less functionnality, but seeing things that way is useful in many situations.

4.2.2 Public and Private Domains

The PTT administrations in all industrial countries are setting up national X.400 public networks, known in the standard as ADMDs (ADministration Management Domain), that will be interconnected. PTT administrations will also interconnect their ADMDs to their existing communication systems (i.e. telex, facsimile, and physical mail).

PTTs will transport x.400 messages for two kinds of clients: users who dispose of a PRMD (PRivate Management Domain), i.e. an internal electronic mail system; and users who are only using the PTT system. In the first category, users dispose of a computer system or network which runs at least one MTA. Users in the second category use a computer running a UA and possibly an MS, but no MTA, or they have solely a terminal and they rent a UA from the PTT. In technical terms, we can say that the first category of clients have P1 access, while the others have either P3 or P7 access, or a simple terminal access. In any case, these clients will generally be connected to the PTT system by an X.25 link, although other possibilities may exist in some countries.

A PRMD can be seen as the electronic equivalent of a company's internal mail system, but it is more than just that. A PRMD can communicate directly with adjacent PRMDs[1]. Indeed, it is technically possible for a company to set up a national or international PRMD (possibly using the X.25 national networks) whose main function would be to interconnect small PRMDs. In this case, the restrictions that apply, if any, are more legal than technical.

The concept of PRMD is interesting for VADS companies, because it allows them to offer their services within the X.400 framework. VADS companies can set up their own PRMD and use the message-store concept to offer mailbox-services in a standard manner. In France, there is already an EDI service that uses this approach. Also, VADS companies may implement a proprietary message-store service and protocol within their PRMD. In doing so, they can open the X.400 world to companies which use proprietary communication solutions. Again, implementations based on this approach are already in existence today.

4.2.3 The Store-and-Forward Concept

X.400 is based on a store-and-forward concept up to the application layer. A message is transferred as a whole from one X.400 node to the next, where it can be stored for several hours if necessary. There is therefore no need to establish an end-to-end session between originator and recipient computers; sessions are set up one by one between adjacent X.400 nodes.

The X.400 network tries to deliver a message to its recipient within a specified time limit. If the message is not delivered (probably because the recipient's computer is not available), the MTS normally returns a non-delivery notification to the sender. This time limit is a function of the message priority; the F.400 series of recommendations, which specify the quality of the message handling service offered by an ADMD, indicates 4 hours for urgent messages, 24 hours for normal messages, and 36 hours for non-urgent ones.

4.2.4 Security of X.400

Users who own their own mailboxes must grant access to their computer to an ADMD, and possibly to several PRMDs, for message transfer. This should represent no serious security threats, for two reasons:

- ADMDs and PRMDs identify themselves through the exchange of passwords;

- the access which is granted is limited to a well-defined protocol which can only perform X.400 services; a remote PRMD therefore cannot directly access the operating system of the host computer, as would be the case with techniques based on remote job entry.

The X.400-1988 recommendations specify a new class of advanced security services that are based mainly on cryptographic techniques. These services, which include message confidentiality and digital signatures, will be invaluable to clarify legal questions within the context of EDI.

5 Standardization Work for EDI/X.400

More and more companies exchanging EDIFACT and other types of EDI messages use or wish to use communication systems based on the X.400 series of recommendations. Indeed, as we mentioned earlier, the universality of this pioneer OSI application layer standard, its world-wide acceptance, its flexibility, as well as its store-and-forward concept, make it a very suitable carrier for a large range of EDI communications.

Unfortunately, the development of EDIFACT and X.400 standards has been done in parallel without coordination between the standardization bodies. As a result, no special user agent class supporting EDI communications was

---

[1] This is explained in ISO documents but not in CCITT documents, the latter being mainly intended for the PTT administrations.

included in the original design. Current X.400 implementations have been designed for electronic mail. They can handle EDI messages, but they do not recognize them as such, and so they cannot do any automatic processing with them.

Several software vendors as well as some determined users, particularly in Europe, have modified existing X.400 implementations to make them more suitable for EDI. But, in the absence of any reference document or any coordination committee, these companies have developed various systems that are often incompatible with one another, defeating the purpose of using a standard such as X.400. This is particularly the case of implementations that arbitrarily make use of X.400 service elements to carry EDI communication parameters.

To improve this situation, the NIST (National Institute for Standards and Technology) in the United States and the CEC (Commission of the European Communities) in Europe have developed extensions to existing X.400 profiles which explain how the X.400 protocols should be used for EDI. Their guidelines are based on very different principles that reflect the different approaches to EDI communication in the U.S.A and in Europe. The CEC has ensured that its guidelines are compatible with those of the NIST through a simple gateway. On this point, it is important to realize that the CEC could not simply endorse the NIST guidelines, because most European EDI users of X.400 were heading in another direction, and would probably have continued to do so.

5.1 The NIST Guidelines: Making Direct Use of the MTS

Presently, X.400 can be seen as hierarchically structured into two levels: the interpersonal messaging service (IPMS) which defines electronic mail functions, and the message transfer system (MTS), which is a general system for transferring any kind of message.

In 1987, experts of the NIST and ANSI X12 analyzed the communication needs of American EDI users. They estimated that the IPMS was not appropriate for EDI, because the IPMS is a system for the exchange of relatively small messages, generally not confidential, between human users. On the other hand, EDI communication is the exchange of large, confidential messages between companies, or more precisely, between central EDI communication agents. *EDI messages*, also called *transaction sets*, are produced by application processes, translated into standard format, and arranged in *functional groups*, which are then directed to the central EDI communication agent. Then, the communication agent puts functional groups together into *interchanges*, and sends these to their recipients over various communication channels. Linking the EDI communication agent to an X.400 MTA presents no special difficulties. Therefore, the NIST concluded that X.400 should be used at the MTS level for EDI communication.

Since no EDI communications agent has been normalized by the CCITT nor the ISO, there is a subtle problem interfacing such a component directly with the message transfer service. In effect, the 1984 version of X.400 (which is the one in use today) specifies that the content type of an MTS envelope (which indicates the UA class for which the envelope content is intended) be simply an integer value; the problem is to decide on a unique integer value to be used for content types not defined by the CCITT nor the ISO[1]. The NIST, having no authority to pick specific integer values for content types, had to use the value zero for EDI, even though this value indicates in fact an undefined content type. This will probably have no serious consequences. Nevertheless, as a result of this choice, the NIST solution has been dubbed *P0* by analogy to the P2 protocol (the only standard content type in use today), although there is no such thing as a P0 protocol. Realizing that it is effectively making use of the P1 protocol and nothing else, some experts prefer to be more precise, and call it *P1/0*.

It is not certain that all current X.400 implementations of the MTS can accept other content types than P2, or have a well defined interface, so it may be difficult for users to interface their EDI communications agent to it. However, an important group of X.400 system developers, united under the banner of the X.400 API Association, are currently working on a series of common interfaces to their systems. Their intention is to make it more easy and more attractive for users and third party software developers to implement communication solutions based on X.400 [12, 22]. Therefore, the work of the API association constitutes a very important complement to the NIST guidelines.

---

[1] The direct use of the MTS for message contents other than content types specifically defined by the standards has been recognised by the CCITT and the ISO; in the 1988 version of X.400, content types can be indicated by object identifiers as well as by integer values.

5.2 The Situation in Europe

EDI communication in Europe is generally based on different principles than in the U.S.A. European users make a minimal use of functional groups; instead of multiplexing EDI messages through central EDI communications agents, they send them directly between final EDI applications. Concretely, this means that they make use of several simple EDI communication agents instead of a complex one. Therefore, European EDI users are looking at the problem of how to use X.400 with a very different point of view from that of the Americans.

It is interesting to note that, in the absence of any guidance, most if not all European pioneer companies that chose to use X.400, decided to use it at the IPMS level. In fact, these users often had very concrete and practical reasons to make such a choice. First, some of them had been using a proprietary electronic mail system as an EDI communication mechanism for some time. Having had a satisfactory experience with it, they found it logical to use X.400 in a similar way. Moreover, essentially for architectural reasons (gateways at the IPMS level, UAs being switched off from time to time inside their company, and so on), it was probably easier for them to migrate to an EDI communication system based on X.400 at the IPMS level than to a system based solely on the MTS.

Other companies decided to use X.400 at the IPMS level because they found it easier to implement an EDI interface that way. In the case of a lack of significant support from X.400 vendors, the idea was to modify an existing X.400 system at the outermost level, making as few changes as possible while maximizing software reuse. For example, the original user interface could be transformed into an EDI communication administrator interface and an application programming interface, while almost everything else would remain unchanged.

Other proponents for the use of X.400 at the IPMS level were the owners and the vendors of personal computers. They benefited from special solutions to get an X.400 access at the IPMS level (along the lines of the message-store concept), or were looking forward to them. Such solutions would not be immediately applicable if X.400 was to be used solely at the MTS level.

Finally, some European EDI users did not see EDI as being a completely automated transfer of structured data between applications. They thought that human intervention in the communication process was tolerable and sometimes even desirable. For them, there was simply no choice to be made.

5.2.1 The TEDIS Guidelines: Using the IPMS

The CEC, which has set up the TEDIS (Trade Electronic Data Interchange Systems) programme to promote and to coordinate the use of EDI in Europe, became alerted to the fact that many European EDI users were implementing X.400 based communication solutions without guidance nor coordination; as a result, they were making different choices for the use of X.400 service elements, such as the subject field, leading to potential incompatibilities between their systems. Another problem was that most implemented solutions were not compatible with the NIST guidelines, making communication between the U.S.A. and Europe very difficult.

During the summer of 1988, the CEC requested proposals for European guidelines on the use of X.400 for EDI; such guidelines would be applicable until an official recommendation is approved by CCITT. In autumn 1988, the CEC organized a meeting with all interested parties, including active users, to determine an official European position. The meeting clearly showed that an overwhelming majority of users were favouring an IPMS based solution. However, it was clear to all participants that it would be very difficult to obtain further agreement on the use of IPMS service elements. Moreover, American delegates, as well as some European users, were concerned that a European solution based on the IPMS would not be compatible with the NIST guidelines. They expressed the wish that Europeans avoid any misuse of IPMS service elements for EDI purposes.

By the end of the meeting, the CEC was able to establish guidelines, thereafter called the TEDIS guidelines [8], which were acceptable to all parties. The use of the IPMS for EDI would be recommended in Europe, but the use of any IPMS (P2) service elements would be discouraged. In this way, EDI communications between Europe and the U.S.A. could take place through a simple gateway. American delegates were therefore satisfied because this was a major improvement on the present situation. The Europeans felt the same because they wanted to use the IPMS mainly for architectural reasons, and generally not for the extra service elements available with it.

The TEDIS guidelines are quite subtle. A confusing fact about them is that they are sometimes dubbed as the *P2 approach*, by analogy to the NIST guidelines which have been dubbed the *P0 approach*. This name is obviously not an ideal choice since the TEDIS guidelines specifically recommend not to take advantage of the services provided by P2. For reasons explained above, it would be more appropriate to speak of the *IPMS approach*.

5.2.2   Demonstrations at CeBit

Only a few months after the meeting convened by the CEC, a demonstration on the theme "OSI and EDI" was held at the CeBit Fair in Hannover. Participants included most if not all major computer and communication software vendors. This was the first occasion to see what kind of X.400 products would be available for EDI in Europe. However, it must be said that this demonstration was organised on very short notice. No strong conclusions should be drawn from it.

The commitment of participants to support EDI in one way or another was very positive. Not surprisingly, all vendors who demonstrated an X.400 solution for EDI came with spin-offs of their original products. Most made minimum changes to their original electronic mail software so that it could automatically handle EDI interchanges. TEDIS guidelines were respected, with one exception: the subject field of the IP-message was used to convey an indication related to the interchange.

The "OSI and EDI" demonstration is to be reconvened at CeBit this year. Participants will probably bring improved versions of the products they demonstrated last year. It will be interesting to see what progress has been made in one year, and whether the TEDIS guidelines are fully respected this time.

5.2.3   Using X.400 for EDI in Europe

Due to the limited demand and also due to the interim nature of the TEDIS guidelines, it is likely that vendors are not ready to do much more than what they showed at CeBit 1989. Interested users will have to negotiate with them for special solutions to their problem, or they will have to write a specific EDI interface themselves (if possible). In that case, they may benefit from the work of the X.400 API Association, although this group clearly gives a higher priority to interfaces at the MTS level than to interfaces at the IPMS level.

Another difficulty that European EDI users will have to face is that European ADMDs are not yet fully interconnected. Since EDI is often used across national borders, they will have to establish PRMD to PRMD direct connections, or to rent the services of a VADS company.

For the next two or three years, using X.400 for EDI will still present some problems. In any case, companies wanting to use EDI must be determined if they intend to succeed.

5.3   New CCITT recommendations

At the end of the 1988 Study Period, the CCITT set up a special Interim Rapporteur Group (IRG) to work on *X.400 support for EDI*.

Exceptionally, participation at IRG meetings was also open to non-CCITT members. As a result there was a large turnout of participants, about 60 persons per meeting, representing not only PTT administrations and computer manufacturers, but also EDI standards organisations (ANSI X.12, UK SITPRO, and United Nations Economic Commission for Europe), VADS providers, and EDI users (in particular, representatives from the EDI users associations EDIFICE and CEFIC). Because of the close collaboration between CCITT and the EDI community, there is good reason to think that the recommendation produced by IRG will be well accepted.

The most important aspects of the recommendation, that have been outlined during the IRG meetings held until now [16,6,7], are listed below:

◊   IRG took quite a conservative approach regarding the most fundamental issues. This approach resulted in a standard which will be a significant evolution from the use of X.400 according to current guidelines, but

A PRMD can be seen as the electronic equivalent of a company's internal mail system, but it is more than just that. A PRMD can communicate directly with adjacent PRMDs[1]. Indeed, it is technically possible for a company to set up a national or international PRMD (possibly using the X.25 national networks) whose main function would be to interconnect small PRMDs. In this case, the restrictions that apply, if any, are more legal than technical.

The concept of PRMD is interesting for VADS companies, because it allows them to offer their services within the X.400 framework. VADS companies can set up their own PRMD and use the message-store concept to offer mailbox-services in a standard manner. In France, there is already an EDI service that uses this approach. Also, VADS companies may implement a proprietary message-store service and protocol within their PRMD. In doing so, they can open the X.400 world to companies which use proprietary communication solutions. Again, implementations based on this approach are already in existence today.

4.2.3 The Store-and-Forward Concept

X.400 is based on a store-and-forward concept up to the application layer. A message is transferred as a whole from one X.400 node to the next, where it can be stored for several hours if necessary. There is therefore no need to establish an end-to-end session between originator and recipient computers; sessions are set up one by one between adjacent X.400 nodes.

The X.400 network tries to deliver a message to its recipient within a specified time limit. If the message is not delivered (probably because the recipient's computer is not available), the MTS normally returns a non-delivery notification to the sender. This time limit is a function of the message priority; the F.400 series of recommendations, which specify the quality of the message handling service offered by an ADMD, indicates 4 hours for urgent messages, 24 hours for normal messages, and 36 hours for non-urgent ones.

4.2.4 Security of X.400

Users who own their own mailboxes must grant access to their computer to an ADMD, and possibly to several PRMDs, for message transfer. This should represent no serious security threats, for two reasons:

- ADMDs and PRMDs identify themselves through the exchange of passwords;

- the access which is granted is limited to a well-defined protocol which can only perform X.400 services; a remote PRMD therefore cannot directly access the operating system of the host computer, as would be the case with techniques based on remote job entry.

The X.400-1988 recommendations specify a new class of advanced security services that are based mainly on cryptographic techniques. These services, which include message confidentiality and digital signatures, will be invaluable to clarify legal questions within the context of EDI.

5 Standardization Work for EDI/X.400

More and more companies exchanging EDIFACT and other types of EDI messages use or wish to use communication systems based on the X.400 series of recommendations. Indeed, as we mentioned earlier, the universality of this pioneer OSI application layer standard, its world-wide acceptance, its flexibility, as well as its store-and-forward concept, make it a very suitable carrier for a large range of EDI communications.

Unfortunately, the development of EDIFACT and X.400 standards has been done in parallel without coordination between the standardization bodies. As a result, no special user agent class supporting EDI communications was

---

[1] This is explained in ISO documents but not in CCITT documents, the latter being mainly intended for the PTT administrations.

included in the original design. Current X.400 implementations have been designed for electronic mail. They can handle EDI messages, but they do not recognize them as such, and so they cannot do any automatic processing with them.

Several software vendors as well as some determined users, particularly in Europe, have modified existing X.400 implementations to make them more suitable for EDI. But, in the absence of any reference document or any coordination committee, these companies have developed various systems that are often incompatible with one another, defeating the purpose of using a standard such as X.400. This is particularly the case of implementations that arbitrarily make use of X.400 service elements to carry EDI communication parameters.

To improve this situation, the NIST (National Institute for Standards and Technology) in the United States and the CEC (Commission of the European Communities) in Europe have developed extensions to existing X.400 profiles which explain how the X.400 protocols should be used for EDI. Their guidelines are based on very different principles that reflect the different approaches to EDI communication in the U.S.A and in Europe. The CEC has ensured that its guidelines are compatible with those of the NIST through a simple gateway. On this point, it is important to realize that the CEC could not simply endorse the NIST guidelines, because most European EDI users of X.400 were heading in another direction, and would probably have continued to do so.

5.1 The NIST Guidelines: Making Direct Use of the MTS

Presently, X.400 can be seen as hierarchically structured into two levels: the interpersonal messaging service (IPMS) which defines electronic mail functions, and the message transfer system (MTS), which is a general system for transferring any kind of message.

In 1987, experts of the NIST and ANSI X12 analyzed the communication needs of American EDI users. They estimated that the IPMS was not appropriate for EDI, because the IPMS is a system for the exchange of relatively small messages, generally not confidential, between human users. On the other hand, EDI communication is the exchange of large, confidential messages between companies, or more precisely, between central EDI communication agents. *EDI messages*, also called *transaction sets*, are produced by application processes, translated into standard format, and arranged in *functional groups*, which are then directed to the central EDI communication agent. Then, the communication agent puts functional groups together into *interchanges*, and sends these to their recipients over various communication channels. Linking the EDI communication agent to an X.400 MTA presents no special difficulties. Therefore, the NIST concluded that X.400 should be used at the MTS level for EDI communication.

Since no EDI communications agent has been normalized by the CCITT nor the ISO, there is a subtle problem interfacing such a component directly with the message transfer service. In effect, the 1984 version of X.400 (which is the one in use today) specifies that the content type of an MTS envelope (which indicates the UA class for which the envelope content is intended) be simply an integer value; the problem is to decide on a unique integer value to be used for content types not defined by the CCITT nor the ISO[1]. The NIST, having no authority to pick specific integer values for content types, had to use the value zero for EDI, even though this value indicates in fact an undefined content type. This will probably have no serious consequences. Nevertheless, as a result of this choice, the NIST solution has been dubbed *P0* by analogy to the P2 protocol (the only standard content type in use today), although there is no such thing as a P0 protocol. Realizing that it is effectively making use of the P1 protocol and nothing else, some experts prefer to be more precise, and call it *P1/0*.

It is not certain that all current X.400 implementations of the MTS can accept other content types than P2, or have a well defined interface, so it may be difficult for users to interface their EDI communications agent to it. However, an important group of X.400 system developers, united under the banner of the X.400 API Association, are currently working on a series of common interfaces to their systems. Their intention is to make it more easy and more attractive for users and third party software developers to implement communication solutions based on X.400 [12, 22]. Therefore, the work of the API association constitutes a very important complement to the NIST guidelines.

---

[1] The direct use of the MTS for message contents other than content types specifically defined by the standards has been recognised by the CCITT and the ISO; in the 1988 version of X.400, content types can be indicated by object identifiers as well as by integer values.

certainly no revolution. For instance, IRG agreed to consider essentially the store-and-forward exchange of trade data meeting the EDIFACT, ANSI X12, and UN/TDI standards, as they are defined today. However, IRG also agreed to keep the standard open ended where possible to accomodate future information types compatible with the service elements included in the protocols.

◊ IRG did consider the possiblity of extending the IPMS to support EDI, but it strongly rejected this approach, mainly because EDI requirements were seen as being essentially different from those of interpersonal messaging. Also, most EDI users clearly expressed their preference that the two services be separated. Nevertheless, IRG did notice that there is also much commonality between the two services.

◊ IRG designed an EDI Messaging System (EDIMS) which is equivalent to the current IPMS; the use of the MTS for EDI is basically the same as it is for IPM, and there is also an EDI UA and an optional EDI MS in the system. Therefore, the architectural advantages of the IPMS, that were deemed important by European EDI users, have been retained.

◊ IRG also attempted to design a protocol which would be as similar as possible to the P2 protocol. At this level, one of the most important contributions of the new protocol is a service element which will convey all essential attributes of an EDI interchange. These typically correspond to the information that can be found in the EDIFACT interchange header today. However, the standard will not give any indication regarding this mapping, so protocol users will have the possibility to send some other EDI content types than just standard interchanges.

◊ There will be at most one EDI interchange within a single X.400 EDI-message (the EDI equivalent of an IP-message). It will be placed in the first body part. Additional body parts will be permitted; they will carry information supplementing that of the interchange, for example, engineering drawings or specifications. This is a simple but significant improvement over current solutions. Furthermore, a cross-referencing mechanism will make it possible for the interchange to reference these additional body parts, whether they are part of the same message, or whether they belong to another X.400 message (which may or may not be an EDI-message).

◊ An area of the IPM protocol that needed complete reconsideration for EDI was the Receipt Notifications. EDI users did not at all like the way these were used in the IPM service. They preferred to call them Responsiblity Notifications, to stress their significance in EDI, and to make it clear that the recipient *must* generate such a notification when it is requested to do so. Another critical question in this area was the interrelation between Responsibility Notifications and the auto-forwarding mechanism of the message-store. In the IPMS, the message-store generates automatically a Non-Receipt Notification when it performs auto-forwarding: EDI users have clearly indicated that such a practice would not be acceptable. The solution that has been retained will provide true end-to-end Responsiblity Notifications between the originator and the final recipient.

The NIST and TEDIS guidelines have been produced for the interim period until a CCITT recommendation is available.This will be the case by the end of this year. In practice, products and services will not be available before two or three years. Because the NIST and TEDIS guidelines were defined independently of the CCITT, the new recommendation will not specify how to interwork between the EDIMS and the two current solutions. However, it seems rather likely that the NIST in the U.S.A, and one of its counterparts in Europe, will produce such specifications.

6 Conclusions

The potential benefits of EDI can represent as much as 7% of shipped goods, but for EDI benefits to be effective, companies need to have EDI exchanges with a significant proportion of their trading partners, whatever their location and their computer equipment may be. This remains a distant goal, in particular because international standards are only beginning to be available for EDI. However, for a lot of companies, it is a good idea to start using EDI now. When doing this, care must be taken to ensure that solutions that work today will remain appropriate tomorrow. In particular, it is very important to use international standards whenever they are adequate. Most EDI experts see in EDIFACT the unique international standard for the specification and the coding of commercial documents. More and more of them realize that X.400 will become the basic method for transporting EDI messages. It is true that the new CCITT standard is not ready yet, and therefore products and services implementing it are several years down the road.

On the other hand, there are interim strategies which are applicable in Europe and in the U.S.A. Looking at the present developments, it is quite clear that the CCITT standard will be an evolution of these schemes rather than a revolution. Therefore, it is quite reasonable to claim that today's X.400 based implementations will be closer to future EDI communication standards than anything else.

Acknowledgements

Nancy Greene (EPFL) made numerous comments, suggestions, corrections, and criticisms which proved invaluable for the writing of this article. Kalliopi Kairi (EPFL) and Roland Tissot (FIDES Informatique) helped us to better understand the translation process and the structure of an EDI application. We also wish to thank members of the EDI and X.400 - CCITT Interim Rapporteur Group, as well as members of the EDIFICE Communications Task Group, for fruitful discussions.

Special thanks to an anonymous referee.

Our work on EDI and X.400 was funded by a Swiss PTT ZBF grant.

Bibliography

[1] ANSI ASC X12, "An Introduction To Electronic Data Interchange".

[2] ANSI ASC X12, "X.400 Communication Guideline for EDI", Doc. no. ANSI/ASC/X12C/TG5/87-052, 1987.

[3] Benjamin, R. I., De Long, D. W., and Scott Morton, M. S., "The Realities of Electronic Data Interchange: How Much Competitive Advantage?", Working Paper 90s: 88-042, Massachussets Institute of Technology, Sloan School of Management.

[4] CCITT Red Book volume VIII - Fascicle VIII.7, "Data Communication Networks, Message Handling Systems", Recommendations X.400 - X.430 (1984).

[5] CCITT Blue Book volume VIII - Fascicle VIII.7, "Data Communication Networks, Message Handling Systems", Recommendations X.400 - X.420 (1988).

[6] CCITT Study Group VII, Interim Rapporteur for EDI and X.400 (Question 18/VII), "Report of the Work During the Interregnum", July 1989.

[7] CCITT Study Group VII, Associate Rapporteur - EDI and X.400 (Question 18/VII), "Report of the Fifth Associate Rapporteur Meeting on EDI and X.400 (Rennes, 9-13 October, 1989)".

[8] DG XIII/D-5 - TEDIS, "Minute of TEDIS Meeting on the Interim Use of X.400 for EDI - Guidelines for P2 Implementation", Brussels 23 November 1988.

[9] ISO, "Basic Reference Model for Open Systems Interconnection", ISO 7498, 1984.

[10] ISO, "Electronic Data Interchange For Administration, Commerce and Transport (EDIFACT) - Application Level Syntax Rules", ISO 9735, 1988.

[11] ISO, "The United Nations Trade Data Elements Directory", ISO 7372, 1984.

[12] Morvan, D., "EDI et API, Echange de Données et Portabilité", Mini & Micros, No 328, October 1989.

[13] NIST, "EDI use of X.400", NBS Implementor's Agreements for X.400, Additions to Chapter 8, Appendix B, 1987.

[14] NORDIPRO, "Creating Legal Security in Electronic Data Interchange: A guide to the UNCID-rules", 4th special paper by NORDIPRO, Hans B. Thomsen editor, published in cooperation with TANO A. S., Oslo.

[15] OSN, "EDI1 - CCITT takes first step to X.400 and EDI convergence", OSN, The Open Systems Newsletter, Volume 2, Issue 7, September 1988.

[16] OSN, "EDI and X.400 - CCITT interim rapporteur group meeting", OSN, The Open Systems Newsletter, Volume 3, Issue 3, March 1989.

[17] OSN, "EDI2 - New tools will ease message design and the convergence of EDI communities", OSN, The Open Systems Newsletter, Volume 2, Issue 7, September 1988.

[18] OSN, "EDI3 - Technical solutions must meet business needs", OSN, The Open Systems Newsletter, Volume 2, Issue 7, September 1988.

[19] UN/ECE, "UN/EDIFACT Message Design Guidelines", UN/ECE TRADE/WP4/R528, 29 June 1988.

[20] UN/ECE, "UN/EDIFACT Syntax Implementation Guidelines", UN/ECE TRADE/WP4/R530/rev.1, 21 December 1988.

[21] UN/ECE, "United Nations Standard Messages (UNSM) - Invoice Message", UN/ECE TRADE/WP4/R527, 24 June 1988.

[22] X.400 API Association, "X.400 Gateway API Specification V 3.0", June 1989.

Telecommunication Services and Distributed Applications

Christian Chabernaud
Bernard Vilain

International standards organizations have actively investigated the problem of heterogeneous system interconnection. This has resulted in the Open System Interconnection (OSI) model. This model is now well structured and its use widely accepted. The International Standards Organization (ISO), which started and worked out this model primarily for data communication needs, has now established close communication and co-operation with the telecommunication world and particularly with the International Consultative Committee for Telephone and Telegraph (CCITT). Most relevant ISO standards have been adopted by the CCITT for telematic services and data transmission needs in the X.200 Series Recommendations.

The OSI model for the six lower layers established, it became obvious that standardizing the seventh (application) layer would lead to greater complexity, first due to the proximity of the application processes and second because of the natural temptation to expand the scope of the standardization, step by step. This article presents a survey of the situation.

Overview

The historical construction of the application layer has led to a proliferation of Application Service Elements (ASEs): ROSE, ACSE, CMISE, RTSE, etc., along with CCR and File Transfer, Access, and Management (FTAM). A quite recent ISO activity, (Upper Layer Architecture) ULA, has set out to organize these ASE's into the application layer structure (ISO 9545 standard): the concepts of ASE, Single Association Functions (SACF) or Multiple Association Functions (MACF) and application context, have been promoted so as to ensure that standards or parts of standards could be used in combination and thus be shared when application layer standards are written. This would avoid a given application layer standard reproducing functional components already available as part of other ASEs. In parallel, other bodies, such as the Standard Promotion Application Group SPAG, POSI, MAP/TOP, etc., have promoted this set of ASEs and classified them into four basic, although not identical, usage profiles:

- FTAM
- Message Handling System (MHS)
- Remote operations or simple client-server service
- Transaction processing

The European Workshop on Open Systems (EWOS), the European Telecommunications Standards Institute (ETSI), and ISO are currently working on a more comprehensive list of functional profiles.

Up to now, each application layer standard has defined its own use of the underlying upper layers (presentation and session). This has resulted in widely different usages, such as FTAM and MHS, while the two other profiles fit in with an application-oriented view of the upper layers and correspond to the current definition of the application layer structure:

- The Remote Operations Service (ROS) model, which is of general application, although primarily developed for office automation
- The OSI Transaction Processing (TP) model, which is also of general application and is better referred to as "program-to-program facilities."

Both deal with the tools for distributed processing.

These two profiles, although complementary, differ in their perception of Distributed Applications (DA). The first is an extension of the Remote Procedure Call (RPC) concept and the structuring of applications into clients and servers. The second provides the general mechanism for message passing and synchronization at the disposal of applications.

Open Distributed Processing and Other Model Status

The temptation within ISO to tackle application interaction problems rather than pure interconnection problems was strong, and new models such as Open Distributed Processing (ODP) were likely to appear. Now there are numerous similar concurrent activities in standardization bodies (e.g., DAF in the CCITT) or as research projects—ISA in the European Economic Community (EEC), ANSA in the U.K., etc. While OSI standards contribute to application distribution from a communication perspective, ODP intends to address distributed applications, with the objective of masking distribution effects from applications.

Open Distributed Processing

ODP is a long-range activity in ISO that is expected to last until 1995 for Draft International Standard (DIS) availability. The ODP Reference Model (ODP-RM) defines five different viewpoints, each of which provides a full description or abstraction of the ODP system [1]:

- The "enterprise" viewpoint focuses on business requirements, structure and organization.
- The "information" viewpoint addresses the exchange of information and models information structure and flows.
- The "computation" viewpoint regards the distributed processing in terms of system components (for example, application components) and their interactions independent of any specific operating or communication system.
- The "engineering" viewpoint concerns configurations, performance, distribution, and the infrastructure.
- The "technology" viewpoint encompasses hardware and software components, such as Input/Output (I/O) devices communication systems, etc.

Each viewpoint corresponds to a particular abstraction of the ODP system. There is no link with phases in a design process, sequence, or hierarchy [2] (see Table I).

The output of the ODP viewpoints is:

- Enterprise → user requirements
- Information → conceptual design and specifications

Table I. Summary of ODP Viewpoints

Viewpoints	Areas of Concern
Enterprise	User interfaces Legal concerns Human and social issues Management/finance
Information	Information models Information flows Information structure
Computation	Data models Application and process design and development
Engineering	Distributed system infrastructure Application support
Technology	Technological constraints

- Computation → software design and development
- Engineering → infrastructure building blocks
- Technology → realized components

Another ODP objective is to harmonize modeling techniques applicable to the five viewpoints. Different approaches are being considered; for example, object-based or object-oriented techniques, entity-relationship model, and the functional approach, although preference is given to object-oriented techniques.

An ODP system may be illustrated by the three component domains [3-5]:

- The distributed application components
- The ODP Support Environment (ODP-SE), which conceals the physical support machine architecture
- The physical support machine, including hardware, operating, and communication systems

The ODP-RM standardization may include all viewpoints, while the ODP-SE standardization concerns particular viewpoints within the ODP-RM. The computation and engineering viewpoints are the most significant ones. More precisely, one could say that ODP-SE should cover support infrastructure for distributed applications, while ODP-RM concerns overall information system modeling.

Major functions of ODP-SE include the provision of distribution transparency, communication support, and security support. Furthermore, the ANSA project proposes an ODP "workbench" as a particular implementation of the engineering viewpoint, the objective being to produce objects containing application component(s) together with an operating system run on a particular physical system [5].

Distributed Applications Framework

DAF intends to produce recommendations in full collaboration with ODP by 1992. DAF work consists of providing a consistent set of tools for the design and specification of distributed applications. DAF shares common objectives with ODP but uses a different approach [6]:

- DAF addresses only the engineering viewpoint aspects.
- DAF has no concept of viewpoints and no intention of putting them to use.
- DAF clearly promotes an object-oriented architecture.

Telecommunication Service Requirements

Communication Aspects

For many reasons, including the parallel development between 1980 and 1988 of ISO model standards with recommendations for Public Switched Telephone Network (PSTN) and Integrated Services Digital Network (ISDN) switching and signaling, the telecommunications world, via the CCITT, produced its own distinct set of standards, which did not fully match the OSI model (although bridging capabilities exist between ISO and CCITT #7).

In addition to the X.200 series of recommendations for "data services world" produced by CCITT Study Group VII, Study Group XI has also produced CCITT #7 protocols that address the need for telecommunication networks PSTN, ISDN, and even Broadband ISDN (BISDN) to offer a specific grade of service (see Figure 1). ISDN, which aims to be a universal network for all kinds of services (telecommunications and data services), and new emerging architectures, such as Intelligent Network (IN), require that full interconnection be possible between various types of nodes.

This situation has prompted a fruitful dialogue between the CCITT and ISO. The question of distributed applications has already been considered, and the definition of the application layer has therefore evolved to something between the CCITT's position (which primarily considered message-passing-based applications) and the ISO's (which proposes use of common services for communication negotiation at the disposal of applications). Nevertheless, specific differences in communication aspects still exist in the telecommunications world when compared to OSI standards:

- CCITT meets its communications needs mainly with connectionless network services.
- Real-time call processing performance requirements may prevent the use of ACSE-like service elements prior to any application process invocation: TCAP assumes that peer application processes have established a predefined context.
- CCITT has specifically designed TCAP for short-lived transactions of a few seconds that consist of a limited number of requests and replies.
- CCITT retains a reduced upper layer model where TCAP directly interfaces connectionless network services to avoid excessive overhead and/or processing time. OSI, however, bases ROSE and ACSE above a presentation connection.

Most of the solutions retained by CCITT are the results of performance aspects, including reliability (MTP should not lose more than 1 in 10^7 messages), short response time (connectionless service provides faster one-shot transactions), and efficient real-time processing (reduced model). These kinds of constraints have also led CCITT to recommend protocols to optimize performances at the application level; in respect to that, TUP and ISUP protocols were designed in such a way that both the protocol aspects and the application process (the call processing) were tailored together. With the release of protocols such as SCCP and TCAP, this trend is now declining, and protocol-independent application processes have been recommended, such as the Mobile Application Part (MAP).

The ISO and CCITT approaches are likely to evolve further in the near future. ISO is already working on the expansion of the Basic Reference Model in order to cover connectionless-mode transmission. Similarly, CCITT is carrying out a study on connection-oriented needs for TCAP.

Intelligent Networks and Distributed Applications

During this study period (1988-1992), CCITT Study Group XI will have to produce recommendations for new switching and signaling techniques such as the IN architecture concept, which entails distributed applications. This concept definitely separates the service logic from traditional call processing functions. Other regional bodies, such as the MVI forum and ETSI, as well as national research centers, are also

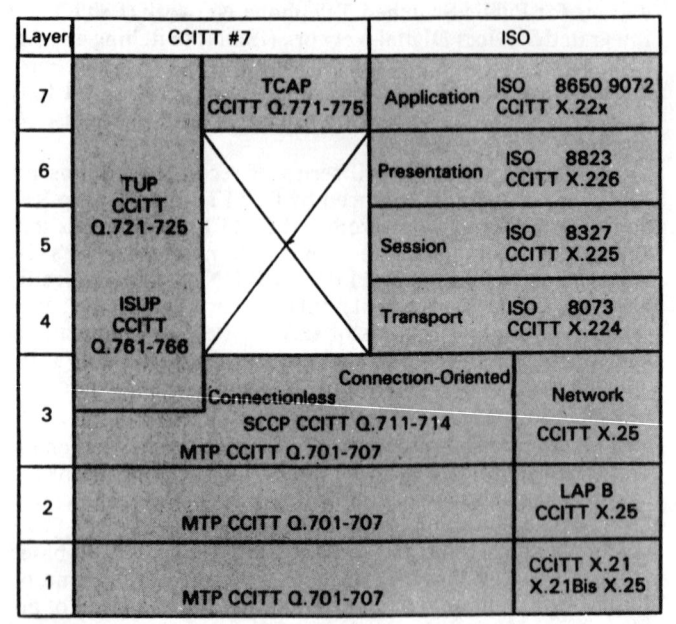

Layer	CCITT #7		ISO	
7	TUP CCITT Q.721-725	TCAP CCITT Q.771-775	Application	ISO 8650 9072 CCITT X.22x
6			Presentation	ISO 8823 CCITT X.226
5			Session	ISO 8327 CCITT X.225
4	ISUP CCITT Q.761-766		Transport	ISO 8073 CCITT X.224
3	Connectionless / Connection-Oriented SCCP CCITT Q.711-714 MTP CCITT Q.701-707		Network	CCITT X.25
2	MTP CCITT Q.701-707		LAP B	CCITT X.25
1	MTP CCITT Q.701-707			CCITT X.21 X.21Bis X.25

ISUP: ISDN User Part
MTP: Message Transfer Part
SCCP: Signalling Connection Control Part
TCAP: Transaction Capability Application Part
TUP: Telephone User Part

Fig. 1. Summary of ISO and CCITT #7 protocols.

working on this issue [7] [8], even in a broader context encompassing Plain Old Telephone Service (POTS), packet, and videotex networks [3] [9]. Other activities in CCITT, such as call-control/connection-control separation, handling of multimedia communications, and telecommunication management network (TMN) [10], have also opened the door for distributed applications [11].

Today, IN seems a promising approach with respect to distributed applications. It is described as a new architecture allowing flexible and rapid service introduction, and assumes vendor and technology independence, network implementation independence, and service implementation independence.

In the context of a PSTN, the purpose of IN is to provide services beyond the basic telephone service in an efficient, cost effective, and flexible manner. Typical IN services include freephone, credit call, credit card call, virtual private network, automatic call distribution, opinion poll, and Wide Area Centrex. The basic architecture of IN relies on the principle of the concentration of the logic of the service on a few dedicated nodes and on slaving the existing call processing of the telephone exchange (now called Service Switching Point—SSP) on this service logic. Because this architecture implies a clearer separation between the application (or service logic) and the transport network (the purpose of the newly slaved call processing being mainly to take care of connection setup and release), this concept is being considered for other types of networks, including the Packet Switched Public Data Network (PSPDN), and broadband and videotex networks. Ongoing discussions highlight the existence of two types of nodes: the Service Control Point (SCP), which deals with the service handling real-time processing; and the Service Management System (SMS), which handles the management activities of the IN, although no firm agreement exists on the details of this structure. Thus, IN would probably be structured in three levels: the service logic (application level), the IN platform (SSF,

SCF, and SMF support functions), and the physical nodes (SSP, SCP, and SMS).

This recent concept, along with transaction-oriented protocols (SCCP and TCAP) already available, provides the basis for a wider debate on the provision of telecommunication services based on distributed processing principles. Although discussion has not yet started in CCITT, TMN is likely to be considered for operation services in INs when preparing detailed specifications of SMS.

Concurrent or Complementary Approaches

The common goal of ISO and CCITT is clearly the standardization of a framework for structuring distributed applications. This is especially true for CCITT's IN studies where service creation is a must. Service creation provides the opportunity for the operator to design new services quickly and deploy them economically into the network, the operator's objective being to satisfy the user's demands in a short time frame.

Therefore, a lot of similarities may be found with the abovementioned ODP-SE. Although not yet standardized in CCITT, service creation relies on principles similar to the distributed system structure, where application components could be com-

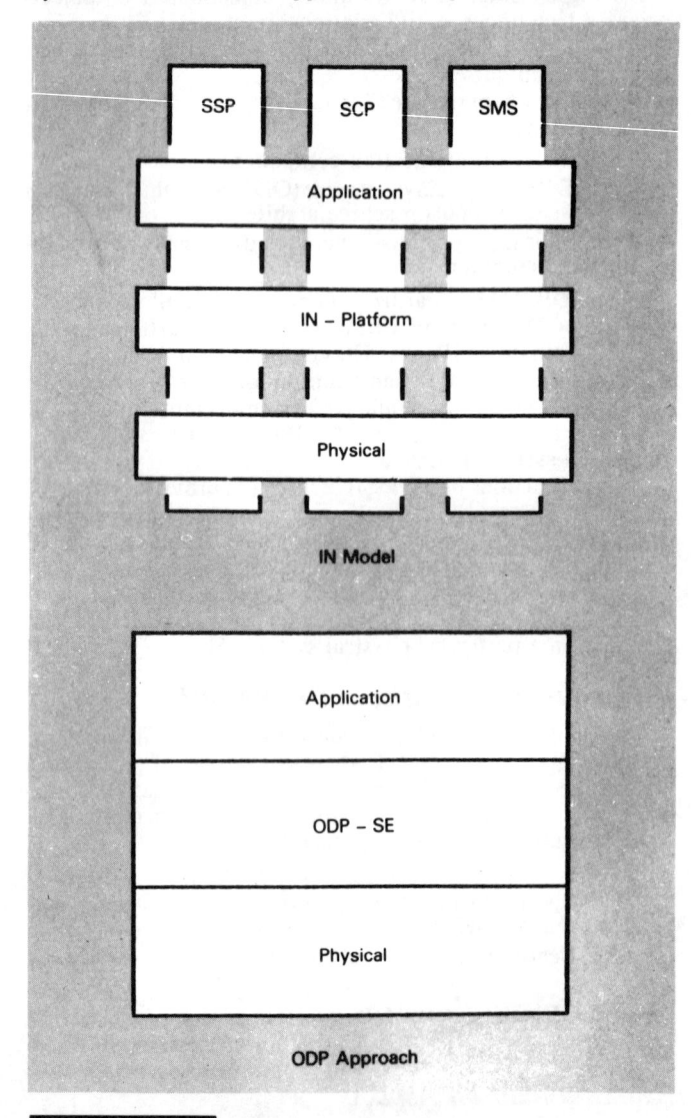

Fig. 2. IN model and ODP approach compared.

pared to the service logic and ODP-SE to the IN platform (see Figure 2).

Furthermore, the IN structure claims a methodology for structure applications. Service creation implicitly relies on the capacity of IN to provide a library of common services, such as authentication, ciphering, etc., and standardized access means to be used in any application. End-user-dependent services would be negotiated when the application is invoked. In the context of charging, similar needs imply that accounting be made independent of the application. Addressing procedures to reach these common services need to be defined independent of the underlying signaling point that hosts them.

Nevertheless, we have seen that ODP relies on the infrastructure provided by the OSI application layer structure, while the telecommunications world is still in the process of analyzing which framework should be used, bearing in mind that the underlying infrastructure is more streamlined and therefore less open. Both underlying infrastructures need to be considered.

Also, telecommunications imply specific needs in terms of performance, as discussed above in the context of communications aspects. The question that arises, therefore, is how far can ODP and other models go to cope with performance aspects? Among the five ODP viewpoints, the engineering viewpoint is a candidate.

Another key problem that INs are being designed to resolve is the dynamic aspect of service creation, namely, the capability to create new application components and new interactions between components. This encompasses both the creation and activation of a new component not necessarily known or even present in the distributed system. Such would be the case of a new IN service that requires new features not yet identified in the IN. Such a situation would also correspond, at the physical level, to the extension of the number of nodes or the introduction of a new node type in the distributed system.

Conclusion

A number of questions still remain to be answered in the ongoing work on ODP and IN. Some of them are listed below:
- Is there place in ODP-SE for non-ISO communications standards?
- How can real-time constraints be taken into account in the modeling activity?
- Do these constraints have an impact on the modeling technique?

Thanks to these points, IN and ODP are two activities that should benefit from each other, especially in the context of telecommunication services with their own set of constraints: ODP will provide the general framework, while IN will bring in a live case study.

References

[1] ISO/IEC JTC1/SC21, nos. 4,019, 4,022, and 4,025, "WG7 Working Documents on ODP," Nov. 1989.
[2] ISO/IEC JTC1/SC21/WG7, no. 116, "Basic Reference Model of Open Distributed Processing," July 1989.
[3] G. Ullmann, "Environment for Distributed Multimedia Application Systems," ALCATEL Austria, TINA-90.
[4] "ECMA Support Environment for Distributed Processing SE-ODP," July 1989.
[5] ANSA Reference Manual, release 01.00, Mar. 1989.
[6] CCITT Com VII Rxx, "Study Group VII Q19/VII (DAF) Report," Feb. 1990.
[7] "Advanced Intelligent Network Release 1, Baseline Architecture," SR-NPL-001555, issue 1, Mar. 1990.
[8] J.-B. Stefani, "On the Notion of Trader in Intelligent Networks," France Telecom, TINA-90.
[9] R. Kung, "Towards Networks and Operations Systems Integration," France Telecom, TINA-90.
[10] R. Drignath, "IN and NM Service Requirements for a Generic Network Model," SEL-ALCATEL, TINA-90.
[11] CCITT Com XI R24, "Report of Working Party XI/4," Mar. 1990.

Biography

Christian Chabernaud was born in Paris, France in 1949, and he is a graduate of the Ecole Centrale Des Arts et Manufactures, Paris. He joined ALCATEL CIT in 1977 as Research and Development Engineer for public switching products, where he managed a development team on subscriber database for ALCATEL E10 System. He is at present Senior Engineer in charge of top-level design for Intelligent Networks, namely data engineering at ALCATEL CIT, Velizy, France.

Bernard Vilain was born in Paris, France in 1953. He is graduate of the Ecole Nationale Superieure des Telecommunications, Paris. After spending seven years at France Telecom's Centre National d'Etudes des Telecommunications (CNET) research center in charge of the product analysis of digital exchanges to prepare the French PSTN for the introduction of ISDN, he joined ALCATEL CIT. Initially, he was Product Manager for pre-Intelligent Network services for the ALCATEL dedicated transit node. At the same time, he chaired functional aspects of digital exchange activity in CCITT Working Party XI/4. He is at present System Design Group Manager for IN, TMN, and mobile radio products at ALCATEL CIT, Velizy, France.

Distributed Multimedia Information Handling and Processing

Gerd Schürmann
Uwe Holzmann-Kaiser

New capabilities in the area of transmission media and the constant expansion of the potential application areas make necessary the availability of suitable communication mechanisms for use in open[1] distributed systems. Communication in distributed systems, without bilateral agreement, can only function on the basis of internationally accepted standards. The development of suitable standardized communication mechanisms and information models, however, is running far behind the technological possibilities.

While the technical constraints of the available bandwidths within public networks have in the past restricted users to relatively simply asynchronous communication relations (except telephone lines and Telex), in the future, the installation of public broadband networks with transmission rates of 140 Mb/s and more will make decentralized synchronous processing of information possible. With narrowband connections, the amount of information to be interchanged had to be kept as small as possible. In the future, fiber optics will permit the real-time transmission of moving pictures and audio sequences, permitting implementation in application areas that, for the presentation of information, have to date served only the traditional presentation forms (text, graphics, and still pictures).

Within the framework of distributed processing, the interchanged information must be available in a form accessible to humans, or in a form suitable to automated processing so that either people or machines can serve as partners. Information in a form accessible to humans is generally associated today with the term "multimedia." Many applications require the integrated processing of information from both categories. The distributed processing of multimedia information cannot be viewed in isolation, but must be seen as a partial aspect of the general problem of distributed applications.

Due to the variety of possible application areas and interfaces between these areas, in the future, instead of static models, a modular-design principle based on information and communications components should guide the modeling of distributed applications. Attempts in this direction have already been made in the multimedia field [1] [2].

Because there is no commonly accepted terminology, the title "Distributed Multimedia Information Handling and Processing," needs some clarification. Multimedia information encompasses (electronic) "documents" as well as remote control of multimedia devices like cameras, security and authorization aspects regarding multimedia information and device access, and the heterogeneity of involved hardware, networks, operating systems, etc. However, only some relevant aspects of distributed processing of multimedia information are discussed in this article, selected according to preference of the authors using the following definition:

Multimedia information comprises common and application-specific information types, i.e., it is intended for visual and auditory perception[2] as well as for automated processing. The information is not restricted to local existence and may, but need not, be presented on different presentation media.

Below, the requirements for such an application-independent construction set and its use in defining distributed applications in open systems are explained. Most developments and standards concentrate upon a relatively restricted area of application and cannot be suitably combined with other developments. For this reason, adequate international standardization activities working towards a reference model for distributed applications are introduced, which support the composition of distributed applications from the basis of generally applicable components. Some relevant functions within the computational and engineering viewpoints in the context of distributed processing of multimedia information are described.

Although there are requirements concerning the lower layer functions of the Open Systems Interconnection (OSI) Basic Reference Model [3], (TMN) Asynchronous Transfer Mode (ATM), or other network technologies, these relations are not described in the context of this paper. Here, the need for integration of isochronous communication is emphasized, and some of the problems to be solved are discussed. Approved international standards and recommendations as well as international standards and recommendations still under development are analyzed in respect to these requirements.

Analysis of Requirements

Requirements for the handling of multimedia information within an open distributed system will be assembled, based upon the application example of "joint editing." Joint editing is understood as a group of users, possibly at different locations, working cooperatively to generate multimedia information, such as a new volume of an electronic handbook. This example covers a broad range of potential requirements, as it deals with operations on multimedia information such as manipulation, transfer and presentation, distribution, and group communication. To begin with, no attempt has been made to classify requirements according to particular model aspects,

---

[1]"Open" here is in the context of Open Distributed Processing (ODP), that is, heterogeneous distributed systems are capable of cooperating to perform some information processing task even if heterogeneous management and control authorities are involved. Therefore, it is necessary to abstract from the restrictions imposed by products from different vendors and technology.

[2]Other types of perception, such as tactile, are currently not considered.

such as distribution in terms of the Open Distributed Processing (ODP) Reference Model or communication in terms of the OSI Basic Reference Model; rather, all requirements are formulated from the standpoint of the user. A mapping onto suitable technical requirements for different components will be made within the approach to a communication model.

Distributed Processing

The most important differentiation with respect to communication requirements is given between asynchronous and synchronous processing.

- In asynchronous processing, without stringent time constraints, autonomy of the working space for each individual is in the forefront, meaning that everyone works mostly within one's "local" (i.e., personal or individual) environment.
- In synchronous processing, a common working space (at the logical, not necessarily physical, level) is necessary, to which all persons or entities participating in the processing must have access.

By distributed processing of information, coordination of the work is of extreme importance. Many publications in this area of "Computer-Supported Cooperative Work" (CSCW), e.g. [4–7] discuss problems of coordination. The behavior of groups communicating with each other may, for example, be described with the aid of the Amigo Activity Model [8].

Common to all forms of processing is the desire to support the "roles" of those participating in the joint processing. "Functions," which may be or should be performed by these roles, must be defined according to suitable "rules." Definition of the possible roles is part of the application and should not be restricted by the model. Examples in traditional document processing are "publisher," "author," "editor," "referee," "designer," "caseworker," and "consumer." For example, the publisher must be able to forbid the author to make changes to the layout. A caseworker may only be permitted to fill in or alter at certain places in the predesigned forms. The editor will have more rights to create or process multimedia information: to control cross-references and bibliographic references, to check the unity of terminology, to write transitions between individual parts, to create an index or table of contests, and to rework the language of the text. Referee commentaries should be recognizable as such and, if necessary, capable of being integrated into the document.

Should joint processing of a document be performed simultaneously, e.g., as part of a joint editorial conference, mechanisms for coordinating the individual participants are necessary. Here a number of requirements appear, with a strong impact on coordination and implicitly on communication, which go well beyond those for asynchronous processing:

- Interactive operations on the information must be able to be performed simultaneously.
- The effects of changes in respect to the content, appearance, or both must be immediately recognizable; this leads to the requirement for fast formatting processes and high transmission rates.
- The time lapse between the alteration of information in a common working space and a consistent view for all participants must be acceptable for the application.
- For the utilization of databases as a source of information, quick response to database queries is necessary in order to ensure uninterrupted work during a meeting.
- In addition to the distribution of information, the distribution of actions and events (e.g., cursor movements and object and region markings) must also be possible. The transmission of information, actions and events from the source to the sinks must be fast enough that it takes place with only a negligible time delay. (The transmission of a 2 Mbyte still picture, for example, at a net transmission rate of 2 Mb/s would still take at least 8 s.)
- For ordered processing as a whole, the administration of authorization (token management) in respect to the individual roles is necessary.
- In order to achieve an imitation of a "real" conference in the form of an electronic one, all events and activities taking place between participants must be reproducible and adjustable by a set of parameters and operations within the specification of an electronic conference.
- Changes within the document must be visible according either to What You See is What I See (WYSIWIS) principal or the What You See Is What I Mean (WYSIWIM) principal. The first capability must be available within a spatially distributed editorial conference, so that the effects of changes to the appearance of information may be jointly judged; however, this requirement restricts the types of possible output devices.

Information and Data Modeling

First, in respect to information modeling, users have the same requirements for the distributed processing of information as they have for local processing. For this reason the requirements will be viewed independent of its handling within a network environment.

Many publications of requirements from various areas of information modeling like databases and multi/hyper media [9–14] show that there are only a few application-specific requirements. In the area of multimedia, there are only a few application-specific requirements. In the area of multimedia, there are various attempts to integrate the traditional presentation forms with application-specific data, for example, from the fields of Computer-Aided Design (CAD), animation, or trade data. Here, it is apparent that the application-specific definition of models for the representation of information can no longer be accepted. In the long term, a general framework for information modeling encompassing different applications is required.

An important characteristic of an information model is the "information types" it supports. The historical development of electronic document processing has produced these information types: character text, geometric graphics, and images (also called still pictures). Technical developments in recent years have made it possible to apply additional information types: moving images, describing sequences of elementary images requiring a minimum temporal frequency for human perception in order to simulate a continuous motion (also called moving pictures or video), and audio. As these information types are used to present information in many application areas, they are considered "presentation information types." Additionally, there are any number of potential "application-specific information types." Examples are product definition data, trade data, descriptions of animation sequences, and experimental data. Based on technical developments, international standardization activities in the area of information processing, such as text and office systems and computer graphics, have also emphasized the importance of these presentation information types.

Information types for the administration of distributed applications—such as standardized and registered attributes for the management of objects in distributed environments, and directory—are called "administration information types." Both the presentation and administration information types are considered "common information types" (see Figure 1). However, it may well be that future developments will lead to additional common information types from areas no longer considered to be application-specific.

From the standpoint of potential users it must be possible to support any information type, and it follows that it must be

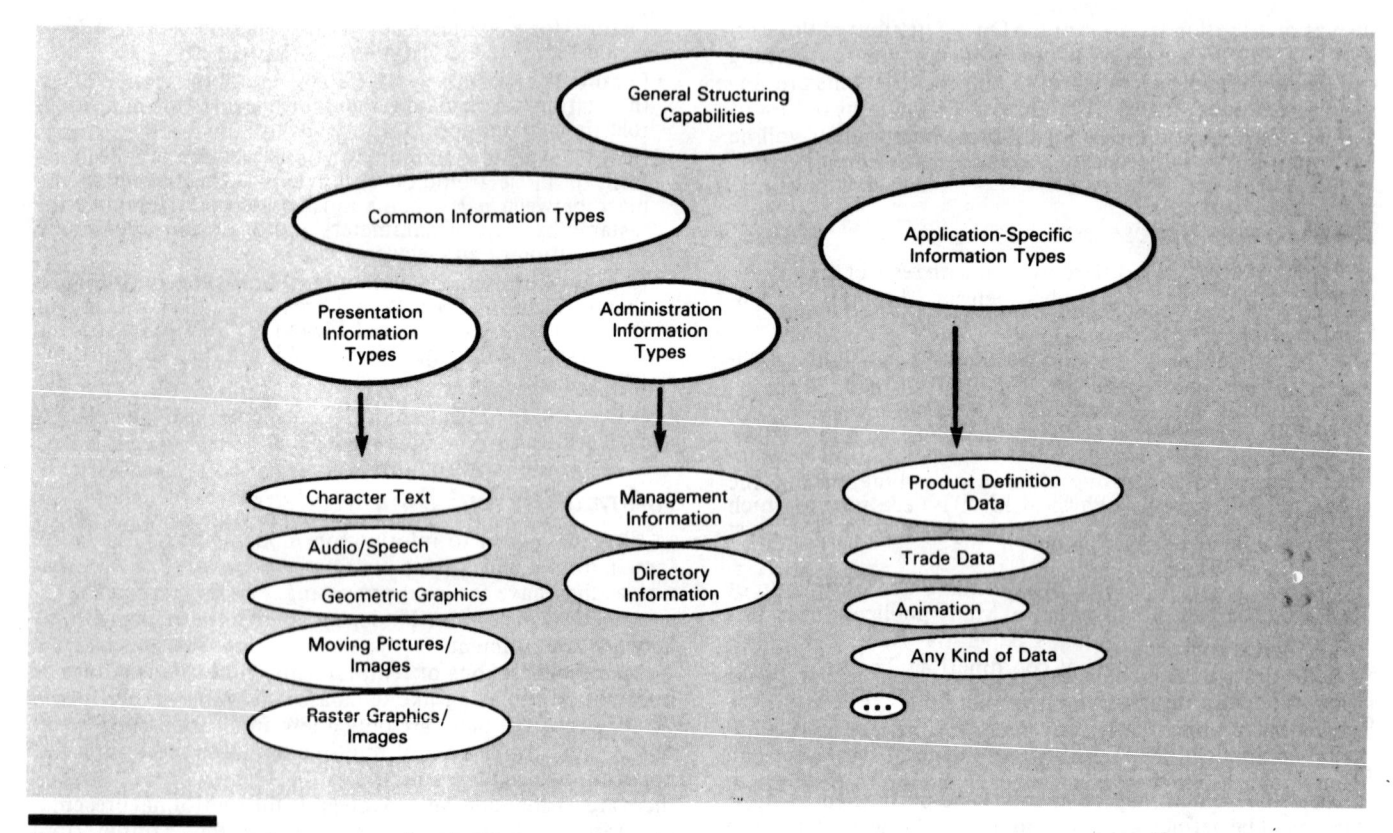

Fig. 1. Information and data structure classification.

possible to integrate into a model new basic information types resulting from current or future development (for example, the presentation of three-dimensional features such as volume imaging). An extensive discussion of these requirements is beyond the scope of this article, and the reader is referred to [12]. Only requirements applicable to more than one information type are discussed in the following sections.

Requirements applicable to more than one information type are generally mechanisms for the structuring of information. These structures—called "general structuring capabilities"—serve for the partitioning of information for the purpose of easier handling and decentralized processing, along with the integration of different information types. Below, the primary requirements in structuring are listed:

- Support for hierarchical and network structures: Structures inherent to traditional documents (sequential and/or hierarchical) must continue to be supported. Beyond this, there are also applications in which it is not necessary to define a unique path through the information. The term browsing describes the ability of the user to "navigate" through information.
- The ability to create several variants of a document with partially the same content and partially different content and versions of a document based on the predecessor, allowing the history of a document to be traced, must exist.
- Support for generation, handling, and retrieval independent of the later presentation form must be provided.
- Support for document classes, which define the rules for repetitive document structures from the available semantically defined structures, must be provided.
- Mechanisms for the synchronization and spatial overlapping of the information to be presented are a necessity.
- The ability to combine any information types in different stages of processing is also needed.

Aspects of information modeling are discussed in more detail in [15].

An Approach to an Integrated Model

A system for the distributed processing of multimedia information can be viewed as a special form of a distributed application or an open, distributed, cooperating system. For the design and construction of an open distributed application, concepts, methods, rules, and guidelines must be defined using common principle. Thereby, with the aid of a basic set of elementary components, advanced applications and services may be specified, available services expanded and joined, and cooperation between participating systems described.

Viewpoints and Aspects

Distributed systems may be observed from different viewpoints [16] [17]. Within these viewpoints, the distributed systems are viewed from different points of emphasis, each focusing on different concerns. One therefore receives a different abstraction of the distributed system, which models the relevant characteristics and ignores the irrelevant. Due to the possibility of concentrating at a given time upon a certain viewpoint within a distributed system, the viewpoint concept is helpful to use when designing and constructing a distributed application. Within ODP, five viewpoints have been identified:

- The "enterprise viewpoint" describes the distributed system in terms of answering the question of what it is required to do for the enterprise or business. The activities that occur within the enterprise in using the system are specified, along with the interaction between the organization, the system, and their environment.
- The "technology viewpoint" concentrates on the technical marginal conditions upon which the distributed systems is constructed. It models the hardware and software used (local operating system, input and output devices, storage, access to communications components, etc.).

The enterprise viewpoint and the technology viewpoint delimit the design space for the designer of distributed applications.

- The "information viewpoint" deals with the information and information processing aspects. Modeled are information structures, constraints, and operations that may be performed upon the information.
- The "computational viewpoint" describes a distributed system as a set of cooperating components or application programs. It deals with the structuring of the applications so that they may be independent of the available computer system and network.
- The "engineering viewpoint" describes a distributed system on the basis of mechanisms to support distributed applications. This viewpoint deals with the aspects resulting from the physical division of the applications, such as measures to ensure the desired characteristics in respect to the throughput and transparency of the distribution.

The viewpoints described are not to be understood as a model for the multilayer modeling of an open distributed system, and not as equivalent to the different phases within a design process. Although the viewpoints are related to one another, no specific order is implied.

With this approach, consistent and complete system models may be described and developed based on concepts and methods still to be designed for the individual viewpoints. An object-based approach is convenient for the modeling of distributed applications in each viewpoint. An extensive discussion of object-based approaches is beyond the scope of this article [18] [19].

The requirements and functions in ODP have been grouped into related categories called "aspects," which allow reasoning about related functions within ODP. The following aspects were considered to be convenient: storage, process, user access, communication, identification, management, and security. These aspects are used for classification of functional components in the computational viewpoint described later.

Aspects of the Computational Model

Among distributed applications, systems for the distributed processing of multimedia information in particular are described from the computational viewpoint by cooperating components. The interactions between the components must be described independent of mechanisms (e.g., interprocess communications or message passing) provided within the engineering viewpoint. Details concerning the description of interaction and cooperation of the components are not within the scope of the article. Below, we sketch the functions of a system for the handling of multimedia information and a functional model approach, including a supporting environment.

Components of a Multimedia Information Handling System

The capabilities of a multimedia information system can be described by the abstract services provided by the different components. The environment of such a system consists of the users of the system and of a supporting environment (set of components) not specific to multimedia. In the computational view of multimedia devices, device drivers and specific operating system software is abstracted, as mentioned earlier.

Below, we describe some important abstract services related to ODP aspects:

Process Aspect

- Generation and processing of multimedia information: The service for the generation and processing of multimedia information supports the distributed creation, manipulation, processing, and deletion of the content and structures of multimedia information.
- Group communication and coordination: A coordination service should support both asynchronous and synchronous processing of information by groups with the aid of suitable mechanisms. For example, during asynchronous joint editing, certain time constraints imposed on the group members' duties must be coordinated (e.g., this may lead to the sending of reminders).

This would also be used for the simultaneous, synchronous processing of a document. Here, access and the authorization to change privilege is controlled. The range of coordination reaches from no support or elementary support (e.g., token control or access control) to complete support, e.g., for a joint editing scenario. Furthermore, coordination can take place by observation and reacting to events or by active user guidance.

One of the most important issues of such a service is the ability to adapt dynamically to changes during life- and/or runtime if such changes happen to the task being supported (e.g., change of group members and roles).

User Access Aspect

- Presentation of multimedia information: The temporal and spatial relations between parts of the information may require simultaneous presentation of several information types at the same or different locations, such as still pictures with speech annotations. Here, the requirements for realtime synchronization of the audio and moving pictures information types must be taken into consideration. "Interaction points" may be integrated between individual presentation parts, giving the user the possibility of any interaction, and thus the ability to control the flow of presentation (for example, to select alternative document content or a multilanguage presentation form).

Storage Aspect

- Storage and retrieval of multimedia information: Private and common storages must be supported for any number of users. Hereby, common group storage for defined (open and closed) user groups and public archives (e.g., databases) with complex structures and different information types are permitted. In respect to the different classes of confidentiality (private to public) and the different concepts, access to stored information may be set and controlled by suitable archive-specific and information-specific mechanisms.

The location, local or remote, and in particular the type of storage, central or distributed, may be hidden from the user. Searching for information is based upon a variety of criteria such as "direct" search, based upon unambiguous identification, or search according to "characteristics," according to "structure," according to "presentation" (e.g., "page 15"), and according to "storage characteristics" (e.g., storage date/time, size, keywords, etc.).

Communication Aspect

- Transmission and distribution of multimedia information: Several different forms of communication are supported for the interchange of information between two or more users (e.g., conversation, multicast, and broadcast). For transmission and distribution, cooperation is necessary from supporting services, such as the identification (directory) and the storage and retrieval service.

Besides explicit sending (sender-initiated), the request for information (receiver-initiated) stored by defined groups and in the private archives of other users, in accordance with the user's access rights, must be supported. If the communications is asynchronous, the information is transmitted and distributed between the users without regard to time; by synchronous processing, e.g., within an online conference system, informa-

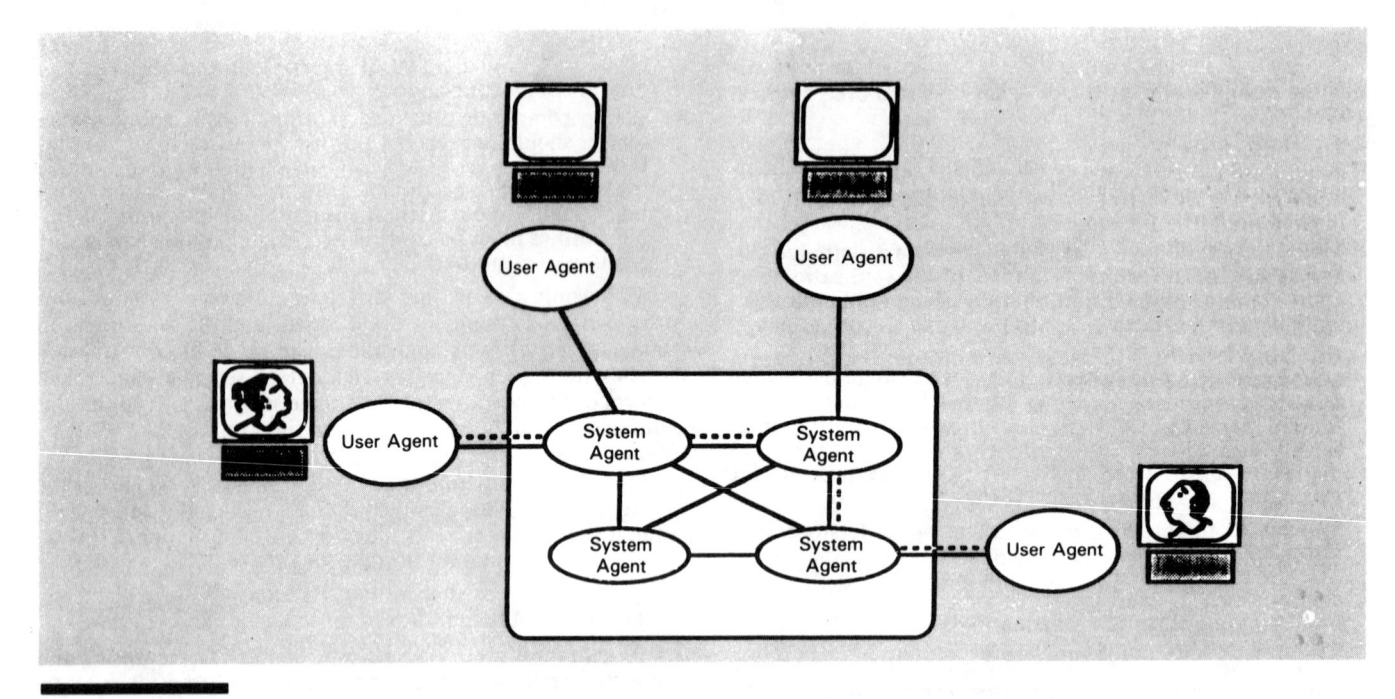

Fig. 2. Functional multimedia information-handling system components.

tion may be interactively processed simultaneously, and so must be interchanged in a timely fashion. There are some experiences in the area of synchronous joint editing, e.g., based on X-windows [20].

Heterogeneity is a major problem due to the possibly inhomogeneous nature of participating systems. This is well discussed in the scope of the ODP work (distribution transparency).

Identification

The identification (directory) provides information concerning the multimedia information, and about user groups that work in a group communication environment. It is based upon services such as Document Filing and Retrieval (DFR) [21] and the Directory [22], and is possibly supported by an information base. Detailed operations must be studied more closely.

The service encompasses the identification of global or context-specific unique object names and localization (e.g., name/address mapping: the name resolution process must be supported, such as name/address resolution).

Management

The management service provides all the mechanisms supporting distributed applications in respect to administration. Network-specific characteristics are hidden from the user; however, the Quality of Service (QoS) requirements (for example, a guaranteed throughput of moving picture information) are supported. The management service support for distributed applications (e.g., distributed storage, distributed processing and group communication) goes beyond OSI management activities, which consider only communication aspects.

Security

This covers the areas of authentication, authorization, audit, and cryptographic support facilities, etc.

These services do not necessarily have to be realized as an entire system, but rather may be combined according to requirements.

Functional Distribution Aspects

As mentioned above, a system for multimedia information handling provides its users (applications) with abstract services. These services are provided by "user agents." A user agent provides a local interface between the service users and the system agents and abstracts from distribution of the system.

The system is realized internally as a set of "system agents," which together provide the abstract services, e.g., for the handling of multimedia information. System agents of the same type possess the same capabilities, and can cooperate with each other. Every user agent can in principle, address every system agent, whereas a system agent can interact with several user agents simultaneously.

Between the functional components, at least two protocols must be differentiated. The "access protocol" defines the interaction between a user agent and a system agent, while the "system protocol" describes the interaction between two systems agents.

A user agent may address any system agent (which in turn may address other system agents via the system protocol for the provision of services) in order to access the system via the access protocol. The cooperation of the functional components is presented by an example in Figure 2. The dotted line shows agents and information flow for a particular connection. The solid lines indicate possible protocols.

An important distribution aspect is the ability to set dynamic configurations for the processing of distributed information [23] [24]. Due to the requirement of heterogeneity, a capability for the development of user agents with different functionalities is required. In order to cooperate, such user agents must have information about the functionality of partner agents. This results either from a query to the directory service or after establishing a connection via a suitable protocol. It is desirable that during a session dynamic functionality may be turned on or off, meaning that the components may be activated or deactivated dynamically.

Supporting Environment

Certain functions offered by a multimedia information-handling system may be provided by cooperation with a set of supporting components of the supporting environment. It should be kept in mind that some supporting components provide very specialized functions, or not all required functions if they are based on standards. So unavailable function and coordination of the supporting components must be realized and developed for a new service from scratch, if necessary. In particular, cooperation with supporting systems must be considered during refinements to the model. The following standards can be used to support or realize the abstract services of a multimedia handling system:

- Directory service [22]: This allows multimedia information to be found and the support of group communication. Note that a directory entry may use an attribute syntax derived from multimedia information such as still pictures. However, this is less relevant in the context of support for multimedia information handling.
- Management encompassing OSI management [25]: The Systems Management Functions specify standard mechanisms for a broad range of management activities [26–28]. The CMIS/CMIP standards are concerned with the set of common services and protocols for transmitting and manipulating management information [29] [30].
- Transmission of multimedia information: This involves Message Handling System (MHS) for store and forward transmission [31], Document Transfer And Manipulation (DTAM) for client-to-client communication [32], Referenced Data Transfer (RDT) for indirect transmission [33], and File Transfer, Access and Management (FTAM) for file transmission and access [34].
- Multimedia information archive system: DFR [21] [35].
- Basic services, including Remote Operations [36], Reliable Transfer Service [37], Association Control Service Element [38], Distributed Transaction Processing [39], and Concurrency Control and Commitment [40].

The interaction of these application-oriented services will be regulated via the Application Layer Structure (ALS) [41], by the results of the activities of Upper Layer Architecture (ULA) [42], and by the modeling approaches of Framework for the support of Distributed Applications (DAF) and ODP.

Integration of Isochronous Communication

A prerequisite for the handling of multimedia information, in addition to the anisochronous, is isochronous communication.[3] This is an important issue from both the computational and engineering viewpoints. For reasons of convenience, we integrate below the engineering aspects within the discussion of the computational model. The following problems must be solved: suitable transport services for isochronous transmission, and synchronization of several isochronous connections and coexistence with anisochronous connections.

Some experience has already been gained in the field of high-speed communication based on circuit and packet-switching networks [43], broadband ISDN [44], and especially on real-time transmission of video and language via digital networks [45–49]. For synchronous digital networks see the CCITT standards [50–53].

The information, which may be interchanged between distributed components of a distributed system in the office field, consists of long block of user data, brief dialogues and brief system commands, answers, and error indicators. Despite different characteristics, such as block length, data volume, and priority, they can not be transmitted isochronously via the same or similar data channels.

This type of transmission is not adequate if the applications contain the video or telephone communication (audio) information types. Isochronous communication, particularly for video, is notable for high transmission rates and requires transport channels that maintain the temporal relations between source and receiver. Undefined delays and jitter out of certain limits are not acceptable. The transmission delay refers to end-to-end and runs from the point in time of creation to the time of presentation. The transmission delay consists of the delay through the preparation of the information (e.g., division into packets and altering the form of representation), plus the transmission via the network and the presentation. Jitter at the sink may be held within limits by making buffers available. The buffer size and handling depends largely upon the coding of the information.

In addition to isochronous user data, control and signaling information must be transmitted. This may also take place via isochronous channels; however, the valuable bandwidth would not be fully utilized. This type of information may also be interchanged via anisochronous channels. Within CCITT, these ideas are being considered in the framework of Integrated Services Digital Network (ISDN) developments by the separation of signaling and user data channels with predetermined bandwidths.

In accordance with the OSI Basic Reference Model and development of distributed applications without dependence upon any individual technology, a transport interface for the support of isochronous and anisochronous communication is necessary, abstracted from network technology (e.g., circuit or packet switching, or asynchronous transfer mode) and network details. These may set by the QoS parameter. The following characteristics of a transport service must be adjustable:

- Selection of different data rates or a dynamic request of bandwidth
- Quality selection in respect to a guaranteed throughput, transmission delay, security, error identification and error handling (as a result, lightweight protocols—e.g., without error recovery or security—are required for isochronous transmission of video and audio)
- A combination of isochronous and anisochronous communication

Independent of the problems of isochronous communications, a transport system must support point-to-point, multipoint, and connectionless communications.

For the distributed processing of multimedia information, it is not only necessary to integrate isochronous and anisochronous communications, but the combination of several isochronous communication (such as video and audio) relations must be possible simultaneously. For this, suitable synchronization mechanisms must be made available. In accordance with OSI Basic Reference Model, such control and synchronization mechanisms will be located in either the session or application layer.

Should speech synchronization be required between audio and moving pictures, this synchronization may be achieved by storing the information at the source upon a common medium, or by encoding audio and moving pictures upon the same connection.

This approach has several disadvantages. Audio and moving pictures have different characteristics, and thus different QoS requirements. With an integrated solution, only one QoS parameter may be set; hence, information-type-specific characteristics are not used to advantage. Another disadvantage is that audio and moving pictures must be available at the same location.

---

[3]See the International Consultative Committee for Telephone and Telegraph (CCITT) Red Book, Vol. X, Fascicle X.1, "Terms and Definitions," 1985: Isochronous: The essential characteristic of a timescale or signal such that the time intervals between consecutive significant instants either have the same duration or durations that are integral multiples of the shortest duration. Note: In practice, variations in the time intervals are constrained within certain limits.

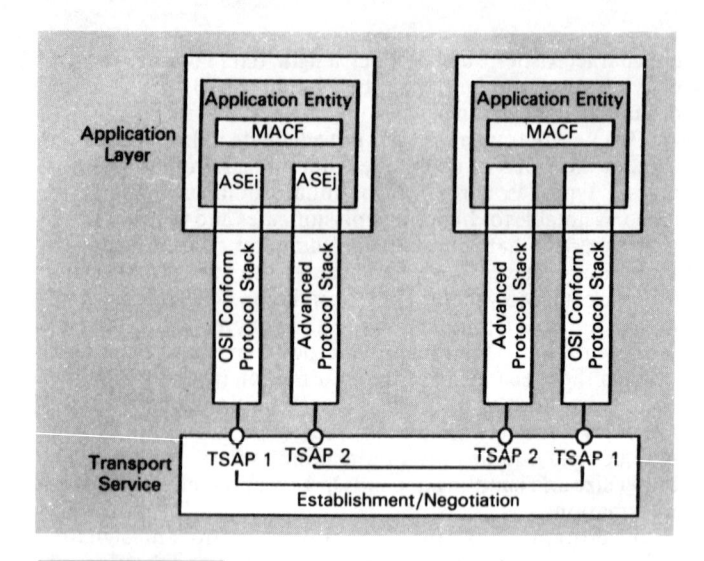

Fig. 3. Isochronous and anisochronous communication in combination for real-time audio and video.

A different approach uses separate virtual connections (e.g., sessions) for the different data streams. Suitable protocols for synchronization must still be developed and require further study. It is important that the receiver should recognize a loss of synchronization and that a suitable response may be undertaken.

To avoid a loss of the chronological order, the various information types are packeted and multiplexed upon a virtual connection [54].

If applications require the functionality of isochronous and anisochronous communication, an adequate modeling approach with respect to coordination and synchronization is required. This combination of advanced and OSI communication profiles is outlined below, but further study is still needed.

From the OSI application layer point of view, two solutions are obvious. The ALS standard [41] supports the modeling of a combination of application entities and application service elements in the OSI application layer and the management of multiple associations. So isochronous and anisochronous communication can be modeled as two application service elements, based on two different associations and protocol stacks. The coordination of the associations is provided by a specific Multiple Association Control Function (MACF). An alternative approach is the use of two different application entities. In the latter case, the associations must be coordinated by the application itself. Figure 3 shows the first alternative.

Two phases must be distinguished: the connection establishment and release phase, and the data transfer phase.

In the establishment phase, the QoS parameters are negotiated (in terms of the application layer, an application context is established); and in the data transfer phase, the protocol stack for isochronous communication (advanced protocol stack) is used for real-time audio or video communication.

Current Standardization Activities

The criteria found in [12] serve as a basis for judgement, and offer the possibility of incorporating the application-oriented standards within a communication model.

In [55], a detailed study has been made of relevant standards within the framework of distributed processing. A major result of this study is the conclusion that there is at present no all-encompassing model for distributed applications and the handling of multimedia information within a heterogeneous broadband environment. Most standards and recommendations cover only a small subset of a future model. As many overlappings in the capabilities exist, the individual developments cannot be united into a consistent model as a whole. This has historical reasons on the one hand, but on the other hand results from a lack of harmonization efforts. Within the committees dealing with application-oriented standards, there is by now recognition of the problems stemming from the multiple development of standards and recommendations. There are efforts being made to harmonize these areas in the future.

Through developments such as directory service [22], MHS [31], DFR [21] [35] and FTAM [34], some aspects of distributed information processing are supported, e.g., storage, distribution, and communication in distributed systems. They do not, however, enable communication between cooperating groups. For this, farther-reaching tools and services are required. Distribution lists and message stores are just a rudimentary approach to the handling of information in a group environment. They do not fulfill the following requirements:

- "$N:M$" multipoint communication, including several modes such as "one-to-many" e.g., for distribution of video, "many-to-one," e.g., for data collection and "many-to-many," e.g., for video conferencing
- Consideration of dynamic group behavior in the form of roles and rules
- Integration of flow-controlled data and data with a guaranteed throughput such as audio and moving pictures
- Synchronous processing of information (e.g., joint editing)

Three areas have been identified that deal not only with subordinate component parts but also with general model concepts, so that concepts and methods developed there could be used as a basis for a general telecommunication model serving different applications. These are the Reference Model of Open Distributed Processing (RM-ODP), DAF and Document Architecture, Transfer And Manipulation (DATAM).

ODP [56] is under development within JTC1/SC21/WG7 of ISO. DAF [57] is under development by Study Group VII of the CCITT. Both developments are intended to define a general framework for distributed processing. A comparison of their objectives shows agreement in many areas. For this reason, despite slight differences of emphasis, both groups are cooperating in joint ISO/CCITT meetings in the area of modeling and functions/infrastructure. While communication aspects were paramount in the development of the OSI Reference Model, the emphasis of the ODP Reference Model is on cooperation within distributed applications (including the aspects of processing, storage, user access, identification, security, and management). For this reason, several basic ODP concepts have been integrated into the conception of the model discussed here. While in ODP a general model is under development, DAF is also concentrating its efforts upon the development or refinement of new or existing standards.

Within the European Computer Manufacturers' Association (ECMA), Task Group 2 of TC32 is engaged in the development of a supporting environment for ODP. Here, distributed processing is viewed primarily from the standpoint of the structure of the application software. Under development are concepts independent of producers to ease the construction, running, and maintenance of distributed heterogeneous software components.

DATAM [58] is the only standard to date that combines a relatively complex information model with services for processing this information in a heterogeneous environment. This is important as many requirements cannot be realized though the independent development of data structures and communications components. The services available to date do not yet take into consideration any of the requirements for the synchronous processing of information and support for different roles, although work continues on additional service definitions.

DATAM is under development by Study Group VIII of CCITT. To describe interchanged information, Office Document Architecture (ODA) [59], developed by SC18 in ISO JTC1, was selected. In the area of information models, ODA was the only standard identified whose concept foresees the description of several information types along with structures combining information types in several processing stages. In the current study period, major extensions of ODA are being undertaken in close cooperation with ISO and CCITT. Included, for example, is the integration of audio, moving pictures, tables, formulae, and data. As ODA was originally developed for traditional documents, several major requirements for a general information model (e.g., network structures and the integration of any application-specific information types desired) have not yet been fulfilled and have not been adequately considered in the expansions.

In addition, the work of the Multimedia and Hypermedia information coding Expert Group (MHEG) of ISO/IEC JTC1/SC2/WG8 should be mentioned at this point, encompassing, first of all, the development of an accurate terminology in the multi/hypermedia area, and second, the development of a common method for representing and coding multimedia and hypermedia information. As such, it is the coded representation of "aggregates" of monomedia information that is of interest, not the coded representation of individual monomedia information. The method is intended to allow for the identification and referencing of component objects within aggregates and their associations, for example, for synchronization purposes. The work of the MHEG is in an early stage of development, and only a few results are available at this time.

Summary

In this article, requirements for distributed processing of multimedia information are summarized and compared with the latest efforts in standardization. An approach towards a communication model is outlined, which can be viewed as a special form of a model for open distributed applications. Additionally, synchronization aspects of isochronous and anisochronous communication are outlined. The model outlined here is still under development. Especially in the areas of formal specification of abstract services and modeling communication protocols, more detailed work still needs to be done.

Acknowledgments

Part of the above work was performed within the framework of the BERKOM project "Multimedia Documents in Broadband ISDN" [60], under a grant from the German Postal Telephone and Telegraph Administration. We would like to thank all our colleagues in this project for their constant availability for discussion, especially E. Moeller, A. Scheller, and K. H. Weiss.

References

[1] M. E. Hodges, R. M. Sasnett, and M. S. Ackerman, "A Construction Set for Multimedia Applications," pp. 37–43, Jan. 1989.
[2] J. S. Sventek, "An Architecture Supporting Multimedia Integration," *Office Automation Symp.*, pp. 46–56, Gaithersburg, MD: Computer Society Press of the IEEE, April 27–29, 1987.
[3] ISO 7498, "Information Processing Systems—Open Systems Interconnection (OSI)—Basic Reference Model," first ed., 1984.
[4] *CSCW '86 Conf. on Comp. Supp. Cooperative Work*, Austin, TX, MCC/ACM, Dec. 1986.
[5] *CSCW '88 Conf. on Comp. Supp. Cooperative Work*, Portland, OR, ACM, Sept. 1988.
[6] *Commun. of the ACM*, Special Issue on Groupware, Jan. 1987.
[7] *EC-CSCW '89 First Euro. Conf. on Comp. Supp. Cooperative Work*, London, England, Sept. 1989.
[8] T. Danielson and U. Pankoke-Babatz, "The AMIGO Activity Model," *Res. into Networks and Dist. Appl., Euro. Teleinformation Conf. (EUTECO)*, Vienna, Austria, April 20–22, 1988.
[9] D. Woelk, W. Kim, and W. Luther, "An Object-Oriented Approach to Multimedia Databases," *Proc. of ACM SIGMOD '86*, pp. 311–325, Washington, D.C., May 28–30, 1986.
[10] F. G. Halasz, "Reflections on NoteCards: Seven Issues for the Next Generation of Hypermedia Systems," *Commun. of the ACM*, vol. 31, no. 7, pp. 836–852, 1988.
[11] S. Christodoulakis, F. Ho, and M. Theodoridou, "The Multimedia Object Presentation Manager of MINOS: A Symmetric Approach," *Proc. of ACM SIGMOD '86*, pp. 295–310, Washington, DC, May 28–30, 1986.
[12] GMD-FOKUS/ZIB, "Multi-Media-Dokumente im ISDN-B—Anforderungsanalyse," version 3.0, Jan. 31, 1989.
[13] ISO/JTC 1/SC18 N1904, "Framework for Future Extension to ODA," May 1989.
[14] W. Klas, E. J. Neuhold, and M. Schrefl, "Visual Databases Need Datamodels for Multimedia Data," *Arbeitspapiere der GMD 346*, Oct. 1988.
[15] E. Moeller, A. Scheller, and G. Schürmann, "Distributed Processing of Multimedia Information," *Proc. of the 10th Int'l. Conf. on Dist. Comp. Syst.*, IEEE.
[16] ISO/TC97/SC21/WG7 N3194 Draft Report, "Basic Reference Model of Open Distributed Processing—Report on Topic 2.3—Framework of Abstractions," Sept. 12, 1988.
[17] A. J. Herbert and J. Monk, eds., *ANSA Reference Manual, Advanced Networked Systems Architecture*, Cambridge, England, 1989.
[18] P. Wegner, "Dimensions of Object-Based Language Design," *OOPSALA '87 Proc.*, Oct. 1987.
[19] P. Wegner and S. B. Zdonik, "Inheritance as an Incremental Modification Mechanism or What Like Is and Isn't Like," *Euro. Conf. on Object-Oriented Programming (ECOOP) '88 Proc.*, Oslo, Norway, Springer Verlag, Aug. 1988.
[20] J. Patterson, "The Good, the Bad, and the Ugly of Window Sharing in X," *4th Annual X Tech. Conf.*, Boston, MA, Jan. 1990.
[21] ISO/IEC JTC1/SC18 N1264, "Information Processing Systems—Text Communication—Document Filing and Retrieval (DFR)," Pt. 1: Abstract Service Definition and Procedures.
[22] CCITT Recommendation X.500, "Open Systems Interconnection (OSI)—The Directory—Overview of Concepts, Models and Services," same as ISO 9594-1, 1989.
[23] T. Danielson and E. Pastor, "Cooperating Intelligent Agents," *Res. into Networks and Dist. Appl.*, EUTECO, Vienna, Austria, April 20–22, 1988.
[24] P. A. Pays, "A Framework for Group Activities," *Res. into Networks and Dist. Appl.*, EUTECO, Vienna, Austria, April 20–22, 1988.
[25] ISO 7498-4, "Information Processing Systems—Open Systems Interconnection (OSI)," Part 4: Management Framework, 1989.
[26] ISO/DIS 10040, "Information Processing Systems—Open Systems Interconnection (OSI)—Systems Management Overview," June 1990.
[27] ISO/DIS 10165, "Information Processing Systems—Open Systems Interconnection (OSI)—Structure of Management Information," June 1990.
[28] ISO/DIS (Part 1–7) 10164, "Information Processing Systems—Open Systems Interconnection (OSI)—Systems Management Functions."
[29] ISO 9595, "Information Processing Systems—Open Systems Interconnection (OSI)—Common Management Information Service Definition," Jan. 1990.
[30] ISO 9596, "Information Processing Systems—Open Systems Interconnection (OSI)—Common Management Information Protocol Specification," Jan. 1990.
[31] CCITT Draft Recommendation X.400, "Message Handling Systems—System and Service Overview," same as ISO 10021-1.
[32] CCITT Draft Recommendation T.430 Series, "Document Transfer, Access and Manipulation (DTAM)—Communication Model."
[33] ISO/DIS 10031-2, "Information Processing Systems—Text Communication—Distributed-Office-Applications Model (DOAM)," Part 2: Referenced Data Transfer (RDT).
[34] ISO 8571, "Information Processing Systems—Open Systems Interconnection (OSI)—File Transfer, Access and Management," 1988.
[35] ISO/IEC JTC1/SC18 N1265, "Information Processing Systems—Text Communication—Document Filing and Retrieval (DFR)," Part 2: Protocol Specification, vol. ECMA/TC32-TG5.
[36] ISO/DIS 9072-1, "Information Processing Systems—Text Communication—Remote Operations," Part 1: Model, Notation and Service Definition, 1987.
[37] ISO/DIS 9066-1, "Information Processing Systems—Text Communication—Reliable Transfer," Part 1: Model and Service Definition, 1987.

[38] ISO/DIS 8649 (formerly 8649-2), "Information Processing Systems—Open Systems Interconnection—Service Definition for the Association Control Service Elements—Association Control," 1987.
[39] ISO/DIS 10026, "Information Processing Systems—Open Systems Interconnection (OSI)—Distributed Transaction Processing."
[40] ISO/DIS 9804 (formerly 8649-3), "Information Processing Systems—Open Systems Interconnection (OSI)—Service Definition for Commitment, Concurrency and Recovery Service Element."
[41] ISO/DIS 9545, "Information Processing Systems—Open Systems Interconnection (OSI)—Application Layer Structure (ALS)," 1989.
[42] ISO/JTC1/SC21 N2823, "Information Retrieval, Transfer and Management for OSI—ULA Topics and Issues," July 27, 1988.
[43] *International Zurich Seminar on Digital Communications*, Zurich, Switzerland, 1986–1990.
[44] R. Popescu-Zeletin, P. Egloff, and B. Butscher, "BERKOM—A Broadband ISDN Project," *Proc. of the Int'l Zurich Sem. on Dig. Commun.*, pp. 77, B5.1, 1987.
[45] S. Ades, R. Want, and R. Calnan, "Protocols for Real-Time Voice Communication on a Packet Local Network," *Proc. of the 8th Int'l. Conf. on Dist. Comp. Syst.*, pp. 525–530, IEEE, June 1988.
[46] A. A. Lazar, A. Patir, T. Takahasi, and M. El Zarki, "MAGNET: Columbias Integrated Network Testbed," pp. 859–871, *IEEE, J. on Sel. Areas in Commun.*, vol. JSAC-3, no. 6, Nov. 1985.
[47] A. A. Lazar and J. S. White, "Packetized Video on MAGNET," Ctr. for Telecommun. Res., Columbia University, NY, July 1987.
[48] R. Want, "Reliable Management of Voice in a Distributed System," Univ. of Cambridge Comp. Lab., July 1988.
[49] D. C. Swinehart, L. C. Stewart, and S. M. Ornstein, "Adding Voice to an Office Computer Network," *Proc. IEEE GLOBECOM 1983, Nov. 1983*; also available as Xerox Palo Alto Res. Ctr. Tech. Rep. CSL-86-1, June 1986.
[50] CCITT Recommendation G.707, "Synchronous Digital Hierarchy Bit Rates," Study Group XVIII Plenary Assembly, Melbourne, Australia, 1988.
[51] CCITT Recommendation G.708, "Network Node Interface for the Synchronous Digital Hierarchy," Study Group XVIII Plenary Assembly, Melbourne, Australia, 1988.
[52] CCITT Recommendation G.709, "Synchronous Multiplexing Structure," Study Group XVII Plenary Assembly, Melbourne, Australia, 1988.
[53] R. Ballart and Y. C. Ching, "SONET: Now It's the Standard Optical Network," *IEEE Commun. Mag.*, pp. 8–15, Mar. 1989.
[54] W. L. Leung *et al.*, "A Set of Operating System Mechanisms to Support Multi-Media Application," *Proc. of the Int'l. Zurich Sem. on Dig. Commun.*, p. 71, B4.1, 1987.
[55] GMD-FOKUS/ZIB, "Multi-Media-Dokumente im ISDN-B—Analyse relevanter Standarisierungsbestrebungen," Version 2.0, May 1989.
[56] ISO/TC97/SC21/WG7 N4883-4888, "Information Processing Systems—Open Systems Interconnection (OSI)—Open Distributed Processing (ODP)," June 1990.
[57] CCITT SG VII/Q19, "Framework for the Support of Distributed Applications (DAF)," Study Group VII Plenary, Geneva, Switzerland, July 1989.
[58] CCITT Draft Recommendation T.400/T.500 Series, "Document Architecture, Transfer And Manipulation (DATAM)."
[59] ISO 8613, "Information Processing—Text and Office Systems—Office Document Architecture (ODA) and Interchange Format," 1989.
[60] "BERKOM Reference Model II," DETECON, Technisches Zentrum Berlin, Vol. 5, Germany, Version 3.1, Sept. 1990.

Biography

Gerd Schürmann graduated from the Technische Universitat Berlin in 1979. After that, he was involved in a research project concerned with the design and implementation of portable compliers and a portable file system. In 1983, he joined the Freie Universitat Berlin, where he was heavily involved within the framework of the German Research Network (DFN) with the development of a distributed GKS based on the ISO Reference Model in an open network. In 1987, he joined the Gesellschaft fur Mathematik und Datenverarbeitung (GMD), where he is responsible for a project developing a multimedia document model and system architecture for a heterogeneous broadband environment. Since 1989, he is responsible for the project area "Architecture and Interactions of Distributed Applications" at the Research Center for Open Communication Systems (FOKUS) of GMD Berlin. He has been active in the field of national and international standardization in the areas of graphics and open distributed processing, and chairs the committee for "Open Distributed Processing" at the Deutsches Institut fur Normung (DIN).

Uwe Holzmann-Kaiser received his M.Sc. in computer science from the Technical University of Berlin in 1988, and afterwards joined the Research Center for Open Communications Systems (FOKUS) of GMD Berlin. There, his main interests are in the area of new architectures for the design of open, distributed application and, since 1989, he has represented FOKUS in ROSA, a project defining an open services architecture for the RACE research program in Europe.

Chapter 7
Glossary

APPLICATION LAYER. Layer 7 of the OSI model. This layer determines the interface of the system with the user.

ASYNCHRONOUS TRANSMISSION. Transmission in which each information character is individually synchronized (usually by the use of start elements and stop elements).

AUTOMATIC REPEAT REQUEST. A feature that automatically initiates a request for retransmission when an error in transmission is detected.

BALANCED TRANSMISSION. A transmission mode in which signals are transmitted as a current that travels down one conductor and returns on the other. For digital signals, this technique is known as differential signaling, with the binary value depending on the voltage difference.

BASEBAND. Transmission of signals without modulation. In a baseband local network, digital signals (1's and 0's) are inserted directly onto the cable as voltage pulses. The entire spectrum of the cable is consumed by the signal. This scheme does not allow frequency-division multiplexing.

BIT STUFFING. The insertion of extra bits into a data stream to avoid the appearance of unintended control sequences.

BRIDGE. A device that links two homogeneous packet-switched local networks. It accepts all packets from each network addressed to devices on the other, buffers them, and retransmits them to the other network.

BROADBAND. The use of coaxial cable for providing data transfer by means of analog or radio-frequency signals. Digital signals are passed through a modem and transmitted over one of the frequency bands of the cable.

BROADCAST. The simultaneous transmission of data to a number of stations.

BROADCAST ADDRESS. An address that designates all entities within a domain (e.g., network, internet).

BUS. A local network topology in which stations are attached to a shared transmission medium. The transmission medium is a linear cable; transmissions propagate the length of the medium and are received by all stations.

CATV. Community Antenna Television. CATV cable is used for broadband local networks, and broadcast TV distribution.

CHECKSUM. An error-detecting code based on a summation operation performed on the bits to be checked.

CIRCUIT SWITCHING. A method of communicating in which a dedicated communications path is established between two devices through one or more intermediate switching nodes. Unlike packet switching, digital data are sent as a continuous stream of bits. Bandwidth is guaranteed, and delay is essentially limited to propagation time. The telephone system uses circuit switching.

COLLISION. A condition in which two packets are being transmitted over a medium at the same time. Their interference makes both unintelligible.

COMMUNICATIONS ARCHITECTURE. The hardware and software structure that implements the communications function.

CONNECTIONLESS DATA TRANSFER. A protocol for exchanging data in an unplanned fashion and without prior coordination (e.g., datagram).

CONNECTION-ORIENTED DATA TRANSFER. A protocol for exchanging data in which a logical connection is established between the endpoints (e.g., virtual circuit).

CONTENTION. The condition when two or more stations attempt to use the same channel at the same time.

CSMA. Carrier Sense Multiple Access. A medium access control technique for multiple-access transmission media. A station wishing to transmit first senses the medium and transmits only if the medium is idle.

CSMA/CD. Carrier Sense Multiple Access with Collision Detection. A refinement of CSMA in which a station ceases transmission if it detects a collision.

CYCLIC REDUNDANCY CHECK. An error detecting code in which the code is the remainder resulting from dividing the bits to be checked by a predetermined binary number.

DATA CIRCUIT-TERMINATING EQUIPMENT. In a data station, the equipment that provides the signal conversion and coding between the data terminal equipment (DTE) and the line. The DCE may be separate equipment or an integral part of the DTE or of intermediate equipment. The DCE may perform other functions that are normally performed at the network end of the line.

DATAGRAM. In packet switching, a self-contained packet, independent of other packets, that does not require acknowledgment, and that carries information sufficient for routing from the originating data terminal equipment (DTE), without relying on earlier exchanges between the DTEs and the network.

DATA LINK LAYER. Layer 2 of the OSI model. Converts an unreliable transmission channel to a reliable one.

DATA TERMINAL EQUIPMENT. That part of a data station that serves as a data source, data sink, or both.

DIFFERENTIAL ENCODING. A means of encoding digital data on a digital signal such that the binary value is determined by a signal change rather than a signal level.

DOD PROTOCOL ARCHITECTURE. A communications architecture that has evolved from the ARPANET project and DOD standardization activities.

ENCAPSULATION. The addition of control information by a protocol entity to data obtained from a protocol user.

ERROR-DETECTING CODE. A code in which each expression conforms to specific rules of construction, so that if certain errors occur in an expression, the resulting expression will not conform to the rules of construction and thus the presence of errors is detected.

FAST SELECT. An option of the X.25 virtual call that allows the inclusion of data in the call setup and call clearing packets.

FLOW CONTROL. The function performed by a receiving entity to limit the amount or rate of data that is sent by a transmitting entity.

FRAME CHECK SEQUENCE. An error-detecting code inserted as a field in a block of data to be transmitted. The code serves to check for errors upon reception of the data.

FULL-DUPLEX TRANSMISSION. Data transmission in both directions at the same time.

GATEWAY. A device that connects two systems, especially if the systems use different protocols. For example, a gateway is needed to connect two independent local networks, or to connect a local network to a long-haul network.

HALF-DUPLEX TRANSMISSION. Data transmission in either direction, one direction at a time.

HEADER. System-defined control information that precedes user data.

INTEGRATED SERVICES DIGITAL NETWORK. A planned worldwide telecommunication service that will use digital transmission and switching technology to support voice and digital data communication.

INTERNET. A collection of packet-switched and broadcast networks that are interconnected via gateways.

INTERNET PROTOCOL. An internetworking protocol that provides connectionless service across multiple packet-switched networks.

INTERNETWORKING. Communication among devices across multiple networks.

MANCHESTER ENCODING. A digital signaling technique in which there is a transition in the middle of each bit time. A 1 is encoded with a high level during the first half of the bit time; a 0 is encoded with a low level during the first half of the bit time.

MEDIUM ACCESS CONTROL (MAC). For broadcast networks, the method of determining which device has access to the transmission medium at any time. CSMA/CD and token are common access methods.

MESSAGE SWITCHING. A switching technique using a message store-and-forward system. No dedicated path is established. Rather, each message contains a destination address and is passed from source to destination through intermediate nodes. At each node, the entire message is received, stored briefly, and then passed on to the next node.

MULTICAST ADDRESS. An address that designates a group of entities within a domain (e.g., network, internet).

MULTIPOINT. A configuration in which more than two stations share a transmission path.

NETWORK LAYER. Layer 3 of the OSI model. Responsible for routing data through a communication network.

PACKET ASSEMBLER/DISASSEMBLER (PAD). A device used with an X.25 network to provide service to asynchronous terminals.

PACKET SWITCHING. A method of transmitting messages through a communications network in which long messages are subdivided into short packets. The packets are then transmitted as in message switching. Usually, packet switching is more efficient and rapid than message switching.

PARITY BIT. A check bit appended to an array of binary digits to make the sum of all the binary digits, including the check bit, always odd or always even.

PHYSICAL LAYER. Layer 1 of the OSI model. Concerned with the electrical, mechanical, and timing aspects of signal transmission over a medium.

PIGGYBACKING. The inclusion of an acknowledgment to a previously received packet in an outgoing data packet.

POINT-TO-POINT. A configuration in which two stations share a transmission path.

PRESENTATION LAYER. Layer 6 of the OSI model. Concerned with data format and display.

PROTOCOL. A set of rules that govern the operation of functional units to achieve communication.

PROTOCOL DATA UNIT. A block of data exchanged between two entities via a protocol.

PUBLIC DATA NETWORK. A government-controlled or national monopoly packet-switched network. This service is publicly available to data processing users.

RING. A local network topology in which stations are attached to repeaters connected in a closed loop. Data are transmitted in one direction around the ring, and can be read by all attached stations.

SERVICE ACCESS POINT. A means of identifying a user of the services of a protocol entity. A protocol entity provides one or more SAPs for use by higher-level entities.

SESSION LAYER. Layer 5 of the OSI model. Manages a logical connection (session) between two communicating processes or applications.

SIMPLEX TRANSMISSION. Data transmission in one preassigned direction only.

SLIDING-WINDOW TECHNIQUE. A method of flow control in which a transmitting station may send numbered packets within a window of numbers. The window changes dynamically to allow additional packets to be sent.

SYNCHRONOUS TRANSMISSION. Data transmission in which the time of occurrence of each signal representing a bit is related to a fixed time frame.

TELETEX. A text communications service that provides message preparation and transmission facilities.

TOKEN BUS. A medium access control technique for bus/tree. Stations form a logical ring around which a token is passed. A station receiving the token may transmit data, and then must pass the token on to the next station in the ring.

TOKEN RING. A medium access control technique for rings. A token circulates around the ring. A station may transmit by seizing the token, inserting a packet onto the ring, and then retransmitting the token.

TOPOLOGY. The structure, consisting of paths and switches, that provides the communications interconnection among nodes of a network.

TRANSPORT LAYER. Layer 4 of the OSI model. Provides reliable, transparent transfer of data between endpoints.

TREE. A local network topology in which stations are attached to a shared transmission medium. The transmission medium is a branching cable emanating from a headend, with no closed circuits. Transmissions propagate throughout all branches of the tree and are received by all stations.

UNBALANCED TRANSMISSION. A transmission mode in which signals are transmitted on a single conductor. Transmitter and receiver share a common ground.

VALUE-ADDED NETWORK. A privately owned, packet-switched network whose services are sold to the public.

VIRTUAL CIRCUIT. A packet-switching service in which a connection (virtual circuit) is established between two stations at the start of transmission. All packets follow the same route, need not carry a complete address, and arrive in sequence.

Chapter 8
Bibliography

The subject of this book is so broad and rapidly evolving that this bibliography can only strive to be thorough and timely. The entries in this section were chosen using the following criteria:

- Relevance: This tutorial is concerned with the principles and evolving standards for communications architectures and protocols, and this is reflected in the bibliography. Few of the references describe proprietary or experimental implementations.
- Currency: Most of the references are of recent origin.
- Representativeness: The interested reader can pursue the topics introduced in this tutorial by consulting the references listed here. They are, however, only representative of the available literature. The articles themselves contain further references for the truly dedicated reader.

ABRA84 Abrams, M. and Cotton, I. *Computer Networks: A Tutorial.* IEEE Computer Society Press, 1984. A collection of reprints plus original material focusing on network applications and management issues, such as network control, security, and planning. Also covers lower level protocols and communications network technology.

ALLA82 Allan, R. "Local-Area Networks Spur Moves to Standardize Data Communications Among Computers and Peripherals." *Electronic Design,* December 23, 1982. A fairly detailed discussion of the IEEE 802 standard.

ANSO90 Anson, C. and Mitchell, C. "Security Defects in CCITT Recommendation X.509—The Directory Authentication Framework." *Computer Communications Review,* April 1990. Security defects to be found in X.509-1988 are described, together with possible solutions.

ASCH86 Aschenbrenner, J. "Open Systems Interconnection." *IBM Systems Journal,* Nos. 3/4, 1986. Discusses the history of the OSI model and the current issues, such as conformance, that are critical to its success. The author also provides an IBM perspective on the relationship between OSI and SNA.

ATKI80 Atkins, J. "Path Control: The Transport Network of SNA." *IEEE Transactions on Communications,* April 1980. Describes the layer of SNA that corresponds to OSI network layer plus part of OSI's data link layer.

BAER83 Baer, D. and Sturch, J. "An SNA Primer for Programmers." *Computerworld,* November 14 and 21, 1983. A lengthy and useful description of IBM's communications architecture.

BALC90 Balcer, R.; Eaves, J.; Legras, J.; McLintock, R.; and Wright, T. "An Overview of Emerging CCITT Recommendations for the Synchronous Digital Hierarchy: Multiplexers, Lines Systems, Management, and Network Aspects." *IEEE Communications Magazine,* August 1990. A review of CCITT G-series recommendations that relate to various issues dealing with high-speed long-distance digital transmission.

BART83a Bartoli, P. "The Application and Presentation Layers of the Reference Model for Open Systems Interconnection." *Proceedings, INFOCOM '83,* 1983. A look at standards at the two highest OSI layers. Included in this tutorial.

BART83b Bartoli, P. "The Application Layer of the Reference Model of Open Systems Interconnection." *Proceedings of the IEEE,* December 1983. A brief description of the ISO application protocol specification.

BBN81 Bolt, Beranek, and Newman Inc. *Specifications for the Interconnection of a Host and an IMP.* Report 1822, December 1981. This report has had a significant influence on the evolution of network access protocols. It specifies the principle network access technique for ARPANET.

BELL84 Bellchambers, W.; Francis, J.; Hummel, E.; and Nickelson, R. "The International Telecommunication Union and Development of Worldwide Telecommunications." *IEEE Communications Magazine,* May 1984. Describes the CCITT and the procedure by which it develops and issues Recommendations.

BEN90 Ben-Artzi, A.; Chandna, A.; and Warrier, U. "Network Management of TCP/IP Networks: Present and Future." *IEEE Network Magazine,* July 1990. Examines alternative approaches to network management for TCP/IP-based networks. One approach is the Simple Network Management Protocol (SNMP), which was designed specifically for TCP/IP. The other is Common Management Information Service over TCP/IP (CMOT), which adapts the OSI network management standards to the TCP/IP environment.

BERT80 Bertine, H. "Physical Level Protocols." *IEEE Transactions on Communications,* April 1980. Discusses principles and gives examples.

BERT81 Bertine, H. "Physical Level Interfaces and Protocols." in *Data Communications Network Interfacing and Protocols,* 1981. A revised version of [BERT80]. Included in this tutorial.

BHUS83 Bhusri, G. "Optimum Implementation of Common Channel Signalling in Local Networks." *Proceedings, INFOCOM 83,* 1983. Compares X.25 and CCITT Signaling System Number 7. The latter is a specification for signaling across a circuit-switched network.

BLAC82 Black, U. "Data Link Controls: The Great Variety Calls for Wise and Careful Choices." *Data Communications,* June 1982. Discusses principles of data link control and examines two IBM protocols: SDLC and BSC.

BLAU84 Blausten, E. "Accessing the Packet Switched Public Data Network—the PAD." *Proceedings, INFOCOM 84,* 1984. A brief summary of the PAD series of standards: X.3, X.28, and X.29, plus a status report on its use.

BOCH90 Bochman, G. and Mondain-Monval, P. "Design Principles for Communication Gateways." *IEEE Journal on Selected Areas in Communications.* January 1990. Provides a survey of various approaches to internetworking. The approaches are grouped into two general categories: service adaptation and protocol conversion.

BODS85 Bodson, D. "The Federal Telecommunication Standards Program." *IEEE Communications Magazine,* January 1985. Describes the procedures by which federal standards are developed and issued.

BORS84 Borsook, P. "U.S. Navy Brings Out Standard for Word Processing Interchange." *Data Communications,* December 1984. A nontechnical description of the development of the Document Interchange Format (DIF) standard.

BOUL89 Boule, R. and Moy, J. "Inside Routers: A Technology Guide for Network Builders." *Data Communications,* September 21, 1989. A tutorial on routers that examines protocols, router mechanisms, and routing algorithms.

BOWE83 Bowers, A. and Connell, E. "A Checklist of Communications Protocol Functions Organized Usng the Open System Interconnection Seven-Layer Reference Model." *Proceedings, COMPCON Fall 83,* 1983. A useful comparison of OSI layers. Included in this tutorial.

BRAB89 Brabner, S. "X.500: A Global Directory Standard." *Telecommunications,* February 1989. A brief introduction to X.500.

BRAN90 Brandwein, R.; Cox, T.; and Dahl, J. "The IEEE 802.6 Physical Layer Convergence Procedures." *IEEE LCS Magazine,* May 1990. Examines the sublayer of the IEEE 802.6 physical layer that maps from the data link layer to the transmission system.

BROD83a Brodd, W. "HDLC, ADCCP, and SDLC: What's the Difference." *Data Communications,* August 1983. Defines and compares two very similar data standards with IBM's version.

BROD83b Brodd, W. and Boudreau, P. "Operational Characteristics: BSC versus SDLC." *Data Communications,* October 1983. Defines and compares IBM's two data link protocols.

BRYS89 Brysh, H. "Security in the OSI Network." *Telecommunications,* February 1989. An overview of the OSI security architecture.

BURG83 Burg, F. "Design Considerations for Using the X.25 Layer in Data Terminal Equipment." *Proceedings, INFOCOM 83,* 1983. A practical discussion of X.25 implementation. Included in this tutorial.

BURG84 Burg, F.; Chen, C.; and Folts, H. "Of Local Networks, Protocols, and the OSI Reference Model." *Data Communications,* November 1984. Describes approaches to internetworking of local networks via X.25.

BURR83 Burr, W. "An Overview of the Proposed American National Standard for Local Distributed Data Interfaces." *Communications of the ACM,* August 1983. Describes the ANSI X3T9.5 standard for high-speed (50 Mbps) local networks. Differs significantly from IEEE 802.

BUSH90 Bush, M.; Rasmussen, K. and Wong, F. "Conformance Testing Methodologies for OSI Protocols." *AT&T Technical Journal,* January/February 1990. Examines and compares the test methods applicable to OSI conformance testing as defined by ISO and CCITT.

CALL83 Callon, R. "Internetwork Protocol." *Proceedings of the IEEE,* December 1983. Discusses a variety of technical issues related to internetworking in the OSI environment, including connection-oriented versus connectionless, quality of service, addressing, fragmentation, error control, flow control, and routing.

CANE86 Caneschi, F. "Hints for the Interpretation of the ISO Session Layer." *Computer Communication Review,* July/August 1986. Discusses and interprets various obscure points in the standard. This is an instructive analysis of the difficulties in interpreting a standards document.

CARG89 Cargill, C. *Information Technology Standardization: Theory, Process, and Organizations.* Bedford, MA: Digital Press, 1989. An examination of standards and the standards-making process.

CARL80 Carlson, D.E. "Bit-Oriented Data Link Control Procedures." *IEEE Transactions on Communications,* April 1980. A thorough discussion of the principles of bit-oriented data link protocols, such as HDLC.

CASS89 Cassel, L.; Partridge, C.; and Wescott, J. "Network Management Architectures and Protocols: Problems and Approaches." *IEEE Journal on Selected Areas in Communications.* September 1989. Discusses resolved issues in network management in the context of the OSI network management architecture.

CERF78 Cerf, V. and Kristein, P.T. "Issues in Packet-Network Interconnection." *Proceedings of the IEEE,* November l978. A lengthy discussion of alternative approaches to internetworking.

CERF83a Cerf, V. and Lyons, R. "Military Requirements for Packet-Switched Networks and Their Implications for Protocol Standardization." *Computer Networks,* October 1983. Discusses the specific requirements that led to the development of the ARPANET protocols and architecture.

CERF83b Cerf, V. and Cain, E. "The DOD Internet Architecture Model." *Computer Networks,* October 1983. Presents the DOD-defined architecture and protocols developed under ARPANET. Included in this tutorial.

CHAP82 Chapin, A. "Connectionless Data Transmission." *Computer Communication Review,* April 1982. Discusses the motivation for, and techniques of, connectionless data transfer. This service is usually associated with the network layer (datagrams), but can be provided at any layer of the architecture.

CHAP83 Chapin, A. "Connections and Connectionless Data Transmission." *Proceedings of the IEEE,* December l983. Discusses and compares connection-oriented and connectionless data transfer in the context of the OSI model.

CHAP87 Chappell, D. "Guide to Transport-Layer Interfaces for UNIX Users." *Data Communications,* July 1987. Describes upper-layer interfaces to ISO TP and TCP.

CHER89a Cheriton, D. and Williamson, C. "VMTP as the Transport Layer for High-Performance Distributed Systems." *IEEE Communications Magazine,* June 1989. Introduces the versatile message Transaction Protocol (VMTP), which is a lightweight transport protocol. The paper describes the basic protocol design and reports the results of performance studies.

CHER89b Cherukuri, R. and Derby, J. "Frame Relay: Protocols and Private Network Applications." *Proceedings, IEEE INFOCOM '89,* April 1989. A detailed look at the frame relay protocol, including details of the protocol mechanisms and formats, and its relationship to higher layers.

CHIL83 Childs, G. "United Kingdom Videotex Service and the European Unified Videotex Standard." *IEEE Journal on Selected Areas in Communications,* February 1983. Describes the European Videotex standard, which has been incorporated into the broader proposed ANSI standard.

CIDO87 Cidon, I. and Rom, R. "Failsafe End-to-End Protocols in Computer Networks with Changing Topology." *IEEE Transactions on Communications,* April 1987. Describes reliable end-to-end protocol mechanisms that would be suitable for a transport protocol.

CLAN82 Clancy, G.J. et al. "The IEEE 802 Committee States Its Case Concerning Its Local Network Standards Efforts." *Data Communications,* April 1982. This instructive article defends the need for standards for local networks. Its line of reasoning is applicable in a broader context.

CLAR85 Clark, G. and Wong, M. "Verifying Conformance to the X.25 Standard." *Data Communications,* April 1985. Describes an on-line facility developed by the National Bureau of Standards to use in verifying vendor conformance to the X.25 standard.

CLAR89 Clark, D.; Jacobson, V.; Romkey, J.; and Salwen, H. "An Analysis of TCP Processing Overhead." *IEEE Communications Magazine,* June 1989. Examines techniques, including header prediction and more efficient error code calculation, that can be used to minimize the overhead of TCP. The authors conclude, and attempt to demonstrate, that TCP can support very high data rates if properly implemented.

COLL83 Collie, B.; Kayser, L.; and Rybczynski, A. "Looking at the ISDN Interfaces: Issues and Answers." *Data Communications,* June 1983. A readable overview of the ISDN standard at the time of writing.

CONA80 Conard, J. "Character-Oriented Data Link Control Protocols." *IEEE Transactions on Communications,* April 1980. Surveys the older (some would say obsolete) type of link control protocols.

CONA83 Conard, J. "Services and Protocols of the Data Link Layer." *Proceedings of the IEEE,* December 1983. A thorough survey of principles. Included in this tutorial.

CONW91 Conway, A. "A Perspective on the Analytical Performance Evaluation of Multilayered Communication Protocol Architectures." *IEEE Journal on Selected Areas in Communications.* January 1991. Considers various approaches that have been taken to evaluating quantitatively the effects of multiple layers of protocol and the associated processing overheads. Methodologies appropriate for OSI are compared.

CORR82 Corrigan, M. "Defense Data Network Protocols." *Proceedings, EASCON 82,* 1982. A brief review of the standards being developed by DOD at all levels of their architecture.

CUNN83 Cunningham, I. "Message Handling Systems and Protocols." *Proceedings of the IEEE,* December 1983. A somewhat formal overview of CCITT message handling systems.

CUNN84 Cunningham, I. "Electronic Mail Standards to Get Rubber-Stamped and Go Worldwide." *Data Communications,* May 1984. A more informal overview of CCITT message handling standards.

CUNN85 Cunningham, I. and Kerr, I. "New Electronic Mail Standards." *Telecommunications,* July 1985. Examines the X.400 family of standards.

CYP578 Cypser, R. *Communications Architecture for Distributed Systems.* Addison-Wesley, 1978. Describes one of the earliest communications architectures to be announced: SNA. Although SNA has evolved since the publication of this book, it remains the most detailed and thorough description of a working architecture.

DALA82 Dalal, Y.K. "Use of Multiple Networks in the Xerox Network System." *Computer,* October 1982. Looks at an internetwork approach taken for Ethernet. Exposes many of the issues a designer must face.

DAVI77 Davidson, J.; Hathaway, W.; Postel, J.; Mimno, N.; Thomas, R.; and Walden, D. "The ARPANET Telnet Protocol: Its Purpose, Principles, Implementation, and Impact on Host Operating System Design." *Proceedings, Fifth Data Communications Symposium,* 1977. Describes one of the earliest virtual terminal protocols. Although Telnet is quite limited, it is one of the few operational protocols.

DAVI79 Davies, D.; Barber, D.; Price, W.; and Solomonides, C. *Computer Networks and Their Protocols.* Wiley, 1979. A textbook on the subject.

DAY80 Day, J. "Terminal Protocols." *IEEE Transactions on Communications,* April 1980. This survey covers much the same ground as [MAGN79]. Included in this tutorial.

DAY83 Day, J. and Zimmermann, H. "The OSI Reference Model." *Proceedings of the IEEE,* December 1983. A formal presentation.

DEAT82 Deaton, G. "OSI and SNA: A Perspective." *Journal of Telecommunication Networks,* Fall 1982. A detailed comparison of OSI to IBM's communications architecture.

DECI82a Decina, M. "Managing ISDN Through International Standards Activities." *IEEE Communications Magazine,* September 1982. Describes CCITT's activities and organization related to ISDN.

DECI82b Decina, M. "Progress Towards User Access Arrangements in Integrated Services Digital Networks." *IEEE Transactions on Communications,* September 1982. Describes the set of ISDN standards. Included in this tutorial.

DHAS86 Dhas, C. and Konangi, U. "X.25: An Interface to Public Packet Networks." *IEEE Communications Magazine,* September 1986. Describes the 1984 version of X.25 in some detail.

DIOT90 Diot, C. and Dang, M. "A High Performance Implementation of OSI Transport Protocol Class 4; Evaluation and Perspectives." *Proceeding, 15th Conference on Local Computer Networks,* October 1990. Describes implementation techniques for TP4 and analyzes the performance improvement achieved.

DOD83a Department of Defense. *Military Standard Internet Protocol,* MIL-STD-1777, August 12, 1983. A specification of DOD's Internet Protocol which, as of this writing, is the only standard internetwork protocol available.

DOD83b Department of Defense. *Military Standard Transmission Control Protocol,* MIL-STD-1778, August 12, 1983. A specification of DOD's TCP, which is functionally equivalent to ISO Class 4 Transport Protocol.

DORR81 Dorros, I. "ISDN." *IEEE Communications Magazine,* March 1981. A general discussion of ISDN. Does not address standards.

DORR83 Dorros, I. "Telephone Nets Go Digital." *IEEE Spectrum,* April 1983. Describes the internal evolution of telecommunications networks that is leading toward the ISDN.

DUC85 Duc, N. and Chew, E. "ISDN Protocol Architecture." *IEEE Communications Magazine,* March 1985. Describes the emerging protocol architecture for ISDN, which encompasses up through the OSI network layer. Architectures for circuit-switching and packet-switching are explained.

EMMO83 Emmons, W. and Chandler, A. "OSI Session Layer Services and Protocols." *Proceedings of the IEEE,* December 1983. A standards-oriented discussion. Included in this tutorial.

ENNI83 Ennis, G. "Development of the DOD Protocol Reference Model." *Proceedings, SIGCOMM '83 Symposium,* 1983. A concise justification for the DOD view of communications architectures and the reasons for their lack of acceptance of the OSI model.

EVAN85 Evans, G. "The U.S. Navy Sets New Standard for Word Processing." *Data Communications,* April 1985. Describes in some detail the Navy's Document Interchange Format (DIF), which may become both a DOD and a FIPS standard. DIF standardized document format to permit interchange of textual data between word processing equipment.

FARO86 Farowich, S. "Communicating in the Technical Office." *IEEE Spectrum,* April 1986. A discussion of TOP (Technical and Office Protocols).

FLET82 Fletcher, J. "An Arithmetic Checksum for Serial Transmissions." *IEEE Transactions on Communications,* January 1982. Describes the "Fletcher Checksum," which is the error-detection algorithm used in the ISO transport protocol and ISO connectionless internet protocol.

FLET84 Fletcher, J. "Serial Link Protocol Design." *Proceedings, SIGCOMM '84,* June 1984. A discussion of technical design principles for link protocols and an analysis of X.25 Level 2 based on those principles. The X.25 protocol is found wanting.

FOLE85 Foley, J. "The Status and Direction of Open Systems Interconnection." *Data Communications,* February 1985. A rather detailed look at the refinements that have been made to the OSI model to accommodate features of protocols that are being developed within the framework of that model.

FOLT80a Folts, H. "Procedures for Circuit-Switched Service in Synchronous Public Data Networks." *IEEE Transactions on Communications,* April 1980. Describes the X.21 standard. Included in this tutorial.

FOLT80b Folts, H. "X.25 Transaction-Oriented Features—Datagram and Fast Select." *IEEE Transactions on Communications,* April 1980. Describes two transaction-oriented services defined for X.25. The datagram service has not been adopted by any major implementer and will be deleted from the standard. The fast select facility, though connection-oriented, provides basically the same service as the datagram standard.

FOLT80c Folts, H. "A Powerful Standard Replaces the Old Interface Standby." *Data Communications,* May 1980. Describes RS-449. Included in this tutorial.

FOLT81 Folts, H. "Coming of Age: A Long-Awaited Standard for Heterogeneous Nets." *Data Communications,* January 1981. Describes the OSI model.

FOLT82 Folts, H. "A Tutorial on the Open Systems Interconnection Reference Model." *OSI Data Transfer,* June 1982. A detailed description. Included in this tutorial.

FONG89 Fong, K. and Reinstedler, J. "The Development of an OSI Application Layer Protocol Interface." *Computer Communications Review,* July 1989. Describes a set of common OSI application protocol interface specifications for high-level-language programmers.

GARL77 Garlick, L.; Rom, R.; and Postel, J. "Reliable Host-to-Host Protocols: Problems and Techniques." *Proceedings, Ftfth Data Communications Symposium,* 1977. Discusses transport protocol principles and describes TCP.

GIEN79 Gien, M. and Zimmermann, H. "Design Principles for Network Interconnection." *Proceedings, Sixth Data Communications Symposium,* 1979. An exhaustive analysis of interconnection issues. Included in this tutorial.

GRAU82 Graube, M. "Local Area Nets: A Pair of Standards." *IEEE Spectrum,* June 1982. A brief overview of the IEEE 802 standard.

GRAY72 Gray, J. "Line Control Procedures." *Proceedings of the IEEE,* November 1972. A discussion of the principles of data link control, published long before the OSI model was developed. The principles haven't changed.

GREE80 Green, P. "An Introduction to Network Architectures and Protocols." *IEEE Transactions on Communications,* April 1980. Discusses the principles of a communications architecture.

GRIF82 Griffiths, J. "ISDN Network Terminating Equipment." *IEEE Transactions on Communications,* September 1982. Looks at the design issues relating to the user-ISDN equipment interface.

GUNN89 Gunningberg, P.; Bjorkman, M.; Nordmark, E.; Pink, S.; Sjodin, P.; and Stromquist, J. "Application Protocols and Performance Benchmarks." *IEEE Communications Magazine,* June 1989. Presents results from performance measures of application services. FTAM and FTP are among the application protocols analyzed.

HALS90 Halsall, F. and Modiri, N. "An Implementation of an OSI Network Management System." *IEEE Network Magazine,* July 1990. Presents a framework and some software tools for implementing network management facilities for an OSI environment.

HAST83 Hastings, T. "Conformance Requirements in the ANSI Videotex/Teletext Interchange Standard (NAPLPS). *Proceedings, COMPCON '83 Fall,* September 1983. Conformance requirements specify exactly what it means to conform to the standard.

HEAT89 Heatley, S. and Stokesberry, D. "Analysis of Transport Measurements Over a Local Area Network." *IEEE Communications Magazine,* June 1989. Reports the end-to-end delay and maximum throughput for a typical implementation of the bottom four layers of OSI, and identifies the factors that affect performance in implementations of those layers.

HEMR84 Hemrick, C. "The Internal Organization of the OSI Network Layer: Concepts, Applications, and Issues." *Journal of Telecommunication Networks,* Summer 1984. A formalized description of the way in which communication networks can be used to provide OSI network layer services. This is related to specified network protocol standards. The issue of internetworking is examined.

HEMR85 Hemrick, C. *The OSI Network Layer Addressing Schemes, Its Implications, and Considerations for Implementation.* National Telecommunications and Information Administration, Report 85-186, November 1985. An examination of the issues surrounding the assignment of unique addresses to hosts in a network or internet environment. The report analyzes a variety of related issues and presents the approach developed for use in the OSI context.

HIND83 Hinden, R.; Haverty, J.; and Sheltzer, A. "The DARPA Internet: Interconnection Heterogeneous Computer Networks with Gateways." *Computer,* September 1983. Describes the implementation of the DOD Internet Protocol. Included in this tutorial.

HOBE80 Hoberecht, V. "SNA Function Management." *IEEE Transactions on Communications,* April 1980. A look at higher-layer protocols within IBM's SNA.

HOLL83 Hollis, L. "OSI Presentation Layer Activities." *Proceedings of the IEEE,* December 1983. A brief discussion of ISO's approach to presentation layer protocol definition.

HOLL85 Holland, G. "NAPLPS Standard Defines Graphics and Text Communications." *EDN,* January 10, 1985. A detailed presentation of the standard.

HORA84a Horak, W. "Concepts of the Document Interchange Protocol for the Telematic Services: CCITT Draft Recommendation S.a." *Computer Networks,* June 1984. Describes document architecture protocols being developed by CCITT.

HORA84b Horak, W. and Kronert, G. "An Object-Oriented Office Document Architecture Model for Processing and Interchange of Documents." *Proceedings, Second ACM-SIGOA Conference on Office Information Systems,* 1984. A clear overview of ECMA's draft document content and document interchange architectures, which are close to those being developed under CCITT.

HORA85 Horak, W. "Office Document Architecture and Office Document Interchange Formats: Current Status of International Standardization." *Computer,* October 1985. Examines the layered set of protocols being developed by ISO and CCITT for document interchange.

HUIT89 Huitema, C. and Doghri, A. "Defining Faster Transfer Syntaxes for the OSI Presentation Protocol." *Computer Communications Review,* October 1989. Presents a lightweight transfer syntax to be used in high-speed networking. This approach is an alternative to the ASN-1 Basic Encoding Rules (BER) which consume considerable processor time.

HUMM85 Hummel, E. "The CCITT." *IEEE Communications Magazine,* January 1985. Describes the standards-making role of CCITT.

IEEE85 "Special Issues on Telecommunications Standards." *IEEE Communications Magazine,* January 1985. This special issue describes the organization and areas of interest of most relevant standards-making organizations.

INAI90 Inai, H.; Nishida, T.; Yokohira, T.; and Miyahara, H. "End-to-End Performance Modeling for Layered Communication Protocol." *Proceedings, IEEE INFOCOM '90,* June 1990. Presents an analytical model for a layered communication architecture. Each layer is modeled by a queueing network. A technique for calculating estimated end-to-end delay is presented.

IORI91 Ioria, M. "Integrating ISDN and OSI: An Example." *IEEE Communications Magazine,* January 1991. Reports on a trial, sponsored by the National Institute of Standards and Technology (NIST), to demonstrate the interoperation of ISDN with traditional OSI data networks, such as LANs and X.25 WANs.

ISRA87 Israel, J. and Weissberger, A. "Communicating Between Heterogeneous Networks." *Data Communications,* February 1987. Examines ways in which the lowest four layers of the OSI model can be used to achieve a variety of connectionless and connection-oriented internetworking strategies.

JABB91 Jabbari, B. "Common Channel Signalling System Number 7 for ISDN and Intelligent Networks." *Proceedings of the IEEE,* February 1991. A detailed introduction to SS7.

JAIN90 Jain, N.,; Schwartz,; and Bashkow, T. "Transport Protocol Processing at Gbps Rates." *Proceedings, SIGCOMM '90 Symposium,* September 1990. Presents an implementation methodology for ISO TP4 that improves performance. In addition, suggestions are made for improving efficiency by making modifications to the protocol that do not compromise functionality.

JOHN80 Johnson, S. "Architectural Evolution: Digital Unveils Its DECNET Phase III." *Data Communications,* March 1980. An overview of DEC's communication architecture, one of the most widely used proprietary architectures.

JOSH83 Joshi, S. and Iyer, V. "New Standards for Local Networks Push Upper Limits for Lightwave Data." *Data Communications,* July 1984. Describes ANSI's proposed standard for fiber ring local networks. Similar to IEEE 802.5 for twisted-pair ring.

KAMI86 Kaminski, M. "Protocols for Communicating in the Factory." *IEEE Spectrum,* April 1986. A discussion of MAP (Manufacturing Automation Protocol).

KANO91 Kano, S.; Kitami, K.; and Kawarasaki, M. "ISDN Standardization." *Proceedings of the IEEE,* February 1991. Summarizes the status of standards for ISDN and broadband ISDN, including the 1988 Blue Book recommendations and the 1990 interim recommendations.

KATZ90 Katz, D. "The Use of Connectionless Network Layer Protocols over FDDI Networks." *Computer Communications Review,* July 1990. Presents techniques for the use of the DOD IP and the ISO connectionless internet protocol over FDDI. Issues specific to the interaction between network layer protocols and FDDI are discussed.

KAWA84 Kawaguchi, K. "Enhancements to Recommendtion X.75 and International Interconnection of Packet-Switched Public Data Networks." *Proceedings, INFOCOM 84,* 1984. Summarizes the changes made to X.75 from the 1980 to the 1984 standard. The paper also looks at procedures for validating international interconnections.

KESS90 Kessler, G. "IEEE 802.6 MAN." *LAN Magazine,* April 1990. An overview of this metropolitan area network standard.

KHEN89 Khendek, F.; Bochmann, G.; and Kant, C. "New Results on Deriving Protocol Specifications from Service Specifications." *Proceedings, SIGCOMM '89 Symposium,* 1989. Summarizes previous work in the derivation of a protocol specification from a formal service specification, and presents a new approach that is more general and powerful.

KNIG83 Knightson, K. "The Transport Layer Standardization." *Proceedings of the IEEE,* December 1983. A brief description of the ISO family of transport protocols.

KONA83 Konangi, V. and Dhas, C. "An Introduction to Network Architectures." *IEEE Communications Magazine,* October 1983. Presents specific example architectures. Included in this tutorial.

KUO81 Kuo, F. *Protocols and Techniques for Data Communication Networks.* Prentice-Hall, 1981. A portion of this book is devoted to higher-layer protocols.

LAM84 Lam, S. *Principles of Communication and Networking Protocols.* IEEE Computer Society Press, 1984. A collection of reprints plus original material focusing on the techniques and protocols used to manage a communications network. Covers packet-radio, packet-switched, and local networks. Algorithm, design and analysis techniques, formal models, and verification methods are also covered.

LAND90 Landweber, L. and Tasman, M. "An ISO-TP4-TP0 Gateway." *Computer Communications Review,* April 1990. Discusses several design alternatives for a gateway between Class 4 and Class 0 ISO transport protocols. These protocols cannot interoperate, necessitating the use of a gateway for a mixed environment.

LANG83 Langsford, A.; Naemura, K.; and Speth, R. "OSI Management and Job Transfer Services." *Proceedings of the IEEE,* December 1983. Briefly describes the concept of network management in the OSI environment. Then describes a protocol for job transfer and manipulation.

LEIN85 Leiner, B.; Postel, J.; Cole, R.; and Mills, D. "The DARPA Internet Protocol Suite." *Proceedings, INFOCOM '85,* 1985. An overview of the DOD-standardized set of protocols.

LEW89 Lew, H. and Robertson, J. "TCP/IP Network Management with an Eye Toward OSI." *Data Communications,* August 1989. Describes the approach being taken to incorporating OSI network management into a TCP/IP architecture. The emphasis is on the layered protocol implications.

LEWA83 Lewan, D. and Long, H. "The OSI File Service." *Proceedings of the IEEE,* December 1983. Looks at the application-level protocol for file transfer. Included in this tutorial.

LIN84 Lin, S.; Costello, D.; and Miller, M. "Automatic Repeat-Request Error-Control Schemes." *IEEE Communications Magazine,* December 1984. A detailed mathematical analysis of ARQ schemes used for error control in data link protocols.

LINI83 Linington, P. "Fundamentals of the Layer Service Definitions and Protocol Specifications." *Proceedings of the IEEE,* December 1983. Describes the terminology and modeling techniques used in the OSI model and related protocol standards. A useful reference for those who want to read the standards documents.

LINN89 Linn, R. "Conformance Evaluation Methodology and Protocol Testing." *IEEE Journal on Selected Areas in Communications.* September 1989. Provides a survey of recent developments in conformance evaluation methodology, including test architectures and a test language which are destined to become international standards, test generation methodology, and application of formal description techniques.

LOHS85 Lohse, E. "The Role of the ISO in Telecommunications and Information Systems Standardization." *IEEE Communications Magazine,* January 1985. Describes the ISO and the procedures by which it develops and issues standards.

LOVE79 Loveland, R. "Putting DECNET into Perspective." *Datamation,* March 1979. A brief overview of DEC's communications architecture.

LOWE83 Lowe, H. "OSI Virtual Terminal Service." *Proceedings of the IEEE,* December 1983. Describes an ISO-defined set of virtual terminal services. The basic model and service commands are presented.

MAGN79 Magnee, F.; Endrizzi, A.; and Day, J. "A Survey of Terminal Protocols." *Computer Networks,* November, 1979. A review of presentation-level virtual terminal protocols. Included in this tutorial.

MARS91 Marsden, P. "Interworking IEEE 802/FDDI LANs Via the ISDN Frame Relay Bearer Service." *Proceedings of the IEEE,* February 1991. Looks at the use of the frame relay standard to support MAC- relay bridges among LANs.

MART81 Martin, J. *Computer Networks and Distributed Processing.* Prentice-Hall, 1981. A readable treatment of most of the topics in this tutorial.

MCCL83 McClelland, F. "Services and Protocols of the Physical Layer." *Proceedings of the IEEE,* December 1983. Provides an overview of the OSI physical layer concept, and then discusses the service specification for a variety of physical layer standards, including X.21, RS-449, and ISDN.

MCFA79 McFarland, R. "Protocols in a Computer Internetworking Environment." *Proceedings, EASCON '79,* 1979. A discussion of communications architecture from DOD's perspective.

MCLE86 McLeod-Reisig, S. and Huber, K. "ISO Virtual Terminal Protocol and Its Relationship to MIL-STD TELNET." *Proceedings of the Computer Networking Symposium,* December 1986. Examines and compares two standards that have been developed for remote terminal access: DOD's TELNET and the ISO VTP.

McQU78 McQuillan, J. and Cerf, V. *Tutorial: A Practical View of Computer Communications Protocols.* IEEE Computer Society Press, 1978. A collection of reprints plus extensive original material on the principles of communication protocols.

MEIJ82 Meijer, A. and Peeters P. *Computer Network Architectures,* Computer Science Press, 1982. This book is primarily devoted to describing specific protocols and architectures, some standard and some proprietary.

MIER82 Mier, E. "High-Level Protocols, Standards, and the OSI Reference Model." *Data Communications,* July 1982. Discusses the direction in higher-level protocols and the role of the various standards organizations.

MILL90 Miller, A. "The Role of LAPD and Frame Relay in ISDN and Private Networks." *Telecommunications,* November 1990. An overview of these two link control protocols.

MINE89 Minet, P. "Performance Evaluation of GAM-T-103 Real-Time Transfer Protocols." *Proceedings, IEEE INFOCOM '89,* April, 1989. Presents the design of a lightweight transport protocol.

MINS91 Minsky, N. "The Imposition of Protocols Over Open Distributed Systems." *IEEE Transactions on Software Engineering,* February 1991. Introduces an architecture and methodology that specifies the implementation of protocols. The intent is to develop formal, implementable laws that enforce the terms of the protocol. This approach appears to have promise in solving interoperability problems and in achieving conformance.

MITC89 Mitchell, C.; Walker, M.; and Rush, D. "CCITT/ISO Standards for Secure Message Handling." *IEEE Journal on Selected Areas in Communications.* May 1989. Examines the security aspects of the 1988 X.400 message handling recommendations.

MODA90 Modarressi, A. and Skoog, R. "Signaling System No. 7: A Tutorial." *IEEE Communications Magazine,* July 1990. An overview of the various components of SS7, with emphasis on its layered protocol architecture.

MOLD81 Moldow, B. "Reality and the Proposed OSI Standard." *Data Communications,* June 1981. A complaint about the restrictiveness of the OSI model in forcing given functions to given layers.

MYER82 Myers, W. "Toward a Local Network Standard." *IEEE Micro,* August 1982. An excellent and quite thorough presentation of the IEEE 802 standard.

NART89 Narten, T. "Internet Routing." *Proceedings, SIGCOMM '89 Symposium,* 1989. An overview of internet routing protocols used in the DARPA internet, including RIP, EGP, and GGP.

NBS80a National Bureau of Standards. *Features of Internetwork Protocol.* ICST/HLNP-80-8, July 1980.

NBS80b National Bureau of Standards. *Features of the Transport and Session Protocols,* ICST/HLNP-80-1, March 1980.

NBS80c National Bureau of Standards. *Features of the File Transfer Protocol (FTP) and the Data Presentation Protocol (DPP).* ICST/HLNP-80-6, 1980. The above three reports are thoughtful analyses of the relevant issues concerning various protocols.

NEME85 Nemeth, K. "Principles of the Document Interchange Protocol for CCITT Telematic Services." *IEEE Communications Magazine,* March 1985. Describes the protocol architecture defined for the document interchange standards.

NETR90 Netravali, A.; Roome, W.; and Sabnani, K. "Design and Implementation of a High-Speed Transport Protocol." *IEEE Transactions on Communications,* November 1990. A detailed presentation of a lightweight transport protocol. This protocol was designed by AT&T specifically for use over broadband ISDN and has been submitted to CCITT as a proposed standard for that purpose.

NEUF89 Neufeld, G. "Descriptive Names in X.500." *Proceedings, SIGCOMM '89 Symposium,* 1989. Describes a descriptive name convention to be used with X.500 to enhance user-friendliness.

NEUF90 Neufeld, G. and Yang, Y. "The Design and Implementation of an ASN.1-C Compiler." *IEEE Transactions on Software Engineering,* October 1990. Describes the use of Abstract Syntax Notation One to develop a tool for defining protocol-related data types in C.

NEUM83 Neumann, J. "OSI Transport and Session Layers: Services and Protocol." *Proceedings, INFOCOM 83,* 1983. A brief overview.

NGUY89 Nguyen, C.; Vialatte, M.; and Rieu, C. "OSI Application Layer Standards Analysis for a Distributed Application Implementation." *Proceedings, 14th Conference on Local Computer Networks,* October 1989. Provides an overview of the structure of the OSI application layer. The paper then examines the way in which existing applications can be modified by incorporating application service entities, so as to conform to OSI.

NINK85 Ninke, W. "Design Considerations of NAPLPS, the Data Syntax for VIDEOTEX and TELETEXT in North America." *Proceedings of the IEEE,* April 1985. Provides an overview of NAPLPS and a discussion of system implementation issues.

NITZ90 Nitzan, R. and Gross, P. "The Role of U.S. GOSIP." *Computer Networks and ISDN Systems,* November 1990. Outlines the content of the U.S. Government OSI Profile (GOSIP) and explains the role and applicability of the GOSIP document.

ONIO90 Onions, J. "Transport Bridging." *Internetworking Research and Experience.* September 1990. Examines the principles and operations of level-four OSI network relays, often referred to as transport service bridges.

PADL83 Padlipsky, M. "A Perspective on the ARPANET Reference Model." *Proceedings, INFOCOM '83,* 1983. Contrasts this model with OSI. Included in this tutorial.

PARK83 Parker, R. "Committees Push to Standardize Disk I/O." *Computer Design,* March 1983. Briefly describes the ANS X3T9.5 standard for high-speed local networks and places it into the context of related I/O standards.

PARU90 Parulkar, G. and Turner, J. "Towards a Framework for High-Speed Communication in a Heterogeneous Networking Environment." *IEEE Network Magazine,* March 1990. Examines current approaches to layer-3 internetworking, and outlines modifications and enhancements needed to deal with high-speed networks.

PIS84 Piscitello, D. and Chapin, L. "An International Internetwork Protocol Standard." *Journal of Telecommunication Networks,* Fall 1983. Describes the functions and mechanisms of ISO's connectionless internetwork protocol.

PISC86 Piscitello, D.; Weissberger, A.; Stein, S.; and Chapin, A. "Internetworking in an OSI Environment." *Data Communications,* May 1986. Examines both connection-oriented and connectionless approaches to internetworking. The authors look at the relative merits of each approach in a variety of environments and assess the requirements of each on the transport protocol.

POPE84a Popescu-Zeletin, R. "Some Critical Considerations on the ISO/OSI RM from a Network Implementation Point of View." *Proceedings, SIGCOMM 84,* June 1984. Discusses the experience and problems in implementing a communications capability using the OSI model. The author concludes that the OSI approach is effective.

POPE84b Pope, A. "Encoding CCITT X.409 Presentation Transfer Syntax." *Computer Communication Review,* October 1984. A somewhat formal description of the presentation level of CCITT's message handling standard.

POST80 Postel, J.B. "Internetwork Protocol Approaches." *IEEE Transactions on Communications,* April 1980. Describes and compares X.75 and DOD's internet protocol. Included in this tutorial.

POST81 Postel, J.B.; Sunshine, C.A.; and Cohen, D. "The ARPA Internet Protocol." *Computer Networks,* 1981. A thorough description of DOD's internet protocol.

POST85 Postel, J. "Internetwork Applications Using the DARPA Protocol Suite." *Proceedings, INFOCOM 85,* 1985. Describes the applications that are part of the DOD protocol architecture, including TELNET, SMTP, and FTP.

POUZ78 Pouzin, L. and Zimmermann, H. "A Tutorial on Protocols." *Proceedings of the IEEE,* November 1978. An enhaustive treatment of protocol functions and characteristics.

RAUC83 Rauch-Hindin, W. "Upper-Level Network Protocols." *Electronic Design,* March 3, 1983. Relates the OSI model to various working protocols and also discusses the role of various standards-making organizations.

ROBI81 Robin, G. and Treves, S. "An Introduction to Integrated Services Digital Networks." *Electrical Communication,* Vol. 56, No. 1, 1981. A good technical discussion of ISDN mechanisms.

ROSS89 Ross, F. "An Overview of FDDI: The Fiber Distributed Data Interface." *IEEE Journal on Selected Areas in Communications.* September 1989. The Fiber Distributed Data Interface (FDDI) is a standard for a 100-Mbps fiber LAN. It encompasses physical and MAC layers. This paper provides a detailed description.

RUTK82 Rutkowski, A. and Marcus, M. "The Integrated Services Digital Network: Developments and Regulatory Issues." *Computer Communications Review,* July/October 1982. A look at the evolving standards and their implications for government regulations. Contrasts U.S. and European approaches.

RUTK86 Rutkowski, A. "An Overview of the Forums for Standards and Regulations for Digital Networks." *Telecommunications,* October 1986. Discusses the role of most of the key organizations, including CCITT, CCIR, ISO, ITU, CEPT, ECMA, FCC, ECSA, ANSI, EIA, IEEE, and COS.

RYBC80 Rybczynski, A. "X.25 Interface and End-to-End Virtual Circuit Service Characteristics." *IEEE Transactions on Communications,* April 1980. A thorough description.

SABN89 Sabnani, K. and Netravali, A. "A High-Speed Transport Protocol for Datagram/Virtual Circuits." *Proceedings, SIGCOMM '89 Symposium,* 1989. Presents the design and a preliminary performance analysis of a lightweight transport protocol.

SAKA82 Sakamoto, R. *CCITT Standards Activity: The Integrated Services Digital Network (ISDN).* Mitre Technical Report MTR-82W00169, September 1982. This is perhaps the most complete description of the ISDN set of standards as it stood in 1982. Although ISDN work has continued to evolve, this remains a worthwhile introduction.

SALT84 Saltzer, T.; Reed, D.; and Clark, D. "End-to-End Arguments in System Design." *ACM Transactions on Computer Systems,* November 1984. Presents a design principle that helps guide placement of functions among modules in a communications architecture. Examples include bit-error recovery, encryption, duplicate message suppression, and delivery acknowledgment.

SAND90 Sanders, R. and Weaver, A. "The Xpress Transfer Protocol (XTP)—A Tutorial." *Computer Communications Review,* October 1990. An overview of one of the best-known and most tested of the lightweight transport protocols.

SAPR84 Sapronov, W. "Gateways Link Long-Haul and Local Networks." *Data Communications,* July 1984. This article emphasizes links between similar local networks.

SCHN83 Schneidewind, N. "Interconnecting Local Networks to Long-Distance Networks." *Computer,* September 1983. Dicusses protocol implications and various technical approaches.

SELV82 Selvaggi, P. "The Department of Defense Data Protocol Standardization Program." *Proceedings, EASCON '82,* 1982. Describes status and plans for DOD protocol standards.

SHEL82 Sheltzer, A.; Hinden, R.; and Brescia, M. "Connecting Different Types of Networks with Gateways." *Data Communications,* August 1982. Describes the DARPA internet.

SELV85 Selvaggi, P. "The Development of Communications Standards in the DOD." *IEEE Communications Magazine,* January 1985. Describes the process by which the DOD develops and promulgates protocol standards.

SHER86 Sherr, S. "ANSI and Information Systems." *Proceedings, Computer Standards Conference,* May 1986. Describes the process by which ANSI develops and promulgates protocol standards.

SHIR90 Shiroshita, T. "A Data Processing Performance Model for the OSI Application Layer Protocols." *Proceedings, SIGCOMM '90 Symposium,* September 1990. Presents a data processing model to analyze the performance of the application data receiving process in the presentation layer. The method is then used to evaluate sample data structures commonly used for document transmission.

SHOC78 Shoch, I "Inter-Network Naming, Addressing, and Routing." *Proceedings COMPCON Fall '78,* 1978. A useful discussion of these issues. A much-referenced paper. Also available in [LAM84].

SHOC79 Shoch, I. "Packet Fragmentation in Inter-Network Protocols." *Computer Networks,* February 1979. Analyzes alternative fragmentation and reassembly techniques.

SIRB85 Sirbu, M. and Zwimpfer, L. "Standards Setting for Computer Communication: The Case of X.25." *IEEE Communications Magazine,* March 1985. Discusses the history of the development of X.25 and the lessons to be learned and applied to other protocol standards.

SKLO89 Sklower, K. "Improving the Efficiency of the OSI Checksum Calculation." *Computer Communication Review,* October 1989.

SKOV89 Skov, M. "Implementation of Physical and Media Access Protocols for High-Speed Networks." *IEEE Communications Magazine,* June 1989.

SOLO85 Solomon, C. "Exploring the Problems of Internetworking." *Data Communications,* June 1985. A survey of internetworking approaches, with a good discussion of mechanisms, including flow control, routing, security, addressing and naming, and fault detection.

SPRO78 Sproull, R. and Cohen, R. "High-Level Protocols." *Proceedings of the IEEE,* November 1978. Discusses principles and implementation strategies for higher-layer protocols. Included in this tutorial.

STAL90a Stallings, W. *Handbook of Computer-Communications Standards, Volume I: The Open Systems Interconnection Model and OSI-Related Standards.* Macmillan, 1990. A description of the OSI model, plus detailed presentation of OSI-related standards at all layers.

STAL90b Stallings, W. *Handbook of Computer-Communications Standards, Volume II: Local Network Standards.* Macmillan, 1990. A detailed examination of the IEEE 802 and FDDI standards.

STAL90c Stallings, W. *Handbook of Computer-Communications Standards, Volume III: Department of Defense (DOD) Protocol Standards.* Macmillan, 1990. A description of the DOD standards, including TCP, IP, TELNET, SMTP, and FTP.

STAL91 Stallings, W. *Data and Computer Communications,* third edition. Macmillan, 1991. A textbook on the subject, structured along the lines of the OSI model.

STUT72 Stutzman, B. "Data Communication Control Procedures." *ACM Computing Surveys,* December 1972. Another (see also [Gray72]) early discussion of data link control that embodies many of the principles found in modern protocols.

SUNS78 Sunshine, C. and Dalal, Y. "Connection Management in Transport Protocols," *Computer Networks,* December 1978. Discusses some of the most important transport protocol mechanisms.

·SUNS81 Sunshine, C. "Transport Protocols for Computer Networks." in *Protocols and Techniques for Data Communication Networks,* edited by F. Kuo, Prentice-Hall, 1981. A functional description of transport protocols. Included in this tutorial.

SVOB90 Svobodova, L.; Janson, P.; and Mumprecht, E. "Heterogeneity and OSI." *IEEE Journal on Selected Areas in Communications.* January 1990. Examines the difficulties in interworking among heterogeneous systems, even when all systems implement OSI. The authors explain the problems that are left unresolved by conformance to OSI and present approaches to solutions.

TANE81a Tanenbaum, A. *Computer Networks.* Prentice-Hall, 1981. A textbook on the subject, structured along the lines of the OSI model.

TANE81b Tanenbaum, A. "Network Protocols." *Computing Surveys,* December 1981. Defines protocols in the context of the OSI model. Included in this tutorial.

THUR83 Thurk, M. and Twaits, L. "Inside DEC's Newest Networking Phase." *Data Communications,* September 1983. An updated look at DNA, DEC's communications architecture.

TYDE82 Tydeman, I.; Lipinski, H.; Adler, R.; Nyhan, M.; and Zwimpfer, L. *Teletext and Videotext in the United States.* McGraw-Hill, 1982. A mostly nontechnical description of Teletext and Videotex.

UNSO82 Unsoy, M. "X.75 Internetworking of Datapac with Other Packet Switched Networks." *Journal of Telecommunication Networks,* Fall 1982. Describes practical experience with X.75. Included in this tutorial.

VARG90 Varghese, G. and Perlman, R. "Transparent Interconnection of Incompatible Local Area Networks Using Bridges." *IEEE Journal on Selected Areas in Communications.* January 1990. Presents a protocol for linking LANs with dissimilar link control protocols.

VOEL86 Voelcker, I. "Helping Computers Communicate." *IEEE Spectrum,* March 1986. Provides an informal overview of the OSI model, and discusses its applicability and status.

WABE82 Waber, K. "Considerations on Customer Access to the ISDN." *IEEE Transactions on Communications,* September 1982. ISDN from the subscriber's point of view.

WARE83 Ware, C. "The OSI Network Layer: Standards to Cope with the Real World." *Proceedings of the IEEE,* December 1983. A somewhat abstract discussion of the ISO network layer standard.

WARN80 Warner, C. "Connecting Local Networks to Long-Haul Networks: Issues in Protocol Design." *Proceedings, Fifth Conference on Local Computer Networks,* 1980. Looks at the difficulties of using an internet protocol across dissimilar networks.

WATS89 Watson, R. "The Delta-T Transport Protocol." *Proceedings, 14th Conference on Local Computer Networks,* October 1989. Provides an overview of the features of a lightweight transport protocol.

WECK80 Wecker, S. "DNA: The Digital Network Architecture." *IEEE Transactions on Communications,* April 1980. A thorough description of DEC's communications architecture.

WEIS83 Weissberger, A. "Bit Oriented Data Link Controls." *Computer Design.* March 1983. Examines functions and formats. Included in this tutorial.

WEIS87 Weissberger, A. and Israel, J. "What the New Internet Working Standards Provide." *Data Communications,* February 1987. Focuses on the issues related to internetworking and presents details of the ISO connectionless internet protocol.

WEIS89 Weissberger, A. "The Evolving Versions of ISDN's Terminal Adapter." *Data Communications,* March 1989. A detailed examination of the CCITT Recommendations dealing with protocol conversion between existing terminal equipment and the ISDN user-network interface standard.

WETH83 Wetherington, J. "The Story of PLP." *IEEE Journal on Selected Areas in Communications.* February 1983. A presentation-level standard for videotex. Included in this tutorial.

WHAL89 Whaley, A. "The X-Press Transfer Protocol." *Proceedings, 14th Conference on Local Computer Networks,* October 1989. A functional overview of a lightweight transport protocol.

WILL89 Williamson, C. and Cheriton, D. "An Overview of the VMTP Transport Protocol." *Proceedings, 14th Conference on Local Computer Networks,* October 1989. A brief overview of VMTP, together with some performance results.

YANO81 Yanoschak, V. "Implementing the X.21 Interface." *Data Communications,* February 1981. A practical discussion of X.21 implementation. Included in this tutorial.

ZIMM80 Zimmermann, H. "OSI Reference Model—The ISO Model of Architecture for Open System Interconnection." *IEEE Transactions on Communications,* April 1980. A rather formal definition of the OSI model.

Author Profile

Dr. William Stallings is an independent consultant with nearly twenty years of experience in data and computer communications. His clients have included major corporations and government agencies in the United States and Europe. Prior to forming his own consulting firm, he has been vice president of CSM Corporation, a firm specializing in data processing and data communications for the health care industry. He has also been Director of Systems Analysis and Design for CTEC, Inc., a firm specializing in command, control, and communications systems.

Dr. Stallings holds a PhD from M.I.T. in Computer Science and a BS from Notre Dame in electrical engineering. He is a frequent lecturer and the author of numerous papers and a dozen books on networking and computers, including *Data and Computer Communications* (Macmillan, 1991) which has become the standard in the field. The popularity of his books is demonstrated by the fact that all but the most recent of these books are in a second or third edition.

Textbooks:
- *Operating Systems,* Macmillan, 1992
- *Data and Computer Communications,* third edition, Macmillan, 1991
- *Business Data Communications,* Macmillan, 1990
- *Computer Organization and Architecture,* second edition, Macmillan, 1990
- *Local Networks, an Introduction,* third edition, Macmillan, 1990
- *ISDN and Broadband ISDN,* Macmillan, 1992

Professional/reference books:
- *Handbook of Computer-Communications Standards, Volume I: The Open Systems Interconnection (OSI) Reference Model and OSI-Related Standards,* second edition, Howard W. Sams, 1990
- *Handbook of Computer-Communications Standards, Volume II: Local Area Network Standards,* second edition, Howard W. Sams, 1990
- *Handbook of Computer-Communications Standards, Volume III: The TCP/IP Protocol Suite,* second edition, Howard W. Sams, 1990
- *The Business Guide to Local Area Networks,* Howard W. Sams, 1990.
- *A Manager's Guide to Local Networks,* Prentice-Hall, 1983

Edited collections of papers:
- *Computer Communications: Architectures, Protocols, and Standards,* third edition, IEEE Computer Society Press, 1990
- *Integrated Services Digital Networks and Broadband ISDN,* IEEE Computer Society Press, 1990
- *Reduced Instruction Set Computers,* second edition, IEEE Computer Society Press, 1989
- *Local Network Technology,* third edition, IEEE Computer Society Press, 1988

IEEE Computer Society Press

Press Activities Board

Vice President: Yale N. Patt, University of Michigan
James H. Aylor, University of Virginia
Mario R. Barbacci, Carnegie Mellon University
Bill D. Carroll, University of Texas
James Farrell, III, VLSI Technology Inc.
Barry W. Johnson, University of Virginia
Duncan H. Lawrie, University of Illinois
Murali Varanasi, University of South Florida
Ben Wah, University of Illinois
Marshall Yovits, Indiana University—Purdue University
Staff Representative: True Seaborn, Publisher

Editorial Board

Editor-in-Chief: Rao Vemuri, University of California, Davis
Oscar N. Garcia, The George Washington University
Joydeep Ghosh, University of Texas, Austin
Uma G. Gupta, University of Central Florida
A.R. Hurson, Pennsylvania State University
Krishna Kavi, University of Texas, Arlington
Ez Nahouraii, IBM
Frederick E. Petry, Tulane University
Dhiraj K. Pradhan, University of Massachusetts
Charles Richter, MCC
David Rine, George Mason University
A.R.K. Sastry, Rockwell International Science Center
Ajit Singh, Siemens Corporate Research
Pradip K. Srimani, Colorado State University
Murali R. Varanasi, University of South Florida
Staff Representative: Henry Ayling, Editorial Director

Press Staff

T. Michael Elliott, Executive Director
True Seaborn, Publisher

Henry Ayling, Editorial Director
Catherine Harris, Production Editor
Anne Copeland, Production Editor
Lisa O'Conner, Production Editor
Robert Werner, Production Editor
Penny Storms, Editorial Production Assistant
Edna Straub, Editorial Production Assistant
Thomas Fink, Advertising/Promotions Manager
Frieda Koester, Marketing/Customer Service Manager
Becky Straub, Marketing/Customer Service Admin. Asst.
Beverly Anthony, Order Processor

Offices of the IEEE Computer Society

Headquarters Office
1730 Massachusetts Avenue, N.W.
Washington, DC 20036-1903
Phone: (202) 371-0101 — Fax: (202) 728-9614

Publications Office
P.O. Box 3014
10662 Los Vaqueros Circle
Los Alamitos, CA 90720-1264
Membership and General Information: (714) 821-8380
Publication Orders: (800) 272-6657 — Fax: (714) 821-4010

European Office
13, avenue de l'Aquilon
B-1200 Brussels, BELGIUM
Phone: 32-2-770-21-98 — Fax: 32-3-770-85-05

Asian Office
Ooshima Building
2-19-1 Minami-Aoyama, Minato-ku
Tokyo 107, JAPAN
Phone: 81-3-408-3118 — Fax: 81-3-408-3553

IEEE Computer Society

IEEE Computer Society Press Publications

Monographs: A monograph is an authored book consisting of 100-percent original material.

Tutorials: A tutorial is a collection of original materials prepared by the editors, and reprints of the best articles published in a subject area. Tutorials must contain at least five percent of original material (although we recommend 15 to 20 percent of original material).

Reprint collections: A reprint collection contains reprints (divided into sections) with a preface, table of contents, and section introductions discussing the reprints and why they were selected. Collections contain less than five percent of original material.

Technology series: Each technology series is a brief reprint collection — approximately 126-136 pages and containing 12 to 13 papers, each paper focusing on a subset of a specific discipline, such as networks, architecture, software, or robotics.

Submission of proposals: For guidelines on preparing CS Press books, write the Editorial Director, IEEE Computer Society Press, PO Box 3014, 10662 Los Vaqueros Circle, Los Alamitos, CA 90720-1264, or telephone (714) 821-8380.

Purpose

The IEEE Computer Society advances the theory and practice of computer science and engineering, promotes the exchange of technical information among 100,000 members worldwide, and provides a wide range of services to members and nonmembers.

Membership

All members receive the acclaimed monthly magazine *Computer*, discounts, and opportunities to serve (all activities are led by volunteer members). Membership is open to all IEEE members, affiliate society members, and others seriously interested in the computer field.

Publications and Activities

Computer **magazine:** An authoritative, easy-to-read magazine containing tutorials and in-depth articles on topics across the computer field, plus news, conference reports, book reviews, calendars, calls for papers, interviews, and new products.

Periodicals: The society publishes six magazines and five research transactions. For more details, refer to our membership application or request information as noted above.

Conference proceedings, tutorial texts, and standards documents: The IEEE Computer Society Press publishes more than 100 titles every year.

Standards working groups: Over 100 of these groups produce IEEE standards used throughout the industrial world.

Technical committees: Over 30 TCs publish newsletters, provide interaction with peers in specialty areas, and directly influence standards, conferences, and education.

Conferences/Education: The society holds about 100 conferences each year and sponsors many educational activities, including computing science accreditation.

Chapters: Regular and student chapters worldwide provide the opportunity to interact with colleagues, hear technical experts, and serve the local professional community.

Other IEEE Computer Society Press Titles by William Stallings

---

Tutorials

Advances in ISDN and Broadband ISDN
Edited by William Stallings.
Catalog No. 2797, ISBN 0-8186-2797-2, 450 pp.

**Integrated Services Digital Networks (ISDN)
2nd edition.**
Edited by William Stallings.
Catalog No. 823, ISBN 0-8186-823-4, 406 pp.

**Local Network Technology
3rd edition.**
Edited by William Stallings.
Catalog No. 825, ISBN 0-8186-0825-0, 512 pp.

**Reduced Instruction Set Computers (RISC)
2nd edition.**
Edited by William Stallings.
Catalog No. 1943, ISBN 0-8186-8943-9, 440 pp.

Videotape Packages

ISDN: A Status Report
By William Stallings.
Catalog No. 823AV, Running Time: 180 min.

**OSI and TCP/IP:
Impact on Software Vendors and Users**
By William Stallings.
Catalog No. 2093AV, Running Time: 180 min.

IEEE Computer Society Press
10662 Los Vaqueros Circle
Los Alamitos, CA 90720
1-800-CS-BOOKS

Notes

Notes

Notes

Notes

Notes

Notes